Advance Praise for

Found in the Wake

Once you start reading *Found in the Wake*, you won't want to stop. It's a riveting page-turner that reads like a thriller novel. It's also a true story about courage, faith, the power of forgiveness, a family's journey from darkness to light, and a young man's determination to turn a personal tragedy into a mission for change.

—**Joe Capozzi,** former reporter (retired),
The Palm Beach Post

Carter shares his traumatic story with tremendous humility and perseverance that inspires and motivates us to have faith and confidence even in adversity. We are so grateful for his friendship and willingness to share his experience.

—**Peg Phillips,** executive director,
National Safe Boating Council

In this heartfelt account of a horrific accident, the Viss family moved me to tears in their moments of triumph—but also in dark times that stretched their faith, livelihoods, and emotional health to the limits. Their story is raw, intimate, and ultimately uplifting.

—**Adriana Barton,** journalist and author of *Wired for Music: A Search for Health and Joy Through the Science of Sound*

FOUND IN THE WAKE

RISING FROM THE DEPTHS OF A DEVASTATING BOAT STRIKE

a memoir

CARTER VISS, LEILA VISS, AND CHUCK VISS

Best wishes to you Scott!

Found in the Wake: Rising from the Depths of a Devastating Boat Strike
by Carter Viss, Leila Viss, and Chuck Viss

Published by the Carter Viss Foundation

Copyright © 2024

All rights reserved. No part of the contents of this book may be reproduced by any means without the written permission of the publisher.

Medical disclaimer: Although the publisher and the author have made every effort to ensure that the information in this book was correct at press time and while this publication is designed to provide accurate information in regard to the subject matter covered, the publisher and the author assume no responsibility for errors, inaccuracies, omissions, or any other inconsistencies herein and hereby disclaim any liability to any party for any loss, damage, or disruption caused by errors or omissions, whether such errors or omissions result from negligence, accident, or any other cause. This publication is meant as a source of valuable information for the reader, however it is not meant as a substitute for direct expert assistance. If such level of assistance is required, the services of a competent professional should be sought.

Content warning: This book includes themes related to mental health, depression, and suicidal ideation, which may be distressing for some readers.

Scripture quotations are from The ESV® Bible (The Holy Bible, English Standard Version®), © 2001 by Crossway, a publishing ministry of Good News Publishers. Used by permission. All rights reserved. Scripture quotations marked (NLT) are taken from the Holy Bible, New Living Translation, copyright ©1996, 2004, 2015 by Tyndale House Foundation. Used by permission of Tyndale House Publishers, Carol Stream, Illinois 60188. All rights reserved.

ISBN: 979-8-9922714-0-9 (paperback)

Publishing and design services: MelindaMartin.me
Editor: Gail Fallen, gail@mesanetworks.net
Cover art: Carter Viss

This book is for anyone facing a hardship
they don't think they can overcome.

Learn more about the Carter Viss Foundation
and its progress, watch videos of Carter playing the piano,
and see his artwork here.

https://cartervissfoundation.org

All proceeds from the sale of this book
will benefit the Carter Viss Foundation.

CONTENTS

Prologue	What Are the Odds?	1
Chapter 1	Braced for Impact	5
Chapter 2	The Call	13
Chapter 3	Impact	17
Chapter 4	Eyewitness Account	21
Chapter 5	News	29
Chapter 6	A Simple Prayer	37
Chapter 7	Communities	39
Chapter 8	Entrance	43
Chapter 9	Backstory	47
Chapter 10	ICU	53
Chapter 11	First Responders	59
Chapter 12	Ventilator	69
Chapter 13	ICU Psychosis	75
Chapter 14	Iggy	77
Chapter 15	Awakening	87
Chapter 16	A Mere Millimeter	91
Chapter 17	New Reality	97
Chapter 18	How Much Does an Arm Cost?	99
Chapter 19	Purple Pig	107
Chapter 20	Upgrade to Step-Down	113
Chapter 21	The Strongest Person I Ever Met	121
Chapter 22	Sinking In	123
Chapter 23	Mourning and Rejoicing	129
Chapter 24	Pain Management	131
Chapter 25	Shit Day	137
Chapter 26	Andy	143
Chapter 27	The Slog	149
Chapter 28	God's Plan	157
Chapter 29	Christmas Gift	161
Chapter 30	Home for the Hospital Days	163

Chapter 31	First Step	171
Chapter 32	Good Samaritans	175
Chapter 33	On the Move	181
Chapter 34	The Perfect Storm	189
Chapter 35	Withdrawal	195
Chapter 36	Second-Floor Condo	199
Chapter 37	Free at Last	205
Chapter 38	Dave and Jodie	211
Chapter 39	A Mother's Lament at 30,000 Feet	215
Chapter 40	Discharged	223
Chapter 41	The Outside World	229
Chapter 42	Ya Mon	235
Chapter 43	Dr. Paley	241
Chapter 44	Dumping In	245
Chapter 45	Steps Back	249
Chapter 46	Wailing Wall	255
Chapter 47	Infection	261
Chapter 48	New Lifelong Friends	265
Chapter 49	Floridafishboyz	271
Chapter 50	Back to Denver	275
Chapter 51	Turning Point	283
Chapter 52	His Day in Court	287
Chapter 53	Let's Make a Difference	299
Chapter 54	Danny	305
Chapter 55	Miracle at Schwartz Lagoon	315
Chapter 56	Kenny	325
Chapter 57	Emily	329
Chapter 58	Alumni Achievement Award	337
Chapter 59	Music and Resilience	343
Chapter 60	Return to St. Mary's	355
Chapter 61	Mourning to Dancing	359
Chapter 62	What Is Found in Loss?	367

Epilogue: The Narrow Path	373
Acknowledgments	381
About the Authors	383
Notes	384

PROLOGUE

What Are the Odds?

*This life, then, isn't for understanding everything;
it's for standing under the mystery.*

—Attributed to Madeleine L'Engle

Leila

There was never any doubt of how the accident happened. It does no good to ask why it happened. And then, there's the question of "what." It's the one that came to mind when our friend Ed, just a few weeks after the incident, took our entire family out for a boat ride on the Atlantic Ocean— so we could idle by the place where the 36-foot triple-engine pleasure craft ran over my son.

The question of what surfaced when we came upon the reef, a snorkeling spot known by locals as Breakers Reef. I imagined the area to be about the size of Sandy Hollow, the pond-sized sandpit I swam in as a kid. That was not the case. Instead, it was a vast area where boats were tethered to buoys so snorkelers could jump in and observe the reef and sea life beneath them. At the same time, jet skis whizzed in circles on the surface. Despite all the boats, Skidoos, and dive flags, the traffic over the popular marine playground appeared sparse amidst the expansive waters. So the question of what is this: What are the odds of a boat striking a snorkeler when there's plenty of ocean? Astounding, astronomical, incalculable odds.

And yet, it happened.

We will never know the answer to what or why. But we do know a little.

We know that our twenty-five-year-old son, Carter Viss, was maimed and nearly killed when he was struck by a boat on Thanksgiving Day 2019, and our lives changed forever. Not only the lives of our immediate family—including our oldest son, Chase; his wife, Brittany; our youngest son, Levi; and his girlfriend, Erin—but also the lives of grandparents, uncles, aunts, cousins, relatives, friends, and even strangers. Strangers who became instant lifetime friends—Andy and Christine (the initial first responders who came to Carter's aid), the dozens of people on the beach who witnessed the aftermath, and the doctors who didn't think Carter would survive.

And as we would learn later, it upended the lives of the man operating the boat that day and his family, leading to an alliance forged by forgiveness and a shared mission to rewrite laws aimed at marine safety.

That's why it's important to document Carter's story. These changes brought about significant heartache. It's impossible to avoid grief on this side of Heaven, and it seems that our experience with permanent loss has reached into and touched the hearts of others who grieve. The accident reminds us that we are not chained to the control we crave. We are fragile mortals with odds that aren't stacked in our favor.

What Are the Odds?

It's our family's mission that neither the odds nor grief win in Carter's story. Instead, his story of forgiveness and resilience must let *change* win. This book serves as a catalyst for this tragic event to make a difference that leads to an unforgettable and enduring impact.

As Carter put it soon after his breathing tube was removed: "I can have more impact now than before the accident."

CHAPTER 1

Braced for Impact

Carter

THE GREATEST FEELING IN THE WORLD IS WAKING UP AND knowing it will be a phenomenal day for snorkeling. I vividly remember feeling this way that morning on Thanksgiving Day in 2019. I rushed out of bed, changed into my swimsuit, ate a quick breakfast of a toasted bagel with peanut butter, grabbed my diving gear, and walked out the door to see Andy waiting for me in his car. During the drive, we discussed the highlights of yesterday's snorkeling adventure, blasted some EDM to get us pumped up for snorkeling, and joked about how busy we would be on Black Friday. We both worked together in the operations department at Loggerhead Marinelife Center (Loggerhead), a nonprofit organization that specializes in the rehabilitation of sea turtles.

Life was good. I remember thinking about what a privilege it was to spend Thanksgiving Day in the water and end it with a relaxing evening in my condo, munching on turkey and stuffing with friends. I was a renter and about to purchase this condo, and it felt like I was taking my first steps into true adulthood. I also felt so lucky to have a job that consisted of working next to sea turtles and in aquariums. Despite the loneliness and occasional depression I battled, I was optimistic about the future and was confident that great things were on the horizon.

We got our first glimpse of the ocean, and it was calm like a lake, with the morning sun shining in the east. The water was so clear you could see the dark spots the reef made in the water in contrast to the bright sand. The sky was blue with no clouds in sight. That feeling I woke up with was confirmed.

Now our only concern in the world was to find a place to park Andy's car on Palm Beach, an island infamous for its lack of public parking. We scoured the neighborhood roads next to the beach and finally found a two-hour parking spot along the side of the road with a short walk to the ocean. We immediately pulled in, breathed a sigh of relief, grabbed our gear, and made our way to the beach access.

We set our towels, shirts, flip-flops, and a bucket with an aerator (for fish that I may catch and want to keep for my personal aquarium at home) where we entered the beach and began walking south toward The Breakers Hotel. This half-mile trek was necessary because there was a submerged pier in front of the hotel that created an astounding artificial reef.

For about two years, Andy and I had the same routine: We swam off the beach in this area to go straight over the pier, and the slight current pulled us north along the rest of the reef, which is parallel to the beach. As soon as we saw our belongings on the beach, we would swim back to shore and call it a day.

Walking toward The Breakers Hotel that day, I had my dive gloves on and was carrying my divers-down flag, my mask and snorkel, my clear vinyl net to catch small fish, and my weight belt that I used to tow my divers-down flag. Andy carried his mask, snorkel, fins, and the contraption we invented called the "Fishing Finger."

Despite its whimsical name, the Fishing Finger was simply a threaded PVC endcap with monofilament fishing line spooled around it and a small lure at the end. We would slide the cap over a finger and jig the lure over the reef. We caught a ton of fish with this device, and it was always fun to see what fish may bite.

Once we reached The Breakers Hotel, we could clearly see the dark area in the water that was the ruined pier. It was time to dive in, and we immediately embarked on our snorkeling journey.

This was obviously not my first time snorkeling the reef; in fact, it was probably my hundredth time. Since I moved to West Palm Beach in 2013 to attend college at Palm Beach Atlantic University (PBA), the Breakers Reef has been a crucial part of my life. I remember the first time I swam up on that sunken pier and was amazed that it was just a short swim off the beach. I explored the rocks and crevices to discover all kinds of marine life living in a beautiful ecosystem. Seeing this gave me confidence that my decision to study marine biology was correct. I knew I had found my happy place.

Throughout the following years, I took several of my college friends and coworkers to the reef to experience its beauty. We would spear and eat snappers and jacks, catch small tropical fish for an aquarium, or simply swim around to appreciate the marine life and take a break from the stresses of college.

I would sometimes go out there alone just to be at peace with nature. But an experience on Christmas Eve of 2018 would teach me the importance of always having a dive buddy.

I was feeling sad and lonely not to be spending the holidays in Denver with my family. I decided to snorkel the Breakers Reef to clear my head because the diving conditions were perfect. I reached the sunken pier and immediately felt at home.

While swimming above the pier, I noticed what appeared to be a five- to six-foot blacktip shark swimming about thirty feet away from me. I had encountered sharks this size in the past, so I didn't panic and kept a sharp eye on its movements. Blacktip sharks migrate annually through South Florida waters during the winter months, so an encounter with one was not uncommon.

After it disappeared, I glanced behind me to see two additional blacktip sharks swimming together. Now my adrenaline was starting to rise, and I did a 360-degree turn to get a grasp of my surroundings. To my shock, at least thirty sharks were circling me, some of them just about ten feet away. I was in the middle of a migrating school of sharks.

My initial reaction was fear, as anyone would expect, but after about ten seconds, I started to calm down because they seemed curious about me and made no aggressive movements toward me. After about a minute of staring these amazing animals down, they all vanished into the vast blue backdrop of the ocean. I breathed an immense sigh of relief but was also amazed I had a close encounter with that many sharks.

I remained near the reef for about another hour, checking my surroundings to see if the sharks would return, but they never did. When I reached the beach, I felt so alive and amped to have experienced that. It was the best Christmas gift I could've asked for. However, I gave myself a humbling reminder that it could've ended much worse, and no one would have been able to assist me because I was out there alone. From then on, I vowed to always bring a dive buddy with me when I snorkel.

Now, back to Thanksgiving of 2019. Andy and I swam up on that familiar pier rubble and were greeted by a large school of grunts and jacks. Andy caught his first fish of the day with the Fishing Finger, and we knew it would be a fun day. We reached the end of the pier and started swimming parallel to the beach on the rest of the Breakers Reef.

The reef was very active that day. We saw a nurse shark hanging out on the bottom, a green sea turtle swimming near the surface, and a guitarfish trying its best to camouflage itself in the sand. I spotted a juvenile queen angelfish (the prize fish I wanted for my personal aquarium) and spent about thirty minutes trying to catch it with my net to no avail.

After I came to terms with my defeat, I heard Andy call my name, telling me to check out what he had just caught. He had hooked a scorpionfish with his Fishing Finger. This fish is notorious for its venomous spines; getting stung by one might result in a trip to the ER.

We were very cautious handling it. Andy managed to remove the small hook from its mouth, and the fish returned to the reef. If I remember correctly, I think we yelled, "That was awesome!" at the exact same time after he released it.

After another hour of snorkeling, we saw our towels and gear on the beach and decided to call it a day. I managed to catch a juvenile French angelfish and a small lionfish that were now in a bait holder next to my dive flag. I was so excited to add them to my personal aquarium.

As I started swimming toward the beach, I heard a rather loud boat engine. This wasn't uncommon because there were a lot of boats out on a holiday, and sound travels about five times further underwater than in air. So a loud engine sound could be coming from a boat that's hundreds of feet away. However, this sound grew significantly louder.

I looked to my right to see a massive boat hull headed straight toward me at a very high speed. My adrenaline immediately kicked in, and I knew whatever maneuvers I made would mean the difference between life and death. I managed to swim as far out of its path I could, but I also knew there was no way I could outswim its size and speed. I tilted my body so my head and torso were as far away from the boat as possible. I made one last desperate push to clear its path.

Then I braced for impact.

The hull of the 36-foot Yellowfin boat named *Talley Girl*
(Photo Credit: Searcy, Denney, Scarola, Barnhart & Shipley Law Firm)

Braced for Impact

The three 400-horsepower Mercury Verado outboard engines with high-performance lower units and five-blade propellers on the *Talley Girl*
(Photo Credit: Searcy, Denney, Scarola, Barnhart & Shipley Law Firm)

Talley Girl beached after the accident
(Photo Credit: Palm Beach Police)

CHAPTER 2

The Call

I'm losing all hope; I am paralyzed with fear.
—Psalm 143:4 NLT

Leila

It was a unanimous decision: no turkey on Thanksgiving. My husband, Chuck, respected by friends and family for his fine cooking, wanted a break from the hullabaloo of brining, trimming, and roasting one. I wasn't crazy about the mess it would make of the oven, and although I love the aroma of turkey while it's roasting, I'm not a fan of the cooked turkey odor lingering when I head to bed. Chase, Brittany, and Levi weren't exceptionally excited about the typical mashed potatoes, green beans, and sweet potatoes. For these reasons, and since no guests were joining us, we didn't default to the traditional turkey dinner. Instead, we chose a Thanksgiving Day meal of ramen. Not the prepackaged noodles with the flavoring packet but a homemade version cooked by our oldest son, Chase, who follows in his dad's culinary footsteps.

The ramen was to be prepared and eaten later in the day, as there was a church service to attend in the morning. Chase and his wife, Brittany, were scheduled to sing and play in the worship team for the special service. It's common for their band to be short on available keyboardists. Because I'm the organist and pianist at a different church that doesn't hold a Thanksgiving service, I was available and volunteered to play piano with their team. It was one of those "mama highs" being able to "jam" with a son on guitar—which he picked up after years of piano lessons—and his wife on flute and vocals.

After the service, Chuck and I wanted to take a walk. So much snow had fallen over the past few days that it was hard to find a snow-free surface in our neck of the woods. So, while we were up north, we headed to Denver's City Park and found paths with only a little ice and snow. My earbuds played Michelle Obama's audible book *Becoming,* and her voice kept me walking at a quick pace amid the frigid air and somewhat slippery conditions.

My phone rang. I checked the screen, and it said Palm Beach, Florida. I've received spam calls from that area before and figured it was just another one. Soon after, the phone rang again, and this time, I was ticked—really, a stubborn telemarketer on Thanksgiving?

When we returned to our car and drove out of the parking lot, I noticed two voice messages on my phone. So I pushed play, and the message came through the car's Bluetooth speaker, so Chuck was listening as he drove.

"Hello, this is Sergeant R-something [I couldn't hear a specific name] of the Palm Beach Police Department. I'm calling for the parents of Carter Viss. If you could return my call, please, I would appreciate it; thank you."

The Call

With a rapid pulse and a sinking heart, I dialed the callback number. We had no idea what the police officer would tell us. My first thought was *What did he do? I hope he's not in too much trouble!*

The officer answered. He told us that Carter had been in an accident. He had been struck by a boat and was taken to St. Mary's Medical Center in West Palm Beach, a Level One Trauma Center. My first thought was one of relief: *Okay, it sounds like he was not at fault for anything.* My next thought was one of panic: *How hurt* was *he?*

The police officer gave us the number for the emergency room at St. Mary's Medical Center. Chuck continued the slow drive back home down Colorado Boulevard. The road was packed with snow and ice, which made it difficult to cruise at a normal speed. I dialed the hospital as we let the information from the officer sink in. We braced ourselves for bad news.

When a trauma nurse answered the phone, and I told her that we were Carter's parents, I distinctly recall her asking, "How much do you know?"

That's when Chuck and I knew the report would be hard to hear. And it was. In a calm voice, the nurse listed Carter's injuries: he lost part of his right arm, his legs sustained severe lacerations, and he was in surgery. After that, I don't remember much more because Chuck was gasping for air and sobbing while trying to find a place to pull over and stop the car in an empty parking lot. I was frozen. My reaction was stuck way deep down inside.

For about five minutes, we sat in bewilderment as traffic buzzed by. Chuck started the car, turned out of the lot onto the slushy road, and announced, "I'm going out to Florida as soon as possible."

I came back with, "Yeah, so am I!"

His use of "I" didn't sit well with me. Of course, *I* was going, too. *We* were going. I didn't like it that he was not including me in his plans. But I know why he said it that way. Usually, my jobs tie me down, things are hard to cancel, and income is lost when I'm not working. This monumental blow meant dropping everything. In fact, it erased the importance of anything that was significant to us just minutes before. Nothing really mattered now except for Carter.

When we arrived home, Levi, son number three, who had recently graduated college and now lived with us until he found a job, heard a distinct gloomy tone in our voices as we called out for him. He rushed out of his room to see what was going on. I told him Carter was in an accident and what we knew of it.

We all stood in the kitchen talking about what to do next and were interrupted by a phone call from Dr. Robert Borrego. He introduced himself as the surgeon on call and explained that he performed Carter's emergency surgery. He informed us that the surgery went as expected. He said Carter was in critical but stable condition and that he was concerned about the condition of Carter's legs.

We all stood by the kitchen sink and hugged and sobbed.

CHAPTER 3

Impact

Carter

THE IMPACT WAS SWIFT. THE PROPELLERS CUT THROUGH MY limbs like a hot knife through butter. My head rose above the water, and I first noticed what was left of my right arm: it was completely severed near the elbow, and I saw my bone sticking out like a broken twig surrounded by my shredded skin and muscle tissue. I also noticed the line to my dive flag was severed, and the bait holder containing my fish was broken into several pieces.

My screams were muffled as my head sank below water, and I caught a glimpse of the rest of my arm sinking down to the reef below. It was eerily similar to a scene out of *Jaws*. Before I could process the shock of what I just saw, I noticed I couldn't keep myself afloat because both of my legs had sustained severe injuries that I couldn't see.

The area I once called my happy place was now hell on earth. The clear water filled with a beautiful reef and many fish was now stained red with my own blood. The nightmarish propeller injuries I saw on deceased sea turtles while working at Loggerhead were now my personal fate. As the red fog of my blood surrounded me, I inhaled saltwater and was sure I was about to drown.

Did this really just happen?

I'm going to die.

What a horrible way to go.

Suddenly, a glimmer of hope arrived. Andy scooped me up and propped my head above the water. He was about as shocked as I was and couldn't believe this was actually happening. To our relief, it appeared the driver of the boat that hit me knew what he had done and immediately turned around to help. The boat slowly backed up toward us, and Andy managed to swim me to the rear platform of the boat.

As Andy and a passenger of the boat hoisted me onto the platform, I screamed with pain and saw the damage that was done to my legs. My left leg was nearly severed by the propellers about halfway down my calf. I saw my bone protruding outward as my foot dangled unusually far to the left. The propeller also cut right through my kneecap on my right leg, and the lower leg was dislocated and hanging unnaturally forward. I remember the worst pain in those moments coming from that injury. I didn't know or feel at the time that my left wrist was also badly broken and nicked by the propellers.

I was screaming profanities and "I'm going to die!" over and over. Then another rescuer arrived. A nearby paddle boarder, who we would later find out was named Christine, saw the boat strike me and immediately came over to help. She had just learned how to tie tourniquets properly in a First Aid course about a week ago and swiftly used the tourniquets from the first aid kit on the boat to tie them around my mangled limbs. At the time, I had lost about half my blood and was on the verge of organ failure. Christine's quick action and knowledge of tying tourniquets were among the many things that saved my life.

Andy and I were now on the boat, and it was headed straight toward the beach, where an ambulance and paramedics were waiting to take me to the hospital. I kept screaming in utter anguish about what had just occurred. My pain was unbearable, and I was certain I would die at any second. Andy was doing his best to comfort me but was also aware of how grave my circumstances were.

As the boat neared the beach, Andy calmly spoke to me, "God is here."

Andy and I never had conversations about our faith or religious beliefs. We were coworkers and friends who loved to fish and dive together, and discussions about deeper topics never really came up. As soon as he spoke those words, I felt a sense of overwhelming peace and perspective that I can only explain as the presence of God. I looked up into the clear blue sky above me and realized that this was all part of God's plan.

I have called myself a Christian from the earliest days of my life, but in the past few years leading up to this, I especially grew in my faith through prayer and studying the Bible. I actively pursued a relationship with Jesus to combat the loneliness I often felt and prayed that He would guide my life down a path to honor Him.

As unlikely as it sounds, I knew this was the answer to my prayers. God was going to use this to help me grow in faith and change the lives of others through what I experienced that day. Andy's words were a catalyst that changed this from a tragic death to a survival story. Andy saw the change in my eyes and demeanor when he said that and understood the power of those words. His life has been forever changed ever since.

The boat finally arrived at the beach, and the paramedics lifted me onto a stretcher. Unfortunately, my new sense of hope did not ease any of the pain I felt as they lifted me up. They got me to the ambulance as quickly as possible, and we were off to the hospital. I remember yelling my dad's cell phone number as loud and clear as I could to the people in the ambulance in a desperate attempt for them to contact my family in Denver. Every bump during that ride meant excruciating pain, especially in my right knee, and what was a ten-minute ride felt like hours.

We finally arrived at the hospital. I was hastily wheeled out on a stretcher and rushed through the halls of the emergency room. I remember the optimistic side of me thinking that they would just bandage me up and send me home so I could spend that relaxing evening at home I initially had planned. They were asking for my name, and I confidently gave them my first and last name as I was wheeled into the operating room.

This was the moment of truth. I was about to go under and give up control of my life. My survival was now in the hands of God and the surgeons. I had no idea if I was going to wake up with any limbs or wake up at all. It was a true step into the unknown, but I knew God was in control, and this was the fate He had planned for me since I was born.

As I stared into the bright operating room light above me, everything faded to black.

CHAPTER 4

Eyewitness Account

Leila

Many people witnessed the horror of that fateful day. Olivia saw our son immediately after the accident, when he was brought to shore, and wrote to me shortly thereafter:

> Leila, I have not reached out previously, but I have followed Carter's journey online and read your CaringBridge updates daily. I was at the beach the day of Carter's accident. My family was spending Thanksgiving weekend at our vacation condo. From our beach with all of the police/fire activity/vehicles, we thought it was maybe a cardiac event because, after all, this is Palm Beach with lots of old people and, therefore, lots of cardiac events. Then maybe the thought of a shark bite as we noted the boat was so close to the shoreline and directly over the reef. When I saw Carter, I knew it was a boat strike. The police actually used the table next to me on our private beach to interview Andy and Christine.
>
> I am a mother. I offered to help the two very young children who were on the boat. I offered to

help Andy and Christine and offered them water, food, and towels, to drive them to the hospital or wherever they needed. They refused it all. They were in shock. I could see the tremendous amount of processing on both of their faces. I heard every word they said to the detective who recorded their statements. I was in shock myself from seeing Carter and realizing and saying out loud, "My God, he is conscious and is just a young kid, so he is healthy and strong and has that in his favor."

As he was transferred and carried from the boat to the rig by the first responders, I was flooded with memories of witnessing a tragic accident involving a close friend decades ago when we were in college. I knew firsthand how Andy and Christine were in for a journey of recovering and healing from the emotional impact of Carter's accident. I asked Christine if she needed a hug, and she accepted. We embraced for a good long while. I saw the young fireman run at Olympic speed with Carter's arm in a big yellow bag to his rig and heard the blaring sirens as he took off toward St. Mary's Medical Center in hopes they could save the arm. There was an army of people who did not know Carter, all trying to save Carter. We prayed right there on the beach for him to be okay.

I sent my husband and young daughter to the swimming pool, as my daughter was scared and too young to understand what was happening. She is six.

I feel as though I know you and your family from following along daily. When my daughter was born and during her first year, we, too, spent many nights/weeks at the Chateau de St. Mary, our family nickname for St. Mary's. She, too, logged hours upon hours for years of pediatric physical and occupational therapy at the Chateau de St. Mary as an outpatient.

When you write from a mother's perspective about mourning, grief, and loss over something for your child, I fully understand. We have different stories, but loss, grief, and pain are universal. Also, always remember in the dark moments of pain and loss that so too love is universal, and Carter was surrounded by love and caring in the moments immediately after the accident, and he continues to be loved and prayed for by total strangers.

I pray for your family daily.

—Olivia

* * *

We knew the story. We had heard it from several angles: Andy's, Christine's, and the Florida Fish and Wildlife Conservation Commission's (FWC). However, we had not heard the story from Carter's perspective. Chuck and I expected that with the breathing tube gone and the sedation lifted, we'd be dealing with an anguished, ballistic son because of his current residence and the state of his body. His "awakening" was the moment that we both dreaded and felt completely unprepared for as distressed parents who couldn't handle the current situation all that well themselves. How would we soothe him when we were gravely concerned about what was to come? How could we reassure him about his condition when we had no idea about how he could heal from such severe injuries and, for that matter, survive them? So it was a complete surprise to us that after Carter passed the nurse's what-day-is-it test, his first unsolicited words were "I swam as fast as I could."

It was clear—we knew that *he* knew what had happened. We asked if he wanted to talk about it. He recounted the horrific chain of events with a calm voice, almost as though he were displaced from himself and rewatching the reel from the balcony seats.

At this point, it's hard to know what Carter remembered the first day he told us the story. We didn't push him for details. The account that follows is one filled in by Carter's retelling of the story to officers, lawyers, friends, and siblings, along with the stories from others—and, of course, Andy—all those who were there with him.

Andy and Carter felt lucky as their day off from Loggerhead Marinelife Center landed on a day with ideal snorkeling conditions. The sea was like glass, and a recent storm had stirred up the ocean, which made it a golden opportunity to spot creatures that were normally hard to find.

Andy picked up Carter, and they arrived at Palm Beach around 9:30 a.m. They left their buckets and backpacks on the beach about a quarter mile north of The Breakers Hotel. And like many others, that day kicked off from that point to swim along the reef. Carter followed the expected protocol of towing a dive flag attached to his dive belt. Andy remained within about twenty-five feet of Carter. Andy is an avid photographer who is always looking for the next best picture. He managed to grab an underwater shot of an octopus and other creatures "unearthed" by the recent storm.

Besides snorkeling, Carter likes to free dive. He holds his breath and dives into deeper waters looking for sea life; he then resurfaces to catch air again. They were swimming and diving along the string of buoys that follow the reef to help them navigate their course. Andy frequently looked for Carter's flag to maintain a close distance—ten to fifteen feet—from Carter. The buoys are there so that captains can tie their boats to them. That way, they don't anchor their boats on the fragile reef.

After two hours of snorkeling and free diving along the reef, Carter and Andy were tired and agreed to head northwest, back to where they had left their stuff on the beach. While snorkeling near the surface, they both popped their heads out of the water and commented on how close a boat swung past them. They kept swimming, and again, they popped their heads up out of the water because of the speed and proximity of the boat. It was headed directly toward them and moving in quickly. Andy was about to shout again how close the boat was when he heard a noise and Carter screaming.

Andy swam as fast as he could, battling huge waves from the boat's wake to reach Carter, who was struggling and hollering in agony. Despite the devastating blow, he somehow kept his head above water until Andy got there. He held Carter beneath the arms to keep his head above the surface as the water turned red. That's when he noticed the missing right arm just below the elbow. Andy screamed toward the beach to call 911.

Many on the beach saw the commotion, got out their phones, and dialed the number, while others grabbed photos and videos of the scene. Some were yelling at the boat captain to turn around. It appeared that the boat was going thirty to forty miles an hour when it hit Carter and did not throttle down until it passed the reef area. In the official FWS report, the 36-foot, three-engine boat was going a little over fifty miles per hour!

The captain slowed after the hit, heard Andy and Carter screaming for help, turned around, and headed back toward them. At the same time, Christine, one of several other snorkelers close to the scene, saw what happened and swam over as fast as she could on her paddle board. She attempted to stop the bleeding by tightly holding Carter's arm. That was not working, so while Andy squeezed the arm and continued to hold Carter above the water, she swam back to her paddle board and grabbed the bungee cord used to strap her gear onto her board. A former FWC officer, Christine had just finished a First Aid course and knew how to apply a tourniquet and managed to wrap one around Carter's arm with the cord while staying afloat in the crimson waves.

Around the same time, the boat arrived at the scene, and a passenger reached out his arm toward Andy to pull him and Carter toward the boat. Christine yelled to put the three-motor boat in neutral, and Andy pleaded for them to turn the craft off so he could hoist Carter on to it. Christine hopped into the boat, and with help from the captain and passengers, Andy loaded Carter onto the back of the boat.

Eyewitness Account

Once they laid Carter on the back of the boat, they noticed Carter's legs. There was a gash to the bone in his left shin, and his right kneecap was exposed and shattered. The shaking captain rushed to get his first aid kit on board and attempted to wrap tourniquets around Carter's legs. Andy then climbed into the boat and attempted to calm Carter.

The paramedics ran knee-deep into the water and lifted Carter out of the boat and onto something that looked like a surfboard. They wrapped his entire body with bandages that resembled a big cocoon. They carried him into the ambulance and rushed him to St. Mary's Medical Center.

A video camera on the roof of The Breakers Hotel recorded the rescue. It took eight minutes from when Carter was hit until the ambulance took off from the beach. Within fourteen minutes, the ambulance arrived at St. Mary's, and Carter underwent his first surgery with Dr. Borrego.

Fire trucks, police cars, and stunned sunbathers remained at the scene as the ambulance sped away. Andy crumpled to the sand, crying as he saw Carter's broken dive flag and its rope wrapped around the boat's propeller. His shock was soon interrupted by police interrogators eager to learn the facts. Christine, the boat captain, boat passengers, and beachgoers out for a nice holiday recounted the gruesome scene to the authorities.

A man on a small boat just offshore who witnessed the accident was called a Good Samaritan for finding the remainder of Carter's right arm. It, too, was rushed to the hospital in hopes that it could be reattached.

CHAPTER 5

News

For some moments in life, there are no words.

—David Seltzer, *Willy Wonka and the Chocolate Factory*

Leila

Seeing Carter as soon as possible was not going to be easy. It was Thanksgiving Day, and airlines had limited flights. Most of them left Denver on Friday morning, which put our arrival time at West Palm Beach around 4 p.m. We simply could not wait that long. So, as Chuck searched for flights that left any time on Thursday, I began an attempt to contact people in Florida who might know more details about the accident.

When no one answered the main number at Loggerhead Marinelife Center where Carter worked, I called the turtle hotline. Sea turtle expert Dr. Charlie answered the phone. I broke down as I told him about Carter and asked if he could let his coworkers know.

Thanks to Dr. Charlie, news of the accident circulated quickly. Carter's boss, Tim, was in Tampa for the holiday and called Caitlin, Loggerhead's CFO. When Caitlin saw Tim's call come in she knew something was up. He's not the type to call and chat, especially on a holiday.

Soon, calls began to trickle in from Loggerhead employees. Yesterday, they were strangers, and now they ranked as concerned best friends. Jack Lighton, president and CEO of Loggerhead, told us that he was in contact with the hospital's CEO to make sure Carter was getting the best possible care.

Between calls, I folded laundry and drank lots of water. I paced the floors listening to Chuck confirming and reconfirming our flight plans through Jet Blue—the one airline with a flight out to West Palm Beach Airport at 10:30 p.m. on Thanksgiving. It seemed like an eternity to wait until then since it was only 12:30 in the afternoon, but at least we didn't have to endure a sleepless night at home. It was best to use that time to travel.

When the number of calls from Florida tapered down, it gave us time to let our family know. My first call was to my parents. Dad answered and, after hearing the news, exclaimed with a nervous laugh, "Our family hasn't had something like this happen before."

It was his way of absorbing the shock of the news, and I understood his reaction but wasn't crazy about it, and it didn't make me feel any better—not that anything would. I really wanted to talk to Mom. She called back shortly after, shocked and stunned.

Next, I called my sister Lorilynn. Her crying got me crying; my emotions were beginning to thaw. Chuck called his sister Judy, as he knew Judy and her husband Dean were hosting Thanksgiving dinner for her family, along with their sister, Jan, and mom, Gert.

After Judy took the call from Chuck, she sat at the table and shared the news with the rest of the family. She thought her little grandkids were busy and not listening to her emotional delivery of the details. Later that evening, she heard that her granddaughter was so shaken by Carter's story that she had trouble sleeping.

Mixed in with the blur of making calls and texts, we continued to receive calls from relatives, nurses, officers from law enforcement agencies investigating the crash, and Carter's friends. Although we had never met or talked with Caitlin, we were both immediately impressed with her frequent, detailed voicemails and our conversations with her. After she got the news from Tim, Caitlin appointed herself as our communication pipeline while we were stuck in Denver. From then on, we called her "Caitlin CFO" to help us remember her name.

Caitlin gathered brief bits of information about the accident. She knew Carter was with Andy, a coworker at Loggerhead, and they had gone out snorkeling at the Breakers Reef. That little piece of information brought an odd sense of relief to us: Carter often dives alone. On this day, he was not alone. That's why he was still alive.

Caitlin told us she'd spoken to Andy, who said, "Carter and I were using a dive flag, as required by Florida law, as we snorkeled around the reef. Yet, somehow, a boat propeller hit Carter. As the boat driver turned around and returned to the scene to help, I kept Carter afloat."

After abandoning her holiday plans, Caitlin spent the entire day looking after Carter's affairs. Each call from Caitlin assured us of the love being poured over Carter's hospital room by a growing village of concerned coworkers and friends. Her "CFO hat" kicked into high gear when she took charge of Carter's finances. Soon, she tracked down his bills that would come due while Carter was recovering and other minuscule yet important details that we hadn't considered. She knew of his second job at the aquarium store and his volunteer job as a bass player at Truth Point Church and notified them. There was no worry about Carter's car, as it was at his apartment because Andy drove to the beach that day. Caitlin hoped to find keys to Carter's apartment and his phone, but she was guessing both were in Andy's car, which was still parked near the accident scene.

Before she returned home to her husband and two small children, Caitlin took time to cover Carter in prayer. In height, Carter is just about twice the size of Caitlin, yet for the initial days after the accident, she played a gigantic role in settling his affairs.

Chase and Brittany arrived around 1 p.m. and already knew Carter had been in an accident but didn't know any details. Apparently, Palm Beach had called Chase while searching for the other Charles Viss in Denver. Chase shares the same name—Charles—as his dad, grandpa, and great-grandpa, which often causes confusion. On their way to our house, Brittany started looking for flights, sensing things were not good.

Although St. Mary's promised direct contact with the trauma team caring for Carter, we had little communication with them. We did learn that Carter was out of surgery, unconscious in the ICU with a breathing tube in his trachea, had lost a lot of blood, and was scheduled for a CT scan. All these hospital terms were familiar but only because we'd seen them on TV shows. Now it was our reality.

Minutes stretched into agonizing hours. It was a struggle to know what to do, what to pack, whom to call, what to eat, and when to eat. Chase and Brittany made the delicious homemade ramen, which served as a distraction for all of us. It was a good thing we didn't have turkey that day. It would have never found its way into the oven. Although the ramen smelled divine, my throat was tight, which made it hard to swallow; my taste buds were numb; and my stomach was in a knot that didn't make much room for food.

After dinner, I received a call from Nancy, the mother of Carter's Florida college friend named Joel. Nancy said she was at St. Mary's and had a medical background. In a calm, steady voice, she gave us a report of what she saw.

"Carter has good color with no scratches on his head, chest, or back. He could wiggle his toes on his left foot, but his right toes didn't seem to respond. His left hand was in a cast."

What? We had not heard that his left hand was injured until now. Our hearts sank just a little lower if that's possible.

It was.

Under a starless black sky, we drove to Denver International Airport (DIA). Few words were exchanged on the 45-minute ride. Chase and Brittany hugged us goodbye. Instead of feeling anticipation for the trip ahead, there was an ominous sense of dread. I've often wondered why people can look so sad in an airport. Why don't they look a little happier? Life can't be *that* bad!

Now I know. Life *can* be that bad.

Our flight was on time, we boarded, and when the plane took off and the lights were dimmed, sleep did not come. Chuck and I sobbed in each other's arms, our bodies physically absorbing the news and fearing what was to come. The dark cabin and the white noise hid our tears and our words from those close by. We both wondered if it would be easier if Carter would die rather than live with his injuries. There was still a chance that his legs could not be saved. How could he live with only one limb, which was almost severed, too?

After the three-hour flight to Boston, we pulled our carry-ons through the empty airport gate and cried off and on as we anticipated what awaited us in Florida. It didn't help that our hopes for securing a cup of coffee were dashed—Starbucks wasn't open at 4 a.m. As we paced the floors with water bottles and waited to board our flight to Palm Beach International Airport, Chuck declared that he had made a deal with God: "If Carter is to live, then You have to let Carter be happy."

When we arrived in Florida, we were met at the passenger pickup area by Jack, CEO of Loggerhead, who had talked to us the day before over the phone. He volunteered to pick us up from the airport and bring us to the hospital, yet he was concerned about the room in his small car. In one of our calls, I assured Jack that we were pretty fit and trim and could squeeze in. Turns out that he wasn't kidding. His two-door Mercedes was tiny but delivered us safely and quickly to St.

Mary's Medical Center. We walked through the sliding doors of the main entrance, stood in a daze as they took our pictures for the guest visitor stickers, and braced ourselves for what awaited us just down the hall.

CHAPTER 6

A Simple Prayer

Chuck

After hearing the news about Carter, we knew we had to get to West Palm Beach as soon as possible. I found some flights and then started packing. What do I take? For sure, just a carry-on, as we'll be back soon. And I may as well take my backpack and work laptop, as I'll have time for work. So we have dinner, jump in the car, and Chase and Brittany drive us to DIA that evening.

Even though we were in total shock, we still navigated DIA just fine, including security lines, trains, concourses, and gates. Not without outbursts, however. Sometimes we were stopped still in our tracks, crumpled to the floor, and cried and moaned and gnashed our teeth. I don't know what it was, but I know I've never done it before. And it was ugly. There were sounds I never heard before, stuff coming out of me randomly. Along with that, I had to blow my nose constantly and dry my eyes, too.

The ugliness continued on the first plane ride to Logan Airport in Boston, Massachusetts. Leila and I were in a row together with one other woman. I'm sure she thought, *I know these two have just been through something horrendous, and I hope they survive,* but nothing was said to us. I often wonder if I was in her position, would I have said something to us? I think I wouldn't have at that time, prior to what we went through. Now, I definitely would.

Two strong thoughts remain with me about that plane ride. First, there were the words from "Is He Worthy?" by Andrew Peterson and Ben Shive, a song our church choir planned to sing that Sunday.

Second, I prayed . . . a very simple prayer. It was not "Lord, please be with the surgeons as they put my son back together" or "Please keep Carter pain-free during this most difficult time" or "Bless all the hospital staff as they strive to keep Carter alive." Nope. Mine was, "God, take him if he can't live a happy life." This, after fifty-six years of being a Christian. All this through the ugly bouts of teeth-gnashing, moaning, and crying (or whatever it was). What kind of father prays that for his son?

After landing in Boston at 3 a.m., the first thing we wanted to do was call the ER at St. Mary's to see if Carter was alive. So we called the trauma center representative, and they were not there, which we figured, but you never know. Then we called the ER directly, spoke with a nurse, told them who we were, and they confirmed that Carter was still alive.

CHAPTER 7

Communities

You're only as happy as your unhappiest child.

—Unknown

Leila

Chuck and I were consumed with Carter's condition the second we got the call from the Palm Beach Police Department. Everything else fell to the side. We gave our sons and daughter-in-law big hugs and left them to fend for themselves. Our bandwidth was at capacity, and they'd have to figure out what to do back home while we looked after Carter. As far as we could tell, the scope of his needs was daunting.

Chase and Brittany slept at their apartment after they dropped us off at the airport. Levi decided to stick with his initial plans and go Black Friday shopping with his friends on Thursday evening to distract himself from reality.

The next morning, they found themselves back at our house. According to reports, their meal plan included freshly baked Pillsbury cinnamon rolls, Goldfish crackers, and leftover muffins. Eating and cooking became less of a priority as the day went on and reality soaked in.

While Chase's grief kept him silent for most of the day, Brittany and Levi decided to set up a CaringBridge site to streamline updates on Carter's condition. Our immediate family and also a growing number of people were interested in Carter's well-being, and this seemed the best line of communication to keep them informed.

After posting the news of Carter's accident on their social media accounts, the kids were inundated with friends asking about what they could do and give. That's when Brittany and Levi decided to set up a GoFundMe account as well. The number of site visits, the supportive comments, and the financial support at both the CaringBridge and the GoFundMe accounts were astounding and virtually hugged our shaken family.

It seems appropriate to pause a moment and give thanks for the steadfast communities that surrounded us, especially our kids, while we looked after our "unhappiest child." I'm not sure where this chapter's opening quote originated. I never forgot it because it's one Chuck and I recounted repeatedly as we parented our boys.

All three attended Denver Christian (DC) from preschool through high school. It's a private Christian school with a Calvinist heritage. Chuck and I were loyal supporters due in part to a lineage of Christian education imprinted on us by our parents. With almost twenty years of driving back and forth to the DC campus, we weren't just supporters; we were friends and are still close friends with many of the faculty members and the student families to this day. In fact, Brittany, our daughter-in-law, teaches there now. The faculty educated, nurtured, coached, and trained all three boys "in the way they should go."

I think it was just as hard for many of our DC friends to absorb the news of Carter's accident as it was for our family. Hope Fellowship, where Chase and Brittany attend, immediately reached out with love and support. Many of their members also have close ties to DC and have known our family for decades. Hope Fellowship is where Chase, Brittany, and I had just played with the worship band on Thanksgiving. Remember my "mama high"?

Then there's the South Sub Church community. I've been their full-time pianist and organist since dear Marilynn handed the position to me when Levi was in kindergarten. For decades, I've sat on the piano bench at choir rehearsals and listened to the prayer concerns of the faithful choir members. They call themselves the biggest small group of the church. It seems each choir member carries a personal story woven with threads of grief—I could fill pages recounting the tragedies, illnesses, and deaths these saints and their families have endured. Yet they continue to be faithful servants and a cloud of witnesses.

Up until now, it appears that our family was immune to any major life disruptions. Things were headed in the expected direction for us. So when things went south on Thanksgiving Day, the choir and the entire congregation of about five hundred members were shocked and heartbroken by the severity of our news. Many congregants have had plenty of practice being pillars of strength when times get tough, and they immediately stepped in with love, prayers, and significant financial help. Our new Floridian friend Ed remarked early on that Chuck and I must have deep roots in Colorado. No one had ever used the phrase "deep roots" to describe what we had taken for granted. Our family tree had sustained a major blow, and now Ed reminded us that our roots remained intact, planted deep in a loving soil.

Meals, gift cards, texts, food, GoFundMe donations, phone calls, visits, and bonus airline miles poured in. Choir director, worship director, and good friend Drew, who could write a playbook on grief, told me that the church would hold my job for me and promised to wait patiently for my return. Our treasured communities wrapped our family in love while Chuck and I rushed to the side of our Florida son.

CHAPTER 8

Entrance

I literally felt as if I was licking the floor of hell.
—Lysa TerKeurst, Facebook, Nov. 9, 2018

Leila

There's no instruction manual for entering your son's ICU room. Before entering the hospital halls, we had to hand over our driver's licenses, pose for a picture, and wait for a sticker to enter Carter's new home. Little did we know that we would need a new sticker every day for the next sixty-eight days. My hands were shaking as I attached mine to my black sweatshirt, one of the few items of clothing I brought with me for our stay.

Chuck and I held each other tight as we processed past the tear-stained and concerned faces of our soon-to-be Florida "first responder" friends who hovered over Carter in our absence. The Florida Fish and Wildlife Conservation Commission officer on duty was eager to get to the bottom of the accident and stood in the waiting room area. Her eyes caught ours. She approached us and requested a chat.

"Not now," Chuck told her as we walked by.

The nurses gently told us to remain calm when we entered room 403, or we would be removed. Hysteria is not allowed in the ICU. As we walked toward his bed, I remember my knees buckling as I moaned from somewhere deep inside. They just about kicked me out, but I stood straight and held on tightly to Chuck.

Together, we studied Carter. He was massive. I thought it was because he's a tall, muscular guy. He looked too big for this bed on wheels, which was true, but we learned that his size also stemmed from his body being swollen from the trauma.

Long "door handles" called external fixators were screwed into his left leg to align and hold the bones together. A tube stuffed down his throat deep into his chest was secured with tape across his lips and face. A black brace strapped around his right knee and thigh locked them in place. Plastic that looked like packing tape clung to his right shin and was connected to what we would later learn to be a wound vac (which stands for a "vacuum-assisted closure" device).

Carter's right arm was missing its wrist, beautiful long fingers, and large nail beds. Blood seeped through the bandages where the arm was severed. His left hand was wrapped in ice and bandages like a boxing glove. Dried blood caked beneath his toenails and gathered around the cuticles.

At this moment, every part of what was wrong with Carter blurred our vision of what was right with him. His beautiful face remained untouched; his large chest, though covered with wires and tape, looked strong and muscular.

The body of our Carter was changed forever.

Entrance

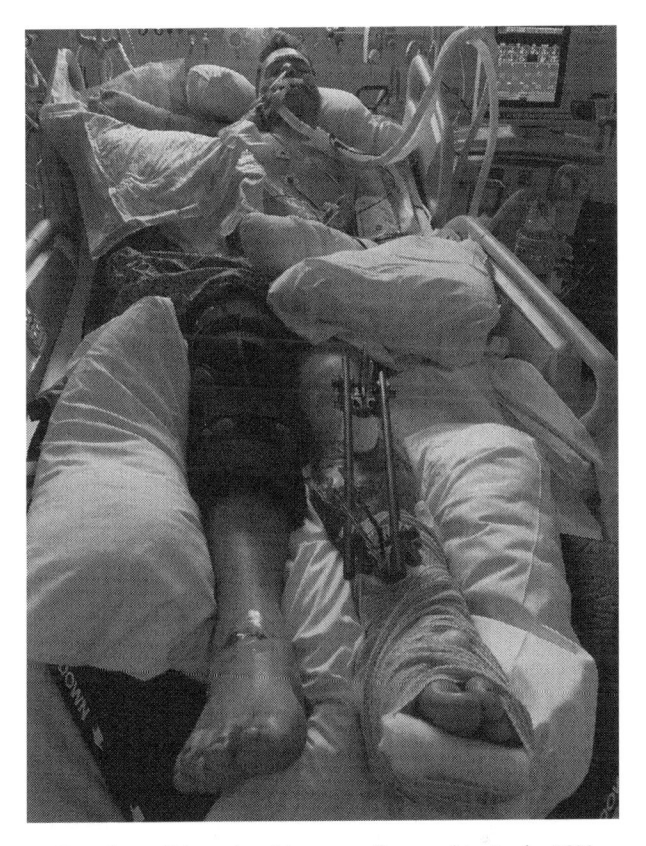

Carter's condition when his parents first saw him in the ICU
(Photo Credit: Viss Family)

Chuck and I exchanged blank stares and no words as we were ushered out. It became clear that as long as Carter was sedated, we'd have the luxury of being as weak as we needed to be. We knew that we'd need to be strong for him when he was slowly taken off the sedation. Neither of us knew how that was going to happen. Outside his room, we collapsed in each other's arms in stunned silence.

CHAPTER 9

Backstory

There are times that we must sink to the bottom of our misery to understand truth, just as we must descend to the bottom of the well to see the stars in broad daylight.

—Vaclav Havel, *The Power of the Powerless*

Leila

It came as no surprise that Carter received a degree in marine biology. A lifelong passion for sea life landed him a job at Loggerhead Marinelife Center right out of college. His fascination with the ocean didn't come immediately, though. At first, our little Carter could not get enough matchbox-sized metal airplanes, which piled up in a huge plastic bin. He'd choose one from his stash, lie on his back, and make zooming noises as his arms whizzed airplane after airplane back and forth across the clear blue sky in his tiny stratosphere.

Maybe it was my attempts to make him a Blue Angel airplane Halloween costume out of boxes and foam paper that tamed his passion for airplanes. I thought he looked adorable in it, but he didn't agree. I guess the costume with a wingspan as wide as he was tall was a bit cumbersome when trick-or-treating. Or maybe time swayed Carter's attention away from airplanes to animals. This may have been partly due to another collection that he, along with his brothers, amassed thanks to a worldwide obsession: Beanie Babies. Unlike many who didn't dare to remove the tag, fearing the plush toys might lose their value, our boys immediately ripped them off after reading the clever name given each one by the manufacturers.

The playtime that Carter and his brothers engineered with their furry friends—mostly a wide selection of reptiles, amphibians, and marine life—was nothing short of spectacular. When Chuck and I would leave the boys with a babysitter for a well-deserved night out, it was not uncommon to come home to twenty, maybe thirty, miniature creatures suspended from the staircase with jump ropes and other paraphernalia. The "hive" would remain in place for days and eventually begin to "crumble." That's when I'd put my foot down and order a demolition.

During summer breaks between elementary school years, the Nelson boys—friends from school in the same grades as Carter and Levi—would come over to walk our neighborhood greenbelt and collect grasshoppers with our boys. Armed with nets and Ziploc bags to hold their catch, the search continued for hours until their moms, happy to have the time to chat while the grasshoppers entertained the kids, finally called off the hunt to eat dinner.

The green bugs lucky enough to survive their trip back home in plastic bag cages were then "trained" by the boys to slide down our swing set slide and perform other amazing "tricks." (I'm hoping that animal rights activists won't be too upset.) Plenty of grasshoppers populated the greenbelt even after the boys' successful poaching season. As moms of rambunctious and curious sons, my friend Donna and I couldn't resist the hours of cheap entertainment and imagination the innocent prey provided.

All the boys were proud of their pets who came and went (okay, *died*) during their grade school days. Critters included an anole lizard, a tree frog, two salamanders named Amanda and Kimmer, goldfish and Koi in the pond out back, a praying mantis (we even watched one lay eggs), a freshwater eel named Lance, garter snakes captured from the backyard, and even a tarantula named Rosie. In fact, we had two tarantulas named Rosie, as the first one died soon after it came to live with us. Chuck faithfully purchased frozen pinkies, baby mice the size of a pinky, for Rosie to eat. We watched Rosie molt and eat its exoskeleton. I confess those weren't my favorite days.

A number of fish tanks took residence at our home. In high school, Carter browsed Craigslist and found a 75-gallon saltwater tank that came with a number of good-sized healthy tropical fish. Since he wasn't into sports, he had plenty of time on his hands to care for a saltwater tank after school, so Chuck and I agreed on the purchase and placed the tank in the basement. Carter took an earnest interest in the aquarium but was unprepared for the sensitive nature of saltwater fish. Soon, all of the fish found their way into the sewer system.

With the empty tank in the basement waiting to be filled with sea life, Carter resolved to level up his dedication to it.

Instead of purchasing more fish, Carter invested in a stingray about twelve inches long and named him Chad.

Chad thrived under Carter's care. When Carter was assigned to make a high-school senior synthesis project that showcased a reflection of his past four years of high school, Chad was the star of the show. Carter channeled his other passion and composed four piano pieces, one for each year of high school. He recorded himself playing each piece and then added the soundtrack to a video of his left hand feeding Chad in the tank.

Because Carter didn't belong to sports teams in high school and Denver Christian was a relatively small school, he had a limited circle of friends. In high school, Carter found a place to hang in the South Sub Church youth group, where he began to play and jam on the bass guitar.

With his mind set on a marine biology degree, it only took one visit to Palm Beach Atlantic University his junior year to determine that it was the place for him. The summer before he attended PBA, Carter spiraled into an all-time low. Throughout his short life, he had a tendency to look at life as a "glass half empty" versus a "glass half full." Plus, it's a rough place to be when high school is finished, college hasn't begun, and there's the itch to leave home, yet the summer drags on.

Not unlike many other parents at this time of life, Chuck and I were concerned about sending our young son across the country all alone. He seemed emotionally unsettled and was arriving at the campus with no friends. But we did it.

While soaking a number of shirts with sweat, we moved Carter into the PBA dorms in mid-August, said our good-byes, and trusted that God and the love of His people would surround and support him. Roommate Joel and later, Ben morphed into friends for life. Ben left to join the army, but Joel and Carter stayed in the same area after they graduated. They hung out, played tennis, watched Nicholas Cage movies, and even attended events with Joel's mom, Nancy. Nancy took pleasure in playing the role of Carter's Florida mom.

After graduation and gaining full-time employment at Loggerhead, and from what Carter shared during bimonthly phone conversations, Chuck and I sensed that he had grown into a young adult who was finding his way and handling life as it came. We respected his tenacity to live alone and make it work financially. He lived frugally and had taken on an extra job at a local aquarium store on his day off from Loggerhead. We just weren't sure about whom he considered his close friends and what, if any, community surrounded him in Florida.

From the calls and texts we received on the day of the accident, we recognized that Carter indeed had a "village" in his new home state. His laid-back demeanor and his daily word limit just didn't let on to how wide his circle was and how much the "villagers" adored him at both Loggerhead and Truth Point Church.

Our worst nightmare had come true. And yet, amid complete darkness, a glimmer of light leaked through the cracks of loss when we witnessed firsthand the dedication of Carter's community. Apparently, that topic was commonly bypassed in our regular bimonthly conversations with him.

We were beyond relieved when we heard from Katie—whom we identified as "Katie Redhead Loggerhead" on our phones to keep track of all the variations of Caitlins, Kates, and Kathys in the "village"—that both she and Joel stayed the night at St. Mary's to be by Carter's side. We marveled at the fact that two twenty-something-year-olds gave up their beds at home and traded them for vinyl couches in an ice-cold waiting room.

As we flew the red-eye headed south, Chuck and I assumed that beyond the trauma doctors and nurses, no one was there to cover the night watch in our absence. The gift that Joel and "Katie Redhead" gave us that evening, along with all the other first responders who gathered around Carter's ICU bed on Thanksgiving Day, was a ray of light in our newfound darkness.

CHAPTER 10

ICU

The pain I feel now is the happiness I had before. That's the deal.
—C.S. Lewis, *A Grief Observed*

Leila

Carter's friend Joel and his mom, Nancy, were eating Thanksgiving dinner when he received a text from Levi: *Carter was in an accident.* Joel was in Tampa enjoying the holiday weekend with family. He immediately jumped in his car and began the four-hour drive to West Palm Beach. Nancy left the turkey dinner dishes in the sink, borrowed her mom's car (because hers was in the shop), and left soon after Joel. On the drive there, Joel relayed updates on Carter to Nancy as he received them from friends at Carter's bedside at St. Mary's.

Despite the fact that Carter's handsome face and broad torso remained untouched, Chuck and I were shocked and then turned numbed by the dismal condition of each limb. The overwhelmingly foreign hospital jargon, doctors and nurses in color-coded scrubs, and various blips and bleeps kept our heads spinning.

Both Joel and Nancy were at the hospital before we arrived, which gave Nancy a chance to assess the situation through the lens of her medical background. She greeted us at Carter's bed with understanding "mom" eyes, an encouraging smile, and warm hugs. She buffered information from the medical staff and the noisy machines hooked to Carter.

In a soothing tone, Nancy coaxed us to look for and find the positives in Carter's condition. It's only because I posted Nancy's observations and the updates on CaringBridge that I can recount Carter's status from hour to hour in those ICU days. Logging the details each evening helped me process the situation. It gave structure to a day where minutes and hours melted into one chaotic blob. There was no beginning and no end.

The first ICU days played out like an endless slideshow in which my brain reluctantly shifted gears: a stoic receiver of information from the doctors, a concerned bystander watching over the shoulder of the nurses, a hostess for the revolving door of visitors, a frightened mother pretending to be strong when comforting an injured son, a wife of a husband who shared an identical grief, and a sobbing mom. Certain images, memories, and observations stuck firmly in my mental photo album of those first days in the ICU.

Nancy thought it was providential that Carter's room was number 403. It served as a reminder that the Father, Son, and Holy Spirit watched over Carter.

Because his feet were so swollen, the caregivers regularly used ultrasound to listen for a pulse in each foot, and even in the first days, we always heard a pulse in both. That meant his legs were in pretty good shape and could be saved.

ICU

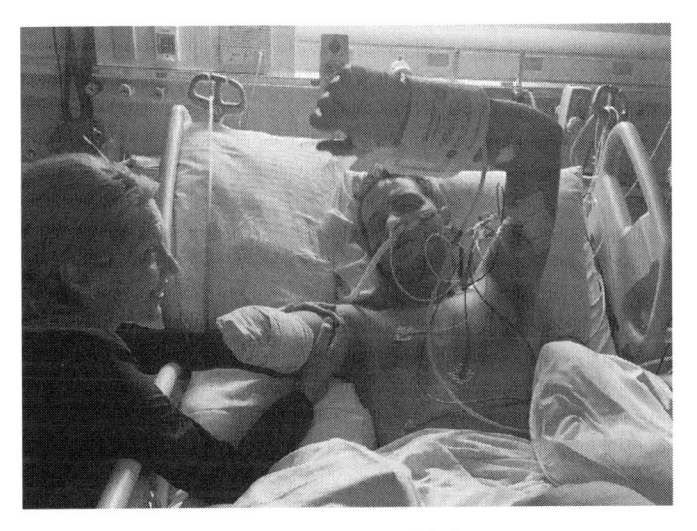

Leila trying to interpret Carter's hallucinations
(Photo Credit: Viss Family)

Two surgeries were dedicated solely to thoroughly washing each wound to keep out nasty infections that could be brought on by warm seawater.

Although we wanted to see Carter's eyes and smile, we cringed when he moved and tried to fight off the breathing tube. It wouldn't serve him well to feel his level-ten pain and the suffocating contraption down his throat. It was important for his body to stay calm and sedated to begin the healing process.

Carter's right arm (I still can't bring myself to say stump) seeped blood and fluids through the bandages. I would stare at it when Carter slept and wonder how he could play piano again. How could he play bass guitar and bait his own hook and cook his favorite Mediterranean meal like he did BA (before accident)? These were passions that identified Carter as *Carter*.

As I studied Carter's face and noticed his dry, cracked lips wrapped around the breathing tube, I thought about what that nasty mouthpiece might do to his teeth. Carter had worn braces, which now served his smile well. With the dire condition of his limbs, it was important to me that his smile and lovely teeth be preserved. I was pleased to see the nurses come in daily to brush his teeth, carefully working their way around the breathing tube to get to every molar. They brushed his teeth to eliminate potentially dangerous bacteria in his mouth, not just to keep up his good hygiene habits. While I was concerned about his teeth, the hospital staff were focused on something much more important now—staving off infection.

While sitting in an oversized, seventy-pound, '70s-style chair that hardly budged and squealed horribly when shoved closer to the bed, both Chuck and I peered out of the glass walls of ICU room 403 into the nurse's station and other ICU rooms and watched in awe. We were privy to the nurses' superhuman responsibilities and saintly tasks. They exemplified doctor-level medical understanding as they wheeled their computer station from room to room to record vital signs and distribute meds. They dutifully submitted to doctors' orders while exhibiting tremendous patience for their patients. They monitored temperatures and blood pressure and then emptied the trash on the way out the door. They lifted and turned frail and uncooperative bodies and tolerated bodily fluids and excretions that most others would cringe at.

ICU

Despite being on a ventilator, Carter still communicated with us—through his eyes, head nods, and facial expressions. Every day, the nurses would raise their voices to cut through Carter's sedation and ask a few questions to check for brain function:

> *What is your name?*
>
> *What year is it right now?*
>
> *What day is it today?*
>
> *How many fingers am I holding up?*
>
> *What did the doctor just tell you?*
>
> *Can you move your toes?*

Somehow, Carter passed each "question test" with correct answers. Quite often, Chuck and I would have to guess what Carter was trying to say, which led to much frustration on his part as we weren't interpreting correctly and quickly enough.

He complained about his mouth being dry. After our pleading, the nurses extended a bit of mercy and brought him a plastic cup of crushed ice. They instructed us to occasionally give him small pieces. He was not to have fluids because they were not sure if he could swallow, and he might aspirate on them.

Every time we walked away from Carter's ICU bed, we felt a tinge of guilt. That guilt quickly faded as we nursed our mental status with short breaks to decompress. Away from room 403 was decent (but not great) hot coffee, pretty good omelets, and downright tasty tuna melts from the hospital coffee shop. We sat in an atrium that we soon named Jurassic Park because of the large statues of dinosaurs and prehistoric creatures meant to entertain kids. We laughed and cried with our newly made Florida friends beside towering dinosaurs and in waiting rooms with other families concerned about a loved one. We found empty hallways and sat on the tile floors to cry with friends and relatives over the phone. We felt the 70-degree morning air and the tinge of heat from the sun as we walked across the hospital campus.

While we navigated the corridors and walkways on the sprawling hospital grounds, both Chuck and I were lost in a maze of emotions and the ICU fog. We managed to maintain a partnership. This partnership came with an innate sense to toggle emotional breakdowns. While one fell apart, the other kept it together. The roles were interchangeable. And they changed like the South Florida breeze.

CHAPTER 11

First Responders

*Lots of people want to ride with you in the limo,
but what you want is someone who will take the bus
with you when the limo breaks down.*

—Oprah Winfrey

Leila

When someone is in distress, it's natural to react. Some stand by and ask, "What can I do for you?" or "Let me know what I can do for you." Others don't ask or wait for an answer; they just *do*. That qualifies a person as a "first responder," and many showed up immediately after Carter's accident.

The critical first responders in this story are Andy, Christine, and others who reacted to Carter's needs in the water, on the beach, in the ambulance, in the operating room . . . and beyond. There are also other types of first responders—those who showed up in our time of need as distraught parents.

One of the very first responders who unknowingly signed up for the job was Aussie piano teacher friend Samantha—her friends call her Sam. We bonded during a 2019 business trip to London and have stayed in touch ever since. She called via

Facebook Messenger on Thanksgiving Day for a casual chat. I thought twice about answering. Did I really want to burden her with our gruesome story that is still hard to tell others who haven't heard about it?

With some reservations, I did answer her call. Somehow, Sam handled the blow of the news, remained calm, and listened. Perhaps because she's a mom and also because she's been steeped in *hesed* from her Jewish heritage. Hesed is the Hebrew word for the simple act of just showing up, being there for others exactly as they are, and lovingly responding to their needs the best they can.[1]

Perhaps it was just a little easier for Sam to chat because my hysterics were frozen, numbed by shock. I credit Sam for her bravery in entering my dark space willingly. Because she knew of our family's turmoil from day one, she became an instrumental sounding board (all puns intended) while I wallowed in grief and self-pity. As our family carried on with the situation, Sam patiently tolerated my tears, emptiness, cursing, and insecurities. Grief messes with your head and shatters realities, and she witnessed it all.

Kate and Katie, on staff at Loggerhead Marinelife Center, were among the first to hear about the accident and rush to the hospital. Both are coworkers and close friends of Carter and Andy. All four are not native to Florida, so over the years, they bonded as they hunkered down during hurricanes and shared "Friendsgiving" meals. Remember that Katie stayed the night with Carter while we flew from Denver to Boston to Palm Beach. Kate was there most of the Thanksgiving Day, and both greeted us when we arrived at St. Mary's Hospital.

Once these gals heard that Chuck and I liked Starbucks, coffee and pastries were delivered regularly. That's until "Gift-Shop Kate"—as I've tagged her in my phone as she is the manager of Loggerhead's gift shop—gave us a Keurig and travel mugs. We found her unexpected gifts worth their weight in gold as we could carry a fresh cup of coffee on our walk to Carter's room early in the morning.

After word got out, the staff and congregation members of Truth Point Church began circling around Carter's bed. "Florida mom" Nancy recalls that a large group of Loggerhead and Truth Point friends stood and prayed over Carter that first night in the ICU.

We discovered through the family grapevine that Chuck's cousin's daughter and son-in-law work at St. Mary's. The son-in-law is an operating room tech who assisted in some of Carter's surgeries, including the first one. Although he unknowingly became a first responder, Chuck and I appreciated hearing this news of a family connection. Florida seemed foreign to us when we first arrived. It made the world seem just a little smaller. There was comfort in that.

J.R. and Laura are what might be called "eternal" friends. Laura and I lived in the same dorm wing during our freshman year of college. We attended their wedding soon after ours some thirty years ago. Laura remembers our early discussions about how many kids we would have and what we would name them. We mourned the loss of their triplets at twenty-three weeks and rejoiced in the birth of their twin girls, Lyndsay and Lauren, who were born weeks before our oldest son, Chase. Their track record with homes is commendable.

They moved at least a dozen times around the country while we've remained at our same address since I was pregnant with Carter. Despite the distance and direction of our lives, we've always remained in contact with them.

For three years, they took up residence in Delray Beach, not far from where Carter attended Palm Beach Atlantic University. This crowned Laura as Carter's first Florida mom. That's why Nancy (another first responder) is considered his second Florida mom, as she came down the pike a short time later in his PBA life. Carter would eagerly take the train to their home on Sunday afternoons for Laura's cooking. Both of their girls were living in Michigan, so during J.R. and Laura's three-year stay in Florida, Carter became theirs. Carter fished off their dock on the Intracoastal Waterway, caught interesting sea creatures, and requested his favorite meals. J.R. and Laura observed firsthand how Carter was growing into a fine young man and enjoyed telling us about it.

Sharing the news about Carter with Laura widened the crack in my heart. Although she now lives in Michigan, she's always treasured the time with Carter in Florida and reserves a special place for him in her heart.

A couple of days after Laura heard the news, she sent one of her Florida friends over to the hospital with a gourmet picnic basket lunch. We sat on the metal tables in St. Mary's version of Jurassic Park and devoured it. The thought and sustenance of the submarine sandwiches known as "Pub Subs" in West Palm Beach were greatly appreciated, even if our pain dulled their flavor.

After trying to keep it together and then crumpling and crying in chorus with Laura over the phone, I attempted to collect myself about twenty minutes later and returned to Carter's room. I arrived to find a first responder who appeared like an angel in our midst: Kathy from Truth Point Church, wearing a pink baseball cap, was standing over Carter's bed praying and playing quiet music on her smartphone. It happened to be "So Will I," a tune that Carter plays with the band at Truth Point and one that I had just helped a piano student arrange as a piano solo.

It startled me to hear music. I had avoided my Spotify playlist, as the power of music triggered emotions that I couldn't spare. But, in that moment, music seemed to pierce the darkness.

Kathy is a nursing professor at PBA, a past chaplain, and a two-time cancer survivor. Her track record has equipped her with impeccable tools as a first responder. Carter was due for surgery, so before Kathy left, she led us in prayer around Carter's bed as we held hands with most of the surgical team.

A day or two later, Kathy returned and sat with me in the waiting room and gave me a white shell bracelet that someone had given her when she was fighting her battles with cancer. It was a gift to remind me that Carter and our family are in the hands of God and His praying people. I wear it every day.

In the midst of our tragedy, Chuck and I were trapped in our frenzied private world of grief. Our son was in the hospital, and we had a responsibility to "fix" what had been broken. We had little time or capacity to think about how this shattering news might impact our parents and our siblings.

That's why a call late on Thanksgiving Day afternoon from my sister Lorilynn and her husband, Ivan, took us by surprise. They told us they had just booked airline tickets to join us in Florida.

We knew the sacrifice they were making. Lorilynn, in particular, was on overload at work and had recently been called to serve on a grand jury, where she was required to report and show up for three days every month for the next twenty-one months. Chuck and I were shocked that they would drop everything to be with us. Little did we know how much their warm hearts, soft shoulders, listening ears, and open arms would mean to us during the first critical days of Carter's fight for life.

Lorilynn and Ivan flew from Raleigh, North Carolina, and arrived at St. Mary's around noon. After long hugs and tears in the ICU waiting room area, Chuck prepared them with a rundown—more like a warning—of Carter's condition.

We all quickly learned the required routine to enter the ICU room. We pushed the button on an intercom to request entry. Each of us held our hands under the hand sanitizer dispenser, and while rubbing the liquid all over our hands, we waited for one of the nurses inside to respond. The massive steel doors swung open once they heard us state who we wanted to visit and viewed us in their camera to verify our ID stickers.

When Lorilynn and Ivan approached his bed, it was almost like seeing Carter for the first time after the accident. They saw for themselves the extent of his wounds. Their initial visit was cut short because soon after they arrived, a team of caregivers wheeled Carter into surgery to clean his wounds and apply fresh dressings.

Beyond the flight, Chuck and I had no plans for our trip to Florida. Lodging and transportation were up in the air. We figured we'd sleep at a hotel or Carter's one-bedroom condo.

While Carter was in surgery, a hospital employee who also attends Truth Point Church reached out to us. With her help, Chuck secured a room for us at the Quantum House on the St. Mary's campus, about a ten-minute walk from the hospital. Something like a Ronald McDonald House, the Quantum House provides an affordable home away from home for families who have children who require major surgery at St. Mary's. Many receive treatment at the Paley Institute, which specializes in orthopedic care. This cozy, home-like motel was intended for families with small children.

Although our son was twenty-five, he needed caregivers there who could advocate for him. The Quantum House opened its doors to us for weeks. Their fine choice of mattresses, pillows, and other comforts of home took the edge off our crisis. We had the option of reserving a room at the Singer Island Marriott with a generously discounted rate offered by a friend of Jack, the CEO of Loggerhead. Chuck was convinced that we needed to be close to the hospital at all times and that we should stay at the Quantum House. I agreed. As there was no room for Lorilynn and Ivan to sleep at the Quantum House, they took up our offer to secure a room for them at the Marriott.

While Carter was in surgery, Chuck stayed at the hospital. Lorilynn, Ivan, and I drove to the hotel to check in. The

Marriott was in party mode when we arrived at their swanky entrance. Guests with drinks and families with small children crowded the lobby, awaiting Santa's arrival.

Just when we had woven our way through the maze of people to the front desk, Santa appeared. The music blared, and the crowd went wild. It was hard to hear the hotel receptionist above the cheers as she handed us the room keys.

To make up for our lack of substantial meals on Friday, Lorilynn and Ivan found a breakfast place on Saturday morning called Sarah's Kitchen that offered takeout. Florida mom Nancy joined us as we ate fluffy French toast and hefty omelets in the dining room area of the Quantum House amidst families with bubbly kids, some in wheelchairs with casts or braces.

Our Southern-style breakfast was interrupted by a call from Loggerhead board member Ed, a first responder, and the boat captain who took us to the accident area. He patched his lawyer friend into our phone call, and we discussed and confirmed a time to meet with him and his partner in their office on Monday.

It baffles me that these memories of first responders and images beyond the hospital doors are more vividly etched in my mind than the first days in the ICU. Why would that be? A defense mechanism? Was it because we had escaped the time warp of the hospital scene and hoped to return to the normal world? Yet this normal wasn't normal! We were hanging with Lorilynn and Ivan in an unfamiliar town during one of the worst times in our lives. Usually, we're with them at a destination of choice, and it's one of the best times in our lives.

First Responders

As much as we were desperate for a respite from the hospital, there was no relief, only ambiguity. To leave the hospital meant we left Carter and his care in the hands of capable yet complete strangers. To step beyond the hospital grounds meant we entered a surreal and foreign land. Despite relying on the love and care of first responders, we found no normal on either side of the walls of St. Mary's.

CHAPTER 12

Ventilator

If you are bitten by a shark, here's the doctor you'll want to see.
—Jorge Milian, *The Palm Beach Post*, April 9, 2015

Leila

Among the many first responders who determined Carter's fate was a world-renowned doctor named Robert Borrego. He is head of trauma at St. Mary's Medical Center and was on duty even though it was a holiday when the paramedics rushed Carter into the emergency room.

When reporter and friend Joe Capozzi interviewed Dr. Borrego for a story in *The Palm Beach Post*, he remembers teasing the doctor with, "Why isn't the head of the trauma unit at home on Thanksgiving Day with his family?"

And Dr. Borrego said, "I try to be the one on duty on holidays so the surgeons under me can be with their families."

Joe thought this said a lot about Dr. B's character.

We agree.

While taking a break from the ICU, we bumped into Dr. Borrego in the waiting room. We assumed he considered Carter a "John Doe" before the operation began. Dr. B was quick to correct us.

"No!" he said. "I asked Carter his name while he was lying on the operating table, and despite his loss of blood and severe injuries, he managed to say: 'Carter Viss!'"

In our unexpected run-in with Dr. Borrego, we learned that he snorkels with his son and daughter. He even googled Carter after the surgery to learn more about him. After we met Dr. Borrego, we did the same and discovered that just like Carter, Dr. Borrego is a fan of sharks and is known as the "shark doctor." The headline from an online article in *The Palm Beach Post* a few years earlier summed up Dr. Borrego: "If you are bitten by a shark, here's the doctor you'll want to see."[1]

At age nine, Dr. Borrego immigrated with his family from Cuba to the States in 1965. He took a break from his long tenure at St. Mary's and spent four months as a combat surgeon in Iraq. He operated in a tent near neighborhoods recently bombed and then secured by US forces.

Back at St. Mary's, the doctor encounters patients with shark bites. He combines his surgical skill to repair the tissue damage with research to help fight the life-threatening infection that stems from the filthy shark teeth. Instead of a broad-spectrum antibiotic, Dr. Borrego and fellow researchers narrowed down the antibiotics to treat specific shark bites from black tip, spinner, and bull sharks so that patients heal more rapidly.

From the first phone call we received from Dr. Borrego while in Colorado, we knew he was concerned about saving Carter's legs. After Friday's surgery, which was dedicated to thoroughly washing Carter's wounds, the surgeon was pleased with the health of the tissue on both legs. With this, the trauma team determined they could move forward with more reparative surgeries the following week.

Their news was good, but things remained complicated by the issues with the ventilator. Carter was intubated before his first surgery to assist his breathing while under anesthesia. The ventilator remained in place after surgery out of precaution. The doctors determined that the severity of his injuries would keep his lungs from providing enough oxygen to his body without assistance. And keeping the ventilator would spare Carter the pain and possible injury of another intubation for the next surgery. However, removing it would allow Carter to breathe on his own, which is always preferred. Carter had a low-grade fever, and his heart rate was high. From all appearances, his body wanted that tube *out*.

For some reason—I'll credit the prayers from around the planet—I was uplifted to a sense of steely calm on the Sunday after Thanksgiving. Resolve or just numb? Unlike Friday and Saturday, I powered through conversations of tremendous sorrow and sentiment for Carter's newfound condition with only a few tears. I sat by Carter's side for hours with Lorilynn and Ivan as the doctors discussed and nurses monitored his numbers, his low-grade fever, his wound drainage, and his obvious frustration with the breathing tube.

Despite another surgery scheduled soon, the doctors were now looking for a window to remove the ventilator. His vitals showed that the unwanted apparatus caused him significant distress. The removal process involved a fine balance of reduced sedation, pain meds, and evidence that Carter could breathe independently.

While my numbness kept me attentively eavesdropping on the doctors' current plan for Carter, the nurses suggested I check on my husband. He was sitting on the floor in the fluorescent-lit hall outside the ICU. Leaning against the wall, hands hanging over bent knees and head down, his tears spilled onto the shiny speckled tiled floor. I did my duty of checking in on him, but there was little I could say. I wasn't okay; Carter wasn't okay. Everything wasn't going to be magically "okay."

As they reduced the sedatives, we saw a part of Carter we had not seen since our arrival at St. Mary's. He repeatedly lifted his right arm (mostly missing) behind his head, perhaps to make his head more comfortable on the pillow. As I recall, that's how he likes to sleep. Frequently, both arms would reach for things in the air, trying to grab something or pull something apart. We weren't sure.

While Carter's friend Kate was visiting, she was certain through head nods that Carter wanted to see Andy. From more intense nods, it was clear he did not want a phone call; he wanted to see Andy in person.

Andy was at the hospital earlier in the day, so we called him back in, but it took twenty minutes for him to return. In the meantime, Carter became extremely agitated; his heartbeat rose to 150. All his vital signs showed he was frustrated and pissed off with the "snake" down his throat. He attempted to pull it out of his mouth, but with one arm gone and the other wrapped in a boxing glove made of bandages, he had no ammunition to fight the battle.

Ventilator

The attending nurse was not pleased and chided us for stirring up Carter with conversation. She then upped the dose of his sedation meds so he would calm down.

This artificial medicinal control of his behavior turned my stomach. Every part of Carter's life was regulated by medical professionals, machines, and drugs. By the end of the day, his medical team decided against removing the tube since he'd be headed to surgery at 5 p.m. on Monday.

Sunday afternoon, we said goodbye to my sister Lorilynn and Ivan, as they needed to catch their flight back to Raleigh. Before they left, Ivan leaned over Carter's bed and read the list he had made on his phone of Carter's wonderful friends he met during their short stay. That slide is etched in my mental photo album, too.

Days after his sedation was lifted, Carter confessed that he didn't remember Lorilynn and Ivan being there. Chuck and I remember that their love and presence pulled us through *the roughest* time in our lives.

I tried to sleep past 5:30 on Monday morning while Chuck slipped out around 5 a.m. to sit by Carter's bedside. We knew it would be another long day of waiting for the scheduled surgery at 5 p.m. We assumed that by the end of this day, we'd have one surgery off the list, with one limb fixed and on its way to healing. We soon learned never to assume *anything* in a hospital trauma setting.

As life in the ICU would have it, some fluid snuck into Carter's lungs, and his fever and heart rate were elevated. The trauma doc—we called him Mario—decided to run a CT scan to double-check all his organs and his brain. The scan showed a little fluid by his lungs but nothing else. So, part of the day, the ICU nurses iced Carter's body, and we covered his forehead with a cold cloth as he fought the fever and the breathing tube.

Despite this setback, or perhaps because of it, the doctors finally decided to remove the breathing tube late Monday afternoon. It turns out that his surgery had been canceled due to a busy day in the OR.

As he prepared to remove the tube, the respiratory doctor was stunned that Carter could talk and even yell with the plastic pipe down his throat. He said it was important to remove it because one day on a ventilator is equivalent to one week of recuperation. He was ecstatic with how the procedure went and remarked that in his thirty years of experience, he'd never seen lungs as strong as Carter's.

Although still under sedation, Carter's mouth and throat were raw yet free to communicate with us for the first time. He thought it was Friday, the day after the accident, and he knew it was 2019. He also said, unprompted, "I swam as fast as I could."

CHAPTER 13

ICU Psychosis

Carter

What I endured over the next few days after Thanksgiving can only be described as a severe case of ICU psychosis. I drifted between what seemed like different versions of reality. I couldn't move in all of them because all my limbs felt like they were on fire.

In one reality, I remember getting discharged from the hospital and going home with my family. Then, I was suddenly transported to a nightmarish world with horrible monsters inflicting pain on me. I tried desperately to teleport back to reality with my family but had no success. I was convinced I had just died and been condemned to hell. Evil creatures held me down with their tentacles as what appeared to be a central figure in this place slowly approached me. It held a sword to my chest and told me that all my family and friends belonged to a cult, and I was now a slave.

Thankfully, I came to a reality where I was back in the hospital. I wasn't quite back to "real" reality yet, but at least I was in a familiar setting.

Despite being covered in bandages, I vividly remember leaving the hospital to go to work at Loggerhead and then driving back to the hospital after I clocked out. This hospital room I returned to felt more like a ward. Other sick patients surrounded me, and several rested their arms or legs on my bed. I would try to get them off but realized I couldn't move my limbs.

I felt trapped and claustrophobic. I wanted this situation to end in one of two ways: death or waking up to the real world.

CHAPTER 14

Iggy

The best in people show up in bad times.
—Palm Beach Marine Police Officer

Leila

THE DRAMA OF THE VENTILATOR AND ITS REMOVAL MET ITS match with unexpected entertainment as Carter came off the sedation meds, anesthesia, and painkillers. When we arrived in Carter's chilly, dark room, we found him carrying a low-grade fever, confused, and talkative:

Are we going to Dairy Queen?

I just want to go home and sleep in.

Mom, can you hold this hammer for me?

Can you wheel me out of this place?

Dad, catch that spider up there. Don't you see it?

Where are my shorts? I'm buck naked.

It doesn't matter at this point in time.

There's twenty bottles of water over there; can I just have one?

While I stayed to watch Carter's first physical therapy appointment, Chuck got more coffee. He thought it would be too difficult to watch.

It had been less than a week since the accident, yet the hospital wasted no time getting patients up and moving once the ventilator is removed. The physical therapist greeted Carter with a warm, lovely smile, seemingly oblivious to his dire condition. She informed him what the plan was and then proceeded.

As I was unfamiliar with fixators, I googled them the night before and discovered they are "a stabilizing frame to hold the broken bones in the proper position."[1] In an external fixator, metal pins or screws are placed into the bone through small incisions into the skin and muscle. The pins and screws are attached to a bar outside the skin.[2]

With swift authority, the therapist grabbed the external fixators like pot-lid handles and swung Carter's legs around to the edge of the bed so he could attempt to sit up. I must have let out a small gasp when the therapist grabbed the fixators. She assured me that her actions were not causing Carter any pain. Then she asked him to move his arms, legs, and feet. He complied with a few tiny motions without even a groan.

The most difficult task for Carter was sitting vertically after remaining horizontal for days, so another male therapist entered the room to provide an assist. He sat behind a woozy

Iggy

Carter and leaned against his back to offer the support he needed to sit up straight. This appointment exhausted Carter (and his mom), yet it lasted only five minutes.

Patience has never been our virtue, and now we understand that in the world of trauma, it's mandatory and must be practiced repeatedly. Time was moving at a turtle's pace. Carter said he was bored and wanted his phone.

Chuck and I both jumped up. The *code!* Ever since we got his phone back from the authorities after the accident, we had been guessing the code to open his phone for days, but we always guessed wrong and got locked out.

With great anticipation, we asked Carter what his phone code was. He thought for a bit and then blurted out four numbers. Chuck said we needed six numbers, and Carter said no, you only need four. Chuck said no, you need six, and then suddenly Carter shouted out all six numbers. The phone was unlocked. Even coming out of a drug fog, Carter's brain seemed capable of remembering and retrieving vital information—that was good news.

Carter also remembered his two guardian angels, Andy and Christine, who dropped by to hang with Carter while he waited. Although strangers just two days before, Andy, Christine, and now Carter had become fast friends because of all the time spent together during and after the accident.

Christine recounted her experience of the boat strike to Carter. Amazingly, despite being a little drug-loopy, Carter remembered everything. He talked with Andy and Christine about what happened and how "it went south."

Chuck and I observed that Carter didn't appear shocked or upset by revisiting the accident scene by scene. Was that hospital fog, or was it a predictor of how Carter would approach his new reality?

Although his memory seemed intact, the drugs kept talking. More Carter quotes:

> *I just want to sleep in for twelve hours in my own bed.*
>
> *I need to get up and go to surgery so I can get out of here.*
>
> *I literally cannot see what I'm holding in my hand anymore.*
>
> *Oh, I guess I need to learn piano again.*
>
> *No, I'm good; I just need to get up. I just need some leverage.*
>
> *I think it's best for my mental health to go sleep at home in my own bed.*

Listening and reacting to Carter's crazy chatter lightened the mood of our wait, as did our first visit by Iggy, a golden retriever. Midmorning, he strolled into the room and sniffed Carter's left foot. Iggy was leashed to the wheelchair of Don Chester, who rolled in with a smile, apologizing for Iggy's enthusiastic greeting.

Don is Iggy's owner and also the assistant administrator at St. Mary's Medical Center. A former triathlete, Don was

Iggy

hit by a car while riding his bike on Christmas Eve in 2004. The impact paralyzed him from the chest down. Don's quiet presence and soft smile were offset by Iggy's eagerness to lick us like we were his best friends.

Sipping my coffee in a cold corner, watching Iggy arrive, I didn't immediately warm up to a dog in the ICU ward. In fact, I was irritated that he was followed by a man in a wheelchair. It was just too much. I wasn't in any mood for more visitors, and I did not want to admit that Carter could find himself in the same place—confined to a wheelchair.

My irritation stemmed from my fatigue from playing "host." So many—*too* many—strangers with kind intentions stopped by, including police officers, even one who lost an arm above the elbow. Both arrived at different times and unannounced. They showed their support for our situation for about the first ten minutes of their visit. Around the ten-minute mark, our conversation shifted from Carter's hardship to theirs.

Although they meant no harm, attempting to serve as a hostess when grief had recently moved in became emotionally exhausting. I felt trapped in a one-sided conversation that appeared self-medicating for my uninvited guests. I owned no extra mental space to absorb their personal stories of tragedy, which I assume they thought would comfort me.

That's why it felt ridiculous to me for a dog to stop by for a visit. And then things got even more ludicrous: Carter's toes poked out of the large bandages that wrapped his swollen feet, and Iggy slobbered affection on each toe.

Although I let out no audible gasps, I was astounded by a shaggy dog generously sharing his germs with Carter. As the hostess of my first ICU room, it felt like the sanitation guidelines were decimated, and it was time to escort our canine guest out the door. That is until I saw Carter attempt to sit up to pet Iggy. The bright look in his eyes and the smile on his face obliterated my efforts to uphold a spic-and-span space.

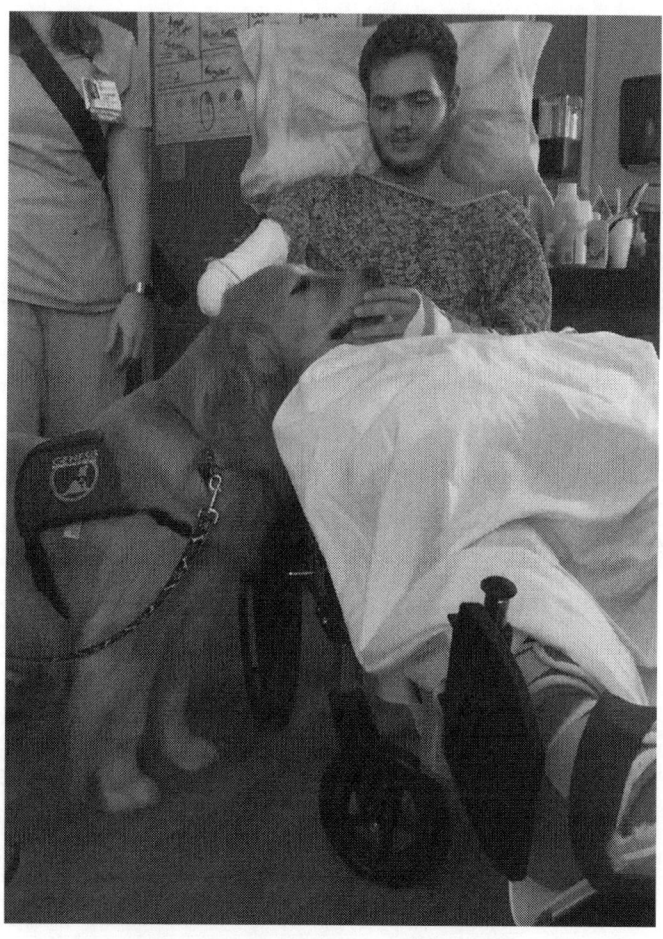

Carter with Iggy in the Rose Kennedy Suite
(Photo Credit: Viss Family)

Iggy

Our family has never owned a dog, and I never quite understood why one may be a good companion. The spark I observed in Carter when Iggy entered the room clarified things.

Don claims that Iggy, trained as a mobility dog, helps him with daily tasks and, perhaps even more importantly, serves as an icebreaker when greeting people for the first time. Iggy steals attention away from the wheelchair and all the stares and questions that come with it.

We learned more about Don's accident—and his miraculous reentry into his life and position at St. Mary's as a quadriplegic—from his wife, Sally, who soon visited us in the hospital almost as much as Don and Iggy. All three of them served as visual aids of what life looks like after surviving a tragedy. Their embedded strength and intuition accumulated over close to twenty years of overcoming their own struggles, providing ample space for them to bear our tears and fears.

Seeing Carter's connection to Iggy, they immediately contacted Genesis Assistance Dogs, where Don has received numerous service dogs, including their beloved Iggy. Carter was placed in the queue to get his own service dog down the road.

Later, during Carter's hospital stay, we visited Don's office. On a shelf sits a framed embroidery of the mantra he claimed since his accident: it reads, "Small Victories."

In an interview with *The Palm Beach Post* in 2005, Don expanded on his new reality:

> What was my attitude going to be and how am I going to do this? I said, these are the things I can

control and these are the things I can't control. I will be in a wheelchair the rest of my life. I won't walk. But I didn't have a head injury. There's still so much more I want to do, that I can do.[3]

There's a quote by the late cookie mogul Wally Amos that goes: "You may not be responsible for getting knocked down. But you're certainly responsible for getting back up."[4]

Iggy and company helped pass the time, but our wait "in line" for Carter's surgery was in vain. Too many traumas trumped his and pushed Carter down the surgery list. In our relatively short time braving the ICU, we discovered that the ICU is like an airport during a snowstorm. Flight times are irrelevant, cancellations are common, and takeoffs only happen when the skies clear.

The hand-specialist surgeon did make time to stop by. His name is Dilhan Abeyewardene (pronounced Ah-bay-WARD-na), but we called him Dr. A. Dr. A explained that once in surgery with the situation assessed, he planned for options A, B, or C. He never implied that he couldn't fix Carter's broken left wrist; he just informed us of the possible options. I made a point of looking into Dr. A's eyes and reminded him that Carter is a pianist and that five working fingers are a must. He understood.

Chuck and I both slept soundly for at least a couple of hours, knowing that Carter was breathing on his own. Our stay at the Quantum House soon fell into a similar pattern to the one Chuck and I had at home. Chuck first climbed out of bed around 5 a.m. Then, with a travel mug of freshly brewed

Iggy

Keurig coffee in his hand, he walked the brisk ten-minute route lit by the moon to Carter's room. After he left, I stayed in bed to think about what to add to the CaringBridge post I had drafted the night before. Once out of bed, I edited a few things and hit publish.

Donning a combination of black leggings, a gray shirt, and a jacket (Carter's room was always freezing!), I made the same trek in sunlight with coffee in hand. The fresh-air stroll with our hot coffee before entering the hospital halls provided time to mentally prepare for the long day ahead.

Surgery on Carter's left wrist was scheduled for 5 p.m. What we didn't know was that our long day of waiting would turn out to be eventful.

CHAPTER 15

Awakening

Carter

FINALLY, AFTER A PERIOD OF PSYCHOSIS THAT FELT LIKE WEEKS, I woke up in the ICU and was sure I was back to reality. I could only hear beeps from the machines next to me and immediately saw all kinds of tubes attached to various places on my body. I was in a haze of drugs and painkillers, but I was awake.

It was the Wednesday after Thanksgiving. I looked in front of me to see that both of my legs were still there. They each had metal external fixators on them and were completely immovable, but my mind was filled with relief—I was sure I would be able to walk again. Before I could mourn the loss of my right arm, I was surprised to see my left forearm heavily bandaged. I couldn't recall anything happening to it during the accident, but after I tried to move my wrist upward, a surge of pain shot through my body, and I knew it was impacted by the boat.

It was an overwhelming moment of humility when I realized I couldn't use any of my limbs. I took a lot of pride in being independent before this happened. I enjoyed living in my own condo and rarely asked for help with tasks. I was proud of my active lifestyle of going on long runs, biking, and swimming for hours at a time. Now, I couldn't perform the most basic essential functions by myself and had to ask the hospital staff for help with everything. God sure knows how to humble the proud.

My parents entered my room. They looked emotionally exhausted but overjoyed to see that I was fully conscious. They began explaining what occurred and why I was there. The vivid memories started flooding my mind, and I couldn't believe I had survived that ordeal.

To their surprise, I interrupted them and said I remembered what had happened to me. My parents then explained what happened while I was unconscious for six days.

They talked about how all my family and friends from work, church, and school had been at my bedside while I fought for my life. They explained how anyone I knew who could not be there in person was also trying to help me in any way they could through financial support and prayers.

Hearing this hit me so hard. While going through those horrible hallucinations, I thought I was alone and abandoned. In reality, all my friends were beside me, and hundreds of people I didn't know were praying for me. Knowing all these people were supporting me was a key factor in my motivation to overcome this. My parents also mentioned that I was all over the news, and the CaringBridge site my family started had already raised tens of thousands of dollars to pay for my medical bills.

It was surreal to think about all the support and attention I was receiving because of this horrible incident. I was simply enjoying the ocean I loved and appreciating all the animals on the reef.

Then, it clicked in my head: I experienced and survived an ordeal that affects marine life on a daily basis. I worked with all those sea turtles with severe boat strike wounds and could now speak as a survivor to advocate for both their safety and for those who go in the water. Now I had the perfect story to share about the importance of water safety.

Carter and Andy helping to move a turtle at Loggerhead Marinelife Center
(Photo Credit: Loggerhead Marinelife Center)

I confidently told my parents, "I can make more of a difference now than I could before."

CHAPTER 16

A Mere Millimeter

Ninety percent of the battle has been won!

—Dr. Borrego

Leila

Carter's drug-induced hallucinations "teleported him to his own bed for a good night of sleep," as he put it. They also had him believing that the staff at Loggerhead kicked him out and no longer wanted him as an employee. Carter was frustrated as he floated in and out of reality and ached to be lucid and in the present, and—though he didn't say it out loud—I bet he just wanted some alone time.

Like Carter, we were grateful for loving supporters. "Host mode" was making us weary. Mandy, our ICU nurse, advised us to limit the number and length of visits. The hospital security noticed an uptick in people inquiring about Carter and implemented a policy where a password was required to visit him. From then on, Chuck and I had to show our license *and* state the password—"Angel 94"—at the reception desk to get a badge to stick on our clothing before we could walk the halls to Carter. As the weeks went on, we got to know the reception desk personnel by name, and they preprinted our stickers for us before we arrived. We were regulars.

Limiting guests was a start, but for one who lives alone and refuels by being alone, a hospital stay offers an unexpected abundance of stimulation. The piercing irregular beeps of monitors near Carter's head, coupled with nurses and docs popping in and out to check on things, frequently aligned with the start of a nap. It was clear that an ICU stay focuses on healing over sleeping.

This became even more clear when a speech pathologist stopped by to check on his swallowing and cognitive skills. Soon after, the orthopedic surgeon dropped in to give an in-depth description of what would be accomplished in the surgery scheduled later that day. At the same time, the physician's assistant entered the room and introduced himself. So, with the nurse, Mom, Dad, and Carter, there were seven people in a small room and the noisy monitors bleeping in the background.

As the crowd stood by, the surgeon we called Dr. A, as we found his last name too hard to pronounce, stepped through his plan to repair Carter's left wrist with a plate. Next, he looked directly into Carter's eyes and stated that the doctors considered taking both legs during the Thanksgiving emergency surgery, and he—Dr. A—held them off and said, "No, we are saving them."

Chuck and I held each other. We were stunned and, at the same time, thankful. Dr. A stood firm in a grim moment and protected the future of our son's ability to walk. Dr. A explained that Carter's left leg was a puzzle to piece together. He was pleased with the condition of his leg tissue and eager to repair the leg with rods and pins.

So, after the overview of the repair to be done later that day, most everyone left while Carter continued working with the speech pathologist. She asked him to repeat what the surgeon had described about the surgery, among other things. Still suffering from some brain fog, Carter did quite well—I'm not sure Chuck and I would have recounted the explanation better than he did.

After all the staff left, Chuck and I took off so Carter could rest in relative peace. And, to be honest, our getaway allowed Chuck and I to find relative peace, too.

On this day and many others, we stopped at Loggerhead Marinelife Center to see the progress of the expansion, the sea turtles swimming in the rehab pools, and the new friends we had made since the accident. We were and still are welcomed like family by the staff and volunteers. We saw Carter and Andy's workshop, got the rundown on their latest projects, and were surprised to learn that Carter fixed the brakes on a four-wheeler. From a YouTube video, Carter and Andy even managed to build a new tank for rescued turtles.

After our Loggerhead visit, which many call "turtle therapy," we headed back to St. Mary's to find a completely lucid, talkative Carter. The fog had cleared, and he had questions.

His finances and how he would pay his bills were his first concerns. We shared how first responder Caitlin immediately swept in, took care of his accounts, and began tracking what bills to pay. We also informed Carter that Caitlin stockpiled paid time off (PTO) from concerned Loggerhead employees.

By giving Carter their PTO, he had three more months of paid time off after he used up his own!

Next, we filled him in on the anonymous donations that poured in, and we showed him the latest total of the GoFundMe account set up by his brothers and sister-in-law. Like us, he had to take it all in and absorb what it means to be part of a loving, worldwide, compassionate community.

Of course, he had other questions about his friends, his condition, his future, how it happened, and why it happened. He discussed the timeline of events with remarkable calm. A considerable mix of trauma, drugs, and anesthesia prompted Carter to believe something terrible happened to Andy on Friday, the day after the accident, and we had to assure him that his hallucination was not true.

Carter's surgery on his left wrist and left leg was scheduled at 5:30 p.m., but it instead began at 9:30 that evening. The left tibia was shattered, and the repair included making an incision above the knee and placing a titanium rod into the center of the bone below his knee. The rod was then secured in place with screws and a plate. There was a big chunk of bone missing in his tibia, so that area was filled with antibiotic cement. The external fixator on his left leg was removed. The doctor predicted that Carter would bear weight on his left leg again but that his mobility would be limited.

The doctor admitted that "someone must have been watching out for Carter." The cut on his left wrist was less than a millimeter away from a central nerve. He was confident that Carter's left hand, his dominant hand, would heal completely with no further issues. Now, the biggest challenge was to manage the infection and pain levels.

The next day, Dr. Borrego stopped in at the ICU to check in on Carter. He was ecstatic about Carter's condition and said, "Ninety percent of the battle has been won!" His enthusiastic declaration and huge smile buoyed us.

Mmm . . . that 90 percent of the battle was major and swiftly won thanks to a stellar medical team. The remaining 10 percent of the battle would be lengthy, considering the tangle of cords and bandages that tethered Carter to his unexpected bed on wheels.

Our question was, could 100 percent of the battle be won?

CHAPTER 17

New Reality

Carter

THE DOCTOR ENTERED THE ROOM AND SAID THEY WOULD DO another surgery on my right arm. I said goodbye to my parents and started bracing myself to go under anesthesia again. I was rolled to the pre-op room and left to wait for my turn.

The room was empty, with bright fluorescent lights above me. About thirty minutes passed, and I could feel my pain meds starting to wear off. The pain and discomfort were truly setting in. I felt excruciating pain as I tried to lift or move any of my limbs. I felt helpless and frozen, desperately waiting for a nurse or surgeon to wheel me into surgery.

Another thirty minutes passed, and no sign of anyone. I was sweating, and the lights above felt like they were getting hotter. It was like I was paralyzed but not numb, so I could only look around to keep my mind off the pain. That's why I started looking around the empty room to keep myself distracted. A clock was on the wall, and I could've sworn the second hand was moving at half speed. Finally, a nurse walked into the room and started wheeling me away. I was so relieved and honestly couldn't wait to be unconscious again.

The nurse ended up wheeling me back to my ICU room. I was completely puzzled about what was happening and in more pain than ever. The nurse gave me some morphine in my IV line and explained that there had been a delay, but I should be going into surgery soon.

The morphine barely eased my pain at the time. The lights above me felt like they were getting even hotter, and a sense of panic settled in. I wanted to roll on my side but couldn't. I wanted to go outside and breathe fresh air but was stuck in this hellhole. I wanted to feel like a normal person again, but I knew my life would never be the same. All I could do was lie there and cry.

About two hours had passed, and the surgeon entered the room and started talking to me. I could barely understand what he was saying because I was so emotionally exhausted and physically uncomfortable, but it sounded like they were ready for surgery. I was hastily wheeled off into the operating room. I could feel myself fading away as the anesthesia was administered. I suddenly entered a restful and coveted state of unconsciousness.

CHAPTER 18

How Much Does an Arm Cost?

You were admitted for drowning . . .
Your admission is not covered.

—UnitedHealthcare® Insurance
Company Correspondence

Leila

Trauma shuts down the prefrontal cortex, which is considered the "mission control" of the brain when it comes to managing logical thoughts and executive skills.[1] So the fact that Chuck had the presence of mind to reserve flights for us on Thanksgiving afternoon, an hour or so after we heard about the accident, is quite remarkable.

The hardest thing to determine was if we should book a return flight or not. Since my studio and the University of Denver position required me to be on the ground and in person, and because important holiday services at church were just around the corner, it was decided that I would fly back to Denver after a week's stay in Florida.

The kids and I gathered for dinner just about every night after my return home to Denver for two weeks in December.

One evening after dinner, I caught up on the stack of snail mail and opened this letter from the insurance company, which read

> Dear Carter Viss,
>
> We received a request to cover an inpatient facility admission. Your admission is not covered.
>
> Physician: Dr. Borrego
>
> Facility Name: St. Mary's Medical Center
>
> Place of Service: In Patient [sic]
>
> Date of service: 11-28-2019 to Discharge
>
> Diagnosis: V90.89X Drowning and submersion due to other accident to unspecified watercraft, initial encounter.
>
> Date(s) determined not to be medically necessary: 11-28-19 to discharge.
>
> The clinical reason for our determination is: Your doctor admitted you to an acute inpatient facility on 11/28/19. You were admitted for drowning. We did not receive enough medical information to make a decision about your admission. The information we have does not show which guidelines to use. We do not have your test results. We do not have reports about your care. Your admission is not covered.

Denial code: Not applicable.

Claim amount (if applicable): Not applicable.

The decision is based on the following information: MCG Care GuidelineMG-SIC . . .

What this mean for you [yes, that's how it was spelled]

We contacted your provider because we didn't receive enough clinical information to determine whether the admission was medically necessary at the time you were in the hospital. Please see the medical rationale section above.

Your provider should not bill you for the cost of the services you received.

Please call us if you receive a bill from your doctor or facility that is associated with the admission request.

Our collective confusion turned to laughter. One phone call with an embarrassed insurance agent assured us that Carter indeed had coverage for his medical care.

An assurance of insurance also comes with an assurance of "stressmares." Notifications continued to trickle in with six-page letters, itemized invoices, emails, and phone calls indicating what our policy covered and what we owed. One letter informed us that one of Carter's emergency room surgeons was out of our insurance company's network; therefore, the surgeon's bills were not covered.

With Carter turning twenty-six in less than a year, we knew his coverage on our insurance plan would end, thanks to the Affordable Care Act. The concern could not be our priority, but the complication loomed. The stack of letters filled the dining room table, so I dumped them in a bag earmarked for insurance papers.

It wasn't only our insurance company that played a major role in Carter's medical soap opera. The drama continued when another insurance company approached Carter with a settlement.

We heard of the settlement through the lawyers we hired. The firm was recommended to us by first responder Ed, the captain who took us on a boat ride to the accident scene. Ed, a board member of Loggerhead Marinelife Center, was one of the first people to walk alongside us after our red-eye flight from Colorado to Florida. A lawyer and a parent himself, Ed called Chuck two days after the accident and told us he was thinking of us and asked if we needed any help. Since he was a commercial property lawyer and not a personal injury lawyer, he couldn't represent us but recommended that we seek representation. Ed declared that if his daughter were injured like Carter, he would turn to his highly esteemed lawyer friend.

Ed offered to take us out for dinner just six days after the accident to share more of his thoughts. It felt strange and maybe a little wrong leaving the hospital, but the promise of a dinner and a cold IPA away from the ICU blips and bleeps was appreciated. Carter was headed to surgery that evening, and there was not much we could do but wait for news of how it went. Little did we know how awful this night was for Carter. He was rolled out of his ICU room only to wait in line for hours: awake, alone, and anxious under the bright lights of the OR waiting room.

Over dinner, Ed recommended his friend's long-standing Florida firm, one highly respected in a community rife with lawsuits, called Searcy, Denney, Scarola, Barnhart, and Shipley, PA. Driving down I-95 from day to day and reading the billboards, it became apparent that shopping for injury lawyers is a regular "thing." To be honest, I didn't recall seeing a billboard on the eight-lane interstate for Ed's recommended firm. Chuck and I figured that was a good sign (pun intended), so we took Ed's suggestion. We were in no mood to shop for a lawyer.

During a visit to the firm near downtown West Palm Beach, we felt transported to an office straight from the set of *Law and Order*. As we waited in our sweatpants and sneakers, we sat in overstuffed chairs with cherrywood legs in a room with dark paneling and slate floors. After hearing Carter's story, the attorneys agreed to take his case, and we retained them within the week after the accident.

We befriended an OR nurse who assisted with Carter's surgery on Thanksgiving Day. We ran into her in the hall, and she hugged us both and whispered in our ears, "Did you get a lawyer, and if so, who?" She sighed with relief, confessed that she was close to one of the judges in the area, and confirmed that we had made the right choice.

While I was in Denver, Carter's attorneys held a conference call with Chuck and me. They informed us that Danny

Stanton, the driver of the boat, and his family were "lawyering up." They hired a high-profile attorney in preparation for the restitution for Carter's injuries—and our grief—could demand.

The family was also in touch with their insurance company. They had wisely protected their considerable assets with a substantial insurance policy. Our lawyers told us that most insurance companies rarely offer a settlement until a thorough investigation occurs and almost never offer a settlement for the full amount promised in a policy. In Carter's case, these rarities happened within weeks after the accident. Our lawyers needed to know what Chuck and I thought of accepting the settlement.

Our conversation with the lawyers eventually led to the tough question: What settlement amount would feel comfortable and fair to Carter? It turns out that my figure had *many* more zeros than Stanton's insurance company was offering. Carter lost an arm, and nothing would come close to replacing it, not even a pricey prosthetic. His arm—*any* body part, for that matter—was something that Chuck and I had nurtured for so long that it felt like *our* arm. How much does an arm *cost*? How can you attach a value to a limb? How could we anticipate the expense of everything we couldn't imagine yet?

There were few signs that Carter could use his legs again, and the hospital bills kept coming. Settling the case just weeks after the accident seemed premature and could shortchange what Carter would need in the future.

How Much Does an Arm Cost?

Our attorneys assured us that this swift gesture by a powerhouse insurance company could be the most money Carter could see. Agreeing to their offer secured a decent outlook for Carter's fragile future. A trial by jury could produce a higher settlement amount, but there were no guarantees.

From the start, we knew that Carter did not want confrontation in a high-profile court case. And so, Chuck and I agreed to consider the settlement. We were encouraged not to share the amount publicly. When the lawyers approached Carter between surgeries, Carter was interested, too.

CHAPTER 19

Purple Pig

Carter

I WOKE UP THE NEXT MORNING IN MY ICU ROOM TO SEE MY dad sitting beside my bed. As I gradually came to my senses, my throat was so dry and scratchy that I couldn't swallow. I felt the thirstiest I'd ever felt in my life.

My dad immediately got me some ice water. Words fall short of describing the amount of relief I felt as I sipped that water. I also had a few sips of chicken broth but knew my body couldn't handle much else. My dad explained that the surgery went well and that 90 percent of my battle to survive was over. Despite the relief I felt after hearing this, I knew I had an extremely long and tough road ahead.

It was Thursday, December 5, exactly one week after the accident. Although it was my first day being fully conscious in the hospital, it was a doozy. I felt less panicked than the night before, but the pain was still overwhelming. It finally registered in my mind that I was at St. Mary's Medical Center and would be there for a while.

Later in the day, Andy visited me with two other friends from Loggerhead. It was the first time I saw Andy while fully conscious since the accident. I could tell he'd been through a lot over the past week but was so glad to see me awake. It felt unbelievable to be having a casual conversation with my friends after all that had happened. It gave me hope that everything would return to normal one day. My optimistic side confidently told them I'd be out of the hospital by Christmas.

The other two friends left the room, and Andy and I had a moment to ourselves. I remember talking to him about all that happened and how hard it was to believe it was real. I assured him that we'd be back out fishing and snorkeling like we used to in no time.

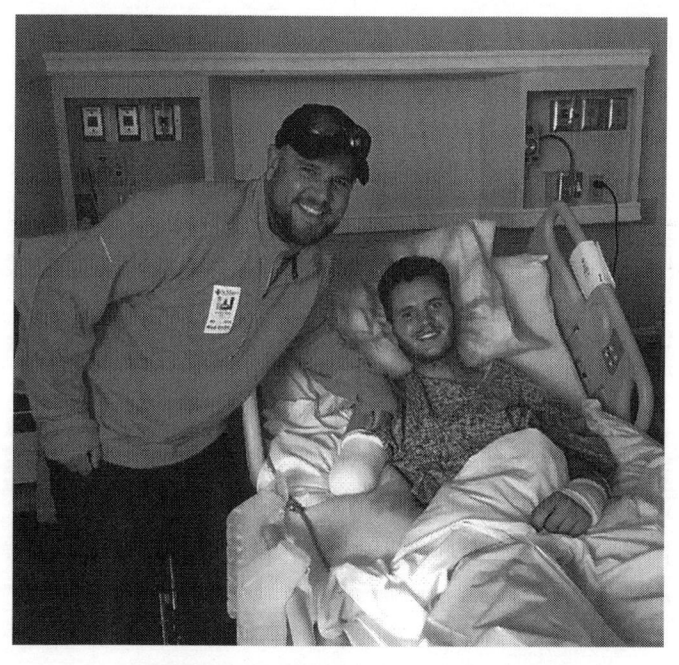

Andy and Carter in the Rose Kennedy Suite
(Photo Credit: Viss Family)

In the evening, a nurse walked into my room and told me they would do a dressing change on my right arm. From what I was told, there was a bad infection in what was left of my right arm. They had to remove some tissue and put me on antibiotics. There was also a symptom they described to me as phantom limb pain, which was pain that occurs from a body part that is no longer there. They started unwrapping the bandage, and a jolt of pain like an electric shock shot from my arm.

I had never felt pain like this before, and they were just getting started. As they took more of the bandage off, I could start to smell my infected arm for the first time. The smell reminded me of rotting meat, and it took my brain a few seconds to process the sight of decaying necrotic tissue on my arm.

The putrid smell made me gag, but that awful odor was quickly replaced by the worst pain I've ever felt. They slowly peeled off the last of the bandage and surges of intense pain seemed like they were shooting from the area my arm used to be. All the previous pain I felt seemed like nothing compared to this. I couldn't stop screaming and my attempts to writhe in pain were ended by the pain in my other limbs.

It was at this moment when I noticed a crucifix above the doorway to my ICU room. While I was enduring this intense state of pain, I couldn't help but think about the pain Jesus endured while on the cross. His limbs must have been in so much pain from those nails and the torture He endured before the cross. I thought to myself that if He could endure all of that, then I could push through the horrible state of pain I was in.

I was distracted from staring at the crucifix enough to briefly get my mind off the pain, and to my relief, the dressing change was finally over. I had a fever after the process was done, and they gave me some morphine to help calm me down.

That night, I ate my first couple of small bites of solid food when a nurse shared some of her lunch with me. My dad also visited to comfort me for a while before I tried to fall asleep.

This was my first night in a fully conscious state since the incident. I thought sleep would come easily because of my exhaustion from the day, but I was wrong. I couldn't get comfortable because of the pain I was in. All the morphine and oxycodone I was on simply wasn't enough, and I kept begging the nurse to give me more. She could only rotate between a dose of morphine and some oxycodone every other hour, so I had a brief moment of relaxation, followed by about fifty minutes of pain.

This went on until 1 or 2 a.m., and I was starting to feel delirious from my pain. I looked up and saw a ceiling vent above me. I had seen this vent many times before, but this time, tentacles started slowly wiggling out of it. These were the exact ones I remember seeing while I was unconscious, but now they were in my reality.

My attention was taken away from the vent when I saw a figure standing in the far-right window of the room. My eyes focused, and I saw the figure's purple, pig-like face with hollow, black eyes. It was tall and skinny, with its long, gangly fingers resting on the base of the window. I told myself that this was that central figure in my horrible stretch of ICU psychosis.

I swiftly turned my head away from the window and peered into the light of the main ICU lobby, but the tentacles and the figure remained in my peripheral vision. I closed my eyes and hoped they would disappear, but they were still there when I cracked open my eyes. I felt entrapped and started doubting if I would ever leave that hellish reality I was in. Thankfully, it was time for another dose of morphine, and I could relax and get the hallucinations off my mind.

I did end up falling asleep that night as I got used to seeing those tentacles in the vent and the figure staring at me with a grin through that window. I woke up about two hours later, and to my surprise, it was seven in the morning. The hallucinations were gone, and I was relieved to make it through the night without losing my sanity. My siblings, who had just arrived in West Palm Beach from Denver, soon entered my room. Seeing familiar faces was the most refreshing feeling in the world and brought me back to reality when it felt like I was slipping away.

That day consisted of visits from doctors and attempts at physical therapy. The main goal in physical therapy was to lift either of my legs up on my own. The shooting pains I endured when I attempted this made me realize how long the road to recovery was ahead of me. It would be a distinct battle to earn back the use of each limb. Since both legs were virtually unusable at this point, I would focus most of my energy on gaining the use of my left hand. My whole wrist and palm were heavily wrapped in bandages, but I could pick up a cup of water and drink it on my own.

I was one step closer to full independence . . . with thousands more to go.

CHAPTER 20

Upgrade to Step-Down

Courage doesn't always roar. Sometimes courage is the little voice at the end of the day that says, "I'll try again tomorrow."

—Mary Anne Radmacher, *Courage Doesn't Always Roar*

Leila

I'll always wonder if I should have left Florida when I did. Even though it gave me time to get my things in order, I left a son in critical condition in the care of complete strangers and a determined yet emotionally overwhelmed husband. This decision and the fact that the accident happened two thousand miles away made things feel disjointed and complicated—like this chapter!

After a few days with the kids at home in Denver, they left me for a quick weekend trip to see Carter. Chase, Brittany, Levi, and his girlfriend, Erin, who flew in from California, managed to book inexpensive flights with Spirit Airlines. They discovered that the aircraft's seat quality reflected the ticket price tag, and no one slept much during the red-eye flight.

Chuck picked them up from their early morning arrival and drove them to the hospital in Carter's 2007 Nissan Xterra, which Carter purchased six months before his accident. After visiting Carter, they took a break to see Loggerhead and received the VIP tour. Carter instructed the boys to feed the fish in the Loggerhead aquariums, as he didn't think they were getting enough food. And, as they walked the Juno Beach Pier, they ran into Christine! Yes, Christine, who, with Andy, had rescued and managed Carter's return to the shore into the hands of the paramedics.

When Chuck and the kids returned to the ICU, they tried several times to see Carter but were not allowed. The nurse informed them that Carter endured a brutal physical therapy session and a change in wound bandages. She reported that his right arm looked infected, and he was running a low-grade temperature. Because of his condition, they had scheduled surgery for the next day to clean his wounds.

When Chuck was finally allowed in Carter's room to say hi, Carter said, "Do you have to go anywhere?"

Chuck said, "Nope."

Carter asked, "Can you just stay here?"

Chuck put his hand on Carter's arm and saw the pain and disappointment in Carter's eyes. He knew that he wasn't out of the woods. His eyes finally closed, and he slept.

The doctors planned for at least two more surgeries after the wound-cleaning surgery—thank goodness for painkillers. One would prepare his right arm for a prosthetic. The other, more complicated surgery would repair his right leg. The strike on his knee broke several bones, including his femur.

The doctors were encouraged that Carter could move his toes on his right foot and that a pulse was found in his ankle.

Upgrade to Step-Down

Every day, the nurses tested where he could feel and what he could move. There were some areas he could not feel in his foot, and when asked to move it in certain ways, he couldn't do it. These symptoms added to our list of worries.

Chuck and the kids went for dinner after the surgery. When they returned to give Carter a snack and tuck him in, the nurse informed the crew that Carter was being wheeled out of the ICU and down the hall to "step-down." This surprise move was typical in hospitals. Step-down is a transition unit for ICU patients headed to the general medical and surgical ward.

They quickly packed up all the stuff Carter had accumulated during his stay. Brittany and Erin started personalizing his new private room. Their efforts may have been in vain as Carter had little concern for the look of his room; he just wanted a room that would give him a really good night of sleep!

* * *

It felt ridiculous to complain about my situation, yet the reentry into home life after enduring a Florida trauma time warp was surreal. My executive functioning skills shut down. My mind easily slid from the task before me into a looping slideshow of the six days in Florida.

It was a serious buzz killer telling our neighbor about Carter as he decorated his house for Christmas and invited me to his party. I quickly grew accustomed to the expression on people's faces after I shared Carter's story. I found a strange sort of comfort when others described the moment they heard about Carter's accident.

Dinner with friends Drew and Sarah found me laughing much more than crying—a typical experience when being with them before the accident, too. They have endured trauma and hospitals too many times to count with their precious daughter, Selah, who was recovering from a major back surgery. Despite our situations, we found that healing comes from humor in the horrific.

I tried to follow my normal Friday routine of practicing the organ and then attending a step class at Lifetime Fitness—my favorite way to exercise. This is no Jane Fonda '80s step class. This is a revamped twenty-first-century step class with Heidi, an instructor who kicks butt. My body and brain didn't seem to jive as they had in the past, but I made it through the workout.

Our family has belonged to the gym for years—one of the reasons why Carter is so strong now. Chuck and I informed friends at Lifetime about Carter's accident a few weeks later. The sweet Wednesday step class posed for a group pic, posted it on Facebook, and tagged us to show their support.

Close friends Dave and Jodie Tinucci treated me to a delicious meal of salmon, rice pilaf, and broccolini. Part of the reason why Carter is a foodie is thanks to the Tinucci family and our "Vissucci" dinners. We dined so often together that we coined a mashup term for Viss-Tinucci shared dinners. As our boys are all grown, it's quite the occasion when all nine of us and significant others hang together for a meal. The two most requested meals are Chuck's calzones or Dave's pizzas baked in his backyard pizza oven.

While I treasured my Vissucci company, Chuck reported that Carter had his best day since the accident. His upgrade

Upgrade to Step-Down

to the step-down unit featured fewer beeps and alarms and allowed him to turn off the lights, close the blinds, and shut the door. The privacy of a dark room, combined with a little fan acquired by Brittany at Target that provided soothing white noise, made for enough peace to sleep.

This newfound peace was interrupted by a visit with the "Fishkateers"—Katie, Kate, and Andy. One of the best things we discovered about Carter after the accident was that he has incredibly faithful friends.

With his left hand still wrapped in thick bandages, Carter had difficulty texting and emailing. And it turned out that the TV in the new room did not have an HDMI port for the Roku Levi had purchased to remedy the situation.

After the kids returned home to Denver, Chuck's sister Jan from California flew in to offer support. Chuck and Jan determined that an iPad may be the best solution for Carter. While at the Apple store, they missed Carter's first trip outside. Not just outside his hospital room in the hallway but outside in the fresh Florida air.

A request for a different TV was not fulfilled, but the hospital did honor Carter's request for a longer bed. As he started feeling better, Carter began to advocate for himself, which never came naturally to him, as he leaned toward the quiet side. According to reliable sources—the nurses who became Chuck's fast friends—Carter was a popular patient because he was pleasant and polite. Carter hid it from the nurses but was often down in the morning when reality sunk deeper. He had access to articles about the accident and read about its impact on so many people.

As the day went on, his spirit improved. His body also improved. His vitals were so strong that the doctors said he did not require hospital care and was ready to move to rehab. The two caveats: before the move, Carter had to be weaned from the pain pump and only reliant on oral pain relievers, plus he had to be able to bear weight on one limb. The doctors were not sure how long this would take.

When we got word of the accident, Carter's needs became Chuck's full-time job. He dipped into his vacation days and began the paperwork for the Family and Medical Leave Act (FMLA) to take a break from his global support position at Oracle.

Instead of solving escalating software problems for corporations worldwide, Chuck filled his "downtime" with expert-level sudoku. He struggled to find a bathroom—apparently, St. Mary's could use more. He declared all nurses are saints. He received flowers intended for Carter that had to remain at the nurse's station or be brought back to the Quantum House. He got his hair cut by someone other than his favorite barber, Chris. Every day he wore the same jacket to stay warm, as Carter liked his room cold. Chuck also discovered that an RN named Patrick gave the best hugs in the hospital hallways.

Now that Carter was free from tubes, Chuck had the privilege of feeding him his first meal in seven days, featuring chicken broth and orange Jello for breakfast and meatloaf for lunch. The next day, a six-inch sub sandwich was Carter's first "real meal."

It seemed strange to be excited that Carter was eating real food, yet it gave us a glimpse of normality. It gave Chuck a sign that his dedication to Carter was helping. It was good news. We learned to take what we could get.

One of the hardest phone calls to make soon after Carter's accident was to close friend and colleague Chee-Hwa Tan, head of Piano Pedagogy at the University of Denver. She developed the Piano Preparatory Program at DU, and now I had to tell her I could not continue as the coordinator of her thriving "baby." But I had the wits about me to offer a ray of hope. I suggested we contact my colleague Matthew because he was steeped in the same pedagogical philosophy and even studied and worked with the same people as Chee-Hwa at Southern Methodist University in Dallas. He also served as director of their Piano Prep Program.

In essence, Matthew was "me" at SMU until a few years ago when he shifted career trajectories. And, as it happened, Matthew was in Denver visiting with a Realtor the day after I had just returned from Florida to put my studio on hold and play for a number of December church services.

Chee-Hwa, Matthew, and I had lunch, which eventually led to Chee-Hwa extending an invitation to Matthew to serve as coordinator for the Piano Prep Program while I took an emergency sabbatical.

* * *

Between settling affairs with Chee-Hwa and my position at the University of Denver, settling things with my studio, and keeping up with Carter's progress, I prepared to play for a festive Sunday morning service. When the day arrived, I felt steel doors slam shut on my emotions. The numbness allowed me to jam with the choir and the worship team.

I stood behind the pulpit and shared Carter's story and our situation with the congregation. They had showered us with love and support. I was told to take as much time off as needed, my pay would continue, and they would hold my position for me. I played for communion with precision and even musicality as I saw congregants wipe away tears.

I assumed that once home, I would crash and fall apart. Instead, I came home to all the kids back from Florida eagerly sharing their stories and conversations with Carter and their time at Loggerhead. After my return to Denver, the heavy, dark cloud was lifted a few inches, maybe even a foot, at least for a little bit.

CHAPTER 21

The Strongest Person I Ever Met

Levi

Spending the first week following Carter's accident in Denver while Carter was in the hospital in West Palm Beach was terrible. Trying to go on living your normal life while knowing that your brother is suffering unimaginably in another state is pretty much impossible.

It felt like I was doing nothing to help the situation, so I was incredibly eager but also nervous to fly a red-eye on Thursday night to finally see him. I wasn't sure what to expect: I didn't know what his coherency would be like (knowing he was heavily drugged over the past few days), and I didn't know what his attitude or mental state would be like either.

I was stunned to walk into his room early on Friday morning and find myself having a normal conversation with my brother. Carter was just himself, not in some sort of panicked state, not loopy on drugs, but rather calm and happy to see Chase, Brittany, and Erin and me. He eventually talked to me about the accident with poise and composure. He mentioned that he remembered everything and that he was now more worried about Andy's mental state than anything he was going through.

We met Andy, and I can confidently say that I'm not surprised he was Carter's lifesaver, as he is an incredibly kind, loving person: someone my family and I will love forever. The fact that Carter was worried for him more than himself speaks to the kind of person Carter is, too.

Seeing Carter in this state made me very sad, but his mental strength, fighting spirit, and kindness to everyone helping him gave me hope that he would be out of that hospital bed in no time.

He continued to surprise my family, the nurses, and pretty much everyone following the situation with how well he's progressed, and I know it's cliché to say this, but he is absolutely the strongest person I've ever met.

CHAPTER 22

Sinking In

Carter

IT'S HARD TO DESCRIBE THE JOY OF GETTING WHEELED OUT OF the ICU. It was the first time I felt victorious since the incident. It felt like I just passed the hardest part of the test, and everything would get easier from there. I remember seeing people eating at the café in the hospital and people going about their regular routines. It was so refreshing to see a glimpse of the normal world, which I had forgotten about, and it assured me that my life would go back to normal someday.

We arrived at the step-down unit, and it was a joy to see the hallways filled with private rooms. I was confident that this traditional hospital setting would accelerate my healing. We entered my room, and I was eager to fall asleep, hoping those hallucinations wouldn't come back to haunt me. I said goodnight to my family and embraced the dark, quiet room. I felt sweaty and uncomfortable for most of the night, but, thankfully, I saw no hallucinations and got a few more hours of sleep than the night before. It was now nine days since my accident, and I had achieved another positive milestone.

The next morning, a doctor came to my room and told me they planned a quick surgery on my right arm to clean the wound and remove any infected tissue. Surgeries felt mundane to me by then, and, honestly, there was a sense of relief knowing I would be sedated and have a break from the pain I was in.

I was wheeled into the pre-op room and left to wait until they were ready for surgery. My patience was tested again as I lay there and stared into the empty room ahead of me. All that time alone with my thoughts gave me time to dwell on some realities that I had avoided thinking about until that point. The most prevalent was the loss of my right arm and living the rest of my life with one hand. I loved my job, especially the work I was doing with fish and aquariums. Now I felt like I would be virtually useless at performing essential tasks and would always need assistance from someone. It was incredibly crushing because I was on track to be the full-time aquarist at work before this happened.

I became even more devastated when I started thinking about all the hobbies and activities I loved to do. The first one that came to mind was playing piano. I had been playing on and off for most of my life, but I had especially gotten into it over the past year. At night, I would sit at my cheap keyboard and learn classical pieces that I loved, from the slow melancholy strains of Beethoven's "Moonlight Sonata" to the fervent passion of Liszt's "Liebestraum No. 3." It was such a relaxing way to end the day, and I had just upgraded to an 88-key electric piano about two weeks before the incident. It crushed me to think that I would never have that hand back and would never be able to play those pieces again.

Sinking In

I sank further when I thought about how I loved to cook, fish, run, bike, and do any other outdoor activity. This all seemed impossible when I looked at my broken body. A nurse came into the room and interrupted my downward spiral. She wheeled me to the operating room, where I started counting back from ten and was promptly put out of my misery.

I woke up later that evening in my room and was told the surgery went well. The antibiotics I was on worked, and doctors removed the infected tissue. I was relieved but still depressed about the realizations I had in pre-op. I made a promise to myself not to dwell on negative thoughts and focus on getting back to doing each and every passion and hobby I was telling myself I couldn't do with one hand. This promise proved very hard to keep in the upcoming months, but I believe this conscious decision was another key to my recovery.

After a decent night of sleep, I said goodbye to my siblings early in the morning and looked forward to a relaxing Sunday in bed. My day was filled with visits from friends as well as naps here and there. It was the first day I felt like I was getting in the "groove" of hospital life. I was still in a lot of pain and could barely move, but the visits and catching up on sleep made the time go by fast.

I did have another surgery the following morning that I was getting nervous about. It was going to focus on repairing my right knee, which I had been told was in rough shape, but I had barely thought about it because of all my other issues. I was told there was extensive nerve damage in the leg, so this operation could be a deciding factor on whether I'd be able to walk again.

That night, I couldn't fall asleep, so I turned on the TV. I noticed there were a lot of commercials displaying holiday cheer. Holiday cheer was the last thing I wanted to see at the time, and I couldn't escape it, no matter how much I flipped through the channels.

I eventually gave in to the holiday mood and left the TV on a channel showing Christmas movies. I was pleasantly distracted by the madness that is *Christmas Vacation* and drifted off to sleep that night with the positivity of *Elf* in the background. I felt a strange sense of peace that I hadn't felt since being in the hospital.

I was wheeled out of my room early in the morning for my next surgery. My dad met me in the pre-op room and comforted me before I went under. There was a sense of hope with this procedure because it had the potential to be my last surgery. My left wrist and leg were put back together, my right arm was cleaned out, and all that was left was fixing up my right knee. I said goodbye to my dad once again and took the plunge back into the darkness.

I woke up that evening and was told the procedure went well. They installed a lot of titanium screws and plates in my knee to keep it together; the hope now was that it would heal according to plan. Then, a surge of optimism overcame me as I was told I could possibly be done with surgeries.

The following days consisted of several visitors from my church and work, eating my first complete meals, and regular attempts at physical therapy. A notable experience in physical therapy was when they moved me from my bed to a table they rolled in. Several nurses had to help slide a large board with handles under me and lift up the board in order to move me. This is the exact procedure I would assist in at work involving critically injured sea turtles. We would slide a board under them and lift them in order to get them out of their hospital tank. I was doing this less than a month ago, and now a group of nurses were doing the same to me because I had the same injuries as several of our turtles.

I couldn't help but laugh out loud and explain this unbelievable irony to the nurses assisting me. During any physical therapy session, they had to pump me full of painkillers just for me to endure even the smallest movements. It was scary to think about the pain I'd have once off pain meds and even scarier to think about all the drugs my body had become dependent on.

CHAPTER 23

Mourning and Rejoicing

Chase

Despite all of the descriptions and images we had previously received, I still almost passed out when we first stepped into Carter's ICU room. Any one of his four limb injuries was enough to take someone out of commission for a long time. To deal with all of them at once was unimaginable. I just had to sit down.

It had been a tumultuous couple of weeks—from getting that first phone call from the Palm Beach Police Department, to not knowing if he was going to keep his legs or even survive, to finally being able to visit him, to learning about his amazing recovery progress, and then having to return home and continue our day-to-day lives. I found myself constantly bouncing back and forth between mourning over that which was lost and rejoicing over all that was spared.

Through everything, Carter's resolve has been nothing short of incredible—both the tenacity to survive that first day and the strength to continue fighting over the following weeks. The scariest part of this ordeal is behind us, but there is still a long and challenging road ahead.

If anyone can do it, Carter can. And the support of the amazing community that surrounds him—in Florida, in Colorado, and throughout the rest of the globe—has been and will continue to be invaluable for his recovery.

CHAPTER 24

Pain Management

I've learned that home is not a place, it's a feeling.
—CECELIA AHERN, *LOVE, ROSIE*

Leila

AFTER MY TWO WEEKS IN DENVER, CHUCK PICKED ME UP from the Fort Lauderdale Airport. We had mixed emotions as we hugged and kissed. Putting yet more miles on Carter's Xterra on the eight-lane I-95 in pouring rain, our face-to-face reunion didn't really make much of a difference. And it certainly did not change the circumstances. Florida reality was something I could avoid when I was thousands of miles away.

But then, as eager as I was to be back, I dreaded what was ahead. And the trip to the airport was an interruption of Chuck's vigil. He had a routine and command of his post. I could tell he felt I might be a distraction to his around-the-clock caregiving. Driving on a moonlit and glistening highway, he reported the details of Carter's latest setback.

While I was in flight to Florida, the medical staff determined that there was no need for Carter to remain in his step-down room, and they rolled him down the hall yet again to the medical/surgical ward (med/surge for short), where most patients recover after surgery or an illness. And because he was improving physically, the doctors removed the pain pump. Now all pain would be managed by oral meds. Initially, the pain was managed by sedation after each surgery or therapy session. Once the ventilator was removed, the pain pump dripped morphine every hour, and Carter could supplement with the pump as needed. It kept him comfortable.

Moving to oral meds felt like a step in the right direction, but it turned out to be a tough balancing act. Carter suffered not only pain without the pump but also a great deal of anxiety. To reduce the anxiety, the doctors tried another drug, which made him nauseous. His clean-living and tattered body reacted to this fresh cocktail of meds, and he couldn't reach the toilet in time. Carter pleaded with them, saying he'd rather feel pain than nausea. It was a humiliating and miserable first night in med/surge for Carter with Chuck by his side.

After we arrived in West Palm Beach, Chuck and I stopped in Carter's room around 11 p.m. I just wanted to touch him. (But I wasn't sure if a twenty-five-year-old even *wants* his mom touching him!) He opened his eyes for a few seconds and didn't seem to mind. Then we headed straight to the Quantum House, which now felt like our second home.

Early the next morning, we stepped into Carter's snail-paced world and, unfortunately, interrupted his sleep. Chuck informed me that the schedule of pain meds and changing his bandages was extremely regimented. Sleep time is segmented and did not come easily. Carter was happy to see me but quiet, fidgety, and fatigued. I asked what his pain level was. About a seven-and-a half, he replied. I asked what his pain was after the meds. About a five or a six, he replied.

Relaunching into the confines of Carter's recovery while I had been free to roam as I pleased unsettled me. Observing Carter's stoic approach to his daily pain was heart-wrenching yet admirable. His tolerance was deeply rooted in his determination to break out of the hospital bed. Just the day before, Carter had told Chuck that he intended to run again.

Between visits from friends, nurses, and a prosthetic representative, Carter dozed or listened to true-crime podcasts. Chuck and I shifted our thoughts toward our children beyond the hospital walls and the upcoming holidays.

The Quantum House had been our home since our first night in Florida. Our room, similar to a hotel room, was just down the hall from a spacious two-dishwasher kitchen, a dining room with ten tables, and a living area with ample seating and a piano. It was ideal for the two of us, but there were no vacant rooms for the kids. The house was filled to capacity with families of children from around the globe awaiting their surgery with world-renowned pediatric orthopedic surgeon Dr. Dror Paley.

Since we wanted our kids with us in Florida at Christmas, preferably all staying in the same place, we decided to make a big ask. Chuck and I approached some of the Loggerhead volunteers who regularly visited Carter to see if they knew of a home or condo where our family could stay over the holidays. Our ask was answered.

A Loggerhead volunteer had a friend named Carolyn who had a second condo just down the hall from her own. She had purchased it for her son and grandchildren when they visited. Her Jewish family planned to gather in January, which meant the condo was available for us. After hearing about our situation, Carolyn generously gave us the keys to the three-bedroom condo that overlooked Clematis Street, the heart of downtown West Palm Beach.

Chuck and I gathered our bags, drove over, and parked the Xterra in the cavernous parking lot with tight corners beneath the 610 Clematis building. The condo was on the fourth floor, so we took the elevator on the way up to carry us and our bags and the stairs on the way down—as they were much faster than the elevator. An oversized brown leather sectional filled the living space and encircled a large coffee table and a media center with a TV, several gaming consoles, and plenty of DVDs. The round dining table sat ten, each bedroom had its own bath, and our bedroom walk-in closet was almost larger than the kitchen.

As we acclimated to the new digs, we discovered that the nightlife on the popular Clematis Street got noisy, so we headed to Target to purchase some fans for white noise. Our new home was a short walk to Starbucks and Rocco's Tacos and Tequila Bar, where they serve the best guacamole in town. The street ended at the West Palm Beach Public Dock, which harbors luxurious yachts and polished boats carrying hefty outboard motors on the Intracoastal Waterway. The sight of them made me gulp back tears, and yet I caught myself studying the propellers frequently as I ran "the loop." The loop became a favorite as we craved a walk or run to distract us from reality. The route followed the trails along the water and crossed the Royal Park Bridge to the elite Palm Beach Island—one of the wealthiest zip codes in the world. Along the Palm Beach "Lake Trail," we passed palm trees, banyan trees, the majestic Kapok tree near the Flagler Museum, and extravagant homes with immaculate landscaping and enormous iguanas guarding their private docks. The Flagler Memorial Bridge closed the loop back to Clematis Street.

Carolyn's generosity was one of many ways that friends and strangers showered our family with love. Another Loggerhead volunteer held a special "loving-kindness" group meditation for Carter.

Somebody took a video, and I stumbled across it on Facebook. It showed complete strangers gathering at sunset for an oceanside prayer meeting for Carter. Kathy, one of those who stood by Carter's ICU bed as we traveled to Florida, held a prayer vigil in her home. Money continued to flow into Carter's GoFundMe account. Others let us know that Carter's CaringBridge was the first thing they checked as they drank their morning coffee. Close friends graciously "took us as we were" and embraced our crying, cursing, laughing, and sighing. These actions wove a "sacred web," a safety net where we could free fall, bounce back, and face the next hour, the next day.

As wonderful as these gifts were, I would have given anything to go back in time and erase our permanent loss. But, like Carter, we grew tolerant of the pain, even if it was still at a level six or seven. And amidst the pain, we found treasures in tragedy.

CHAPTER 25

Shit Day

The hospital feels that Carter should be moved out.

—Dr. Claude Oster

Leila

Not long after Carter moved to the medical/surgical ward, we received a visit from Steve, our lawyer's top paralegal. He specializes in dealing with insurance companies after settlements are granted. I'll never forget Steve's bedside manner. It felt like he was one of the first strangers since we rushed to Florida who really saw us . . . saw our pain as parents. His gentle, soothing, and affirming tone delivered a sense of calm to two parents who were drained of fuel and hope.

It was in this same tone that Steve informed us that our insurance company had a right to Carter's settlement money.

Whoa! *What?*

Yep. Because he received a settlement, our insurance company could ask for their money back—it's in the fine print of every policy! Carter could potentially have to pay back the insurance company the hundreds of thousands of dollars billed to them by St. Mary's Medical Center.

This ruling is called ERISA, the Employee Retirement Income Security Act of 1974. It means an employee with health insurance through an employer is governed by ERISA. The health insurance policy contains a "subrogation" provision granting the insurer (our insurance company) the right to be reimbursed for all medical bills in the event that an employee receives a personal injury recovery from a third party (in our case, Stanton's insurance company).[1] Steve assured us he would contact our insurance company and represent our cause. He cautioned us that from his vast experience with these types of cases, it required a diplomatic approach and loads of patience.

If there was anyone you wanted on your side in a situation like this, it was Steve. And yet, his comforting bedside manner did little to lighten the blow of his stomach-dropping news. It felt like everything gained from a settlement for Carter's future could now be taken away by the cost of healing his body in the present. We thanked Steve for his visit and his efforts as an ambassador for Carter's assets with heavy, frustrated hearts.

While we were still reeling from Steve's news, a doctor we had never met walked into Carter's room. He introduced himself as Dr. Claude Oster, the head of the rehabilitation unit at St. Mary's Medical Center. With a strong accent and a scratchy throat that he kept clearing with little success, he announced, "The hospital feels that Carter should be moved out [of St. Mary's] for a different level of care."

He reasoned, "Carter cannot put weight on any of his extremities, and since he needs at least one limb to be

Shit Day

weight-bearing before acute rehabilitation can formally begin, it would be best for him to transfer to a critical care unit in a different hospital unless you [Chuck and I] could provide Carter with twenty-four-seven home care. Carter would return to the St. Mary's rehab unit when his body was ready for rehab."

Next, the doctor stated, "Someone will stop by to give you a virtual tour of his recommended hospital that offers critical care."

Chuck and I were stunned, immediately defensive, but not fooled. We put two and two together and figured that Carter was being downgraded to a nursing home.

The unexpected entrance and upsetting announcement from a doctor we had just met threw all of us for a loop. We were working with multiple doctors and had just changed rooms, *again*. Now this?

So Chuck asked, "Why not stay here?"

Then, we got to the bottom of the issue.

The doctor said, "Under the guidelines of the hospital and the insurance company, you cannot keep a patient for a long period of time."

Chuck asked, "Who determines that?"

And the doctor replied, "It's the agency and the insurance company's decision."

Chuck: "Who communicates this to us?"

Doctor: "Your case manager; I'm just relaying the message to you."

Chuck: "I'm not sure if we've made that decision yet . . . or has the decision been made *for* us?"

Doctor: "The decision has been made for you, by your case manager."

Chuck and Leila: "We just talked to our case manager and told her that we do not live here. She did not mention this to us."

Chuck: "With respect, we need to talk with the manager of case management."

Doctor: "They will keep pushing to get Carter out. The hospital will not let him stay here."

This is one of only a few conversations I remember word for word because I recorded it with Voice Memo on my phone. I was going to get into the habit of doing this more and happened to catch this one.

* * *

Carter was clearly upset and did not want to move from St. Mary's. After we let the news sink in, Chuck and I resolutely walked to the nurse's station and asked for our case manager. We had words with her, and I'm pretty sure the entire floor heard those words as our anxiety levels rose.

Soon after the confrontation, while we were simmering down in Carter's room, one of Carter's occupational therapists stopped in. She overheard the entire exchange with the case manager and understood our frustration. She empathized and validated our desire to keep Carter's care at St. Mary's. We were caught between hospital policy and insurance company demands. Carter had become an expensive liability for each, and they wanted him out.

Around 4 p.m. that day, all of Carter's caregivers—the trauma docs, surgeons, nurses, therapists, and the case manager—huddled for a team meeting. Chuck and I were invited to join them about twenty minutes into the meeting. They explained to us that the rehab unit's main requirement for Carter to be transferred depended on his ability to bear weight on one limb. Then they encouraged us to voice our opinions.

One of our main concerns was an interruption in Carter's care from caregivers who knew his situation and whom we trusted in a facility that now felt like "home" to us. Another concern was for Carter's mental and emotional health. After numerous moves within St. Mary's, most of them being anything but smooth, a transfer to a foreign facility could trigger more trauma. Plus, Carter has always been highly sensitive to change and suffered considerable sensory integration issues as a child. The occupational therapists' eyes lit up with understanding when we mentioned Carter's past and confirmed their concern for Carter. They, too, were on his side and knew it was in Carter's best interest to stay put.

Later that day, "the "powers that be" determined that Carter would stay at St. Mary's. His renewed "pass" to stay longer at St. Mary's resulted in a "free" upgrade to yet another new room.

By the end of the day, Carter rolled a few doors down from a cramped room with a broken TV and a door that almost swung into his bed to a spacious corner room with a table and chairs and a working TV. We soon learned that this wasn't just any room; this was the Rose Kennedy Suite, a luxurious room where the matriarch of the Kennedy dynasty, including President John F. Kennedy, Senator Robert F. Kennedy, and Senator Ted Kennedy, resided when she required medical attention.

Chuck and I named this day "Shit Day" as we climbed into bed. We didn't want to forget the day that threw us into unexpected boxing matches with our insurance company and the hospital. It ended with a small but mighty victory where the power and humanity of the caregivers defeated the bureaucracy of institution regulations. We would have to count on Steve to win the battle with our insurance company, but today, "good" won this round.

CHAPTER 26

Andy

If you save a life, you are responsible for that life.
—Chinese Proverb

Leila

Although there were many uncertainties after the accident, the one thing Carter could count on was Andy. Andy showed up at St. Mary's just about every day to check on Carter. As we learned during one of his regular visits, he was just starting his own healing process.

As Carter slept in the Rose Kennedy Suite, the three of us sat in folding camp chairs that Chuck and I had imported from our Clematis condo. (Even the Rose Kennedy Suite didn't have enough chairs for Carter's visitors.) In a matter-of-fact hushed tone, Andy recounted his experience from that awful day—and we quickly realized he was battling personal demons of his own:

> After the ambulance sped off with sirens blaring as it rushed Carter to the hospital, I sat at a cement picnic table next to the beach entrance with investigators from the Palm Beach Police Department and Florida

Fish and Wildlife Conservation Commission (FWC). I still wore my swim trunks and a T-shirt stained with Carter's blood. I spoke for three intense hours, often breaking down in tears as I recounted the details of the accident.

When I finally finished my statement, I walked back to my car and sat frozen in the driver's seat. That's when my demons tried to haunt me. Anxiety boiled through my chest and nearly convinced me that a stiff drink would "kill the feel." To ward off the temptation, I picked up my phone to call a friend, a sober friend.

In a bloodied T-shirt and swim trunks, I drove myself to St. Mary's to await word of Carter's condition after surgery.

Andy stepped back to fill us in on how he landed in Florida, at Loggerhead Marinelife Center, and at Carter's side at the right time, at the right place.

In 2013, I recognized that I needed help. Since high school, I drank, smoked pot, and partied nightly with friends back in my hometown in Illinois. It was the culture I knew best, and it was nothing all that unusual in my circle. I remained loyal to my job as a CNC technician while feeding my addiction after work.

After recognizing that life had to change, I found a rehab place in Florida and signed up. I always liked water, fishing, and sea life, and Florida sounded like a good place to find help. After months of treatment, I returned to Illinois, went back to work, and eventually circled back to my addiction. With the urging of friends and family, I headed again to the same rehabilitation center in Florida a year or so later for another round of therapy. Again, I returned home only to be overpowered by my addiction to alcohol. I confess that I did not put the work into making the change when I checked in for recovery both times. My depleted self-control let me slip back to the bottle and back to the bottom of the barrel again.

In 2017, I realized I didn't want to live and didn't want to die. I found a new rehab center in Florida and committed to their program. The third time was the charm, and part of the reason was my visit to Loggerhead Marinelife Center while I resided at a designated sober house.

As part of their recovery program, I was encouraged to serve others, so I volunteered at Loggerhead. It was the highlight of my week as I saw my own brokenness and healing reflected firsthand in the center's mission of rescuing sea turtles.

Soon, I was appointed a docent, sharing my expertise on all things turtles with visitors. My commitment to Loggerhead eventually landed me a part-time position at Loggerhead. I began to stroll the breezeways with Carter, fixing things, maintaining operations, and "entertaining" volunteers at the front desk while decorating for the holidays and doing other such chores.

A full-time job in maintenance operations opened, and I was elevated to the position. As the center continued to grow, Carter also moved into full-time work after he graduated from Palm Beach Atlantic University. Carter and I built new tanks for turtles, cared for the aquariums, assembled desks, set up for parties, and fixed planks on the Juno Beach Pier. It didn't take long for a friendship to blossom. I saw Carter as the "young Andy" I always wanted to be—a marine biology major with a passion for sea life. We both set up fish tanks in our small apartments and liked diving.

The accident on a sunny morning at the Breakers Reef catapulted our casual friendship into an unexpected "godly" realm. I never considered myself a religious person or a person of faith, but the event revealed God or one greater than ourselves... The One or Higher Being I was encouraged to find as a recovering alcoholic. On Thanksgiving 2019, I encountered the most profound spiritual moment I have ever experienced.

While a brutally mangled Carter declared, "I'm done, it's over," as he lay bleeding on the boat that struck him, I reminded him, "God is here, Carter, God is with us."

Along with the boat captain, I handed off Carter to the paramedics, who waded waist-deep to greet us when the boat got to the beach. My strength to get Carter to shore disappeared the minute the ambulance left. I fell to my knees on the beach and began to sob and screamed, "Holy shit, my friend just about died in my arms."

My brain looped the horrible scene of the incident, and this led to powerful symptoms of PTSD or post-traumatic stress disorder. I was treated with EMDR (eye movement and desensitization and reprocessing), which dampened the emotions connected to a tragedy. As hard as the accident is to erase, I have been able to flip the lens and reflect on the fact that I experienced and now "understand" the power of God: I now know it's real. No doubt about it.

Carter's good days and setbacks as he recovers directly affect my mood and my own progress. My sensitivity makes me feel like I live vicariously through Carter's recovery. His progress is mine, too.

I see providence in the fact that I am an alcoholic. If I hadn't gotten treatment, I wouldn't be down in Florida. Everything I've done in my life led up to the moment of Carter's accident.

As I fight my battles with post-traumatic stress disorder and the temptation of numbing with alcohol, I see a reason for being sober by tapping into the power of God.

It feels good.

As we absorbed Andy's story in the Rose Kennedy Suite, something came to me. Andy's courage to dramatically change his condition after two failed attempts must have had an influence on Carter's tenacity, which we witness each day. As I see it, both of them are obligated to each other. Andy chose to live, and through the power of serendipity, he was there to save Carter's life. Now it's Carter's turn to muster up the courage to change his condition.

Chuck and I wept with Andy as Carter slept, and that evening, Andy moved up the ranks to our fourth son.

CHAPTER 27

The Slog

Falling down is part of life. Getting back up is living.
—José N. Harris Brushing, *MI VIDA*

Leila

The word "slog" was added to my vocabulary when Dr. A stopped by to check on the condition of Carter's limbs. The word, which means "to toil or to keep your nose to the grindstone,"[1] reminded me of the drawbridges we encountered on the roads along the downtown West Palm Beach waterfront. Chuck soon memorized the bridge schedule and planned our trips around it. Inevitably, we would get caught and roll our eyes when we'd see the lights flash, traffic stop, and the decks (or leaves) majestically rise and break apart to let vessels pass in the water beneath—for about fifteen minutes, time stood still. We felt trapped and helpless and resigned to waiting until the leaves would gracefully drop and join as one to let us continue with our day.

Watching the drawbridges was similar to watching Carter's wounds heal. The long and crooked incisions were stapled or sewn to bring the tissue on both sides of the wound closer to mending and healing. As Dr. A said, we must "slog" through this time and be patient as cells regenerate and come together.

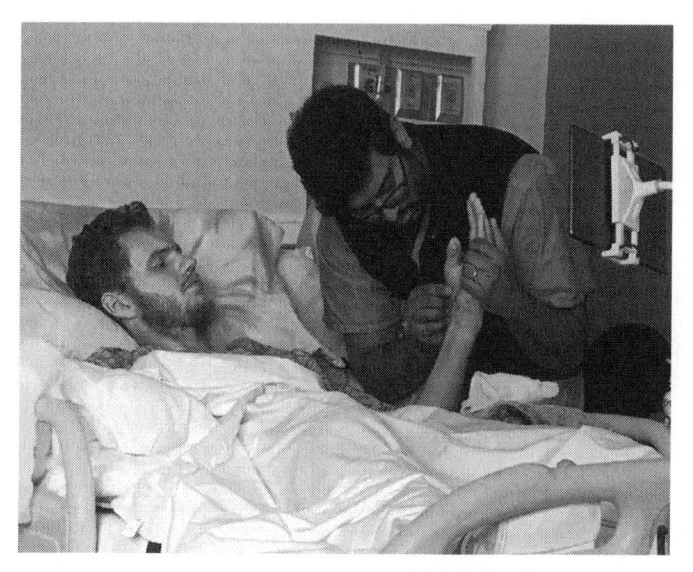

Dr. A inspecting the wound on Carter's left hand
(Photo Credit: Viss Family)

Fortunately, Carter's slog was now taking place in the spacious Rose Kennedy Suite, bathed in natural light from the floor-length corner windows. The room was just what the doctor ordered. (Pun intended!)

The slog was broken up by binging *The Office* and having a jam-packed visitor schedule, including a visit by Stephen Schwartz, Carter's fishing buddy. The last time Stephen visited St. Mary's, Carter was hooked to a breathing tube in the ICU. He beamed at the vast improvement since then. Stephen declared that Carter holds the title of the luckiest fisherman on his boat because Carter caught a fish that most people travel the world to catch: a bonefish.

Physical therapists began work on Carter's feet, pushing them gently forward to build up strength and loosen Carter's tight calf muscles. Chuck and I donned latex gloves and learned to do this, too. It became a therapeutic ritual for Chuck as well as for Carter. It was something Chuck did every night before we left for the evening.

Chuck got kicked out of a physical therapy session because he got a little jumpy when Carter looked like he would fall over when sitting up in bed. Shortly after, I got kicked out when Carter told me I made him nervous by moving around and taking pictures with my phone.

Sitting up was hard for Carter as it took great effort, and he had no healthy limbs to lean on. This caused his blood pressure to skyrocket and made him lightheaded. Carter weighed approximately 190 pounds before Thanksgiving; now, three weeks later, he'd trimmed down to 170. The goal was to strengthen Carter by importing protein to the Rose Kennedy Suite.

Chuck began bringing protein-packed smoothies, made at the condo, every morning to Carter. We picked up a sausage and egg bagel from Makebs—Carter's favorite breakfast place while attending Palm Beach Atlantic University. Loggerhead volunteers brought chicken and pasta from C.R. Chicks, Carter's favorite Italian restaurant.

Along with the pasta, they gave us #CarterStrong T-shirts ordered to help raise funds for Carter at the upcoming Loggerhead Christmas party. Carter frequently requested pork souvlaki and falafels from his favorite Greek restaurant called Souvlaki Grill. And like before the accident, every night, Carter finished a bag of raw spinach, munching a few leaves at a time.

Although his appetite was improving, Carter's bowel activity was not. Things get messed up with all the drugs, anesthesia, inactivity, loss of appetite, etc. So irregularity became an ongoing issue along with everything else. Any pride or privacy that Carter had left was checked at the door.

It had been two weeks since the last surgery, so a doctor stopped by to remove staples and stitches. With large tweezers, he lifted out the staples—I was shocked to see they looked just like the ones from the office supply store! He used scissors to cut and pull out the stitches sewn over Carter's deep cuts.

One wound had previously been a large gash with missing tissue and bone. Somehow, they stitched together skin to form a cover over the flesh. Unfortunately, a large hematoma formed in this area. As some of the stitches were snipped, the pool of excess blood from the hematoma began to seep, and the doctor gently pushed it out. That's when I left the bedside and checked my phone for a diversion. The pain meds occasionally brought Carter's pain down to a level five, but usually, it hung around a six or seven. Carter winced only a couple of times during the entire procedure. The doctor admitted he's one tough guy.

Each hint of progress made the slog tolerable. Sitting became easier thanks to therapy and his protein-packed diet.

Soon, Carter sat in his wheelchair for over three hours. He showed more strength in his left leg, and Dr. Mario Rueda, the attending trauma doctor, was very pleased to see his toes move on both feet.

Carter's left hand, in a splint, could hold a spoon and a water bottle; he could also use it to text on his iPad. The big hematoma on his left leg disappeared. His right arm had gone down in swelling, and the stitches were healing but tender. Physical therapists moved Carter to the edge of the bed with both feet on the floor and bent his left knee while the right leg remained in a brace. Each "bend" was measured with a protractor-like ruler. The PT's "flexion" goal was to break the seventy mark. Carter made it to seventy-nine—and it was hard to watch as his sutures seemed so fresh.

I made an attempt at trimming his fingernails. Although I got the job done, I apparently didn't cut them nearly short enough at first, and Carter thought that my idea of filing them was "dumb." I didn't mind Carter taking out his frustrations on me. He had every right to be frustrated.

Dr. Borrego stopped by to check on Carter's progress. An L-shaped area of numbness remained on his foot, which gradually receded, indicating that his bruised nerves were healing. And yet, Carter struggled to move his right toes toward his nose. When he attempted to do this, Dr. Borrego was pleased that he could feel the nerves pulsing or firing on the ball of Carter's foot. He claimed, "The signal is there, but the connection between the brain and the nerve is not quite strong enough. Be patient, as nerves regenerate one millimeter a day."

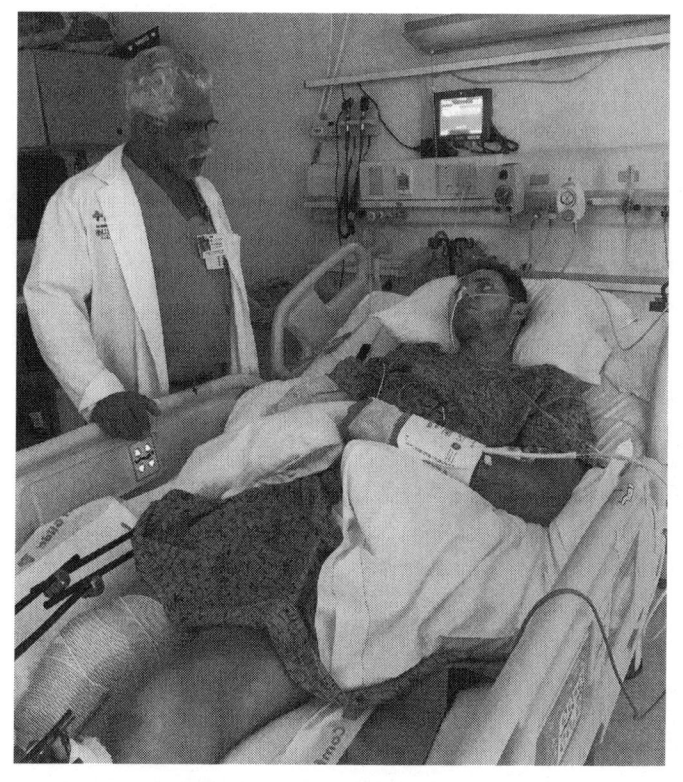

Dr. B speaking to Carter while he was in the ICU
(Photo Credit: Viss Family)

Chuck was concerned about his right foot, so he extended his nightly ritual of rubbing Carter's foot a couple of times a day. He removed the boot and gently pushed his toes forward to stretch Carter's calf. The foot brace made Carter's feet smell, so Chuck rubbed them with frankincense essential oil for the room diffuser. The sensation calmed Carter as he watched *Parks and Rec*—he had finished all the seasons of *The Office*.

During these calf stretches, Chuck pondered to himself why God would allow such severe physical damage to Carter. At the same time, he prayed to the Great Physician to bring back all movement and sensations in Carter's right leg and foot.

This routine was one of many Chuck initiated after the accident—he functioned better with structure. He would leave me behind to sleep and visit Carter first thing in the morning. Carter likes his coffee the same way Chuck does—strong and dark. Each morning, he brought Carter coffee and Starbucks' pumpkin bread. They used the alone time to discuss pre-accident life, post-accident life, health, housing, finances, dreams, and schedules. It was something that Chuck declared each father and son should do more often.

Every ounce of mobility and strength gained in the countless hours of Chuck's massages and the physical and occupational therapy depended on Carter's determination to power through the pain. One therapist joked that PT stands for "pain and torture" and OT stands for "other torture."

CHAPTER 28

God's Plan

Carter

The days in the Rose Kennedy Suite were filled with gradual improvements. I could use my left hand for a majority of basic tasks and was able to roll on my side without assistance. It usually took three physical therapists to maneuver me into my wheelchair and roll me around the hospital. This was the first time I was "mobile" since arriving at the hospital, and my first request was to spend some time outside.

The therapist wheeled me through the sliding front doors, and I'll never forget the feeling of the sun shining on my pale, broken body. It was like a dose of a medicine I desperately needed.

She placed me near a bench so I could enjoy the outdoors again. I watched lizards running through the grass, birds flying from tree to tree, and small insects walking on the pavement. A gentle breeze blew across my face, and although we were in a grimy hospital parking lot, it felt like I was experiencing the most beautiful, majestic natural habitat God's world had to offer. It was like being reintroduced to a world I had all but forgotten.

After about an hour of soaking in the sights and sounds of the outdoors, the therapist wheeled me through the front doors, and it was back to life on the inside.

I would anticipate my dad's arrival to the Kennedy Suite at seven sharp every morning. He would arrive with Starbucks coffee and hand me my order. We would discuss what was going on that day, who was visiting, what time I had therapy, and any updates from friends and family in the outside world. These visits gave my life structure again. I always had a daily routine throughout college and the years after. It kept my mind healthy to keep a routine, and I thought routines would be lost after the accident.

We also had time to talk and reflect during these visits. I was barely able to have a relationship with him before the accident because I lived so far away. Even though I lost so much in the accident, this was the first time I realized I had gained something from this in the form of a closer relationship with my family.

A topic that came up several times in my dad's visits was the situation involving the boat driver that hit me. A civil case was going on, and a lawyer would frequent my room to update me on its progress.

This was the first time I really started thinking about the driver. All I had heard about him was that he was very remorseful about what happened, and this incident devastated him and his family. Throughout my stay at the hospital, the thought of *I'm here because of him* never dwelled in my mind. Although there is truth to this, I avoided this thought so as to not harbor anger or hatred toward this person. I believed that would only hinder my recovery. I truly wanted this case to end quickly and with a fair outcome so I could move on with my life.

Instead, *I'm here because of God* often crossed my mind. This made me angry at God sometimes, but it also helped me accept and embrace the situation God placed me in. This was the plan God had for my life since I was born.

CHAPTER 29

Christmas Gift

Carter

CHRISTMAS DAY REARED ITS HEAD BEFORE I KNEW IT. My optimistic attitude of being discharged by Christmas in the ICU was completely wrong. I wasn't even close at that point. However, I made progress in physical therapy by sitting in a wheelchair for about three hours a day and improving the bend in my left knee. In occupational therapy, I was working on desensitizing the nerves in my right arm, which proved to be very painful. Also, the civil case with the driver of the boat was settled fairly, which was a relief for me.

On Christmas Eve night, I watched *Die Hard*, the perfect Christmas movie, with my siblings, and on Christmas morning, my entire family entered my room with fresh, homemade cinnamon rolls.

Having my family join me in the hospital for Christmas was an invaluable blessing. My favorite hospital companion, Iggy, the golden retriever, also appeared and licked some cinnamon roll icing off my fingers.

That afternoon, I got the ultimate gift: eighty-five staples were removed from my wounds. This slow, tedious process took the nurse about two and a half hours. I remember the small jolts of pain as each staple was plucked from my skin. I talked to the nurse during this process and gave her details about the incident and my injuries. This was the first time I explained the accident to someone I didn't know, and I couldn't believe the words coming out of my mouth. I breathed a sigh of relief when she pulled out the last staple; that meant I had the rest of the afternoon to myself.

That evening, my family came to my room for Christmas dinner. We ate Thai food, played several trivia-based games, and opened gifts. It felt like we were at home and not the hospital.

That night, going to sleep, I couldn't help but compare that Christmas to the previous year. Although my shark encounter on the Breakers Reef was quite a gift, I felt very lonely and isolated. To have all my family here meant the world to me, and I likely wouldn't have seen them for Christmas that year if the Thanksgiving Day incident hadn't happened. I was so grateful to experience this Christmas with them, and it was a true example of how God brings people together through tragedy.

CHAPTER 30

Home for the Hospital Days

*Grief unexpectedly cancels and changes
any anticipated holiday and future plans.*

—Leila and the Grief Monster

Chuck

My father passed away in July 2019. At Dad's hospital bedside before he passed, we listened to Chris Tomlin during some gut-wrenchingly tough but also strikingly beautiful moments. Ever since, I have replayed my Chris Tomlin playlist on Spotify over and over and over. But since Thanksgiving, I have been unable to listen to music. It's pretty ironic considering I'm a musician, and it's the Christmas season.

Leila

The accident shattered routines. Chuck and I abandoned our jobs and our home. Our world whittled down to the four walls of a hospital room. Our kids juggled their jobs and absorbed the questions, love, and support on the Denver home front. We all felt divided and depleted. The best course of action was a gathering in Florida for the holiday season.

At the start of Brittany's school winter break, Chase and Brittany hopped on a plane and arrived around 2:30 a.m. They rented a minivan to drive from the Fort Lauderdale Airport. It was too dark, and they were too tired to notice that the van had not been cleaned after the previous renters. It became a pattern. There was an issue with every rental car experience—an excessive wait at the counter, a heated steering wheel that couldn't be turned off, a rude employee, a Camaro instead of the promised Camry. Nonetheless, moonlight and Google Maps guided the weary travelers to their new sleeping quarters. They parked the minivan at 610 Clematis and fell into bed.

After Chase and Brittany stopped in to say hi to Carter, and while he powered through another physical therapy session, the four of us snuck away for some retail therapy at The Gardens Mall in Palm Beach Gardens. We had to return an iPad cover that did not work for Carter's new device. And we wanted to check out the Give Back Event that the Kendra Scott jewelry store was holding for Carter. The store frequently partners with Loggerhead Marinelife Center, and when they heard about Carter's accident, they gave 20 percent of the proceeds from their sales between 2 and 5 p.m. to Carter! It was a touching act of generosity and an excuse for Brittany and me to buy some new earrings.

Shopping was a welcome break, yet it felt odd to "enjoy" the moment. It rattled my hospital brain, as did the sight of students of a local piano and vocal studio performing

Christmas music in the mall. The lineup of students in their holiday best and their smiling teacher reminded me of what I had been doing just a month earlier. Surprisingly, the jolt back to my past reality didn't bring me to tears. Numbness replaced any passion I had for teaching. Life before the accident seemed inconsequential.

Hospital food did not satisfy Carter's refined palette, so we developed a mandatory takeout rotation from Carter's favorite restaurants. After Chase and Brittany made a trip back to the Fort Lauderdale Airport to pick up Levi and Erin (in a cleaner van), they picked up Greek food in keeping with the cuisine calendar. That let Chuck and me off the hook for bringing Carter his dinner, so we accepted an invitation to dine with Loggerhead friends. The lovely wine and a delicious dinner at a restaurant in the heart of West Palm Beach pulled us away from our self-designated bedside posts. The shopping and dining made it feel like we escaped the walls of our navel-gazing and laser focus on Carter, at least for a little while.

Chase, Brittany, Levi, and Erin established their own routines during their stay at the condo. They, too, ran around the drawbridge-swanky-zip-code loop and kept an eye out for the three-foot-long orange iguana sunning on the private docks. They strolled down to the Clematis Street Starbucks for coffee before they embedded themselves in Carter's slog. Every day, he could sit just a little longer in the wheelchair, so they made a point of wheeling Carter outside to enjoy some sunshine.

One day, we left Carter to his "slog torture chamber" in the Rose Kennedy Suite, and the six of us headed to a meeting with financial advisors at a large trust company. We were unsure how much money Carter would have from the settlement. Steve, the paralegal from our attorney's office, continued his patient diplomacy with our insurance company as they debated how much to cash in from Carter's misfortune. (Of all the events in this horrific situation, nothing infuriated me more than the fear that Carter could be left with financial insecurity thanks to a law passed thirty years ago.) Regardless, Ed assured us that Carter would have enough money to be managed by professionals. Ed recommended this private bank because of prior dealings with it and set up a meeting to discuss Carter's options.

As we sat around the table in our sweats—the only clothes we brought to Florida—we were served ice water in goblets, and each received an iPad to view the bank's plan. We looked out of place compared to the sharply dressed financial advisors across the table from us—some in dark suits, others in dresses with nylons and spiked heels. Their lofty presentation of bar graphs, tables, and pie charts was commendable. Although the visuals were meant to inform us "laypeople," the terms and numbers were far above my comprehension. And while we were impressed by the formal affair and the slippery white marble floor and matching walls with gold trim, Ed walked out disappointed. He was unhappy with the percentage the bank would charge for their services and felt they had overcomplicated Carter's options.

Tracking the micro milestones of Carter's recovery and securing a safe place for his settlement funds blurred the days. The world surrounded us with the holiday spirit, but we were distracted by grief and uncertainty. Signs that reminded

Home for the Hospital Days

us Christmas was around the corner were the kids in Florida—"home for the hospital days"—and Carter's empty therapy calendar. All the therapists had taken time off. In their absence, friends filled the time and imported a Christmas tree and trays of sweets. At one point, nine people were bringing Christmas cheer to the Rose Kennedy Suite.

Andy came by with Christine, the woman on the paddle board who used a bungee cord as a tourniquet to stop the bleeding on Carter's arm. Although Christine had visited Carter once in the ICU, he did not remember it. They stayed for a few hours recounting the timeline of Thanksgiving Day.

Chuck's cousin Carol and her husband, Daryl, stopped by, and we played "Dutch Bingo." Daryl's mom, Gertrude, was a dear friend and cousin of my grandma Hannah. This means that Daryl is a first cousin once removed from my dad, so he's my second cousin once removed.

Daryl and Carol were visiting their daughter and her family, who live in West Palm Beach. What made this visit stand out is that their daughter's husband, their son-in-law, is an operating room tech at St. Mary's Medical Center and was in Carter's first emergency surgery along with one other surgery. He did not know Carter's name during the first surgery; if he did, he would have recognized that he was distantly related.

When Christmas Day rolled around, it felt like any other day. It had been almost four weeks since the accident, which meant that Chuck had been in Florida since then, too. He missed home. We imported home to St. Mary's with a family Christmas tradition of homemade cinnamon rolls smothered in cream cheese frosting. Levi and Erin volunteered for the baking duty and discovered no rolling pin in the condo, so they rolled the dough with a wine bottle instead. Don, Sally, and Iggy arrived to a roomful of Carter's siblings gobbling up the warm, gooey rolls. Iggy couldn't stop licking Carter's frosted-covered fingers and almost ate the last one.

Don and Sally's presence showed us that light can be found at the end of an agonizing tunnel. Christmas Eve of 2019 marked fifteen years since Don's accident. Don and Sally became friends, examples, advocates, mentors, coaches, and cheerleaders. Good things trickled down to us during our hospital stay, thanks to Don. Sally validated and guided our thoughts so we could prepare for what the future would hold. They were and still are an integral part of Carter's recovery and our family's healing.

We sorted stacks of cards with endearing sentiments; touching, lovely blessings; and generous support. The encouragement Carter received from the cards and the comments on his CaringBridge gave him an overwhelming sense of gratitude. Not knowing how to thank everyone troubled him.

The family agreed that there would be no gifts that year, yet everyone came bearing gifts, including Carter. He had Facetimed Kate at the Loggerhead gift shop and picked out gifts for each of us. One more gift? In the cuisine rotation, Thai food was up next. Carter's favorite Thai restaurant was open on Christmas Day.

After dinner, we played a game that Carter's friend Kate had given him. The game, called Smart Ass, tests your knowledge of trivia. Despite a bum tummy, level-six-plus pain, and pain-med fog, Carter won just about every round. He's a trivia fan and plays it weekly at his favorite hangouts. From page one of this unfortunate chapter, our friend Ed marveled at Carter's strength and called him a badass. Now we know that Carter's also a "smart-ass."

In the midst of mourning and missing Christmas, we recognized and cherished priceless gifts that could not be wrapped in a bow:

- Andy, a recent addition to our family;
- Christine—who also saved Carter's life with a bungee cord;
- Dr. Borrego's availability to operate on Carter when he arrived at the ER;
- Dr. A's determination to save Carter's legs;
- the fact that, like his grandpa Wil, Carter is left-handed;
- saying goodbye to the breathing tube and the ICU;
- pain blockers that kept Carter's pain down to a level five or six instead of a ten plus and Carter's determination to wean himself from them;
- the outstanding community—family—at Loggerhead Marinelife Center;
- the loving support of the Truth Point congregation, including Jeremy, Eric, and Kathy;
- the doctors, nurses, nursing assistants, and physical and occupational therapists who watched over and cared for Carter;
- an upgrade to the Rose Kennedy Suite so our family could hang together for the holidays;

- the spacious three-bedroom condo generously provided by Carolyn;
- the unimaginable outpouring of love and financial support we received from our local communities and the global virtual community;
- CaringBridge for supplying a strong platform that helped us efficiently track and spread the word about Carter's story;
- three sons who surpassed our wildest expectations as parents; and
- Andy's profound words to Carter, "God is here," which echo the message of Christmas—"Immanuel . . . God with us" (see Matt. 1:23).

CHAPTER 31

First Step

Carter

THE NEW YEAR APPROACHED, AND I WAS EAGER TO LEAVE 2019 behind. I expected 2020 to bring recovery and an eventual return to normal life.

Just a few days after the new year, I was transferred out of the Rose Kennedy Suite and into the rehabilitation area of the hospital, where I needed to "graduate" before getting discharged. Although my new room was a lot smaller and not as nice as my previous room, I had my "new year, new me" optimism with me and was ready to move forward. Little did I know that this would be my most difficult stretch of hospital life.

My first days in rehab were filled with rigorous occupational and physical therapy. In occupational therapy, I would work on strengthening my left wrist and arm. I would feel tremendous pain whenever I would move my wrist forward or backward. In physical therapy, the first goal for me was to move in my wheelchair on my own. This was very difficult because my right arm was obviously useless, as well as my right leg, in which my knee could only bend to about 30 degrees at the time. I could only use my extremely weak left hand to turn the wheel and my even weaker left leg to push off the ground. I was soaked in sweat and reeling in pain after moving about twenty feet on my own. I remember thinking I would never be able to walk if moving in a wheelchair was this painful.

Another daily event in rehab was recreational therapy. This involved playing games, doing puzzles, painting, or just sitting outside with a therapist. Painting was obviously my favorite of the three therapies, and it was the first time I had been able to express myself artistically since the accident. I am incredibly grateful that I was born left-handed, and I was easily able to get back into drawing and painting, even with my very weak wrist. Painting brought me out of my current situation and placed me into a state of mind where everything was okay. It was a temporary release from the vigor of recovery and the push to get back to a normal life.

Near the end of my first week in rehab, I was making a lot of progress with moving in the wheelchair by myself. At the beginning of the week, I could barely move twenty feet in it, but now I could comfortably go down an entire hallway and back without much pain. This was the first time I thought of the phrase "time and repetition." Each time I tried moving in the wheelchair, it got a little less painful, and each time I attempted this, I moved a little more distance than the previous day. I figured that if I applied these two simple concepts to other factors in my recovery, I could get back to a normal life.

I clung to this phrase from then on. Time and repetition inspired hope and pushed me through the deepest valleys I encountered throughout my recovery.

First Step

The next step in my physical therapy program was standing up. I was incredibly nervous when my therapist announced that he would help me stand. I thought my legs would snap if I put my body weight on them. The therapist wrapped his arms under my armpits and slowly started lifting me. My torso rose up, and before I knew it, I was standing again. My life was horizontal for over a month, and the feeling of being vertical again gave me a rush of adrenaline I hadn't felt since the day of the incident.

But before I could do anything else while standing, the pain started surging in both my legs, and it felt like they would break. I hastily told the therapist to help me down, and he slowly lowered me back into my wheelchair. This was clearly a step in the right direction for me, and this had to get better with time and repetition.

About a week and a half into rehab, it was time to take my first steps. This was a "moment of truth" in my recovery. The doctors were not sure if I would be able to walk again when I was in the ICU, and I had been determined to prove them wrong ever since.

My therapist hoisted me up and out of my wheelchair, and I stood again. My left hand was grasping a walker, and the therapist had both of his hands on my side to keep me steady. I slowly lifted my left foot and felt a jolt of pain as all my body weight was on my right leg. I quickly put my left foot down about six inches forward from where I originally had it, moved my walker about a foot forward, and slid my right foot so it was in line with my left foot. I had officially stepped forward. I attempted another step with my right foot in the lead but promptly had to sit down due to severe pain in my left ankle.

I couldn't believe it. I had just taken my first step only forty days after I was run over by a boat and it wasn't nearly as bad as I thought it would be. My frail legs were aching, and I had beads of sweat on my face, but all I could think about was attempting that again. I insisted that my therapist hoist me back up, and I managed to take about a dozen steps that day.

When I was in bed that evening, I felt confident that I had this whole situation under control. Although I had a long recovery ahead, it seemed like everything was going according to the "plan" I had conceived in my head. This plan involved leaving the hospital in a couple of weeks, getting used to life on the outside again, and returning to a normal life of living independently and working by April or May of that year. What I didn't know was that my plan was obviously fleeting in the scope of God's master plan, and I was about to learn that the hard way.

CHAPTER 32

Good Samaritans

*Everyone may have a disability,
but it's up to you to choose what you do with it. The only
handicap we have is the one we create on our own.*

—Michael Dreamchaser Smith,
in the *Fort Cavazos Sentinel*, Aug. 16, 2018[1]

Leila

Carter had watched part of his twenty-five-year-old body float to the ocean floor and disappear as the water turned murky red. A man dubbed a Good Samaritan by the press was passing by in his boat soon after the accident. He assumed—like any charitable or helpful person—that rescuing Carter's arm was the right thing to do. Carter felt differently about his lightly tanned right elbow, wrist, palm, and five fingers instantly amputated by spinning, wicked-sharp blades. He wished his limb would have remained lost at sea and become part of the ocean. We learned later that despite the Good Samaritan's best intentions, the recovered arm was trashed in the hospital's biohazard waste pile.

In one of his six surgeries, the surgeons amputated his arm further above the elbow to reroute the nerves into muscles, a process called "targeted muscle reinnervation" (TMR, for short). The procedure can reduce phantom pain.[2] However, the doctors decided against TMR as there was too much risk of infection. Instead, they removed more bone and sewed up the skin into a flap around the bone so there was no exposed tissue.

For weeks, what was left of his right arm (to this day, I cannot call it a stump) wished the rest of his arm back as much as we did. Severed nerve endings tortured Carter by sending excruciating electrical shocks up and back down the limb. Occupational therapists would gently rub textures like a washcloth and the soft bristles of a toothbrush over the arm to help desensitize it. Carter tolerated the therapy but held back tears as the therapist struggled to place the snug compression sock back around the tender skin.

Chuck and I were shown how to compress and gently stretch open his arm toward his head. From Carter's eyes and sweaty brow, it was clear that the pain from this therapy was far worse than most of the other pain he experienced. Unfortunately, he soon found that removing the stitches ranked even higher on the pain meter. Managing the pain and the phantom pain was a top priority.

One day, I asked Carter what could be worse than what he was enduring at that moment. He immediately replied that the boat could have struck his back or head, or he could have died. He looked me in the eye and stated firmly: "This is God's plan for me."

Many wondered why the surgeons did not attempt to reattach his limb. Years ago, a longtime family friend and highly respected hand surgeon explained to Chuck and me that reattaching a finger usually doesn't work. We assumed an arm would be even more difficult to reattach, and a prosthetic was the best alternative.

From an uninvited guest, we learned that prosthetics are not always the preferred choice of amputees. One morning, as I sat in the corner of Carter's darkened ICU room, attempting to decompress from hours of too many visitors, tears, and fears, a woman with a missing arm suddenly appeared in the room to say hi. Although she came as a Good Samaritan to encourage Carter, I was stunned that she waltzed into his room unannounced and without an arm! The sight of her made me cringe and froze my welcome. I didn't care that she had adjusted to one arm and saw no need for a prosthetic. My grief couldn't stomach a "Hallmark greeting card" with an "everything-will-be-all right'" message.

A few weeks later, another Good Samaritan, this time *with* an invitation, confirmed that reattaching a severed arm doesn't usually work and that prosthetics are not always the best work-around. Michael Smith was a recent acquaintance of Christine, the woman considered Carter and Andy's unexpected new friend since Thanksgiving Day.

Michael is the only active-duty serviceman in the US military to serve with an above-the-elbow amputation. Over a decade of service in the US military, Michael was never injured. While on leave, he was hit by a car while riding his motorcycle.

The driver didn't stop.

Michael always carries a tourniquet in his motorcycle jacket just in case he needs to tie one, as many people do not know how to apply one properly. He told the nurse who happened to come to his aid at the accident scene about the tourniquet, and with it, she helped to stop the bleeding while they waited for the paramedics to arrive. His arm was found and reattached, but after twenty-two surgeries and several infections, it was removed. He lost his arm, over seventy pounds, and nearly lost a kidney as well.[3]

Christine first encountered Michael while subbing as a swim coach at a large swim training facility in early 2020. Michael was with Darla and her husband, who run the training facility. Darla had recently met Michael at Palm Beach International Airport, where she works for American Airlines. Michael's bike was lost, and she was helping him locate it at baggage claim. They became fast friends.

Michael trains as a professional triathlete for the US Army in Colorado Springs. He opted to train for the swimming portion in Florida with Darla's husband as his swim coach. Michael needed a place to stay, and Darla invited him to stay at her house on the spot.

When Darla took Michael on a tour of the swimming facilities, they bumped into Christine. Michael was surprised at the way Christine froze when she saw him and stared at his missing limb. In tears, she told Darla and Michael about Carter and her part in his rescue.

Christine checked to see if Carter would be open to a visit from Michael. He stopped by with Darla and spent forty-five minutes with Carter. When we met Michael, we understood why Christine wanted Carter to meet him.

After saying our goodbyes, we immediately googled Michael—he goes by Michael Dreamchaser Smith. Today, he motivates people of all ages and people like him—with one arm less than most. Although he has a prosthetic, he chooses not to use it, as his arm is too sensitive, and it gets in the way of all his physical activities as a Paralympian. He did say that Carter could borrow his prosthetic if he liked, as it hangs in his garage, and that it would match Carter's skin tone. Michael is African American, and when he was fitted for his prosthetic, there weren't options in skin colors.

Carter was encouraged and impressed with Michael and was also like-minded—determined to walk, swim, run, and work as before. By the end of his visit, Michael challenged Carter to participate in the Operation 300 open water swim and 5K or 10K event in June of 2020. Even if he had to push Carter in a wheelchair, they both planned to be there.

Unfortunately, COVID-19 put the kibosh on those plans.

CHAPTER 33

On the Move

Leila

THE DAY AFTER THE ACCIDENT, WE RECEIVED CARTER'S KEYS and phone, which had been retrieved from Andy's car by the FWC officer investigating the case. We wanted Carter to have his phone, and we needed his keys to get his car so we could have a vehicle. Lorilynn and Ivan, who flew down after the accident, gave us a ride in their rental car to Carter's condo. The used Nissan Xterra was a purchase made with great pride by Carter that replaced a rusty 1999 two-door Acura. The condo was another source of pride, representing Carter's graduation from dorm life to bachelor pad.

After a year in the freshmen dorms, Carter moved into an off-campus apartment with friends for his sophomore and junior years at PBA. As a senior, he shared a two-bedroom condo with three others. Four tall guys squeezed into small bedrooms and slept on twin beds—not even the extended twin-size. By graduation day, Carter was ready to bust out and move into his own place. He knew it would be expensive to live alone, but he was ready to make the financial commitment and pay for the peace and solitude. His introverted nature was screaming for space.

He discovered that rent for a second-floor, one-bedroom condo in a complex on the Intracoastal Waterway was a reach based on his Loggerhead salary. Still, with the extra income from his part-time work at Atlantic Blue Aquariums, he could squeak by.

With careful budgeting, his Florida bachelor pad was a dream come true. Around September 2019, the condo owner offered to sell it, and Carter jumped on the opportunity. The paperwork had begun, but the accident put a stop to it.

Chuck and I saw the place for the first time in the spring of 2019 during a quick visit on the way to a music conference. Although we enthusiastically offered, Carter declined our help to "deep clean" and "make it a home." It was clear that he enjoyed living independently and wasn't interested in or didn't need Mom and Dad's janitorial services.

With the keys to his condo in hand, we took the narrow stairs up to his second-floor unit. The steep incline had us doubting that he could ever return to his home. Opening the door with the key took a special jolt and twist. It required two hands, not just one.

Each of the following visits we made to his place felt like space frozen in time. We walked past his newly purchased digital piano with sheet music open to Beethoven's "Adagio." An aquarium lined the same wall. Clean dishes leaned on a drying rack by the side of the sink. The fridge stored his favorite Mediterranean chicken in plastic containers. Carter had gotten into the routine of batching meals for the week and living off the leftovers. Extra dive gear was stored near the window. Everything Carter cherished was housed in a space that he could no longer access.

The Quantum House was cozy and convenient but had no room for the kids. The spacious three-bed, three-bath fully furnished condo at 610 Clematis was available for only two weeks over the holiday season. That meant that Chuck and I had to find a new landing place during the rest of Carter's hospital stay. And we also had to find a new home for Carter when he was released. Although we were proud of Carter's independence and excited that he was on his way to home ownership, his one-bedroom rental was not the first place we wanted to call our home as we took up temporary residence in Florida and attended to Carter's needs.

Volunteers from Carter's church had generously stepped in to clean the condo, but in his parents' opinion, the place needed deeper cleaning and some upgrades. A futon served for a couch, a small TV with a gaming system was perched on a wobbly table, the shower needed a major scrub, the toilet had trouble flushing, diving equipment crowded the bulky dining room table and chairs, the vinyl floors were coated with sand, the mattress dipped in the middle, and the pillows were lumpy. The bachelor pad was simply substandard for us fifty-something-year-olds accustomed to things clean and comfy. And for grieving parents, this time-warp travel triggered an excruciating reminder that our son's past could no longer be his future.

On one of my many walks around "the loop," I encountered a woman I'll call Rita, who was in a wheelchair donned with American flags and a sign with her name on it. My heart sank. I looked at her differently now that our own son could well be limited to a wheelchair. She was waving to cars as they passed by and was clearly on a campaign trail for a local election.

We stopped and began to chat. She lost the use of her legs when an SUV failed to stop and hit her as she was crossing the street. I was unusually open that day and shared Carter's story and our current living situation with her, and soon I had an invitation to come and visit her home near Mar-a-Lago. It was a large property, and she offered to let us stay in the vacant gatehouse next door while we found a new home for Carter.

Chase and Brittany returned to Denver, but Levi and Erin stayed a few days past the holidays, so they joined Chuck and me in Carter's Xterra to meet Rita. Of course, they also looked forward to getting as close as possible to the heavily guarded Mar-a-Lago, Donald Trump's home away from the White House.

We followed Rita's directions, and when we reached the guards standing by the cement brigades blocking the way to the elite neighborhood, we said the magic word "Rita," and they quickly let us pass.

Rita graciously welcomed us and wheeled around the back of her spacious home to give us a tour of the gatehouse. The step down onto the main floor kept Rita from entering the small living area appointed with floral couches and wicker chairs. A steep set of stairs led up to the bedroom area. She confessed that the Wi-Fi was spotty. The kitchenette included a small sink and a microwave. The space just didn't feel right for a long-term stay. But perhaps the biggest reason why Rita's generous offer would not work was due to Rita and her stories.

After she invited us to sit in her living room decorated with glass tables and marble floors, our conversation focused on Rita's escapades and heritage. She had escaped Hurricane Irene by taking a flight to Chicago. When she arrived, she found herself on the streets and homeless. Apparently, her ancestors were into ancient medicine, and she was opening a mushroom university to honor the tradition. Rita was on fire to make changes in the local government to support the homeless and faithfully campaigned from her wheelchair. She was proud that she shook hands with Donald Trump and showed us pictures of the two posing for the camera.

As the four of us sat on the slightly worn floral couches, we were befuddled by her continuous stream of somewhat unbelievable stories. We glanced at each other when she mentioned that she needed a campaign manager and a web designer. She was looking for free help. We realized it was time to make our way back to St. Mary's.

We rose from her floral couches as a group. We felt the need to galvanize our departure to avoid being permanently trapped by Rita's stories. It turns out that we couldn't leave without Rita, though. She announced she was headed to a campaign rally, but her transportation fell through. Could we give her a ride? Of *course!*

This required Chuck to pick up Rita out of her wheelchair and place her in the front seat of the Xterra. Doing his best to accommodate her motionless legs, he lifted her a little too high, and she caught the side of her head on the car roof. She smiled and said she was fine. Levi and Erin managed to fold the wheelchair and place it in the back.

After a ten-minute ride, Chuck gently lifted Rita from the Xterra without bumping her head. He placed Rita back in her wheelchair, and she eagerly rolled herself over to a small gathering of campaigners who lined the street. She turned to say thank you and waved goodbye with a smile. We did the same and then quickly hopped back in the car.

The minute we took off, we all took a collective deep breath and could say little else but, "Whoa! What *was* that?"

It was clear that Rita's generous option was not viable because of the distance from St. Mary's Medical Center, spotty Wi-Fi, and, well, it just didn't *feel* right! We needed a place to hang while we found a permanent home for Carter. And the location and the amenities of his bachelor pad were looking better and better until we could find an alternative solution. So, between insurance issues, appointments with lawyers, meetings with financial planners, and hospital visits, one item rose to the top of our to-do list: contact a Realtor to help us find a first-floor condo for Carter.

A trip to the front desk at 610 Clematis resulted in a stack of Realtors' business cards. As I called each number and repeated the story of why we needed a condo and what we were looking for, the one contact who actually answered the phone and stood out among the rest was named Cat. Cat listened attentively and showed immediate and authentic interest in helping us.

About a week later, she took us on a tour through five possible units. After walking through her strategic lineup of "maybes," the last one was the clear winner. With a new tile floor, hurricane-proof windows, and one hundred steps from the world's most gorgeous beach, we were ready to sign on the dotted line. Of course, it came with a hefty rental fee, but the substantial GoFundMe account would cover it for the time being.

The condo would not be ready for occupancy until the end of January, so Chuck and I resolved to hang out at Carter's bachelor pad for a month. We added three more things to our growing to-do list:

1. Purchase a mattress to replace Carter's current mattress.
2. Hire a plumber to fix the toilet.
3. Buy rubber gloves for some deep cleaning.

CHAPTER 34

The Perfect Storm

The ultimate measure of a man is not where he stands in moments of comfort and convenience, but where he stands at times of challenge and controversy.

—Martin Luther King Jr., *Strength to Love*

Leila

We boarded the plane on Thanksgiving night, knowing that Carter had lost most of his right arm and his legs were injured. We did not know that a blade slashed Carter's left hand and wrist. After stabilizing the wrist, Dr. A was hopeful that the hand would be restored to full function.

Despite Dr. A's positivity, seeing the formidable six-inch gash down the middle of Carter's palm and wrist zigzagged with stitches still made us wonder how it could serve him the way it did before.

For weeks, we had to feed Carter because his hand was three times the size wrapped in layers of Ace bandages. It was a major milestone when he could grab a water bottle and control his hospital bed with his left-hand fingers. Once the bandages were completely removed, he could finally fully use the hand, and the numbness dissipated quickly. Because of Dr. A's handiwork, Carter had one functioning hand left, and it happened to be the *right* one.

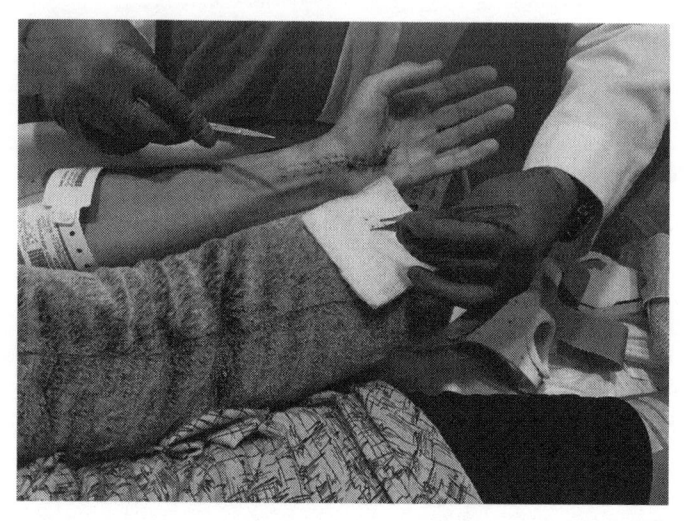

Dr. A removing stitches from Carter's left hand
(Photo Credit: Viss Family)

The fact that one limb was restored was nullified by a setback with the right arm. The suture area was not healing as expected, so surgery to clean and drain it was scheduled on Martin Luther King Day. A series of events on the Monday holiday stirred up a perfect storm.

It started when we learned that Carter refused the fentanyl patch against the doctor's order on the Saturday before MLK Day. He had received his first transdermal patch to manage pain in step-down after he was weaned from a morphine pump. Fentanyl kept the pain at bay and simultaneously kept him in a fog with nausea.

The Perfect Storm

The demotion to a noticeably smaller room meant a promotion to more rigorous therapy. It was required that Carter have at least one limb strong enough to endure this new level of therapy, and his left hand met the prerequisite. Although the therapy was tough, it broke up his day. Adjusting to another new room, powering through withdrawal, the looming surgery, and no weekend therapy to get him active and out of bed gave Carter ample time to worry.

Although his surgery was scheduled for 9 a.m., the brightly lit pre-op room is similar to waiting in line on the tarmac for a flight to take off. Your bed is rolled in, and you wait as preoccupied doctors and nurses in caps and gowns rush to prep the next "victim." And there's no guarantee when surgery will happen, and it may not happen if other operations take precedence.

Carter dreaded the pre-op runway as a tenured surgery patient. In addition, the effects on the gut that follow anesthesia make for an uncomfortable week or more. So anticipating the surgery made him anxious and fidgety with no appetite—all typical withdrawal symptoms from fentanyl.

Even before we got to the hospital on the morning of Martin Luther King Day, things felt particularly unsettled due to what Chuck and I encountered as we left our new residence—Carter's condo—and headed toward his Nissan Xterra. We had been out for dinner the night before, with my family visiting for the weekend. Chuck and I figure that's where a hit-and-run damaged the front end of the Xterra.

When we got to St. Mary's, Carter was "hangry," as he couldn't eat breakfast because of the upcoming surgery.

Always a fan of an agenda, he despised not knowing when he'd be rolled into pre-op. He was not in a mood to hang with his two parents, who were on edge, wondering how to show support after their own rough morning. That's one of the reasons why we decided to spare Carter the news of his damaged vehicle. There was no need to contribute to the storm already brewing.

To our relief, Carter was rolled to the pre-op room around 9 a.m. as promised. We tagged along, so they offered chairs for us to sit in next to Carter's bed. The curtains separating the patients in the room did not provide all that much privacy. The patient to the right of Carter appeared to be a grandma with family members hovering nearby. I noticed that the ankle of the patient on the other side of us was cuffed to the bed. That explained why there were so many security guards pacing the room.

The OR nurse asked if Carter had undergone any previous surgeries, if he had any rods or plates in his body, and if he was on any drugs. While Carter patiently answered the questions, I discreetly rolled my eyes. Was this information not already logged into their records after his residing at their institution for two months? Not to mention that if you looked at him, it's pretty obvious he's had a few surgeries recently.

Yes, it's all protocol. I was impressed with Carter's acquiescence. My sarcastic and cynical side was seething beneath a fragile calm.

Nurses attempted four times to insert the catheter for the IV in Carter's arm and then tried his left hand. The fifth time, it was successfully placed in a tiny vein on the top of his one freshly healed hand—the only hand he had left. Carter writhed in pain during each attempt and was clearly distraught. He usually didn't visibly react to pain, so we knew it hurt.

Chuck and I were too stunned to offer much support as we watched the disturbing procedure. We were relieved to see Dr. A arrive. Carter was wheeled into the OR, and we were released from our bedside duties, more than ready to bust out of pre-op.

Over Carter's sixty-eight-day stay in the hospital, Chuck and I became experts on suffocating our guilt. We were torn by how cruel it felt to abandon our son and let him fend for himself as he faced needles, scalpels, anesthesia, etc. In a bewildered state, we straddled our anguish over his agony and our relief to walk away. Eventually, the triple whammy of trauma, grief, and loss kicked in, and our brains self-medicated with a strong dose of numbness to dull the pain.

The operation went as expected. Dr. A drained a small abscess, removed some tissue, cleaned the area, and declared that Carter's right arm was free of infection. We found Carter groggy and upset because his right arm was tethered to a wound-vac machine that helps with healing, and he couldn't use his left hand because the IV catheter taped to his hand was too painful. The news that the IV needed to remain in place for at least three days to deliver antibiotics to protect against further infection pushed Carter over the edge. The annoying IV, which kept him from using his one functioning limb, combined with the fog of anesthesia and fentanyl withdrawal, brought on tears. The three of us cried in each other's arms—or at least we tried, but Carter really didn't have any *arms* left! It was our "perfect storm" on Martin Luther King Day.

After desperate talks with the doctors about Carter's situation, a nurse named Patrick—again, the one who, according to Chuck, gave the best hallway hugs—passed by as we were taking a break from Carter's room. Wiping away our tears, we explained the situation. Within minutes, Patrick removed Carter's IV from his hand and inserted a new one using ultrasonic guidance—with relatively little pain—into his upper left arm. Now, Carter was back to at least one hand again.

CHAPTER 35

Withdrawal

Carter

About two weeks into my stay at the rehab ward, doctors told me that I was on track to be discharged from St. Mary's on January 31. Again, I had been there since Thanksgiving Day. So January 31 was like a light at the end of the tunnel. There was an exact date I was leaving this place, and I couldn't be happier that it was only two weeks away.

I was also motivated to get off pain meds before I left, and the first one I wanted to remove from my regimen was the fentanyl patch. It was a small patch, about the size of a quarter, and I started wearing it when I was in the Rose Kennedy Suite to help with the intense phantom pain I had in my right arm. It was replaced every couple of days. In my state of confidence, I decided not to wean off the drug and went full cold turkey. It was a decision I would soon regret.

On the same day, one of my surgeons visited to look at my right arm. There was concern about an infection lingering, and after he looked at it, he decided it was best to do another surgery to clean it. I was mildly frustrated with this but figured it would be a minor inconvenience.

The surgery was scheduled for Monday, and that Sunday, I felt incredibly clammy, anxious, and didn't have an appetite. I couldn't tell if these feelings were the symptoms of fentanyl withdrawal I was warned about or anxiety for my upcoming surgery, but I was sure I would feel better when this surgery was over.

I woke up that morning and only felt worse. I was in a horrible mood, nauseous, and didn't want to talk to anyone. I was rolled into the dreaded pre-op room where my parents met me and stayed by my side.

A nurse came to my bed and attempted to put an IV line in my left arm. After multiple failed attempts, I was getting very agitated and praying she would get in one of my veins. She then moved down to my left hand and tried the veins on the back of my hand. I vividly remember each failed poke with the needle as I writhed in pain and started shivering in my bed. She finally got the line in a vein and proceeded to clear the line with saline solution, I screamed out in pain. I could see my vein expanding as she injected the fluid. It felt like she had just lit my hand on fire.

I begged her to pull it out and try again on my upper arm, but she told me it was too late because I'd be going into surgery soon. She also said they would most likely move the IV line to my upper arm during surgery. This was my only limb in "usable" shape, and it seemed like they were trying to take it away from me.

I was rolled into the operating room, and they started administering anesthesia through my IV line. This burned even more than the saline solution. Thankfully, my screams were cut short as I fell unconscious.

A couple of hours later, I returned to consciousness in a fog. I felt extremely nauseous and clammy. My vision cleared, and I immediately noticed a wound vac attached to my right arm. I then glanced at my left hand to see that damn IV line still in the back of my hand. I was enraged! What kind of idiots would see my condition and think, *He'll be fine with that on his only limb that's not wrapped in bandages*?

I tried lifting my hand only to be hit with excruciating pain. I felt the catheter moving around in my hand and inflicting pain on my healing wrist. I then heard that the infection in my right arm was cleared, but I would need to be on IV antibiotics for at least three days.

Hearing that this IV line had to stay in my hand until further notice broke me. The combination of not being able to use my only good limb mixed with my fentanyl withdrawal plunged me into a dark place I had never been before. I remember just lying in my room crying, desperately trying not to vomit, and wishing this would all just end.

My parents came into my room and started crying with me when they saw I could barely move my left hand. They pleaded with the doctors and nurses to relocate it and finally contacted an IV specialist they met in the early hospital days. He promptly came to my room, removed the IV from my hand, and professionally installed a PICC line in my upper left arm. The relief I felt when I comfortably moved my wrist was truly indescribable. I cried tears again.

That night, I was physically and emotionally exhausted. I remember sitting in my room with my parents, attempting to eat a Publix turkey sub they brought me. My nausea was still severe, my entire body was covered in cold sweat, and I couldn't get my mind out of the dark place where I had immersed myself. We were all reflecting on what a horrible day it was and hoping there would only be improvements from here.

The combination of the beeping from the antibiotic pump and the constant nausea made sleep impossible. When the morning came, I felt a little less nauseous and exhausted but was ready to press forward. My discharge date of January 31 was at the forefront of my mind.

CHAPTER 36

Second-Floor Condo

Carter will be a motivational speaker to inspire others because of his relentless coping abilities.

—Dr. Bella Choksi

Leila

Days later, Carter's attending rehabilitation doctor, Dr. Bella Choksi (Dr. C), gently "chided" him for going "cold turkey" and refusing to wear his fentanyl patch prescribed in the step-down unit to reduce his pain. She would have preferred to exchange the patch with a lower dose to make the withdrawal more tolerable. Dr. C also stated how impressed she was by Carter's remarkable ability to compartmentalize what had happened to him and what needed to be done to recover. She remarked on his compliance to complete any task in therapy while working through the pain to achieve the next goal. She predicted that Carter would be a motivational speaker to inspire others because of his relentless coping abilities. Of course, we were proud, though the word "proud" seemed trite considering what he'd overcome.

Dr. C's encouraging words parted the clouds, as did the news that the HOA approved Chuck and Carter's application for the seaside first-floor, two-bedroom condo that our Realtor, Cat, had found for us a few weeks prior. Move-in day was set for Friday, but Carter would miss out. Before vacating St. Mary's, he had to meet a substantial physical goal. With a little help from others, Carter had to be able to transfer himself from the wheelchair to the car and anywhere else.

It seemed questionable, but there was progress from the slog, and therapy was strengthening his legs. It was still painful to carry weight on his left leg and difficult for him to bend his right knee enough to be of much support. And yet, when hoisted out of the wheelchair by pulling on a belt around his waist, his battered legs in removable casts could stand and shuffle across the floor for about one hundred feet.

We witnessed Carter's resolve to walk when we wheeled him to the therapy gym. He did not have an official therapy session but was allowed to complete his assigned exercises, so we assisted him with the needed equipment and watched. For his final exercise, Carter sat on the edge of a raised mat, and Chuck and I took turns holding Carter's right leg straight and then applying pressure to bend it just a little closer to 90 degrees.

With his legs gaining mobility and strength, the next hurdle was his right arm. A wound vac had been placed over the fresh sutures on his right arm after his last surgery. VACs pull the wound's edges together, which gently reduces fluid, eases swelling, keeps it clean, and removes bacteria. The sutures were dressed in gauze and covered with an adhesive film that connected to a portable pump. In other words, Carter was tethered to a machine with what looked like clear packing tape. Carter reported that it felt just like sticky tape being ripped off his skin as it was removed. It was an unpleasant event that Chuck and I, fortunately, missed seeing.

One more hurdle to overcome was eliminating the possibility of infection. Carter was on antibiotics delivered intravenously until the end of that week. This was particularly annoying to him because it required that the nurse wake him at 3 a.m. to administer one of the doses through his PICC line. This procedure lasted about fifteen minutes. When the machine beeped, signaling that the treatment had been completed, Carter had to ring for the nurse to come and remove the syringe. Then it was on him to fall back to sleep.

If all these physical goals were met—no more wound vac and IV PICC plus one strong limb—Carter would be released from his unexpected residence of two months and see his new place on January 31.

As he worked toward his goals, Chuck and I focused on our move from 610 Clematis to Carter's second-floor condo in North Palm Beach, next to the Intracoastal Waterway. Our move required an important purchase: a mattress. Carter's present one had expired—we rolled to the middle when we lay on it. Since sleep was already hard to come by for both of us, a fresh mattress was a priority. So we went mattress shopping!

After lying on several models, we chose one and learned from the store manager that it was the queen selected by hoteliers at The Breakers, the luxurious Palm Beach hotel. Surely, it must be good.

After the mattress was delivered up the narrow outdoor stairs to the bedroom, I eagerly made the bed with newly washed sheets and a fluffy mattress pad. The bed felt quite sturdy. In fact, it hardly made an impression when we sat on the edge of the mattress, and it almost felt like a sturdy dining table.

When we rolled onto the bed, we were jolted by the firmness, maybe even alarmed! My shoulders hurt when I slept on my side—my preferred sleep position. Chuck seemed to embrace it—it was better than the old, lumpy one. Lesson learned: don't buy a mattress when life gets hard—the mattress may inadvertently reflect the present state of affairs!

Cleaning became a daily chore. We emptied the fridge of the leftovers that had sat on the shelves for over a month. A plumber fixed the toilet, and Chuck scrubbed the shower to a new shade of beige. After washing the sheets, it was clear that the dryer vent had not been emptied for months. (Maybe even years?) It could be that Carter was unaware of this important task.

Chuck logged into our Xfinity account so we could watch Netflix and the Australian Open—a January tradition for Chuck. Carter had gotten me hooked on *Parks and Rec*; I watched that as I packed Carter's clothes and dive equipment. Would he ever use the flippers again? He owned an extra pair of gloves, but now he only needed the left glove. Binging episodes helped me keep a distance from the reality of what I was doing.

The dining room became our desks where we tended to bills and emails. While Chuck patiently talked with a credit agent about an issue that was getting in the way of moving forward on Carter's new apartment lease, I tried to pay my quarterly estimated taxes. I failed to finish the job because the important login information in my "secret notebook" was back in Denver.

Shopping was a daily task as we prepared to move to the seaside condo. Carter's second-floor condo came fully furnished, meaning he owned very few household items and not much furniture. As our list got longer, Chuck's patience got shorter. I distinctly recall a spat in the flatware aisle of Costco—I was taking too long to decide on a set.

One day, while in the lightbulb aisle in Target, Chuck answered a call from a doctor who could approve and prescribe medical marijuana for Carter. After consulting with Carter, we agreed it was a safer alternative than continuing his prescription drugs for easing pain and inducing sleep. In the coming months, Carter found that the $250 ten-minute chat with the doctor was worth it.

During the same Target run, while strolling the Magnolia section (my favorite!), Chuck received a call from Levi in Colorado. Levi was making soup and wondered what pot to use. As we drove off the Target parking lot, Chuck had tears streaming down his cheeks. He would have liked to be making soup with Levi. (There was a day early in our marriage when Chuck enjoyed shopping. Chuck didn't like shopping anymore.)

Grocery shopping has never been my thing, but Chuck could tolerate Publix. As we settled in, our grocery list transformed from Colorado gourmet to Florida quick and easy.

Instead of picking out fresh fish or a filet mignon to grill, our meal of choice was deli turkey sliced thick and cut into cubes tossed with a bag of premixed salad greens and the accompanying dressing and sliced nuts.

Gin and white wine always landed in the cart, too.

CHAPTER 37

Free at Last

Carter

After the surgery, I gradually got back to physical therapy and was able to take about twenty steps before needing to sit down. The wound vac attached to my right arm was very annoying, but my therapist and I figured out ways to work around it. I could feel the withdrawal symptoms starting to fade, and I was regaining my appetite.

However, I had developed a ton of paranoia that I could not shake off. I started thinking the nurses were not looking out for my best interest and were forcing me to take meds that I did not need. I thought they were purposely trying to keep me in the hospital forever. I felt this was a combination of withdrawal symptoms, the incident with the IV line in my left hand, and simply being in the hospital for about two months.

By Friday of that week, I got the wound vac off my right arm, and the symptoms of withdrawals were pretty much gone. It was exactly one week until my discharge date, and I was rallying myself to push through this final stretch. Unfortunately, I was still on IV antibiotics, and it sounded like I would stay on them for a while to ensure the infection didn't return. This also meant they would do daily lab work on my blood to check for signs of infection.

Lab technicians would visit my room once or twice daily to draw a blood sample. Ideally, they would have drawn the sample through my PICC line; however, it would almost never work, so they had to poke my arm. My veins are small, so it almost always took two or more pokes with a needle to draw the sample.

These "vampires" would come to my room at any hour of the night to take a sample. This made sleeping and relaxing at night very difficult because I was anticipating their arrival. Their timing always seemed to be right after I fell asleep.

Despite my issues with sleep, I was making progress in physical therapy. I could walk across the physical therapy "gym" with my walker. I also was very mobile in my wheelchair. I would go around the rehab area in my chair to get exercise and feel minimal pain while doing so. It was a night and day difference from three weeks ago when I first entered rehab.

However, the most difficult hurdle was standing up out of my wheelchair or from any sitting position. My right knee could still barely bend, so I had to rely completely on my left leg and wrist to push my body up, which both were nowhere near strong enough to do so. I essentially put this battle on the waitlist and focused on the battles I was winning.

It was now January 30, one day until my release from what felt like a prison. The thoughts of life on the outside flooded my mind with excitement, and I don't think I've been more eager for something in my entire life. I had practiced getting into my car during physical therapy, and I couldn't wait to see the new first-story condo my parents had just finished moving into.

The nurse entered my room and took my temperature as part of the normal morning routine. It turned out I had a low fever of about 100 degrees. They did not know what was causing this and informed me that I could not be discharged within twenty-four hours of having a fever. I was mortified. The fact that my rehab doctor would not be in until Monday meant I would definitely be spending the weekend in the hospital. All I could do was hope and pray that this fever would disappear by Monday. I remember getting extremely nervous every time my temperature was taken from then on.

All my temperature readings were below 99 degrees starting Sunday, so on Monday, they could proceed with discharging me. An immense wave of relief swept over me when I was given that news. However, the process of getting discharged proved to be very difficult. While my dad was handling all the logistics, I continued with my normal physical therapy schedule.

Finally, around 5 p.m. on Monday, I was ready to be discharged. Andy came to the hospital and assisted my dad with grabbing all my stuff.

As we left my room for the last time, I waved goodbye to the nurses and some patients I met while in the rehab ward. We rode the elevator down for the last time and entered the main lobby to see some staff clapping for me as we approached the exit. I felt so grateful that this day had finally come and was exhilarated to experience the outside world again. That final trip out of St. Mary's in my wheelchair felt like a perfect victory lap.

Upon leaving the hospital's front doors, a local TV reporter and news crew were waiting in the parking lot to interview me. Having them waiting for me like I was some celebrity was such a surreal feeling. I was hoping they wouldn't follow me around as I adjusted to life on the outside.

They rushed to me as my dad and Andy were loading stuff into my car and asked questions about my accident, recovery, and what was next. This all felt like a blur to me, and all I remember talking about was how happy I was to be out of the hospital. The news crew left as soon as they got their story, and I managed to get in my car with the help of my dad and Andy.

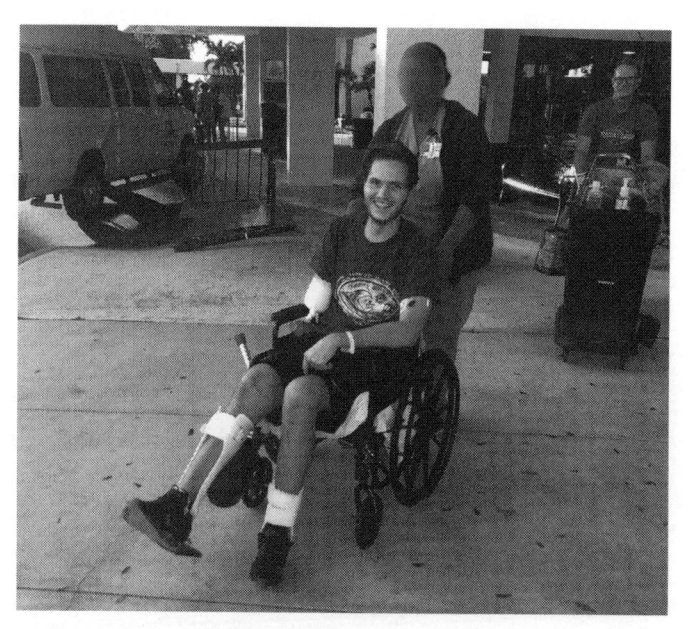

Carter as he was getting wheeled out of the hospital
(Photo Credit: Viss Family)

That drive out of the hospital was one that I will never forget. We got on US Highway 1 and headed north to the new condo. I saw all the usual buildings and stores I drove by on my commute to work, but now they looked like beautiful structures that reminded me of normal life. I remember being happy to see traffic jams, pedestrians, and people going about their regular lives. It felt like I hadn't seen any of this in years, and everything that once seemed mundane in the real world was beautiful.

A couple of tears rolled down my face as we drove by Loggerhead. That place grew into somewhere so much more than work to me because of this. I couldn't help but think of the community that supported me while I was in the hospital, and it all stemmed from my time spent in that building.

We pulled into the new condo complex about a mile down the road from Loggerhead. It was such a weird feeling pulling up to the building and knowing all my stuff had already been moved from my old condo. Andy rolled me up to the front door, and I got my first glimpse at my new home. It was so spacious compared to my old place, and my parents did a great job of making it feel like a home.

After having pizza for dinner and a visit from a nurse who taught my dad how to administer my IV antibiotics, I was ready to go to bed. My dad helped me into bed, and I could see the relief on his face as we said goodnight. I was finally in a peaceful and quiet place. No beeps from machines surrounding me. No nurses intruding to do routine check-ups. No "vampires" coming to take blood samples. Just peace and undisturbed rest.

I fell asleep with joy and hope.

CHAPTER 38

Dave and Jodie

A friend who can be silent with us in a moment of confusion or despair, who can stay with us in an hour of grief and bereavement, who can tolerate not knowing, not curing, not healing . . . that is a friend who cares.

—Henri Nouwen, *Out of Solitude*

Leila

The last week of January, Chuck and I moved into the seaside condo, and a day later, we welcomed longtime friends Dave and Jodie Tinucci (the wonderful half of our "Vissucci" dinner clan) to Carter's new place. They flew from Denver primarily to see Carter and help us get the place in shipshape for Carter's homecoming.

Between trips to Home Depot and Target, Dave and Jodie removed glass doors in Carter's shower so he could move in and out of the small space more easily. After morning barefoot strolls with coffee in hand along Jupiter Beach, they helped us assemble bedframes and shelving and hung pictures on the walls.

During their short stay, we introduced them to Doris, a local Italian market that prompted five-star dinners featuring risotto, fresh greens, Italian sausage, and red wine. After weeks of Florida quick-and-easy meals, Colorado gourmet was divine.

We met the Tinuccis at a company picnic twenty-some years ago. Their two boys and our three were around the same age, and they became fast friends—more like instant cousins. Since that first encounter, world-class, homemade food; fine wine; and the challenge of launching our sons have connected our families. Our friendship led to camping weekends, ski trips to Winter Park, and graduation celebrations in Mexico.

We've coined our family gatherings as Vissucci events. In fact, last Christmas, Chuck got both families and all the significant others Yeti mugs personalized with the Vissucci name. In essence, Dave and Jodie count as family; their companionship and support as we settled Carter into his new reality was an important step toward healing.

Their weekend stay in Jupiter happened to dovetail with my return to Colorado. It became clear that it didn't take two of us to care for Carter. Although it was unspoken at first, we both knew Chuck would stay and be Carter's main caregiver until Carter was self-sufficient. Chuck called it his tour of duty. He can work from anywhere with a laptop and excels at taking charge when situations escalate. Never did he realize his skills would be put to the test in this way.

After filing for unpaid leave from work for the first few weeks, Chuck got permission to work remotely beginning in February. That meant I could reboot life in Colorado after

Dave and Jodie

seeing Carter released from the hospital. The Tinuccis would stay one more day than I to help Chuck and Carter settle in.

Those plans fell apart when Carter came down with a fever. Carter practiced the transfer to the back seat of his Nissan Xterra, stood upright, shuffled, and maneuvered himself with fierce determination through major pain. He passed the test, yet his doctors refused to release him until the fever was gone. So the night before my early-morning flight back home, Carter and I said our goodbyes at St. Mary's. Incarceration by a fever slipped him into disappointment, frustration, and depression. I couldn't blame him, as I felt the same. It was an empty and helpless goodbye. As Dave drove all of us back to the condo, the starless, late-night ride home was devoid of words.

The next morning, Chuck drove me to the Fort Lauderdale Airport while Dave and Jodie continued their work on Carter's bathroom shower. As we took the on-ramp to I-95, Chuck told me he wouldn't miss me being around. It didn't surprise me or hurt my feelings. For Chuck, I was a liability. My emotional flair-ups (I did go bananas one late afternoon in a park—it was ugly) and our "spats" and "tiffs" over flatware and area rugs were a distraction. Eliminating my presence would help him focus on his tour of duty.

Although I trusted Chuck's ability to manage what was to come, I worried about him and felt left out. I had come to love our new "Florida family" and leaving behind our pain in paradise was hard. The last time I left Florida—two weeks after the accident—were some of the best and the worst times Carter experienced in the hospital.

CHAPTER 39

A Mother's Lament at 30,000 Feet

*I can't find a ledge to hold on to.
Instead, I slide down the edges and pout about it.*

—Leila

Leila

Although I wanted to stay in Florida, I knew Chuck was perfectly capable of managing Carter's home care. And my work required me to be on the ground in Colorado.

Recent hospital and insurance issues had pushed all my buttons the wrong way—it wasn't pretty. By the time I left Florida, I had spiraled down to another low tide.

Most of the following "lament" was written at 30,000 feet on my long flight home to Denver. A stranger who sat next to me on the flight reached out to me via Facebook Messenger. He confessed that he read my post over my shoulder while I typed. As the document was labeled "Carter Blogs," he figured it was for public consumption. He went home, googled Carter, and found his CaringBridge site and my grief blogs.

I have to credit him for being honest, but my SRDs (shitty rough drafts) are *never* for public consumption. In his lengthy message, he meant well by offering words of support. However, they came across as advice to "buck up" rather than expressions of comfort.

In my short yet intense relationship with grief and conversations with fellow grievers, I notice that our culture rushes the grief process. Most articles I find are not written by people going through grief in real time. They're usually written in hindsight of grief. The dark side of life is just as prevalent as the bright side, yet most prefer the dark side to stay in the dark. Bad things remind us of our fragility, and that's painful. As you can tell, it's impossible for me to maintain a sense of peace while my insides are shattered and my heart is torn. I'm banking on the fact that the dark side will eventually help me see the light.

After I landed in Denver, after a run and listening to some podcasts and tunes, a little bit of light snuck into the darkness of my SRD, as seen in my blog post of February 8, 2020, below:

> It seems that I've exchanged my faith for fear. It's as though I sent my faith back to the manufacturer for repair, and it's gotten lost in the mail.
>
> How did my neatly wrapped package of faith disappear?
>
> I've been scraping the bottom of the barrel looking for it, and I've only come up with splinters under my fingernails. I can't find a ledge to hold on to. Instead, I slide down the edges and pout about it.
>
> The fear of the unknown, the absence of faith, and this pouting are compounded by the ache of

A Mother's Lament at 30,000 Feet

a mother's heart for our son Carter and his present condition. His determination should inspire me, and yet, my fear clamps down on my hope and my stamina to see this through. I'm unsure what we'll see on the other end of this tunnel. The clouds have blocked my view of the horizon and the possibilities beyond it.

The medical professionals who have cared for Carter have seen patients like him come and go. They know what the horizon looks like, and they're accustomed to patiently following the road map to get there. The warning signs, sharp curves, and detours never seem to faze them—the beeps and buzzers that alarm (and annoy!), the bruised nerves that keep feet from flexing, the unforeseen extra surgery that sets back healing, the needles that prick and bruise, the sticky bandages that irritate oozing wounds when removed, the course of another antibiotic that delays a discharge. The caregivers have witnessed the roadblocks, yet they've safely arrived at the final destination over and over.

Throughout Carter's sixty-eight-day hospital stay, they occasionally attempted to lift my spirits by sharing stories of patients who now lead fulfilling and satisfying lives. At the same time, they advised me to take one moment, one day at a time. I wonder if their intention is to help me zoom in on the slow-motion progress and then zoom out to the promising life yet to come so that it blurs the current brutal reality.

Frankly, I found little comfort in either perspective because the present moments and a considerable amount of the sixty-eight days have sucked—no other word fits here.

As Carter is twenty-five, most communication for his care was directed toward him first. From what I saw as a parent who observed and avoided interjecting more than necessary except when I just couldn't hold my tongue and wanted to explode, it seemed they knew Carter as a patient in a room with a number first, then as a person. It's just the way it is at a busy hospital. They are oblivious to what Carter enjoyed doing before the accident. Much of what he did is directly impacted by his injuries. How will dealing with his limitations lead to a satisfying life for him?

As much as I appreciate Carter's dedicated caregivers and their actions to save and preserve his life and limbs, the hospital system struggled to walk alongside our grief. It's not a surprise considering our nation's current state of healthcare and overworked staff. To add salt to the wound—a poignant cliché—Carter continues receiving bills from the insurance company because many doctors who cared for him are not in our plan's network. When Carter was rolled in from the ambulance, there was no time to check to see if the emergency surgeons, Drs. A and B, were in our network, but they're not. But thank God they were both on call that day. Our overstay at the

A Mother's Lament at 30,000 Feet

hospital and crazy interactions with the insurance company (and many other things) have shoved my reasoning and package of faith further down to the bottom of the barrel.

I learned from Kate Bowler's *Everything Happens* podcast episode featuring BJ Miller that my grieving correlates with my love for Carter.[1] This makes sense. This accident is the *last* thing I wanted for our son when he was born twenty-five years ago, and yet, it is what it is—I despise that phrase, but it's true.

The grief monster has gridlocked my perspective. It's cast a shadow on my ability to appreciate Carter's tremendous progress and how pleased the doctors are. It also tempered my gratitude for Carter's resolve and resiliency to overcome his physical hurdles and make an impact with his story.

Our family's foundation was rocked on Thanksgiving 2019. It's forced me to search for a faith that went missing, face a future packed with uncertainties, address the fear of what Carter must yet endure as his body heals, and forge my way back to stability in a self-made career.

> "Life is a series of losses."[2]
> —Kate Bowler

Our family's list of losses is long. I'm failing at dealing with this list right now. I'm in a funk and can't get out.

Where did my resolve go that I used to have?

Where did my ability to compartmentalize go?

Where did that glimmer of hope go that used to pull me back up and make me strong enough to face a day with determination?

It's as though they've all abandoned me or have been lost in the mail. My husband seems steady and lives with hope for the future by saying over and over: "I only want the best for Carter. I'll do what it takes. This is only temporary. It's a tour of duty. What else but faith can we rely on?"

Why can't I plug into this mindset? Where's my grit? When will I dig my heels in and take a fist to this gloom? Every part of me wants to resist acceptance of this new chapter. Why can't I close the door on yesterday?

The only solace I find is when I tamp down the pain and default to numbness. Recognizing and writing down why I'm lamenting has revealed my own disconnect. My intellect tells me to be strong, hopeful, and courageous and reminds me of all the marvelous support I'm receiving from so many. My emotions tell me something different.

I've got to get a grip and kick this grief monster in the butt, as its fear-inducing power has paralyzed me. It's time to unlock this heavy heart and rescue my grit, determination, and faith. They haven't been shipped to the wrong address. They're all waiting for me to build the strength to untangle them.

A Mother's Lament at 30,000 Feet

I believe the best way I'll reunite with my faith begins with practicing a sense of hope each day, even if I don't feel like it or have any of it.

Before the accident, I took up the challenge of memorizing Brahms' "Rhapsody in G Minor." Despite the trauma, my brain still worked enough to continue memorizing it. I practiced most nights on Carter's digital piano in his one-bedroom condo in Florida. It's memorized but not fluently—yet. All the information has been entered, and now the memory will become more solid with many repetitions here in Colorado.

I've got to use strategies similar to my memorization tactics to override the powerful fear that floods my heart and replace it with faith and the hope that comes with it. Adjusting to life's new road map will be more difficult than memorizing the Brahms' piece. Like my work at the piano, I won't expect perfection from my practice, but I expect progress, little by little.

In her book *Help, Thanks, Wow*, Anne Lamott claims there are three essential prayers to pray:

1. Help
2. Thanks
3. Wow[3]

I'll start with help and assume that practicing this one first will help me say the other two prayers in time.

Unfortunately, there's no Amazon Prime two-day shipping for the hope, resolve, strength, and determination that come with faith. They've been hiding in bubble wrap deep down inside. I've got to dig deeper, find the package, and open it up. It's going to take practice to rip the packing tape and tear up the brown paper.

Off to the practice room.

CHAPTER 40

Discharged

Okay . . .

—Marty Byrde, *Ozark*[1]

Chuck

On February 3, not the hoped-for January 31 date, Carter was discharged, after a tortuous day of waiting. I had never been through that before (I'll say that a lot). We quickly came to know that the person who would approve Carter's discharge was not his rehab doc, not his orthopedic doc, not the trauma doc, not the internal medicine doc, but the infectious disease doc. Of course, that was because he was in the warm ocean with open wounds for a long period of time.

All the other docs make their rounds first thing in the morning, as early as 7 a.m. Not the infectious disease doc. Sometimes they don't show up until after noon or even later. This particular day was later, around 4 p.m.

It was a long day for Carter and me. We had several prescriptions to take home, so Walgreens agreed to deliver them to the hospital, which was very nice.

In Carter's case, home health care was prescribed for nurse care, OT, and PT. When the home health care agency called me as I waited with Carter for the discharge papers, they asked me how comfortable I was administering meds via the PICC line and changing wound dressing. I told them I had never done meds, but I had some history with wounds before (we had raised three boys). They said they could arrange for someone to come in four times a day to administer meds, or they could teach me how to do it. Immediately, I said I would do it, as I didn't want to see someone else in our condo that many times a day.

The wait for the release from St. Mary's was filled with calls and notifications—home health care, Walgreens, news reporters, hospital press releases telling me I couldn't meet with reporters . . . you know, the normal things. I also got a call from Carter's first home health nurse, whom I pretty much fired on the spot without even meeting. She first confirmed that I would administer meds through the PICC line. I said yes, I wanted to learn that. She asked me what the meds were. I said I didn't know because we hadn't gone through that yet with discharge instructions. She chided me for not knowing and said I had to find out. Frustrated, I told her, "I will find out, I know I will, I just don't know what they are at . . . this . . . *moment!*

My ire was rising.

She was to meet us at the condo around 6 p.m. (if we ever got discharged!), so I told her what to do at the condo gate in order for us to let her in. She said something to the effect of "Oh, well, that's something I need to know" in a really snotty way, like I should have told her that first.

Discharged

My gut feeling was that she was putting me on the defensive right away, and I didn't deserve any of that. But I figured I'd roll with it until after I called the agency and let them know my reaction to the nurse interactions. They really appreciated my feedback and asked if I would still work with the original nurse, and I said yes. Then, much to my surprise, I got a call from her supervisor, who said she was no longer assigned to our case and that they would assign a new one for tomorrow. He himself (the supervisor) would come over to the condo that evening to teach me how to administer the meds.

When we finally got discharged, a local TV reporter was there and got our exit from the hospital all on film! (Sorry, St. Mary's, I let her in on the time and place.) Carter was on the news again that night.

I have to say I was a little nostalgic about leaving the hospital. I mean, Carter wasn't the only one who had been there for sixty-eight days. I was there every single day. I even had the staff discount at the cafeteria. There were so many people who became family to me at St. Mary's: countless nurses, doctors, people who put in PICC lines, therapists, and other patients. But it was time to look forward to the next stage of Carter's recovery.

Andy was there for the discharge as well, for which I was very thankful, as Carter had accumulated quite a few things to haul from the hospital room to the condo. Many items, called durable medical equipment, were provided to make the condo a combo of the hospital room and rehab center. They included a wheelchair, shower seat, walker, toilet extension (something to sit over the toilet), transfer board (a heavy polished piece of wood with tapered sides to assist getting Carter from one surface to another), an ice machine for his knee, and a lifting belt (a belt he wore around his waist so I could help him stand up to move from one place to another).

The nurse arrived and showed me how to administer the meds through the PICC line. It wasn't difficult at all. The difficult part was keeping the schedule of IV drugs four times a day, plus his other meds in the form of pills. I believe it was somewhere close to seventeen different pills he was taking, some four times a day, some twice a day. I remember getting some mega pill boxes from Walgreens and thinking, *Is this really happening?*

It was.

I had a notebook, and each page in the notebook represented one day in our lives: the meds, the doctor appointments, OT, PT, phone numbers, reminders, etc. I still have that notebook and will open it sometimes to a random page and usually get shivers down my spine thinking of that specific day.

I remember ordering pizza for dinner that night after Carter's discharge from the hospital, somewhere around 9 p.m. It was a long, tiring, and exhausting day, but it was so good to be out of the hospital.

After Carter went to bed, I walked along the path by the beach. I walked to the pier and back, a total of one mile. I ended up doing this every night unless the rain was too strong. Many times I was in tears the entire walk. The gravity of the day would set in, and I would be at the end of my rope.

I would put Carter to bed, say goodnight, and tell him that I loved him; he would tell me he loved me, and I would close his door and again think, *Is this really happening?*

My walk would always settle me down.

When I got back, I would pour a strong drink, turn on Netflix, and get lost in a series, usually a violent one. For some reason, the more violent, the better. I think I just needed to see something worse than what I was going through.

I watched the entire series of *Ozark*, and I related to Marty Byrde, the character played by Jason Bateman. His life quickly became a series of very unfortunate events, and each time something devastating happened, Marty Byrde would just close his lips, sport a slight smile, say to himself, "Mmm-hmm," and continue on. Nothing phased him.

That was me. I had been in fight-or-flight mode since Thanksgiving Day of 2019 and would continue to be until June of 2020, when I would return to Denver for the very first time. Of course, I didn't know this at the time it was happening, but I would come to learn a lot about trauma and the nervous system by reading some key books and going through years of therapy.

CHAPTER 41

The Outside World

Carter

On my first day on the outside, my main goal was to see the ocean. My dad rolled me along the path to the beach just across the street from the condo, and it was a short stroll to the Juno Beach Pier.

It's hard to describe my feelings when I saw the ocean for the first time that day. The joy of seeing the blue water I loved so much was weighed down by the fresh memory of the last time I was in the ocean getting chopped up by a boat. I wondered: *How will I ever enjoy the water after this? Will I ever be able to physically swim in water again? How will I respond to seeing a speeding boat?* For now, these questions were unanswerable. I just decided to focus on how much I loved the ocean and its inhabitants.

The first couple of days on the outside consisted of in-home physical and occupational therapy and lots of doctors' appointments. I kept making progress with walking and strengthening my left leg and arm.

About a week after I was discharged, a red bump appeared and grew on the scar in my right knee, and my dad insisted we go to the ER at St. Mary's to get it checked. I was extremely apprehensive about this because it could mean getting readmitted.

As we drove there, I could feel panic set in, and I started shaking all over. When we arrived, I could barely speak because of my anxiety. Thankfully, I was seen promptly after arrival, and they determined it was just an abscess that needed to be cleared. They brought me into an operating room, numbed the area, cleared the abscess, and after about an hour, I was free to go.

I was so relieved it was a simple procedure, and we got home just in time to eat dinner. Unfortunately, every hospital visit after that wouldn't be as simple.

Despite the quick hospital visit, life was great on the outside. My dad and I visited Loggerhead during a turtle release, and it was my first time there since the incident. It was an incredible feeling getting rolled through the facility again. Entering those front doors felt like returning home after a long time away.

My visit was unannounced, so there were several extremely surprised staff and volunteers. Andy rolled me through the facility and explained all the changes that happened since I was last there. Seeing the aquariums I cared for and all the fish made me very emotional. It was such a vivid flashback to the way things were before Thanksgiving. They (the turtles and the fish) all looked about the same since I last saw them in November, and I wished I could get out of my wheelchair to feed them like I used to. They were the perfect motivation to keep pushing through the challenges ahead.

At the condo, I had several hobbies and sources of entertainment to keep my mind busy. Andy helped me assemble the 32-gallon saltwater tank I had in my old condo. I had plenty of TV shows, video games to attempt with one hand, and puzzles to work on. I also listened to many albums and discovered a lot of new music. An album that I frequently came back to was Radiohead's *Kid A*. Its cold, distant, and abstract atmosphere perfectly captured what I was feeling at the time. It made me feel like I was placed in a strange new world where I had to get used to my new way of life.

In the second half of February, I finally got my PICC line out, and I could almost stand up on my own and walk around the condo independently. Things were moving in the right direction.

Then, suddenly, on Presidents' Day weekend, I broke out in a bad rash. It started on my chest and moved to most parts of my body. We made the prompt decision to go to the ER to get it checked out. My anxiety on the way there was ten times worse than our first trip a couple of weeks ago. The mystery of not knowing what was causing this rash made it so much worse.

We arrived at the ER, and I felt panic set in, as there was a high potential I would be readmitted. The doctors looked at it and were not sure what was causing it, but they thought it could be from getting off the antibiotics. They then broke the news to me that I would be spending the night at the hospital for observation.

I broke down sobbing upon hearing this. It felt like all my freedom was being taken away from me again, and I was back where I had started. Although they said it would likely be one night, my mind was too flooded with negative thoughts and sadness to compartmentalize my situation. In hindsight, it was rather a small inconvenience to my recovery, but in the moment, it absolutely devastated my mental state.

I said goodnight to my dad and older brother, Chase (who was visiting then), and was rolled to another hospital room. I got in my bed, and a horrible sense of déjà vu came over me. Did I even leave the hospital? Was getting discharged just a dream?

In the morning, my rash looked like it was calming down. Still uncertain of its cause, the doctors monitored my vitals, and if everything seemed normal, I would be discharged later in the day. Thankfully, all my vitals didn't change, and they began the discharge process.

As usual, the discharge process took a lot longer than needed, and late that evening, I took my second victorious ride out of those front hospital doors. Chase picked up Indian food (one of my favorites), and we all ate dinner at the condo. I was beyond relieved to sleep in my bed that night, and the rash had almost disappeared.

Outside life returned to normal after that short hiccup. Near the end of February, I had gotten used to my new condo and the routine my dad and I had established.

One day, after an appointment, Dad had to run to my old condo one last time to grab the last of my stuff. February was officially the last month of my lease there. We pulled into the complex, and a wave of emotions hit me. This was the first time I'd seen this area since the accident. I really missed driving through there after getting off work. I was reminded of the simple life I used to live and how dramatically everything had changed.

My dad pulled into my parking spot and walked up the stairs to my condo. There was no way I could make it up the stairs, so I had to wait in the car. Tears started streaming down my face, as this was the first time I saw where I lived since the accident and now the last time I'd ever see it. It then hit me how quickly my life was stripped away from me. God had other plans than the life I was creating for myself and yanked them away before I could ever say goodbye. If only I had known it was the last time I rushed out the door that Thanksgiving morning. I wished I had savored those last moments in my home.

CHAPTER 42

Ya Mon

Chuck

THE FIRST TWO WEEKS IN THE CONDO WERE TWO WEEKS OF adjustments: Carter getting used to living with his dad again, me getting used to living with Carter again. It's not a natural thing for a twenty-five-year-old who was living independently to suddenly be living with his father in a new condo, unable to perform most daily living activities. It's also not a natural thing for me to be living in Florida, away from my home, caring for my adult son. But I chose to do it and took on the challenge.

Carter could not move himself from one place to another, so you can imagine what that meant. Getting him out of bed into his wheelchair, from the wheelchair to the couch, from the couch to the toilet, from the toilet to the couch, from the couch to the shower, from the shower to the couch, from the couch to the bed . . . you get the picture. The lifting belt needed to be around his waist, not too tight but not too loose, Carter bracing to stand on his left leg, me lifting him up, him moaning in pain by being up on his leg, then gently getting him into the next destination. We took some of those portable urinals from the hospital, so that saved *many* trips to the bathroom. And they came in handy at night so Carter (and I) did not have to get up when he had to pee in the middle of the night.

Carter had to be assessed by both the OT and PT agencies, so we got that completed. He had to have a primary care doctor for meds. He also had to meet with his ortho doctor for surgery follow-ups. So we did it.

Every time we had to leave for a doctor's appointment, we had to get him into the wheelchair using the lifting belt, get the wheelchair to the car, and lift him out of the wheelchair. He would then scooch in on the board Leila and I purchased from Home Depot that we set on the back seat of Carter's Xterra. Then I would disassemble the wheelchair, lift the wheelchair into the trunk, drive to the appointment location, pull the wheelchair from the truck, assemble it, get Carter into the wheelchair, and continue to the appointment. It was exhausting, and my back was aching due to all the lifting and straining.

Once at the appointment, we waited and waited. We got used to waiting. We waited in the lobby, we waited in the examination room; in fact, we waited everywhere we went. We spent a lot of time together.

I loved home health care. I didn't have to go anywhere, and someone else would be watching Carter. During these visits, I would usually take off on a run, go to the beach, and get groceries. We had a very nice nurse who would come and take Carter's vitals and a blood sample, then check his wounds. We had an OT who would review the condo facilities and teach Carter how to do things one-handed. The

OT also ordered several pieces of equipment to assist Carter with DLAs (disability living allowances), like a cutting board with spikes on it to hold an onion so you could slice it with one hand.

I started doing things one-handed to empathize and also to teach Carter what I learned. I would always use my right hand, my dominant hand, and try to cook everything without using my other hand. It worked. It took a lot more effort, time, and thinking, but it worked.

I will never forget our PT, whose name was Sherman. Sherman was a very large and muscular man who spoke with a heavy Jamaican accent. His job was to get Carter moving. Often, he would call me before each visit and request that I go get another piece of equipment, such as a quad cane. So I would run to Walgreens and get a quad cane. Every time I went to Walgreens I felt so young, as there is a high-density population of older people in southern Florida.

Sherman would effortlessly lift Carter up from the couch and guide him to the barstool he placed against the wall. Carter would then practice moving from the barstool to standing on his own, transferring his own weight by himself rather than relying on others.

After Carter was standing, Sherman would stand behind him, hold the belt, and have Carter walk. By this time, his left leg was fairly pain-free, and he could put quite a bit of weight on it. His right leg, however, was complicated. He had a drop foot, so he had to wear a brace to keep his foot up. His right knee could only bend at about 40 degrees, so he also had to compensate a lot for the lack of mobility.

When Carter walked, his right hip would come up each time he would take a step with his right leg. Sherman would keep his hand on Carter's right hip and say, "Keep it down." When Carter finally was performing to Sherman's liking, Sherman would smile really big and say, "Ya mon" in his heavy accent.

I cried the first time he said it, every time he said it after that, and even now I cry each time I hear a Jamaican "Ya mon." He would always look at me when Carter crossed a hurdle and say, "You see dat, Daddy?"

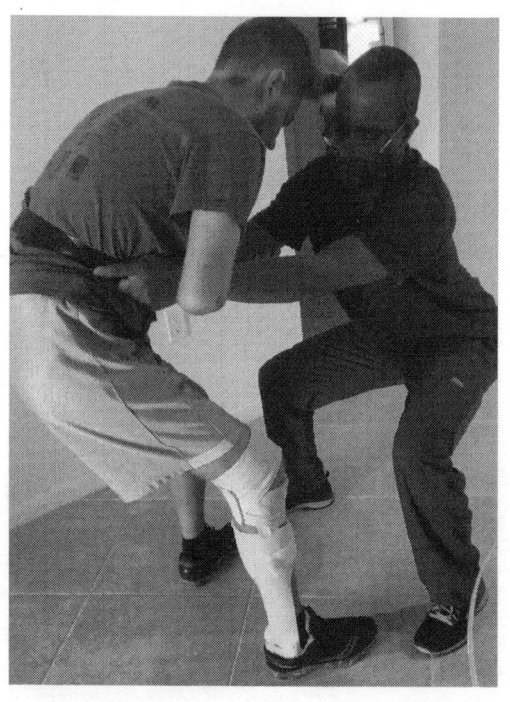

Sherman helping Carter relearn how to stand
(Photo Credit: Viss Family)

Sherman told me that by week two, he would have Carter walking outside on the beach path and doing stairs. We didn't know if Carter was ever going to walk again, and now he's going to be doing stairs!

The fact that we had to get a new apartment for him because his old one was only accessible by stairs was the first thing I thought of when he told me that. Sherman was right, they were walking outside by week two *and* doing stairs. Carter said going up the stairs was a lot easier than coming down the stairs.

Sherman also taught me how to properly walk Carter and gave me permission to walk him outside. So not only was I teaching Carter how to cook with one hand, but I was also teaching him how to walk again. I would take Carter on the beach path, lifting belt in hand, and so many people would say hi to us and encourage us as we inched our way down the path. Every time a stranger said something nice to us, I cried.

I cried a lot, actually. This trauma, while taking a huge toll on Carter, had affected so many people in so many ways. Personally, I had put myself aside and focused solely on Carter. While being away from home, I knew I needed help psychologically, but I couldn't take the time to seek help. I also was nursing a really bad toothache, and my regular shoulder cortisone shot was months overdue, which made lifting Carter and the wheelchair that much more painful. My shoulder hurt so badly that I could barely pull the covers over myself in bed with my right arm without a tremendous amount of pain.

I felt like I was falling apart, and I was. But I just closed my lips, smiled, and, like Marty Byrde, said, "Mmm-hmm," and went on.

CHAPTER 43

Dr. Paley

Chuck

REFLECTING ON FEBRUARY 2020, A FEW MORE THINGS COME to mind. First, I started working again. Fortunately, I had brought my work laptop with me on Thanksgiving Day. I was in contact with work the first few weeks, then went on unpaid leave, as the situation was very unclear as to when I would be able to start work again.

As we settled into a nice routine in February, I was granted the opportunity to work remotely; I was reviewed quarterly by our leadership. Then COVID-19 happened, and I was no longer an exception, as we all went to remote work.

On February 14, Carter and I made a trip to our lawyers' office. We had received the news that the settlement from the civil case was free to be transferred to Carter's newly created brokerage account. I can't reveal many details about the settlement. But I can say it was a very amicable experience between the two parties.

After transferring the funds, I looked to our lawyer and said, "It looks like dinner is on Carter tonight." He cracked a smile, which didn't happen very often either.

That first month in the condo was tough on me. Not only were we still dealing with the civil case, but the criminal case investigation continued. So did calls from news reporters. It was a lot.

I was also *the* caretaker. Being a caretaker takes a big toll on anyone, and this situation was much more than being a caretaker. I myself was suffering from PTSD and had symptoms of body aches, terrible anxiety, gut issues, depression, and, for the first time in my life, suicidal thoughts and sleepwalking. I also had this overwhelming fear that I would harm or maybe kill my son during those sleepwalking events or through an overdose of drugs. That's why I wrote down everything in my notebook—in case something *did* happen to him, at least I had a record of everything I had given him.

During the few weeks of home health care, Carter had a few crucial doctor appointments that we went to. The two I remember most are both orthopedic doctors, the first with Dr. A, who performed most of his surgeries.

When we first arrived and checked in, the receptionist gave me a form to sign, which basically said we would pay for anything that the insurance didn't pay for out of our own pocket. I said I would not sign it but seek advice from our lawyers and my insurance company.

Unfortunately, Dr. A and his office were not a preferred provider under our health insurance. They, therefore, had *zero* coverage for us, but under emergency situations, our insurance agreed to reimburse the doctors under the preferred provider rate, which was much less than what is billed out.

Ultimately, the doctor's office sought hundreds of thousands of dollars from us. I'm pretty sure they knew a settlement was paid out to Carter, so they were seeking payment from that settlement, just as our insurance company was (look up "subrogation," which I think the Devil invented).

Needless to say, the whole situation was awkward and stressful. Dr. A and I had become very close. That last visit to his office was a "goodbye" visit due to a lack of insurance coverage. We said goodbye, hugged, and cried.

The second orthopedic doc visit was at the Paley Institute, a world-renowned orthopedic center of excellence located on the campus of St. Mary's Medical Center. Our rehab doc got us a visit with the clinic's namesake—Dr. Dror Paley—in about a week, which is almost unheard of. Normally, it's at least a two- to three-month wait.

We arrived on "clinic" day—when the doctors saw patients, as they were not in surgery on those days. Clinic days are hell days. There are so many people hanging around, waiting to see the docs, and the crowded conditions were not only horrible for a patient in a wheelchair but also horrible for his father, who is trying to calm the patient. If the doctors are not an hour behind the scheduled visit, it's a good clinic day.

After that first visit, we always asked for the very earliest appointment of that day that was open to avoid so many waiting periods.

When Dr. Paley saw Carter, he looked him over along with the X-rays they had just taken, had him stand and sit on the table, rolled him to one side, and had him perform a few movements. He said some big names of surgical procedures, then looked at me and said, "Who is going to do the nerve decompression for his right leg?"

I said, "Can you do it?"

He confirmed he and his team would perform the surgery, along with either a right distal femur cleanup or a full quadricepsplasty—a risky procedure to release tendons to allow a full bend in Carter's knee.

I cried when he said he would do the surgery, and I felt like he honestly cared about Carter and his quality of life after this horrible accident. The quadricepsplasty surgery sounded intense, and he looked at Carter and said, "Don't let anyone else but me do that surgery should you have to have it done."

Carter quickly replied, "Okay, Dr. Paley."

We were able to get the surgery scheduled for March 30, 2020, which quickly got canceled when COVID-19 shut down the world and all elective surgeries.

CHAPTER 44

Dumping In

Being human is not hard because you're doing it wrong; it's hard because you're doing it right. You will never change the fact that being human is hard, so you must change your idea that it was ever supposed to be easy.

—GLENNON DOYLE, *UNTAMED*

Leila

IN MARCH 2020, A MICRO MONSTER FORCED LIFE AROUND the world into a holding pattern. Normality was erased. As institutions and businesses decided how to protect themselves, the COVID-19 virus whittled away, hour by hour, any hope for attending future events on our spring calendars.

When my March music teachers' conference in Chicago was canceled, I redirected flights and planned to be with Chuck and Carter in Florida for two weeks. Days after, those plans were canceled, too. Chuck continued his work remotely from Carter's condo, and I remained in Colorado, morphing my home-based piano lessons into a virtual studio on Zoom.

It was disappointing on so many levels being stuck in Colorado. I wanted to check in to see if the emotional dust had settled since Carter's release from the hospital. I was eager to see and relieve Chuck of his caregiving duties. And, of course, I wanted to see Carter, especially how his right knee was faring, as it had been the number one source of concern since his hospital stay.

Though Dr. Paley planned to operate on the knee on March 30, the procedure was postponed until April 30 due to COVID-19-related restrictions on nonessential surgeries at St. Mary's. During the long weeks of lockdown and isolation, Carter and Chuck had time to work up plenty of angst about the upcoming surgery, which meant returning to a hospital building. Both were banking on the doctor's promise that it would be outpatient and that they could return home within a day.

But that would not happen. What the doctor intended as an outpatient procedure turned into a surprise six-hour surgery and a four-night stay in the hospital. The surgical team found a significant infection in Carter's knee, removed the hardware from his femur, and checked the condition of the nerve behind his knee that controls the dorsal flex motion in his foot. The surgery left two long rows of stitches on either side of his knee. The doctor deemed it a success, especially since it revealed the mysterious infection that had plagued Carter since the accident. Despite no fever, Carter's blood tests showed infected cells. The cause of that infection had been found.

As good as the surgery was for inching Carter's recovery forward, the anxiety it caused both Chuck and Carter before and after took a major toll on both. The anticipation that

Dumping In

there would be no hospital stay made the event tolerable. But when Carter awoke to the news that he could not go home, he was understandably devastated.

With COVID-19 restrictions in place, Carter was to have no visitors. Because Chuck was Carter's caregiver, he was given permission by Dr. Paley to visit Carter and bring him meals. Looking back, Chuck's not sure it was the best thing for either of them to be granted this visitation privilege. The anesthesia and painkillers triggered high anxiety and extreme lows in Carter. He pleaded to go home, claimed his life was over, and said there was no reason to live. Chuck was hanging on to emotional threads himself, and both "dumped in" on each other.

Soon after the accident, a friend shared a blog post about how to care for loved ones who are sick or injured. The premise is that the patient is in the middle of the circle, his closest family members and friends (caregivers) are just outside the circle, the family and friends of the caregivers are in the next circle, etc. This circular formation carries one significant rule: No dumping *in*, only dumping *out*.[1] In other words, Carter has permission to dump out as much as he wants to anyone. Chuck can dump on others outside his circle, but he cannot dump in on Carter.

While at the hospital, Chuck texted me a confession: He had just "dumped in." Frustrated with how to respond to Carter's desperation, he called him a "poopshit." I absolved him. (Now, I'm not sure I would have come up with poopshit, but I bet I would have dumped in, too. Hospitals have a tendency to bring out the worst when things are bad already.)

The first signs of Carter's darkness became apparent in January, the day we labeled "Shit Day." The powerful effect of drugs, coupled with his realization of what happened to his body and the life changes ahead, shook Carter to his core. Chuck and I have determined that it was necessary for Carter to hit bottom occasionally. If not, his grief may uncontrollably boil up at some point. In general, we've been amazed by Carter's healing maintenance plan he's prescribed for himself. His checklist includes patience and courage, which keeps us grounded as well.

Chase and Brittany heard that things were rough after surgery. Armed with homemade face masks, they braved the COVID-19 airline travel restrictions and hopped on a plane the next day. Their presence was the much-needed distraction for Chuck and Carter to get through another hospital-brain detox. Chase had work-from-home status, and Brittany somehow figured out how to teach preschool online, so they continued their jobs while at Carter's condo. They grocery shopped, cooked, cleaned, and offered company to the weary father-and-son duo.

CHAPTER 45

Steps Back

Carter

March had now arrived, and I had weaned off all my pain medications. I was only using medical marijuana and Advil. I felt myself gaining more energy and was determined to do more activities.

One of my first goals was to walk to the Juno Beach Pier and back from the condo—roughly a one-mile walk. My left leg was getting stronger, and I had a good Ankle Foot Orthosis (AFO) brace for my right foot.

The first half of the walk went great, but during the second half, I was starting to feel pain and discomfort. I remember my dad was walking with me and encouraging me to press on. After what felt to me like I'd just run ten miles, we finally made it back. I was so proud of myself, and it was a testament to the effect of time and repetition during my recovery.

Another old hobby I was determined to apply time and repetition to was playing the piano. It had felt hopeless to me that I could do much with one hand on the piano. Not to mention, the pieces I could learn would be very limited. Despite these thoughts, I decided to sit at the piano again and just start playing.

It was very frustrating at first. It felt like there were so many more notes I needed to play, but physically, I was unable to. My right knee also didn't bend enough to sit straight on at the piano, so I had to sit with my body awkwardly shifting to the left to hit the sustain pedal.

I eventually got used to it and started working on an arrangement of the hymn "It Is Well" for the left hand. It was an encouraging return to piano, but I knew it would require an immense amount of time and repetition.

A new hobby I picked up during my recovery was drawing. I had always enjoyed art in school but never dedicated much of my free time to it. In the hospital, my cousin Kassy gave me a sketchbook and a ton of other art supplies as gifts. She showed me some cool tips for drawing in the sketchbook, and I wanted to try them once I felt up for it.

I sat down at my new desk that my dad and I put together and started drawing different species of fish. They are animals that I love and know a lot about. It was such a great way to keep my mind occupied, and I could see the gradual improvements in my technique with each fish I drew. This newfound hobby made the time fly by.

In the middle of March, the entire world shut down because of COVID-19. It was such a bizarre shift in reality. Everyone was basically confined to their homes, and there was so much uncertainty about what the future would look like. However, my life barely changed because of this. I would still go to physical therapy at the Paley Institute and spend the rest of the day hanging around the condo. I remember the roads being eerily empty every time my dad and I would make that drive to PT.

Steps Back

Although the fact that the world changed in a matter of days gave most people, including myself, a sense of dread and anxiety, it also brought me an odd sense of comfort. It felt like the world was now on the same page as me. My life had been uprooted on Thanksgiving of 2019, just like everyone's life changed in mid-March. I was confined indoors because of my physical limitations while everyone was ordered to shelter in place. I was no longer missing "regular" life on the outside because "regular" was suspended indefinitely.

I often broke some of the COVID-19 guidelines back then by going for walks along the beach. I could now walk independently and without a cane. It always brought me so much joy to experience the sights and sounds of the outdoors, and most days there was barely anyone outside.

I remember all the beaches and the Juno Beach Pier were closed. I would occasionally see a jogger pass by and immediately get jealous of them. I wished I still had legs like theirs and could run for miles at a time. It made me think about how much of a gift two healthy legs are and how many people, myself included, took them for granted. Despite this jealousy, I would often feel I was still incredibly grateful to be walking at all after what I had experienced.

As April approached, I got news that the upcoming surgery on my right knee was postponed to April 30 due to COVID-19. I was so relieved to hear this because it meant a longer amount of time until I had to return to the hospital. However, there was a bit of disappointment since this was likely my final surgery, and I could get on with my life sooner if I could get it over with.

Although the anxiety from this surgery was building as the weeks went by, I was also getting the itch to go out fishing again. I called Andy, and we went to a local canal just to see what I would be able to do. It turned out that I could handle a fishing rod just fine with one hand. Andy would have to bait the hook for me, but I could easily cast the line and reel it in by tucking the end of the rod into my right armpit.

I caught three fish that day. I recall it was probably the happiest I've felt since the incident. Andy and I were filled with a sense of optimism after this and planned a daylong fishing trip for the following week.

As my surgery approached, I kept making progress on the outside. I went on frequent long walks by myself. I was starting to do more strengthening workouts. I relearned "Prelude No. 1 in C Major" by Bach, which was meant for two hands. And I spent a lot of time drawing fish.

Andy and I also headed to Fort Lauderdale for a fishing trip at some freshwater canals. I caught an invasive bullseye snakehead, a large fish I had been trying to catch before the incident, and was ecstatic. I remembered a brief moment of forgetting I was ever injured, and we were out having fun fishing just like we did before.

Although I felt like I was enjoying life again, fear was welling up in me, as it was now the week of my surgery. My dad and I had a pre-op appointment with Dr. Paley, which ended with optimism as he said this would most likely be an outpatient procedure. I felt a little more confident about going back under the knife.

Early Thursday morning, the day of the surgery, my dad and I arrived at a very empty hospital. I said goodbye to him

Steps Back

and walked into the infamous pre-op room. Fortunately, there wasn't a long wait, and I was put under anesthesia in less than an hour.

I woke up disoriented, confused, and very nauseous. I looked down and noticed a PICC line was installed on my upper left arm, and my right knee had a wound vac. I looked at the clock on the other side of the post-op room, and it was about 6 p.m. They had told me this procedure would just take two or three hours; it had actually taken more than eight hours. I was also told I had to stay at the hospital for a couple of days. The surgery went well, they said, but they discovered an infection in my knee, so it ended up being far more invasive than planned. I was absolutely mortified when I heard this news, and it sank me into a dark place I had not been since the early days in the hospital.

My dad miraculously was allowed to visit me despite the extremely stringent COVID-19 rules in the hospital. He brought me a smoothie that night, and we talked for a bit about my situation. He was definitely optimistic that the surgery went well, but no matter how much he tried, he couldn't improve my attitude about being in the hospital again. I remember vomiting multiple times that night and could barely sleep because of my nausea.

I'm not completely sure why I immediately found myself in that very dark place during those days in the hospital. Maybe it was because of the PTSD I had from my previous hospital experiences. Maybe it was because I started taking pain meds again. Or maybe it was because there were potential setbacks in my recovery. It felt like I was taking two steps back instead of forward. All I knew was that I couldn't get out of this place while I was in the hospital. It was a time when I wished I had prayed more instead of wallowing in my sadness.

There was also a quiet, vacant atmosphere in the hospital then. Since no visitors were allowed, the hallways were empty except for an occasional nurse walking by. This was not the St. Mary's I remembered, and it felt like I was at a different facility. The solitude of having no visitors besides my dad also took a heavy toll on me.

Monday had arrived, and thankfully, everything worked out—I was discharged that evening. I could feel the weight of the darkness lifting off my shoulders as soon as we went out those front doors. I felt so much relief as I reentered the condo and was greeted by Chase and Brittany, who were visiting to help my dad.

I remember sleeping like a baby that night. I was so glad that surgery was over and hospital stays were potentially a thing of the past.

CHAPTER 46

Wailing Wall

Chuck

As the therapies continued at home, I was very hopeful that Carter would make a full recovery. Then I saw the right leg develop a bump. A boil-like thing was developing on one of his surgical scars, just above the knee on the inside of his leg. We marked it with a pen to see if it was growing. It was. It was red around the outside and looked like it would pop if I poked a needle into it.

I checked in with his surgeon, sent some pics, and finally, we decided the trauma center should look at it. So we went back to the ER at St. Mary's. It was February 10, about a week after he was released from the hospital.

Understandably, Carter had anxiety to the point that I hardly knew who he was. He wanted to leave so badly. We were seen very quickly when we got to the ER (Carter was pretty famous at St. Mary's by now), and we saw trauma docs who knew us and our journey. They incised the growth, said it didn't look very deep, but they wanted us to come back to the trauma center the next day to have it reviewed by more docs.

We returned the next day, and they showed me how to care for the wound. Ultimately, it would never heal. It was always leaking fluid. The doctors would test this fluid, and nothing ever came back definitive for infection. We ended up at Dr. M's office several times; he was our infectious disease specialist. It was a mystery. That right leg haunted me.

At the beginning of March, Carter's home health care quickly turned to outpatient PT and OT. This was truly the beginning of Carter's comeback. We often had five visits each week, three PT and two OT. He worked very hard at therapy and hard when he came home, too. He was now walking alone to the pier and back, even with his full drop foot. He did get a nice new brace for his foot, which made him look a bit sexier, in my opinion. I always worried about him when he went out, crossed the busy street to get to the beach path, walked a mile, and came back home. I once asked how it was to cross the street (people often do not stop for pedestrians), and he said that people always stopped for him because he had extra sympathy points when they saw him.

When COVID-19 happened, we still were able to go to therapies. We had our temperature checked each time, wore masks, and continued with the exercises. When Carter was in therapy, I would either work on my laptop or go for a walk or run outside. I felt like I was out of my usual shape and wanted to lose a few pounds by being more active.

Often, on my walks outside, I would go to my "Wailing Wall," which was the area between two cement buildings on the hospital grounds in the back of the facilities, which were very isolated.

The very first day we arrived, I found that spot and yelled at the top of my lungs to the God I thought I knew—profanities included—for several minutes at a time. I would crumple beside one wall, stare at the other, and curse at God. This happened several times daily during the first two weeks and often after that.

I wasn't proud of it, but I had reached the end of my rope, and that's the only thing that came to mind. I didn't yell when I revisited the wall, but my anger was (and is) still present.

COVID-19 really didn't change the lifestyle that Carter and I settled into those first months of 2020. We pretty much stayed at home anyway.

One very unfortunate thing that happened was the beaches were closed. The beach was my getaway place. Every day after work at 4 p.m., I'd pack some beer in the cooler, take my chair and blanket, tell Carter I'd be gone for a few hours (but had my phone for emergencies), and would go to the beach. This was my escape place, which was ironic in many ways. Carter was in the ocean when he got hit, and there I was, sitting by the ocean during his recovery. Every time I saw a boat, chills went down my spine. There were many boats, too.

For me, the hotter the weather, the better. And the rougher the waves, the better, too. I would get in the water and just let the waves crash against my body. Did that make me feel alive? Is this a result of my trauma? Why did I like the constant pressure of the water and waves on me? I'm not really sure, but it always gave me enough of something to pack up my beach stuff, go back to the condo, clean up, and figure out what we were going to have for dinner that night.

By the end of April, some elective surgeries were being allowed again. We got a call from Paley, and they said we could come in for a pre-op appointment and get something scheduled for surgery for the end of April. Both Carter and I were very anxious about what they would suggest. We were both afraid of the quadricepsplasty. Basically, that involved cutting away all the scar tissue on Carter's right leg to allow him to pretty much bend the knee fully so he could touch his foot to his butt. But the recovery is awful—one full week in the hospital on a traction machine. Neither Carter nor I wanted to endure that.

During the pre-op, Dr. Paley was present remotely (due to COVID-19 restrictions), and Dr. Claire Shannon was there in person. Ultimately, they were happy with Carter's progress at that point and didn't want a major surgery like quadricepsplasty to set him back. So they decided on an outpatient surgery to clean up his wounds, see what was causing the fluid to come out of his right leg, and decompress the perineal nerve in his right leg. We were very happy with their decision.

Then, the surgery happened.

I dropped Carter off at 6 a.m. and then went back to the condo (I could not go in with him because of COVID-19). I cooked, did yoga, went for a run, and tried to do anything but think of the surgery. I started to receive texts from the Paley staff about how well the surgery was going and how well Carter was doing. I was so anxious and nervous, just like when Carter was having surgery while in St. Mary's.

I finally got a call from Dr. Paley and Dr. Shannon, and they told me what had happened and why Carter would have to recover in the hospital. Carter had an infection from skin to bone, so they cleaned it all out. They found a hole in his femur that was previously undetected, so they filled that up with cement. They removed some of the no longer-needed hardware that helped his bone heal. They worked on his perineal nerve that had been stretched (like when you stretch licorice and it doesn't have the same original shape), and during this procedure, they did notice that his foot moved when they activated his nerve. There was hope that Carter's drop foot would resolve!

I knew Carter would wake up in a hospital room and find out he had to stay for a few days. This was not the news we were hoping for. I packed a bag for him and included a note to try to pick up his spirits. I cried so hard writing that note. This guy has had to endure so much, and now this, too. I ran it to the hospital and gave it to the front desk.

I saw one of Carter's nurses from step-down, called her over, explained what was happening, and just burst into tears, as did she. She promised to check in with him from time to time. I called Dr. A, and he also promised to check in on him when he was doing his rounds. I called Dr. Shannon and asked if I could get "caretaker status" and be able to visit Carter in the hospital during COVID-19. She texted me a few hours later and said it was approved and I could visit Carter.

Surgery was on a Thursday, and Carter was discharged on Monday. I'm pretty sure it was the lowest I've seen him. He was barely himself, full of PTSD and anxiety. I was glad I could visit, but it was awful to see him in that state.

Again, it was Dr. M, the infectious disease doc, who approved Carter's exit from St. Mary's, but he would have to go on IV meds again, have another PICC line installed (the first one was removed in March), and Nurse Chuck would again have to tend to his wounds.

CHAPTER 47

Infection

Chuck

With new meds to administer and more wounds to care for at home, we were assigned a new home health nurse. When I first heard the nurse's name, I knew it was the first one assigned to us that I had "fired" before I met her. The thought of asking for a different nurse crossed my mind, but I decided just to go with it. I knew if it didn't work out, I could ask for a replacement. We ended up getting along just fine, although Leila, Brittany, and I had some experiences with her that were a bit questionable. Nonetheless, we were able to work through it.

The first time I would administer any new meds, the nurse had to stick around for a few hours afterward to see if there were any bad effects.

She should have stayed an hour longer.

It was a late night, as Carter wasn't discharged until late afternoon. Then, we had to get the meds, arrange for the nurse to arrive, administer the meds, and wait for a reaction. I think the nurse left around 8:30 p.m., then Carter got ready for bed . . . he was excited to sleep at home again. I poured my stiff drink and turned on Netflix, only to hear a violent commotion in the room next door. Carter threw up every single bit of dinner he ate that night (beef nachos) and more.

Vomit was everywhere: in the bed, on the floor, on the wall, and by the sink on the other side of the room. Carter even got out of bed on his own and made it to the toilet to finish up. The fact that he got up and was able to walk was actually a good sign . . . before that, he never walked without his brace. But his room was a disaster.

I put the bedding in the washer, scraped up the nacho pieces, helped Carter get to the shower (since he had a PICC line, it had to be covered up for the shower), deep-cleaned the floor and the walls, and put on new bedding so Carter could get some rest.

He obviously had a bad reaction to the antibiotics.

The next day we called Dr. M and told him what happened. Although he felt terrible for Carter, he insisted that we stick with the drug for three more days. We argued profusely, but he was adamant. Carter never threw up again, but he felt miserable for three days and hardly ate anything.

We called Dr. M again, and he told us about this new antibiotic that was supposed to be good for skin infections. The downside? Most insurance companies would not cover it due to the cost. I told him to try with my insurance company, as I had good coverage (as long as you used in-network providers).

Sure enough, the new med was approved, and we started over again. While the new med was hard to find, eventually, Walgreens came through.

The nurse returned to the condo, and we administered the medication, and we settled in to wait. Fortunately, there

Infection

was no reaction this time. Phew. It cost around $14,000 a month. Fortunately, I had met all my deductibles, and it cost us nothing.

The best news was that it actually seemed to be working! Carter had his blood drawn weekly to check for infection markers, and it was a huge relief to see that C-reactive protein fall from over sixty to two in a few months.

This surgery started a new trend in Carter's recovery. They wanted him back at therapy as soon as he was released from the hospital, so I got to revisit the whole wheelchair/car/hurt-my-back routine. But it was worth it. Soon he was bending his knee more, walking better, and had slight movement in his foot. Could it be coming back? Was there motion there now that hadn't been there before? If Carter got his dorsal flex back, then he would no longer have a drop foot and would be able to walk normally again without his foot orthotic.

One morning, about a month after the surgery, I heard something from his room I had never heard before. I heard the dresser drawer opening. I thought about going in there, but I think he would have let me know if there was an issue.

Pretty soon, Carter walked out on his own, all dressed, with socks on. He had walked over to the dresser, gotten some socks and clothes, and put them on all by himself. His drop foot was definitely going away, and his right knee could bend enough that he could put his socks on.

This was a big deal. Every morning before that, I helped him get dressed. I never helped him after that day.

Could this be a sign that he could be totally independent again?

CHAPTER 48

New Lifelong Friends

Dance in the moment.

—Ichiro Kishimi and Fumitake Koga,
The Courage to Be Disliked

Leila

Chase and Brittany's trip from Denver to West Palm Beach inspired me. It proved that I could make my way there safely, too, so three and a half months after leaving Florida, I returned (of course, wearing a mask due to COVID-19 requirements) in May.

I strategically sat in an aisle seat. No one asked to sit in the window seat in the same row, and no one was allowed to sit in the middle seat. I was free and clear of neighbors the entire flight.

After greeting me at the airport with a long hug and kiss, Chuck took me back to Carter's oceanside condo. Reuniting with Chuck and Carter was something to treasure, yet it was also a painful throwback to what life was before I left Florida. I'm not sure if there are words to describe the visit and my emotions. Good? Glad? Sad?

When I opened the door, Carter stood up from his favorite couch to give me a hug. He seemed even taller and thinner than I remembered, but perhaps that was because he was usually in a hospital bed or wheelchair when I saw him last.

It was some time ago since I'd seen the condition of his limbs, so I took an inventory throughout my visit. Despite a long scar beginning mid-palm and ending above his wrist, his left hand and arm seemed completely healed. His left leg appeared sturdy, thanks to a piece of cement planted below his knee, which made his shin bone feel strangely crooked, although the leg looked straight. The leg, along with his ankle that's held together by screws and rods, carried most of his weight with little to no pain.

A pink scar wrapped halfway around what was left of his right arm. There was still a large red bruise on the tip of his arm. He claimed it didn't hurt, but Carter hollered some choice words when Chuck placed the compression sock on his arm and pulled it up a little too snugly against the spot.

Carter's left hand took a severe blow from the blade of a motor, yet Carter regained full functionality with it. I'll never forget the day in early March when Chuck texted me that Carter was testing his left hand at the piano despite the absence of his other hand.

Now that I was back in Florida, I was eager to hear and watch Carter play, yet the moment was bittersweet. As a pianist, I would have struggled to reunite with a beloved instrument I adore playing with two hands. Carter had just purchased a new digital piano weeks before the accident. All the repertoire by Beethoven, Liszt, and Chopin he had worked on before was written for two hands.

New Lifelong Friends

His reconciliation with the piano and one hand began with a setting of "It Is Well" by my friend and colleague, Daniel Light. Soon after, he challenged himself to Bach's "Prelude for Cello in G." His dynamic musicality was just as impressive—and perhaps even more so—despite one less hand. Sigh ... the magnetic power of music had won—he couldn't help but return to it.

As expected, I became privy to and helped with the routine that evolved over the months of recovery at home.

Once awake around 9 a.m., Carter calls for Chuck, who pauses work at his laptop to begin the drill. The ice wrap is removed from the knee, and the water from the ice tank is poured over the patio plants. Urinals are emptied, a clean T-shirt is chosen from the closet, and shorts are already on from the night before. Chuck helps to put on the compression socks, size 13 running shoes, and an AFO since Carter cannot bend his right knee quite enough to do it himself.

Coffee and two mini muffins are served to Carter after he moves from bed to couch. A breakfast of a fried egg with sausage on an English muffin, grapefruit juice, a peeled orange, and a few meds is served about an hour after Carter gets out of bed.

In between meals, Carter listens to podcasts, sends texts, watches fish videos, reads fish-related books, plays piano, draws at his desk, and cares for his fish tank. Dinner is served around 7:30 p.m., and soon after, Carter gets in the shower with a little help from Chuck.

After he chooses some clean shorts, he gets in bed, and Chuck returns to wrap the ice pack around his knee, prop up his right foot with pillows, and give Carter a few meds. We also added one more step to his regimen. His scars needed some attention, so we found some oil, and Carter liked it when others rubbed the oil on each of his scars. As painful as it was to see them, it's one of the most tender moments I've had with my twenty-five-year-old son since he was a baby.

When the in-home care nurse stopped by to check the PICC line, she chided us for putting anything on Carter's wounds, as it could cause infection. Our ritual was short-lived, but we'll never forget it.

One evening, Carter cooked his favorite Mediterranean-inspired meal that included baked marinated chicken, jasmine rice, greens, and homemade hummus whipped up in his Ninja blender. There are some things that Carter cannot do with one hand, like open a garbanzo bean can with a can opener, hold down the blender lid while pushing the pulse button, and cut a lemon in half. He did manage to scoop yogurt out of a container by bending over and securing the carton with his right arm while scooping with his left. He easily squeezed a number of lemons with a juicer, gripping with his left hand only.

His confidence in the kitchen has inspired me to follow his recipe. The challenge will be to make it as delicious as his.

During my visit, Carter had a special appointment at Hanger Clinic. Many reps from the clinic had visited Carter during his stay in the hospital, coaxing him to consider a prosthetic.

After several appointments, his made-to-order prosthetic was in, and it was time to try it on. Connecting what's left of his limb to the six-pound black robotic arm requires suction and tight straps around his upper torso. If both are not just right, the prosthetic won't stay on or work. After two hours, Carter left, owning one arm and wearing another.

We headed to the aquarium store where he used to work. Carter selected some new sea life for his fish tank. He continues to add certain fish and coral with intention and purpose to his pristine tank. The time it took for him to shop and decide on his purchases reminded me of the time I spent waiting for my mom in a fabric store as a kid. Chuck and I waited cheerfully and enjoyed watching Carter in his element.

On the same day as the prosthetic appointment and the stop at the fish store, Andy and Christine came over for a dinner of make-your-own tacos. This reunion of five people who did not know each other before Thanksgiving was a long time coming.

Christine brought homemade angel food cake and fresh strawberries for dessert despite the fact that we did not ask her to bring a thing. The cake was transported in a Rubbermaid cake holder strapped on the back of her motorcycle.

As she washed her hands when she arrived, she apologized for her dirty fingernails. She had just fixed the axle on her Subaru.

Strangely, this circle of five people are now lifelong friends due to an accident. There's a feeling of sincere gratitude for their part in saving Carter's life and also a feeling of sorrow, as all of us have suffered dramatically from this trauma.

As I come to grips with the gravity of the friendships and Carter's return to his beloved piano playing, a phrase comes to mind from a book called *The Courage to Be Disliked*. It states that there is no past, there is no future, there is only the present, and one must "dance in the moment."[1] I think this phrase helps me wrap my head around such a tragic way to cherish new lifelong friends and the healing power of music.

CHAPTER 49

Floridafishboyz

Carter

On May 10, I got my wound vac removed from my knee and could walk on my own again. I didn't feel much pain in my right knee, and it seemed to be healing as planned. My blood work showed that there were still signs of infection present, so my doctor switched me to another antibiotic. This proved to be disastrous, as I was vomiting the entire night after I was switched.

Over the next few days, I felt more nauseous than I had ever felt in my life and could barely move or turn over in bed without wanting to vomit.

I had to endure about four days of this until I could switch to another antibiotic. Those days were absolutely miserable for me, but I was still grateful to be in the comfort of home. Once I was switched to a different antibiotic, the nausea went away.

Near the end of May—roughly half a year after the incident—I was back to doing the same activities before surgery. My right knee could bend to about 90 degrees (the bend was barely over 60 degrees before the surgery), and the nerve in my right foot was beginning to activate. This meant I could start to lift my toes upward on my own.

Before the surgery, I had no upward movement in that foot, but with this glimmer of hope, there was a real possibility I wouldn't need to wear an AFO for the rest of my life. Everything kept improving, and near the middle of June, I decided I was well enough to return to work at Loggerhead.

It was such an unreal feeling getting ready for work that first day I went back. I was only going to work on the aquariums and would only be there for a few hours. Putting that "staff" shirt back on made it all feel real again. I couldn't believe I would be back at work after all I'd been through.

My dad dropped me off, and I met up with Andy at the workshop in the back. We walked around campus just like we used to and ended up at the front aquariums. I started cleaning the aquariums, and it immediately felt natural to me. It was almost therapeutic to do after lying around so much. I had no problem climbing up the short ladders to clean them, and soon, everything didn't seem so hard having just one hand.

I remember telling myself while I was in the hospital that I wouldn't be able to work with aquariums again; in fact, I said it so often that I started to believe it. It was only after actually trying that I could prove otherwise.

I returned home after a couple of hours, definitely needing to sit down for a while, but my body wasn't too sore. I knew, just like everything else throughout my recovery, simple time and repetition would be key to the healing process.

In mid-June, my dad decided to go back to Denver for a couple of weeks while Chase and Brittany stayed with me. I was so glad he was finally able to get home, and he deserved some time away from me. He had been by my side since the day after Thanksgiving. It's very difficult to describe the depth of my respect and love for him as he took care of me and ran my life while I recovered.

The weeks passed, and I finally got my PICC line out and was able to switch to oral antibiotics. This meant I was officially free to live on my own again.

In late July, my parents headed down to the Keys while I would try a night all on my own. It passed with no problems, and I felt like I could easily get used to that. My dad still stayed with me for a while until late August. We decided I should try living a couple of weeks on my own and see how it went. It was a huge deal to live by myself again, and I was ready to embrace it.

In the meantime, Andy and I spent most of our free time fishing. This led us to start an Instagram account called "Floridafishboyz." Its purpose was to show all the different species of native and non-native fish we caught in freshwater and saltwater.

We posted pictures of all the different fish we caught. This motivated us to explore new fishing spots and search for certain areas to catch particular species. We would go on all-day fishing trips, driving around South Florida and catching all the species we could locate. Nothing could beat the thrill of finding a spot that was a gold mine for fish. It was the perfect way to heal mentally, as it got us out doing what we did before the incident.

CHAPTER 50

Back to Denver

Chuck

With COVID-19 in full force, travel actually became affordable and joyfully uncrowded, so Carter and I began to host Denver visitors again. Chase and Brittany arrived at the end of May. Of course, they wanted to visit, but they also were determined to give me a break so that I could go back to Denver for a few weeks. We went through the schedule of each day; I taught them how to administer meds via the PICC line, gave them all the essential numbers to know, and all sorts of other things. For two weeks, I wouldn't have to do anything related to Carter, or so I thought.

I flew to Denver in early June and went to my office for the first time in seven months. That's when a huge anxiety attack hit me. I was home, in my office, which was Carter's old bedroom. There were things of his everywhere, which brought on a flood of emotions on my part. My heart was pounding, my palms were sweating, and my eyes were a mess. At that time, I knew I needed the help of a mental health professional, so I looked up my insurance, found a provider just over a mile away from our house, and set up an appointment for the following week.

Before that appointment, I had my annual physical with my primary care physician, whom I have seen for years, and I thoroughly adore him. I told him about what happened to our son, what happened to me, what happened to me when I came home, and we're crying through these COVID-19 masks that we just can't seem to get used to. Our glasses were fogging up, too.

We finally settled down; he completed his exam, gave me a script for something I could take if I had another panic attack, and on the way out, without even any prompts, we hugged each other for about a minute.

I also drove to Vail to see my shoulder doctor. I had surgery in January of 2019 to repair a torn labrum, and after months of physical therapy, the pain was still at a level that it was before surgery. Of course, I had to tell him and his staff about the accident and recovery, and we all ended up crying together in the exam room. I told them that being at their orthopedic clinic had been very triggering for me, and they totally understood.

I ended up getting a steroid shot in my shoulder. My doctor said I could have shots as long as they were effective, and once they were no longer effective, I would need a shoulder replacement. I'm trying to put that off as long as I can.

Finally, my appointment with the psychologist arrived. I had no idea what to expect. I had never even thought of seeing a shrink before. But then, I knew I needed one. I blabbered out the entire story in about thirty minutes, used a whole box of tissue, and I don't think he said more than a few sentences.

In the end, we both agreed that I should see a therapist in Florida. So I found an amazing therapist in Jupiter through my insurance network and started meeting with him on Friday nights at 6 p.m. We connected instantly.

We had several sessions where I told him my story, and just having someone who generally cared and was not connected in any other way was very helpful. He was also a Christian, having gone through a psych program at PBA (another reason I chose him). We had some very good heart-to-heart talks, and he did some EMDR—eye movement desensitization and reprocessing—therapy on me to alleviate some of the PTSD symptoms I was having. It was from him that I learned about the rest and digestion phase of my nervous system response.

When the accident happened, my sympathetic nervous system kicked in, and I was in a stellar fight-or-flight response for months. When I returned home to Denver, my parasympathetic nervous system kicked in, and I finally hit "rest and digest," which, in my case, caused a panic attack. Surely, I had these responses before in my life, but *never* to the degree that I was experiencing them at that point. I was off the charts on both ends and needed help regulating both responses.

We had our last in-person session the week of Thanksgiving 2020—a year after Carter's incident—and agreed to try online sessions once I moved back to Denver. The online sessions were not the same, so we both decided that I would have to find another therapist in Denver to continue my mental healing. I found somebody and had my first session with him in January 2021. We also established a strong connection very quickly, and I'm still seeing him at the time of this writing (summer 2023).

I didn't think I would need therapy *that* long! At the most, I figured maybe six more months after the six months in Florida. But the depression set in quickly and dramatically. I was prescribed antidepressants to cope with life. I had more suicidal thoughts.

The first ones were in Florida whenever I walked over a drawbridge. I would look at the water below and think, *If I jumped, it would be all over.* But then I would think of Carter and the rest of my family and know that it would make things tougher on them. Back home in Colorado, those same thoughts would usually crop up when I was driving over a bridge.

I worked closely with my therapist and my primary care physician for just the right dosage of meds to keep me going. It was not and still is not an easy journey. All this while I'm holding down a job, working on being a husband again, and trying to reenter into my Denver life.

I could probably write a whole book on my experiences with PTSD, anxiety, depression, and the treatments I sought out. For now, I can tell you it has been one of the toughest experiences I have ever gone through, and I've been through a few. But now, I definitely see the light at the end of the tunnel.

* * *

Back in June of 2020, I went back to Florida and realized how much I *love* the summer heat and humidity there. It made me feel alive, just like the waves hitting against my body—another insight into how trauma affects the body and the mind. I would go out for a run at 2 p.m. and come back and not stop sweating for an hour. Everyone warned me how brutal it was, and I thought it was *great*.

Carter continued to get stronger and do more things on his own. He had gone back to work part time and also started driving again. We started working out together at the gym.

Levi, Erin, and Leila came at the end of June, so we were all in Florida together. I arranged to have the condo next door available for us for July, and that worked out well for all the visitors. Things were definitely heading in the right direction.

Carter still had the PICC line in, so Leila learned how to administer his meds. It was kind of a pain because it had to be covered in waterproof tape every time Carter wanted to shower, but we worked it out.

In the middle of July, the doctor said the PICC line could come out, and Carter could start taking oral antibiotics. That PICC line was my anchor, and now my anchor was lifting!

Leila and I decided to drive to Key West to celebrate our anniversary so Carter could test out how it would be to live alone again. He did just fine without us, a true sign that independence was coming.

For the months of August, September, and October, Carter and I decided I would split my time between Florida and Colorado. Of course, switching back and forth was not easy for me, but I was thankful for the time in both locations.

While in Florida, I would clean and cook and help Carter assemble things, etc. I remember that when I was there in

October, he had an important appointment with Dr. Paley. I asked Carter if he wanted me to go with him. He said no, he would go on his own. I was a nervous wreck, and I thought he would have to have another surgery.

Carter came home and reported that the X-rays looked great; they were not concerned about the wound on his right knee leaking fluid, and Carter could even get in the water again (as long as it wasn't murky water)! Okay, if they were not concerned about the fluid, I shouldn't be, right?

I wish it were that easy.

We said our goodbyes in October, knowing we'd see each other in November for the court hearing during the week of Thanksgiving.

I remember visiting Carter alone in October of 2021. I had some things to take care of. My teeth were still hurting, so I wanted to see the dentist for all my records. I wanted to meet my Florida therapist for tea to catch up, as we had become very close during our therapy sessions. I wanted to see Carter. I missed him. We spent a lot of time together during the previous year. I also missed Florida. I made Florida home when I lived there.

One afternoon during that visit, I remember packing the cooler with beer and going to the beach alone, just like I did during my caretaker days. I sat there, alone, looking out at the ocean and the waves and the boats, thinking to myself, *Did this really happen?* just like I constantly said to myself "Is this really happening?" for several months after the accident. Of course, it did happen.

Another thought was that Carter had been living independently for a whole year. It was always our goal to have him live a completely independent life, with one arm and damaged legs. And he is doing that! I know he had a ton of help along the way, but the help I offered was something that was needed desperately—someone to live with him, someone to care for his wounds, someone to administer meds, someone to dress him, someone to feed him, someone to get him to all of his appointments, and so many other things. It was like I had reraised my son. And I thought to myself, *I did it! I fucking did it!*

That fact is still sinking in.

CHAPTER 51

Turning Point

Carter

Going into September, life was pretty much back to the "normal" I remembered. I was working about three times a week, I could drive myself to physical therapy and doctor appointments, and I was regularly fishing with Andy.

After a checkup appointment with Dr. Paley, it was determined that I was healed enough to get back in the water. I knew I wasn't ready to get back in the ocean, but I was eager to start swimming laps in the pool at the condo. With time and repetition, I eventually got used to swimming with one arm, and it became my favorite form of exercise.

When October came, a big subject on my mind was the upcoming court hearing with the driver of the boat. He was potentially facing time in prison, and I had a meeting with a state attorney to discuss a possible plea deal.

I never gave much thought to the kind of punishment I thought the driver should get. Instead, I focused on ways I could prevent this from happening again and ways to make the ocean safer. Rather than demanding the driver spend years or months behind bars, I wondered if the driver could instead help me campaign for an improvement in the standard divers-down flag I had the day I was hit or for more speed restriction zones for boats.

During the meeting with the attorney, I communicated this, and we came up with a plea deal I was satisfied with. Instead of going to prison, the driver would spend the next year helping me lobby for a new law requiring divers to have a three-dimensional divers-down device instead of a flag. He would help produce a video with the FWC to educate the public on the importance of a divers-down device. There was also a fine and community service with an organization specializing in ocean conservation or safety. The court hearing was ironically scheduled for the Monday of the week of Thanksgiving.

At the beginning of November, I was asked to speak during a chapel service at Palm Beach Atlantic University. I accepted but was incredibly nervous to talk about my experience in front of a crowd. I figured this could be a healing experience for me to talk about it.

On the morning I was scheduled to speak, I entered the chapel building and felt an incredible sense of comfort. This was the same place I attended dozens of chapels as a student, and it was the first time I'd seen it since I graduated.

When chapel started, the crowd sang a couple of worship songs, and then it was my turn to take the stage. I walked up there nervously and proceeded to tell my story. I broke down crying a few times, especially when I talked about my family receiving the news of the incident, but I continued reliving the past year in front of many college students. I used terms like "time and repetition" and "I could make a bigger difference than I could before" to describe my strength and motivation during my recovery.

After I was caught up to the present moment in my story, I announced to the crowd that I had the court hearing with the driver in two weeks. I told them I wasn't sure how I'd react to seeing the driver in person for the first time. I was nervous about getting angry when I met him. I just told the crowd to pray for me.

When I was finished telling my story, I asked if anyone had any questions. A girl immediately stood up and asked if I could play piano. This caught me off guard, but a rush of confidence came to me. I said yes and sat down at the piano that was already on stage. I played Bach's "Prelude No.1 in G Major" for the cello, as I had learned a version for the piano not long ago. I finished and received a standing ovation from the crowd. I then said a prayer, and the chapel was over.

This was one of the major turning points of my life. It was when I realized how much God had been working since the incident. I put my trust in Him before going under when I first got to the hospital, and He has shown me His control over everything.

I was so close to losing myself to defeat in the hospital while I was in my dark place, but my faith in God led me to the light. It felt like God gave me a reason to play piano now instead of taking it away from me. He gave me the perfect opportunity to show that to others. I felt healed after talking at the chapel and grateful for all God has done in my life.

CHAPTER 52

His Day in Court

Overall, I want nothing but positive outcomes to emerge from this tragic accident, and working toward productive changes in marine safety is where I want to start.

—CARTER

Leila

THERE'S NO INSTRUCTION MANUAL ON HOW TO WALK PAST THE boat driver who left our son chronically single-handed.

Daniel Stanton stood with his mother and lawyer in the corridor as our family paraded past them toward the courtroom. By default, both families avoided eye contact yet managed a peek at each other while the other wasn't looking.

I couldn't help but occasionally glance at the three of them. I was surprised by how tall and thin Daniel, who goes by Danny, looked in his dark suit and tie. The only picture of him we had seen before was the one of him in the papers sporting swim trunks, a visor, and a white polo sprinkled with Carter's blood.

We peered out the floor-to-ceiling windows on the third or fourth floor of the Palm Beach County Courthouse, attempting to mask our indifference that our two families were just yards away from each other. And there, off in the distance, stood the prestigious Breakers Hotel. The sight was an unexpected and cruel reminder of why we were at the courthouse. It was The Breakers' beachfront, with its world-class reef, where the accident occurred—and the hotel's cameras caught it all on video.

From his first conscious moments in his hospital bed, Carter was adamant that this catastrophic collision must be turned into something good. In October 2020, the assistant state attorney, Joe Kadis, sat down with Carter, Chuck, and me. He wanted to be clear on our desired outcome of this case.

He pushed us hard as he questioned our leniency toward Danny. He was charged with one count of willful and reckless operation of a vessel. The attorney explained that this was a first-degree misdemeanor punishable by up to one year in jail. Our civil lawyers informed us of this possible maximum penalty, as they assumed we might want to seek a harsh sentence. The FWC officer in charge of the investigation expressed her frustration with maritime laws and the fact that Danny's negligence was considered a mere misdemeanor. She apologetically informed us there was little chance of jail time because alcohol was not involved.

Carter wanted a resolution, not a confrontation. From a legal perspective, Carter and our family had every right to push for charges, yet it seemed fruitless, so finding a way to make good of the bad made sense to us.

It didn't take long for a carefully designed plea agreement to be reached between the state attorney and the lawyer representing Danny. Per our request, the plea hearing was scheduled for November 23, the Monday before Thanksgiving 2020.

Our entire family met in Joe's office, and then we followed him to the courtroom up a couple of floors. The halls were quiet due to the COVID-19 quarantine restrictions. From all appearances, it looked like Carter's case was the only one to be heard on this first day of a slow holiday week. That's why we couldn't avoid spotting the Stantons in the building.

Looking back, it seems remarkable that it was held in person because at the time, so many court hearings were held via Zoom (due to COVID-19 safety protocols). Had Carter's hearing been held via Zoom, we wouldn't have seen the Stantons up close, and Carter's transformative actions would not have happened after the hearing. It's why we couldn't avoid spotting the Stantons in the building.

When we first received our parents' worst-nightmare call that Carter was involved in an accident, Chuck and I panicked for a split second: "I hope he didn't cause it!" When we learned what went down that day, our thoughts went to who *did* cause it. It was clear that whoever was driving the boat made a rotten choice and one that would be hard to live with. But the captain had a name. Danny was a human, someone's son, someone's brother. I almost . . . not quite, but *almost* . . . felt as sorry for him as I did for Carter.

I put myself in his place and pondered:

How does he wake up each morning knowing that he operated his recently outfitted, 36-foot pleasure craft named after his girlfriend at fifty miles an hour while clearly too close to a paradise for sea life, divers, and snorkelers?

How does he process the fact that he "failed to maintain a proper lookout in crystal clear waters with no chop," as reported by the FWC?

How did he feel when he put the boat in reverse and idled back to see the carnage caused by his triple-engine boat built for speed?

How did he feel as he helped to load Carter's mangled body up past the propeller blades onto his boat's pristine rear platform gleaming in the hot sun?

How did he feel when Christine applied a tourniquet from his own first aid kit to stop the bleeding from Carter's limbs?

How did he feel when the ambulance took off from the beach and headed to St. Mary's Medical Center?

How did he feel knowing that his mistake couldn't be mended by a misdemeanor on his record, a jail sentence, or even all the money in the world?

Those questions stuck with me as we watched Carter roll in and out of surgery. I knew the answers might feel equivalent to a life sentence in prison.

Because of strict COVID-19 restrictions, the presiding judge, Robert Panse, limited the courtroom capacity to fifteen people. As we waited in the hall, the bailiff checked our names and relationship to the case and escorted us one by one into the room. The bailiff carried a tough exterior and frightened me until he approached me and asked my name and my relationship to this case. I was about to say Carter's mom when he suggested, "Sister?" I smiled and took the compliment.

His Day in Court

Seats were assigned when we entered the courtroom. In front of the judge, Carter and the state attorney sat at one table. Danny and his attorney sat at another, six feet away. Chuck and I sat on a wooden bench, which was tiny like a church pew, about eight feet in front of Danny's mother. On other benches sat the FWC officer in charge of the investigation, a news reporter, and a cameraman. The bailiff stood in the back of the room, and two court assistants and the judge sat up high behind a long, regal desk.

Although they hoped to sit inside the courtroom, Chase, Brittany, Levi, and Erin were not allowed in and had to watch the proceedings on Zoom in the hallway outside the courtroom. Along with Carter's civil attorney, Danny's father attended via Zoom due to health reasons. We saw them from a monitor secured to a wall just right of the judge.

Even though the agreement was set prior to the hearing, Judge Panse made it clear that he thought the terms were too lenient. The judge emphatically stated that the amount of evidence could sway a jury to charge Danny with a crime and sentence him to one year of prison and a $1,000 fine.

Chuck and I sat rigid on the wooden pews, wondering if all the work we put into the plea agreement would be overturned. The judge looked directly at Carter and asked more than once if the terms were acceptable. As Carter sat with a slight slouch to accommodate the limited bend in his right knee, he assured the judge that he was satisfied with the agreement as planned.

Next, the judge asked both sides if they wished to make a statement. Danny stood and walked to a microphone first.

His skin color seemed pale gray, his face somewhat gaunt, hiding behind his face mask. His dark suit seemed roomy on him, and the knot on his tie was a little crooked. He read his statement in a deep, clear voice, looked intently into Carter's eyes, and turned toward us occasionally. He apologized, expressed regret and remorse about Carter's injuries, a determination to change maritime laws, and asked for forgiveness. His words obviously came from the heart:

> Good afternoon, Judge. Thank you for giving me this opportunity to share my statement.
>
> Carter, I would like to first speak to you and your family for a moment. I am so sorry that this happened to you. I cannot fathom the physical and emotional pain you and your family have endured. You have been in my thoughts and prayers every day for the last year. Your strength, bravery, and positivity that you have shown in the face of such loss and hardship is truly amazing and inspiring.
>
> Over the last year, I have routinely tried to envision our meeting. I so regret that it is in this formal court setting. I look forward to working with you on seeking to make changes to the dive flag rules and regulations. I also hope, given the opportunity, that one day we might become friends.
>
> I look forward to pursuing work on dive flag safety reform so that no one ever has to experience the tragedy that happened in this case.
>
> Thank you.

His Day in Court

A few moments later, Carter slowly rose, putting weight on his left leg to bring the right leg beneath him, as it couldn't bend enough to assist. He approached the microphone, where there was no lectern for him to set his statement on. It was printed on two pages and stapled together.

I'm not sure why he didn't choose the double-sided option on his printer. I would have advised that, but neither Chuck nor I were consulted when Carter prepared and printed his statement. At this point, why would he? Carter didn't need us hovering over his every move. He managed fine without us now. He was walking with just a slightly crooked gait; he was off all antibiotics, cooked his favorite Mediterranean meals, drove himself to work, and had recently given a speech and played piano at a chapel service at his alma mater, Palm Beach Atlantic University.

Yet, as Carter confidently delivered his statement, our parental instincts kicked in. We wanted to jump in to help when he headed to page two. We repressed our urges—as did the rest of the room—and remained in our seats and watched him successfully flip to the next page with one hand.

His impact statement was direct and to the point:

> Imagine yourself doing the thing you love the most. It is a perfect day for doing this, and out of the hundreds of times you have done this responsibly, today is particularly exceptional.
>
> After hours of enjoyment, you decide to call it a day and head back home. Then, in a matter of seconds, your joy and contentment are interrupted by

a sudden impact. The next thing you notice is your arm on the ground about twenty feet away from you. Before you can process the absolute shock of that sight, you notice both your legs are dangling from your body, and your ability to move effortlessly is nothing but a distant memory. As you start to inhale your own blood infused with saltwater, you start to sink until you cannot breathe, and all you can see is red. This is not a story from a war zone or battlefield but from an area you once called your happy place.

I am not the only person permanently traumatized by this experience. My family and friends were severely affected and will likely never be the same. Not only has my ability to dive been hindered to a point where it feels impossible, but I can also no longer express myself like I used to through the piano or enjoy a calm day of fishing without frustrations about my physical condition. I had to painfully relearn all of my physical functions and learn to live with the constant pain in all of my limbs.

However, I believe everything happens for a reason, and all the pieces of this case are in place to make positive changes for marine safety. I moved to Florida seven years ago in pursuit of my passion for the ocean, and this is my prime opportunity to fulfill my goals of protecting life in the ocean. I believe that efforts to prevent boats from speeding through the Breakers Reef will be a substantial start in protecting divers who love to experience the ocean and marine life that is vulnerable to boat strikes. Once this goal is achieved, it could start a chain reaction of protecting beloved areas for divers around the world. I also believe that improvements to the standard dive flag would create a safer environment for divers and notify boaters of their presence before it is too late to avoid them.

Overall, I want nothing but positive outcomes to emerge from this tragic accident, and working toward productive changes in marine safety is where I want to start.

Judge Panse then invited Chuck and me an opportunity to give our impact statements. Chuck took up the invitation, and although he spoke powerful words, we both wished that the hearing would have ended with Carter's statement.

* * *

Years of experience in compartmentalizing emotions allowed me to scan the room in a mode of neutral observation. In about seventy-five minutes, we experienced the justice system at work—just like *Law and Order*.

From what I could tell, Carter's case was handled fairly and given its due time. Daniel pleaded guilty and was charged with willful and wanton reckless operation of a boat and sentenced to one year of probation and a $1,000 fine. His sentence included seventy-five hours of community service. His service would be dedicated to ocean conservation, a video about boating safety, and a revision of the dive flag design.

Carter was adamant that he, along with Danny, would be an integral part of the efforts.

After the proceeding, Carter leaned on the table to help him again release his long stiff legs from beneath the table and rise to his feet. The intimidating bailiff walked resolutely over to Carter. In a firm voice, he told Carter that he was an inspiration. Since then, I've learned that bailiffs almost never approach someone like that in a courtroom. If I ever meet that bailiff again, I'd like to give him a big hug.

We were so proud of and impressed by Carter as he stood and read his dynamic statement after enduring months of devastating agony. But as good as I was in fighting back the tears during the proceedings, they were unleashed when we witnessed Carter's next action.

After the affirmation from the bailiff, Carter limped over to shake Danny's hand and told him that . . . well . . . I forgot what he said because I was a mess as I eavesdropped. Both Danny and Carter looked each other in the eyes over their masks and agreed that they would work together to make a difference.

Carter's courageous decision to break the ice toppled the wall that kept our families apart since the accident. After Chuck and I hugged the kids outside the courtroom, Daniel's mom, Mary, approached me. She explained that she had prepared a statement to read but that the judge didn't offer her a chance to read it. Now, standing in the hallway outside the courtroom, she asked if she could read it to me, mom to mom. I remember she wore a black lace dress and pearl earrings.

His Day in Court

As she read her words through her red-framed reading glasses, she shared how she had silently walked alongside us since the accident. She experienced firsthand the ache of a mother's heart because of Danny's battle with cancer. It was our first and unexpected peek into their personal lives.

As sorry as I've felt for our situation since day one, I've always felt compassion for the Stanton family. Despite COVID-19 regulations with masks in place, Chuck and I hugged Daniel and his mom, and through intense conversation and tears, we made a connection and set intentions to move past the suffering and on to the next chapter.

Danny's attorney, Doug Duncan, made it clear that this courtroom experience was a powerful human moment when he told us: "I can tell you that having done criminal defense work for forty years, I never witnessed what happened after court was adjourned."

CHAPTER 53

Let's Make a Difference

Carter

THE DAY OF THE COURT HEARING HAD ARRIVED. TO FIGHT MY anxiety, I prayed to God for most of that morning. I prayed for strength and peace of mind during the hearing. I honestly couldn't wait to get it over with, as I felt it was the final step in my recovery.

We arrived at the courthouse and took the elevator to the assigned courtroom. Walking out of the elevator, I was surprised to see the magnificent view of Palm Beach Island outside the window. I could see The Breakers Hotel and the ocean. I could almost pinpoint the spot where I was hit by the boat. I greeted my siblings, who had flown in with my parents the night before. At the other end of the room, I noticed the driver, Danny, standing with his family. I felt my stomach sink and couldn't make eye contact with him or his family. I knew this court hearing had to be over before I could interact with him.

Due to COVID-19 restrictions, only a few were allowed in the courtroom. This included my parents but not my siblings. When I entered the courtroom, I remember sitting in a chair at the front, feeling very uncomfortable and sweaty.

Doubts were swirling through my mind, like, *Is it too early to be seeing the driver of the boat? Would I be able to compose myself while reading my victim impact statement?*

I found comfort in reminding myself of God's plan. When Andy said "God is here" on the boat, it reminded me of God's presence, and those words echoed in my head while sitting in the courtroom. It felt like everything was coming full circle from that day, and now was the time to be a peacemaker. The world would want me to take my anger out on him. I had every right to. But God had plans for me. He knew this was my moment to show His grace to a world that values retaliation. I knew what I had to do.

The hearing began with the judge asking me if this plea deal was sufficient for me. He mentioned that I could push for up to a year in prison if I wanted to. I was given one last chance to go back on the deal I made and seek a harsh punishment. It didn't take me long to reply and confidently say I was sure of my terms.

Danny then took the stand to give his statement. He turned toward me and maintained eye contact with my family and me throughout the entire statement. I could see the remorse in his eyes and the anxiety he felt while speaking to me. He finished, and it was my turn to take the stand. I read my statement firmly and felt good about what I communicated to Danny. My dad then took the stand and read a statement. After a few other proceedings, court was dismissed. Now, it was on me to approach Danny and break the tension in the room.

I immediately walked toward him and extended my hand. We shared a firm handshake, and I said, "Let's make a difference; I forgive you."

The tension in the room dissipated as I was shaking his hand, and Danny's parents started interacting with my parents. I felt such a weight lifted off my shoulders when I said that. My anxiety was gone, and I was optimistic about the future. This was God's way of healing me, in addition to healing my family. It was hard for me to think of anything else to say to Danny then, but we exchanged a few more words and walked out of the courtroom.

When I exited, news stations were outside the door waiting to interview me. I gave a quick interview, but I really wanted to talk to my family and the Stantons. We all talked for a bit and left the courthouse. I remember walking down the street after that, feeling so happy and free. I was free from the burden of resentment toward Danny and ready to move on with my life. It was hard to think about us ever becoming good friends, but I knew he would play an important role in my goal of promoting water safety.

Thanksgiving arrived a few days after the court hearing, and it was officially one year since the incident. I got out of bed feeling incredibly grateful to God for where He led my life and was happy to be alive. My dad made me a sausage and egg sandwich for breakfast and said he was incredibly proud of me. I could sense the genuine tone in his voice, and that statement meant so much to me.

During the day, I went with my siblings to a natural area to walk around and fish. Afterward, we returned to the condo where my family was staying and enjoyed a Thanksgiving feast featuring ribs as the main course (my favorite). I kept comparing the circumstances of that day to where I was one year ago. It stunned me to think about the condition I was in and how I'm now living an independent life. It warmed my heart to think about my family celebrating Thanksgiving with me compared to the horrible news they received last year. I fell asleep that night so happy and content.

In the summer of 2021, Danny and I met at a video production studio in West Palm Beach to film the FWC video mandated by the plea agreement. Accompanying us were several FWC officers and our lawyers.

In a small room filled with cameras and a green screen, I volunteered to tell my experience in front of the camera first. This was followed by Danny telling his experience of that fateful day. The camera crew then took us to shoot "B roll," scenes of Danny and me walking together outside and chatting at a table. While talking at the table, Danny respectfully asked me if I wanted to grab a couple beers when this was all done. I was somewhat relieved when he asked this because I really wanted to talk to him in a normal setting.

After the video shoot was done, Danny and I agreed to continue our day together at a local brew pub, Civil Society. We sat at a high top near the back of the brewery and finally got to talk one on one without lawyers present. We chatted about our day-to-day lives and how much things had changed since that Thanksgiving Day.

There were a few moments where I felt like I was talking to a friend and forgot about the circumstances in which we met. This was very healing for me.

We continued speaking for another hour, finished up our beers, and said goodbye. Although we haven't gotten beers together since, it was the experience that truly made me feel at peace with him.

CHAPTER 54

Danny

I can't believe we couldn't see anyone.

—Danny

Leila

In early July of 2021, Danny and I chatted over the phone for about ninety minutes. One would think that this could have been an awkward conversation. It was anything but.

I pushed Carter's permanent losses aside and leaned into my curiosity about Danny's background and current situation. Perhaps it was that I desperately wanted answers to all of those questions circling in my mind during those long days at the hospital. In our conversation, Danny remained open to sharing his side of the story—an integral and important part of the full story.

Early on, Danny said, "Throughout the process, we were always on opposite sides—all I wanted to do was form a relationship with you guys—it was so frustrating."

I understood Danny's frustration and told him, "You and Carter are both good souls who collided in a sea of incalculable odds."

After Danny's friends heard the news of the accident, they couldn't believe it happened to him, of all people, of all the boat owners. They know Danny to be one of the most responsible boaters, with years of experience, significant training, and a captain's license to prove it.

Danny's interest in water didn't start in his suburban hometown of Ridgewood, New Jersey. That's where he lived with his mom, dad, and two sisters—one older and one younger—for most of his first eight years of school. He spent his free time playing video games while his mom worked as a registered nurse, and his dad commuted forty-five minutes to Manhattan for his job as an executive at Goldman Sachs.

His passion for the ocean developed after his parents retired and moved to Florida just before Danny's sophomore year in high school. Their home backed to the Intracoastal Waterway. Tied to their dock was a 22-foot Boston Whaler. Danny was the only person who operated it, and he wove the vessel through the canals to his buddies' homes long before he got his license to drive a car. He spent many weekends cruising to the Bahamas with his friends and their parents. His immersion in an elite nautical social life led to his considerable fascination with boats.

With a second family home on Martha's Vineyard, Danny spent his summers working as a golf caddy and boat driver. At eighteen years old, he accumulated the required 360 days on the water, took a month's worth of classes, and earned his captain's license. After that, he spent his summers as a captain for a yacht club in Martha's Vineyard.

Danny

A ruptured appendix derailed Danny's first year at Georgetown University. It wasn't the rupture that kept him from completing his first semester. Instead, it was the postoperative checkup that found a rare (only five thousand cases in the US every year) carcinoid tumor on the edge of his appendix. If his appendix hadn't ruptured, the tumor could have gone unnoticed and eventually been terminal. Coincidentally, Georgetown was the best hospital to treat this type of cancer.

After numerous tests and balancing the risks, a surgeon performed a right colectomy and removed one-third of Danny's large intestine and twenty-three lymph nodes. The surgery kept him in the hospital for a week, and it took two to three months for him to get back on his feet cancer-free and back to classes.

Because of a missed semester, Danny added a fifth year to his Georgetown education and graduated with a double major in finance and management. He followed his college mates who finished a year before him and spent three years on Wall Street. With his friends, he launched a wealth management business. It grew from six employees to fifteen, with offices in New York and Florida, where Danny eventually took up full-time residence.

In 2005, when they began manufacturing Yellowfins, Danny declared, "I'm gonna buy that boat someday." When he had saved up enough money, he bought a 2008 36-foot craft known for its high-speed performance from a man in Louisiana. It needed major structural and mechanical improvements and a cosmetic facelift. Danny special ordered the facelift to reflect the "embodiment" of his then-girlfriend, named Talley. *Talley Girl* was this captain's dream come true with its three shiny engines, each with a five-blade propeller built for optimal performance.

About a year and a half before the accident, the refit was complete, and the vessel returned to Danny's capable hands. He was itching to test how it cruised at fifty-five miles an hour with impressive fuel efficiency, so he frequently ran it to the Bahamas to free dive and spearfish.

On the eve of his collision with Carter, he had taken his friends for a ride. Danny was so excited about how the boat performed the night before that he invited his dad, brother-in-law, and his brother-in-law's two kids for another test drive on Thanksgiving morning before lunch. It was rare that such a nice day on the ocean landed on a holiday, so they eagerly agreed to go for a ride.

Danny's story makes me wonder (as I did at the beginning of the book): What are the odds? What are the odds that Danny discovers a rare cancer due to an unrelated appendix rupture? What are the odds that he receives a possible terminal diagnosis, yet timing allows for a complete recovery? What are the odds that prime ocean conditions and fine weather line up on a national holiday? What are the odds that out of the million or so boat owners in Florida, it would be Captain Danny with years of experience who cruised by the Breakers Reef on the wrong day at the wrong time? Unfortunately, the odds were stacked in Danny's *dis*favor when he decided to take his newly outfitted pleasure craft for a spin.

Danny

It was common for Danny to cruise just off the beach and past the Breakers Reef. As his slick Yellowfin glided through the calm seas, he passed another boat with a divers-down flag. The 20" x 24" flag was easy to spot as it flew from the highest point of the vessel. It signaled that divers were in the water or under the surface. He took every precaution to give them a wide berth.

As he approached the soccer-ball-sized buoys along the Breakers Reef, he noticed boats tethered to them and steered clear of them, too, as it meant divers were beneath the surface. As Danny scanned his route from nine o'clock to three o'clock, his dad was talking with his granddaughter while on the lookout for people in the water. The craft was running with the wind and the wind added a texture to the surface. The required 12" x 12" dive flags for snorkelers are stiffened with wires yet are nearly invisible—pencil-thin—when they fly *with* the wind.

Danny planned to turn around in about forty seconds to steer clear of divers at the popular spot. He rarely encountered divers on the southern tip of the reef and didn't expect to see any on this day. Neither he nor his dad saw any dive flags until they were perpendicular to the divers.

As he came upon people, he quickly turned to the left and backed off on the throttle, which meant there were seconds where Danny had little control of the boat's speed or direction. Because the boat was planing and the bow of the craft was pointing upward, it blocked his view of the water, and he wasn't aware that someone was right in front of the boat. Even though the craft was slowing down, there was no emergency brake to stop its momentum from coasting at fifty miles an hour. Carter's efforts to push himself away from the boat's path weren't enough, and his snorkeling line, dive flag, and limbs became tangled up in the propeller blades of the three engines.

It wasn't until the boat came to an idle that the captain and passengers could survey the scene. Danny was initially unaware of what happened, as he felt nothing when *Talley Girl* struck Carter, but he sensed the situation's urgency. As he turned the boat around, his heart stopped, and his adrenaline surged as he heard Carter screaming. His brother-in-law called 911 and herded his two kids up onto the bow to shield them from the gruesome scene.

Although Danny offered to share the details of Carter's rescue and the short boat ride to the beach, I just didn't have it in me to listen. And, for the most part, I already knew them and didn't need a refresher.

Danny admitted, "All I wanted to do was walk over and give you all a hug, but I followed the advice of my attorneys and kept my distance."

When the boat slid onto the beach, Danny was surrounded by authorities. They asked for his papers and his statement. As he waited for more interrogations with the FWC, he collapsed by a wall on the beach, sat with his mom in the sand, and cried.

In the following weeks, Danny's address became public record, and the media came knocking. He felt vilified by the relentless reporters who wouldn't leave his doorstep. To avoid them, he camped out at his parents' home.

Danny

Danny defaulted to a rational frame of mind to help him cope with what happened. He claims that if he had been distracted by his phone, in a conversation with someone, messing with the navigation system, or playing with the radio, he would carry a deep sense of personal guilt that would be too heavy to overcome. Danny came upon an unexpected group of divers in the water where he had never seen them before. Although he took precautions, he was caught off guard. The fact that he was captaining a boat the way he usually did and that the odds just happened to be against him that day seemed to help lighten the guilt over the gravity of Carter's current condition.

The Stanton family wanted to reach out to us, especially at Christmas, as they knew our holiday would be spent in St. Mary's. Their lawyer advised them not to.

Soon after the accident, it appears that word got out about the incident in the Goldman Sachs circles, as Carter's GoFundMe account balance suddenly grew. It was one way their family could rally around ours.

Danny renamed *Talley Girl* and refurbished it, but he couldn't look at it for months. He finally boarded the speedboat of his dreams in April of 2020. As he watched dozens of vessels cruise at the same distance from the shore as he was on Thanksgiving 2019, he wonders why an accident like this hadn't happened sooner. He knows the collision could have been avoided if he could have seen the current required dive flags. Right now, and contrary to logic, dive flags must be much larger on boats than the ones divers use when in the water. A larger, three-dimensional design could eliminate the chance of a diver being hit by a boat again.

But it's not just a change in dive flags that will prevent future accidents. The root of the problem starts with who's behind the steering wheel.

Years ago, those who operated a boat were properly trained and knew the water and navigation rules. When Danny bought his boat, it was the fastest thing out there. He was excited about it and, with years of experience under his belt, was ready to manage the speed until he came upon a nearly invisible dive flag.

Today, there are cigarette boats that go twice the speed. When someone scores a bonus at work and has money to burn for a slick watercraft, they are tempted by the latest models that top ninety to one hundred miles an hour. Heaps of high-performance models on the market with more inexperienced drivers cruising at top speeds make for a lethal combination. The ocean is an unregulated frontier with no lanes and no speed limit. It's a toxic freeway destined for more deadly collisions.

As part of his plea agreement, Danny campaigned for a law that requires divers to use three-dimensional dive flags. He admits that the diving community could see the inflatable and sizable flags as a burden due to the cost, but the expense seems minuscule compared to the lives they could save. As there's no political agenda with this bill, Danny is confident it will pass as a bipartisan law.

Danny looked quite different at the court hearing than in the photos taken at the accident scene. While Danny did reunite with his boat, he renamed it when his relationship with Talley ended. The breakup, the accident, and the

Danny

COVID-19 lockdown offered time for introspection and a fitness kick. Danny borrowed a suit for the plea hearing, as he shed fifty pounds and didn't own one that fit. Currently, he resides in both Florida and New York and hopes to move down to Florida permanently.

Chuck envisions Danny and Carter on the steps of the Florida State Capitol in Tallahassee someday. Danny hopes to fish with Carter someday.

CHAPTER 55

Miracle at Schwartz Lagoon

Carter

ANDY AND I TALKED A LOT ABOUT GETTING BACK TO snorkeling after the incident, but there was an unspoken fear in both of us about reentering the ocean. We loved exploring the near-shore reefs so much, but our experience left a permanent stain in our memories related to the ocean. There was a fear we would panic whenever a boat passed by or that the same thing would happen again.

As a compromise, we decided to try snorkeling again in an enclosed area, where boats cannot go and there is very little human traffic. This spot was an area we called the "Schwartz Lagoon."

The lagoon was named after Stephen Schwartz, a long-time volunteer at Loggerhead. We became friends with him over our interest in fish and he took us inshore or on deep sea fishing trips several times on his boat. The lagoon was located right behind his condo on Singer Island. In the lagoon, there was a dock with a lot of fish living under it as well as a seawall teaming with life.

In late February of 2021, Andy and I went on our first snorkeling trip since the incident at the lagoon. We met up with Stephen and enjoyed a morning of clear water with plenty of fish to see. Although I got nervous whenever I heard the sound of a boat far away, it was so great to be back in the water. I couldn't believe I was back snorkeling after all I've been through. It felt like I was meant to be there.

After we left that day, Andy and I got a call from Stephen. Little did we know we were about to have the best snorkeling experience of our lives. I could try to share that experience in my own words, but it was nicely summed up by a local independent journalist who a year earlier had written about my incident for the local newspaper, *The Palm Beach Post*.

What follows is the story about my truly memorable—and positive—snorkeling experience.

> Miracle at 'Schwartz Lagoon:' A lost and found tale about sunken treasure and the bond of friendship
>
> by Joe Capozzi, March 16, 2021
>
> **DESPAIR SWEPT OVER STEPHEN** Schwartz like the waves in which he'd just been swimming.
>
> Not even 30 minutes after snorkeling in the Intracoastal Waterway behind his Singer Island home, the retired lighting salesman made a horrifying discovery: His wedding ring, the gold band that hugged his finger for the past 51 years, was gone.
>
> Schwartz knew where it went.

Sitting on his back patio, his gaze drifted from the white tan line on his ringless finger to the vast waterway at the end of his yard, stretching to the distant Blue Heron Bridge and, beyond it, Peanut Island, the Palm Beach Inlet, and the Atlantic Ocean.

"I almost fainted," he recalled. "I couldn't believe it. It was a scary moment."

There was no point of even trying to hide the news from his wife, Diane: She was sitting right there when her husband realized the precious ring was missing.

"I didn't know what to do," Schwartz, 77, said. "I called the boys."

The "boys" are Andy Earl and Carter Viss, longtime friends Schwartz met after he started volunteering at Loggerhead Marinelife Center in Juno Beach eight years ago.

Earl, 36, and Viss, 26, are technicians at Loggerhead, where the three men bonded through a shared love of the ocean and marine life.

"For me, having young friends like that is keeping me young," Schwartz said with a laugh. "I became sort of like a father figure to them because their parents live out of town."

They go fishing on Schwartz's boat. And they often snorkel together at Phil Foster Park under the Blue Heron Bridge, known for its colorful array of tropical fish.

One of their favorite places to enter the Intracoastal is north of the bridge, behind Schwartz's house on the west side of Singer Island, a spot they nicknamed "Schwartz Lagoon."

On Feb. 28, the three men enjoyed another great day of snorkeling. When they finished, Earl and Viss said good-bye and headed home, and Schwartz retreated to the back patio to relax with his wife.

"You know when you have a ring, you touch it all the time? I was doing that and felt something strange. I looked down and there was no ring."

Drowning in despair, he dialed Earl and Viss.

"They were still in the car," Schwartz recalled. "Immediately, they said, 'We are coming back. We're going to find that ring for you. We know what it means to you.'"

Schwartz tried to tell them to not bother, to just keep going home, but the boys wouldn't listen.

"I told them, 'You guys are crazy. You're insane. We were in so much water, and the size of that ring . . .'

"They came back and looked and they didn't find it and I thought that was the end of it."

IN THE ENSUING DAYS, Schwartz started coming to terms with the likelihood that the ring was history, either carried away in the currents and swept out to sea or embedded in sand somewhere near North Palm Beach.

To his relief, his wife took the news "amazingly well," he said. "She was upset, but she didn't freak out."

It was Diane who picked out the ring before they were married in July 1969, two years after Schwartz worked up the nerve to ask her to dance after he first saw her on Long Island, "this hot-looking girl" in a red sweater pulling a kite along the beach in Montauk Point.

The ring symbolized not just their marriage but their life. They raised a son while Stephen built a successful lighting sales business before he retired with Diane to Singer Island.

Days after the ring disappeared in the Intracoastal, Diane suggested a backup plan: Wear your father's wedding ring, which he did the first week in March.

Then, the following Sunday, his phone rang.

It was Viss announcing that he'd purchased an underwater metal detector and that he and Earl were on their way to "Schwartz Lagoon" to resume their search.

"We are going to find that ring," Viss told him. "This is our mission."

At first, Schwartz wanted to tell them not to bother. Seven days had gone by, with bad weather and fast-moving currents. The ring was long gone, he told them.

But he relented.

"I did not want to crush their enthusiasm," he said. "They had been through enough with the tragedy that had happened."

On Thanksgiving Day 2019, Viss and Earl were snorkeling off Palm Beach when a speeding motorboat failed to see their red diver-down flag. The boat ran over Viss, its propellers severing his right arm and badly injuring his three other limbs.

Earl was the first rescuer to reach him; he kept Viss's head above water until the boat that hit Viss returned to ferry him to a waiting ambulance.

Schwartz and his wife were among the dozens of friends and relatives who kept vigil at Viss's bedside the first week after the accident, when doctors weren't sure he'd survive.

After seven surgeries, 68 days in the hospital and countless prayers, Viss recovered. He has returned to work at Loggerhead and has gone snorkeling again.

And on March 7, with Earl following, he purposefully marched across Schwartz's back yard with his new underwater metal detector.

"Filled with nothing but optimism, we hit the water," Earl recalled.

It was too cold that day for Schwartz. "I took my chair and just sat and watched them," he said.

For about 90 minutes, off and on, the metal detector dinged, each time signaling hope that only

Miracle at Schwartz Lagoon

fizzled to the sad reality of crushed cans, rusted nails, and a corroded pipe.

"We were happy the detector was working, but discouraging thoughts started to creep into both our minds," Earl recalled.

The water was 15 feet deep and the boys kept diving, hoping for a miracle.

"After an hour and a half, I said, 'Guys! Enough already! I'm freezing out here!'" Schwartz recalled.

They started swimming toward Schwartz and reached a rocky bottom near the ladder to his property, where the water is about 2 feet deep.

"Let's look one more time by this rock pile," they yelled.

Again, the boys pulled up a few more pieces of trash. Schwartz, by now resigned to enduring disappointment, had stopped watching them.

After several old, unidentified metal objects, Carter got one last "hit" on the metal detector.

Buried about three-quarters of the way under the sand, they saw a glittering gold band.

"There it was!" Earl said to himself. "We had found it!"

Earl climbed the ladder and extended his closed hand toward Schwartz. "Stephen, we found it," he said.

Yeah, right, Schwartz thought, assuming Earl was joking.

"Then Carter pops up," Schwartz recalled. "I see him smiling like crazy. Andy opened his hand and there was my ring."

At first, the boys thought maybe they found someone else's ring. But after a quick inspection, Schwartz confirmed it was his.

"Oh, my God!" he yelled.

"We went crazy. We were screaming, yelling," he said. "(Neighbors) were coming out because they thought something had happened. There was my ring. And it's so freaky. I mean, if you are in that amount of water . . .

"It's just incomprehensible. It's just miraculous. You know that saying 'a needle in a haystack'? This was bigger than that. You didn't just have the haystack, you had currents and tides."

Schwartz, who said he recently lost 10 pounds, thinks maybe the ring was loose and got pulled off by the strap of his snorkel mask.

A few days later, Schwartz said he asked Viss how much he paid for the metal detector.

"What are you talking about?" Viss protested, interrupting Schwartz before he could offer to help pay for it. "I don't want any money from you. I'm going to use this thing."

Schwartz plans to share the experience when giving tours at Loggerhead, "so kids can relate to it as a lesson to never giving up."

"That's what's so beautiful about the story, in my mind," he said. "What those two guys went through. They have such grit and determination, especially Carter."

The boys also learned a lesson from the experience.

"Miracles happen to everyone," Earl said. "Sometimes you just got to put a little footwork in for them to come full circle."[1]

CHAPTER 56

Kenny

How could I ever say no to this?

—Deanna

Leila

Working for the Loggerhead Marinelife Center operations department, Carter and Andy were popular with the hundreds of volunteers. Docents appreciated their efforts to repair the turtle and fish tanks. The pair "entertained" those at the front desk as they climbed ladders to clean aquariums and hang a Santa hat on the giant turtle sculpture suspended from the ceiling.

After the accident, the volunteers brought dinners to Carter in the hospital and organized a fundraiser for him at their annual Christmas party. They designed T-shirts with #CarterStrong in bold red letters, and everyone wore them to the party.

During one of our visits to Florida after Carter's recovery, Chuck and I had dinner with a volunteer named Deanna at our favorite restaurant, The Food Shack. This particular visit to Jupiter included our first meet-up with "Kenny," Carter's new dog, a goldendoodle puppy. Kenny and Carter connected, thanks to Deanna.

As we waited for our table, Deanna told us how Kenny made his way into Carter's life. I pressed the record button on my Voice Memo app so I wouldn't miss a thing.

Deanna and a volunteer friend named Betsy were chatting about Carter after he returned to work. Betsy claimed, "Carter really needs a dog and a girlfriend."

She repeated herself: "Deanna, Carter really needs a dog, and it's a two-year wait for him to get a trained service dog!"

Deanna picked up on Betsy's nudge, pondered the idea, and replied, "Okay, I can get Carter a dog; I've always wanted to do something for Carter, and I've trained a million dogs. But I can't be in charge of the girlfriend. I have my own son who needs a girlfriend!"

Carter was open to the idea. He already had his name on the Genesis waitlist for a trained service dog—the same place that paired Iggy with Don from St. Mary's Medical Center—but he had heard nothing from them in over a year.

Deanna took the cue from Carter that he liked golden retrievers, so she contacted her friends at rescue shelters and let them know she was looking for a golden retriever or a Lab. One of the rescue centers called Deanna and said, "I know you're looking for a Lab or a retriever, but I have a goldendoodle puppy in Tampa pulled from a bad breeding situation. He's twelve weeks old, and he needs a home."

Deanna admitted, "I did not sign up to raise a puppy!"

But then she heard the story.

Kenny

Seventy puppies were rescued from a goldendoodle breeding facility—there were puppies everywhere. The last dog to get a home was Kenny's mother. They took her to the vet to be spayed, and two puppies fell out of her. One was dead, and one was Kenny.

The Humane Society agents took him home and bottle-fed him until he was eight weeks old. Then, Kenny was cared for by a foster-to-adopt home. The day before the family was going to adopt Kenny, they backed out and said, "We don't think we want to keep the dog. He's really bitey—he's very smart—but not affectionate."

Deanna caved, saying, "How could I ever say *no* to this?! The dog has gone through the same story as Carter—the cards were stacked against him!!"

After Deanna traveled to Tampa to pick up the pup, Carter was worried, asking, "What if he doesn't like me?"

Deanna assured him, "If the puppy doesn't like you, he can live with me."

Carter called to tell us that he was about to become a dog owner and was considering names. He asked for ideas from the music world. His skink—think lizard with a blue tongue and a long scaly body like a snake—was named Ennio after the late Ennio Morricone, Carter's favorite composer. Of course, there were common names like Beethoven, Mozart, or Wolfgang, but none seemed to resonate with Carter.

After seeing the curly pup, Carter immediately knew his name had to be Kenny. Chuck and I were puzzled—Kenny Loggins? Kenny G? Where is Kenny coming from? The name had nothing to do with music and everything to do with Loggerhead.

Soon after Carter began working at the turtle rescue center, his coworker passed away. He was a single dad and left behind a nine-year-old daughter. In fact, Carter was hired to a full-time position after the father's unexpected passing. His name was Kenny.

Although he's not red, our first encounter with Kenny reminded Chuck and me of Clifford the Big Red Dog. Our bedroom door in Carter's place never quite closes. Once released from his kennel in the morning, the eighty-pound puppy hopped on our bed. As he attempted to walk around the bed to lick us, sliding his paws between our arms and legs, we giggled and covered our bodies with the sheets so he couldn't scratch us and his furiously wagging tail wouldn't whack us in the eye.

The entire family gushed over the jumbo puppy with endless legs and a bark for everyone who knocked on the door. Ennio took second fiddle once the hairy canine arrived but tolerates sharing Carter's affections.

Kenny's arrival meant Carter was halfway toward realizing Betsy's recommendation. Now, he just needed to find a girlfriend.

CHAPTER 57

Emily

You should know: Nothing I do is random. It's all plotted!

—Emily

Leila

AFTER A LOVE-HATE RELATIONSHIP WITH DATING APPS DUE TO numerous first-date-only encounters, Carter reluctantly downloaded Hinge in the summer of 2019 to "try again."

For those of you who have not experienced the twenty-first-century method for meeting a mate, Hinge is one of many platforms where people fill out details about their lives and preferences on food, religion, hobbies, activities, etc. A sophisticated algorithm pairs people with similar interests.

Chuck and I heard little of Carter's dating life, so when he announced that he was bringing Emily to Colorado, we arranged for a Vissucci meet-up—this was an event none of us wanted to miss! We expected that both Emily and Carter would have a unique perspective on their courtship, and I didn't want to miss a thing, so I recorded both accounts on my Voice Memo app.

According to Carter, the platform churned the facts and declared Emily and Carter a match. Carter initiated a conversation and asked if she wanted to get drinks sometime. Emily ghosted him. Again, for those not familiar with dating app lingo, it is a term for never responding.

Then, the accident happened.

About a year later, around Christmas of 2020, Carter logged into Hinge, and the two matched again, but they never connected.

In August of 2021, Hinge did the math and connected them *again*! Carter was determined to go on at least one date with Emily this time. She finally agreed to meet, so on August 23, they grabbed a drink at the Square Grouper.

We couldn't wait to hear Emily's take, which she happily provided.

Apparently, in the summer of 2019, she downloaded Hinge to numb the pain of a horrible breakup. When Carter reached out and asked to go for drinks, it felt too soon; she wasn't ready, didn't reply, and deleted the app.

In November 2019, the article about Carter's accident fell into Emily's Facebook feed. The photo the media used of Carter was the same one that he posted on Hinge, and she panicked. "That's the guy I met on Hinge! What if I would have said yes to this guy? Then he would have spent Thanksgiving with my family, and he wouldn't have been in the water!"

Now, it felt strange to reach out; it just didn't seem appropriate.

In July of 2021, Emily spent a weekend caring for a fifteen-year-old named Hudson, who had been in a boating

Emily

accident and almost lost a leg. His parents, who are close family friends, had to go out of town for the weekend, so Emily agreed to stay with him.

She learned that Hudson had followed Carter's story and also the Floridafishboyz—Carter and Andy—on Instagram. After hearing this, Emily followed them, too, hoping that Carter would, in her words, "remember me, too, and slide into my DMs!" (DM stands for "Direct Messages" for those not fluent in twenty-first-century app lingo.)

Carter did notice Emily's "follow" and recognized her profile but figured it was a random coincidence. Emily admitted with a smile, "You should know—nothing I do is random. It's all plotted!"

Emily's conversations with Hudson about his horrific accident requiring twenty-some surgeries to save his leg, combined with Carter's story of survival, sparked a fire in her: "I'm meeting Carter; I don't care what it takes."

After multiple deletions of Hinge from her phone, Emily downloaded it one more time. Whenever she deleted it, she had to set up a new profile with the same information as the last time, and Hinge would refresh the search for the perfect match.

Emily waited for the fancy couple calculator to pair her with Carter. She had no choice but to wait, as the app does not allow you to reach out and initiate a conversation with anyone unless you are matched with a person and both of you "like" each other.

Algorithms don't lie, and eventually, science did not disappoint. The numbers matched Emily with Carter again. She quickly "liked" Carter, and then waited for him to like her back. It took about a month!

When he finally responded to her "poke," Emily immediately called her mom and exclaimed, "Mom, we matched! It's gonna happen!"

First on her agenda was to make sure they began chatting in the app, so Emily asked Carter a question to start a conversation thread, saying, "Happy Sunday, what are you doin' today?"

It didn't take long for Carter to reply and catch on; indeed, Emily was genuinely interested in meeting him. But before the initial date at Square Grouper, Emily changed her mind and decided she wouldn't go. She was wary of yet another first-date flop.

With a gentle nudge from her mom, she met Carter at Square Grouper. It obviously went well, and a second date was scheduled. That date was supposed to be at the beach. But Emily was committed to watching a friend's two-year-old for the weekend. Carter said okay, that's fine, so the couple spent their second date with a toddler. Emily's mom thought this was a good sign.

A couple of dates later, Carter invited Emily for dinner to meet his brother Levi and his girlfriend Erin, who were visiting from Denver. Carter had forgotten that he had a prior commitment to go gecko hunting that same night and didn't want to miss the chance. So he let Emily know of the planned activity after dinner and extended an invitation to come along. Emily took him up on the offer and embarked on her first-ever gecko hunt. Levi and Erin thought that this was a good sign.

Emily

It appeared that Carter and Emily were an item, and we certainly had reasons to believe that Carter and Emily could well be partners for life. They planned to fly out to visit us during Christmas 2021. Their flights were rebooked when COVID-19 reared its ugly head, and they both tested positive. This delayed their visit until late January 2022. It was the first time Chuck and I met Emily, unlike the kids—they had met her over Thanksgiving while we visited Lorilynn and Ivan and Mom and Dad in North Carolina. The kids returned home and reported that Emily was definitely a "thing."

After many hikes in the snow and an evening spent with the Vissucci clan, Carter and Emily flew to California with Chuck to visit Chuck's mom, Gert. Later that year, Carter and Emily returned to Denver and joined the family on a road trip to Iowa to meet my mom and dad, Jo and Will. To celebrate their one-year anniversary in August of the same year, they booked a trip to the Bahamas. After two visits to Denver, meeting the grandparents in California and Iowa, and dining with the Tinuccis, we couldn't help but wonder if an engagement might be part of their August getaway.

Not yet.

About a month later, as Chuck and I rolled the car into the garage after running errands, Carter called to let us know that he was going to propose to Emily. There was a hint of a question when he told us—wanting to know if we approved. Of course, we did! We gushed on and on about his decision—*their* decision.

Although there was no ring on a finger, Carter admitted that the two had already gone ring shopping, chosen a date, and even booked a venue. Time went by without any engagement news. Brittany and Erin noticed that Emily's nails were always beautifully polished on her Instagram posts. They assumed the nail upkeep was in anticipation of Carter popping the question.

Weeks later, Carter called and informed us that a ring was on order and a proposal date had been set. Carter was in cahoots with Emily's mom, Peg, and they masterminded the big ask during a fall trip with Emily's parents to Grandfather Mountain in North Carolina.

On the morning of October 25, Carter and Emily set out on what she thought was going to be a hike. When they arrived at the peak of Grandfather Mountain, there was a woman nearby grabbing photos of the magnificent view. She was actually a prearranged photographer hired to capture the moment Carter kneeled to propose.

As he bent down on a knee that the doctors considered amputating three short years ago, he opened a small box carrying a beautiful diamond ring. The photographer snapped the camera at the moment when Emily realized the time had come.

It's hard to tell with her hands at her mouth, stooped over to see the ring on her hand, and hair blowing in the wind if Emily's reaction was one of surprise by the unexpected proposal, the ring, or the excitement of the moment after she said yes. From all appearances, it had to have been all three.

After the engagement came wedding planning and something else that didn't happen before getting married when Chuck and I tied the knot! Emily rented a condo, and Carter had recently purchased his. Now, it was time to combine households and find a home.

They found one in Jupiter Farms, not far from Emily's parents, with plenty of room for the dogs to roam. The only thing missing from their sprawling ranch was the one-hundred-step walkway to the ocean that Chuck and I cherished whenever we visited the condo. It held a special place in our hearts, as it was the home we found and made for Carter's recovery.

It was bittersweet saying goodbye to the seaside residence, but it marked the end of a chapter. There was a new one to begin with Emily in the picture—and her dog, Kaia, too. She was worth leaving the space and all its lament behind.

CHAPTER 58

Alumni Achievement Award

It is well with my soul.

—Horatio Spafford, lyricist,
"It Is Well with My Soul," (1876)

Leila

We hadn't expected to jump out of our car in the middle of a small and packed parking lot to hug Carter, Emily, Andy, and his baby, Rylan. Yet that's what we did when we noticed that both Emily and Andy's cars were ahead of ours. We had all followed the GPS instructions given to us by Palm Beach Atlantic University for parking so we could attend the special chapel and award luncheon for Carter. It was clear that we all had arrived at the wrong lot, so we hopped back into our cars and caravaned along the campus streets to the correct parking lot with reserved spots just for us for this particular day.

It was the Monday of Thanksgiving week 2022, and PBA was honoring Carter with the Alumni Achievement Award. Chase, Brittany, Levi, Erin, Chuck, and I flew to Jupiter from Colorado around 12:30 a.m. for the special day.

The university had scheduled the event to coincide with their Homecoming week in September. Chuck, Chase, Levi, and Erin had eagerly secured flights to attend the event, but I would be missing out and staying home, as the timing didn't jive with my schedule.

As Hurricane Ian would have it, I didn't miss a thing, as flights and all university events were canceled because the storm threatened to land near West Palm Beach. With a recently purchased navy suit specially tailored for Carter's missing right arm, an anticipated visit from family, and a prepared speech crafted for the occasion, the cancellation was terribly disappointing. PBA was open to Carter's request to reschedule the event on the Monday of Thanksgiving when he informed them that his parents had planned months ago to be in town for the week. Teaching schedules had kept Brittany and me from coming out in September. We had suffered severe bouts of FOMO (fear of missing out). This change in timing allowed for our entire family to attend, and even Colorado friends Dean and Dee, who now reside in Florida for the winter, could be there, too.

Perhaps PBA's efforts to grant Carter's request to reschedule during the week of Thanksgiving were partly thanks to a friend we unknowingly had in the PBA. Patricia, a longtime Colorado friend who we had lost contact with for years, lived in Florida. She reached out during Carter's stay at St. Mary's in 2019. In September of 2022, Patricia texted us, as she heard about Carter's award. She also told me she landed a job in the PBA Advancement Office and would attend the luncheon! We couldn't wait to attend the event and reconnect.

Alumni Achievement Award

Ian wreaked havoc on parts of Florida, but in our case, plan A, ruined by the powerful storm, made for an ideal plan B.

After Carter received the elegantly inscribed glass award given to him by the president of PBA, Dr. Debra A. Schwinn, he began his speech. It's one that Carter continues to develop as the invitations to speak keep coming. This was the first time Chuck and I had heard him speak in person. As we sat in reserved second-row seats, tears streamed down our cheeks as Carter recounted the accident, his loss, and his determination to make good out of something so devastatingly bad.

In a situation like this, it's as if the writer or the reporter in me steps out of the "mom role." Just like seeing Carter in the ICU bed tethered to a breathing tube and bones pinned in place with external fixators, I sensed the need to capture the moment with photos so I would never forget the details. So I grabbed my iPhone and snapped shots of the worship band, the choir, and Carter regally pacing back and forth in his navy suit as he shared his story and gestured with the same hand that held the remote to change slides.

It took all I could muster not to turn around to see the people gathered behind us. From the robust singing and energy in the room, it felt like every seat was taken. As soon as Carter was introduced, a hush fell over the crowd.

After his speech, Carter sat down at the piano to play "It Is Well with My Soul," arranged by Daniel Light. The house immediately stood to cheer and applaud as Carter rose from the bench.

After the PBA chaplain closed in prayer, Chuck and I took a deep breath and collected our soggy tissues. Before we stood, a young woman tapped Chuck's shoulder and asked if he was Carter's dad. Then she asked if she could pray for us. Somehow, she sensed the impact, the struggle, and the depth of sorrow and healing that came with this milestone in the life of Carter's parents, especially his dad.

Chuck and I greeted those who had become dear friends since the accident and took the time to attend the special chapel to honor Carter. Chuck couldn't help but hold eight-month-old Rylan, Andy's son, blessed with Andy's dimples and his mom Natalie's dark eyes. The baby firmly gripped a Pokémon card, and we predict that Rylan will soon take on the Pokémon obsession of his dad and "uncle" Carter.

Along with Stephen and his wife (remember the lost wedding ring story?), we spent time with Don and Sally—the owners of Iggy—the dog that strolled into Carter's ICU room with Don in his wheelchair. Iggy gently licked Carter's ten toes and five fingers and gets full credit for the first smile from Carter after the accident.

Chuck, Carter, and I were the last three to be escorted from the chapel auditorium to the extravagant boardroom with portraits of past university presidents. A twenty-foot-long marble table was set with tasteful placemats, flatware, and PBA merch. The university had generously offered Carter the opportunity to invite whom he pleased to the luncheon.

They served a generous meal of Caesar salad, rolls, turkey, mashed potatoes, cranberry sauce, and roasted vegetables. The guest list even included three of his favorite professors from his school days. Carter dwarfed the three women as they lined up and posed for pictures.

After Laura Bishop, executive vice president of advancement, shared some final words about Carter, I felt compelled to stand and express my gratitude—a feeling I've been hesitant to let myself feel over the past three years. I shared the story of Kathy McKinnon, who descended—like an angel—upon Carter's bedside immediately after the accident. She attended Truth Point Church, where Carter played bass guitar, and was a professor of nursing at PBA. I'll never forget when she asked the surgeons and nurses prepping Carter for his next surgery to circle around his bed to pray. This angel sporting a pink visor to commemorate her survival of thyroid cancer and breast cancer sat beside me in the waiting room as I wept. She slipped a shell bracelet from her wrist, secured it around mine, and said it was a reminder that others were praying for me.

Through my story, I wanted to assure the leaders of PBA that the university's sacred spirit was present in every hallway, at every bedside, and in every operating room. During the months of Carter's stay at St. Mary's, we learned that most of the nurses were graduates of PBA and shepherded by Kathy, whom they all adored.

The intention for our trip to Florida over the Thanksgiving week was not only to see Carter receive his award; that was a bonus. Our trip also gave us a chance to celebrate Carter's fiancé, Emily! We enjoyed a dinner at Hog Snappers and witnessed Carter and Emily asking Chase, Brittany, Levi, and Erin to stand as attendants at their June wedding in Key Largo. And the girls and I, along with Emily's mom and friends, came along on the quest to say yes to the dress. As seems pretty typical with brides-to-be, Emily said yes to the first one she tried on.

At the end of this trip, I found gratefulness bubbling up. I couldn't tamp it down or push it away anymore.

CHAPTER 59

Music and Resilience

Music seems to understand without saying a word.

—Leila

Leila

Attending annual music teacher conferences has been a priority for over twenty years. At first, I registered to learn and network and didn't know a soul. Now, I eagerly attend to get inspired and meet up with dear friends and colleagues worldwide.

It's also been one of my passions to present at these functions. I've been fortunate to have a number of my submissions accepted over the years. It's been a privilege sharing ideas about apps for music teaching and getting creative at the piano.

In 2020, it became important to me to present a session on a topic I never imagined. I felt compelled to tell my family's story of trauma, loss, grief, and the healing power of music. While it's common for conference sessions to cover how to teach or play music, it's rare for sessions to focus on the healing power of music. My desire to share the story emerged from my need to make meaning out of permanent loss. I also wanted to help my music teacher colleagues see that their work significantly impacts mental health and well-being.

I was blessed to share my thoughts with music teachers at the Music Teachers National Association in 2020 and then again at the National Conference of Keyboard Pedagogy (NCKP) in 2021—both moved online when COVID-19 shut down live events. It was a special honor that NCKP asked me to present my session as a twenty-minute PEDx (think TED Talk in the world of piano pedagogy) that would be shared with all attendees.

Below is a slight revision of my PEDx talk titled "Keeping It Together When Life Falls Apart":

> Our family fell into the arms of despair and secured a permanent relationship with grief. I recognize that our family is not alone, especially when the unimaginable pandemic dropped in for an extended stay. The world as we knew it was ripped from our arms and tossed into the firm grip of a micro monster. We idled in a wilderness, wondering when the good of yesterday would be back in our grasp. The world soon learned that the good of yesterday was a pipe dream. Coupled with COVID-19 came devastating fires, destructive floods, war, and the loss of loved ones. As humans, musicians, and teachers, we share the collective grief of ambiguous loss.
>
> Most are familiar with the five stages of grief identified by Elizabeth Kübler-Ross: denial, anger,

bargaining, depression, and acceptance.[1] I have a hard time with the acceptance stage and may never embrace it. David Kessler, another expert on grief, recently released a book that shares his discovery of a sixth stage of grief: finding meaning.[2] This stage resonates with me. I'm determined to find meaning in our brokenness and loss. I aim to find meaning personally, communally, and musically.

Personally, I claim a matriarchal duty. By sharing Carter's story, I can help his initiatives as a marine biologist to accelerate a change in dive flags and maritime laws.

Communally, collectively, we ache to find purpose and good in what's been lost. I intend that by sharing details about our family's experience, others may open up and share and practice reciprocity. Reciprocity is the art of exchanging things with others for mutual benefit. It's holding space for others in your mind and your heart, being truly heard and seen by people, and feeling that we are held in someone else's mind and heart.

And last, musically, from my experience, I know that music is a powerful coping mechanism that restores and heals. Chuck and Carter came to the same conclusion.

My journey with grief and music made me curious. I began to dig deeper into what research shows about music and the brain. Keep in mind I'm not a scientist. But nearly everything I found in Google searches, books, and YouTube backed my experiences and speculations as a longtime musician and a recently heartbroken mom.

Two weeks before the accident, I was fortunate to hear Renée Fleming speak on "Music and the Mind" at the University of Colorado Boulder Medical Campus. Through my research after the accident, I found Renée and her *Music and the Mind* episodes produced by the Kennedy Center on YouTube. One of her guests was Daniel Levitin, author of *This Is Your Brain on Music*. He explained that brain scans show that music lights up both sides of the brain. Even just *listening* to music activates the entire brain.[3] In my search to learn more about the brain and music, I stumbled across additional facts:

- Some people are more prone to getting goosebumps when listening to music.[4]
- Neurons from the front of the brain or the prefrontal cortex fire together and wire together with neurons from the back of the brain. When they activate in unison, this is called mental synthesis or what we call imagination.[5]
- The brain is malleable. When there's a loss of function or if the brain is damaged, it can be remapped or corrected by rerouting signals along a different pathway.[6]
- Gray matter cells are responsible for the movement of muscles. Professional keyboard players have thicker gray matter.[7]

In a nutshell, music activates the brain.

I also dug up facts about the triple threat of trauma, loss, and grief on the brain:

- The amygdala (emotion processor) hijacks the brain.
- The prefrontal cortex (cognitive processing) shuts down.
- The stress hormone cortisol levels rise to constant fight or flight.
- The hippocampus, the memory storage place, burns out.[8]

When someone experiencing trauma says "I think I've lost my mind," that's actually true! While music activates the brain, trauma triggers the fire alarm and switches systems to lockdown mode.[9] That's why I speculate that Chuck and I could not listen to music for weeks after the accident. Physically, our brains were offline. Emotionally, music felt like a sharp knife piercing our souls, like salt in a wound.

The height of the Christmas season was two weeks away after the accident, so I returned to Denver to report for duty for my church job, as important services were coming up. At this point, grief moved in as a permanent resident and fatigue set in, which led to numbness. I was, as my good friend calls it, emotionally constipated. While the congregation listened to me play during the services, they wept. I felt nothing.

My aversion toward music slowly wore off, and music evolved into an intervention as I trudged through the stages of grief. A piece by Norwegian composer Ola Gjeilo called "Still" broke the silence. My husband and I have been fans of his music ever since our choir sang his piece "The Ground." I wrote this to Mr. Gjeilo when asking him for permission to play his piece for this talk:

> Every one of my walks or runs begins with listening to "Still." I believe it's because it connects with my emotions and allows them a place to land. Your music seems to "understand" without having to say a thing.

Although religious, I couldn't stomach hearing scripture quoted to me unless David Baloche, Casting Crowns, or Chris Tomlin sang it. New additions to my Spotify grief playlist coincided with the state of Carter's condition. As he improved, music became more tolerable.

During high school, Carter enjoyed playing video games but also rose to the challenge of playing Beethoven and Chopin. Since his move to his one-bedroom condo after graduating from Palm Beach Atlantic University, Carter had been putting up with a used digital piano keyboard he bought off Craigslist. He really wanted and *needed* (!) a piano with better touch and sound quality. Weeks before the accident, I helped Carter choose and purchase a new digital piano. I was thrilled that he wanted a piano and excited for him that he would have a decent instrument on which to play.

While camping out in Carter's one-bedroom condo during his hospital stay, I walked past his piano most days without touching it. I couldn't look at it. It didn't seem right. If he couldn't play, then neither could I.

One night, while Chuck was watching tennis, I couldn't resist: I pushed the power button and began playing Brahms' "Rhapsody in G Minor" to see what I could remember. Over the next few days, I began to explore and play by ear the music I was listening to on my walks. That mental synthesis or imagination began to kick in again, and fresh patterns surfaced. But my improvisations didn't reflect feelings of lament. Instead, a musical reenactment of the accident appeared through the eyes of Carter and Andy. My emotions orbited around the story. Making music was a visceral place to hold the emotions and carry the slideshow of the accident in my mind.

My musical retelling of their story morphed into a composition called "Angel 94." It's titled after the passcode we used to see Carter in the hospital because his room had to be protected from too many visitors. The password came to us quickly, as Carter adores angelfish, and he was born in 1994.

It was devastating that Carter's left hand was wrapped up in bandages when we first crumpled at his ICU bedside. No right arm? Maybe no legs? How much function would be left in his left arm? Dr. A, the surgeon who operated on Carter's hand, said the surgery was successful. This gave us hope that Carter would use his hand again. But will he be able to play piano, too?

Dr. Anita Collins, an expert on brain development and music learning and well known for her viral TED Talk "How Playing an Instrument Benefits Your Brain" says that when you listen to music, multiple areas of your brain become engaged and active. But when you actually play an instrument, that activity becomes more like a full-body brain workout.[10]

In a podcast episode with Tim Topham, Dr. Collins argues that when parents let their child quit a musical instrument because things—the full-body brain workout—get hard, their child is missing out on learning an important life skill. Playing a musical instrument builds resilience in musicians who stick with an instrument even when the going gets tough. Collins claimed that we are "breeding resilience out of our children."[11]

Dr. Collin's powerful statements made me curious. After Carter was struck by a boat, we watched him cope with being confined to a hospital bed for months and learning how to walk again on two legs considered almost irreparable. He adapted to losing an arm. Did Carter's efforts to play the piano and the bass guitar for over twenty years have something to do with his remarkable resilience? I don't know if there is scientific evidence to prove my theory yet. However, after listening to Dr. Collins, knowing Carter's passion for playing the piano and witnessing his dramatic recovery, I claim, to some degree, that being a musician helped Carter power through and overcome staggering odds.

As he heals, Carter is between identities. He's been the desperate victim and then the brave patient and done the hard work to get better physically. Now he faces the next challenge of getting better emotionally, and he'd rather not be solely identified as an inspiration, a feel-good story, or an amputee. He's seeking an identity that makes meaning from his loss and resilience. He aches to be a musician at the piano and is determined to impact the behavior of humans in our oceans.

Because I dropped everything on Thanksgiving 2019 to be in Florida with Carter, I told my studio families that I was stopping lessons and didn't know when they would resume. While Chuck stayed behind to care for Carter in Florida, I began teaching again in February 2020 back in Denver. Then, of course, I moved to online lessons in March when the COVID-19 lockdown began. Most student families waited for my return, but three quit. A junior in high school named Lilly, who opted out of lessons in December, sent me this email in mid-February, soon after I reopened my studio:

Dear Ms. Leila,

At the beginning of the year, I made a super hard decision to take a small break from piano. I miss having you and piano in my life, and I truly regret making my decision so rashly. There is nothing I would enjoy more than to come back. If you are willing to take me back, I know in my heart that I would work very hard to practice my skills and give it my all. I miss you and piano so, so much and have been thinking about you a lot.

—Lilly

It wasn't until Lilly abandoned the piano that she discovered it was too important for it to be put on the back burner. Lilly identified as a pianist, and now she missed that part of herself. Lilly, like Carter, realized that part of her identity went missing. Both pianists couldn't deny the magnetic pull of music.

If music teachers are grooming future humans who identify as pianists, then it seems appropriate to ask these questions of music teachers:

- Who are *you*?
- How are you taking care of *yourself*?
- What is *your identity*?

My hope is that at least once in your lifetime, you receive a love letter like I did from Lilly—a reminder

Music and Resilience

of the important role that you and music serve in the lives of your students.

Commit to self-compassion, and when (not if) loss happens, embrace your grief. It's the loss you despise, not the grief. It's a necessary process. Cherish the gift of music-making and let it serve as an intervention. Find your voice in music and give your thoughts and feelings a place to land.

Show reciprocity. Truly hear and see those around you. Carry them in your heart and mind and heart. No doctor can write a prescription for friendship and love.

Empathize with "minority bodies" (those whose bodies are "different") and don't minimize the possibilities.

Broaden the perspective of your identity as a piano teacher. Yes, you are a business owner, an organizer, a bookkeeper, a cheerleader, a practice drill sergeant, a corrector of mistakes, and a coach prepping for the next performance. And you are

- a trainer that activates full-body workouts for the brain,
- a breeder of resilience,
- a guide to a place where emotions can land, and
- an instigator of imagination.

You are a key holder. You have the potential to unlock the passion for music in others and help establish their identity as musicians. Their identity wrapped up in their passion may offer a coping mechanism, an intervention, and the resilience to help them keep it together when life falls apart.

CHAPTER 60

Return to St. Mary's

Carter

IN DECEMBER OF 2022, A CASE MANAGER FROM ST. MARY'S contacted me and asked for my help. They had a patient who just had his hand amputated and was not doing well mentally. She was wondering if I could visit him and give him some encouragement. I was a little hesitant at first, because I would still get anxious around hospitals, but I knew I had to go.

On December 23, I arrived at St. Mary's in the late afternoon. I walked through the familiar front doors and checked in at the desk, undergoing the same steps dozens of people went through to visit me.

Once checked in, I decided to take a few moments to walk around the main floor. I'd been wheeled through this area so much but never got the chance to walk around it by myself. The hallways were mostly empty due to the holidays, and the evening sun was starting to shine brightly through the large windows. I couldn't believe I was back where I spent my hardest days.

I took a moment to reflect on all the darkness I experienced there and how far I've come in a couple of years.

Whether I like it or not, this place had been my "home" for a couple of months, and I couldn't help but feel glad I could reflect on my time there.

I eventually made my way to the main elevator and went to the third floor. I made an immediate left toward the surgical step-down unit and started searching for the correct room number. My search led me to the corner of a very familiar hallway, and I saw the room number I was looking for on the door.

I was then hit with a sinking feeling in my stomach. I knew exactly what this room was. It was the Rose Kennedy Suite. I was absolutely shaken when I realized this, and I couldn't believe I was about to reenter this room. Now, it was really time to step into the past. My clammy hand gently knocked on the door, and I began to open it.

The patient's mom greeted me as I walked in. I felt uneasy as I exchanged a greeting with her because my mind was consumed with the fact that I was now standing in the Rose Kennedy Suite. I immediately recognized the pinkish walls, the table and chairs by the door, and the spacious area for the hospital bed. It felt like I was taking in my surroundings for at least a minute when, in reality, it was just a couple of seconds. My mind snapped back into focus, and I introduced myself to the patient. The first thing I said to him was, "This is the exact room I stayed in!"

He then told me about the car accident he was in and how he lost his hand. I could tell the trauma from the incident was still fresh and difficult for him to talk about. He had a lot of the same negative thoughts I had when I faced the reality of losing an arm.

I confidently assured him that life would return to normal again: that he would be able to do anything he wanted to with one arm, that he will discover so many new abilities and skills he would've never thought of with two arms. I also told him about my incident and my recovery process. I hoped he could see that I was telling the truth when I told him his life would only get better.

Meanwhile, it was still hard to process the fact that I was encouraging an amputee in the same hospital room I was confined to. Exactly three years ago, I was in that same hospital bed and barely able to move. I was lying in that bed thinking I wouldn't be able to do any activity I loved anymore. While I was feeling down, I was visited by an arm amputee, Michael, who encouraged me that life would get back to normal.

Now it feels like everything has come full circle. It's my turn to encourage and build up someone facing loss, as someone did for me several years ago.

We talked for about an hour until the nurse came in and announced he was ready to be discharged from the hospital. It was perfect timing that I could talk to him right before he was discharged. I could see the excitement and optimism in him, as he had been at St. Mary's for well over a month. I couldn't help but feel so happy that he would be home soon. I wanted to give him some space as he was getting ready to leave, so I said goodbye and assured him that he would do great things through his experience.

I walked out of the Rose Kennedy Suite with a new outlook of the room itself. Instead of it being the room where I was confined to a bed and in constant pain, it was a room that demonstrated a full circle of encouragement throughout the healing process.

I left St. Mary's that day feeling like God had healed a wound in my soul. It was a wound that festered fear and anxiety when I would enter a hospital. It was a wound that I ignored and tried to cover up. However, God took me right back to where I suffered the most to teach me that the most profound healing comes from helping and encouraging others.

CHAPTER 61

Mourning to Dancing

You have turned my mourning into joyful dancing.

—Psalm 30:11

Leila

June 3 marks dear Grandpa Charlie Viss's birthday, who passed in 2019. Chase and Brittany were married in her hometown of Picture Butte, Alberta, Canada, on June 3, 2016. Because the Key Largo venue Emily and Carter preferred was available on June 3, 2023, the date is permanently packed with significance.

We had already grown to love Emily for her instant smile and, of course, her adoration for Carter. The wedding allowed us to see Emily's stellar aptitude for event planning. Our admiration was soon raised several more notches.

We became privy to her skills when Emily asked Erin and Brittany to be bridesmaids, and Carter asked Chase and Levi to be groomsmen. They all received boxes with personalized beverage glasses, tropical shades, and scented candles. The girls also received a card that informed them of their assigned dress color and a QR code for the website to choose a favorite style and order it in time for the big day. Brittany was asked to wear watermelon and Erin, canary yellow. Emily explained there would be eight bridesmaids, and all of them would be in shades of a Key Largo sunset.

As neutrals are the current trend, we all wondered how that array of colors would turn out. We learned not to doubt Emily's vision as she wholeheartedly devoted every waking moment she wasn't working to the day of her dreams.

Emily's precision trickled down to minute details like matching robes for the bridesmaids and moms to lounge in as they awaited their turn for hair and makeup. I don't believe I'll ever take that much time and investment to look that glamorous ever again. Many prayers were lifted for a day without rain. Emily must have had a direct line to God, as the skies remained clear. He could have delivered a little bit more of a breeze, but all things considered, even the weather checked the box on Emily's list.

The guest list was limited, and when tier-one invites were declined, tier-two invites were pulled up in rank and received an invitation. Most everyone we could have hoped for made it to the wedding, including Grandma Gert, Grandpa Wil, and Grandma Joe; Chuck's sisters, Lorilynn and Ivan and their family; the Tinuccis; and all the dear friends and family of Carter and Emily.

Steel drums echoed across the private bay as guests sipped on cool beverages as they waited for the wedding party processional to begin. The muscular wedding planner, sporting toned arms and decked in running shoes and athleisure wear, efficiently escorted the brightly dressed guests to their white folding-chair seats lined up on the crusty white sand beach. A keyboardist accompanied by a violinist serenaded the procession of parents, bridesmaids, and groomsmen down a long, sun-bleached plank path toward a white trellis adorned with roses, hydrangeas, and bird of paradise that popped against the dreamy blue sky and ocean.

Seated guests donned sunglasses and cooled themselves with the wicker fans placed on each chair (another minuscule and thoughtful Emily touch) and turned to stand as Emily strolled down the wooden path. A crown of blonde braids with a curly ponytail hiding beneath a simple veil complemented her "yes-to-the-dress" gown. The plunging neckline, strappy back, and a train stitched with an embossed tropical floral design shimmered as it flowed over the gray planks and glistening sand. One hand held a vibrant bouquet echoing the trellis flowers, and the other clung to her handsome father's arm. As they approached the preacher and Carter standing beneath the trellis, she giggled, looked back, and said, "Hi, everybody!"

Emily's unbridled greeting brought on laughter, lightening the mood and signaling us to be seated. The ceremony began.

With two brothers, Carter was hard-pressed to decide on a best man but leaned toward Andy. Both Chuck and I agreed that Andy, our declared "fourth son," was the man best suited to take on that role. Andy assumed his first position in the lineup of groomsmen. They stood like statues as sweat dripped and seeped into their crisp white shirts, navy tuxes, and coral-colored ties.

There may have been a dry eye or two as Emily and her dad made their way down toward the rocky beach edge; however, when Carter laid eyes on his bride, his lower lip quivered, which brought on a stream of tears and several choked-backed sobs. The crowd of about 120 friends and family quickly joined Carter and attempted to fan away their tears as they sat and perspired on the picture-perfect beach.

Thankfully, I had my fresh hanky with the words "For happy tears! Love, Carter" in hand. From then on, it was a constant battle to dab and keep the tears from smearing the "art" professionally painted on my face earlier in the day. Chuck's hanky was as soaked as mine.

Emily's mom and dad, Peg and Jim Forgan, had prayed feverishly that there would be no rain the night of the wedding. God held back the rain threatened by most forecasters and supplied a generous amount of sun rays uninterrupted by clouds as Carter and Emily read their handwritten vows.

Emily's Vows

Carter,

> Ever since I was a little girl, I dreamed of getting married and being someone's wife. Around when I turned eighteen, I really longed for that, and from then into my mid-twenties, I really started praying about my husband and that God would bring him to me at just the right time.
>
> I prayed the man I would marry would be generous, patient, funny, kind, love his family, and most importantly, love the Lord.

Mourning to Dancing

I had no idea that during the many years I was praying that prayer that it was about you. But God knew all along.

He truly carried out His promise in Ephesians 3:20 because you truly exceeded all my hopes, dreams, and expectations of who my husband would be.

Not only are you all the things I prayed for, but you're also tenderhearted, forgiving, intentional, the best dog dad to our fur babies, and very, very handsome. And tall, too; that is a great bonus!

As we stand here today committing ourselves to one another before our friends, family, and God, I vow to always remember you are the answer to my prayer, and I will never take you for granted.

As your wife, I promise to be patient, kind, and give you the very best of me each day. I promise to cherish you, love you unconditionally, and remember that God loves you so much more than I ever could. I promise to remind you that you are a child of God and made perfectly in His image.

I promise to point our marriage toward Christ and to remind us our marriage is built on His firm foundation.

I promise to be your biggest cheerleader and supporter, always encouraging you to chase your God-given dreams. I promise to laugh with you, cry with you, and hold you close on the mountaintops and in the valleys.

I promise to continue trying new adventures with you, even if it means putting on a pair of boots and going mucking in a sketchy canal.

I promise to be excited every time you find a new fish . . . or frog . . . or lizard.

I promise to support your love of reptiles and welcome new critters into our home, but I do have to draw the line with spiders.

Carter Viss, I promise to love you with everything I have and will love you each and every day until the good Lord calls us home.

I can't wait to start this new chapter with you, and I know God has a beautiful story written for us. I love you so much.

Carter's Vows

Emily,

Today is the happiest day of my life. It is the day that marks the beginning of our beautiful journey together. And on this day, I give you my heart in its whole and unwavering love.

The privilege to call you my wife is a blessing I can only start to comprehend. And with this blessing comes vows and guarantees that I will hold sacred.

I promise to be your best friend, your number-one supporter, your loyal teammate, and, most importantly, your faithful and loving husband.

You have brought so much beauty into my life and are truly my greatest gift from God.

Ever since I met you, you have shown yourself to be a joyful beacon to others, and I promise to help you illuminate others and show them what a special gift to the world you are. I will build our marriage on the firm foundation of God's word and pray for God to be the center of our thriving marriage.

I will walk beside you through whatever life may bring our way.

Even in the darkest of times, I will stay beside you and strive toward seeing the light God places in any situation. So, to put this all into a couple words that I will repeat to myself every day, you are my person, my love, my life: today and always.

Chuck and I intentionally soaked in every moment and toggled between Carter's situation just three and a half short years ago and the scene playing out before us.

We had wondered how Carter could thrive with a missing arm and severely injured legs. We knew he wanted a lifetime companion, but our hope was in short supply, and it was hard to let ourselves imagine Carter matching up with Emily. Yet Carter's determination, resilience, prayers from around the world, an app called Hinge, Emily's friend named Hudson, a nudge from Emily's mom to go on the first date, and God's will overpowered our doubts. The dichotomy of the evening wasn't lost on Chuck or me or all the family and friends who made extraordinary efforts to make their way to Key Largo.

Grateful is a start in describing how we felt toward those who made the trek to the Florida Keys to witness the wedding in person—grandparents, aunts, uncles, cousins, lifelong friends, and work friends. We also felt the presence of our

CaringBridge village at every memorable moment. From best man Andy's toast to the choreographed dance performed like pros by Emily and her dad, the evening was unforgettable.

A decadent and abundant Cuban-inspired smorgasbord, a photo booth van for a guest book, the well-stocked tiki hut bar, and the coffee martini trailer kept the party rocking. The foam "lightsabers" ignited free-form epic dance moves.

All, and I mean *all*, our mourning turned into serious dancing.

Emily and Carter at their wedding ceremony
(Photo Credit: Viss Family)

CHAPTER 62

What Is Found in Loss?

The first and often the only person to be healed by forgiveness is the person who does the forgiveness. When we genuinely forgive, we set a prisoner free and then discover that the prisoner we set free is us.

—Lewis Smedes, in *What's So Amazing About Grace* by Philip Yancy

Leila

And they lived happily ever after.

That's how we like books to end.

But we know life happens.

Happy comes and goes. What sticks around is change, which comes bundled with uncertainty. The odds were not in Carter's favor that Thanksgiving Day in 2019, and grief hit us hard. Now we live *changed* ever after because of the decisions that were made.

Chuck and I flew to Florida to wrap our arms around a son who almost lost four limbs. The doctors agreed to keep Carter's legs. Hosts of friends and relatives took time away from their busy lives to gather around his bedside.

Dr. Borrego's biggest concern was that Carter would have chronic pain and slip into addiction. Carter denied himself addictive painkillers, leaned into the slog, and currently lives pain-free. Chuck stayed to care for Carter, which no doubt sped up the recovery process.

And perhaps the most notable decision came from a heart that knows the love of a forgiving God. Carter decided to forgive Danny and make meaning out of a horrific collision. We were all healed by forgiveness.

As we eagerly await changes in maritime laws, another change comes to mind. With permanent loss comes a change in perspective. It hurts the eyes—like squinting in the sun—when crawling out of a hellish tunnel of loss.

Now that I've crawled back into the light, it still feels right to retreat to the shade and reminisce about the pain. Now, I see that the darkness of the past enlightens the path of the future. Through loss, we found gains. Most I never dared to hope for.

The accident shook the foundation of our family's faith and, I'll be honest, my personal relationship with God. Grief bruises and leaves scars. Yet even when the grief monster moved in for good, my faith never walked alone. The faith of others filled in the gap when lament lingered. And when my faith falls short (as it still does!), God's hands hold my tears, and His grace withstands my doubt.

This quote from William Sloane Coffin summarizes how I have reconciled my relationship with Him: "We see in Jesus that God gives us minimum protection, but maximum support."[1]

What Is Found in Loss?

The accident also schooled me on Paul's words to the Corinthians: "So now faith, hope, and love abide, these three; but the greatest of these is love (1 Cor. 13:13 ESV).

Now, I view faith as the foundation of the past, hope as the anchor of the future, and love as the blanket of the present.

In grief, I found company, in fact, *good* company. I discovered that lingering in lament is biblical and beneficial and brings new and lasting friendships. It's because of one simple truth: behind every loving face, there is secret sorrow.

Living with permanent loss and walking this earth in a minority body significantly shifted Carter's focus. Instead of caring for tanks at Loggerhead Marinelife Center, he now heads up the Carter Viss Foundation (https://cartervissfoundation.org). The board of directors, which includes Carter, Emily, Andy, Christine, and wedding-ring-story Stephen, aims to support individuals with limb trauma resulting from boating incidents and promote safe boating and diving practices.

Carter receives regular invitations to speak and, with Emily's help, sets up booths at fairs and conferences to promote his cause. His display includes T-shirts with his colored-pencil drawings of fish printed on the back and three-dimensional inflatable dive flags.

Someday, he and Danny will celebrate on the steps of the Capitol in Tallahassee when a bill passes that protects divers and boaters from future collisions.

As he predicted soon after his breathing tube was removed, he has more impact *now* than before the accident.

Of all the glorious wedding moments, there is one that I treasure the most, although I admit that I'm projecting feelings on my son. His tears erupted at the first sight of his beautiful bride. As I gazed at him through the blurry lens of my own tears, I believe his bubbled up from deep within. They had been pooling for decades far beneath his "badass" exterior. Yes, they were tears of unfathomable love for Emily as she processed down the beach alongside her loving dad, but they were also

- tears of relief, knowing that his years of searching and longing for a lifetime companion had ended;
- tears for the arm lost at sea that will never wrap around his wife and future children;
- tears swept aside during the torturous hours of the ICU and surgeries;
- tears from the bright light after months in the wretched dark slog of recovery;
- tears of gratitude to a global village that supported him when he didn't have the strength to say thank you;
- tears of anguish for how Thanksgiving Day 2019 scarred his friends, relatives, siblings, and parents;
- tears of wonder at how a hospital room could morph into sacred ground;
- tears of hope that were in short supply as the recovery slog inched by;
- tears of forgiveness for a deed that some would deem unforgivable;
- tears of triumph that he overcame incredible odds to be present and stand on two legs at the altar with Emily;

What Is Found in Loss?

- tears of faith in a God who—as Andy reminded Carter on the bloody boat floor—"is with us";
- tears of gratefulness for not being left or lost in the wake but found; and
- tears of joy because change won despite permanent loss.

May we all find ourselves living *changed* ever after.

Carter and his family on Thanksgiving Day of 2018
(Photo Credit: Viss Family)

EPILOGUE

The Narrow Path

Carter

I AM WRITING THIS AT THE END OF 2023. THE INCIDENT happened more than four years ago, and my life has changed to the point where the events of my stay in the hospital and recovery feel like a distant shadow of the past. I had the best day of my life getting married to my beautiful wife a few months ago. We bought a spacious house with a great yard for our dogs to run around in. We plan on starting a family soon and are embracing our new lives together as one. I am truly amazed at what God has done in my life over the past few years.

I continued to apply time and repetition to my hobbies and interests. I didn't give up on playing piano and can now perform most of the pieces I used to play with two hands. I had even learned classical pieces I labeled "too hard" when I had two hands, including "Etude Opus No. 25 (Ocean)." I plan on continuing to push the boundaries of what can be done with one hand on the piano and strive to be an inspiration for other musicians facing adversity. I also never gave up my hobby of drawing fish. It will be a lifetime hobby, and I aim to be a scientific illustrator.

In addition to maintaining my hobbies, I also live a very active lifestyle. I run at least once a week and just ran my first half marathon ever in December. I can swim a mile easily and feel more proficient in the water than I did before the incident. I also got a recumbent tricycle that's easy to control with one hand. It also makes pedaling very easy on my legs because my right knee seems to never get past a 90-degree bend. I hope to combine all these exercises by doing a triathlon next year. I also have continued doing many recreational activities. I've been scuba diving a few times, I play a lot of tennis, I've been on several fishing trips, and I love to go on long hikes.

Another goal I am still working toward is making a bigger difference than I could before, as I stated just days after the incident. The video I made with Danny did very well upon its release. I've also been able to share my story at boating safety conferences, churches, schools, and several company functions. I end each of my talks by playing the piano for the crowd. My goal one day is to do a TED Talk on my story.

I left Loggerhead in December of 2022 after years of working as an aquarist and started a 501(c)(3) nonprofit called the Carter Viss Foundation in early 2023 to continue my goals of making a bigger difference. Its mission is to support individuals with limb trauma from boating incidents and promote safe boating and diving practices. I plan to use this foundation to make three-dimensional divers-down devices available to everyone in dive shops. This is the most immediate impact I can make on diving safety. I will also use this foundation to educate the public on the importance of going slow while boating near a beach. I hope to establish some rules and guidelines to enforce that.

Although I've chosen to let this incident define my life in a positive way, there is no way to avoid the painful memories and gruesome flashbacks of that day.

In 2021, I had several symptoms of PTSD and decided to seek help. After years of therapy and medication, I can say that most of my symptoms are gone, besides infrequent feelings of intense anxiety. The most vivid memory that triggers my anxiety is the moment I realized my arm was chopped off. However, when I look past the gruesome details, my mind often focuses on how great snorkeling was that day and how much fun we had out there. It felt like the perfect way to spend the last moments of my life before everything changed.

I have yet to return to the Breakers Reef, which I once called my happy place. I miss it dearly, but the memories still haunt me, and I feel unsettled thinking about swimming in those waters. Perhaps I would return one day after I've made a substantial change in boating and diving safety to the point where I would feel safer snorkeling there.

While I reflect on the incident and my recovery, it's very easy to think about what I lost. I lost my right arm, the regular function of my legs, my sense of safety while in the water, my happy place, and my entire old way of life. I also remember the pain and suffering I endured in the hospital, the horrible hallucinations I saw, and the dark place I would often get stuck in.

However, the passing years have shifted my mind for me to see all that I have found through this experience. I found community through all the support I received in the hospital. I found a closer relationship with my family. I found an opportunity to make a difference in the boating and diving world. I found a testimony to share and use to impact other lives. And, most importantly, I found a beautiful wife whom I love dearly. These are all just a few examples of how God works through tragedy to create beauty.

Instead of dwelling on the horrors of my hospital stay, I now think back to all the quality time I had with family and friends. Despite the tears, there were many laughs with friends and inside jokes with nurses. Instead of mourning the loss of my right arm, I embrace life with one arm and love to make jokes regarding my missing arm. Instead of seeking vengeance and retribution toward the driver, I practiced forgiveness through faith in God. I've seen the power of forgiveness firsthand and share its importance every time I tell my story.

One time, after telling my story at a church, an elderly man came to me with tears in his eyes and told me that was exactly what he needed to hear. He didn't explain his situation to me, but I'm confident he chose forgiveness and got to experience its life-changing power.

Despite all the positive memories I've experienced over the years, there are still some that will always be negative to me. The main one is how the incident affected my family. I break down whenever I think about my parents getting that call on Thanksgiving morning. I can't imagine the mood in the house as my parents were about to leave to see me, not knowing if I would be dead or alive the next morning. I continue to pray for healing in them. I feel like this incident damaged them

The Narrow Path

more emotionally than me. I hope to live my life to the fullest and be the happiest I can be to promote their healing.

A question I frequently asked myself, especially in the early days, was, "Why me?" Why did this happen to me and not someone else out there that day? Why is it that I was using a dive flag and got hit while so many divers don't use them and don't get hit? Focusing on this question sank me into a victim mentality. I would get more depressed in this mental state and lose my motivation to recover. I would ultimately end up in my dark place and need God to pull me out. I knew this cycle needed to change.

Over the years, I've started asking myself "Why *not* me?" Why should I wish this happened to someone else when this is God's plan for my life? Why should I feel like a victim when I have the perfect opportunity to make a difference? Focusing on *this* question raised me to my feet and got me moving. This is the path God led me on, and it's my duty to make it to the other side through faith.

My choice between "Why me?" and "Why not me?" as a way to handle the incident reminds me of my favorite part of Jesus's Sermon on the Mount:

> Enter by the narrow gate. For the gate is wide, and the way is easy that leads to destruction, and those who enter it are many. For the gate is narrow and the way is hard that leads to life, and those who find it are few. (Matt. 7:13–14)

The easy path for me would be feeling sorry for myself, numbing myself with all kinds of medications, and harboring anger about my circumstances. I've leaned toward this path many times since the incident. The hard path has been embracing the life God has planned for me, getting back to doing all I love, and choosing forgiveness where the world would choose vengeance. I often stumbled off this path during my recovery and ended up on the easy path. Fortunately, my faith in God would bring me back to the narrow path, and I had to trust Him to remain on track. When this pathway becomes treacherous or shrouded in darkness, I must cling to God to make it through.

An experience that exemplifies this concept to me was the last run I went on just a week before Thanksgiving of 2019. It was a cold, gloomy November evening (very rare for Florida), and I had just gotten off work. It was about 5 p.m., and due to the recent time change, the sun set around 5:30.

Once a week, I would run through the Juno Dunes Natural Area across the street from Loggerhead after work. It was something I looked forward to every week. I could clear my head, pray to God, and appreciate nature during these runs. The fact that it got dark around 6 p.m. did not prevent me from running because I usually was done by then. However, on this day, I started running and noticed it was significantly darker because of how cloudy it was.

By the time I was halfway done, it was almost completely dark, and I still had a couple of miles until I would be out of the natural area. With only tiny remnants of natural light left to guide me, I continued running through the cold, quiet, wooded area.

One might expect fear to kick in while I was in the dark, but all I felt was peace. I trusted my feet were familiar with

The Narrow Path

the trail I had run on dozens of times. I felt the presence of God all around me and was comforted by His guidance.

I saw a glimpse of streetlights straight ahead and started running faster. I could see faint traces of the trail as I got closer. I finally reached the streetlights of the main road and continued running back to where I was parked.

After finishing, I remember thinking that it was an amazing experience. It felt like I was putting my complete trust in God because I couldn't see. God guided me through the darkness and got me on the right path. I believe this is the right or narrow path Jesus speaks of in the sermon: the path that is only crossed by walking by faith, not by sight.

Little did I know God was about to guide me through my darkest valley just a week later, where my limits would be tested, and I would experience true horror—where I needed to put all my faith in God to recover fully and where God would teach me lessons on forgiveness and how to effect change in the lives of others.

I overcame this incident by walking by faith and not by sight. I believe this is how anyone can overcome any obstacle or setback. I believe God has a master plan for everyone, and you should place all your trust in Him when you are passing through a valley so you don't lose your strength. I hope to keep this faith as I continue to pass through valleys in life. I hope to remain strong during the rest of my life and stay on the narrow path.

I know God has made me stronger through this experience, and I know faith in God will make *you* stronger.

ACKNOWLEDGMENTS

We want to extend our deep appreciation to all those who stood with us—and by us—throughout this life-changing journey and beyond. You have become our extended family and will always have a place in our hearts.

After the accident, we shared updates on Carter's condition with family and friends through the CaringBridge website. The site allowed us to connect with a global community and receive much-needed support through thousands of comments and prayers, which inspired us to continue posting. My journal entries on CaringBridge became the framework for this book, which began when there was little else to do, thanks to COVID-19. Instead of playing for church services on Sunday mornings, I grabbed coffee and my laptop, returned to bed, and pieced together this unfathomable yet true story.

The early chapters may not have seen the light of day if it weren't for Joe Capozzi, a journalist who diligently tracked and documented Carter's recovery. Joe and his wife agreed to read the rough drafts and encouraged me to keep writing. Joe's expertise in storytelling assisted me in compiling a potential page-turner. When it seemed too difficult for me to transcribe Chuck's perspective, Chuck wrote his raw narrative, which differed from mine. Carter later decided to contribute chapters, and it became clear that weaving together three distinct voices would complete the book and set it apart.

Donna Berger wrote to us while Carter was in the hospital to show her support and share her insights on loss and grief. In 2022, she published *Living Through Loss: A Memoir of Recovering Joy After Cumulative Grief.* She highly recommended her editor, Gail Fallen, and book designer, Melinda Martin, who, along with hundreds of expectant readers, were instrumental in making *Found in the Wake* a reality.

We are eternally grateful to you all.

—Leila

ABOUT THE AUTHORS

Carter Viss

Carter Viss is a marine biologist who lives in Jupiter, Florida. After recovering from the gruesome injuries he sustained when he was struck by a boat, he has dedicated his life to inspiring others. His gripping account of overcoming this incident through faith and resilience is a shining example of how God can create beauty out of tragedy.

Leila Viss

Leila Viss, mother of Carter Viss, is an accomplished pianist, organist, composer, author, presenter, and piano teacher who shares her passion for faith, honesty, and music-making in *Found in the Wake*. Her candid storytelling offers insights into navigating a parent's worst nightmare, grappling with dilapidated hope, and discovering recalibrated courage.

Chuck Viss

Charles (Chuck) Viss, father of Carter Viss, is an IT professional who lives in Centennial, Colorado. Chuck took a leave of absence from his job to take on the role of Carter's caretaker, navigating the complicated system of healthcare and insurance. He shares his gripping experience of rehabbing his son, along with his unexpected personal interactions with trauma.

NOTES

CHAPTER 11

1. Ray Clendenen, "Hebrew Word Study: Hesed," Christian Standard Bible online, July 30,2021, https://csbible.com/hebrew-word-study-hesed/.

CHAPTER 12

1. Jorge Milian, "If You Are Bitten by a Shark, Here's the Doctor You'll Want to See," *The Palm Beach Post,* updated September 24, 2016, https://www.palmbeachpost.com/story/news/2015/04/09/if-you-are-bitten-by/6774479007/.

CHAPTER 14

1. Jason A. Lowe, "Internal Fixation for Fractures," OrthoInfo, accessed August 4, 2024, https://orthoinfo.aaos.org/en/treatment/internal-fixation-for-fractures/#:~:text=An%20external%20fixator%20 acts%20as,a%20bar%20outside%20the%20skin.
2. Major Trauma Team, St. Georges' University Hospitals NHS Foundation Trust, "External Fixators," After Trauma, accessed August 10, 2024, https://www.aftertrauma.org/diagnosis-and-treatment/external-fixators#:~:text=An%20external%20fixator%20is%20 a,a%20bar%20outside%20the%20skin.
3. Rachel Sauer, "From the Archives | The Year of Quiet Strength," *The Palm Beach Post,* updated December 18, 2014, https://www.palmbeachpost.com/story/news/local/2014/12/18/from-archives-year-quiet-strength/7661943007/.
4. See Michael Edmondson, "How Often Do You Take the Responsibility to Get Back Up?" Navigate the Chaos, accessed August 9, 2024, https://www.navigatethechaos.com/post/do-you-realize-you-are-responsible-for-getting-back-up.

CHAPTER 18

1. David Eagleman, *The Brain: The Story of You*, rep. ed., (New York: Vintage, 2015), Kindle.

CHAPTER 25

1. Cassie Springer Ayeni, "Personal Injury Subrogation Claims Under ERISA: Hawaii Does the Work, and the Ninth Circuit Gets ERISA Right," American Bar Association, December 9, 2019: Holiday 2019 Issue, https://www.americanbar.org/groups/labor_law/publications/ebc_news_archive/holiday- -issue/personal-injury-subrogation-claims/.

CHAPTER 27

1. *New Oxford American Dictionary*, s.v. "slog."

CHAPTER 32

1. Michelle DeGuzman-Watson, Army News Service, "Accident Drives Recruiter to Become World-Class Athlete," in the *Fort Cavazos Sentinel*, August 16, 2018, http://www.forthoodsentinel.com/sports/accident-drives-recruiter-to-become-world-class-athlete/article_0bc6a02a-a0ba-11e8-a57b-338747f4b809.html.
2. "What Is Targeted Muscle Reinnervation (TMR)? [Infographic]," Northwestern Medicine, https://www.nm.org/healthbeat/medical-advances/new-therapies-and-drug-trials/What-Is-Targeted-Muscle-Reinnervation-TMR-Infographic.
3. Kim Constantinesco, "Michael Smith Is on a Quest to Become First Above-the-Elbow Amputee Skeleton Racer at the Olympics," Purpose2Play, December 10, 2015, https://purpose2play.com/2015/12/10/michael-smith-is-on-a-quest-to-become-first-above-the-elbow-amputee-skeleton-racer-at-the-olympics/.

CHAPTER 39

1. Kate Bowler (host) with BJ Miller (guest), "Loving What Is" in *Everything Happens for a Reason*, Season 3, Episode 5, podcast, mp3, 30:05, https://katebowler.com/podcasts/bj-miller-loving-what-is/.
2. "Loving What Is."
3. Anne LaMott, *Help, Thanks, Wow: The Three Essential Prayers* (New York: Riverhead Books, 2012), Kindle.

CHAPTER 40

1. "The Byrdes Are All In," in "Characters—Marty Byrde," Ozark Wiki, accessed July 31, 2024, https://ozark-netflix.fandom.com/wiki/Marty_Byrde.

CHAPTER 44

1. Elana Premack Sandler, "Ring Theory Helps Us Bring Comfort In," *Psychology Today,* May 30, 2017, https://www.psychologytoday.com/us/blog/promoting-hope-preventing-suicide/201705/ring-theory-helps-us-bring-comfort-in.

CHAPTER 48

1. Ichiro Kishimi and Fumitake Koga, *The Courage to Be Disliked* (New York: Atria Books, 2018), Kindle.

CHAPTER 55

1. Joe Capozzi, "Miracle at 'Schwartz Lagoon': A Lost and Found Tale about Sunken Treasure and the Bond of Friendship," ByJoeCapozzi.com, March 16, 2021, https://www.byjoecapozzi.com/post/miracle-at-schwartz-lagoon-a-lost-and-found-tale-about-sunken-treasure-and-the-bond-of-friendship?fbclid=IwAR13L1uj4x27KQgmNbi-r0Jx27XvrDwhtRQY9ww3aCzxg49CEbK7QsCNpyo. Used by permission.

CHAPTER 59

1. Elisabeth Kübler-Ross, *On Death and Dying: What the Dying Have to Teach Doctors, Nurses, Clergy, and Their Own Families* (New York: Scribner, 2011), Kindle.
2. David Kessler, *Finding Meaning: The Sixth Stage of Grief* (New York: Scribner, 2019), Kindle.
3. *Music and Mind LIVE with Renée Fleming*, Episode 6: Dan Levitin and Victor Wooten, "How and Why to Engage with Music Now," June 23, 2020, YouTube Video, 46:57, https://www.youtube.com/watch?v=wzS0XdciHwY.
4. Reuben Westmaas, "What Getting Chills from Music Says about Your Brain, *Discovery*, August 1, 2019, https://www.discovery.com/science/Getting-Chills-from-Music.

5. "What's Happening in The Brain When Your Imagination Is Active?" Mindshift, December 29, 2016, https://www.kqed.org/mindshift/47125/whats-happening-in-the-brain-when-your-imagination-is-active. (Includes TED-Ed video of "The Science of Imagination" by Andrey Vyshedskiy.)
6. "Neuroplasticity," *Psychology Today,* accessed August 5, 2024, https://www.psychologytoday.com/us/basics/neuroplasticity.
7. Lutz Jäncke, "Music Drives Brain Plasticity," *F1000 Biology Reports,* 1, no. 78, https://www.ncbi.nlm.nih.gov/pmc/articles/PMC2948283/.
8. Traci Pederson, "What Does Grief Do to Your Brain?" PsychCentral, updated May 6, 2022, https://psychcentral.com/lib/your-health-and-grief#how-grief-affects-the-brain.
9. "A Therapist Explains Why We Shut Down When Flooded with Big Emotions," UnityPoint Health, accessed August 10, 2024, https://www.unitypoint.org/news-and-articles/a-therapist-explains-why-we-shut-down-when-flooded-with-big-emotions.
10. Anita Collins, "How Playing and Instrument Benefits Your Brain," TED-Ed, July 22, 2014, Video, 4:44, https://ed.ted.com/lessons/how-playing-an-instrument-benefits-your-brain-anita-collins.
11. Tim Topham, "How Neuroscience Relates to Students Who Quit Music Lessons," February 16, 2021, YouTube Video, 7:01, https://www.youtube.com/watch?v=2MRknLa_YTw.

CHAPTER 62

1. William Sloane Coffin, "Eulogy for Alex," Beliefnet, accessed August 9, 2024, https://www.beliefnet.com/love-family/1999/12/eulogy-for-alex.aspx.

Scoundrels & Spitballers

Writers and Hollywood in the 1930s

PHILIPPE GARNIER

BLACK POOL
PRODUCTIONS

Scoundrels & Spitballers
Writers and Hollywood in the 1930s

© 2020 by Philippe Garnier

Second printing, 2021

Editor and Publisher: Eddie Muller

Book and Cover Design: Michael Kronenberg

Production and Proofreading: Daryl Sparks

All rights reserved. No part of this book may be reproduced in any form or by any electronic or mechanical means, including information storage and retrieval systems, without permission in writing from the publisher, except by a reviewer who may quote brief passages in a review. Scanning, uploading, and electronic distribution of this book or the facilitation of such without the permission of the publisher is prohibited. Please purchase only authorized electronic editions and do not participate in or encourage piracy of copyrighted materials. Your support of the author's rights is appreciated. Any member of educational institutions wishing to photocopy part or all of the work for classroom use, or anthology, should submit a permissions request to blackpoolproductions@gmail.com.

Published in the United States of America

Library of Congress Control Number: 2020934187

ISBN 978-0-578-65369-3

Black Pool Productions
An Eddie Muller Enterprise
Alameda, CA

blackpoolproductions.com

Front cover images: Writers at work — (top) Graham Baker and Gene Towne, (bottom) Niven Busch

Back cover image: Edward Anderson in Hollywood, late 1930s

To the Living

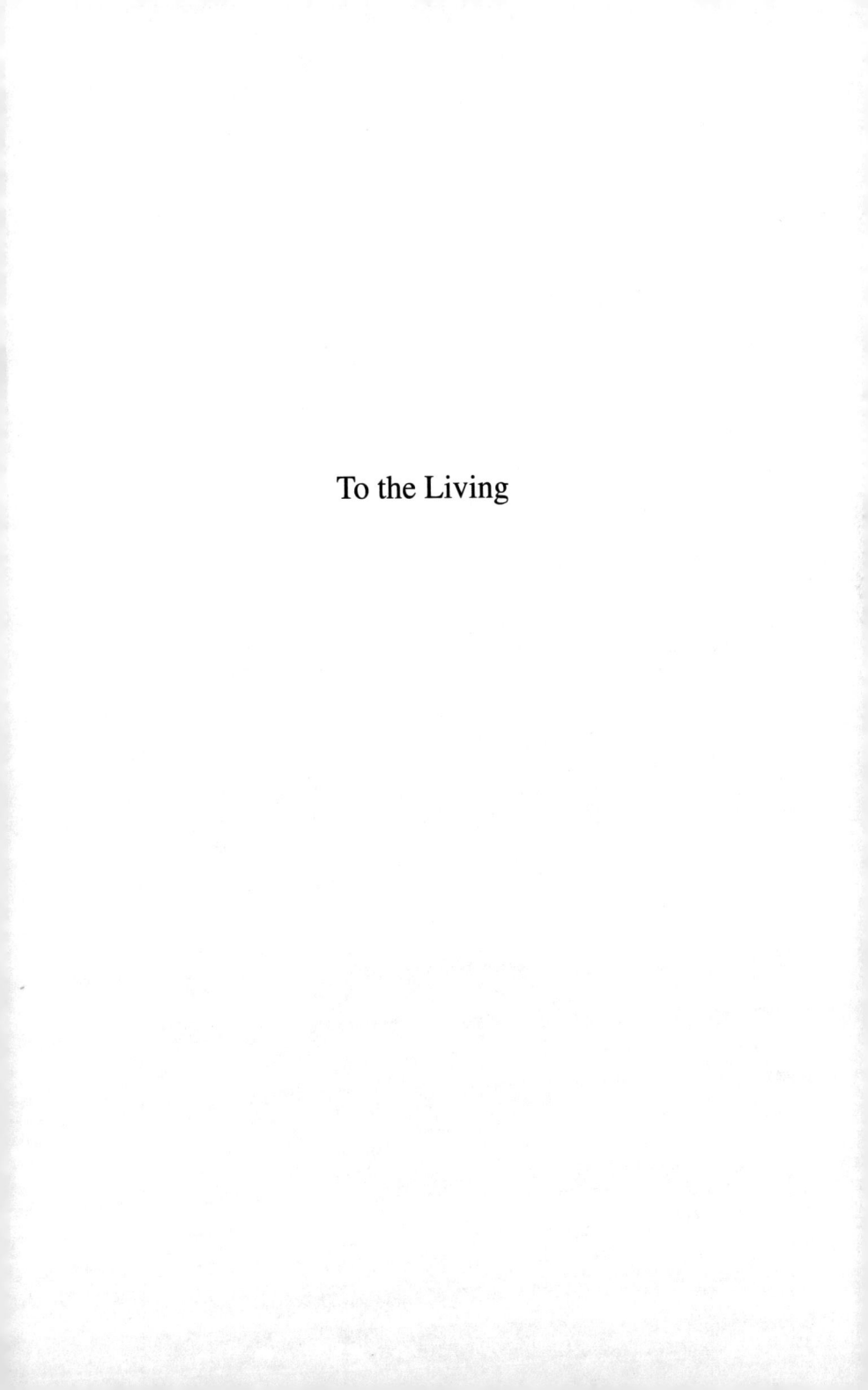

FOREWORD

I love this book. It mines, deeply and with great amusement, two aspects of cinema history dear to me.

First, it has keen appreciation and respect for writers. It ignores the slavish devotion to directors that has characterized film scholarship since the *auteur* theory seduced cinephiles back in the 1960s. Philippe Garnier understands that narrative cinema begins with *writers*. He displays in picaresque fashion that the work of a writer doesn't always begin in a courageous confrontation with the blank page—it can start with the quick-witted spinning of a yarn, conjured instantly out of experience and imagination, with no grander motivation than the need for some dough to spend on women, horses, and top-shelf hooch. The writers profiled here had *lived*. They had stories to tell, and to them the picture-making business was what the Gold Rush had been for prospectors. These were constructionists and fantasists, truth-tellers and bullshit slingers, and collectively they laid the foundation on which the Dream Factory was built.

Of course, when they came to Hollywood it was not yet an actual factory. That's the other thing I adore about this book: it depicts an era, the early years of talking pictures, when the industry was as much a playground as it was a business. Rogues, artists, knaves, hustlers, and geniuses all had a chance to make their mark in this sunny Southern California sandbox, before Wall Street assumed complete control and set the rules in stone.

Garnier also dares to subvert the conventional "wisdom" that has long branded Hollywood as a quagmire that callously consumes and destroys literary talent. He shows that, at least in its formative years, storytellers thrived or perished due largely to their own savvy or self-destructiveness.

The world depicted in these pages is long gone. We'll never again experience an adventurous frontier like Hollywood in the 1930s. So it's a thrilling pleasure to ramble through its streets and studio sets, its parlors and barrooms and bookstores, with Philippe Garnier as our guide. We drink, carouse, and witness modern American culture being created before our eyes by an amazing assortment of men and women who believed that nothing in life—*nothing*—was better than telling a good story.

–Eddie Muller

Screenwriter and soon-to-be Hollywood columnist Sidney Skolsky on the set of Busby Berkeley's 1937 musical *Ready, Willing and Able*

The kid said: "I don't like drunks in the first place, and in the second place I don't like them getting drunk in here, and in the third place I don't like them in the first place."

"Warner Brothers could use that," I said.

"They did."

—Raymond Chandler,
"Red Wind"

They (filmmakers, producers, directors) were a gaudy company, rambunctious and engrossed. What they produced was a phenomenon, teeming with vitality and ardor, as indigenous as our cars or skyscrapers or highways, and as *irrefutable*. Generations to come, looking back over the years, are bound to find that the best, most solid creative effort of our decades was spent in the movies, and it's time someone came clean and said so.

—Daniel Fuchs,
"Writing for the Movies"
Commentary,
February 1962

Henry King directs Gregory Peck and Deborah Kerr in *Beloved Infidel*

A NOTE ON TRUTH IN HOLLYWOOD HISTORY

THE ORIGINAL FRENCH VERSION of this book, published in 1996 by Éditions Grasset, was (to the chagrin of the publisher and a great many readers) titled *Honi Soit Qui Malibu*. It was filched from a F. Scott Fitzgerald *bon mot* which found its way into *Note-book E—Epigrams, Wisecracks and Jokes*, a posthumous volume edited by Edmund Wilson. It's a rather abstruse witticism that seemed to enchant no one but me.

Nevertheless, it is revealing of the spirit in which I wrote this book to know that Fitzgerald's quip came to me not through Wilson's scholarly book, but through a mediocre movie starring Gregory Peck; "Honi Soit Qui Malibu," coined from the motto *"Honi Soit Qui Mal Y Pense"* emblazoned on every British citizen's passport, was painted on a shingle nailed to Fitzgerald's rented Malibu bungalow in *Beloved Infidel*—a 1959 20th Century–Fox production about the writer's last years in California. The hoary tale was based on a memoir of the same title by his paramour, Hollywood columnist Sheilah Graham, and flaccidly directed by Henry King, but somehow this pun-on-a-shingle forever convinced me that even Hollywood screenwriters have souls. In this case, *someone* had done his (or her) homework, and it could not be the gossip hag, who didn't mention it in the book about her affair with the great man. It sounded more like something Oscar Levant would ad-lib in a movie, likely while tickling the ivories—except he wasn't around. Could it be Sy Bartlett, the lone writer credited on the script? Bartlett was an established figure at 20th Century–Fox, specializing in Air Force pictures like *Twelve O'Clock High* and *A Gathering of Eagles*. He was also Gregory Peck's man when it came to polishing dialogue. But with Jerry Wald in charge of the *Beloved Infidel* production, who's to know? The man, great producer though he was, had a reputation for picking brains everywhere and shuffling writers like playing cards on any given project.

I don't remember much about *Beloved Infidel*. Deborah Kerr was fine as Sheilah, probably more than the real-life subject deserved, but, as Fitzgerald, Peck was hopelessly miscast: with all that health and brooding handsomeness he looked like a shiny new penny, not the pasty-faced ghost the great author had become. Fredric March—a dead ringer for the novelist at the end of his reel—was available at the time, which makes this casting blunder all the more unforgiveable: March was as depressed and dyspeptic as Fitzgerald—"all used up," as Marlene Dietrich would say in a more memorable movie.

Many of the facts and details hauled in for this book have been trawled and sifted from similarly oddball sources ranging from original research and personal interviews to strangely boring publications like *Screen Writer*, the monthly magazine of the Screen Writers Guild, as well as the trade journals and fan magazines of the period. The details are all true, verified as much as humanly possible. But in spite of these efforts, when it comes to truth in Hollywood—who's to know for sure? Was the picture shot on location or in front of a matte painting? Hollywood anecdotes, especially the good ones, should always be enjoyed with the proverbial grain of salt.

Abraham Polonsky tipped me to this early, between takes as it were, when I was filming an interview with him on the old Enterprise lot (now Raleigh Studios, across from Paramount). At the behest of actor John Garfield, Polonsky had made his debut there in 1948, both as a screenwriter and director, and he hadn't been back to these soundstages in over forty years. While we were reloading film, I mentioned my book project. He gave me a look and nodded wearily. "Let me tell you about biography," he said.

"Two years ago, a friend of mine calls me from New York. Seems that a university professor is doing research for a biography of Paul Goodman, and he's doing the rounds, interviewing people. Goodman, my friend and I, all three of us, went to the same school, City College of New York.

Now my friend is embarrassed. He made up a few details, he says over the phone. Like he said it was Goodman who turned me on to Proust. 'Why would you say that?' I asked, 'You know it isn't true.' 'I know, I know,' he says, 'but I had to say *something!*' The professor wanted to know what influence Goodman had had on his college friends. And he *did* influence me, but not concerning Proust, I guarantee you! But my friend asked me to go along with what he said, should the question come up, and I did. What does it matter? Now it's probably in the book, black and white on the page, like gospel. But from this time on, I've been wondering if it is not the same with all the biographies you read, if it's not just a heap of little white lies, as silly and innocuous as this one. Take Spartacus. One day—this was before the Kubrick movie—Yul Brynner asked me to write him a script about Spartacus. So I locked myself for months in the New York Public Library, and all I could find that had been written by a contemporary of his was this one line: 'Led by a man named Spartacus.' That's all there is, the rest was invented a hundred years later. Same with the 'Boston Massacre.' There was never any massacre, only two men killed, and only one was from Boston. But I can't even begin to tell you how many books were written about it."

The other conceit of the present work is a matter of casting and emphasis. When I started my research, a good number of books had been published in English on the subject of writers in Hollywood—Tom Dardis' *Some Time in the Sun,* for one—and, at first, I too started rounding up the usual suspects, some of whom had by that time become the subject of full-blown biographies. But in the exclusive hush of the Huntington Library it one day dawned on me that what was detritus to one biographer could be gold for another. Jay Martin, the author of a fine biography of Nathanael West published in 1970, had donated his notes and research material to the library. It took some doing to obtain permission to rake through it, but once I was in, the staff was superb. Martin had used a nifty but hopelessly obsolete miniature reel-to-reel tape recorder for his interviews, and it took the librarians three months to find the proper machine on which I could play the tapes. The effort was worth it. The most interesting interviews, for me at least, were the Hollywood ones. Martin, greatly qualified as a literary scholar, was out of his depth when it came to movies and the film industry. Or let us say that he wasn't overly interested; he wouldn't necessarily follow up about Burt Kelly or Rowland Brown or Wells Root when they were mentioned by S. J. (Sid) Perelman. And who was this fellow Tasker? These names meant nothing to me either at this point, but I became intrigued.

Later, when good luck brought me in contact with the likes of Niven Busch, John Sanford, and Samuel Gilson Brown, or with booksellers Louis Epstein or Edward Gilbert, I knew enough to ask the right questions. More crucially, I was able to cast and shape my book so it would not be a rehash of things already published by others, albeit in another language. All this accounts for the elliptical slant of this book and its crazy-quilt structure—it's a book that peers into little-seen corners, rather than staring squarely at its subject, a book more concerned with colorful second fiddles than with the tenors. So—no Ben Hecht, no Charles MacArthur, no Dudley Nichols, no Anita Loos or Dorothy Parker. James M. Cain only cooks ducks here, William Faulkner figures only insofar as he drank, one dry weekend, all the hair tonic in Buzz Bezzerides' wife's bathroom. Sometimes the sources themselves unexpectedly drift into the foreground, briefly becoming more beguiling to me than the people they're telling me about. This happened many times, so often I started cultivating this kind of bank-shot approach. Sometimes the tension this produced (unqualified admiration, jealousy, whatever) added up to drama. But above all I wanted to stress the vibrancy and free-for-all giddiness of a period when the film industry was young, and its workers even younger. And, perhaps, along the way these tales might define the important and not-always-negative role Hollywood played in the literary life of the 1930s. Hollywood broke a few writers' souls, but it also helped many—and definitely inspired a few. It could even have a profound effect on a writer living two-thousand miles away.

This is why *Scoundrels & Spitballers* is to be read more as a book about writers *and* Hollywood, rather than one about screenwriters *in* Hollywood.

NINE LIVES

ON APRIL 3, 1933, WILSON MIZNER expired in his room at the Ambassador Hotel. "I'm dying above my means," he reportedly moaned, a wit to the end. That same year, Achmed Abdullah pitched his tent for good in Hollywood, having just published his improbable autobiography, *The Cat Had Nine Lives*.

Even for the hardcore cinephile, these two names do not immediately jump to mind when the words "screenwriters" or "Hollywood writers" are mentioned. But it is one of the many idiosyncrasies of this work that it steers away as much as possible from the typical Hollywood Reel, even though the history of the place has by now been set in bronze and tends to play out as a succession of received truths and indestructible anecdotes—the facts be damned. The figure of the Hollywood Writer sometimes seems to come straight from Central Casting: overqualified, overpaid, constantly kibitzing but ultimately meek, with wives, children, bookies, horses, and ulcers to feed. Even the Coen Brothers, usually pretty savvy about their poaching, succumbed to such clichés when they wrote *Barton Fink*, a major misstep for them. Their hero was bad enough, loosely based on George S. Kaufman and Clifford Odets, but the veteran Southern writer based on William Faulkner was a shocking clown (as we shall see, the great man had himself a gypsy good time in Hollywood).

All of which is a shame, for one could not imagine a more colorful and varied breed to stoke the dream machine than these storytellers, especially those who plied their trade when Hollywood hadn't quite coalesced into the well-oiled studio system it would become by mid-century. In the late twenties and early thirties, there were more adventurers than artists at play in Hollywood, and the biographies of these men and women were often more interesting than the films they were assigned to write.

The silent era had its share of such adventurers, but they were directors and actors, or the moguls themselves—rarely the writers. The screenwriting profession was then dominated by gagmen and fan magazine writers, or women who all seemed to share the same pedigree: California-born, WASPish, all with strong social connections. A few of these names remained in the top-tier well into the forties, almost always a sign of quality: Lenore Coffee, Anita Loos, Mary C. McCall Jr., Jane Murfin, the great Zoe Akins and Frances Marion were a sort of *noblesse de cour* in the studios. Among them, Marion was the most astonishing, chalking up 140 pictures over 50 years, drawing salaries unthinkable even for the likes of Ben Hecht. Marion felt as much at home among cowboys (she married one) as with the *nouveaux riche* at Pickfair and San Simeon; she wrote for Mary Pickford and Marion Davies, as well as for her great friend and admirer Irving Thalberg. Many of these important women came from money, like Zoe Akins, Dorothy Arzner's favorite collaborator (*Anybody's Woman, Christopher Strong*). The Akinses from St. Louis were important Missouri Republicans. Zoe Akins was also a lesbian, like Arzner, and like Arzner had the kind of "fuck-you money" which assured her relative independence from studio bosses. Besides being a sought-after scenario writer, her plays were often adapted to the screen, sometimes twice, as was *The Greeks Had a Word for It*, which, besides a 1932 Samuel Goldwyn production helmed by Lowell Sherman, was the source for *How to Marry a Millionaire* in 1953. Other ladies in the trade had delicious Victorian names like Zelda Sears, Helen Logan or Gladys Lehman, and although they have become more obscure with time, each was proficient and highly successful. In fact, one could reasonably claim that these women were the true pillars of the early Hollywood scenario—along with solid "constructionists" like Benjamin Glazer, Casey Robinson, Edwin Justus Mayer, Norman Krasna, John Lee Mahin, Seton I. Miller, Robert Riskin, Sidney Buchman, Samson Raphaelson, Garson Kanin, Dudley Nichols, Wells Root and a dozen others—all esteemed practitioners but historically ignored, either because their lives were relatively bland or because they did not leave behind poisoned memoirs. There was some fanfare for constructive teams like Wilder and Brackett (or Wilder

"America's Sweetheart," Mary Pickford, with one of the young industry's most prolific screenwriters, Frances Marion

and Diamond), but few trumpets for Frances Goodrich and Albert Hackett, brothers Charles and Jules Furthman, or the Epstein twins, Philip and Julius.

Instead of going for an illusory composite sketch of the Hollywood screenwriter, this book will try instead to examine—sometimes under its most eccentric facets—the part Hollywood played in American Literature during the Depression years; the way Hollywood (its resources and its wiles) affected the lives and work of various writers. This effect would be ephemeral and superficial for some, crucial for others, for Hollywood at the time recruited far and wide. The calling card could be a Broadway hit or a story in *The Saturday Evening Post*. A published novel was usually enough to secure a railroad ticket and a try-out contract. A well-placed brother-in-law could do the trick just as well, or a reputation as a newpaperman, or (more often than one would think) a few years spent doing press relations for a movie star or a studio publicity department. Hollywood agents found journalists the easiest to place: they rarely had expectations, they were hardboiled and cynical enough to be glad of the windfall; they took the job for what it was.

Dinner

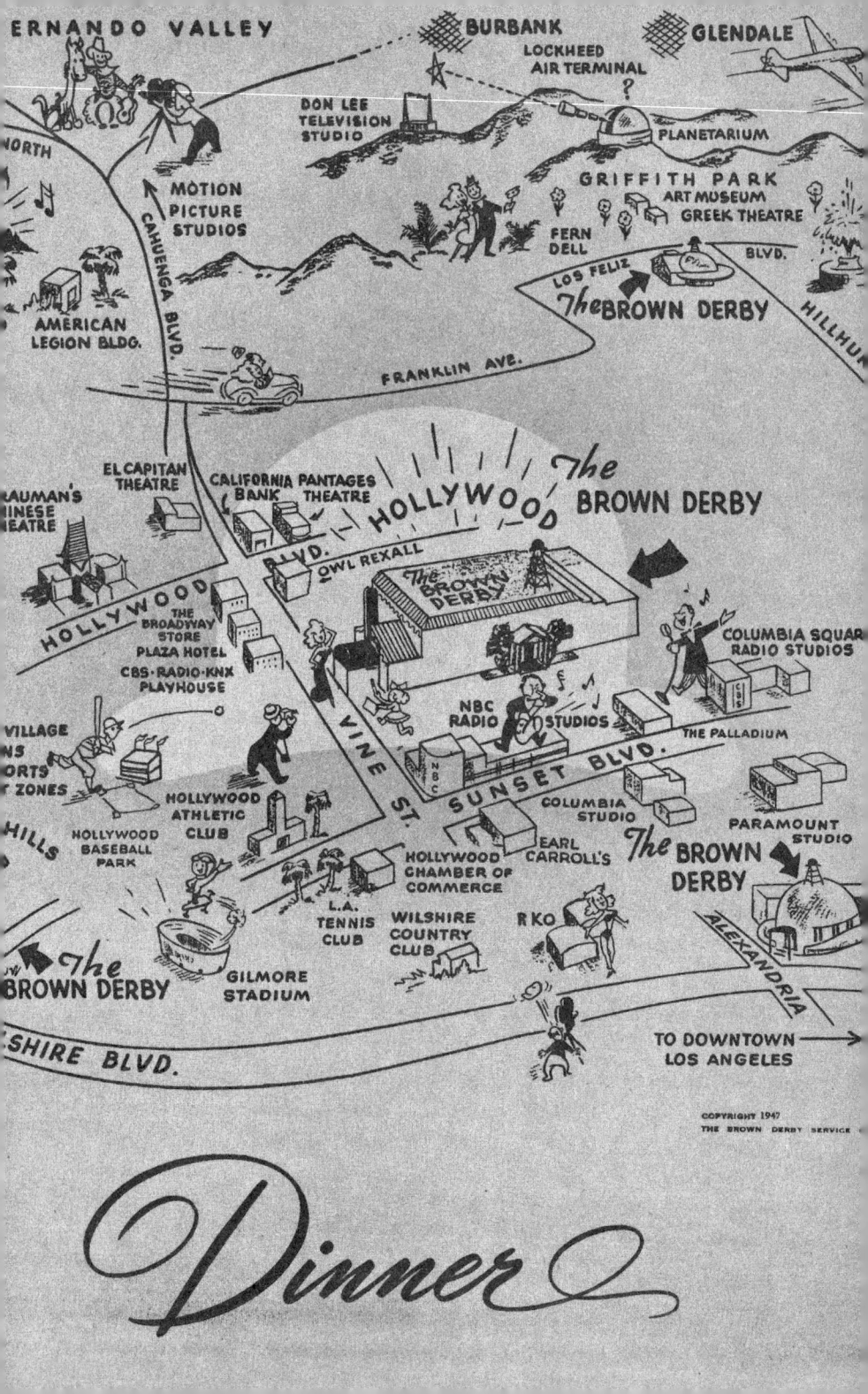

A solid sense of humor was essential to survive, or even prosper. Glad for those mind-boggling weekly salaries, newspapermen rarely saw Hollywood with stars in their eyes, or came with too much ambition. Fitzgerald made that mistake, believing he could apply his talent for writing fiction to this new narrative medium. It nearly killed him. But he was the tragic exception rather than the rule, even if the exception has become durably emblematic.

Still others went to Hollywood as one goes on a water cure or to the zoo. Most of the early clichés about the place, as James M. Cain once remarked in an *American Mercury* article, came from famous writers who barely stayed long enough to write windy dismissals afterwards, much as they did after visiting Soviet Moscow and Leningrad in the 1930s. These hasty and shallow impressions come to us mostly from those who never worked in Hollywood, or ever so little: H. L. Mencken, Theodore Dreiser, Evelyn Waugh, Blaise Cendrars and a host of others, who all viewed the place with a caustic book already in mind.

There was still another kind of writer at that time who never put a word to paper, but was essential to the business nonetheless. They rarely figured in those skimpy on-screen credits of the early 1930s, and they appear even less in film histories. But the moguls knew enough to retain these relics from the silent days, even if they kept on treating them as gagmen and rarely gave them a desk to sleep at. For these birds, being a "studio writer" meant impressing the boss once a week with an idea, some scenario switcheroo that would save the day. These were the plumbers of the "stuck" production. The most famous was Robert E. Hopkins, whom everybody on the Metro lot called "Hoppy." He rarely left the studio commissary. When a production was stuck, someone came and fetched him.

No one (except Kevin Brownlow) has paid much attention to title writers of the silent days, but when you compare a line from Marc Connelly's script of the wonderful 1926 comedy *Exit Smiling*, starring that great clown Beatrice Lillie, with the card eventually written by Joe Farnham, you can measure their importance. In this story of a traveling show, Beatrice Lillie's character was introduced by Connelly: "Violet, the patsy of the show. Born and raised on the stage. She knew life only as the stage reflected it." Farnham's card: "Violet, the drudge of the troupe. Who also played parts like Nothing in *Much Ado About Nothing*."

Joseph Farnham was also a film editor (under Thalberg's orders, he notoriously reduced Erich von Stroheim down to size, shearing *Greed* from eight hours to two and a half), but most of these men had been gagmen or writers. They all seem to have been Irish as well: Ralph Spence (who wrote for Keaton), James Kevin McGuinness, Malcolm Stuart Boylan, George Marion Jr. (also an actor, he wrote titles for Clara Bow, Colleen Moore and Mary Pickford) and, of course, "Hoppy" Hopkins. Of all those, only Farnham ever won an Oscar® for his trouble—at the first Academy Awards ceremony in 1929, after which the category for title writers was abolished forever.

Nevertheless, these guys were prized by MGM production chief Irving Thalberg, almost as much as dependable studio workhorses like Frances Marion, writers who could structure a whole movie and write intertitles and dialogue to boot. Having been gagmen, guys like Hopkins thought visually. "Hoppy," for instance, came up with the idea for the movie *San Francisco*, earthquake and all, and this one time he was kept on the project long enough to be credited for the story—a rarity for men of his ilk.

Then there was yet a newer breed of screenwriter. They'd waltz into the office of Zanuck or Goldwyn and start spinning a yarn, impersonating characters, telling the boss a smashing story—which they'd more often than not forget on their way to the track as the ink was drying on the check. In Hollywood, this high-wire act was called "spitballing." The men who practiced it (Rowland Brown, Gene Fowler, and the writing team Towne and Baker were the most notorious) were valued by studio bosses as much for their company as for the ideas they peddled; after all, the push cart, card table and nickelodeon days weren't far behind for most of these movie moguls; they still enjoyed a good con when they saw one. These early writers often were carnies or vaudevillians; all were gambling men, some outright crooks. They were the real Gold Diggers of 1933, soon to be replaced by blander but more solid "constructionists," dialogue writers, and other stalwarts of industry. Given a chance to become something else and shine for a spell, as in the case of Rowland Brown, they would sooner die than be promoted to the rank of producer, a fate reserved for the more sedate type of writer who would come later, like Nunnally Johnson. Still, for people like Wilson Mizner

Spitballers Graham Baker (left) and Gene Towne, who according to producer Walter Wanger, wrote scripts on rolls of toilet paper

or Achmed Abdullah, Hollywood was truly the end of the road, a mere codicil to an already full life. They had *lived*, truly lived, some of them nine lives or more. They may not have left much on the screen to be remembered by, but with lives like theirs, one wonders if they could have spun movie stories any better than their (possibly bogus) studio biographies.

When he died of a heart attack in 1945 at the age of 64, Achmed Abdullah had already left Hollywood behind. His last rooms in Manhattan were on the top floor of the Hotel des Artistes on W. 67th Street, just off the Park. Noel Coward, Fannie Hurst, Isadora Duncan and Norman Rockwell had lived behind the same gothic façade at one time or another. The wallpaper in Abdullah's rooms was green and gold—properly exotic for a man who left behind more than 27 volumes bearing overheated titles like

Steel and Jade, *Deliver Us From Evil*, and *Shadow of the Master*. He had a Chinese valet and drank Turkish coffee exclusively, but his impeccable manners and the crucifix dangling from his fob-chain made him look more like an Oxford don than a sheik. Although he studied the Koran at Al-Azhar College in Cairo, and in 1926 published an article in *Collier's* called *Why I Am a Mohammedan*, he still converted to Catholicism in 1936.

But then contradiction and duality were second nature to Achmed Abdullah, whose real name was Alexander Nicholayevitch Romanoff. He was born in Yalta in 1881, a city of holidays and treaties, where Roosevelt, Churchill and Stalin would later divide Europe among themselves in prevision of a victory over the Axis. His father, the Grand Duke Nicholas, was Tsar Nicholas II's first cousin; his mother, Princess Nourmahal, the daughter of an Afghan emir. The Romanoffs having imposed a separation between his parents for political reasons, Alexander was raised by the emir, Rahman Khan, and renamed "Allah's Beloved," which didn't prevent young Achmed from being baptized a Christian in an orthodox church during one of his father's visits to St. Petersburg (Leopold of Belgium stood as his godfather). After cosmopolitan studies at the Lycée Louis-le-Grand, Eton and Oxford, Achmed Abdullah joined the British Army. For seventeen years, he served in the Balkans, France, Mesopotamia, as well as Africa and China. He then joined the British-Indian Army and obtained the rank of colonel. He is also rumored of having spent one year in the Turkish army as a British spy. He first visited the United States as a low-level diplomat just before the first World War. By this time, he was already writing commercially in English, French and German. Between 1915 and 1924, he published two books a year, things like *The Blue-Eyed Manchu*, *The Trail of the Beast*, and *The Mating of the Blades*. Sometimes he would write treatises, such as the one he published in Calcutta in 1902, "A Grammar of Little-Known Bantu Dialects." It might be that his mottled lineage condemned him to the *n'importe quoi*—"mixed signals" was his middle name.

In the mid-twenties, he took a stab at prospecting in Nevada, but soon found himself in Reno dealing faro. His real strike came a few years later—on Broadway. He became a favorite of the Shuberts and David Belasco, who recycled his adventures (real and invented) in thriller shows like *The Hon-*

Achmed Abdullah, in mufti, spinning out another far-flung tale of adventure

ourable Mr. Wong, The Grand Duke, or Toto. Could the latter (or Achmed himself) be the model for "Toto" (Sig Arno), the coaster of mysterious origin and dialect who attaches himself to Mary Astor in *The Palm Beach Story?* At any rate, *The Honourable Mr. Wong* would be adapted at Warner Bros. in 1932 as *The Hatchet Man*, with Edward G. Robinson in the title role and a defeated William Wellman at the helm. In 1927, Merian C. Cooper and Ernest B. Schoedsack used the title of one of his many novels for their semi-documentary picture, *Chang*. Once in Hollywood, Abdullah's presence was both ubiquitous and spectral. He signed the novelization of Doug Fairbanks' last success, *The Thief of Bagdad*, while still writing pulp fiction for the likes of *Detective Story Magazine*, where he first published "Fear" in 1919. In 1935, he was called upon by Paramount to adapt *The Lives of a Bengal Lancer*, a title that could well have applied to our man. But, as one wag put it at the time, the studio mustered more writers than lancers on this production, rendering Abdullah's contribution moot, at best. The picture, however, was a crackling success, leading to the vogue for Old Empire yarns in Hollywood. This made Abdullah an expert consultant on all things British, from uniforms to coats of arms, club ties, flags and scabbards. He only left his station by Ronald Colman's stirrup or C. Aubrey Smith's High Command to go whip up a Foreign Legion yarn at MGM or Columbia. He became part of the lawn-bowling and polo-playing set, even though he was by then so decrepit he was relegated to the bleachers with old Indian Army buzzards like Sir Guy Standing and Lumsden Hare—minor character actors whose rank (at least in the movies) never sank below Major.

On occasion, one of Abdullah's earlier lives was specifically called forth, as with *British Agent*, a 1934 spy story set in Soviet Russia featuring Leslie Howard, whose role was loosely based on real-life British diplomat R. H. Bruce Lockhart. Kay Francis was his love interest, working for a Soviet secret service man played by future blacklisted director Irving Pichel. Anything can happen in a picture where J. Carrol Naish plays Commissioner of War Leon Trotsky, especially if the film is directed by Michael Curtiz, never a man to be bothered with historical accuracy. But the Warner ledgers do indicate that "Captain Abdullah," as he was known on this production, worked five weeks at the royal rate of $1,000 per. Wrong or right, Hollywood seems to have taken for granted the man's improbable military and social register pedigree. And why not? Who, in a company town lousy with impostors and snake-oil merchants, would have bothered to invent such a preposterous biography for himself?

Wilson Mizner's eventful life is more solidly documented. A line William Powell delivers in Tay Garnett's 1932 picture *One Way Passage* aptly encapsules it, and it's one Mizner probably wrote himself: "I went a long way and I walked a wide mile." But in 1926, when he repaired to Hollywood, settling into an outside bungalow at the Ambassador Hotel, Mizner was at the end of the line. That line had taken him far and wide all right. The youngest son of a San Francisco diplomat, Mizner went rogue early. Family tradition called for every generation to produce at least one priest, one physician, one lawyer, one architect, one businessman and one miscreant. Mizner's five older brothers had all done their duty, and then some: among them was a manager of the Alaska Commercial Company, and young Wilson's favorite brother was an architect almost single-handedly responsible for the "neo-Spanish" craze that struck California and Florida in the twenties; Addison Mizner had built most of Palm Beach and Boca Raton, but had to abandon the latter development rather hurriedly, and ignominiously, because of an enormous real estate scandal in which brother Wilson figured prominently. Fleeing victims and flustered investors, Wilson Mizner one day simply appeared at the gates of Los Angeles' Ambassador Hotel, behind the wheel of an enormous Packard town car.

Mizner's dodgy career had started early, nurtured by boyhood days spent on the Barbary Coast. San Francisco was then wide open, as were the arms and bed of this young fop, a giant-sized dandy who had a way with the dames. His motto was "Always treat society ladies like whores and whores like ladies." In 1897, as a young man of 21, he sailed north to try his luck in the Klondike gold fields. There he rubbed elbows with men he'd encounter again much later in show business, such as authors Rex Beach and Jack London, and Alexander Pantages and Sid Grauman, who would build legendary movie palaces in Hollywood. Mizner was the first to admit that he spent more time in Alaska handling marked cards than picks and shovels. Grauman

Wilson Mizner

always maintained that Mizner had managed a brothel in Nome.

We next find our man, still on the gold trail, in Nevada, where he worked for a time with Wyatt Earp, (who, like Mizner, would play out his string in Hollywood). Our man also worked as a "greyhound," part of a pack of professional gamblers operating on ocean liners, fleecing passengers and fellow card sharks alike—just like Charles Coburn and Melville Cooper at the beginning of *The Lady Eve*, before Barbara Stanwyck cramps their style. Mizner also managed fighters, among them puncher extraordinaire Ruby Robert Fitzsimmons, and world middleweight champion Stanley Ketchel ("The Michigan Assassin"). When Ketchel was found murdered at a Missouri ranch in October 1910, his ex-manager famously quipped: "Tell them to start counting ten over him. He'll get up."

Later, on Broadway, Mizner would know legendary gamblers like Arnold Rothstein and Diamond Jim Brady, as well as old roustabouts, ex-cons and embezzlers like William Sydney Porter, otherwise known as short story scribe O. Henry. While in Manhattan, Mizner ran an art gallery, mostly flogging forgeries to credulous rich folks. A couple of Broadway plays were based on his experiences, *Alias Jimmy Valentine* and *The Deep Purple*. The latter became a 1915 silent movie starring Milton Sills, and its 1920 remake was directed by Raoul Walsh (Mizner is credited as the playwright).

In spite of those early splashes, Mizner was mostly remembered for his larger-than-life personality, appetites, and gumption proportional to his uncommon physical size (he was 6' 5"). Those traits were also his downfall. He had to flee New York in a hurry because of some murky business with a rich widow he'd tried to take to the cleaners. Boca Raton was his last swindle of note. For months Mizner had sweet-talked gullible New Yorkers into buying parcels of a tropical paradise that was mostly malarial. As brother Addison drew mirific plans and sketches (which today figure in coffee table books lauding his architectural work), brother Wilson was back in New York flogging acres and acres of Florida mosquitoes to the highest bidder.

Once in Hollywood, his health declining, Mizner lived a somewhat more sedate existence, a fact that left him depressed. Mizner had rapidly become part of what passed for "café society" in Hollywood—if such a thing ever existed. One night while dining at the Ambassador's restaurant with

The original Brown Derby on Wilshire, brainchild of Wilson Mizner and his second home

Jack Warner, Sid Grauman and Herbert K. Somborn (president of Equity Pictures Corporation and the second of Gloria Swanson's many husbands), Mizner deplored, more bitterly than usual, the lack of night life in Los Angeles. Sure, there were roadhouses in Culver City, gambling boats off Santa Monica, even blackjack tables on the Sunset Strip—but no restaurant worthy of the name. Or at least, no clubby place open late at night, like the many show business restaurants he had known in New York. Somborn happened to own a plot on the Miracle Mile, just opposite the Ambassador. Mizner would only have to cross Wilshire to amuse himself at night. Jack Warner agreed to be a silent partner. The Brown Derby was born. Its success was immediate, more for the social life within its cramped confines than for its food—the place was a glorified luncheonette that stayed open at night, serving a simple, uncomplicated menu, nothing more elaborate than chili and hamburgers. But it came on china plates, amid exciting surroundings and star-studded regulars. The Derby could seat a hundred people, either at the central circular counter or the numbered booths lining the walls, each of which was adorned with a hanging light fixture in the shape of a derby hat. Worse than merely mellowing out, Mizner played doggie in the window, quickly becoming a featured attraction at the Derby, lording it over the rubes from his throne at Table 50, dispensing insults and *bons mots* in equal measure. In spite of the modest menu and the hokey decor, the Derby rapidly became one of the hubs of Hollywood life: a sort of annex to the Cocoanut Grove, the ritzy supper club within the Ambassador Hotel, directly across the street. Mizner fit in so well that when his associates decided to open another Derby on Vine, Mizner bought a few shares.

Meanwhile, he found another place to hang his hat when an old Broadway pal, Lew Lipton, got him hired at RKO to work on *Gambling Ship*, an early Cary Grant picture about the floating casinos that since 1928 were moored three miles off the Santa Monica shore. The movie was based on Paul Cain's *Black Mask* stories (later made into Cain's only novel, *Fast One*), but the film had little of the original's hardness or terrific pace. Mizner then moved onto the Burbank lot, hired by Jack Warner, who in spite of Mizner's frequent insults couldn't get enough of the old man. Maybe the youngest Warner brother envied his pal's reputation as a swindler. For Mizner, the appointment was timely. Beyond the weekly $500 he earned, he needed a reason to get up in the morning, and a place to hang his hat besides the Brown Derby. The studio put him in the patient care of Robert Lord, a young Zanuck collaborator who would later become a producer, notably for Humphrey Bogart's production company, Santana. They were supposed to be a team, but Lord did all the writing and typing. Mizner took to a big red armchair in which he slumbered all day long like a doge. He also had, according to Lord, an unsettling habit of tipping cigarette ashes in his hat, a huge Stetson he set by the chair. Despite all this, Mizner could be counted upon to inject some authenticity or wit in whatever prison or gangster yarn the studio was churning out, be it *Little Caesar, Five Star Final* or *20,000 Years in Sing Sing*.

Inevitably, Mizner ended up in a Hollywood picture as a character, in a film to which he made crucial contributions. According to its director, Tay Garnett, Mizner was even pegged to play the *S. S. Maloa*'s barman in *One Way Passage*, but he was already too sick to do so. Roscoe Karns took over behind the plank to make two more Paradise Cocktails for the fateful couple played by William Powell and Kay Francis. "Death is not tough

WILLIAM POWELL-KAY FRANCIS in "ONE WAY PASSAGE" - A Warner Bros. & Vitaphone Picture

enough," reflects his friend, confidence woman "Barrelhouse Betty" (Aline MacMahon), "he had to fall in love." *One Way Passage* was a romanticized version of Mizner's many close calls with the law. Powell's elegant-but-tough stance in the face of adversity came naturally to Mizner, who contributed many of the movie's best lines.

Lord and Mizner left a few other memorable gems behind, notably their script for *Heroes for Sale*, a particularly dry and violent attack on the American legal system, curtly directed by William Wellman. In this, one of Wellman's best films, the writers pleaded the case of WWI veterans who returned home addicted to morphine, a habit contracted in VA hospitals. It was the first time this problem was addressed in a Hollywood picture, and the writers pulled no punches deploring hero Richard Barthelmess' desperate fate.

At the other end of the entertainment spectrum, Lord and Mizner also turned out *Hard to Handle*, a Cagney vehicle directed by Mervyn LeRoy. It was typical Cagney fare, suited to his rat-a-tat delivery and cocky personality. He plays a man who can sell anything to anyone. "Grapefruits? Never heard of them." But when Mizner had Cagney drumming business for some phantom Grapefruit Estates in Florida and being indicted for real estate fraud by the DA, it was practically a private joke. On the other hand, a year after *The Public Enemy*, movie audiences were used to grapefruit jokes in Warner Bros. pictures. But this one took the cake: in *Hard to Handle*, Cagney was left holding the bag by the Florida promoter. He weasels his way out of trouble by launching a publicity campaign for a weight-loss diet entirely based on grapefruit, and ends up being awarded the Golden Grapefruit by something called the Florida Citrus Growers Association. *Hard to Handle* was all fluff and fun, but the movie's first reel, showing Cagney promoting and hosting a dance marathon, packed more wallop and grit than the entire two hours of *They Shoot Horses, Don't They?*, the laborious adaptation of Horace McCoy's famous novel that Sydney Pollack would make thirty-six years later. One even fantasizes that McCoy might be in the crowd scenes, as he was employed as an extra in 1933, when he could get the work...

There are many apocryphal stories about Mizner, as befits a man of his stature. "I'm dying above my means" is likely one of them. Mizner did not have the elegance of Arthur Caesar, Zanuck's favorite buffoon and screenwriter, whose Last Will and Testament stipulated he should be buried at 9 a.m., "so my friends and colleagues won't miss the first race at Santa Anita." Mizner would have approved, but his will simply left his estate to an old girlfriend. He came back from the dead three years later, however, in the guise of... Clark Gable. Anita Loos, the main writer of MGM's tremendous hit *San Francisco*, always admitted that Blackie, the gambler pitted against Spencer Tracy's priest, was based on Mizner. Loos knew him, of course, from many nights at the Brown Derby, but it is Bob Hopkins who furnished her with first-hand testimonies of Mizner in his Barbary Coast days. At the time of the San Francisco 1906 earthquake, Hopkins had been a groom in one of the city's best hotels, and he'd seen Mizner paint the town red on many occasions or burn through his entire roll at the gambling tables. He remembered the swath Mizner cut, the spring in his stride, and his incredible charm—something Loos would have been at pains to recognize in the decrepit form of the "Sage of Booth 50" at the Brown Derby.

THE PICTURE DESTINED TO STARTLE THE WORLD!
KING KONG
with
FAY WRAY · ROB'T ARMSTRONG · BRUCE CABOT
A COOPER-SCHOEDSACK PRODUCTION—AN RKO RADIO PICTURE—of course!
From a Story by Edgar Wallace and Merian C. Cooper—David O. Selznick, Executive Producer
RKO RADIO PICTURES • RKO BUILDING • RADIO CITY • NEW YORK

MARCH 1933
The Three Days That Almost Shook Hollywood

ACCORDING TO A 1933 *Motion Picture Herald* poll of movie exhibitors across the country, America's favorite stars that year were not Harlow, Garbo, Crawford, Montgomery or Cooper, even less Dietrich or Mae West—but Marie Dressler, Will Rogers, Janet Gaynor, Eddie Cantor and Wallace Beery. Respectively: an old battle axe, a nail-keg philosopher, a dime-store angel, a Jewish vaudevillian, and a blowhard. This decidedly unglamorous pantheon may seem surprising, but it also gives a pretty good idea of the sour stiffness of the period: Middle America is lowbrow and likes it that way. The jazz-babies are all washed up, Shirley Temple is in. The country has no more patience for New York sophisticates, with their monkey suits and endless cocktail parties. The most striking moving picture of 1933 is *King Kong*, deep down an all-out attack on the Metropolis and its vanities. When Kong climbs the Empire State Building, this emblem of unbridled development and speculation is brand new, its 102 floors three-quarters empty.

King Kong premiered at Radio City Music Hall on March 2, 1933, two days before the inauguration of the new President of the United States. In *Variety*, a full-page ad shows Mickey Mouse tipping his top hat "to the Leader"—but Disney is hailing the great monkey, "Leader of the box office," not Franklin Delano Roosevelt. In the ensuing historic week, not even the state-mandated closing of the banks could stop some 180,000 New Yorkers from watching Kong destroy half of Manhattan. More than $100,000 was dropped into the Roxy and Radio City cash registers.

In his inaugural speech on Saturday, March 4, FDR once again exhorted the nation to fear nothing but fear itself, even as California Governor

James Rolph ordered all banks in the state to close indefinitely. Wednesday was traditionally payday in Hollywood, but come March 8, MGM was the only studio that could meet its payroll. Employees were paid in cash, and cash was scarse. Newspapers were already hinting that companies might temporarily resort to scrip, monkey money issued by employers, as mine owners had done in earlier decades. Studio heads were hinting of either stopping movie production altogether, or radically reducing overhead and salaries. Some, like MGM's Louis B. Mayer, wanted the entire movie industry to accept brutal and "voluntary" salary cuts, as much as fifty percent, all down the line, top to bottom. During these tense days, ensconsed in the penthouse of the Roosevelt Hotel in Hollywood, captains of the motion picture industry held talks on how to confront the "national catastrophy," searching not only for ways to cope, but for how these dire events might be turned to their advantage. Specifically, they wanted to subjugate the only union in existence in Hollywood at the time, the International Alliance of Theatrical Stage Employees (IATSE), which defended the intererests of grips, carpenters and laborers on the lots.

On Thursday, March 9, half-a-million people watched an impressive U.S. Navy parade in Long Beach and San Pedro, the fleet visiting from San Diego. The following day, at 5:54 p.m., a violent earthquake destroyed much of Long Beach and its nearby boroughs. Had it struck a day earlier, there would have been thousands of casualties, instead of "only" 120 victims. The Hollywood premiere of *King Kong* was scheduled for that night at the Grauman Theatre, but Sid Grauman postponed it at the last minute, claiming his dancing and singing prologue ("with a thousand and one bongos," according to the ads) was not quite ready. Had he stuck to the schedule, the promotor would have offered his unsuspecting patrons an early and natural version of Sensurround. Aftershocks lasted well into the following morning. During the night, squadrons of Marines went ashore to help with the wounded and prevent looting. John Fante, who was in Long Beach that day, recounted the events in a striking chapter of his 1939 novel *Ask the Dust*, and for years afterwards shunned all brick buildings, according to his widow.

Still, as early as Saturday, the Hollywood community was celebrat-

Rose and Anaheim Avenues in Long Beach, being dug out after the big quake of 1933

ing that the studios had escaped any serious damages. Friday's aftershocks were barely felt in Burbank, for instance, where on Stage 2 Busby Berkeley blithely went on rehearsing 60 chorus girls for his famous luminous violin sequence in *Gold Diggers of 1933*, shot from the stage rafters. The tragedy even seemed to have a beneficial effect on the stubborn studio heads at the Roosevelt still holding out for drastic salary cuts: as early as Monday, they announced that work would resume at all the studios, and that a compromise had been reached with the Academy of Motion Picture Arts and Sciences, the inadequate in-house mediator that supposedly represented the interests of writers, actors and directors alike. The proposed cuts were also toned down: only those earning more than $100 a week would see their paycheck reduced by half during the period of adjustment. Salaries below $50 would remain unchanged, and those in between would be pro-rated down. In spite of staunch opposition from IATSE and a few stars (Maurice Chevalier, for one), 2,000 employees went back to work at Paramount the next Wednesday. A few days later it was business as usual in Hollywood.

In this spirit, on Monday, March 13, as a complete list of the quake victims blackened the front pages of local papers, *The Film Daily* in New York ran a huge banner braying: NO DAMAGE TO THE FILM COLONY. The quake's toll was 120 killed, thousands injured, and an estimated $50,000,000 in damages, but for *The Film Daily* the only casualty of note was James Brodie, assistant manager at the Imperial Theater, a movie house in Long Beach. He was killed when a canopy fell on him. In Hollywood proper, the same parochial cynicism prevailed. On the radio, comic El Brendel quipped in his famous Swedish-moronic accent: "It took dat to get de banks to open." Not to be outdone, Eddie Sutherland and W.C. Fields claimed to have footage of the quake hitting the sets of the picture they were making, *International House*. The scene is in the picture, the claim was widely believed in Hollywood, and it figures in many film histories, but the director later admitted it had been a hoax: they'd ordered their set to be put on rollers and vigorously shaken by a team of grips. As we will see, many filmmakers tried to capitalize on the catastrophe, and references to or recreations of the 1933 Long Beach quake would figure in many pictures to come.

But for sheer cold-blooded opportunism of another kind, few could top Fox's Sol Wurtzel. On March 11, a press release announced that he would immediately start production on a motion picture called *The American*, based on the life of Chicago Mayor Anton Cermak, whose corpse had just reached Chicago where it was to be buried with State's honors. Three weeks prior, on February 15, FDR had been in Florida for his first official presidential visit. During his post-parade speech, a Calabrese immigrant named Giuseppe Zangara attempted to assassinate the president, but instead shot Cermak, who had moments earlier joined Roosevelt on the stand. At least this is what the Administration and the press claimed. In fact, Zangara, a degenerate gambler, had been coerced by the Chicago Outfit into killing Cermak, who had been causing a lot of trouble for the Italian mob, much to the benefit of Cermak's political allies, Teddy Newberry and his North Side Irish Mob. The Democratic National Convention had been held in the Windy City six months earlier, and Cermak, an immigrant from

Scoundrels & Spitballers: Writers and Hollywood in the 1930s

Giuseppe Zangara

Bohemia who had built himself a real estate and political empire with the help of "white" (read non-Italian) gangsters, had thrown his weight and money behind FDR's primary rival, three-time loser Catholic Presidential candidate Al Smith. He also had campaigned on bogus promises to clean up the city administration. The Outfit ('Curly' Humphreys, Tony Accardo and Johnny Torrio) had supported Roosevelt with large campaign contributions and wholesale, often fraudulent voting blocks. So, unbeknownst to most Americans at the time, Roosevelt's Florida parade had been used to camouflage a Mob hit against a Chicago rival. Zangara had been a sharp shooter in the Army and would never have missed. Roosevelt even acknowledged in later years that he was not the target that day. Yet Cermak, who died March 6 of complications from the shooting, was brought back to Chicago where he was lain in state, lionized as an upright citizen, the victim of a swarthy anarchist. Hollywood would soon enshrine that myth when *The American*, hastily retitled *The Man Who Dared*, was released on June 30, less than four months after the Cermak's death. Helmed by hack director Hamilton MacFadden, it starred the then-little-known Preston Foster, properly mustachioed as Cermak ("Jan Novak" in the picture), and actress

Zita Johann, a D.W. Griffith regular. It caused barely a ripple at the box office, but even Darryl F. Zanuck (who, as production chief at Warner Bros., prided himself on picking stories hot from the presses) had not thought of this one, busy as he was taking over a new company, Joe Schenck's 20th Century Pictures, soon to merge with Fox.

The producer of *The Man Who Dared*, Sol Wurtzel, had been William Fox's secretary before taking charge of programmers at his studio on Western Ave. and Sunset Blvd. But the idea of making a film of the "tragic" life of Anton Cermak, now conveniently in the public domain, really came from an obscure reader at the story department named Lamar Trotti. This was a time when biographies were not yet the rage in Hollywood—Universal's Preston Sturges-scripted *The Power and the Glory* would be released in August, and *Wilson* still eleven years off. A native of Atlanta and a journalist, Trotti was given his chance at scriptwriting, but as he was new to the trade, he was teamed with Dudley Nichols, who, at 48 and with eleven credits to his name, passed for a veteran. Nichols was from Ohio and had worked in New York for ten years on the *New York Evening Post* and the *New York World*. His first Hollywood writing credit was on a John Ford submarine picture called *Men Without Women* in 1930. In spite of the negligible success of *The Man Who Dared*, Nichols and Trotti were to remain partners at Zanuck's 20th Century–Fox on seven pictures, including two for Ford (*Judge Priest* and *Steamboat Around the Bend*). On his own, Trotti quickly became the resident go-to man for all things Southern, first at Fox, then with Zanuck. Trotti's name is on countless 20th Century–Fox opulent (if not all memorable) productions like *Young Mister Lincoln*, *Drums Along the Mohawk*, *The Ox-Bow Incident*, *Wilson*, and *Brigham Young*.

Once, when someone asked him why David O. Selznick did not call upon him to work on *Gone with the Wind*—in spite of fellow-Atlantan Margaret Mitchell urging him to do so—Trotti quietly replied that during the three years it took Selznick to produce his epic, he had time to write no less than eighteen pictures. By the time Trotti died in 1952, he had written 52 films, not counting the unproduced ones. Trotti was rather affable, not exactly the acerbic figure Dick Powell cut in *The Bad and the Beautiful*, although Charles Schnee and Vincente Minnelli must have had him in mind

**OAKIE'S *a Scream!*
TRACY'S *a Panic!*
together they're a RIOT!**

They must have been a couple of other fellows before an inspiration teamed them up in this three-mile-a-minute comedy that even an earthquake can't slow up. It's a laugh a second...and a second laugh after that!

JOSEPH M. SCHENCK
presents
Spencer **TRACY**
Jack **OAKIE**
in
Looking for Trouble
with
CONSTANCE CUMMINGS
ARLINE JUDGE • JUDITH WOOD
Directed by William Wellman
a DARRYL F. ZANUCK Production

One year after the big quake, Zanuck played it for laughs and a big finish in this 20th Century Pictures production, directed by William Wellman

for the James Lee Bartlow character in the picture—a Southerner and a scholar married to his pipe and Gloria Grahame. During his twenty years in the trade, in spite of his professional stature, Trotti had many occasions to personally verify what Wurtzel, his first employer, told him when he started in 1933. As Trotti was angered by the changes made in his dialogue for *The Man Who Dared*, Wurtzel gave him the lay of the land. The production chief fixed Trotti through his thick horn-rimmed glasses and said: "Young man, today we broke your heart, but understand that we will continue to do so, every day you spend on the lot."

On March 20, a mere 33 days after his crime, Giuseppe Zangara's life joined that of Anton Cermak in the public domain when he was executed in the electric chair. Justice in the United States was swift then, especially in places like Raiford, Florida. The national press shed no tears. Newspapers described the 2,300 volts that snuffed out the life of the "swarthy immigrant." Nobody took offence either that "After the autopsy, four forensic examiners verified that his brain was perfectly normal." This *after* he got the jolt. *The Front Page*'s Walter Burns would have rejoiced. Not that Zangara did anything to rate sympathy from anyone: showing no remorse whatsoever, he dined "copiously" and sat calmly on the chair with no restraint from the guards. But when he learned from the warden that his last wish would not be granted—he'd asked his execution to be filmed by Fox's Movietone News—Zangara became agitated and swore mightily against "capitalist swines" and "swindling bastards," finally dying to the shouts of "*Viva Italia!*" and "*Viva Camorra!*"—hardly the black flag the press insisted he was flying under.

Not one to be outdone by Sol Wurtzel in the Topical Department, Zanuck made a lively picture with Spencer Tracy and comedian Jack Oakie about two telephone repairmen that included a spectacularly vivid earthquake scene set in Long Beach: *Looking for Trouble*, directed by the ever-steady William Wellman, which opened in March 1934, exactly one year after the Long Beach temblor. In the thrilling finale, Tracy walks in on tough-as-nails and blonde-all-over Judith Wood and starts roughing her up, trying to get her to clear his girlfriend of a murder rap. As she pulls a gun on him, the apartment starts shaking and the back wall suddenly cracks open. Then, on rather realistic sets, there is a recreation of the quake as walls and electrical wires fall on Tracy, Oakie, and the girl, who is seen fleeing in the street, only to be buried under falling bricks. She is near death, but One-Track-Mind Tracy jumps on a fallen utility pole, and, among the crackling live wires, connects his repairman's phone to the line to call his office in Los Angeles. He asks the superintendent to hook up the phone to a dictaphone, and manages to record the girl's expurgating last words as she expires under half a ton of bricks. One can clearly detect Zanuck's hand in this over-the-top flourish. He clearly loved, at this point in his career, jazzing up stories with gags like this—as he did with Rowland Brown's *Blood Money*, which includes a trick eightball that explodes on a billiard table.

It had taken Zanuck nearly a year to come up with *Looking for Trouble*. But as early as September 1933, he had hastily instructed his writers to inject an earthquake scene in a flaccid Lee Tracy newsroom programmer, where it clearly did not belong. The cheapy was called *Advice to the Lovelorn*, a watered-down adaptation of Nathanael West's *Miss Lonelyhearts*. The scene was perfunctory, not spectacular—just a newsroom built on a stage deck rocked by several grips—but who's to say West did not remember this five years later when he wrote the scene of an earthquake striking the Waterloo movie set in *The Day of the Locust*?

Clark Gable is more interested in Carole Lombard's gams than books in *No Man of Her Own* (1932), but when studios needed to fill faux library shelves it was manna for Hollywood booksellers

BOOKS BY THE YARD
A Short History of Hollywood Bookstores

CHANCES ARE EDWARD GILBERT would not have become a bookseller had his sister Florence not been a dead ringer for Mary Pickford, at least in the eyes of their stage-struck mother. Nor would Louis Epstein have lasted so long as "Bookseller to the Stars" had he not sometimes rented books by the yard to one or another studio around town. As with writers, the story of Hollywood booksellers is closely linked to the motion picture business.

Born in Chicago, Gilbert was only five when his family moved to Los Angeles in 1918. His sister was fourteen, old enough to be dragged by her mother to the gates of Triangle, Christie, Sennett, Famous Players-Lasky and other studios. By 1926, young Eddie was enrolled at Hollywood High, at Sunset and Highland, but his grades were fatally affected by his devouring passion for Tarzan—and all the other books Edgar Rice Burroughs was then churning out of his Tarzana studio in the San Fernando Valley. The American Jules Verne was the reigning tycoon of escapism, producing books and serials by the bushels, with the help of many ghostwriters in his employ. Eddie Gilbert collected gilt editions of Tarzan's adventures, and to fund this ruinous habit he hired on as errand boy for two booksellers who had set up shop on Hudson Street, between his school and Hollywood Boulevard. The two men were named N. M. Gordon and Stanley Rose. The pair recruited a third partner, Murray Ward, to open another shop next to the second Brown Derby that was opening on Vine Street. The restaurant was a curious structure, ochre-colored stucco and terra cotta tiles, with fake balconies reminiscent of a *Zorro* set. With good reason: to save money, co-owner Jack Warner had the head of his studio art

The Satyr Book Shop, adjacent to the second Brown Derby restaurant on Vine St.

department, Carl Weyl, design the building, which was conspicuously more luxurious than the original glorified shack on Wilshire. A rather impressive bar lined one wall, facing a series of booths usually reserved for VIPs. The famed Bamboo Bar did not exist yet, nor did Eddie Vitch's caricatures cover the walls. Outside, a gray-green canopy led from the sidewalk to the entrance, permanently lined with photographers and autograph seekers. To the left was the Eddie Cantor Gift Shop. To the right, a two-lane driveway to the parking lot behind the restaurant. Next door was The Satyr Book Shop, sporting its own little canopy and two windows: one looking out on the street, the other under the arcade—which was important, as the books on display were likely to attract the eye of automobile passengers going in and out. This opening of a second Derby on Vine was truly inspired because, beyond the restaurant's immediate success, the area took on a life of its own: not only did film stars and professionals pack the place to have lunch and conduct business, but a great many agents, managers and lawyers had offices in either the nearby Taft Building, at Hollywood and Vine, or in the Equitable Building across the street. In the evening, the Satyr benefited from the crowds exiting the picture palaces and legit theatres nearby, as well as the boxing fanciers coming back from the Hollywood Legion. Producers, writers, directors and actors opened accounts at the Satyr, and Eddie Gilbert spent his Saturdays and weekday evenings after school delivering books to the Beverly Hills homes of Ginger Rogers, Lew Ayres and George Cukor, among others. He also recalled a later, more voracious, client who lived nearby on Ivar: not-yet-director Preston Sturges.

Ex-libris stamps of The Satyr Book Shop and the Stanley Rose Bookshop, two former partners turned rival Hollywood booksellers

The two main partners of The Satyr Book Shop complemented each other: "Mac" Gordon was the business head, neat and prudent. Stanley Rose was already the spendthrift for which he would become legend, one of the crucial personalities that made this end of Hollywood a magnet for artists and writers during the thirties and forties. Originally from Matador, a cow town in the Texas Panhandle, Rose had once worked as a pest exterminator before enlisting and shipping out to France in 1917 to practice his craft on the Jerries. Whether or not he was a mustard gas casualty, as he claimed, remains a moot point; returning home, he was nevertheless interned in a VA sanatorium near Stanford, where he acquired his taste for books and modern literature—an intellectual penchant he always fiercely denied, hiding it behind his roustabout exterior. Ash-blond, built like a safe without an ounce of fat, the Texan professed a horror of physical exercise, bookkeeping, and intellectual conversation. Never the sort to wait for walk-ins at the store, Rose often packed two suitcases full of the lastest novels and went door-to-door like a drummer, visiting all the story departments and writers buildings around town. As he didn't drive—a blessing, given his usual state of ebriety—Eddie Gilbert chauffeured him to Goldwyn and Paramount studios in Hollywood, or to MGM in Culver City. Rose may have been a drunk and an autodidact, but he could peruse a publisher's autumn list and instinctively pick which books had a chance at the gate, a bit like a tout decoding the *Racing Form*. His tastes ran to the newer kind of writer, those not yet discovered or recognized, like William Faulkner, Nathanael West, William Saroyan, or John Steinbeck. During my conversations with surviving studio writers of that era, many showed me first editions of *The Grapes of Wrath* that Stanley Rose had sold to them out of his famous suitcases.

Many have hinted in print that out of those same suitcases Rose provided writers and producers with booze and pornography. His brother Jack had been a bootlegger in Texas during Prohibition, but the tinkling sounds probably came from his own stash; Rose was known to down more than a fifth of bourbon a day. As to the "erotica," as it was called then, every book seller worth his salt sold it to make the rent—and it was all rather innocuous fare, illustrated editions of Pierre Louÿs and the like, or less literary naughty stuff. During my research, however, I was to hear more about the mezzanine of a later Stanley Rose store, one that—if you believed the stories—made him a sort of A. G. Geiger, the smut peddler in *The Big Sleep*. Nothing could be further from the truth, as I was to discover from first-hand sources.

With The Satyr Book Shop, Stanley Rose and Mac Gordon had practically the entire Hollywood territory all to themselves, which wasn't saying much. Until the early thirties, Hollywood's need for intellectual nourishment was limited, and the Hollywood Bookshop had been enough to fill it. Situated opposite the famous Hollywood Hotel on Highland Blvd., the place was managed by a character named Stoddy, who sold mostly religious books. Bookstores in Los Angeles were traditionally concentrated downtown around Sixth Street, a twenty-minute and five-cent trolley ride from Hollywood. There were Holmes, Powner's, Parker's, Dawson's, and the Argonaut. At the corner of W. Sixth and S. Grand stood Jake Zeitlin's shop, already a magnet for bibliophiles and collectors statewide. A bit further on, Louis Epstein, future owner of Pickwick Bookshop on Hollywood Blvd. in the forties, sold used books on W. Eighth Street.

In 1934, an incident occured, inoccuous in itself, but which would soon have momentous consequences for the nightlife along the boulevard and push Stanley Rose towards his singular destiny. The Satyr Book Shop had published a pirate edition of a harmless—if a bit crude—little book by vaudevillian Chic Sale. *The Specialist* was based on a play about an outhouse builder, and was merely outhouse humor, sold for a dollar. At the time, book piracy was commonly practiced and usually ignored, but a female employee of The Satyr had been caught trying to sell this pirate edition at a department store. Somebody pressed charges, and Rose gallantly agreed to take the rap. He even spent a short time in jail. His associates must have made him a few unkept promises, however, because upon his release Rose abruptly sold his shares of the Satyr—only to open his own store across the street on Vine,

Louis Epstein's Pickwick Bookshop on Hollywood Boulevard

next to an eatery owned by Al Levy. At the time, every bookseller had as a publicity ploy his own ex-libris, a small removeable stamp inside each volume. "At the Sign of the Satyr" naturally featured Pan blowing his flute. For his new store, Stanley Rose came up with an art deco Sagittarius in terra cotta hues, whose arrow always pointed towards his former partners across the street. At least you would have reached this conclusion when hearing the loud, profane and frequent invective the Texan aimed at them over the traffic noise, especially when he was liquored up, which was often.

But the first Stanley Rose store was short-lived; at the end of 1935, Al Levy bought him out to expand his deli and open a cocktail lounge. That's when Rose moved fifteen blocks east, setting up shop at 6661 1/2 Hollywood Blvd., two doors from the town's most famous eating and drinking emporium, Musso & Frank Grill. The establishment, started in 1919 (originally at a different location) by Joseph Musso, Frank Toulet and Jean Rue, then offered above-average brasserie fare and a serious bar that still has a reputation today.

On the opposite side of the boulevard stood the Shane Building, where the Screen Writers Guild first had its headquarters. The ornate art deco building also had a bar in its lower depths called the Circus that could only be accessed by a single lift—if owner Frank Averill let you in. The place was famous for its discretion, its personnel carefully screened from the swankiest places, like the Montmartre or Texas Guinan's. The Circus' decor was more frivolous than Musso's somber wood paneling, with pink elephants stuck to the friezes above the bar, along with toucans, monkeys and zebras. Colors were peach, orange and ivory. George Raft was known to frequent the joint, as did other slumming stars. But any writer spotted on his way down from a Guild meeting earned the lasting, if not eternal, scorn of Stanley Rose and his friends, who were not all writers.

Rose had democratic ways and could make himself accepted by all sorts. His attitude never varied, whether he was at a bookmaker's or in the office of Louis B. Mayer, and if agents, painters, producers, writers and a few actors frequented his bookstore, Rose himself cottoned to pimps, track touts, cowboys, acrobats and cockfighters—the boulevard *demimonde*. As for the store, the place may not have lasted many years, but it stayed in the minds of those who were part of the scene—many of whom left written memoirs about it. As with all legendary places, these records contain many contradictory details, if not outright falsehoods. I've only seen two photographs of the bookstore, one of those for a mere thirty seconds. Although the main entrance of the shop was on the boulevard, most regulars entered through the backdoor, directly from the parking lot it shared with Musso & Frank. Writers would meet their dates in the bookstore, then conveniently slip out through the back and into the restaurant. This rather obvious *manège* was described to me by women who would have known, for often they were the dates: John Fante's wife Joyce (although, according to her, she was not always his date), Meta Carpenter (Faulkner's mistress in Hollywood) and Yetive Moss (more about her later).

Every regular I managed to talk to had their own take on the place, yet their descriptions rarely matched: there was a mezzanine, no there wasn't. There was a back room, for sure, often used as a makeshift art gallery. The same haziness applied to the restaurant next door: many described it as if today's main dining room existed at that time, but for years Musso's had only one long dark room stretching from the street entrance, its wooden booths going all the way to the back. On the left, where the bathrooms are now, but reaching much further into the building next door, was the famous backroom, where a select group of writers did their drinking. The bar, with its distinctive lozenge motif on the panels, is now in the added main dining room. But at the time, the backroom was sufficiently famous for Edmund Wilson to have written, in 1940, a particularly uninformed (and unappreciative) article on hardboiled writers titled *The Boys in the Backroom*. The place's reputation had at least reached New York.

Regardless of the East Coast snobbery, Musso & Frank and the Stanley Rose Bookshop were a real scene, the nearest thing Los Angeles had to Montparnasse, all things being relative. Musso's was where the Warner writers went every weekday to have their liquid lunch, since alcohol was a strict no-no at the Burbank commissary. At night, it was more like a salon. But the backroom was at once exclusive and egalitarian; it was one of the rare places where a highly paid scriptwriter could *not* lord it over a barely published but talented novelist. There were institutions drinking at the bar, such as Faulkner and Frederick Faust (author of Westerns and the Dr. Kildare stories, under his pseudonym Max Brand), but intempestive new bloods like William Saroyan, or marginal but respected ones like Nathanael West or even John Fante, were allowed to rub elbows with the celebrities. Two or three stories published in the *The American Mercury* or *STORY* magazine often counted for more than a hefty weekly salary at Warner Bros. The same reverse snobbism applied two doors down at the book store—only more so.

The Stanley Rose Bookshop was ensconsed between Norman's Art Shop, which promised "harmonic" [sic] frames, and the Gainsborough Beauty Shop. A bank and a drugstore stood at the nearby corner. Almost from the start, Rose employed a struggling musician named Yetive Moss, although his Texan upbringing made him doubt the propriety of having a girl so young working in such a place; the book store stayed open very late (midnight), and the clients were sometimes randy and rowdy, especially after a drinking session next door. But Moss, speaking with me forty years later, said she never had problems with "the boys." In her presence, Stanley

William Faulkner with his Hollywood muse and mistress, Meta Carpenter

forbade any rough stuff, even bad language. She never knew, for instance, what went on in the mezzanine where the erotica was kept and sold. She thought it was merely an office. But Joyce Fante remembered going upstairs with her husband and seeing "racy stuff."

Yetive Moss had come to Hollywood very young, hoping to find work as a violinist in one of the many orchestras employed by the studios or the many movie theatres offering live accompaniment for silent films. The coming of sound had changed all that. Thirty-five years after Stanley Rose's bankruptcy, she was still selling books, which is how I found her in a Westwood bookstore in the mid-1980s. As a girl, she was shy, but had been seduced by the night scene at Stanley Rose's. She didn't always understand what went on, she admitted, and some of the more outrageous shenanigans were kept from her. But she knew about the writers meeting their secretaries in the shop, and was amused by their obviousness. Women arrived early and alone. The "boys" joined them a bit later, often in bunches, already lit by whatever stimulating conversations or drinks they had shared. Many of these rendezvous were, of course, illicit. Moss especially remembered Faulkner joining Meta Carpenter in the store before going off to dinner with her. He was then living at the Knickerbocker Hotel, seven blocks away. Carpenter was employed by his friend Howard Hawks as a secretary, and would soon become a script supervisor for Hawks and many other directors. Her magnolia manners and speech enchanted the writer and made him forget his homesickness. Brownie snapshots she took of the novelist—in his room at the Knickerbocker, on the beach in Santa Monica, in front of the Hollywood Studio Club where she lived—leave little doubt that Faulkner's detestation of his stints in Hollywood have been greatly exaggerated, as was his so-called "mistreatment" by the studios. The only time he was grossly underpaid was during the war, a bad agent being responsible for his low salary at Warner Bros. Otherwise, thanks in no small part to Howard Hawks, Faulkner had earned as much as $1,000 a week in the thirties—a fortune during the Depression, especially for a writer whose books never sold much until the mid-fifties.

According to Yetive Moss, there always were men returning to the store after dinner, with or without their women, and always a client or two would wait until Yetive closed up safely before slipping next door for a nightcap. Moss was also in charge of dressing the window. Once, Rose let her do a small exhibition of the antique sheet music she collected. On rare occasions, Rose would push a novel he liked, usually written by a friend he admired. Yetive particularly remembered when the window went flaming red with copies of *The Day of the Locust*. But instead of exulting, its author Nathanael West also saw red, since he found the dust jackets particularly hideous: against a blood-red background was a yellow "Mickey Mouse" Mitchell camera, and rolls of black film spewing praise from his friends Dorothy Parker, Dashiell Hammett and the like. In fact, West had been so incensed by this jacket that he had wired his publisher, Bennett Cerf at Random House, asking him to recall the original 3,000 print run of the jackets so he could have them redone at his own expense. All in vain, of course. *The Day of the Locust*, among the three best novels ever written about Los Angeles, sold a mere 1,464 copies. It was also at Rose's bookstore, Yetive Moss recalled, that in the eleventh hour West sought a better title for his Hollywood novel. Six months earlier, Random House had accepted it under the title *The Cheated*. Now West wavered between *Cry Wolf*, *The Grass Eaters*, and *Days to Come*. West and Yetive pored over a volume of Shakespearean quotations, before settling on the Book of Revelation and its Exodus episode.

Even in the early 1980s, Moss remained protective and close-mouthed about her "boys." Only once during our many meetings did she volunteer any artifacts. One was a small snapshot of the storefront, which she would not part with, not even for an hour to let me reproduce it. The other was a god-awful painting author Horace McCoy had given her as a birthday gift in the 1950s, when he'd taken up the brushes. It showed a kind of fortress in red bricks with an eye in the middle, and McCoy had written "Yetive's House" on it, maybe a reference to her prim and guarded ways. According to Moss, the writer, then riding high on the late success of his worst novel (*Scalpel*), confessed that it had been painted "in an alcoholic haze."

The only other visual reference for Stanley Rose's Bookshop is a picture by John Swope (page 52) taken in 1935, just before he started working for the agent and future producer Leland Howard.[1] The photo is taken from the mezzanine and shows the store brightly lit with many browsing patrons, among whom, dead-center, is noted vagabond author Jim Tully, amid a coterie of admirers. To the side, actor Norman Lloyd is recognizable, arching his back against a stack of books. The clientele is strictly masculine, with a lot of pipe smokers.

In spite of the bohemian atmosphere he liked to encourage, Rose ran a serious bookstore: he stored art books in equal quantities with modern literature. Art books were stacked on shelves that formed a sort of half-wall that separated the main area from what was called the "backroom," which at one time was as famous as the one at Musso & Frank. The backroom at Stanley Rose's was also used as a makeshift art gallery where one could find affordable lithographs, etchings, or even paintings by Chirico, Klee, Lurçat, Masson or Kandinsky, as well as pieces by Calder or Brâncuși. In this, Rose also exercised his innate taste, though he greatly benefited from the advice and contacts of Howard Putzel, who owned a gallery a few blocks up the boulevard, opposite the Egyptian Theatre. Rose's main clients for art were the usual suspects—Edward G. Robinson, Vincent Price, and later Billy Wilder, but also writer Harry Kurnitz. Kurnitz not only collected art, he made a pile of money writing a series of crime novels and plays set in the

---

1 The photograph is reproduced in *Los Angeles, Portrait of a City*, published by Taschen in 2009. It originally appeared in Swope's 1939 book *Camera Over Hollywood*, an insider's look at the film community.

art world, or among bibliophiles, as was his *Fast Company*. These books featured a couple à la Nick and Nora Charles (although unmarried) who were breezy and wickedly funny. Kurnitz cashed in when MGM bought his novels to stock up on what they saw as a much-needed replacement for the soon-to-be-tapped-out Dashiell Hammett cash cow—their celebrated *Thin Man* series. Strangely enough, the "Fast" series never used the same actors twice; *Fast Company* had Melvyn Douglas and Florence Rice, *Fast and Loose* Robert Montgomery and Rosalind Russell, *Fast and Furious* Franchot Tone and Ann Sothern. Maybe for that reason, or because they were too sophisticated, or because they lacked the all-important tail-wagging terrier, they never really caught on with the American public, while the *Thin Man* series limped along until 1947 (Kurnitz even wrote one installment, *Shadow of the Thin Man*).

High-browed, hook-nosed, and sporting Harold Lloyd glasses, Kurnitz cut a memorable figure in California, even though he remained essentially what he had been in the East, a patrician Philadelphia snob, not about to let Hollywood chink his armor. He generally moved in circles more exclusive and exalted than the average Stanley Rose browser. Moss Hart, Cole Porter, the Gershwins, John Huston, Billy Wilder and Mike Romanoff were among those who sought his company and savage wit (he once refused to climb into Lillian Hellman's Volkswagen, famously prostesting: "I've been in bigger women than this!") He was always in demand for bridge games or to brighten cocktail parties, with or without his violin, which he always brought along anyway. He was considered an excellent scriptwriter, when he could be bothered, and had a reputation for working fast. According to Maurice Zolotow, Kurnitz declared that writing for Billy Wilder on *Witness for the Prosecution* was like toiling for two people: "Mr. Hyde and Mr. Hyde." Most of the filmmakers who hired him did so as much for his company as for his craft, like Howard Hawks, who while in France at the Plaza Athénée put Kurnitz on *Land of the Pharaohs*, along with a hapless Faulkner and a young writer named Harold Jack Bloom, who came up with the original idea of the film—which in spite of its commercial failure (and Hawks badmouthing it accordingly)—remains an interesting picture.

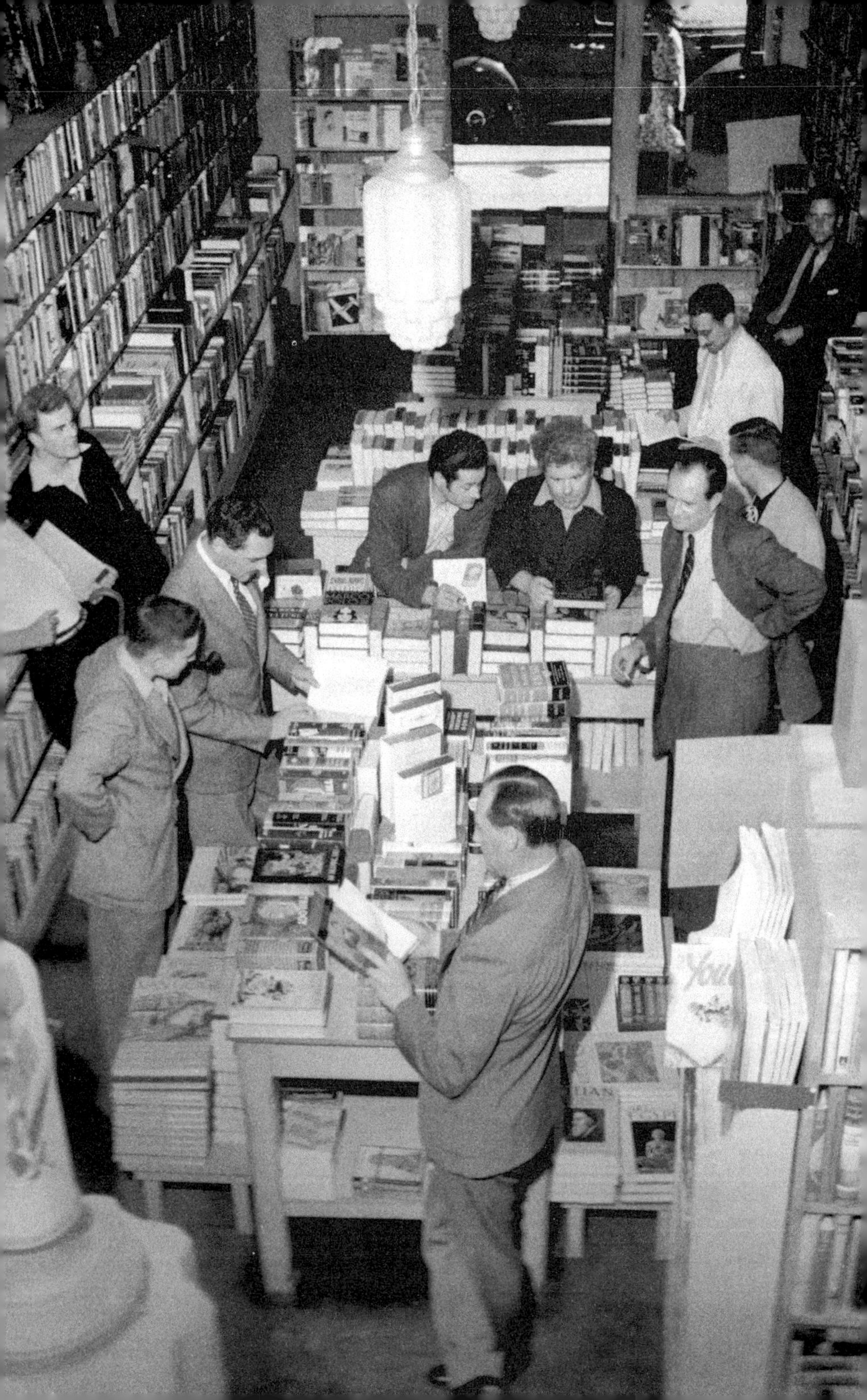

Stanley Rose never let himself be impressed by big-shot clients. Like the time E. G. Robinson asked for a discount. Granted, he had piles of expensive art books stacked on the counter. Yet as Yetive Moss went to inquire, Rose bellowed from the mezzanine for everybody to hear: "Tell Mr. Robinson that if he can't afford those books, it will be my pleasure to offer them to him." But in spite of his store's reputation and the loyalty of his patrons, Rose was never very far from bankruptcy. After several close calls, he sold the business to his primary one-stop wholesaler, the Los Angeles News Company—although he remained on as manager.

Rose was a victim of both his generosity and his carelessness. Stealing was endemic in the store. As he was often drinking next door during the quiet afternoon hours, Rose would ask *anyone* to keep an eye on the till, sometimes people he'd never seen before. Patrons often would leave with books, calling out, "put this on my tab," even if they did not have credit. In spite of this, Rose was always good for a touch. Any writer he liked could eat lambchops on-the-cuff next door, on his tab. For years he let a particularly unlucky and impoverished agent, Ben Medford, squat in his office and use the phone. Rose lived in a minuscule two-room studio above a garage at 1337 N. Formosa Avenue, but he was rarely alone in it, always offering shelter to somebody. He was on good terms with lots of people, with booze as the usual mixer: Gene Fowler, Bill Saroyan, the painter Fletcher Martin and the Irish actor Thomas Mitchell were his regular companions. Apart from Saroyan, they all had hollow legs. Martin, who later would find fame with his illustrations for *Life*, his horrible portraits of Charles Laughton and Sylvia Sidney, and his boxing tableaux for *Sports Illustrated*, was then employed at Earl Hays, a printer whose main clients were in the film industry. Whenever a production needed a poster, a Civil War gazette, or an engraved invitation to the ball, they called Hays. As a painter on his own time, Fletcher worked in the populist vein then in vogue, led by Grant Wood, George Bellows and Thomas Hart Benton. As for Thomas Mitchell, his friendship with Rose would have been surprising, given the blanket contempt in which the Texan held all thespians and movie folk. But Tommy Mitchell was no matinee idol; he had started as a newspaperman and come to acting rather late, always playing drunks for the likes of John

Ford or Frank Capra. And he was a pure-blooded Mick, which for Rose meant immediate absolution of all other failings. Saroyan often recounted a fishing day on the Malibu Pier where the two men spent more time feeding the fish than catching them, so bad was their hangover. Other writers always wanted Rose to come with them on hunting trips, even if he could hardly afford it. With Faulkner, he went after boar on the Channel Islands. In the winter, he drove south to Mexico with Wells Root and Nathanael West, hunting quail and partridges. Any pretext to desert the bookstore and go drinking.

For these very reasons, Rose hired in 1937 a young man whose name still is found on the boulevard, when all the others are long gone and forgotten. Ironically, he died before all of them. Larry Edmunds, born Lawrence O'Connell Edmunds in 1906, had studied geodesic engineering and was occasionally working as a land surveyor when Rose met him. Their association was as brief as it was explosive. Larry Edmunds was, of course, black Irish, and from all accounts incredibly handsome. His association with Rose did not survive their binges and bickerings for very long. In the fall of 1938, after a particularly violent row with his boss, Edmunds stalked off to go work for Milton Luboviski, a boy his age who had a leftist bookstore on La Brea. Book of the Day was no more than a bungalow turned into a store, and it sold radical literature almost exclusively. Sometimes, when he came to open the store at ten in the morning, Luboviski found Edmunds on the front steps, dead drunk. But Larry Edmunds could also turn on the charm, and he had incredible connections. He was said to have seduced half of the female stars in Hollywood, furnished Marlene Dietrich with pornography, and flooded Southern California with contraband volumes of *Tropic of Cancer*, which he brought in (according to legend) on banana boats via the Panama Canal. These tall tales are still in circulation today, even though denied by all his friends and associates. Edmunds can't confirm or deny, for on August 31, 1941, he was found lying on the linoleum floor of his kitchen, his head in the gas oven. Alerted by the police, Luboviski went to the small apartment on Gordon Street. The walls were pocked with holes made with a hunting knife, which Edmunds had thrown many times, maniacally. A note he left explained this final act: "Too many little green men. Couldn't kill them all. Time to go." The six diaphragms found carefully aligned at the bottom of a bedside drawer should have confirmed his reputation as a ladies' man, but according to his friend Milton, the rubber was dried and cracked, a sign that this sort of life was a thing of Edmunds' past.

Only a year earlier, he had experienced the biggest day of his life, a Sunday in September when he was doing inventory with his associates Luboviski and Janet McFarlane at the store, which they had just moved to the corner of Selma and Cahuenga. A gnomish, bald-pated man knocked at the door. The sign read CLOSED, but the man kept banging on the glass. Luboviski kept shouting back "*Inventory!*," until finally the guy held a crumpled piece of paper against the glass, on which he had written: HENRY MILLER. There was no inventory that day, nor during the three following. For the young trio (Edmunds was 34, the other two 27), Henry Miller was the greatest writer of their generation. They all had read *Tropic of Cancer*, proud owners (collectively) of two copies of the Obelisk Press edition, with the famous crab cover designed by Jack Kahane's 15-year old son, Maurice Girodias. The books had been smuggled from Paris by a friend, not on a banana boat. Miller had heard of the bookstore through a friend in New York just before setting off on the car trip through the States that would a year later result in *The Air-Conditioned Nightmare*. That night the trio took Miller to dinner, on their dime. For once, they were with a writer even more broke than they were. Generally, they had to accept the hard-to-swallow fact that, while they allowed themselves $15 or $30 a week for living expenses, most of their scriptwriter clients drew $300, $500, sometimes $2,000 a week—which did not stop them from running very long tabs at the store. Forty years later, Luboviski was still rattled that Dalton Trumbo's tab once reached $950.

After their partner's death, Luboviski and McFarlane kept the bookstore going until Milton was drafted and sent to the Pacific. Then in March 1946, one marriage, one divorce and two lease changes later, Luboviski reopened the shop on N. Cahuenga, renaming it the Larry Edmunds Bookshop in memory of his mercurial friend. In 1952 he moved again, this time on the boulevard proper, across the street from Musso & Frank, the store progressively becoming, if not the best specialty house in town, at least the most well known—with clients ranging from Antonioni to Truffaut. Totally against his will, Luboviski acknowledged that by 1982 the store was specializing in cinema books, movie posters and lobby cards. Gone were the modern first editions and the radical literature.

Stanley Rose's store did not last half that long. In the thirties, he was the only bookseller on the boulevard, but by the end of the decade Louis Epstein had opened his store, in front of the Egyptian. There had been another bookseller, in the arcade of the theatre—a German refugee named Braun; and a used and discount book shop run by a man named Salop, on Vine Street. And Verne Chute, author of *Flight of an Angel*, ran a bookstore further east, on Vermont. But Epstein's Pickwick Books was assuredly Rose's main competitor, even if the two men remained friends to the end. In fact, as time went by, Rose relied more and more on Epstein to get his books, as one by one his suppliers refused him credit. If Stanley Rose remains in history as the writers' bookstore, Epstein's was "Bookstore of the Stars," at least in his advertisements and on the store's canopy. After all, as Epstein once recounted to me, he'd had Marlene Dietrich as a saleslady for a night. It was during the Christmas rush, the lines were long, and the actress simply took over the wrapping desk, without fuss or remuneration. A few lucky dogs even went away with "Sold by Marlene Dietrich" inscribed on their purchases. On the other hand, scriptwriter-producer Adrian Scott was always being importuned by customers because of his resemblance to one of the regular salesmen.

The movies helped Epstein in still another way: his Paramount account easily totaled over a thousand dollars a month. And the studios weren't only buying those books to fill their research library or to meet the story departments' voracious needs. Sometimes, they bought books by the yard. When their requirements exceeded the prop department's capacity, they called Epstein. Once, in 1932, when he was still selling used books on Eighth Street, Paramount put in an order for 15,000 volumes, which they wanted overnight. It was for *No Man of Her Own,* a Wesley Ruggles comedy mostly notable for co-starring Clark Gable and Carole Lombard, who were not married at the time but were already an item (it's the only picture they would make together). In the story, Lombard is on the lam and hides in an upstate New York town, hiring on quite improbably as a librarian. Gable is after her and bothers her between the stacks. Epstein had had to beg, borrow and steal from his colleagues to gather enough books, loading them in moving vans during the night—only to learn the next morning that the shooting schedule had changed; the books wouldn't be needed until the following week. But at seven cents a book, plus a penny each day for the delay, during the worst of the Depression, this was a lucky break worth a little frustration.

The movies also came to the rescue for Stanley Rose, but too late to matter. His difficulties seemed to grow in the same proportion as his reputation on the boulevard, and his alcohol consumption. After a first bankruptcy in 1939, he had to close for good two years later. William Saroyan tried to help by officially making Stanley Rose his agent, having him rep *The Human Comedy* to MGM. Saroyan went so far as to offer Rose a higher commission than was the norm. This was, of course, a joke: Rose was the last man you'd want in your camp in a negotiation, and the self-assured, cocky Saroyan did not really need an agent. According to Sam Marx, who headed MGM's story department at the time, Saroyan had already completely flummoxed Louis B. Mayer when he related the climax of his tale, an unabashedly manipulative scene involving a telegraph boy bringing a Chicano family news of their soldier son's death. Mayer was in tears and ordered a check for $50,000 to be immediately cut. Rose hadn't uttered a word, but still got his ten-grand percentage. Mayer was so taken with Saroyan he hired him as the scriptwriter to develop the adaptation, produce, and even direct his play. Saroyan was to first cut his teeth on a short film for which he'd have complete freedom. He took one of his old stories about a fruitcart peddler and started filming *Jazz* in Pershing Square in downtown Los Angeles, using real people. Besides its much touted "technical innovations" (this was when Saroyan could make people believe he had invented the wheel), there was a scene where a woman dropped a watermelon "into her cleavage." Reportedly, when Mayer saw the short he decided to hand over the direction of *The Human Comedy* to an experienced movie man, Clarence Brown.

During all his dealings with Mayer, Saroyan insisted that his "agent" Stanley Rose be present. But Frank Orsatti, brother of agent Victor Orsatti and an ex-bootlegger (he'd been Mayer's personal booze purveyor), was instructed to intercept Rose as soon as he walked on the lot, and take him away for drinks. The one time Saroyan put his foot down, insisting that his "agent" be present in Mayer's office for the "contract negotiations," Rose promptly fell asleep in his chair. Truth be told, Rose only ever had one client of note as an agent, the female bullfighter Patricia McCormick. That was in the last year of his life, when he repped her memoir *Lady Bullfighter*. Quite fitting for the only agent ever to come from Matador, Texas.

Of all the writers Rose had supported with money and connections, Saroyan was probably the only one to repay him. In 1937, humorist Sid Perelman did wire Random House with instructions to transfer the royalties of his last book to Stanley Rose. Should the total be under $250, he asked his editor, Donald Klopfer, to consider it a loan against future earnings. But the book was not called *Strictly from Hunger* for nothing. A year after publication, it had earned the royal sum of $12; at least this was the figure Random House cabled back to Perelman. The writer, who had come to Hollywood to work primarily for the Marx Brothers, was grateful to Rose not so much for his help and friendship, but for the support the Texan always showed Perelman's brother-in-law, Nathanael West. Their friendship went beyond admiration, as the two men shared the same taste for the boulevard's *demimonde*. West was particularly attracted to Mexicans, and he and Rose sometimes went to cockfights at the top of Beachwood Canyon or at Pismo Beach when they drove back from a hunting day. West was genuinely drawn to the criminal element, often claiming that a bank robber was more honest than a banker—a notion he tried to develop in his novel *A Cool Million*, a satire of the Horatio Alger hero. Which did not prevent the sly screenwriter from flogging the story to Columbia as an original and walking away with ten grand. (The picture, given to Sidney Buchman to adapt, was never made.) Whatever their ideological differences, Rose and West spent a lot of time together and made a cartoonish duo on the boulevard. Friends usually called West by his nickname, "Pep," a derisive reference to the writer's gait and manners: he was as clumsy as a possum and slow as a panda. But in Rose,

West had found his match, as Rose, too, moved as slowly as molasses. West soon took to calling his friend "Jeeter," after a character in Erskine Caldwell's *Tobacco Road*. (Caldwell was also in Hollywood at the time and frequented Rose's store.) Rose countered with his own special nickname for West, calling him "Tweedy," for the heavy Brooks Brothers suits the writer insisted on wearing under the California sun.

After the store's closing in 1939, Rose still had a few good years. He even managed to marry and produce a son. He and his wife Maude lived in relative (for him) luxury on Woodrow Wilson Drive in the Hollywood Hills. But Rose soon started drinking even more than usual; his friends avoided him, fearing a touch. At the end of the war, his wife left him, taking the child to her parents' home in San Bernardino. Rose ended up back on the boulevard, taking a room in a run-down hotel on N. Las Palmas, the next block over from Don the Beachcomber, the Polynesian nightspot on N. McCadden Place, right behind his old rival Pickwick Books (the hotel, still standing, is now famous in tourist guides as a location in *Pretty Woman*—Julia Roberts' fleabag hotel). According to Louis Epstein, his old friend came often to the store to gab and borrow money. Once Rose even asked him for a job at the desk. Epstein agreed, with more shame than regret. Rose did not last the day.

When he finally died on October 17, 1954, of a throat hemmorage, Stanley Rose was practically indigent. Yet there were a few people at his funeral: his mother Kate, who came all the way from Matador; Louis Epstein, his old friend; and Yetive Moss. Of all the writers, scriptwriters and artists he had helped along the years, only Gene Fowler showed up. This did not prevent a surprisingly large number of authors from later writing about their boozy patron saint and his famous bookstore—among them Saroyan, Budd Schulberg, John O'Hara, Erskine Caldwell, labor historian Carey McWilliams, Lester Cole, John Bright and John Fante—chapters, articles and reminiscences as fond as they are, for the most part, inaccurate.

THE HOLLYWOOD FLAGELLANT

THE MAN HAD BEEN TALKING to us about his friend Nathanael West for half an hour when, during a pause requested by the soundman, he suddenly mused aloud: "I wonder if Pep would have done the same thing for me. Over the years, I must have given ten or twelve interviews about him to biographers, or for documentaries like the one you people are doing. I wonder if he would have bothered…"

One had the distinct and uneasy feeling that not only did John Sanford ask himself this question often, but that he also knew the answer. His wife, who up until then had merely tolerated us, was listening from the kitchen. She readily furnished the answer, probably not for the first time, either. She let out a dry chuckle, not without tenderness: "Pep? He didn't even read your books when you gave them to him."

At the time, we should have paid more attention to the set-up between the two, and to this stiff but exceptionally spry octogenarian—the fury that sometimes broke through his professionally staid voice; the rueful way he told us upon our arrival, waving towards the opulent mansion, the well-kept grounds, the yellow Jaguar sticking out of the open garage: "Don't mind this," he said, "nothing is mine, it all belongs to my wife." A remark all the more puzzling in that it came unprompted. We had, in fact, wanted nothing more from him than the stories he could tell us about his old friend West—as he knew all too well. We did not know then that this was precisely the story of his curious life: that of a man from whom nothing was ever asked, but who had spent his entire existence explaining himself to the world—in dozens of diaries he'd kept since childhood and in haughty volumes few had bothered to read, at least until his ripe old age.

At the time we were making this documentary on Nathanael West for French television, Sanford had not yet published his five-volume memoir. We couldn't have known that the ten-year-old yellow Type-E Jag would soon be replaced by a breathtaking silver $35,000 model, the first of the many Jaguars that his wife, screenwriter Marguerite Roberts, finally managed to put in her husband's name after a half-century of marriage. Maybe she sensed she had only a few years left to live. Maybe she also realized it was her husband's absurd fate to survive a great deal longer in their golden Montecito retreat in the hills of Santa Barbara—a rare species of mollycoddled anchorite, a bellicose witness to a century that never wanted him.

Young Nathanael West

For thirty years, he'd patterned his life after Nathanael West's, whom he first knew as Nathan Weinstein: like him, he rejected his social milieu to become a writer; like West he went to Hollywood. Instead of becoming a screenwriter like West, he did the next best thing: married one who earned enough money at MGM to support five relatives, and keep racing horses, to boot. After West's untimely death in December 1940, Sanford spent the following fifty years proving to himself that he was as worthy a writer as his gifted friend, and that (as his wife always said, in her Nebraskan hardscrabble way) West was no longer "a stone in his shoe." Volume after volume, sometimes printed privately at his wife's expense, Sanford would pick and gnaw at his life's central conundrum: that he was a man who, in spite of his artistic ambitions and political gestures, never had the slightest grip on the world around him. He seemed condemned to always watch the world's events pass him by, his nose against the window. He never went to war, never went to jail. He seemed to write his books in expiation. His membership to the American Communist Party fell short of earning him even a footnote in the history of the blacklist. Instead, his wife would pay for him.

Still, John Sanford, born Julian Shapiro in 1904, seemed cursed by an implacable luck, which, far from making him happy, pushed him to obstinately document his life in every detail, in books that offer a precious take on two lives more interesting than his: those of Nathanael West and Marguerite Roberts. Indirectly, his writings also shed a light on the singular and not-always-negative role that Hollywood played in modern American literature.

During our filmed interview in 1986, even as Sanford claimed he couldn't do justice to West's brilliance and eloquence, you couldn't help but admire the clarity of thought and elocution of this old man, whom time seemed to have spared so unkindly, a clarity which might have come from his formative years as a lawyer. On the other hand, nothing could explain the vivacity in his voice as he recounted episodes of his friendship with West—memories that seemed to singe his brain, even fifty years later. We knew nothing of John Sanford or why he acted like this.

"I knew Pep, I must have been ten years old, and so was he. His family lived in the same building as one of my aunts, Seventh Avenue and 119th Street, in Harlem. I believe his father had built the apartment building—for that is what he was in, old man Weinstein, rental buildings. As a real estate promoter, he even had a rather big business at one time. Pep was still Nathan Weinstein then, and I Julian Shapiro. I never saw him play like kids did in our neighborhood. I still see him sitting on his front steps, looking at us playing marbles, with disdain. We went to the same school, DeWitt Clinton, but he was one class above me, so it is much later, in 1925, that our paths crossed again. This happened one summer in Asbury Park, on a golf course. We hadn't seen each other for a dozen years, and what he told me that day changed my life. I was asking him what he was doing. "I'm writing a book," he said. I was stunned. Writing a book, for me, was inconceiveable. But immediately it looked to me the noblest thing I could dedicate my life to. From then on, the little enthusiasm I had for becoming a lawyer completely vanished. I had sleepwalked through law school and had joined my father's firm, but even when his practice failed and my family needed my financial support, I quit everything to write.

Scandalously. Selfishly. I never did anything in my life but write."

In spite of his striking declaration of intent in 1925, Nathan Weinstein was still six years away from publishing his first book. In the meantime, he would change his name, take the *de rigueur* trip to Paris, absorb all that Dada and the Surrealist movement had to offer, and acquire the annoying habit of dropping Marie Laurencin's or George Grosz's names in his conversations. He also collaborated with William Carlos Williams in *Contact*, the literary review founded in Paris by Robert McAlmon, which two New York booksellers, David Moss and Martin Kamin, had just taken over. It was under their short-lived imprint (PARIS-NEW YORK, said the title page) that his first book, *The Dream Life of Balso Snell*, finally appeared in the spring of 1931, under white and sky-blue wrappers. The intellectual cachet of this limited but decidedly tony first publication was more nose-thumbing than anything else for West; he was still enamoured of canards, impostures, and all things Dada. As it was, this *Contact* publication was rather tardy—in fact it was the last book of the imprint, bringing to a close a particularly fecund period of literary experimentation by people much better known than he was: Gertrude Stein, Hemingway, Robert Coates, all had published in *Contact*. At the time, this confidential publication (500 copies per issue) was merely a coda to West's former life. He had been at work for at least a year on *Miss Lonelyhearts* and already knew one crucial thing about his future as a writer: he would always need a day job to make a living. The family business provided him with a sort of sinecure, a low-paying but ideal position for a writer, as assistant director of Kenmore Hall, a residence hotel on East 23th Street that had fallen into the Weinstein's receivership. Later, he would hold a similar job at the Sutton, higher in Manhattan, lower still in reputation. This position would nonetheless give him a certain standing among his choice circle of fellow writers, as he was able to help them out on occasion: inviting them to lunch, to the hotel pool, or letting them use one of the empty rooms in the afternoon for less socially acceptable but more pleasant activities.

"Pep was infinitely more sophisticated than I was," Sanford told us that day in Montecito. "I had everything to learn. He, on the other hand, had read enormously; the Russians, French symbolist poets, all the avant-garde

Nathanael West and John Sanford

movements. He knew all the names you had to know in music and art, and of course in literature. Jarry, Kafka ... He felt a deep contempt for his social milieu, rejected his family's vulgarity and lack of culture. He was not ashamed of being a Jew, as people often say to explain his change of name. But he detested certain aspects of Jewish life in New York, people who talked loud, like his father Max. Or the Fanny Brice sort of humor, everything that had to do with Broadway. He certainly was a snob: in college, he was always changing names, identities. Changing shells, really, for these were all protective. Just before he sailed for Paris in the fall of 1926, he asked me to go downtown with him. He had to pledge some sort of allegiance for his passport, and he needed a witness. He was already calling himself Nathanael West, but this made it official. A name which, by the way, says a lot about his love for putting people on: if he really had wanted to hide his Jewish origins and pass for good New England stock—well, with his looks, I doubt it would have worked!—he could have at least kept the Christian name in Nathaniel West—there was a renowned merchant navy captain in Boston by that name. Instead, Pep made a point of keeping the Biblical spelling, Nathanael. Nathaniel is the Puritan deformation of Nathanael."

Sanford may have been disdained somewhat by his friend, but he nevertheless contributed to the difficult birth of *Balso Snell*, proofreading no less than four times the provocative novel, which related the adventures the eponymous hero had in the anus of the Trojan horse. For his trouble, West gave him copy #2 of the hardcover limited run of fifteen. In contrast with the already scarce folio edition, these copies had gold lettering on a white field, framed between two light blue vertical bands. They were all signed, but Sanford's copy was inscribed "For Julian, with affection. Nathanael West." According to Sanford, West had first wanted to dedicate his Trojan story: "From one horse's ass to another." On the other hand, it seems typical of their one-way friendship that Sanford had to buy West's three subsequent novels at Stanley Rose's bookstore.

In the summer of 1931, however, the two were still close enough to go vacationing upstate together, purportedly to work on their respective novels. They stayed for two months in a lodge at Viele Pond, a place Sanford knew near Warrensburg in the Adirondacks. Having previously acquired, for $195, a Ford all too obviously stolen, they piled in fishing rods, rifles, ammunition, canned goods and survival manuals, and drove up along the Hudson River, full of excitement and expectations. "Two Jews from Harlem into the wilderness," as Sanford would jocularly put it years later in front of our camera. The lodge, rented sight unseen, was beyond their wildest dreams: for $25 a month they had the run of seven furnished rooms and 2,500 acres of woods, pastures, ponds and mountains. The owner only wanted the place occupied to discourage poachers. Sanford often used this idyllic sojourn to Viele Pond as material for his novels. According to him, West was no Natty Bumppo, not by a long shot. He showed the same ineptitude in hunting as in fishing, which did not prevent him from dispensing advice on the art of building a campfire, or gutting a lake perch. "One day he pointed a loaded shotgun against my stomach. The safety wasn't even on… Save for writing, he had no coordination in anything whatsoever: he needed both hands to light his cigarette without singeing his mustache. At the wheel of a car, when he signaled right, he turned left. I have always believed that at that crossroads near El Centro where he was killed, he always intended to stop. But when Pep thought stop, he stepped on the gas."

Between fishing and long walks through the woods, Shapiro worked on what would become his first novel, *The Water Wheel*, and West on *Miss Lonelyhearts*. The only drawback for Sanford was that his friend needed to read aloud what he had just written. "He was constantly revising, and he did not know how to work otherwise: he had to hear the words to determine if they were the ones he was after."

It had been several years since Sid Perelman, West's brother-in-law, had given him these lonelyhearts letters, which he'd gotten from a female columnist at the *Brooklyn Eagle*. Strangeley enough, the humorist and future Marx

Brothers dialogue writer never knew what to make of them. West, on the other hand, was haunted by these pathetic calls for help, and from them he eked out what is possibly his most accomplished novel—his most cruel at any rate. Still under the influence of William Carlos Williams (*In the American Grain*, in particular), he was tempted to incorporate heterogenous and non-literary elements in his novel. In fact, he saw *Miss Lonelyhearts* as a comic-strip, one that would start as hilarious satire and end in tragedy.

Julian Shapiro, for his part, was still writing the inevitable coming of age novel, half defiant, half confessional. His hero was named John B. Sanford, which he later took as a pen name for his subsequent books. Sanford's hapless shadowing of West had already started. For instance, he kept up an active correspondence with William Carlos Williams (which he eventually published, of course), long after West had broken with the doctor-poet from Rutherford, New Jersey. West had no use for patrons or models, however flattering and prestigious. By contrast, when Sanford had gone to London (as always, in West's footsteps), he had wrestled a short interview with T. S. Eliot to show him some of his writings, and brought back a letter from the great man, which he could not resist framing and hanging in his office. On seeing it, West told him: "This is not a good letter. You ought to put it away." Sanford had refused to read between the lines, not realizing that Eliot's excessively polite words made very clear what he really thought of Sanford and his writing.

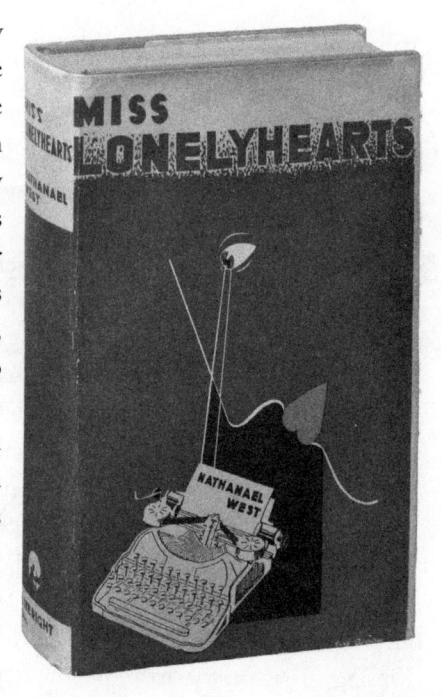

When *The Water Wheel* was finished, West asked to read it. "The only time this happened," Sanford made a point of saying, sixty years later. After reading it, West said nothing about the novel, its worth or its style. He just remarked, in no uncertain terms: "This girl, you'll have to change her. I recognized her." Unlike Hemingway or John O'Hara, West was not the sort to adorn his novels with sexual trophies. He was very clear about what one could and couldn't do. Yet, Sanford claimed that his friend's chivalry and sense of propriety were highly selective. "He never swore, but he was no prude. He had sexual relations like everybody else, but he kept it very discreet. Around the time he published *Balso*, he was engaged to a sensational girl, Alice Shepard. She's the *A. S.* in the dedication of *Balso*. She corresponded to his ideal when it came to women. He liked them tall, WASP, horsey. Alice was all this, and more. She was the favorite model of Elizabeth Hawes, the clothing designer and fashion critic. Pep and Alice were to get married. He already worked at the Sutton by then—this is when he comped Lillian Hellman and Dashiell Hammett. Hammett locked himself in one of the hotel's tiny rooms, trying to finish *The Thin Man*. One night, Pep, Alice and Lillian went out together. Afterwards, they walked Alice to Grand Central, where she took her train for New Rochelle, where she lived. And I don't quite know what happened, but all night long Alice tried to reach Pep on the phone at the Sutton, and he never answered. Now, he may have been drunk in some bar, I don't want to insinuate anything. I only know that the next day they had a fight, and Alice broke their engagement. This was an enormous shock to Pep, because this marriage was very important to him. Alice had been introduced to him by his sister Laura, and when you know what Laura was to Pep..."

Others were less circumspect than Sanford, and jumped to conclusions. Jay Martin, West's biographer, already had this story (probably from Perelman), even though he chose not to use it—one of the frequent cases where a biographer has to mince-step over the minefield of people's feelings, especially when someone as litigious as Lillian Hellman was involved. After her death, however, several Hellman biographers wrote how she had simply offered Pep to spend the night with her—one of these one-night stands she often had in a vain attempt to stir up Hammett's jealousy.

In the summer of 1935, when West found himself in Hollywood with no work, he was in such desperate straits (not to mention a very painful case of gonorrhea) that he called on Hammett to get him hired at MGM. The detective-turned-successful-writer was at the time spending most of his days drunk and unproductive in the penthouse he rented at the Beverly Wilshire, but he was still in a position to help. Even though Hammett's contributions to the succesful Nick and Nora series largely stopped after the first movie (he provided the story treatment for the sequel, *After the Thin Man*), he still held prestige and influence with the studio. But, according to West, Hammett chose to humiliate the man who had helped him at the Sutton when he was trying to finish *The Thin Man*. After inviting West to a party, Hammett told him, loud enough for everyone to hear, that he had no money on him that night, and to come back the next week. Aware of West's embarrassing medical condition, Hammett could not resist telling a female guest who was trying to put the make on West: "Forget it, this guy doesn't have a pot to piss in." This is not merely Hollywood gossip. The letters West sent to New York that summer leave no doubt as to his resentment of Hammett: "He made me eat the carpet," he wrote to a friend.

Sanford, for one, did not seem surprised by this harshness, when told about it. "In Hollywood, writers did not help each other, even if they were friends elsewhere. Here they were rivals, enemies. There was just too much money involved. This sort of thing would never happen between two novelists. What is there to compete for? A handful of readers somewhere? One of those paltry advances publishers gave you? But in Hollywood, yes, this was a job, and a salary that at the time, in the middle of the Depression, was almost inconceiveable."

Sanford had arrived three years later than West, but the two started in Hollywood at the same entry level, with a salary of $350 a week, six months guaranteed, and a paid return train ticket—just in case. Both had been invited for tryouts on the strength of their novels; neither *Miss Lonelyhearts* nor *The Old Man's Place* had sold many copies, but both received good notices, and that was enough. The Hollywood manna was timely, as both men were hard-up.

West joined Columbia's junior writers pool in the summer of 1933, a few months after his novel was published. As always with him, the happy event was fraught with almost comical catastrophies: *Miss Lonelyhearts* was barely out and receiving encouraging notices when his publisher, Liveright, went under. Nearly 2,000 copies of the 2,200 initial run were seized by creditors. Horace Liveright, whom his colleague Bennett Cerf once called "the John Barrymore of publishing," had already been pushed out, and died soon after. By the time Harcourt, Brace & Company bought the plates and re-released the novel, its good notices had been forgotten. West had to be satisfied with a *succès d'estime*. The movie sale to Darryl Zanuck ($4,000 less commissions) and the Columbia job were his only solace. Staying with his sister Laura and Sid Perelman in their faux-provençal house on Cazaux Drive in the Hollywood Hills, West was immediately put to work and not a little shocked, as he had heard stories about writers being brought in on obscene salaries, only to do nothing but wait. This didn't apply, however, to $300-a-week junior writers, especially at Columbia. "They're not fooling here," West wrote his friend Josephine Herbst back East, "All the writers are in their cubicles typing like mad, and God help you if you stop for a minute, because as soon as you do, some guy pops his head into the door checking on you to see if you're really thinking. Otherwise, it's like the hotel business."

Only West could come up with this last analogy, but all in all on his first try he did not find the dream factory any more demeaning than what he'd been doing in New York; and, even at this beginner level, it paid infinitely better. Besides, just as he had at the Sutton, where he observed the shenanigans of his lowlife clients (going so far as steaming open their mail, with the eager help of Lillian Hellman), he would find Hollywood an equally fascinating cesspool. He was never attracted to the glamour and glitter of it, being more interested in the service doors and back alleys. But it would have to wait two years before his return, because, come winter, Columbia did not pick up his contract. He was already on the train to New York on December 13 when 20th Century Pictures, Zanuck's upstart company (following his departure from Warner), released *Advice to the Lovelorn*. Even if West received credit for the story, it was based on *Miss Lonelyhearts* only nominally, being more of the typical newspaper yarn they churned out almost monthly. Still, motormouth Lee Tracy was entertaining as the reporter demoted to the lonelyhearts desk, and so was Alfred Werker's movie, in its crass way. It was in any case much better than the respectful but turgid version Dore Schary would make of it at MGM in 1958. Given the savage humor of the novel, it comes as no surprise that it could not be adapted to the screen in any meaningful way. Still, West may have been set straight right off the bat: he was intrigued and beguiled enough to keep paying his Screen Writers Guild dues.

John Sanford's tryout was equally fruitless, but he was even more grateful than West for the opportunity. He had been sponging off his ruined father for a few years, but the well had run dry. Sanford remembered that when he went to the New York Paramount office to negotiate his contract with Bill Auerbach, he had to borrow cab fare from the Leland Hayward Agency employee who had been sent to represent him. Hollywood was calling because of his first novel under his new name, *The Old Man's Place*, which Charles Boni had just published. It had not sold many copies, but the violent vein and rural setting of the story were in vogue at the time, and reviewers had been impressed. A Hollywood contract was almost automatic in such a case. From studio moguls to story editors, they were all poker players, and it was the equivalent of a "call" bet. It was a cheap practice, the famous seven-year step-contracts obligating only the writer, never the studio, which could let him go at almost any time. If the man was good, he was theirs for a relative pittance, at least for a few good years. If not, the writer was merely sent back home on the Super Chief. Given what Sanford had to offer the studios ("absolutely nothing," he liked to say), he had been somewhat lucky.

First of all, Paramount was a slightly different factory from the others: there was a veneer of country-club atmosphere. Employees did not punch clocks, as most did at Warner. You did not have supervisors and producers watching you constantly. Still, Sanford's first assignment confirmed his prejudices and the weirdness of the profession. He was immediately teamed with an experienced writer to graft a glib, commercial *Saturday Evening Post* story onto Humphrey Cobb's novel *Paths of Glory* (the same one Kubrick would adapt in the 1950s). The enterprise was already doubtful, but the partnership was the sinker: "Here we were, a Jew from Harlem and a Cherokee half-breed from Oklahoma, toiling over a pacifist story set in the trenches of WWI on the French front..." Collaborator Lynn Riggs was no ordinary Okie (a play of his would later become the basis for the musical *Oklahoma!*), but he *was* one-quarter Cherokee; and three-quarters homosexual, as he liked to say. As a front, he was conveniently associated with Jean Muir, an actress. For this reason alone, Sanford, though a cipher in the Writers Building, enjoyed a few months in the heady company of Franchot Tone and Joan Crawford, a close friend of Muir's. This social contact would get him, two years later, a brief and undeserved job at MGM, when Crawford demanded of producer Joe Mankiewicz that Sanford be hired to adapt *The Shining Hour*, the fashionable play she'd designed to be her next picture. In retrospect, Sanford sussed out that Crawford wanted him around mainly to keep Franchot from drinking too much. Whatever the case, the writer did not last long on the Culver City lot, but long enough to get some insights into the Hollywood process, which he later related in one of his memoirs. The skill he brought to these recollections would almost be enough to make one doubt his self-avowed lack of talent as a dialogue writer.

Before *The Shining Hour* job, Sanford had met Mankiewicz on one occasion, when the latter asked to read in galley proofs what would become Sanford's third (and best) novel, *Seventy Times Seven*. The request had surprised Sanford, but less than the sharp and constructive remarks the producer-writer made on his novel. Typically, Sanford did not heed *any* of the notes, but he never forgot Mankiewicz's parting words that day: "Don't look so surprised. Not everybody here is a moron. You know how to write books, I'll grant you that. But we know how to write movies, and something tells me it's not your case." Sanford was let go after turning in one draft of *The Shining Hour*.

Sanford met Marguerite Roberts during his short tryout at Paramount in the summer of 1936, as he toiled half-heartedly on a new adaptation of *The Great Gatsby*. First taken aback by his haughty coldness, then frankly irritated, she nonetheless became curious about this difficult man in whom she saw such obvious self-hatred. She was slightly older than he was, and vastly more experienced in both life and sex, and she eventually got him to let his guard down. They often met after work at Oblath's, the restaurant on Marathon just outside the Bronson Gate, which was one of the studio's watering holes (Lucey's was another, across Melrose). Small of limbs and height, short-haired, round and dainty as a Dresden porcelain, Roberts cut a peculiar figure in Hollywood. She had been a scriptwriter since 1933 and remained fully employed, first at Fox, then at Paramount; she would soon become a pillar of the MGM Writers Building. But, unlike most women writers in the business, she did not come from a genteel background and consequently she seemed to be always working on stories featuring roustabout sailors or legionnaires. Her scripts went to "manly" directors like Raoul Walsh or Louis Gasnier rather than, say, George Cukor. There was a reason for this: in spite of the tight-fitting work suits and high-heeled shoes she sported, Roberts could not have been more different from the ex-columnists or novelists who made up the majority of the female writing force. When seen driving her Phaeton roadster or atop one of the five horses she kept at the Pickwick Stables in Burbank, it was hard to believe she'd been born Maggie Azota Smith in a boiled-cardboard-and-tarpaper shack on the Platte River in Nebraska, the oldest of a brood of six she would soon bring to Hollywood and support. One of her brothers was a rodeo rider. Her younger sisters had names like Pearl Arizona or Bijou Arissa; like her own (Azota), their father found their names not in the calendar of saints but on cigar bands.

    She got a good Hollywood job the hard and usual way, through men, and she made no bones about it. The "Roberts" of her professional name came from one of the first men she hooked up with, a Colorado accountant always ready to up and leave town. Together they scoured the American West, making a living selling fake pearls in the lobbies of the hotels where they'd stopped. Both the landscapes and the men she met during this period would come in handy in her later script work, whether she was writing *Honky Tonk* or some other Clark Gable vehicle. Finally, she and Roberts ended up in El Centro, a sleepy border town in the Imperial Valley. There, not far south from the crossroads where Nathanael West and his wife would perish in a car crash years later, the couple spent a year; he as a working stiff in a cannery, she at the desk of the local newspaper. Then, desperate to escape this dead-end life, she wrote the Fox Company in Hollywood, asking for a job. Such a blind request in 1931 (or any other time) had one chance in a million to get results. But a man answered, telling her to come to the studio on Western Avenue for a test. She went, though she entertained no illusions of an acting career. She also knew she would have to sleep with the man. Jonathan Cecil Alphington-Wiggins had worked for Sennett, one of a contingent of ex-officers of the British Army who were then ekeing out a living in Hollywood. The screen test was a tradition as well established as the casting couch, and Maggie took both in stride, vaguely amused. All her life she kept her test film in its tin box, making Sanford promise to never look at it—which of course he did as soon as she was dead, even going so far as to have it transferred to video tape.

According to Maggie Smith Roberts, Wiggins was married, had an iron plate in his skull, and could be violent in bed—none of which fazed a hardened pioneer's daughter like her. One day, Wiggins lost his job at Fox and disappeared from her life forever. She had already worked, and probably slept, her way to a better job, becoming secretary to Fox's production chief Winfield Sheehan, before she moved on to scriptwriting. Her first produced scenario was *Sailor's Luck*, a rowdy, belabored and sometimes racist comedy directed by Raoul Walsh. In its only mildly funny scene, taking place in a fleabag hotel, a brutish sailor named "Bilge" (Frank Moran) simultaneously ate a banana, sucked on a beer bottle, all the while reading *The American Mercury*.

As soon as she could afford it, Roberts brought her whole family to California and sheltered the "pioneers," as she called the clan, in a big house she had built on an old apricot orchard next to the Los Angeles River, beneath the Colfax bridge. She paid her brother Dan, now crippled from a rodeo accident, to train the two thoroughbreds she raced at Santa Anita or Agua Caliente. The good life would soon hit the wall, however, because in 1938 she married John Sanford, just as he was joining the Communist Party. Nevertheless, there were still a few good years ahead.

Nathanael West's re-entry into the movie business had been less vicarious and more laborious. In July 1935, following the commercial failure of his third novel, *A Cool Million*, West was back in Hollywood, hat in hand. This time there was no paid train fare, no Hammett parties, and no job. He would have to wait more than eight months before he landed one, in January 1936, at "Repulsive Studio," as he soon would be calling Republic. During these unemployed months, he lived mostly off the Perelmans. He boarded at the Parva-Sed Apta apartments, a depressing dump at the top of Ivar, two blocks up from Hollywood Blvd., which nevertheless enchanted him for the colorful lowlifes he got to meet: prostitutes, drummers, touts, movie Eskimos, a whole gamut of burnt-out Midwestern dreamers who would more often than not end their days on a street bench, like Homer Simpson at *The Day of the Locust*'s conclusion. In the novel, the Parva-Sed Apta would become the San Bernardino Arms, otherwise known by its tenants as the San Berdoo. West also placed his fictional Château Mirabella on Ivar—the building his young hero Tod Hackett first checks into. While living at the Parva-Sed Apta, West witnessed a scene he placed at the Mirabella in one of the novel's early chapters. One morning he saw the occupant in the next room throw what looked like a heap of dirty laundry into the corridor and slam the door behind her. A dwarf soon emerged from the pile, screaming obscenities. He would become one of the most vivid figures in West's Hollywood bestiary: Abe Kusich. In reality, the man was a tout and, on occasion, a pimp. In his book, West has him hand out calling cards, which, besides announcing "Honest Abe Kusich," also bear a warm recommendation by Stanley Rose—a private joke, and a funny one at that, given the spotty reputation of the Hollywood bookseller.

West also pulled material from the trades and the fan magazines. It is hard to believe, for example, that he never read this breathless *Modern Screen* account of the Hollywood premiere of *Strange Interlude* at the Grauman Theatre, on July 15, 1932: "*The crowds arrived early in the afternoon to make sure to be able to see Norma Shearer, Thalberg and Clark Gable. A girl in glasses in the first row was trampled on. This terrifying crowd beat all the records, even* Hell's Angels, *for its rowdiness and enthusiasm. Fifty policemen were not enough to contain them. Two hilarious* [sic] *women were pushed under a car and crushed!*" Similarly, West must have been aware of Ray Wise's story when he wrote about the Gingo family, a group of Eskimo extras stranded at the San Berdoo. In 1935, Wise was on the bill of a weak imitation of *Tabu: A Story of the South Seas* released by MGM, called *Last of the Pagans*.

Wise started in movies in 1928, indirectly because of F. W. Murnau. The newly arrived German director had in mind a mix of fiction and documentary about a walrus hunter in Alaska he wanted to call *Frozen Justice*, and Fox had sent a crew to Point Barrow in Alaska (where the Gingos are from in West's novel) to photograph what walrus, whale hunting and upturned kayaks they could find. Wise had been hired as assistant cameraman and interpreter. One of the expedition's two planes was lost and never found; neither were the passengers. The rest of the crew, including Wise, got back after a three-month ordeal, only to learn that Murnau had lost interest in the project. Fox would eventually try to recoup the losses by using some of the Alaska footage in an early talky, a hoary dance-hall story set in the Yukon, directed by Allan Dwan, which, of course, they called *Frozen Justice*.[1] Ray Wise, nevertheless, stayed in Hollywood hoping to become Eskimo-in-residence. But it happened only once, when in 1933 the roustabout director W. S. "Woody" Van Dyke made him the star of a big MGM production called *Eskimo*. Ray was renamed "Mala" to make it more authentic, and audiences liked him so much that producer Hunt Stromberg put him under contract at MGM. Eskimo parts being scarse, however, Mala played his share of Malays in sarongs or Tahitians in grass skirts—as in *Last of the Pagans*.

In January 1935, West finally found employment at Republic. For him it was both the worst and the best of luck: Herbert J. Yates' newly created studio was undeniably the lower rung of the ladder in terms of prestige and salary, but its total lack of class also presented one advantage for West: at a place like this, he was in no danger of ever thinking it possible to do great work. This turned out to be a blessing, as West was always able to separate his film work from his art. Besides, the hack work at Republic offered a release for the writer's whackier side. Whereas he wrote his novels slowly and painstakingly revised them, almost to a nub, his studio work let his

---

[1] Kevin Brownlow told the story of this misguided trip in much more detail in his priceless 1979 book *The War, The West and The Wilderness*.

imagination run wickedly wild, tackling hare-brained stories of lost pilots, gangsters, and musical aquatics. He would take savage pleasure in making these yarns as extreme as he could.

Yates was by all accounts a stupid man and a bean counter, but day-to-day production at Republic was run by a capable manager named Burt Kelly. Republic was, in reality, a merger of two B-movie and serial factories, Mascot and Monogram, both indebted to Yates' photographic labs. In 1935, when Yates took over the business, the other Hollywood studios were embroiled in a fight with the Screen Writers Guild over contracts. Kelly was able to quietly negotiate with the Guild to give its members the terms they demanded, and would obtain eventually from the majors, only much later. This explains why lowly Republic could employ experienced and capable writers like Wells Root (an MGM veteran), Horace McCoy, Lester Cole and Sam Ornitz. West was first teamed with Cole, who in his autobiography, *Hollywood Red*, relates that the day after West's arrival at the studio, furious at the shrikes nesting in a tree outside his office window, West bought a BB gun and killed all the birds one by one, before sitting down to work. In the two years he was at the studio, West worked on no less than twelve pictures, each with different collaborators. One of them, Wells Root, understood West's hatred of shrikes. A hunter himself, he didn't care either for these birds who kill their prey by impaling it on a spiky object, and sometimes kill other birds as well. West found them simply "against nature"—a rather outlandish claim—and named his cynical City Desk editor in *Miss Lonelyhearts* Shrike. Usually quiet and dignified, West was sometimes seized by such fits of anger, like the time he used his car to run down (a frightful thought, given the way he drove) a pair of prominent scriptwriters who had trashed a duck blind he was foolish enough to recommend. These were two established writers who could have been of help to him someday, but West did not care about this sort of thing. Otherwise, he impressed his colleagues with his self-contained manner, and his quiet determination to keep on with his literary work. For this, he was fully respected by his peers, no matter how low his salary at Republic. And he would find a rare balance in his film work. At first disdainful of it, he soon took a diabolical pleasure in the absurd things he was asked to write. He started to relax. Once his option was renewed, he would often go on hunting weekends with Root or Faulkner. He had sexual affairs, but remained discreet about his partners. Root, when interviewd in 1986 in his Pacific Palisades home, remembered only one of his women, a model. West told him that for one particular sitting she had to pose in the nude, her body entirely covered with gold paint. She could only stand it for four hours at a stretch. West found this sort of detail so irresistible that, for once, he had broken his personal code and told the story to Root. He also had a liaison with a woman who would later become one of Beverly Hills' most prominent realtors; contacted by phone in 1986 for our documentary on West, she still spoke of "Pep" with affection, but declined a filmed interview: "Honey, you don't want to see me on film," she said to me.

West had also found a secretary, Jo Conway, a fat girl who, according to Root, tended to West "with the devotion of a Cocker Spaniel." She took his laundry to the cleaner, paid his bills, took care of his check books and tax returns, got his over-and-unders back from the gunsmith; but more crucially, she read the addled material the studio gave him to adapt. "Pep went hunting all weekend," recalled Root, "and come Monday morning Jo briefed him on the stuff. She was good at it, she had a good movie sense." West was not unlike the über-scriptwriter played by Humphrey Bogart in Nicholas Ray's *In a Lonely Place*, who did not read anything if he could help it. And soon West wouldn't write either, leaving his collaborator of the moment to type and construct the actual script, while he paced the room and let his imagination fly.

After two years at Republic, West refused to stay, turning down a raise in salary. All through 1938 he waited for another offer, until in desperation he had to accept a job at RKO at his established rate of $350 a week. But in the meantime, he had made useful friends and partners in crime: there was Wells Root, of course, through whom he managed to sell a story idea to MGM for $7,500—a script for Gable on John J. Audubon's life, which was never produced. There was Joseph Schrank, another Metro writer, with whom West would write a play, *Good Hunting*, which bombed in New York in November 1938. It was a ferocious satire about inept Allied generals in WWI. But his most congenial collaborator was Boris Ingster. It is difficult to imagine a more bizarre team than West and this Russian émigré, who had been Sergei Eisenstein's assistant in Hollywood during his ¡Que viva México! interlude. After the Soviet director's departure, Ingster stayed behind to become known in the business as a "constructionist" and idea man.

He also admired West's novels enormously, and told him so. West, for his part, was almost alarmed by Ingster's energy. "You could run an excavator on it," he wrote his sister Laura. But he was also fascinated by his new friend's crooked schemes, his gall and his negotiation skills, thinking he might have more financial success if he hooked up with the Russian. The only drawback was that this time around West had to do the typing, Ingster's English not being up to the task. West first teamed with him at RKO on a film called *Five Came Back*, a good enough adventure yarn, ably directed by John Farrow, starring Chester Morris and John Carradine. Impressed by the surprisingly good notices the picture received upon its release, the front office put the winning team on *Before the Fact*, a British crime novel nobody at RKO had so far managed to adapt to anyone's satisfaction, although the studio had tried for years. After Louis Hayward and Robert Montgomery, it was now Laurence Olivier who was slated to play the criminal husband. In the novel, the wife knew she was going to be killed for her money, but, knowing herself pregnant, she lets herself be killed to "prevent the monster to reproduce." There was no chance of keeping this in a Hollywood movie, of course, but for West it was an opportunity to work on an A-picture for the first time. And RKO was pleased with the 133-page script he and Ingster swiftly turned in, as well as with the solution they had come up with: the woman was telling the whole story in flashback after she'd killed her husband *in extremis*. Unfortunately for West, the actress who was to be Olivier's co-star got pregnant for real, and the picture was postponed. Alfred Hitchcock took advantage of this delay to co-opt the project, which became *Suspicion*, with altogether different actors (Cary Grant and Joan Fontaine). He had the script rewritten to his specifications by Samson Raphaelson, Joan Harrison and his wife Alma, but contrary to what he later claimed (notably in his published interviews with Truffaut), Hitchcock never had the least intention to "go back to the book." His memos to RKO clearly indicate that from the start he was after something lighter than the novel *Before the Fact*, or Ingster and West's script—which he had deemed "perfect" upon coming aboard. This is probably why he hired Raphaelson, for his lighter touch, short of the Lubitsch touch. As to the regrets he later vented about the picture, they were typical "after the fact" Hitchcock gripes—a way of not admitting that he had been wrong all along.

Hitchcock had not yet shot a reel of film on *Suspicion* when Nathanael West died in December 1940; in the meantime, West had written three more movies.

John Sanford joined the Communist Party in 1938. His wife followed suit a few years later, still keeping her counsel about the members of their "gilded cell" who would more often than not hold meetings at their house in the Valley, just to use the pool. She could not help noticing that their fellow members did not take her husband seriously. And when the witch hunt got going in earnest in the early fifties, Sanford bitterly resented the fact that the House Committee on Un-American Activities *never* interviewed him. He was deemed a lightweight even by the anti-communists. He simply did not matter.

His wife, on the other hand, as a valued and highly paid writer at MGM, was fair game. In 1951, even though everyone in the front office begged her to comply and come clean, Marguerite Roberts refused to explain herself and was effectively blacklisted and forbidden from working. She had been well liked at the studio, where for eleven years she wrote robust adventure stories for Clark Gable, Robert Taylor, Greer Garson and Ava Gardner. At Metro, though, her union with John Sanford remained a puzzle. The man had a real talent, his father used to say, for losing the few friendships he had. There was always the cutting remark. Roberts financially supported not only her own family, but Sanford and his father, as well. Her husband's only task, besides writing his lofty novels, was to look over her contracts, something he was very good at. But this time, when it came to negotiate with the likes of Benny Thau, she asked her husband to wait outside in the car. She was sensible, pleasant, a genuine success in a profession she loved—without illusions, but without condescention either. By contrast, Sanford was "viewy," as his mother-in-law used to say: a dreamer but also a lesson-giver, a lover of history who had no practical sense of life or in his own chosen field. Yet, maybe feeling that at least he was a keeper, Roberts had gone for him without reservation. Their adoration of each other, through thick and thin, was undeniable. Nothing was too good for him, nothing was too good for her. Never mind that it was her money in either case. His books did not sell? He couldn't find a publisher for his novel *A Man Without Shoes* after six years of trying? In 1951, Roberts would have 2,000 numbered copies privately printed, at a cost of $7,000. Fifty years later, the initial run had still not sold.

Marguerite Roberts did not suffer from the guilt many Hollywood writers felt at being overpaid—a guilt which they often compensated for by drinking or through political activism. First, she thought she was worth every dollar she made. But more importantly, she also felt she was doing it for art. *His* art. As for Sanford, he ceaselessly repeats in his autobiographical books that he had no scruples about letting her support both him and his father. When Sanford joined the Communist Party in 1938, it was not a form of expiation, as was the case for many others in Hollywood. He had no illusions. He simply could not stand missing the boat one more time. All his life he had been a watcher, with no understanding of what was going on. All his life he would write books to repair that mistake. Finding himself in Madrid during the 1931 riots of the popular front, his only reaction to such a golden opportunity for a writer was to hop the first train out to Paris. During the drive to free Sacco and Vanzetti, Sanford shocked even his friend West by his ignorance of the events. Years later, he would try to make up for it by writing about Sacco and Vanzetti in *A Man Without Shoes*—at a time when nobody cared anymore.

His political commitment looked suspect even to his fellow cell members, who were leery of him and his motives. To them, Sanford remained the "unpleasant egotist" he had been called in 1933 by a *New York Times* critic reviewing his first book. To no avail did Sanford complain to V. J. Jerome or to recruiter Martin Berkeley (a fellow writer who would name him and his wife in front of a HUAC committee in 1951, among hundreds of others), that the Party had assigned him to a "housewives cell," which included not a single writer or screenwriter. They did not even let him teach his Marxist interpretation of American history at the Little Red School House on Highland Avenue, where many Communist writers volunteered their time. When war was declared, Sanford went to Washington and joined the first team Frank Capra put together to make his series of propaganda films, *Why We Fight*. Sanford wrote the first draft of what would become (under Anthony Veiller's credit) the notorious *The Battle of Russia*, the picture which years later would cause Capra so much embarrassment. The director later wrote about the episode with the same revisionism he applied to so many things in his autobiography, *The Name Above the Title*. But, contrary to what he claims, Capra did not exactly "get rid of this bunch of Reds." Instead, he sent Sanford back to Hollywood to await his marching papers and the reserve lieutenant promotion for which he'd been recommended. It was denied by the military secret services (G2), since belonging to the Communist Party triggered an automatic refusal. At least this is what Capra said in his letter of apology, and it is what Sanford wanted to believe.

Just as he was denied his war, he was denied his blacklist. Naturally enough, Sanford had not been deemed sufficiently important to be called in the first round of inquiries HUAC chairman J. Parnell Thomas conducted in the fall of 1947. Typically, our man was in Manhattan just when the sentences for contempt of Congress were being pronounced; he was even at the Hall of Justice to see the Hollywood Ten being led away in handcuffs. "Why not me?" he writes in his journal. Sanford *was* later subponaed and asked to testify with his wife in front of HUAC in April 1951, but he only became a victim of the blacklist by proxy. Marguerite Roberts became one of the most extraordinary (and least known) of the pariahs. The first time HUAC agents attempted to serve them with subponaes, the Sanfords were not in their large Encino property, but in Louisville, Kentucky, buying horses. Which should not have been surprising: they were often seen at the stables on Riverside Drive where Louis B. Mayer had his horses trained; one of the Sanford's mares even sired a colt by a stallion that belonged to Mayer.

Marguerite Roberts' dismissal from MGM in September 1951 was on

Marguerite Roberts

par with this kind of socio-political surrealism. Even though she could truly say she was not at that time a member of the Communist Party, Roberts, like so many others, opted for the Fifth Amendment when it came to answering questions put to her by HUAC. This fierce attitude caused no end of embarrassment among the MGM brass: not only was Roberts working on two productions at the time (including the intriguing *My Man and I* from a story by John Fante), but Sanford had just negotiated an advantageous five-year contract renewal for his wife, without options. This meant that the Sanfords could live out their exile from Hollywood on $3,000-plus a week for several years. Ironically, the "liberal" Dore Schary, who had just started as head of production at the studio—coming over from RKO, where he had championed such intolerance busters as *Crossfire* and *The Boy with Green Hair*—was the one at MGM who showed the least sympathy towards Marguerite Roberts, according to her husband. Schary had shown no scruples when, just a few months earlier, he tried to persuade the Screen Writers Guild to abandon the unrepentant Hollywood Ten, so that "the witch hunters would leave Hollywood alone" (such were his words). But Roberts had powerful allies at MGM, notably VP Benny Thau, who more than anyone knew what Roberts was worth to the studio: not only was she a most capable and versatile writer, she was also never loath to "clean up after someone else" and play script doctor on the side. The front office bent over backwards trying to persuade her to do a minimum amount of groveling, so she could stay at MGM. Even during the weeks she was questioned by HUAC, the studio kept paying her salary so she could finish, at night and at home, a script she was preparing for Armand Deutsch, an Elizabeth Taylor vehicle called *The Girl Who Had Everything*. When her answers to the Committee were deemed too negative, Eddie Mannix went so far as to negotiate with HUAC, suggesting that Roberts write a letter to the Committee, giving her his personal assurance that it would never leave his desk drawer. When she refused out of principle, the studio had no other choice than to show her the door. She was so well liked and respected that the MGM executives did not even try to use the famous "morals clause" to void her contract. As Sanford later wrote in one of his memoirs, "a certain amount of dollars were offered."

Thus, Marguerite Roberts was paid by MGM a quarter of a million dollars not to work for the studio anymore. In this, Metro lived up to its reputation of always doing everything bigger and classier than the other studios, even when it came to infamy. Still, Roberts' exile, lined in gold though it was—and her material sacrifices remaining relative (the race horses were sold)—was truly devastating for this woman who had considered MGM her second home. Being deprived of the work she loved so much was even worse than being deprived of her passport, as she was for several months. The Sanfords then left Hollywood, first for Carmel, then for Europe where they immediately bought a spiffy little MG and started their grand tour. *The Black List on three grand a week*, Sanford liked to quip, exaggerating only slightly.

It was eleven years before Roberts could work again—this time at Columbia, and for salaries as substantial as those she had known at Metro. She had to kick-start her career with some Pat Boone pap (*The Main Attraction*), some Robert Mitchum insanity (*Rampage*) and some pineapple king muck starring Charlton Heston (*Diamond Head*), but soon she was off and running. Curiously, for two different studios, she wrote crusty old Henry Hathaway's last three Westerns, including his worst (*5 Card Stud*) and one of his most revered (*True Grit*). It is not known whether John Wayne ever knew that a blacklisted woman wrote the role for which he earned his only Best Actor Oscar®, or if he cared. Sanford once told publisher and editor Steve Wasserman, when he was heading the book section of the *Los Angeles Times*, that The Duke had agreed to star in the Hathaway picture only if Marguerite Roberts wrote the script. One wonders.

In Hollywood, John Sanford and Nathanael West knew each other, but were far from intimate. They still called each other "Pep" and "Scotty" as they had done in their youth, but their friendship had cooled, if it had ever been warm. A game of pool with Fante and Saroyan in a dive on Las Palmas, a quick hello in the Stanley Rose Bookshop, that was all. Once, Sanford went with West to the premiere of a Republic picture his friend had co-written called *The President's Mystery*. Sanford, ever so tactful, declared afterwards that the story was stupid and the production values almost non-existent.

"What do you know about the picture business?" snarled West, all the more upset because the producer was standing right behind them. "Nothing," said Sanford, who always wore his obtuse mind like a badge of honor.

Most of the time, West treated his old school chum like the cypher he was, in just about everything: as a scenario writer, as a Communist, even as a novelist. The amused affection he'd shown him in the past wasn't there anymore. Sanford attributed the estrangement to an episode he pinned down to the winter of 1932, which in effect snuffed out any warmth there might have been in their friendship. This was a period when Sanford took advantage, as many other writers did, of West's largess with the free board at the Sutton. For some reason, Sanford was peeved at West because a story of his had been turned down by *Contact*. Sanford held his friend responsible, mistakingly, as he later found out. In any case, Sanford (still Shapiro) bided his time until one night, in a restaurant after a show, West insulted a prostitute who propositioned him. Shapiro let him have it, telling him to take on someone his own size. "Like you, Scotty?" railed West, "Oh no, I would be too afraid to measure wits with you, afraid you'd show me for what I am."

"What you are, Pep," Shapiro said calmly, "is a Kike in a Brooks Brothers suit. I knew you when your name had two syllables." In the deadly silence that followed, Sanford realized that nothing between them would ever be the same again. He reckoned in his memoirs that West had taken it on the chin, as calmly as he could. He also recognized that he had bushwacked his friend, hitting him with the most hurtful sarcasm he could think of. Although he would regret this moment for the rest of his life, Sanford got good literary mileage out of it. Later, he owned up to the fact that he always measured himself against West not out of admiration, but because he wanted to be better than West.

When West died in that car accident just before Chrismas in 1940, Sanford's wife asked him: "Are you going to keep on writing against a dead man?" In a sense, this is exactly what he did, stubbornly stacking up no less than twenty published volumes against his dead rival's thin output of four. As a writer, Sanford was not without talent: a few of his books have striking passages (as in his stark and very violent Depression-era novel

The last photo taken of Eileen McKenney West and her dog, Julie, before the fatal car crash with husband Nathanael West in El Centro, CA, on December 22, 1940

Seventy Times Seven). His dialogue is often excellent. But most of his books give the impression of being about nothing—like pages of repeated lines a schoolboy is ordered to write in a notebook as punishment. *The Day of the Locust*, on the other hand, showed that West had found himself as a novelist, and that instead of dooming him to cushy mediocrity and compromise, Hollywood could nurture his work with vivid and original material. In this, he fared much better than Fitzgerald, whose *The Last Tycoon* is, in the end, less successful.

As early as the fall of 1939, despite his last novel's commercial failure, everything seemed to fall into place for Nathanael West. The salaries were getting better, as was his life in general. He met the girl he would marry the following spring—a girl built the way he liked: tall, big-boned, and a *shiksa* for good measure. Her name was Eileen, and she was the Eileen of the very successful play soon to open on Broadway, *My Sister Eileen*, based on the autobiographical stories her sister Ruth McKenney had written in the *New Yorker*. Better still, she was always keen to go hunting with him. According to Wells Root, who often went with them, Eileen killed more game than the two men combined, while professing only a mild taste for hunting. During that December of 1940, the couple had just moved into a big rustic house on Magnolia Boulevard in the San Fernando Valley. West seemed to thrive as a husband, playing father to the little boy Eileen had from a previous marriage. The weekend before Christmas, they were supposed to go quail hunting around Mexicali in Root's station wagon, and Root would be at the wheel. But something came up and the Wests went on their own instead, with their dog Julie, in the family's Ford station wagon, a late-model Woody.

The car crash took place on their return from Mexico, on the road to El Centro, in circumstances that in some ways West would have surely put in one of his novels, a mix of the sordid and the surreal. Like the $150 he had on him that disappeared on the way to the hospital. The night before, they had stayed in the Hotel De Anza on the American side of the border, and had cashed a check in the morning. West knew the road perfectly, and could see from afar the black Pontiac on the Yuma road approaching the crossing. Joseph Dowless, the 27-year-old field hand who was driving west with his wife and daughter, also knew the road and that a stop sign gave him priority. West, that "great spasmodic," as Sanford called him, lived up to his reputation as the world's worst driver, never even slowing down at the stop sign. Eileen died in the ambulance. West succumbed of multiple skull fractures in the hospital. The three people in the Pontiac were only slightly hurt. Julie, the West's bitch, took off when she heard the police and ambulance sirens. As his last novel did, West's life ended up in a howl of sirens.

Sanford's, on the other hand, was just beginning—at least in his real calling. Three years after his friend's death, he would dedicate his fourth novel, *The People from Heaven*, "To Nathanael West, 1903-1940," ultimately convinced his "friend" would not have bothered to read this one either. And he went on beating his chest in print until the end of the century (Sanford died in 2003), in the comfort of his house in Montecito, finally acquiring a small reputation as a singular memoirist. More voluminous now that he had a willing publisher (mostly Black Sparrow, and other Santa Barbara small presses), his books filled up his shelves, bound in expensive leather. They stood next to West's novels in his library. Only one volume (sky-blue and white, a signed hardbound edition, #2 of a special run of five) remained locked in his bank safe, too precious or too painful to contemplate, as it was not one of his.

Robert Tasker

THEY MADE ME A SCREENWRITER

IN THE 1937 WARNER BROS. picture *San Quentin*, Pat O'Brien plays a military captain newly appointed warden. Midway through, he is seen visiting prisoners. One, "Simpson," is known in the joint as "the writer." He has a typewriter in his cell and is played by a good-looking actor, Dennis Moore.

> O'BRIEN
> Writing, eh? How's the story going?
>
> SIMPSON
> Fine, Captain. I'm about finished. Here, read this.
>
> O'BRIEN
> Well, I'll wait till after it's published. You know, I never could understand how a man with your brains would ever end up in a place like this.
>
> SIMPSON
> Well, I couldn't live on rejection slips.
> I didn't start getting accepted until I got in here.
>
> O'BRIEN
> Mmm. Maybe the address impressed them.

In the next shot, the warden stops in front of "Dorgan," in for forgery.

> DORGAN
> I'm a writer, too.
>
> O'BRIEN
> Oh, I think I remember now, it's writing other people's names on checks now, is it?
>
> DORGAN
> Right, Captain. Trouble is, I retired so long, I got out of practice.

No fewer than eight writers were put to work on *San Quentin*. The purchase price of the story was expensive: $18,901—almost as much as what the star of the picture was getting, and certainly more than what the other featured players cost ($2,750 for Humphrey Bogart, a paltry $450 for Ann Sheridan, who even sang for her supper in this one). Screenplay credit for this routine Lloyd Bacon picture went to Humphrey Cobb and Peter Milne, but the original story was by John Bright and Robert Tasker. Bright was the better known of the two. In the early 1930s, he and his partner, Kubec Glasmon, had been so successful writing stories for James Cagney that Warner Bros. featured their names prominently on publicity materials, a practice unheard of at the time. But then, Cagney's *The Public Enemy* had been a huge hit in 1931, and Bright went on writing for the actor until he ran afoul of Warner Bros. production chief Darryl F. Zanuck, who fired him for "personal reasons."

If the cocky young Bright knew the underworld only vicariously (through Glasmon, an ex-pharmacist whose drugstore had been a gangster hangout in Chicago), his new partner, Tasker, was the real deal. He based the jailbird writer in *San Quentin* on himself.

There was a time, between 1927 and 1929, when he and fellow inmate Ernest Granville Booth had such a grasp on the Hollywood market for crime stories that they'd had to split the pie between them—Tasker sticking to prison stories, Booth to knockover yarns filled with gunfire and babes. While imprisoned, Booth made more than $28,000 from Hollywood. The gravy was so thick that other cons, in both Q and Folsom, wanted in: a scrawny ex-jockey named Joe Mackin, doing a 15-year jolt for highway robbery, already showed promise, according to a report in *The American Mercury*.

The jailhouse writing craze got so out of hand the authorities had to clamp down. A March 29, 1928 article in the *San Francisco Examiner* opened with an exasperated quote from Judge C. E. McLaughlin, Sacramento member of the State Board of Prison Directors: "We're running prisons, not literary bureaus. The board has no time or disposition to read this material and see that it is in proper shape."

Stricter regulations did not prevent cons from writing in their spare time, the report went on, but it did prevent them from submitting their stories outside while still in stir. "Both Booth and Tasker, who are serving life terms at Folsom for robbery after a botched escape from San Quentin, have recently been taken under the literary wing of H. L. Mencken, editor of *The American Mercury*. Warden Smith disclosed today that three motion picture concerns are now negotiating for film rights to one Booth *Mercury* article entitled 'We Rob a Bank.' And Warden Holohan at San Quentin confirmed that a dozen convicts were preparing material with an eye on the outside market. "It all started with the *Bulletin*, and that short-story contest in which Tasker won first prize out of 400 entries from prisoners."

The *Bulletin*, Q's inmate-edited journal, kept on going well after the ban, but it declined sharply after its two luminaries got sprung by their famous literary mentor. It was scrapped for good in June of 1936, on decision from Court Smith, the new warden: "It had become too intellectual and superior for some time now, less and less inmates read it. The funds allowed to the *Bulletin* will go to the *Sport News* instead, and to the organization of boxing matches."

Of the California penal system's two star writers, Ernest Granville Booth is certainly the more colorful, even if he left a lesser mark on film history than fellow inmate Robert Tasker. We know Tasker, if at all, through the romantic image painted by his old partner John Bright in his writings and interviews. Tasker's name is found in newspaper society columns as well as on more than a dozen film credits. By contrast, Ernest Booth—alias Ernest G. Granville, alias Roy W. Reeves, alias Ray Reeves— cut a swath mainly on police blotters. He switched jailhouse numbers like others do post office boxes: 44016 was his number at the Los Angeles City Jail, 349077 at the county jail; to the FBI he was suspect number 12558; at San Quentin he was prisoner 42601, at Folsom 13332, at the Oakland City Jail he was 9530, in Portland 3192, in Stockton 4258, and in Berkeley 497. These were the numbers of a career criminal, which even Mencken ultimately found "discouraging."

Born in 1899, Booth started his career at 14 with a break-in that earned him a two-year juvie stretch in Ione, near Sacramento. Soon after turning 18, he was arrested in Oroville for stealing a car. In 1924, on the day

ERNEST G. BOOTH
Held In Mystery Slaying
—Los Angeles Examiner photo

he married Valdera Miliken, he knocked over a bank in Oakland, threatening the clerks with what the local press called an "ammonia bomb." He spent his honeymoon in Folsom, alone. He was ultimately sentenced to a 20-to-life term. He got transferred to San Quentin, where he met Tasker, who by this time was editor of the *Bulletin*. Both were soon writing for Mencken, who loved the romance of rough trade even more than discovering new talent. Although Mencken privately thought Tasker "much lighter stuff than Booth," he also found him a better writer and prospect for parole.

Pulling strings with "a few governors he knew," Mencken managed to have Tasker released on parole in December 1929. He still had doubts about the more hardened Booth. In November 1931, Booth's wife Valdera, his brother, and an old cellmate named Warren Mulvey were arrested in the prison administration building in Sacramento attempting to steal and replace Booth's prison record with a fake one. The dim plot landed the brother in prison for ten months. Valdera got a suspended sentence, and Mulvey went back to Folsom for another five years.

Writer John Fante, who was living in nearby Roseville at the time, knew the prison doctor at Folsom and wrote to Mencken about another of Booth's spectacularly inept capers: "It seems Booth has been trying to convince the medicos that he belongs to the TB ward. According to the doc, he went so far as to bring to the hospital the sputum of a bona fide sufferer, claiming it to be his own, but the deception was discovered. Now, ironically enough, Booth *has* got tuberculosis! The doc is not very sympathetic, feeling that, now that Booth is a sick man, the best place for him is Folsom."

The parole bureau thought otherwise, releasing him in the spring of 1937. Reporting on this, the Oakland *Tribune* ran a picture of him with the caption HE'LL BE BACK. Booth settled in Placerville with Valdera and wrote "treatments" for Warner Bros. But he found this tough going, and the paltry $50-a-week checks he sometimes got from Burbank were a startling change from the heady days of the late 1920s, when Paramount-Publix had shelled out $15,000 for his story "Ladies of the Mob" (William A. Wellman made the film in 1928, starring Clara Bow and Richard Arlen). In 1930, Metro had bought the rights to his published autobiography, *Stealing Through Life*, which Rowland Brown adapted, intending to direct (the film was never made).

Pick-up, the picture Paramount made in 1933 out of his story "Ladies in Stir" was such a success for director Marion Gering and star Sylvia Sidney that the pair went on to make five more together for B. P. Schulberg. But in 1937, the terms of his parole forbade Booth from writing about the only thing he knew: crime and prison. Instead he slaved on desultory assignments like *Fremont the Pathfinder*. A year later, however, his parole over, he was living on Russell Avenue in Hollywood churning out yarns with telltale names like *This Man Must Die* and *You Might Be Next*. He served as technical adviser on *Men of San Quentin* (1942), and fellow studio hack Horace McCoy wrote a script from Booth's play *Women Without Names*, which Robert Florey directed in 1940 for Paramount. But during all this, Booth was supplementing his movie income the only way he knew how. In 1941, he was questioned about the murder of a dowager bludgeoned to death and robbed in her Pasadena home. He was released, after spending two days in jail for carrying a gun. But by 1947 the jig was up, as this March 18 flash in the *Daily Police Bulletin* indicated:

Suspect in company of John J. Sedlak—probably driving Studebaker sedan, 1946; registered to Eulah Sedlak, used on several hold-ups. Suspect uses narcotics and is armed with a .32 or .38 caliber blue steel revolver. Known associates are in Hollywood and around Third and Figueroa— Hold—We will extradite.

Booth was finally arrested by the FBI at Musso & Frank. His police description reads like something out of Ellroy:

WMA – 48 years old, 5 foot 11, 160 lbs – blue eyes, brown-gray hair, receding hairline, high forehead, slender build, hollow cheeks (TB), dimple in chin, turkey neck, slightly stooped, walks with slight limp. Usually wears blue pin-striped suits. When operating, talks with gruff voice. Has been employed by Warner Bros. studio and as camera repairman for Don Bleitz Camera Shop in Hollywood. Has habit of flashing large bills.

Booth had been wanted for questioning on an old 1943 case, a burglary at the Portland Cement Company involving $250,000 in stolen bearer bonds. But the police found he'd also been behind a series of bank robberies in and around Los Angeles, including the Atlas Federal Savings and Loan in Pasadena, from which he took $2,100. A judge set his bail at $50,000, and as early as July 1947, he was "BACK IN ALMA MATER," as several newspaper banners screamed. Ernest Granville Booth didn't finish his latest 20-year stretch. He died of tuberculosis in a prison in Washington in 1959. Upon his last arrest—his 26th—the *New York Mirror* wrote quite convincingly: "E. G. Booth always had difficulty deciding whether to write about crime or go out and commit one. He tried both, and both occupations paid him well."

Upon acceptance of his initial short story, "My First Day," Robert Tasker sent Mencken the requested capsule-biography: "Born in North Dakota on November 13, 1903, raised in Canada, finished high-school in Portland in 1921. One year later I'm in California, go through

Robert Tasker appears as a hired gun named "Lefty" in *Quick Millions* (1931), adopting a pose with which he was not unfamiliar in real life

a bad patch, buy a gun—there you have it. I'm now serving a five-to-life sentence in San Quentin for armed robbery ... Don't hesitate to call me whatever you want: thief, hood, knock-over artist. It's all the same to me. As to where I'm from, I can't really say—except maybe from here." This was signed Robert Joyce Tasker, #39962, S.Q., Cal.

Tasker had robbed the Sauer's Dance Palace in Oakland on Valentine's Day, 1924. He had thrown a handful of bills into a tablecloth and left, but he was easy for the police to find because he'd just walked a few blocks and waited; the gun they found on him was empty. The caper had all the hallmarks of a rebellious gesture, and years later his writing partner John Bright did not hesitate to paint Tasker as a romantic hero of the class wars. But this was the year of the Leopold and Loeb case, and the national press was up in arms against "psycho-crimes." The judge threw the book at Tasker. In the novel he wrote based upon his friend, *It's Cleaner on the Inside*, Bright claims Tasker robbed the dance hall merely to enrage his rich conservative father. Tasker did cut a romantic figure, with the smooth good looks of a matinee idol (Lew Cody, say), but he was no Robin Hood. In another letter to Mencken, he asked him to send the payment for his story "A Man is Hanged" directly to his father in Waterville, Ontario, adding: "I'm rather fond of the old chap, and I can think of no nicer manner of sending information of another success." This and other checkable facts establish Bright as a notoriously unreliable witness of his times, both in interviews and in his otherwise entertaining unpublished[1] memoir, *Arsenic and Old Faces*.

In September 1927, author Jim Tully visited several prisoners in San Quentin, including *cause célèbre* Tom Mooney and actor Paul Kelly, in for beating another actor to death over actress Dorothy Mackaye. Recounting his visit in *The American Mercury*, Tully described Tasker as "24, tall, good looking, a sheik type for society girls and stenographers, with black hair carefully combed." Tully was lucky he wrote about caged men: inside, he'd have gotten his ticket punched for a lesser offense than calling an inmate "a sheik type for stenographers." But Tasker *was* slumming, in a way. His prison novel *Grimhaven* was published by Knopf in 1928, and a year later he was released on parole. Mencken had even finagled him a bogus job at *Photoplay*, one of the leading fan magazines of the period. The terms of his parole forbade him from writing about crime for another two years, but in April 1931, a lobby card displayed in theatres across the nation showed Tasker handcuffed to a garage door. Rowland Brown, a screenwriter making his first picture at Fox, had given him a small part in *Quick Millions*. Brown, an important but forgotten artist of the early talkies, was a connoisseur of crusty characters and criminals. In his native Ohio, he had rubbed elbows with members of the Purple Gang, and he was the first director to dress gangsters like princes and give George Raft a good part (before 1932's *Scarface*). In *Quick Millions*, Raft plays the smooth lieutenant of racketeer Spencer Tracy, who has him killed by a shifty-looking bird named Lefty (Tasker). He has only two lines, delivered in a garage while filing the serial number off a gun. He then hands over the "lam" money to Raft—before shooting him in the back. The police have been tipped off, however, and

---

[1] It was eventually published by Scarecrow Press in December 2002, under the title *Worms in the Winecup: A Memoir*.

Lucey's Restaurant on Melrose, across from Paramount, where Tasker and writing partner John Bright would hatch many unfulfilled projects

Lefty is handcuffed and hauled away.

Even before this, Tasker probably had a hand in another, more "prestigious" crime picture. According to Bright, Tasker had written *The Big House* (1930) with veteran writer Frances Marion, who had Thalberg's ear at Metro. Typically, Bright also claimed that the dapper Tasker did more than help her on the script, which is possible, as she was then between husbands (she'd soon wed George Hill, director of *The Big House*). If true, the slight was all the more galling for Tasker, as Marion won the Oscar® for Best Screenplay in 1931 for this picture. In her memoir, *Off With Their Heads!*, Marion mentions a "research visit" to San Quentin, which lasted all of three hours and was mostly a photo opportunity for publicity purposes. A trustee with a stammer did present Miss Marion with flowers, perhaps giving her the idea for the Roscoe Ates character. But then, stammering was one of Roscoe Ates' main schticks on-screen. It is a fact that San Quentin's Warden Holohan, upon watching the picture, was flabbergasted at Marion's accuracy and sense of detail, which she must have gotten somewhere, or from someone. Tasker's obits in both *Daily Variety* and the *San Quentin News* credit him for *The Big House*, so let's just leave it at that.

Tasker could have used that Oscar® in early 1931, as his debut on the outside had been laborious, at best. His second novel had been rejected by Knopf, and he was without a studio job. By December 1931, however, he was in clover, married to Lucille Morrison, whom the society pages described as "an actress and socialite". Bright branded her a "catastrophe," and Tasker called her his "shit-pill heiress" (Lucille's father manufactured the famed laxative Fletcher's Castoria). The couple moved into a swank bungalow at the Mi Casa, a deluxe apartment building on Havenhurst, next to the Colonial House, where William Powell, Carole Lombard and other movie stars lived. Hired by RKO in 1932, Tasker, along with Samuel Ornitz, helped Rowland Brown prepare *Hell's Highway* (1932), a penitentiary picture. He also wrote *Secrets of the French Police* (1932) and *The Great Jasper* (1933) with Ornitz, who introduced him to Bright. "Between us," said Bright later, referring to the future "hostile witness" and blacklisted writer, "we completed Tasker's radical education."

In effect, Tasker was replacing what Bright had lost a few years earlier—his partner Kubec Glasmon. But he and Tasker were more sympatico: they were the same age, had the same politics, and liked the same things, namely Mexican girls and gambling. Together they freelanced around town, placed a story at Fox with the Sol Wurtzel unit, and wrote two pictures at Universal (*A Notorious Gentleman* [1935] and *The Accusing Finger* [1936]). They were at Warner Bros. writing *San Quentin* when they asked their agent, Zeppo Marx, to get them out of their contract: ex-Paramount chief-of-production B. P. Schulberg, now an independent, had suddenly gone radical and wanted to line up a number of "socially significant" projects with the likes of Lillian Hellman and Clifford Odets. (All this according to John Bright.) Schulberg eventually brought in William Saroyan to work with Bright and Tasker. After ten months, they only had the lackluster *John Meade's Woman* (1937) to show for all those grandiose plans, and that was the end of this particularly cockeyed (even for Hollywood) episode. Mostly, Bright and Tasker had taken a page from their new boss' book, whose creative credo, according to them, was "nags, gin and cunts." By day they drank at Lucey's, scheming to adapt great proletarian novels like B. Traven's *The Death Ship* and by night they were at the Clover Club or the Century, the other gambling joint on the Strip.

Tasker had shed his heiress by 1934, and was now going out with a sensational-looking Mexican girl. The partners then embarked on another epic adventure, which could be called "From Castoria to Astoria": they had been tapped by William K. Howard to write the script for *Back Door to Heaven* (1939), which was to be the director's comeback picture, but turned out to be his somewhat muffled swan song. Howard had been a big man once, holding his own at Fox with the likes of Ford, Hawks and Borzage. A personal friend of F. W. Murnau when he was in Hollywood, Howard had been one of the pallbearers at his funeral, and his 1931 hit *Transatlantic* owed Murnau a big artistic debt. He'd earned salaries of up to $4,000 a week, and Korda had recently brought him to England, where he toiled over a version of *Lawrence of Arabia*, an intriguing project which was finally aborted. In 1938, however, he was more or less finished in Hollywood. But his old pal Johnny Walker, an actor he used in four Fox Westerns in the silent days, came to him with a gem of a deal. A bunch of Wall Street financiers, headed by businessman Floyd Odlum, wanted to front a big production made in New York and revamp its film industry. Hard to believe, but Johnny Walker had the ear of a few of these gentlemen. This is how *Backdoor to Heaven* came to pass—one of the strangest alliances in the history of American movies: a bleaker-than-bleak story written by a Communist (Bright) and a jailbird (Tasker), directed by an over-the-hill big-shot director, with actors mostly from the Broadway stage, augmented by a posse of Howard's old alky pals, all financed by "progressive" Wall Street moneybags.

For Howard, this was to be a sentimental but uncompromisingly downbeat journey back to his hometown of St. Marys, in Western Ohio, where he went to school with men like future hobo-writer Jim Tully and Dillinger gangmember Charles Makley. The central character in *Backdoor to Heaven*, Frankie, is based on Makley, a "good guy" whose only crime was to have been born on the wrong side of the tracks. A striking scene patterned after Makley's real-life escape from death row, using a gun carved from a bar of soap and painted with black shoe-polish, was cut from the picture by its now-horrified backers before the movie's release.

A specific part of the initial deal, considerably adding to the oddity, was having Howard recreate his Western Ohio hometown in the Bronx, on various stages in the old Biograph studio, with transparency plates filmed in Cleveland. The actors, who include a young Van Heflin (playing a failed lawyer), Wallace Ford (fresh from his *Of Mice and Men* triumph on Broadway), and child actor Jimmy Lydon, all speak as if on Quaaludes. Howard's slow-paced and laconic direction deprives the viewer of any bit of excitement (a break-in, a stickup, a murder and a prison break, all take place off-screen), and as such the movie is reminiscent of Rowland Brown's easy grace and humor in films like *Quick Millions*. *Backdoor to Heaven* was so personal that Howard himself plays the no-nonsense district attorney who sends Frankie to the chair.

The ending revolves around a class reunion, which the production clearly was for Howard, who brought in old lefty collaborators like Hal Mohr (then president of Local 659, the West Coast cinematographers' union) and any number of his drinking buddies. Odlum had morality clauses put into everyone's contracts, but the bourbon was concealed in Coca-Cola bottles, and the work got slow in the afternoon. Leading lady Patricia Ellis was the director's girl friend at the time and could drink anybody under the table; the only one who didn't partake, ironically, was Johnny Walker (who played a prison trustee), but his epilepsy fits proved more disruptive on set than the booze. As Frankie, Wallace Ford gives a haunting, low-key performance that makes Henry Fonda's in Lang's *You Only Live Once* seem fake in comparison. The film may seem creaky at times, the jail-bird humor from Bright and Tasker gets tedious, but *Back Door to Heaven* is nevertheless a heartfelt and strangely affecting film, and can be seen as Howard's last Bronx cheer to Hollywood. In sentiment, it is not far from Nicolas Ray's *They Live by Night*. There is even a sequence prefiguring the "I'm a stranger here myself" opening of another Ray movie, *The Lusty Men*, when Frankie revisits his childhood house, now occupied by a black family—except that in feel and look and just plain doped-up weirdness, Howard's film plays more like a socially-minded *Detour*.

The production went way over its $340,000 budget, the Wall Street backers squawked but could do nothing (the downbeat aspect was structural as well as inbred and no amount of editing could brighten it up), and

Backdoor to Heaven was a dismal flop that did nothing to rekindle New York film production, nor the respective careers of William K. Howard, John Bright, or Robert Tasker.

Tasker's own death was typically dramatic and fraught with rumor. Drafted at the start of the war, he went south to do nominal work for Nelson Rockefeller's goodwill program in Latin America, and essentially forgot to come back from Mexico City. Several Mexican pictures bear his name, including *La dama de las camelias* (1944) and *Los miserables* (1943). On December 8, 1942, *Daily Variety* wrote that Tasker, 43, had been found dead in the swanky Chapultepec palace where he'd been living. An empty vial of Seconal was found by the bed. The day before, according to Gladys Flores, "grand-daughter of the former president of Costa Rica," they had quarreled and he had threatened to kill himself. Rumors flared up on the increasingly busy Hollywood-Mexico City shuttle.

According to Sam Brown, his brother Rowland was one of the last people to see Tasker alive. He claimed Tasker was very frightened because days earlier he had beaten up his wife's lover, an important man very close to the chief of police in Mexico City. He knew they were going to come for him, he told Brown, and he had sworn long ago he would never go back to jail, least of all a Mexican pit. Bright always maintained that he had it "from a famous homosexual Mexican actor" that Tasker had been smothered with a pillow.

The *San Quentin News* was the only paper to mourn "Robert J. Tasker, famous San Quentin author," adding that Tasker had made the *San Quentin Bulletin* into a literary magazine "of splendid intellectual appeal."

KNOW YOUR MOVIES

By
Welford Beaton

It is my pleasure to commend KNOW YOUR MOVIES to you. Whatever your interest in pictures, you will find in it much that will prove of value to you and nothing that is not worth reading and considering carefully.

Cecil B. de Mille

KNOW YOUR MOVIES

By WELFORD BEATON

Price $2.00

ONE OF US: WELFORD BEATON

HE **COULD GO ON THE LOT** at any studio and get the ear not only of the movie directors, whom he lauded or mocked at will, but also of moguls such as Jesse L. Lasky, Winfield R. Sheehan or Cecil B. DeMille. For nearly thirty years he was Hollywood's Jiminy Cricket, the strangest figure in the industry. In his time he was called "a lone voice of honesty and common sense." Starting in the mid-twenties with his bi-weekly *The Film Spectator*, which soon was "published every Saturday," Beaton eventually could not resist putting his name above the title, recasting his publication as *Welford Beaton's Hollywood Spectator*.

Wealthy enough to rub shoulders with movie moguls on their own turf, and educated enough to hold his own with what passed for *intelligentsia* under the palms, Beaton cut a recognizable figure on movie sets, with his prematurely white hair, white sport coats and shirts, and white tennis or buck shoes. Beaton was a Canadian who had moved to Seattle and become a magazine writer and editor. In the early twenties, he had come to Hollywood to write for the pictures, but soon became a critic. He was often hard-hitting in print, but also spoke a language the moguls could understand. Always argumentative, even pompously so, he never defended or attacked something in the name of art, but always for the sake of the box office, and common sense. His publication had nothing to do with the trades, either: Beaton was first and foremost a movie critic, the only one in town who took picture making seriously enough to earn the grudging respect of creative people like Lubitsch, Chaplin or DeMille, all of whom, plus Mary Pickord, blurbed *Know Your Movies*, Beaton's only known book. Published in 1932, it is a digest of theories he had elaborated in the preceding decade. Typical of this one-man army was the book being published by a local firm, Howard Hill (6362 Hollywood Boulevard - Hollywood, California), whose address of course was none other than the *Spectator* office, ensconsed in the elegant Palmer Building, three blocks west of Vine. *Know Your Movies* could have passed for typical movie-fan fare, albeit for the long subtitle, which reads more like a Situationist tract:

> **The Theory and Practice of Motion Picture Production**
> *The fundamentals of screen art as they affect the box-office; an analysis of the condition of the film business in 1932, with constructive suggestions for its improvement, together with discussions of the principal features of picture production and the knowledge one must acquire if he is to succeed in screen work.*

Mixing common sense, long-winded arguments and prudery, Beaton played Don Quixote against the Hollywood windmills, always in the name of economy. He had weird dislikes, such as Zeppelins, close-ups, and D.W. Griffith. His views on talking pictures, when they came, were not much different than most held at the time, but he also knew when he went wrong. Initially enthusiastic about sound, in 1932 he was advocating a return to silent movies in a long piece called "Why fight a losing fight?," which concluded that the only one who had used sound wisely and succesfully was Walt Disney. He railed savagely against "stupid producers" then importing writers and players from Broadway, and against directors who forgot all too quickly the art of silent pictures in exchange for "miles of dull dialogues and cacophony," finally advocating for a new art of talking pictures "which would not talk more than silents."

Beaton may have been a sententious windbag most of the time; the *Spectator* nevertheless makes for captivating reading, as it brings to life this rich and chaotic transition period in Hollywood. For all his debunking of the corrupt practices of the press and the trades (the going bribery rate for a prominent *Los Angeles Times* critic, he brazingly reveals, "is now five hundred dollars"), Beaton was not above a little racketeering himself. As early as 1928, when his rag is only in its second year, he solicits advertisements for the *Spectator*'s "Fiftieth Anniversary Issue" (due in early 1976). The gag works well enough: Frank Tuttle responds, "Put me down for ten pages." Others, like Edward Everett Horton or Tay Garnett, take a full page to advertise what they are up to, a play on Vine Street and a script just sold, respectively. George Sidney gripes in a letter to the editor: "I don't mind the nine dollars, Welford, but *Gott im himmel* spell my name right."

His likes and dislikes may have had the same fiduciary origins, but in general he was better disposed toward Winfield Sheehan at Fox or Joe Schenck at United Artists than towards MGM's Louis B. Mayer, or even the saintly Thalberg. *A Woman of Affairs* is good, he writes, "even though it is a Metro production." He goes on to elaborate that "the picture is good only because Clarence Brown has a clause in his contract that provides that no one is to interfere with him while he is making a picture." Which doesn't sound much like what we know of MGM. More than the indiscriminate use of close-ups, Beaton hates carnality and kissing. He likes *A Woman of Affairs* well enough and praises it, but when it comes to the kiss he loses it: "Possibly the most disgusting kisses of this fall season are those exchanged by Greta Garbo and Jack Gilbert in *A Woman of Affairs*. You can see Greta's upper lip curl backward and her jaw recede until it bends her ears. It's enough to turn one's stomach. They could not call it *The Green Hat* for it is supposed to be an immoral book, but they put things in the picture more filthy and disgusting than Arlen ever dreamed of." Similarly, after praising Clarence Badger's *Red Hair* and commending Clara Bow for her performance, he deplores a scene at the end of reel six in which Clara takes off her clothes at a party and dives into a pond. "This makes three I've seen disrobe in the presence of a crowd of men, Corinne Griffith, Billie Dove and now Clara Bow. Each scene is ridiculous, vulgar and stupid and caters to degenerate minds."

Beaton never minces words; therefore, his longevity in Hollywood remains a mystery. He calls studio heads "pimps," at least those who loan out their contract players at exorbitant prices and keep the extra money, badgering Carl Laemmle Jr. and others for the "disgraceful" practice.

Only Joe Schenck at UA, in his eyes, remains honorable: he bargains hard to get the highest price for his actors, but they get to keep the money. He also loves being vindicated. Having spotted the early work of "Willie" Wyler at Universal in a no-name Western (Beaton does not like Westerns), he crows in his review of the subsequent *The Shakedown*: "Out at Universal they'll soon be calling Willie Wyler William," adding: "I feel grateful to him for helping to maintain my status as a prophet." One wonders if Beaton was not writing for movie people alone, such is the familiarity shown in the ads they place in his magazine. One anniversary issue displays an ad from Walt Disney in which Mickey Mouse is being ransomed at gunpoint by a black-hatted Beaton. Ben Schulberg takes out one, too, asking wrily, "OK now, am I good for a year's worth of good reviews?" Paramount's head of production on occasion penned long-winded articles in the *Spectator*, like the time he protested in print against Carl Laemmle Jr.'s "folly" at buying *The Power and the Glory* from Preston Sturges, ready-made, as he would a Broadway play. The title of his piece vents an opinion that prevailed then: "Two Writers (or More) Are Better Than One." He must have been heard because his fellow moguls soon pulled rank and the practice did not reappear until the Sixties.

If the *Spectator* was more or less a one-man show, Beaton did have collaborators. Early on, his teenaged son Donald provided a dissonant voice as "the Junior Critic," a *vox populi* that may reflect the tastes of the paying public. Beaton, for instance, praised a Reinhardt production of Joe May's *Homecoming*, deploring only the deliberate pace of this European import. Junior's judgment is not so effete, thrashing the picture as any red-blooded American would: "The German must be a peculiar people, anyway," he writes, "in this country, if a man comes home and discovers his best friend living with his wife, he picks up a chair and bounces it on the friend's cranium. But the man in this picture just sat around heavily and moaned. Then he departed and got a job on a ship, leaving his wife to the friend." Donald would have been fit to be tied in front of art movies like von Sternberg's calling card in Hollywood, *The Salvation Hunters*.

Late in the life of the *Spectator*, in 1933, Beaton acquired yet another contributor, a not-so-young Colorado native who worked at the Davis Perfection Bakery in order to feed his widowed mother and her brood, while trying to make a start of it in the movie business. He worked nightshifts downtown at the bakery on N. Beaudry and Mignonette, which left him the daylight hours to study social unrest, unionism, and to write the occasional short story or magazine piece. *International Detective Magazine* was the only taker for his fiction output, but in late '33 a piece he'd written on Chaplin caught Beaton's eye, who promptly hired him as managing editor. The White Knight rarely could pay his $50 salary, but a few months around the lots bearing the colors of the *Spectator* convinced Dalton Trumbo he'd been making the wrong kind of bread all along. In 1935, after a short stint as a reader, he became a junior writer at Warner Bros. It is interesting to note that in his articles, in keeping with the *Spectator* editorial policy, Trumbo focused almost exclusively on the economic aspects of the industry. In the rare instances he ventured cinephilic opinions, they were aligned with those of Welford Beaton: no film should cost more than $100,000 (tell this to the King Bros., who would later employ him at the beginning of the blacklist to script *Gun Crazy*); a whisper from Charlie Farrell was worth more than all the Jack Barrymores in the world, etc. Still, the future scenarist of *Spartacus* was not as categorical as his employer, who in 1930 had been one of the few unimpressed by *The Big Trail*, Raoul Walsh's big screen spectacle filmed in the Grandeur process. His review was called "The Wide Screen Idiocy." In it, the irrepressible Beaton pontificated that "the motion picture industry needs broad minds, not wide screens."

Welford Beaton died in December 1951, at age 77. He had ceased activities well before this, but once he stopped no one stepped up to fill his white buck shoes. There were plenty of movie critics, reviewers, columnists and gossip witches (Beaton once described a Hollywood party in which a collection plate was passed around and then handed to one of the column-hags, who blithely pocketed the bribe)—but no one else came along who enjoyed Beaton's peculiar mix of familiarity and independence, from both directors and studio heads. He may have been a sententious, self-centered boor, but reading his *Spectator* today (small doses are advised) one gets a rare glimpse of how this industry town really worked, at least in the late twenties and thirties.

Jean Harlow gets eyeballed in a police lineup in *The Beast of the City*, written by W. R. Burnett and directed by Charles Brabin

1932-1933:
VIGILANTE PICTURES
AND THE FASCIST ATTRACTION

THERE EXISTS A BODY of Hollywood films made in 1932-1933—a narrow window just before and after F.D.R's election—that reflected the deep despair of the American people confronted with Mob power and corruption at all political levels, and their temptation to take matters into their own hands. This type of populist vigilante film never happened again, except possibly in the early 1970s, fueled by hits like *Dirty Harry* and *Death Wish*. In MGM's wonderful *The Beast of the City* (directed by Charles Brabin, from a W. R. Burnett story), Irish police captain Walter Huston had to shoot it out with the Mob in a speakeasy, a kamikaze finale worthy of *The Wild Bunch*. Gregory La Cava's political fable *Gabriel Over the White House* showed a corrupt Washington being swept out by the big broom of the same Huston, a suddenly awakened President, but the film had fascist overtones betraying the fascination Mussolini exercised over Hollywood's weaker minds. The picture was not only initiated by W. R. Hearst and produced by his Cosmopolitan Productions, but some say the Chief wrote portions of Huston's speeches in the later part of the film. Even an indie programmer like Charles E. Roberts' *Corruption* (with Preston Foster as an honest lawyer) reflected the same public sentiment of helplessness: that no matter what the police did, the press, judges, mayors and DAs were in the pockets of the racketeers, and that something had to be done about it, even outside the law.

Tay Garnett's entertaining *Okay, America!* (1932) started as a zippy pre-Code comedy and abruptly pulled the rug out from under the audience: Lew Ayres played newspaperman Larry Wayne (clearly based on Walter Winchell, who was even pegged to play the part at one time), notorious for exposing High Society's extra-marital peccadilloes in his column. Shown at first as nothing but a smart-ass scandal-mongerer, Wayne surprises us when he's able to use his contacts with the Mob to intervene in a kidnapping case. Edward Arnold is delightful as the supine, Dickens-addled top mobster, and the ending of the film is quite shocking—in keeping with *The Beast of the City* kamikaze finale. Playwright William Anthony McGuire wrote the crackling dialogue for this Universal gem.

Produced, like *Okay, America!*, by the unjustly reviled Carl Laemmle Jr. at Universal, Edward L. Cahn's *Afraid to Talk* was based on a student play by Albert Maltz and George Sklar. The film did not quite walk the talk of its original material, copping out with an obligatory happy ending. But as a political *La Ronde* (*Merry-Go-Round* was its original title), this was as hard hitting as anything in early W. R. Burnett novels. When a bellhop witnesses a mob killing that could embarrass local politicos (as it concerns a payoff), smarmy Assistant DA Louis Calhern has him railroaded for the murder. Wide-eyed Eric Linden (who plays the bellhop) may be a liability to any movie, but the rogue's gallery he's up against was impressive and effective: besides Calhern, there's Edward Arnold, Robert Warwick and Berton Churchill (as the Mayor) all writhing in a craven, unholy alliance rarely shown on-screen.

Cahn matches this toughness with several stylistic flourishes of his own, as in the horrific scene in which cops swarm over hapless Linden, who shrinks in the frame as their shadows loom against the wall. Rarely has the third degree been depicted with such raw power in the movies. The director of photography was none other than Karl Freund, who had worked with Lang and Murnau in Germany before joining Universal.

Strangely, for such a notorious kibitzer (at least according to his Warner Bros. wartime colleague A. I. Bezzerides), Albert Maltz never complained about the "Hollywood treatment" his play received. He wrote it with Sklar when they were both enrolled at the Yale School of Drama, and Maltz, for one, later dismissed *Merry-Go-Round* as "juvenile" and "politically naive"—probably meaning it wasn't dialectical and Stalinist enough. In their short-lived New York production of the play, the curtain dropped on a darkly lit prison cell in which the young bellhop was found hanging.

Even the weirder-than-weird Cahn couldn't get as bleak as this in 1932. Still, when one sees the picture today, it seems inexplicable that Cahn chose the path he did: from promising, even ambitious artist to director of shorts at MGM, only to follow the downward spiral from B-movie director to provider for the Hollywood grind at places like PRC, Allied Artists, and American-International Pictures.

Rowland (left) and Sam Brown, with Rowland's son and Sam's daughter, Moya

TWO BROTHERS FROM OHIO

These days I have been endlessly intrigued by the Edelman theory about how the brain functions. Memories are not filed away, like a motion picture in a can, which you can watch again at the pressing of a button; rather, it is recreated, like a play, which explains why it is never quite like the preceding performances. The interpretation also weakens. Inevitably.

Gore Vidal's answer to "A Day in the World,"
special issue of *Le Nouvel Observateur*, April 29, 1994

he old man has beautiful smooth features: healthy pink skin, hair fine and perfectly white. His gray eyes are practically unseeing. When he tilts his head back to laugh or to reel back a name from the past, you see him in luminous black-and-white, whiter than black, one of those exalted close-ups in Borzage silent pictures, maybe. If Sam Gilson Brown's eyes are so gray, it is not only because his diabetes is clouding them, but also because, dredging up the past as he has been these past few days, a little muck has also risen. Try as he might to tell you about his older brother Rowland in glowing terms, how he was more important than Orson Welles for the development of Hollywood in the thirties, how his brother launched careers such as George Raft's or Barry Sullivan's, Sam can't help bringing up his own life, measuring it against his more famous sibling's until it becomes one complex continuum, one long interwoven story.

It is also the story of a family, not only the life of a man who cut a wide swath in his time and left many tracks in the newspapers of his day. There will be other voices than Sam Brown's in this story, other voices warning that one should not always believe him.

For me, at first, Sam Brown—a retired prop-man and sometime scriptwriter—was a mere source of information on his director-writer brother, Rowland. Each time I heard him veer off course and mention his own career I would, like a rude nurse, put him back on track. But later, listening to the tapes, his mentions of Tom Mix, Murnau, and Tahiti alerted me to the fact that maybe the real story was there, *that I had to go back to Azuza, where Brown lived in the house of his daughter Moya; go back to hear* his *story, not Rowland's, and measure what tied them together, and what drew them apart. Sam Brown was 88 at the time of these long interviews, when the sun was always streaming through the windows because he liked to "bake his old bones," as he said, chuckling. His brother Rowland was born in the 19th century, on November 16, 1900 and he died on May 6, 1963. Sam, his junior by six years, passed away on September 10, 1991.*

SAM: When we were kids we were all taken by Horatio Alger's stories. My mother read his books to us, four kids under the covers in one big bed. Rowland never lost a word of them. They all told the same story: become rich, and everything will be all right. A theory that turned out to be built on mud because all of a sudden one day we had nothing. When he was alive, my father had been rich. He was a real estate developer. At one time, he owned 41% of Cleveland Heights, which is still one of the finest suburbs there. Rowland idolized my father; his world was a world of men. My father was strong and tough, like all of us. One day I saw him punch a man. I never thought a man could fly so far. He was an agnostic, but he insisted we go to church. Rowland was like him in every way, and of course he was his favorite. His full name was Rowland Chauncey Brown, after the famous singer Chauncey Olcott, a friend of my father's. Needless to say, this Little Lord Fauntleroy middle name owed Rowland quite a few fights in the school yard. If anything, it made him tougher. My idol was Rowland; he was six years older than me, so he did not take me with him very often. He was not religious, not a believer, and yet all his stories, all his films have

Studio portrait photo of Rowland Brown, early 1930s

religious references and overtones. Even his titles, there's always a hell, or a devil, or angels with dirty faces! Me, I had faith, always had, from the beginning. When I was very little, you'd find me up a tree, the highest I could climb, singing the loudest I could, my face turned up towards the sky. Where these words I sang came from, I never knew. My mother was Welsh, very religious, a believer through and through. She was very gay and lighthearted, even after my father died in 1913. Within a year, his fortune had vanished; she'd been rooked by my father's partners, by the lawyers, all those people she used to see around the house and considered her friends. Rowland was twelve then; I was six. But the household remained cheerful, we had a good life, even if growing up in Canton, Ohio, was not obvious for any kid. Canton was a tough town.

MOYA, Sam's daughter: They were rich twice during their lives, the Brown brothers. Their mother dressed all of her children in white, with wide collars, girls and boys alike. They all had blond hair, very fine, almost white. We still have a picture from that time, the whole family in their Sunday best, taken at a picnic. In a graveyard, if you can believe this! Toots was the oldest. She was the pillar of the family after the father died. When Rowland quarreled with the family, he went and joined her in Los Angeles, where she'd been living. She died of an infected goiter, very young. She was twenty-two. The other sister was Jean. Rowland and she did not speak to each other. Anna, their mother, was always very positive, very cheerful. Always hanging out at Harold Lloyd's house after they moved to Los Angeles. She was in the Assistance League. Neither she nor Aunt Jean ever had to work in their lives. Me, I knew Uncle Rowland mostly from the time he was with his third wife, Karen. They lived like gypsies, one day riding in a Cadillac, the next in a Greyhound bus. One time, I was little but I remember, they arrived at our house in the middle of the night. The previous year they had been living at the Garden of Allah; they weren't married, but they had a child, Stephen. They were coming to live with us because they'd run out of money, which happened often over the years. I remember this strange child, white-haired like all of them, but skinny, probably from malnutrition. That was Rowland in a nutshell: from the relative luxury of the Garden of Allah, the famous bungalow hotel on Sunset, to a trundle bed at our house. A year later, they were moving around in a brand-new Thunderbird.

SAM: Of all of us, Rowland was the wildest and the most emancipated. Like my father, he had to measure up against everybody. He knew everybody in all those Ohio towns, he knew all the gangs, Jewish, Italian... even the Purple Gang, the Jewish crew that had all the rackets in Detroit. They were not killing each other yet. They were just young, like we were. We could have been like them. Rowland understood them, and later he knew how to portray them better than anyone. Very soon he had a reputation, mostly in the sporting world. He boxed some, but he wasn't very good because he never trained. One time, though, he sparred with Jack Dempsey and did three rounds with him; he even knocked him down. Probably an accident. He was better as an artist. He drew cartoons for the sports sheets. He opened a speakeasy in Detroit, which took off immediately. People came to see you, if you were known, even a little. Rowland did the remodeling [and] the decor in his club. He could do anything.

He had met his first wife in art school. She was five years older and was already an established illustrator. She worked for all the ad agencies. Soon he was as good as she was. It was with her that he went to Los Angeles for the first time in 1922. Her parents lived there. Then he went back a second time to join our older sister. In Los Angeles, he did a bit of everything: sold cars, real estate. ... I was sending him letters, giving him news of the family. I was a sophomore in college, and he always boasted that he had a little brother with a gift for writing; he showed my letters to his friends, and one day one of them told him he should bring me over, I could maybe get a job writing cards for the silents, or write stories for the movies. And so he did send for me. Of course, I did not find any writing work, but during our first five years there I supported Rowland while he was trying to make it in the movie business. I found a job as a ditch digger, and then as a grip on the Fox lot. I was giving Rowland one dollar a day out of my earnings. He had written one or two short plays that were produced in little theatres, but otherwise he was not doing so well. He was always taking the side streets when he walked somewhere, for fear of meeting someone who'd ask how things were going for him.

MOYA: Aunt Jean claims that half the stories Sam tells about Rowland are pure inventions; like this speakeasy story, or the fact that he supported Rowland for five years in the beginning. I don't know, it is possible. I only know that my father has a saint complex, he always wants to see himself as a savior for his family, always ready to sacrifice himself. There is a lot of bitterness in all his talk: Sam never let his hair down in his life, he always tried to be perfect, always afraid of doing something sinful. Uncle Rowland was the opposite, he always did as he pleased. And he never complained, even when things did not fall right for him. He always found a way to bounce back, or to make do until he did. Once, in the fifties, he even wrote for a comic-book company! Earning just enough to be able to go to the track. My father, on the other hand, the family is an obsession with him. He left instructions for his body to be shipped to Girard, Ohio, to be buried between his father and Rowland. Why does he need to have his body shipped over there, when his whole family is here? Even Rowland died in California. He even wanted to dig up Toots, from where she'd been in Colorado for thirty years. On the other hand, his mother is at Forest Lawn, without a stone or nothing. She is in an unmarked grave, not far from where Tom Mix is.

SAM: Rowland at that time lived in a little one-room apartment above a garage, corner of Gower and Sunset, which he shared with the man who taught him how to write. His name was George Hull, and he was the best Western writer in Hollywood at one time. Did all these movies with John Ford and Harry Carey at Universal. George lived on one quart of whisky and one quart of milk a day, and was on his way down. It was there that Rhea, Rowland's first wife, came to look him up. They had separated. She'd been earning a lot of money as an illustrator, and he did not, so there were tensions. This, and she was the kind to correct him when he said "ain't." She did it for his own good, because she loved him, but he could not stand it. And yet he never loved a woman like he loved her. So that time, Rhea was staying at the Ambassador. She never drank, and neither did Rowland.

Rowland Brown looked every bit the American gangster when he transferred his filmmaking career to England

A glass of sherry, socially, that was all. But because she was so nervous that day when she went to see him at his little apartment, she had a drink or two, to brace herself. When she got there, Rowland told her she reeked of booze, called her all kinds of names, called her a tramp. She ran away, in tears. Later, when he became famous, he wanted to marry her again. But one week before he asked her, she'd married John Bauer, who did all those covers for *The Saturday Evening Post.* She wanted a father for the child she'd had with my brother, Rowland Jr. After this, Rowland was never the same again, he became harder, more cynical. He remained a bachelor in his good years. He had plenty of women, but was never in love with any of them. It was not Rhea's fault, though, more like his. They stayed friends. But besides my father's death, this breakup is what changed him the most.

Rowland was still knocking on doors in Hollywood. He was a gag-man at Warner's for a spell. At that time, he was living in a small hotel on Sunset and Van Ness, just in front of where the old Warner lot was. Clark Gable, who was just a bit-player then, stayed at the same dump, which was called the Kenmore... But after five years trying, Rowland finally wrote two one-act plays, out of which he cobbled a story called *A Handful of Clouds.* Which was a slang expression for a gunshot. He had a friend who was a reader at Warner, Carl Erickson, and Carl showed the story to Zanuck. Zanuck was head of production at Burbank, and he told Rowland to come and see him. He offered him $5,000 for the story. Now, my brother was skint at the time, but he grabbed the manuscript and tore it in half in front of Zanuck. He was furious. "It's the best story I've ever written!" And he stormed out of the office. When he told my mother, she just laughed. This was so like Rowland. Flat broke, but still refusing to be taken avantage of, even if the money was a considerable sum for him at the time. The next day he was beginning to have second thoughts about his gesture! But that day the phone rang in the hotel corridor. It was for him. It was Zanuck. "Come on over, you crazy fool, let's make a movie." Rowland was offered more money, I can't recall just how much. And this became *The Doorway to Hell,* which made tons of money for Warner and gave Zanuck a big head—because naturally he claimed responsibility for all of the script. Except that there was something about Rowland's stuff, you always recognized his mark. A certain sensibility, a way of doing things. He had a very peculiar sense of humor, very dry, almost elusive. The audience had to work, he did not chew it for you.

The Doorway to Hell script was credited to actor-writer George Rosener (shilling for Zanuck), but nonetheless it did launch Rowland Brown's Hollywood career. Which his brother Sam found ironic: "I had been working for the movies for years already, I had become a prop man at Fox. First for Tom Mix, then for Murnau. I had come to Hollywood to write, and it was Rowland who became the scenario writer! Yet, if ever someone was not cut out to be a writer, it was my brother. He wrote in telegraphic style, mostly. His secretaries had to deal with it. He could hardly write, or spell. Nobody knew this, except his collaborators, who were more his typists than anything. But he knew how to tell a story, and play all the parts in front of producers as good as any Barrymore. But boy, when he was thinking about a story and cooking something up, you'd better not be around. He was a horror. He had to know how it ended. Once he had the ending, he wrote the thing very fast. You can always spot an ending cooked up by Rowland: the hat rolling in the gutter (*Quick Millions*), Cagney pretending he's yellow on his way to the gas chamber (*Angels with Dirty Faces*) ... And he was the first to write visually for talking pictures, which at the time was still mostly filmed theater. You watch his pictures, even if the techniques are still crude the action flows, there is a naturalness to it that contemporary movies didn't have yet. And they are very loose, very casual. Rowland didn't write in dramatic terms. He did not care about structure, he only wrote bits of scenes, little pieces of throwaway business that accumulated and gave you a character. The plot was secondary.

"Zanuck liked Rowland. He gave him a leg up in the business. He let him work as a gagman for Archie Mayo, the big zero who directed *The Doorway to Hell*. Zanuck's script is very different from Rowland's original. His was full of little details that showed he knew criminals and how they thought and behaved. He had information Zanuck couldn't have had. Like for instance, Mileaway's lawyer was a black man, which might sound surprising for the times. But in the twenties, the best criminal lawyer in Chicago, named De Priest, was black.

"The character played by Cagney in the picture was called Mileaway Thomas, because he was always miles aways from the corpse, the rare times a corpse was found. There were a lot of Mileaways in his pictures. Lew Ayres was the star of *The Doorway to Hell*—he'd just made *All Quiet on the Western Front* at Universal; but Rowland had spotted Cagney and liked him so much that on the set he kept suggesting bits of business to Mayo, to beef up Cagney's part. Him and my brother remained pals for a long time."

"Big Zero" Mayo actually didn't direct *The Doorway to Hell* with two left feet, as he did many pictures in his long career; it's actually a seminal gangster film, and a forerunner of Brown's own directorial debut, *Quick Millions*. Zanuck's fingerprints can be found here and there (a prison breakout is a bit hokey, if well filmed), but the leisurely pace is all Brown's. Or it may just be something endemic to good early sound pictures: no music to speak of, characters dragging their words—Lew Ayres especially, but also Robert Elliott, who plays "Pat O'Grady," a police detective with an understanding of criminals—verging on empathy—and one of Rowland Brown's best creations. This laconic cop knows what's going on. Early on he pays the two principals a friendly visit, to warn them. He actually likes the mugs, Louie Ricarno (Ayres) and Mileaway Thomas (Cagney), two-bit crooks on their way up, with O'Grady lying in wait for them. The casting of Ayres is a liability. Although fine for the most part, he just isn't tough enough. He is supposed to organize the Chicago mob into a semi-legitimate business, and does it so well that all the other hoods come to depend on him. They balk when he decides to leave the rackets to Mileaway in order to "retire" with his wife (a bland Dorothy Mathews), who is two-timing him with Cagney. O'Grady knows all this, but keeps quiet until he can use it against them. Robert Elliott is especially fine. A leading man in the silents since 1916 (he was in von Stroheim's *Greed*), he then played flatfoot cops, judges or prison wardens in hundreds of pictures from the 1930s until 1942 (when he played an uncredited cop in the first version of *My Sister Eileen*).

SAM: So Rowland was doing all right, but one day Zanuck was supposed to buy a story my brother had told him, and he didn't. I don't know what happened exactly, but Rowland told me he went to see Zanuck, looked him straight in the eyes and told him, "You know Darryl, you've got rat's teeth. You look like a rat. And the fact is, you *are* a rat!" Well, that didn't go down so well; after this, he wasn't welcome at the studio. But not much later, after Zanuck left Warner to head Century Pictures for Joe Schenck (before they merged with Fox), he called on my brother to make a picture there. Zanuck was in a fix because he had bragged to the shareholders he could produce a slate of six pictures before the end of the year, and he had only six months left. He told Rowland, "Come on over, you son-of-a-bitch, I need you, and you need me." And he was right: if only those two had been able to stand each other, they would have become the best team in Hollywood. Zanuck always knew how to make other people work at their best, you can't take that from him. So Rowland went over and he made *Blood Money* for Zanuck. And still later, Zanuck called him in again to fix *Johnny Apollo*, although there were a lot of writers on that one. Zanuck was good at structure, but he was above all a showman, and he could be tacky sometimes. So, of course, he had to meddle with *Blood Money*. After Rowland was done shooting, Zanuck wrote another ending, which has Darryl written all over it: a bomb is concealed inside the eightball, and they play pool! Rowland refused to shoot that. He walked away. Lefty Hough, his assistant and prop man (he was also Ford's at the time), shot that scene with the eightball. Still, Zanuck appreciated my brother's qualities, mostly his originality. But it is not easy to forget that someone once called you a rat.

"Rowland's career really took off when William Wilkerson launched his trade publication, *The Hollywood Reporter*, which at least in the beginning was just a racket. He had started all those restaurants and clubs, the Vendome, then the Trocadero, later Ciro's, and there was a guaranteed plug in his paper if you were seen in one of those places. You were a publicist or a producer and you wanted to plant a story, you just reserved for six at the Vendome, which was just a block away from the *Reporter* on Sunset. But Wilkerson really liked Rowland, and he plugged him like crazy; they wrote that he was signed here, that he was starting on a project there. Most of the time it was just bunk: up till then, the only screen credit Rowland had was the script he wrote in 1929 for a Hoot Gibson Western at Universal [*Points West*, Arthur Rosson], and the story credit Zanuck let him have for *The*

Brown's casual, informal handling of *Quick Millions* initially scared Fox executives, but the film quickly won raves for the insouciance of its performances and direction

Doorway to Hell. But there was someone else who liked Rowland, Harry Leon Wilson, an old newspaper editor who wrote books and was working at Fox at the time. He wrote *Ruggles of Red Gap*, the novel, not the movie. Also *Merton of the Movies*. Rowland's first directing job happened in a funny way. He was at Fox working as a gagman on a William Beaudine picture, and he had grown this pencil mustache because he wanted to look older, to be taken more seriously. But you couldn't say it was very becoming. One day in the studio parking lot at the corner of Sunset and Western, Wilson sees him and says: listen, you promise me you'll shave this horror, I'll get you a picture to direct. Of course, Wilson knew what he was doing, he'd noticed all those visual ideas Rowland had. This is why they had him as a gagman, because they could pump him for all sorts of ideas. Still, it was a time when things like this could happen to you. We were all young.

"So Rowland made *Quick Millions*. He wrote the script with a very good reporter named Courtenay Terrett, who like many newspapermen was a drunk and ruined his career because of that. Gene Fowler was another one. Terrett knew the subject he was writing about very well, he knew gangsters and cops, but as far as writing, it was all Rowland. Terrett could not remember a single name. He called people by what they were driving. You rode in a Caddy, he called you Cadillac. Or Mr. Pierce-Arrow. I knew him, I ghosted for him once or twice. He used to spitball an idea in some producer's office and got an advance from him to write it; then he called me. "Sam, you can do it, it's all here." I did it once, twice, but he never paid me. But Rowland, I saw to it that he should be well protected. I'd been working at Fox for years, so I picked his crew, and they were all aces. Joseph August for photography, Harold Schuster for editing, who'd done *Sunrise* for Murnau. Even the script girl was the best on the lot; later she became a scriptwriter for Zanuck. And it was a good thing he had a good, experienced crew because Rowland shot very little film, and he printed even less. The brass at Fox saw the rushes, they went balistic: Rowland was not covering himself at all. If they'd given him Tom Mix's editor, for instance, he'd never have known what to do with the material. But Schuster knew. And once the film was cut, and they showed it to the brass at Fox, everybody raved about it. All the Fox directors watched it, even Mr. Ford. Because it was really new, what he'd done. First, it was natural. And there was this casualness, this way to tell things, very flat, almost laconic. Very subtle, sometimes you did not even spot the humor. And it looked real. Rowland knew a lot of people, and he brought in Raft, and Robert Tasker, who was just out of jail on parole. He could smell the real article. Tasker was way over his head in that one, same as Raft—he had never acted before. You couldn't show people being killed in those days, at least the killer doing it in the same shot as the victim. So Rowland had this long scene in the garage, the only thing you saw of Raft was the hem of his coat, and his shoes, and you heard the shots. It was very evocative and very scary. Tasker and my brother were attracted to each other because of their backgrounds. He knew a lot of people that Rowland wanted to know. Tasker was not a bad man. Rowland saw a nice guy in him. A very good-looking man.

Even (Spencer) Tracy ... Tracy was glad to be playing a gangster, becaue he could do it with very little make-up. He hated make-up. He'd just done *Up the River* for Ford, but otherwise he hadn't done much yet. George Raft—Rowland didn't give him many lines, because it was his first picture, but he had him do what he always did best: look good and dance. So he gave him little bits of business, like when you see him dressed to go out. At one point, he opens a drawer and he selects a handgun, like you would a handkerchief or a tie. As if he wanted the gun to match his cufflinks! And that dance he does at the party, it seems like it just happens, spur of the moment. It's at the hotel where Bugs Raymond (Tracy) gives a cocktail party. There is this black piano player, and George starts sliding, but his body remains straight, like his legs are not moving. It was marvelous the way he'd hike his jacket sleeves and pant legs. So smooth. It was the first time in pictures gangsters were shown right, dressed like princes in $500 suits, not like pimps. And the reason Rowland did this was not because he was in awe of them, but because he wanted to show that the rich, the capitalists, the high society people, were not much better than the hoods. There is this scene where Raymond explains to this banker or politician (John Wray) that their rackets are not much different. This is why he would be so interested in [Edward Anderson's] *Thieves Like Us* later on, a book saying that bankers are worse than bank robbers. And that was something that took a lot of nerve at the time. Rowland was harder on the craven politicians and industrialists than he was on Bugs Raymond, even if he kills him at the end. He sees Bugs as a good Joe, but with a criminal turn of mind. And the way he shows how Bugs becomes a racketeer is different than the usual psychological pap they have in other movies. There are no bad parents, no social reasons: just logic. When Bugs loses his trucking job because of the rackets, he just sits and thinks it over, and he goes for another career, a racket of his own. Rowland equated American capitalism and the underworld, the way it was organized and structured. And this forty-one years before *The Godfather*!

"At the time we had communist ideas, my brother and I: Russia for us looked like a panacea. Once, Rowland even wanted to send me there, so that I could learn first-hand what was going on. All this is to say that Rowland had advanced ideas, progressive ideas. Like Anderson said in his novel *Thieves Like Us*, which my brother later bought to adapt: bankers are much better thieves than bank robbers.

BUGS RAYMOND

A parasite, you say? No, no, you don't get it. I'm just a brainy guy, too nervous to steal, too lazy to work. I do the dirty work for people, and they get to appreciate it... All the laws are made by man to protect honest people, but how many you think can claim they are honest? The rackets, it's just a way to put your hands on something someone else owns. In a nice way.

SAM: The picture was not a success. Reviews were good; the people at Fox were so pleased they gave Rowland a thousand dollar bonus and a paid trip to Europe on top of that. But nobody in the country wanted to see this picture. It was too new, too loose, people didn't know what to make of it."

As always, Welford Beaton, of *The Film Spectator*, had something sharp to say about it:

> *The Public Enemy* is without a doubt the most realistic and the most dramatic portrait of a gangster's career this reporter has ever seen, but nevertheless it remains realistic in a dramatic way ... Artistically, that is to say fundamentally, it isn't much more than the remarkable criminal personality James Cagney gave us in other pictures. I see no reason to look for any hidden genius behind it. Wellman's direction is volcanic and well paced. This is a topical story, coming directly from a newspaper column. But not much more. By contrast, *Quick Millions*, a much better picture artistically, was ignored and doomed to oblivion. Many called it awkward, episodic, incoherent. The truth is, it had the fastest direction, the best editing and the most original dialogue this industry has ever known. *The Public Enemy* is a good crowd-pleaser, but the real connoisseurs will prefer *Quick Millions*.

SAM: So, Rowland went to Paris at Fox's expense, and when he returned they wanted him to direct *The Yellow Ticket*, a story set in Paris. But Rowland refused and slammed the door behind him. He had already made a deal with Carl Laemmle Jr. He was under contract at Universal for two or three years, and he never made a film there! He preferred being loaned out here and there. Contracts never meant much to Rowland. ... David Selznick had just become head of production at RKO and he wanted him to direct *State's Attorney*. Mostly because he knew my brother was an intimate of Jack Barrymore. Rowland had brought him to Madame Francis for his first time—Hollywood's most famous brothel. At RKO, he was partnered with Gene Fowler to write the script. It got off rather inauspiciously. Rowland had a girlfirend at the time, Marcella Sayres, and she'd done something he didn't like, so he took this great big bottle of perfume she had, and poured it all over her. Well, of course, he got some on himself, too. So, when he met Gene in Selznick's office, the whole place reeked. Gene didn't quite know what to make of it, thinking Rowland was a poof or something. They used to joke about it afterwards when they became friends. The only problem they had was my brother didn't drink, so that was a problem for Gene."

Selznick and studio producer Pandro Berman also had a problem with Gene: when Fowler presented himself to the studio for the first time, he was refused entrance by the guard, not used to seeing any RKO employee arriving on a bicycle. Fowler went back to his hotel and stayed there a few days until Berman located him and made arrangements with the gate personnel. And other arrangements: Fowler insisted on having his office entirely renovated, his wish list including bare white walls, an Underwood #5, and a hat rack. He refused to have a secretary, but demanded that the studio rent him a small apartment on an adjacent street so that he could go out for his frequent naps and other forms of "relaxation." Apparently, he did not know about the many girls who could be had for the same kind of daytime sport in the upstairs rooms of the Tudor building just in front of the Paramount lot (the two blocks on Melrose have since been annexed by the studio, but the building with the Tudor decorative beams can still be seen on the new lot). So, on the surface, Fowler and Brown seemed unlikely partners. But the two men loved boxing. Brown had his own gym in the new bachelor pad he'd taken just above the Sunset Strip; he drove a Pierce-Arrow, had a Chinese valet, was seen in the clubs with the Countess di Frasso or Estelle Taylor. And there was this story about him decking Dempsey in training. Other than this, the two men couldn't have been more different. Fowler was one of Hollywood's most prodigious drinkers, associating with legendary lushes like W. C. Fields, John Barrymore and Gregory La Cava. Brown spent his money exclusively on women, gambling, tailored clothes, and a particular type of cookie he had the disconcerting habit of storing in an umbrella stand behind his office door. In spite of these differences, Fowler and Brown got along like thieves, and although *State's Attorney* was eventually directed by George Archainbaud, it bears Brown's unmistakable mark in many ways:

Item: corrupt laywer Barrymore meets with his gangster client in the locker room of a sauna for more privacy. Watching the latter's posterior being massaged by a mechanical strap, he notices a gun sticking out of his back pocket and quips: "Careful with this, you could blow your brains out."

Item: a girl tries to coax Barrymore into accepting candies instead of a strong drink. "They say candy produces alcohol in the stomach," she ventures. "It better be true," grumbles Barrymore, not at all convinced.

In spite of its excruciatingly slow pace, this pre-Code picture abounds in such delights and throwaway lines. Who else but Rowland Brown would come up with "sending for eye-witnesses in Milwaukee?" This is typical of Brown's view of the criminal life, his prosaic approach, his dry humor (which sometimes went unnoticed), and above all a fond complicity with these men, which may have turned some audiences off but makes Brown so remarkable today.

SAM: Rowland was set to direct *State's Attorney*, he was going to be paid $50,000 to make this picture. He was to start on a Monday, this was on Friday, but at the last moment the front office refused to give him the crew he wanted. Once again, it was a case of friendship and loyalty. Lee Garmes had just been suspended by Paramount, to please [von] Sternberg, because people everywhere said that Lee was responsible for the "Sternberg look," not Joe. So, Rowland wanted to hire Lee to help him out of being blackballed. But Selznick refused because all these guys were a close club, all these moguls knew each other, played high stakes poker together, tennis on the weekend, went to the races together. ... If a guy was blackballed, it was tough to break because the bosses closed ranks. So, Rowland left the picture at the last moment. Leo Tover was the photographer, in the end. For Rowland, it was a question of principles. But this is when he started to get the reputation, what the press called him for a long time, "the man who never finishes a picture." At RKO, he did direct *Hell's Highway*, but it is true he did not finish it, in a way, because he did not agree with the moralizing ending the studio wanted to tag on the picture, with Dix coming back from escaping the prison camp so he can clear his little brother, and the prison administrator who gets caught and ends up doing time for sadism and negligence of duty. Which was a laugh, these things never happened, and Rowland knew it. But in these cases, he never insisted, never made a scene. He just shrugged and walked away. John Cromwell shot those last scenes, he was on it for three or four days.

Set photographs in the RKO archives confirm this: one cannot mistake Rowland Brown's massive shoulders and the intimidating biceps under his rolled-up shirtsleeves with the thin and frail director one sees on another set of photographs next to Eddie Cronjager, the director of photography. The picture, supposed to take place in a state other than California, was shot in some Hollywood Hills canyon, where a makeshift prison camp was built. The chain-gang convicts all wear curious uniforms with targets painted on the back—typical of Brown's peculiar gallows humor. From the very opening of the picture we know we are with a social critic of another stripe, when, coming into the prison camp, a sign reads "LIBERTY ROAD, soon open to the public." Just as he denounced capitalist businessmen in *Quick Millions*, here Brown exposes the many States then exploiting prisoners as slave labor, prison boards in cahoots with political cronies, and officials who skimped on convict food and pocketed the savings. This was a time when a number of motion pictures protested such practices and advocated prison reforms: from the weirder-than-weird Edward Cahn adaptation of Jim Tully's lugubrious book *Laughter in Hell* (in which convicts were kept in cells on wheels so they could be easily shipped to dispose of corpses in a town decimated by yellow fever) to the truly admirable *I Was a Fugitive from a Chain Gang*, the Warner Bros. picture which totally eclipsed *Hell's Highway* at the box-office and in film history books. Based on the famous and controversial book by prison reformer Robert E. Burns, the film benefitted from a superior performance by Paul Muni and the energetic direction of Mervyn LeRoy. Still, *Hell's Highway* can be appreciated today for many sequences, such as the one in which a deaf and dumb escaped convict is shot down because he can't hear the warnings. There are also more lighthearted moments: Brown made good use of his cartoonist talents to tell us, graphically, what is being done to "Popeye," the cuckolded guard, through a series of cartoons supposedly drawn by a black convict, while his colored brothers sing lustily snippets of "Frankie and Johnny": "*He was her man / but he done her wrong.*" For once, the obligatory Negro spiritual was for-

Rowland Brown (center) directing *Hell's Highway*, which he chose not to finish due to studio interference: "I wasn't making convict pictures for choirboys"

feited for something more spiritual. In a similar vein, a religious nutcase (in for polygamy) complained: "Hitting a bank is nothing: try to make three women happy at the same time." Or another convict, the forever boasting "Romeo," who receives signed pictures of Constance Bennett, which fan magazines then peddled by the thousands. When another inmate asks if he really knew her, he replies, indignantly: "They're signed, ain't they?" It is funny, but also non-judgmental; the cook is clearly a nance, but there is no cruelty or derision in the depiction. It is a way of seeing things you find in all of Brown's pictures, and, in spurts, in his scripts directed by others.

Brown had been shooting for a month when he left *Liberty Road*, as it was still called (the studio chickened out on the cheeky title). He seems to have shot many "additional" scenes, mostly off-the-cuff bits of business. His style was clearly incremental, and in this, very unusual for Hollywood, where only a few creators were allowed their peculiarities, provided they made money. La Cava was one, Leo McCarey, and to a certain extent, Edmund Goulding (Thalberg at MGM sometimes let him shoot without a finished script). The RKO archives indicate that Cromwell took over from Brown after a short hiatus, and shot for another week. The archives are also instructive on the salary scale of the various professions: Richard Dix, still a big star at the time, was signed for a $60,000 straight fee. Samuel Ornitz, ex-con Robert Tasker and Rowland Brown earned, respectively, $4,416, $1,237 and $3,833 for their work on the script. Brown's rate for directing was $1,000 a week, which netted him $7,000. In spite of all this, Brown did not hesitate to go to the press about his leaving the picture, declaring: "The studio wanted me to make so many changes in the ending, it just wasn't the story I wanted to tell. I told them I wasn't making convict pictures for choirboys."

SAM: When Rowland was barred from a studio, he often came back in through the window, like when they needed him for *What Price Hollywood?* at RKO. This was right after the snafu over *State's Attorney*, Selznick had told Rowland he'd never set foot on the RKO lot again. But it was Pandro Berman's first production for the studio, and they couldn't lick the story. Jane Murfin and all the others had been on it for six months, but she didn't know Hollywood like we did, from the street. When Berman called

Rowland, my brother said he couldn't help him because he'd been barred from the studio. Pandro said, "Let me worry about that." And two weeks later, Rowland had an office on the lot. He laid on the bed for an hour or so—yes, he had a bed in his office—then he told Gene, 'I think I got it.' Which with him meant he had the ending. He and Fowler wrote *What Price Hollywood?* in five weeks. This story of the Brown Derby waitress who marries her alcoholic mentor because he gave her a leg-up to stardom as an actress—this is the quintessential Hollywood story, remade many times—*A Star Is Born* and all that.

"By 1933, Rowland lived on Pinehurst Road. He liked it there because of the location. Right above Franklin, but still close to everything in Hollywood. At the same time, it was very quiet. He should have bought the house. It belonged to Leon Ames, who was a fine actor. Leon had a bit part in *Quick Millions*, when he was still named Leon Waycoff. And Rowland had cast him in *State's Attorney*, too. At that time, Rowland often picked me up in his Packard, and he would ask, "Want to go for a ride?" We would always have to make a detour to the corner of Hollywood and Cahuenga, where there was this little apple seller. This was the Depression, there were a lot of them in the streets. But he would always go to the same one and buy his apples, paid way over price for them. He was his lucky piece for the races. Driving, he would ask me what I thought of such and such story, or about a scene he'd just come up with. More often than not, I'd say it was no good, or plain awful, and I'd explain why. And he would always shake his head, smiling and saying: 'You'll never learn, you're just a kid.' It is true his ideas never seemed very good to me at first. But when you thought about them for five minutes, you started seeing the possibilities. He saw them right from the start, of course. They were very original ideas that had never been tried before. Today, of course, they would seem run-of-the-mill. Like the ending of *Angels with Dirty Faces*. He had this peculiar way to tell you a story in reverse because this is how he worked it out."

By 1933, Brown did not need William Wilkerson's good graces to have his name in the press, even though some of the items in *The Hollywood Reporter* might have been planted. In January, the Howard Hughes organization announced it would film a remake of *The Racket*, a gangster picture Lewis Milestone had made for him in 1928 as a silent. Rowland Brown was set to write the scenario. Two days later the millionnaire changed his mind and announced that Brown would instead pen a sequel to *Scarface* for him, with Edward Arnold starring. As often happened with Hughes' projects, nothing came of it. Come February, Brown was at MGM, supposed to write a legionnaire story for Wallace Beery and Clark Gable called *Man Stands Alone*, but nothing came of that either. Then he and Fowler sold RKO a story idea cheekily called *The Great Hollywood Robbery*—which really was what they were doing, in a minor and routine way. Rowland Brown's name was now sufficiently known to make the gossip columns, like that night in July when he was spotted at the Cocoanut Grove with Estelle Taylor. Two tables down sat Jack Dempsey, whom she had just divorced, showing off with his new squeeze and future wife, Broadway singer Hannah Williams. No KO this time around.

On September 19, 1933, at last, the *Los Angeles Herald* announced something that stuck:

> Hollywood's "bad boy" has finally redeemed himself. Rowland Brown has finished a picture at last, and everybody agrees it is a winner. On top of that, Brown finished shooting four days ahead of schedule and $40,000 under budget. Darryl Zanuck is so pleased he picked up his contract option. Brown should be at work on a new picture within two months. Within two or three years Brown has acquired a curious position here in Hollywood. He is generally considered an ingenious writer and a great director, but at the same time is known as the man who left the most productions than anyone in the business. "But I always had good reasons for doing so," says Brown, who will spend the next month in Europe.

Blood Money, a modest picture in terms of both story and budget, nevertheless showed the qualities that would have made Brown a great director had he been able to develop. It is a leisurely paced picture in which plot is largely beside the point. Rather, it is an accumulation of little bits of busi-

George Bancroft plays bailbondsman Bill Bailey in Brown's unsentimental and hardboiled *Blood Money*

ness and throwaway scenes which ends up bringing half-a-dozen characters to life. "All my life I wanted to meet a dame who likes raw scallions," says Bill Bailey to Elaine, a young socialite who is slumming in his criminal *demimonde*. In just one sentence, the bailbondsman played by George Bancroft is fully drawn. Bailey's partner and lover is a nightclub owner named Ruby Darling, played by Judith Anderson at her toughest. But she is clearly on her way out when Elaine (a thrill-seeking minx played by an uncharacteristically bitchy Frances Dee) comes to Bailey for a bond; she has been caught and arrested for petty theft. Bailey falls hard for her, in spite of the ever-understanding Ruby's warnings, and the plot (barely) thickens when Elaine's no-good brother steals the bonds she gave Bailey as collateral.

Blood Money: Frances Dee and Chick Chandler getting up to no good. Dee described her character as "a kleptomaniac, a nymphomaniac, and anything in-between"

Elaine skips, and Bailey is $50,000 out of pocket. After a few improbable plot turns (including the hokey eightball gag concocted by Zanuck), Bailey goes back to Ruby.

According to Sam Brown, the script was written in just a few days, so desperate was Zanuck for product that year. Hal Long, whose first movie credit (for "Continuity") this is, would end up furnishing the story for *Johnny Apollo*, which Brown co-wrote in 1940. "Hal Long was the sweetest boy," said Sam. "He was a reader at Warner. He and another one, Carl Erickson, those two were responsible for making Zanuck read Rowland's play *A Handful of Clouds,* which started his career, really."

In *Blood Money*, the story is inconsequential. The tone is everything, playful and pleasantly hardboiled. When they break up, Bailey explains to

Ruby that "everybody sooner or later outgrows his friends, same as people outgrow their clothes." Judith Anderson, making her first appearance in a full-length picture (*Rebecca* was still a little more than six years away), replies with her nicotine-soaked voice: "Yes, and it usually begins with the hat." There were also added treats, like the Queen of Syncopation herself, Blossom Seeley, singing "Melancholy Baby."

Regardless, the picture was met with largely lukewarm reviews, and the public stayed away in droves. Mordaunt Hall of *The New York Times*, sneered as was his wont: "This whimsical little tale of thievery, thuggery and attempted slaughter was mistaken for entertainment by Darryl Zanuck." It took a modern critic like Stephen Zito to recognize, decades later, that *Blood Money* both appalled and impressed: "The plot," he writes, "almost completely devoid of violence, is cynical and relativistic (sic). It's about dog racing, nymphomania, kleptomania, prostitution, golf, civic indifference, political corruption, and the various injustices of American jurisprudence: a gangster film about the middleman, in this case the bailbondsman. The film's lack of sentiment and charity, its coldness, moral indifference, is what makes it appealingly modern today."

Once again, Welford Beaton was about the only contemporary critic to recognize Rowland Brown's originality; he marveled about the fluidity of his cinematic style, praised his prosaic but witty dialogues. Even better, Brown worked his magic mostly in master shots and long takes, eschewing the flashy cutting and close-ups that so riled Beaton. But this time, he let his new collaborator Dalton Trumbo carry the torch in *The Spectator* review.

> Rowland Brown had an idea for a story. With [Hal] Long he made it into a script. Brown is an ingenious director, with a sense of what is commercial, but this is not the main reason why *Blood Money* is a success. The picture is good because it has creative unity. The idea flows directly from Brown's brain onto the screen. There is no detour, no intermediary in the concept. Under these conditions, even a mediocre theme can be successfully presented. The writer-director is one of the solutions to remedy what is wrong with motion pictures today.
>
> *Blood Money*'s principal virtues are as follows: a logical plot, a

growing suspense, bright dialogue ... Frances Dee, who until now has never been properly directed, had to wait to meet hardboiled Rowland Brown, supposed to know how to direct only men, to give the best performance of her career as a thrill-seeking little bitch.

By then, Brown was in England, earning big by flogging movie ideas to Irving Asher, in charge of producing "quota pictures" for Warner Bros. at Teddington Studios. Because of the protectionist laws passed by Britain in 1927, American firms could only show their wares in the United Kingdom if 20% of them were "British." To qualify as such, at least 75% of salaries had to go to British citizens. Consequently, American studios were making these bogus productions to meet the quotas and rarely bothered to show them, at least in the U. S. Fox made theirs at Wembley, Warner at Teddington. When by a miracle someone was noticed in one of these ten-day wonders—like Errol Flynn, who made his European debut in one of them—they were quickly shipped to Hollywood and put under contract.

Irving Asher, who at Burbank had been a technician well versed in all aspects of the business except publicity, had initially been sent to London by Warner to teach the Brits how to cope with sound. He ended up staying and producing the whole slate of quota films for Warner Bros. American directors, writers, and actors came and went, usually when they wanted to finance a pleasure trip. Allan Dwan, Monty Banks, Ralph Ince, all made quota films in England. Sometimes a British newcomer got his first crack at pictures this way, like Michael Powell and *Something Always Happens*, a lightweight comedy with a happy-go-lucky lad played by Ian Hunter.

Rowland Brown wrote three scripts for Asher (that we know of): *What Happened to Harkness?*, *Widow's Might*, and *Leave It to Blanche*. The latter was directed by Harold Young, Alexander Korda's film editor, who would soon replace Rowland Brown on a much more prestigious picture, *The Scarlet Pimpernel*. *Widow's Might* featured fading star Laura La Plante, who had married Irving Asher on a trip to London. Brown himself was slated to direct a film version of *The Twelve Chairs* from the same Russian novel Mel Brooks would adapt in 1970. Monty Banks made a quota cheapie of it in England in 1937 (*Keep Your Seats Please*). But soon, Alex Korda was calling on Brown to direct *The Scarlet Pimpernel*.

Baroness Orczy's famous adventure story set during the Terror phase of the French Revolution seemed an odd choice to entrust to a decidedly American and modern director such as Brown, and it can only testify to the stature he had built so quickly in the movie business. Korda had a lot riding on the project, coming from the costly flop he made with *The Private Life of Don Juan*, starring a grossly miscast and over-the-hill Douglas Fairbanks. Korda spared no expense in order to secure a success on the American market with his next production, hiring Robert Sherwood and S.N. Behrman to work on the script, in addition to his staff writers Lajos Biró and Arthur Wimperis. Starting in July, long before actual shooting was to begin, difficulties immediately arose between Brown and Korda, who did not share the same conception of the spectacle they were going to make. Brown walked out of the Borehamwood facilities only a few days into the shoot, first replaced by Korda at the helm, then by editor Harold Young.

SAM: Korda wanted to direct this picture right from the start, but did not want to admit it. For Rowland, it was a great lost opportunity to branch out. But walking out he also knew what he was doing: Irving Thalberg was about to come back to Hollywood after the long European trip he took to recuperate from his heart attack. He would not be head of production any longer, but an independent working on the lot, and Thalberg liked Rowland, unlike Mayer. Together they almost made *Stealing Through Life*, which was based on the prison memoir of Ernest Booth, an ex-con who briefly became a scriptwriter. Thalberg and Rowland also sold a script to MGM called *The Toughest Guy on Earth*, which was the story of a G-Man who must arrest a corrupt judge, except he's in love with his daughter. There was already the idea of the guys who grow up together and end up on different sides of the law, which is in *Angels with Dirty Faces*. Rowland even wanted to tell both careers simultaneously, a premature version of the split-screen technique. He always had those visual ideas. But to come back to Thalberg, one time Rowland asked me to act as his agent with Thalberg. He was changing agents like he changed shirts, and he must have been short. Anyway, Thalberg had me the next morning with his orange juice.

I was so petrified, he ate me alive. I never could utter the sum Rowland wanted me to ask for, which was $50,000. Later, Thalberg told Rowland, "You know, I like that new agent of yours. Real tough guy..." They had a good laugh over that. But I think Rowland had to make do with just $25,000 that time. He got along fine with all those studio heads. Even Harry Cohn. He liked him personally, they went to the races together, but he always refused to work for Cohn. Maybe this is why the relationship lasted until Cohn's death. The real reason all the studio heads refused to see him after a while was not because he was too difficult or because he punched one of them, as people always say. It was because Rowland was always borrowing money from them, and never gave it back, or not always. Rowland, he borrowed two hundred and he gave one back, maybe. Even with me, his own brother.

The time he punched an executive at MGM, which is a famous story, it was all a set-up from the head office. Eddie Mannix was a good friend of my brother, and he was sick having to do it to him, but he did, and it worked. This happened in 1936, Rowland had written a story called *The Devil Is a Sissy* and he directed it for MGM. A rich kid (Freddie Bartholomew) is forced to go live in the Lower East Side with a bunch of hoodlum kids like Jackie Cooper and Mickey Rooney. This was very much like Rowland, a combination of toughness and sentimentality, and it was a good little picture. But they had one problem: no name big enough to put on the poster, no star (Rooney wasn't big yet). So, the front office had the rich idea to put Woody Van Dyke's name up, instead of Rowland's, as the director of the picture. Van Dyke was their star director at the time. They had Rowland come to the studio to explain this to him. But they knew my brother, they knew what was going to happen. And sure enough, when Mannix told him what they had in mind, Rowland struck his face with a telephone book, or the script, I can't recall which. But now they had good reason to fire him, and that's what they wanted all along. The picture was Rowland's, from beginning to end. Not one scene was shot by Van Dyke.

This may have been what Brown told his brother, and the MGM archives confirm it, but only up to a point. The original story was Brown's, without a single doubt. A 49-page treatment dated September 1935 bears his name on the title page. Brown seems to have worked alone at first, then Frank Fenton joined him around April 1936. Their draft was revised, through June and July, by John Lee Mahin and Richard Schayer. The shoot started at the beginning of July, with Brown acting as the sole director for about three weeks. The "striking" incident, if it really happened, took place around July 20, when Woody Van Dyke was still preparing to shoot *Love on the Run*, a comedy teaming Gable and Crawford and Franchot Tone (it got made). A *Daily Variety* item dated August 4 is the first inkling of a replacement on *The Devil Is a Sissy*, the article going so far as to claim in suspiciously strong and damaging terms that "Brown's work will be junked, and with the exception of two scenes, the three week's work Brown did on the picture will be re-shot by W. S. Van Dyke. Metro hoped to be able to use most of this footage, but after seeing Van Dyke's first daily rushes the front office decided that the difference in style was too obvious."

This, of course, could have been a smear campaign engineered by the studio in a trade publication notorious for its dependence on movie promotion. Still, the last pieces in the MGM archives show that Van Dyke did shoot quite a bit of the film and worked on it for at least ten days beginning on August 11, during which several studio drones like Cyril Hume (off his usual *Tarzan* duties) produced eleven pages of rewrites. The dialogue continuity by one Tom Held is dated September 9 to October 9. So Van Dyke could have shot for most of August. Sam Brown, who was in England at the time, only knew what his brother told him. Which doesn't mean Rowland Brown never smacked Eddie Mannix in July 1936, or that he wrote and directed the film alone; it only means that if the Devil is a sissy, Truth is very often a tramp.

Rowland Brown had also already acquired a reputation for giving his scripts to his brother to finish, and for sometimes selling the same story twice to different studios. One can track his rather cavalier practices just by reading *Variety*'s reports of his lawsuits. In winter 1938, for instance, the MGM story department realized that the script they had just bought from Brown, *Ten Penny Crosses*, was so close to the story for which he would receive an Oscar® nomination that same year (Warner's *Angels with Dirty Faces*) that the Metro brass decided to shelve it and write it off to experience. A 1937 Monogram picture, *Boys of the Street,* bears Rowland Brown's name on the screen—a story Sam Brown swears he wrote all alone.

SAM: It came to a point where Rowland would pick me up in the morning in his Packard, we would stop at such and such studio, he went in to see a supervisor or a story editor there and spitballed a story while I remained in the car. Most of the time he'd come out with a check, enough to go to the track that afternoon. Soon the word got around: "If you hire Rowland Brown, be careful not to end up with Junior."

On January 22, 1938, Hal Wallis sent this telegram to two Warner executives:

JUST BOUGHT SUPERB STORY FOR JIMMY CAGNEY AND PAT O'BRIEN CALLED ANGELS WITH DIRTY FACES, WRITTEN BY ROWLAND BROWN, AUTHOR OF THE DOORWAY TO HELL, ETC STOP A VERY GOOD STORY, PERFECT TO PUT CAGNEY BACK TO THE PLACE HE DESERVES

In fact, Brown had written the story a year earlier for Mervyn LeRoy, who needed a yarn for the Dead End Kids, whom he'd just put under personal contract. In typical fashion, Brown had refused to let LeRoy have it for what he was offering to pay, and instead made the rounds of the studios with it, Paramount and Universal among them, even picking up option money at several places. He finally sold the story to First National through his good friend Cagney, who intended to make his "comeback" with it after a protracted dispute with Warner. Wallis, in buying the whole package for $12,500, was going against the advice of most of the supervisors at Warner. Sam Bischoff, for one, opined: "As you know, I was the first one to champion this story when it was told to me. But after reading the script, I wouldn't give a nickel for it. It may be worth $2,000, just for the idea." Lou Edelman agreed: "In its present state, I wouldn't touch these angels with a barge pole. If we can buy the script very cheap, it may serve as the basis for something, but if you want to shoot it as is, good luck."

Rowland Brown directing Spencer Tracy in *Quick Millions*

After the enormous success of *Angels with Dirty Faces*, which was directed by Mike Curtiz, Brown tried to get co-credit for the scenario, in spite of John Wexley and Warren Duff's vehement protests. Brown's script was 120-pages long, theirs ran to 160. Let's just say that Brown had nothing to do with the extra 40 pages. Come Oscar® time, both Brown and Cagney lost to Dory Schary and Spencer Tracy for *Boy's Town*, an MGM picture similar in theme. One might say that, had Curtiz filmed Rowland Brown's script (and only his), the picture might have been more successful, or at least more delightful today, if only for this pedagogic exchange between boys gone wrong: "I bet you don't even know what glands are," says one of the Dead End Kids. "Sure," replies another, "little sponges that regulate the personality." As for determining how much of *Angels with Dirty Faces* was Brown's, Fred McEwen, head of legal services at Warner, responded to Brown's authorship claims before the movie's release in typical Warner Bros. fashion: "He should have asked this before, now we'd have to redo all the publicity..." Pat O'Brien, for one, never had any doubts who wrote the picture. As late as 1975, he maintained: "Brown wrote it, no doubt about this. He was sort of a genius, that guy. He hung around on the set, he was a pal of Cagney. He talked to you like a stevedore would, in plain old everyday American. Brown was a swell guy. I don't know what became of him. Maybe he's dead."

The only thing Sam Brown did not want to talk about was what happened with *Thieves Like Us*. "A tragedy," was all he'd say. In March 1939, Rowland Brown bought the rights to the novel from its author, Edward Anderson, a man who'd just tried his luck as a screenwriter, with no success at all. Brown had easily made him accept the modest purchase price of $500, promising him further employment in the company he was about to create with his friend, actor Joel McCrea. The project fell through when the star could not get out of his contract with Paramount. Still, one can believe Brown had been sincere in his transactions with the Texas writer. Save for Anderson's drinking problem, the two men were of the same cloth, born to get along. Brown's adaptation of *Thieves Like Us*, which he subsequently sold to RKO, is proof enough that he had real sentiment for the book and respected its unique tone. More, at least, than any studio readers and producers at that time. Since the winter of 1936, the Brandt & Brandt Literary Agents had been circulating the novel in galley form. A reader's report at RKO is typical of the way it was received: "Second-rate hard-boiled crime novel, with some philosophy about most of the world being thieves of one kind or other. Not very new."

Brown knew better and would try for two more years to get his script produced. In 1941, he finally sold the rights to the novel and his script to RKO for $10,000, still hoping he'd get to direct the picture. But the project would stay buried at the studio until John Houseman and Nicholas Ray resurrected it in February 1947 to make it as *They Live by Night*. Curiously, Brown's script showed many affinities with Ray's approach: his taste

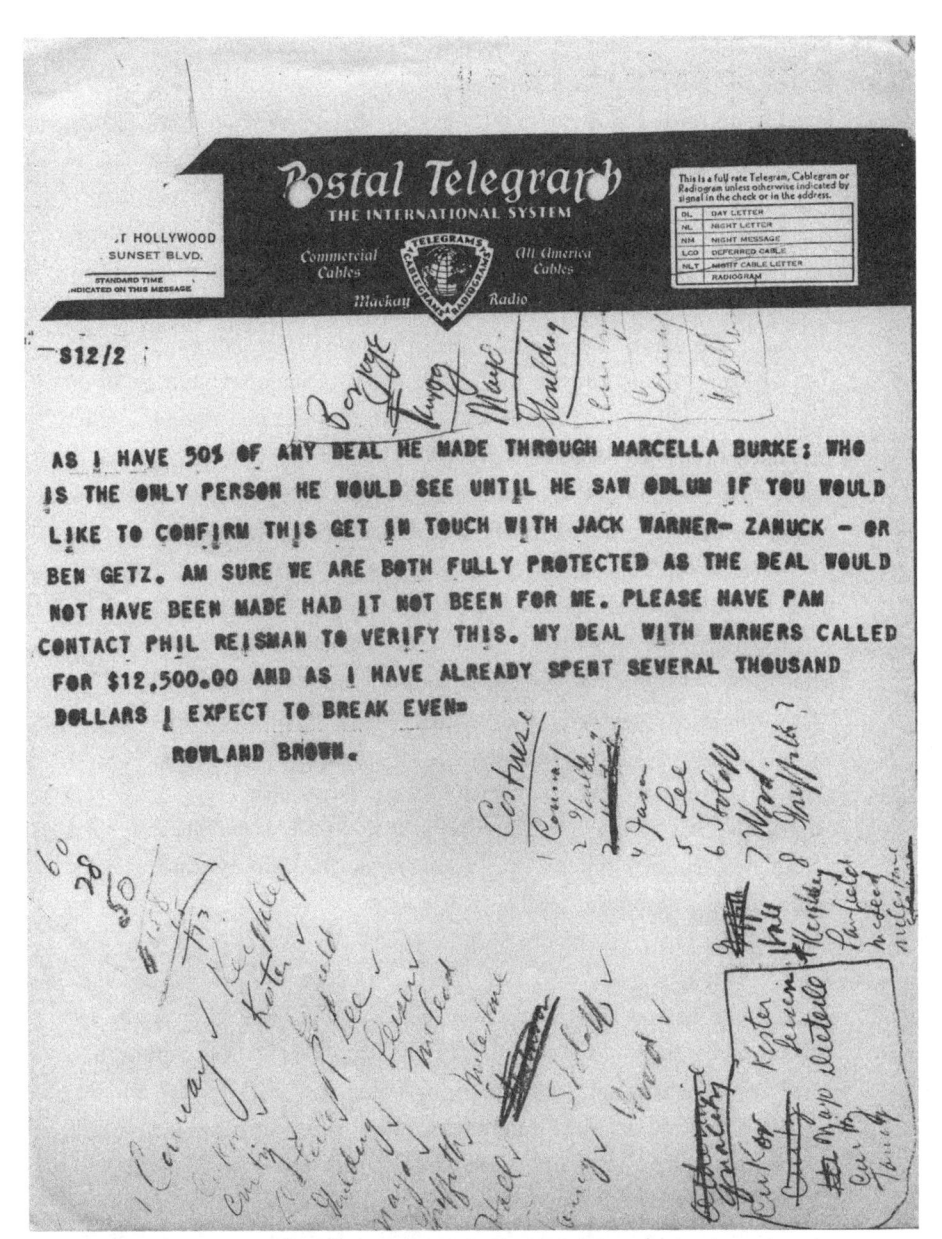

Scoundrels & Spitballers: Writers and Hollywood in the 1930s

> **Postal Telegraph** — THE INTERNATIONAL SYSTEM
>
> S12/2
>
> AS I HAVE 50% OF ANY DEAL HE MADE THROUGH MARCELLA BURKE; WHO IS THE ONLY PERSON HE WOULD SEE UNTIL HE SAW ODLUM IF YOU WOULD LIKE TO CONFIRM THIS GET IN TOUCH WITH JACK WARNER— ZANUCK — OR BEN GETZ. AM SURE WE ARE BOTH FULLY PROTECTED AS THE DEAL WOULD NOT HAVE BEEN MADE HAD IT NOT BEEN FOR ME. PLEASE HAVE PAM CONTACT PHIL REISMAN TO VERIFY THIS. MY DEAL WITH WARNERS CALLED FOR $12,500.00 AND AS I HAVE ALREADY SPENT SEVERAL THOUSAND DOLLARS I EXPECT TO BREAK EVEN=
>
> ROWLAND BROWN.

A 1938 telegram from Brown to agent Walter Kane, festooned with production notes, showed his ire over not getting co-credit for scripting *Angels with Dirty Faces*

for folklore (in his script, a railroad man sings "The Midnight Special"), for colored folks, and for his way of always siding with the young fugitive lovers, with no ambiguity or compromise for the censors. But the two men veered in a crucial way in the treatment of the characters: Ray sought at all costs to explain and excuse the lovers' behavior through psychology and social antecedents, while Brown refused to explain or justify them. Brown was also going for a very modern, if misguided, way of distancing the viewer from the story—a quasi-Brechtian didactic approach which takes the form of religion. He invents a character called "the sign-painter" who "All through the picture we will see ... painting religious inscription on wall, rocks and houses. Everytime tragedy strikes. No one among the other characters ever notices these inscriptions, except Bowie, and not always. It is just a way to remind the viewer that crime doesn't pay. This character is typical of rough and tumble preachers one sees everywhere on the roads in the Middle West." It was also, of course, a good way to mock the righteous, while reassuring the studio about his intent and placating the censors.

If he was true to the book's spirit, Brown did not hesitate to invent. There is an amusing mud-bath scene with the three escaped convicts. And he devised an ingenious ending. After springing Elmo Mobley, Bowie stops at a store and buys a phonograph and a brace of Mexican records for Keechie ("She loves that spic music," he says to the storekeeper). He also buys a *Mother Goose* record. Then he returns to the Alamo Plaza Courts and the two lovers reunite. He plays her the Mother Goose record, starting with "The Farmer in the Dell" ("This'll be me," says Bowie), followed by "Mary had a Little Lamb" ("This'll be you"). Bowie asks her if she wants a real cold soda and she says, "Yes." At the door, he sees the Sheriff's men fanning out around the motel court. Bowie ducks back in but does not pull out his gun, as in the novel. He only asks Keechie, very calmly, "Do you mind if I don't go get it just now? Some people I'd rather not see, outside." We hear warnings shouted through a megaphone. Bowie rewinds the phonograph. The record plays while outside the Sheriff counts ten. Then we hear gunshots outside, while the nursery rhyme keeps playing. Keechie asks, "Bowie, the two thieves who died with Jesus, were they like us?" Bowie kisses her. "Yes, Keechie, thieves like us." A swarm of bullets blasts through the door, through the windows and the thin wall. The music volume is cranked up, blending with the din of machine gun fire.

In spite of his growing reputation as a liability, Brown still had Zanuck's ear as late as 1941. A transcript of a story conference between the two men indicates that if Rowland Brown's blend of Irish Midwestern sentimentality and tough-guy talk was on the wane, Zanuck hadn't changed much since his Warner days.

> You must concentrate most of your efforts on the third act, which until now is the weakest point of the story. In this third act you must crystalize your theme and come up with a sensational ending, like that of *Little Caesar* or *The Doorway to Hell*.

Curiously, the story discussed was very close to that of *Angels with Dirty Faces*: a grumpy Mick with a heart of gold (Tracy, say) wants to prevent a bunch of neighborhood kids from turning bad and runs for District Attorney. The year before, Brown had worked on the script of *Johnny Apollo*, from a story idea by Hal Long. The yarn had punch, even if it was another father-and-son relationship, and the milieu was the world of high finance and the carceral. Directed by Henry Hathaway, it was one of Tyrone Power's few good pictures at 20th Century–Fox. Later, Brown's name will be credited on *Nocturne*, a George Raft vehicle considerably enlivened by Jonathan Latimer's dialogue; but Brown's touch can be spotted here and there, as when Raft gets a dancing lesson from an exasperated girl instructor he wants to bed. In 1952, he still puts his mark on Phil Karlson's very good and original *Kansas City Confidential*. Until his death, Rowland Brown would keep on writing and spitballing movie ideas. But the very titles of some of these scripts indicate that Brown had lost touch with the times: *Ricochet, Dust Was His Name, Let the Eagle Scream!* (a Mafia story written with Frank Fenton), *On Leave From Heaven, The Devil Answered Their Prayers, Stick Up, Bright Future* ("a Hollywood story"), *Jacob and the Angel, Out of the Clouds, Law and Order, Inc., S. S. Apocalypse, Pardon My Halo, That's My Pop, Sinner's Luck, Fame, The Magnificent Torso, Tom

Brown on a Tijuana vacation with his new bride, heiress Marie "Sugar" Adrienne and her family, a short-lived union that would almost ruin him

Murdock's Left Ear. A whirl of titles that were submitted to the studios by about as many agents (Victor Orsatti, Walter Kane, Jules Goldstone, Kenneth Feldman), which suggests that Brown, in spite of his Packard, his valets and his flashy suits, had remained stuck somewhere in Ohio: fathers and sons, angels and demons, good and evil, red or black, repair or impair, *passe* or *manqué*. His personal life followed in the same mode, either good or evil, red or black, odd or even, high or low.

SAM: Rowland had been living as a bachelor for some time already, but at the end of the 1930s he married Sugar. Her real name was Marie Adrienne, but we called her Adriana, or Sugar. Truth be told, Rowland's main attraction to her was that she was an arch-millionaire's daughter. The father was a Greek, and he hated Rowland's guts. When he died, he had something like a hundred-and-sixty-million dollars, most of which did not belong to him, but that's another story. He had been one of Huey Long's shills in the past, some murky oil business in Louisiana. When Long was murdered, the Greek ended up with all this illegal dough. Rowland liked luxury and the idea that some day he would get some of this money. The funny thing is, he never got even a whif of it! He shelled out for everything. Sugar had a monthly stipend of two grand from her father, but she never paid for anything. She couldn't have children, so she never went anywhere without her mother and sister. Rowland paid for everyone! He spent lavishly, thinking that one day Sugar would be in the pink.

MOYA: When I was a kid, these two seemed like from another world. She had these long, long nails, and enormous rings on her hands. Always limousines or Cadillacs. At first they moved into the guest house of Winfield Sheehan, who had been head of the studio at Fox when Rowland was there. Then they bought the whole property for $120,000. It was in Benedict Canyon. Sugar got the house when they divorced.

SAM: Sugar was not a bad girl, but her family was horrible. This could not last very long. Rowland was ruined because of this marriage. They divorced in 1943. What happened was Rowland met Karen in New York when he was doing his play, *Johnny 2X4*. It was his second try on Broadway. Three years before he had written a play called *This is Our Day*, but never found backing for it. This one took him back to the speakeasy days; he produced it himself in 1942. He had a terrific cast: Barry Sullivan, in his first **gangster** role, Jack Lambert (already as a henchman), and a newcomer named Betty Bacall. The play could have been a hit, but the war started and it was not a good time to have something on Broadway. Karen was Lauren Bacall's understudy. In reality, she was a dancer, she'd been in the Ballets Jooss in England. She and Rowland had an affair at that time, and she got pregnant. They came back to Hollywood together, and this pretty much ended the marriage with Sugar. Rowland and Karen stayed at the Garden of Allah for a time. Later, Karen used to say that Rowland pretty much ruined her career, promising her a lot of things, but she really loved him. She stayed with him through thick and thin until he died. And from the fifties on, times were hard for them. Rowland was blacklisted. Not for political reasons, like many, but for his supposed anti-Semitism—which was a laugh, when you knew him. Three women, including one who had been his mistress, started circulating these stories. When we lived on Fairfax and he was staying with us, Rowland had Christmas trees for all the neighborhood kids. He loved Christmas, and he said just because you're Jewish is no reason not to have a tree and presents. Or not to have two New Year's holidays! It is true that he punched a guy once who was Jewish, but in Hollywood the odds are pretty high, as there are a lot of Jewish people in the business.

Another Hollywood story, and I ask you if an anti-Semite would have acted like this: Eddie Small, an old-time agent who'd become a very successful independent producer, bought a synopsis from some guy for $10,000. Eddie asked him who wrote this story, and the guy said he did. "In a pig's eye," Eddie said, "this is a Rowland Brown story." So he calls Rowland to find out, and sure enough, my brother had sold the story to the guy for a grand, just to go to the track. Eddie gave Rowland the ten thousand directly. This was the *Kansas City Confidential* story. Now, do you think Eddie Small, who couldn't have been more Jewish, would have acted like this with a dirty bigot? But the smear campaign worked, and Rowland was blackballed. It affected me, too. All of a sudden, I could not sell anything anywhere. I had to give up writing and go back into the business through the back door. I worked in the National Screen editing rooms for nineteen years.[1]

[The man Brown punched, who made him pay dearly for it, was a press agent named Epstein, much in the mold of the "demon press agent" Matt Libby, played by Lionel Stander in the 1937 *A Star Is Born*.]

SAM: He was blackballed, yes, but his troubles had started well before this. Rowland burned all his bridges, he owed everybody. Good and evil, it was all the same to him, he never stopped to consider the consequences of his actions. Let's say that he was very cavalier when it came to money. The horses were his religion. He even sold a racing story to Paramount, a gambling picture that got made with George Raft. It was called *The Lady's*

---

1 National Screen Service was a company formed in 1920 to produce and distribute movie trailers for the studios. From the 1940s to the 80s, it also consolidated the business of promotional material and posters for exhibitors.

from Kentucky. Raft was one of many who dropped Rowland when he was on the skids. All the people my brother had helped on the way up, including Cagney. Only one came through for him, a man named George Bag, who'd been treasurer at Fox. Later, he was on the board of the Motion Picture Home, and he managed to get Rowland some sort of pension for the last four years of his life. But the others… Jimmy Cagney and he had a falling out when Rowland kept the money he made on *Angels with Dirty Faces*. Just because it had been written for him, Jimmy thought that the story belonged to him. Sure, he made Warner buy it from Rowland, but still. Cagney was always a bit of a tight wad. And yet, the picture brought him back to stardom.

But you would never hear Rowland whine or complain during all this bad period. He was all washed up, he didn't even try to work anymore. He'd screwed too many people, and it came back to haunt him. Also, he had lived hard. Look at me, I am 80-years old. He looked like me when he died, at 63. He'd been one of Hollywood's handsomest men. There was only another pair of brothers like us in Hollywood: Myron and David O. Selznick. They also let it all go away. David was one of the biggest producers, but an inveterate gambler, like Rowland. Still, compared to Selznick, Rowland was not that extravagant. On a good year, he'd make about $100,000. And he never paid any income tax, which caused him a lot of trouble later. He had his cars, his Chinese valet, Tom, his bachelor pads. We had a picture of him taken at San Simeon during a party with William Randolph Hearst. It was in a scrapbook full of pictures of stars, every one of them signed to Rowland. Someone stole it, unfortunately.

> Sam Gilson Brown wasn't born before the turn of the 20th century like his brother, and may not have left as many tracks in Hollywood, but he had his share of adventures and worked with the greatest.

SAM: When I started working in pictures, this was at a time when two men could do absolutely what they wanted at Fox: Tom Mix and Murnau. I was their designated propman, both of them. I was Tom Mix's propman for four years, and then sound came. Tom was going to Paramount, but he still owed Fox a picture. But he couldn't make up his mind. Meanwhile, Murnau was making *Sunrise*, and I helped a little on this. One night his propman was out of commission, dead drunk in a ditch, just when he was supposed to fire up six-thousand Roman candles to create a wall of flames. So I did it, and Murnau was satisfied. He asked for me for *4 Devils*, but Tom Mix refused to do without me. I made [Mix's] picture and came back just in time for *4 Devils*. Murnau was very nice. When he was pleased with something, he let you know.

Later, he asked me if I'd like to go to Tahiti with him to make a picture, but I had to be approved by Robert Flaherty, who was co-producing. I went to see him in Long Beach and he gave me the job. I had to gather all the equipment to make *Tabu*, and all I had to go by were twelve bits of paper Flaherty had given me. But I managed. We had a lab over there in Tahiti; you had to do everything yourself. But I was used to it because with Tom Mix we always shot on location, often near his ranch in Arizona, near Prescott. He had the best of everything there to make movies. This experience helped me a lot in Papeete, I can tell you that! Murnau and Flaherty's brother sailed ahead in a yacht, and we followed on a cargo ship. On board, someone asked me if I knew Murnau was queer. But although I was 25 at the time, I was as innocent as a lamb. A nymphomaniac for me was maybe a girl who stole things in department stores. So you can imagine what I thought a queer was! Sure enough, in Tahiti Murnau lived with a local boy, but I never made the connection. He never bothered me. Once, though, he told me, "You know, Sam, I have a bad reputation in Hollywood." Maybe he was sending me a feeler, but I said, "Oh, I know, they say your pictures don't make money." He looked at me and he must have realized what a rube I was. But he also knew he could trust me. He had to be careful—people always wanted to blackmail him because of his personal life. *Tabu* only cost $75,000. I was making $95 a week with a bonus at the end.

One day, we'd been back in Hollywood for weeks or months, someone rang me: "Mr. Murnau owes you money." This was Rose Kearin, his secretary. Murnau was like this, always above-board. He wanted to take me to Paris to make *La Bohème*. But the picture was never made because he killed himself in an automobile accident on his way to Santa Barbara. He was going to a sneak preview of *Tabu*, I believe. I'd gone to Paris to join Rowland. When I got there he told me, "You know what happened to Mr. Murnau? Well, he's dead."

I started writing scripts when I was a propman. For me, it wasn't more attractive or glamorous than anything else, just a way to make a little money. I never earned a lot from writing. My rate never went above $500 a week. Sometimes Rowland gave me a script to write, like *Navy Blue and Gold*, which he signed, but which I wrote. At the very beginning, when I was still living on the corner of Western and Franklin, I was churning out sometimes two stories a week. And I *walked* to Warner Bros. to deliver them. They had left the Sunset location, they were already in Burbank, so it was a long walk. It is during this period that I met Frank Fenton and John Fante, who were struggling, just like me. I was about to join Rowland in England, who needed me for *The Scarlet Pimpernel*, which he was just preparing. I had written a synopsis based on a true story—a woman who worked for Tom Mix, who prepared his income tax returns: Tom forced her to cheat on what she declared and, when they got caught, he put the whole blame on her. She had a little boy and she lost custody, at least for a while. Of course, I made it heavier, made it into a melodrama. I didn't have time to write the script, so I gave it to Fenton and Fante, so they could sell it. I knew Fenton through Rowland—he was around the studios, he could get a meeting. Fante had nothing to do with the movies, but he had a name; he had a reputation as a writer of fiction because of his stories in the *The American Mercury*. So, finally, they sold the script to Warner and it became a picture called *Dinky*, a Jackie Cooper weepie, with Mary Astor playing the mother. I have a co-credit for the story. Fenton got the money; he gave some to Fante and he gave me $500 when I got back from England, but it took some doing to get it. This was the first money I ever got as a writer. Later, Fenton went the way my brother did—he made the same mistakes, but big time. He lost everything gambling, and on top of that he drank.

When I got to England, my brother was about to leave. He'd quit the Korda picture, but I stayed. I met my wife Nora there. We almost starved at first because I did not have a work permit. Finally, I got a job shooting newsreels for Fox-Movietone, all over Europe. And while I was at it, I also shot a lot of stock footage for different studios; the stuff they used for the plates in process shots—all the cathedrals, boulevards, all the sights that immediately identify a city. All the capitals of Europe. It's funny, sometimes I spot one that I shot in a Hitchcock movie, or one by Hathaway. ... And later, they used some of that footage in the RAF for bombing Germany. I went back there after the war, everything had been razed, all the bridges gone. This is when I paid a visit to Murnau's brother, Robert Plumpe Murnau, in East Germany. He was destitute.

MOYA: When Sam saw Murnau's brother eating out of garbage cans, he gave him everything he had on his back, coat, umbrella, probably also money. [Robert] Plumpe Murnau gave him the deed of a piece of property he had in Santa Maria (north of Santa Barbara), probably for him to sell at some point. I don't quite know what happened, except that Sam for years kept sending money orders to East Germany, and kept paying the property taxes so it wouldn't be sold by the county. Sam also brought back several prints of *Tabu* with the intention of distributing the picture in America. Some time later, Sam got some inheritance from an uncle, a rather large sum, and he founded a production company called Golden Bough with the idea of going back to Tahiti, to see what happened since he was there. Or maybe he wanted to do a remake, I don't know; I was twelve at the time, I did not really care. It must have been in 1956. One thing I remember vividly is the day my father took us to San Pedro to see a big ship he wanted to rent to make the picture. He wanted to sail to Tahiti on that big yacht. And I don't know what really happen, but it involved Uncle Rowland. My father had brought him in on that deal because his brother was broke as usual, and Rowland must have signed the wrong papers to the wrong people. Anyway, he got rooked by one of those crooked lawyers. The Browns lost the film rights or something. Later, a print of *Tabu* fell into the hands of some guys who ran a nudie house on Fairfax. They showed dirty movies, or rather naughty movies, because most of the time all the dirt was on the poster only. Still, they ran Murnau's movie as a nudie, and advertised it with stills of bare-breasted Tahitian women as a come-on. Up until then, when Sam and Rowland had shown the picture, they had presented it as an artistic film, like in art houses or film clubs. I remember one show they had at the Ebell Theatre, a Jewish cultural place on Wilshire. When Rowland heard what was going on on Fairfax, he felt responsible so he went there to take the print away from them. But at the theater they ganged up on him, the projectionist and other guys, and beat him up. The next day, my father, whose nickname wasn't Sam "Buster" Brown for nothing—and he was even bigger than his brother—went back with Rowland and this time they beat *them* up! But this is only one episode of the sad association our family had with *Tabu*. Even today, Karen, Rowland's widow, doesn't want to hear of it and claims this whole thing ruined the family, that *Tabu* is really bad luck. All I know is that Uncle Rowland was very upset, and that was not his style at all to be upset by anything.

Karen Brown and Moya Ashdown are not the only ones to think *Tabu* was bad ju-ju. A lot has been written about Murnau's arrogance—and its consequences—when he insisted on filming on an island that was considered taboo by the Tahitians: an islet called Motu Tapu, in sight of Bora Bora. The locals always attributed the many accidents during the production to this transgression: an assistant badly burned by magnesium torches, several pearl divers drowning, cameras falling into the sea. Even the superb house Murnau had built in Puna'auia, north of Papeete, burned down in 1935. And of course, Murnau's death.

Sam Brown never mentioned these bizarre accidents and coincidences, only saying that they had "a lot of trouble" making the picture. For instance, they had to replace the first cameraman, Floyd Crosby, because of some "woman trouble" over there. It's slightly suspicious that Brown never said a bad word about Murnau, except to mention that Flaherty had a quality Murnau lacked entirely: "human warmth." According to Brown, under his gruff exterior Flaherty was "a puffcake," kind and sentimental, "like most Irish men." Flaherty slowly distanced himself from the project when the company backing the picture withdrew its funding. Originally, *Tabu* was to be shot in color in a process developed by Colorart, and the company had promised to invest $75,000 in the picture. But the color stock never arrived, or it wasn't satisfactory, and relations between Murnau and Colorart became tense. After a while, Murnau decided to make the picture in black-and-white, and since Murnau was putting his own money into it, it became his film exclusively.

What Sam Brown forgot to mention in his account was that he did not stay in Tahiti for the end of the shoot. He never told his family this, either. But recently published letters by Rose Kearin, Murnau's secretary at the time, who had stayed behind in Los Angeles, indicate without a doubt that Brown was back in California by the summer of 1929. Murnau kept shooting till at least July. Something may indeed have happened in Tahiti to make him hightail it back prematurely[2]. In a letter to her boss dated May 13, 1930, Kearin announces the arrival of the "negative girl" to the island (film editor Martha Dresback), whom she is sending him post haste. She also tells him that Sam Brown would contact him directly with a proposition. Apparently, Sam had already undertaken the task of finding distribution for *Tabu*. He would go back to Papeete to watch the picture, and on his return to Los Angeles he was "reasonably sure" of convincing Zanuck to buy the picture for distribution. While making clear that she has nothing to do with this idea, Kearin mentions in passing that "Sam's brother is well introduced at Warner, and has Zanuck's ear." One has to read between the lines of this correspondence, as Murnau's return letters to Kearin have not survived. But the secretary's defensive tone, when she touches on the subject in subsequent letters, indicates what Murnau's reaction must have been. Yet, two months later, in a letter dated July 7, 1930, Kearin writes again in Brown's defense, but also hints at some unwholesome incident that could have hastened Sam's departure from Papeete:

> *Sam Brown happened to give me a hurried call, asking if I thought you would permit him to go to Papeete (his brother paying the expenses) and see the picture and then try to fix it with Zanuck. You will one day realize how sincere he is … and I would never for a minute be afraid of*

---

2 A manifest of the *S.S Maunganui* dated August 21, 1929, lists not only Sam, but his "friend" Lotus Long (real name Lotus Pearl Shibata). This was apparently not all of the "woman trouble" cargo, as Jeanette Flaherty was also on board. Robert Flaherty's brother, David, had very publicly and rancorously split from his wife because of an affair she had on the island. I thank film historian Janet Bergstrom for sharing this manifest with me.

him turning traitor.

He was terribly hurt when he came back and you know what the majority of fellows would have done, but he stuck for you all, praised you to the highest ... until he was kidded unjustly. And then he stopped talking entirely, but even now, when I hear from him (which is very seldom), he mentions always some of your good qualities, and that "genius" in you that appealed to him.

They all discuss your faults, but they forget to mention your good qualities.

I do not see Sam ever.

In his conversation with Carl Laemmle Jr. you and your picture were discussed. I don't know details.

It might seem incredible today that a 25-year-old propman would entertain business notions of such scale, but it is further proof of his brother's stature in the 1930s. Also, Hollywood structures were not as rigid, the industry was still young, and the studio system a few years away. Rogue "geniuses" like Rowland Brown or Preston Sturges could still make a splash and find support from a Carl Laemmle Jr. or a Darryl F. Zanuck.

In that same May 13 letter, Kearin mentions to Murnau that her office is besieged by another admirer of his offering similar good samaritan services, a certain Edgar Ulmer ("whom you surely know"), who proposes to do the same as what Sam Brown had in mind, but through Eddie Small—who was still an agent at the time. "He estimates that your best chances lay at Warner, Paramount, or United Artists, and he claims to have connections in these studios. Ulmer is very obstinate, and it is very difficult to say no to him." Then Kearin permits herself an opinion, in understandable (when one knows Ulmer's famous mythomania) but still striking terms: "I smell a nigger in the woodpile," she writes.

Further letters tell of Murnau's ruses to prevent Colorart from confiscating the film reels. Instead of shipping them to Los Angeles, they transited through San Francisco. Finally, Colorart dropped its claim and the picture was released through Paramount in March 1931.

In his account, Sam Brown also neglected to mention that he did not assemble the lab in Tahiti on his own; the production manager, Tony Bambridge, had done most of the work, and for good reasons. Bambridge (whose brother Bill is featured in *Tabu*, as the policeman playing the accordion) was the scion of one of the original white families on the island, and he had earlier worked for Flaherty. A good part of the lab and material from *White Shadows in the South Seas* had remained behind and was used on *Tabu*.

And it is now certain that Sam Brown was not as innocent as he claimed. For instance, his naiveté regarding Murnau's homosexuality seems highly suspect, and Rose Kearin's veiled references to the blackmail Sam could have engaged in if he had not been so admiring of [Murnau] all but confirm this. A short time after our many-afternoon interviews, Sam, aged 87, fell victim to pneumonia. He died on September 10, 1991, at the Motion Picture Home hospital in Calabasas, where he and his wife Nora had spent their last years battling illness. But the story did not end with his passing.

MOYA: We discovered many things about my father after he died. It is true he always helped everybody in the family, even outside the family. But he was no saint. For instance, we discovered that a family friend we all knew, Lotus Long, was, in reality, an old mistress of his. He'd met her in Tahiti. Lotus was not Tahitian, but Indochinese. In Papeete, she'd worked like the devil to dance like the girls out there, just to get a part, but she never could manage it. Maybe she's an extra in it, in the background. But later she came to Hollywood and had a minor career, playing in the Fu Manchu movies. I remember her; she often came to the house, my mother never knew what happened between her and Sam. She was not alone, mind you: the house was always full of passing Tahitians! Anna Chevalier, the half-breed who played Reri in *Tabu*, came after the war. And Charlie Mauu, another Tahitian who tried to make it in the movies. He was in an Esther Williams musical, *Pagan Love Song*, and other things. Then he became fat, his nose was all flat and his pores were so large they were like holes in his skin. He and his wife stayed a while, then nobody wanted them. Another of those sad Hollywood stories.

A few months before the French publication of this book in 1996, a photograph came in the mail, a beautiful black-and-white snapshot taken on the deck of the cargo ship taking Flaherty and part of the *Tabu* crew to Tahiti. It is an overhead shot, four men and two women in fur coats are standing on the deck, or sitting on movie-set canvas chairs. Only one of the women is identified: Patsy R. Miller, surely not the actress, possibly the script supervisor. Tripods and cameras stand against the bulwark, next to a lifebuoy, suitcases and crates lay at the feet of the passengers. Next to them, back to the ship's rail, stands a young Samuel Gilson Brown, one hand holding his head, the other one on the cables. In his own handwriting is the caption: "Registering sea-sickness. We stayed on this tub nearly two weeks."

Moya had sent a note with the picture: "It's on his way to Tahiti on that boat that his skin got badly burned I think. Years later he started having skin cancer, it peeled and had spots, which we'd burn with liquid nitrogen, till finally they cut off bits of one ear, almost a third, bits of his lips. That's the *Tabu* legacy, as far as I'm concerned." Soon after this, Moya gathered all the paper concerning the *Tabu* business—contracts, scripts and every Golden Bough document—and burned the whole lot, putting an end to the link between the Brown family and the accursed *Tabu*.

In the same letter, Moya still had a few things to add about her Uncle Rowland: "He came to stay with us, in the last years. We kids loved him because he would never judge us. Once he walked in on me and my boyfriend, we were on the living room sofa. The lamps were not on. Later, he talked to me alone. He only told me: "Moya, darkness is the Devil's kitchen." And that was all. He was strange that way—he was not a believer, but his movies were all full of priests, devils and paradise. I still see him today, his gait, his posture, like someone important. Not unpleasantly, just like someone who knew his worth. Or someone who liked himself. I think that this is what distinguished him from my father. Uncle Rowland liked himself. He never refused himself anything. He died like his father, from a massive heart attack. High blood pressure, both of them. But what they said in the papers, that it happened on his way back from the movies, this was completely invented. In fact, he had gone to the police precinct to spring his daughter. Daphne, the daughter he had with Karen, was going out with a gang of surfers and they'd all been busted in a raid for marijuana. They were living in Costa Mesa by then. Rowland had gone to pay her bail, and on the way back he had his heart attack. Of course, the family did not want this known."

This was an end perfectly befitting the man who wrote stories about angels with dirty faces and who warned his niece, with no illusion, about the dangers of the Devil's kitchen. But instead, newspapers like the *Orange County Register* published an obit, on May 7, 1963, that was larded with inaccuracies, in which one could almost feel the hand of a scriptwriter (possibly Sam's):

COSTA MESA—The "1930s Orson Welles" is dead. Rowland Brown, generally credited for having started a cycle of gangster pictures in the early 1930s, apparently collapsed of a heart attack at 10 pm Monday at 1808 Iowa Street, as he was coming back from the movies with his family, who live at 1808 Iowa Street.

A writer and a director, he gave George Raft his first part, and gave their first chance to Lauren Bacall, Barry Sullivan and Barry Greco in the Broadway production of his play *Johnny Two-By-Four*. ... Some of his scripts sold for more than $50,000. Before television killed the motion picture industry, he was under contract at $1500 a week.

Mr. Brown and his wife, the German actress Karen Van Ryn, settled in Costa Mesa in 1957. Mr Brown was preparing a television series with Gene Fowler J. and William Kozlenko based on *Young Man From Denver*, Gene Fowler's autobiography about his newspaper years. ... A five-time Oscar® nominee, he acquired his stature as a director on the Dead End Kids movie series.

Sam's passing would see him join his brother in the realm of the specious, his death getting almost as much column space as his illustrious brother's, but in many more publications: *Daily Variety, The Hollywood Reporter,* the *Los Angeles Times,* the *Daily News,* all reported the death of

Samuel "Buster" Brown in the established tradition of fanciful obituaries. He was described, for instance, as the film editor of such pictures as *4 Devils*, *Tabu*, and even *Moana*, the picture Robert Flaherty made in 1925—which would have made Sam Brown the youngest film editor in history.

Brown finally decided to be laid to rest with his wife Nora, who died a year ahead of him—and not in Girard, Ohio, as he'd always wanted, between his father and brother. Maybe his decision was inspired by Nora having bought a plot at the Queen of Heaven Cemetery, just south of Covina, on a knoll listed in the land registry as Rowland Heights.

STORY

35¢

SEPTEMBER 1934

DEVOTED SOLELY TO THE SHORT STORY

Fire in the Bush . . . JAMES WARWICK
Reunion . . . . PARE LORENTZ
Hero, Leander and the Shepherd . . . I. A. KUPRIN
Gangster's Girl . . . . . . LOU WYLIE
Hotel Room in Chartres . . . MALCOLM LOWRY
Lift in Wyoming . . . . . . BIP HANSON
One of the Leaders . . . ARTHUR CALDER-MARSHALL
Dear Life . . . . SARA HAARDT
Major Croydon . . . . . RICHMOND PAGE
Fratres in Collegio . . . ALAN MARSHALL
Boy in the Birches . . . MARY B. POST

SEVENTY THOUSAND ASSYRIANS CAN'T BE WRONG

AT THE ONSET OF THE 1930S, old literary lions like Sherwood Anderson, Theodore Dreiser, Ford Madox Ford and Sinclair Lewis kept on publishing, like the living dead. The "Moderns"—Ernest Hemingway, William Carlos Williams, F. Scott Fitzgerald, John Dos Passos and others—had already arrived and conquered. But there was a new ferment in the literary boondocks: Alvah Bessie in Vermont, William Saroyan in Fresno and San Francisco, Nelson Algren in south Texas near the Rio Grande, Edward Anderson in New Orleans, John Fante in Roseville and Los Angeles, James Ross in North Carolina, to name just a few.

For these as-yet-unknowns, there was a review with a magic name, its importance immeasurably larger than its modest circulation: *STORY*, the name spread across the cover in bold caps. It suited a magazine claiming to be "devoted solely to the short story," as was stated under the name. There was something sporty and defiant in this declaration of intent. In just a few issues, *STORY* fast became a sort of metaphoric boxing ring in which writers had to prove themselves, or at least last a few rounds against recognized heavyweights like William Faulkner and Sherwood Anderson—who themselves were not above contributing to *STORY* on occasion. There is a fervor in the pages of this strange review, at least in the first half of the decade, which you don't find in the literary publications of any other period.

STORY was born to fill a vacuum. Until then, there always had been an important market for short stories—generally recognized, above all else, as *the* American form. Besides the slicks—popular weeklies with huge circulations like the *The Saturday Evening Post*—there were any number of small magazines and literary reviews open to experimentation, which often served as nurseries or laboratories for the mainstream publishing houses. In 1925, as H. L. Mencken and George Jean Nathan abandoned *The Smart Set* and announced that their new magazine, *The American Mercury*, would be of a more journalistic bent, Eugène Jolas in Paris was starting his small but vastly influential *transition*, in which authors like Hemingway, Kay Boyle, Djuna Barnes, Kenneth Fearing, Robert Coates and Josephine Herbst could experiment with new forms. *transition* also helped many European writers become known in America.

But in 1930, Jolas and a few of his collaborators (including Samuel Beckett), veering left under the influence of the Surrealist movement and the left, announced in a manifesto that *transition* would no longer publish fiction of any length. This left the field to Mencken, who relented and started to publish short stories in the *Mercury*. But they were all by "his boys," young men he recruited far and wide, preferably from the seamier walks of life. But if Mencken remained a formidable force in the business and was known for exploding old ways and prejudices, he was also, deep down, conservative in his literary tastes. *STORY* was created to fill this gap, a little magazine haphazardedly edited by and for writers who had no place else to call home.

As had so many Americans between the world wars, *STORY*'s founders, Whit Burnett and Martha Foley, had cut their teeth in Paris. Fiction writers *de coeur*, journalists by trade and necessity, they both worked at the *Herald*. Although professionnally they had access to the Parisian-American bohemian circles which were fast becoming institutionalized, if not dessicated, they were not part of it. They frequented Le Pharamond more than the Le Select, Jolas more than Joyce, Joyce more than Stein. Sometimes Whit Burnett placed a story in *transition*. William Bird, backer of the Three Mountain Press and first publisher of Hemingway, was the couple's most solid associate. Bird was also in charge of an American news agency's European bureaus, and so in 1930 Burnett became the Vienna bureau chief for Consolidated Press. The couple settled near the Wienerwald, in the same street as Arthur Schnitzler, then the only significant Austrian author known in America. Burnett and Foley of course hung out at the famous Louvre

Stammtisch, a restaurant and cafe where all the ex-patriates and correspondents gathered, such as John Gunther or William Shirer, future author of *The Rise and Fall of the Third Reich*. Burnett and Foley started sending dispatches on Vienna and the Balkans to Mencken's *American Mercury*.

In 1931, despairing of finding somewhere to send their artistic output, Burnett and Foley decided to launch *STORY*. The original concept was more a "book of galleys" (their term) than a regular review, more for the use of publishers and magazine editors than for the general public. Authors, for instance, retained the rights to their stories and could later place them in more established publications. The first issue was simply mimeographed, a run of 167 copies which in three year's time would fetch up to $500 on the bibliophile market. The inaugural issue (April 1931) sported a cover made of stiff orange cardboard. The eight titles of the published stories were each followed by their authors, the most striking of which was "Rest Cure" by Kay Boyle. Soon the fledging editors discovered that the money Mencken wired for one of their articles, $150, would cover the cost of not one but two issues of *STORY*, which would be hand-printed on marvelous rag paper by an old local artisan, in a run of 600 copies each. They were flabbergasted at the enthusiasm with which the close-knit English-speaking literary world responded to their admittedly amateurish effort, proof that their small review filled a void felt by all, at all levels, from Paris to New York.

From Baltimore came Mencken's accolades, as well as more checks, and from Oxford the congratulations of Edward J. O'Brien, the influential editor of the annual *Best American Short Stories*. An ex-patriate Bostonian whose job was to oversee Rhodes scholars sent to Oxford, O'Brien, soon after the series' debut in 1915, had become the primary arbiter for all practitioners of the exacting art of the short story. His approval and encouragement certainly mattered much more to Foley and Burnett than the great honor Robert Musil bestowed upon them, submitting a humoristic fable for their second issue. As with most parochial Americans (ex-pats though they were), Foley and Burnett knew nothing of this man their Austrian friends kept referring to as "the great Musil." Nevertheless, they had the gumption to like what the author was submitting, and to publish his sour Kafkaesque fable, "Catastrophe."

In 1932, Burnett and Foley married, had a son, and lost their day jobs at the news agency, all pretty much simultaneously. Having to leave Vienna in a hurry, they decided to go to Majorca, where they had friends who might help them. Once there, however, they discovered to their dismay that the island's lone typographer was only able to print four pages at a time on his antique press. Worse, they soon had to reckon with the fact that the letter *W* does not exist in the Spanish alphabet—and certainly not in the local printer's thin inventory. Before the first Majorcan issue of *STORY* could be put together, not only did Foley and Burnett have to order a boxful of brand new *W*s in different fonts, but they and their friends had to stomp on them, file and rub them in sand so they'd have the same degree of decrepitude as the other blocks used by the old typographer.

In spite of the precarious conditions of its fabrication, the isolation and the unpredictable Spanish mail service, *STORY* became increasingly known among writers and publishers. Even the great Robert McAlmon, Joyce's one-time patron and founder of the review *Contact*, paid Foley and Burnett a visit, even though the fledgling *Contact* was markedly more European—even dada—in tone and content than *STORY*. Contributions started to come in, from none other than William Faulkner, as well as Conrad Aiken, Erskine Caldwell and Gertrude Stein. Granted, they all were sending material they hadn't been able to place elsewhere, but this recognition from the "old guard" brought about the inevitable—what Burnett and Foley had been striving for all along. Within a year, the three founding partners of Random House, Bennett Cerf, Donald Klopfer, and Harry Scherman, invited *STORY* to set up shop in their 57th Street offices in Manhattan.

Now a monthly publication, its fabrication would be handled by the Random House printers, and the review only cost 50¢ (later dropped to 25¢). Nominally, Martha Foley and Whit Burnett lost none of their independence, but it is obvious that from then on Random House considered *STORY* their private nursery, and a cheap one at that. And indeed there was as much osmosis between the two entities as there was between *The American Mercury* and Alfred A. Knopf's house. Mencken never ceased to plug and push his protégés, and instead of seeing *STORY* as an interloper on the scene, he welcomed it. He was about to relinquish the directorship of his magazine anyway. In true Mencken style, the sage of Baltimore invited the couple to lunch at the Algonquin—but in his room, not at the Round Table, the fabled institution he always made a point of snubbing.

The first American issue of *STORY* came out in March of 1933, the day before the nation's banks were ordered closed. It contained eleven stories, including "My Mother's Goofy Song," one of John Fante's best short stories, and "Convalescence," by the perennially under-the-weather Kay Boyle. In effect, this first issue was a passing of the torch: Fante was a *Mercury* transfuge—along with James M. Cain and George Milburn, he was one of the contributors Mencken published the most. This was the populist, regional and ethnic vein brilliantly mined by Mencken, who liked his subjects to be specifically American, and his writers radically isolated (sometimes incarcerated), either geographically or socially—at any rate working far away from New York and its literary coteries. In this same vein, *STORY* would publish a great many sons of Greek, Armenian, Italian and Hungarian immigrants—even an African American named Edward Lucher McDaniels, an illiterate man who operated an elevator in a San Francisco hotel and whose stories had to be taken down by a stenographer. In this intellectual landscape, Kay Boyle was a link with the past wave, the Moderns of the 1920s, whose stories were infinitely more intimate and personal.

STORY enjoyed its most successful and fertile period during the four years that followed this debut, its circulation going from 600 to 20,000 in that short a time. From a marginal *succès d'estime*, *STORY* almost became a newstand staple. The cover colors varied from red, orange, yellow, or gray, but the title still slashed in a diagonal banner, and the declaration of intent remained unchanged ("Devoted Solely to the Short Story"). The editorial content, however, thickened; so did the ads. The specific fervor of those years is found today in *STORY*'s yellowed pages of advertisements: you could rent a portable Remington for 10¢ a day, with the manual teaching touch typing in two weeks coming free of charge. Writing contests abounded in Burnett and Foley's pages. The first books by *STORY* alumni were proudly announced, months before publication: Saroyan, Milburn, Caldwell, José María Vargas Vila. There was a sort of headiness involved, a romance, which seemed to matter much more than the $25 paid for each story. Even after they became famous and widely published, authors like Caldwell, Saroyan and James T. Farrell kept on sending material to *STORY*.

Martha Foley was the one opening the mail and dealing with manuscripts, sending back letters of either acceptance or rejection, always with encouragements. Burnett's end was business and fabrication. In the 57th Street offices, they met with a constant flow of writers, often broke and discouraged. One of the shadows who dropped by one day lived nearby, a man named Cornell Woolrich. He had been semi-famous once for his Jazz Age novels *Children of the Ritz* and *Manhattan Love Song*, and he'd even had a stint in Hollywood, but he hadn't placed anything anywhere for a long time. Foley warmly accepted a piece of his, "The Night Reveals," a short thriller in a totally different manner for the author, and assuredly for *STORY*. The reactions were good and prompted Woolrich to persevere in this vein. He soon started to write for the pulps and the slicks, becoming the prolific author we now know under various pseudonyms, such as William Irish and George Hopley.

Malcolm Lowry was another wreck that came crashing into the *STORY* office. Not yet under the volcano, the British writer was already building his personal hells, like a bird feathers a nest. He had come to New York, a city he detested, because he could not live far from Jan Gabrial, his problematic wife, even though he clearly could not live with her either. Lowry's manuscripts were rejected all over Manhattan, except by the editors of *STORY*, who published two of his pieces, including "Hotel Room in Chartres." A few months later, after his taxing sojourn at Bellevue, Lowry offered another story to Burnett, called "The Last Address," inspired by what happened to him in the psych ward. Burnett accepted it, but just as he was leaving for Hollywood (still following Jan Gabrial), Lowry asked the editor to give him his story back so he could revise it once more. This was, of course, what would become, copiously augmented and a hundred times rewritten, *Lunar Caustic*, which would only be published posthumously in 1963, six years after the author died, in another journal with a transAtlantic vocation, *The Paris Review*.

Erskine Caldwell, who was in New York often because of his obscenity trial for *God's Little Acre*, was also a frequent visitor. The novel would earn him a fortune, but that was still half a year away, and the author often had to borrow train fare to get back home to Maine, where he and his family subsisted largely on a diet of beans and not much else.

Nelson Algren was also knee deep in beans, or rather, peas. But he was shelling them. His first publication, "So Help Me," was written at a gas station in the armpit of south Texas, twelve miles from Rio Hondo, where he survived by shelling and canning bushells upon bushells of black-eyed peas for a shady partner who later was involved in a failed bank robbery. Like many young men during the Depression, the Chicagoan had drifted from town to town, working or hustling his way to New Orleans. In the Crescent City, he got by for a spell as a door-to-door salesman, hustling housewives with some sort of Miracle Perm kit. Things broke bad somehow and he had to leave town in a hurry. This is how he had found himself pumping gas in the middle of Nowhere, Texas. "So Help Me" was actually a letter he had written to a friend in Chicago, but before he had time to mail it, Algren found himself in jail, arrested in Alpine, Texas, for stealing a Royal DeLuxe typewriter. Four months in stir for theft of a Royal DeLuxe—this was irresistible stuff for a bio-caption on any book-jacket flap. And sure enough, in the summer of 1933, Algren sent his piece to *STORY*. The biographical notice mentions only that "Nelson Algren Abraham, who is Jewish and Swedish, is already back in Chicago." His drifting days were over, or about to be. Thanks to "So Help Me," Algren received a letter from Vanguard Press, asking him if he was at work on something. The writer hitched a ride to New York and met James Henle at Vanguard, who promptly sent him back to Texas to write his book. Henle's encouragements were most spartan, however; he'd given him ten dollars for the road, with promises to send him money orders every three month or so, totaling no more than ninety dollars. After the total failure of this first book for Vanguard, *Somebody in Boots*, Algren would publish nothing for five years, a period when he worked for the Federal Government editing (with Richard Wright) the State of Illinois Writing Project. One often finds this alternative for writers in the 1930s—this or Hollywood. Another variant, equally nefarious, was to be awarded a Guggenheim.

STORY soon became a rite of passage where writers could lose their literary cherry in good company: Tennessee Williams, John Cheever, and a 19-year-old girl who in 1936 signed her first story for the magazine: Carson Smith—the future Carson McCullers. In addition to prestigious European contributions from the likes of Graham Greene, André Malraux, Aldous Huxley and Pirandello, Burnett and Foley could pride themselves for having published, over the years, Frank O'Connor, Peter De Vries, Wallace Stegner, Frederic Prokosch, Richard Wright, Edward Anderson, James Ross, Daniel Fuchs, Alvah Bessie, Albert Maltz, and even Charles Bukowski (as early as 1944, a good ten years before he became known as a poet). Come the end of the decade, two-thirds of these people would be working in Hollywood.

But with this success, *STORY* also lost its original identity, as well as its primary objective. Dropped by Random House in 1936, Burnett and Foley had to stoke up their finances with book clubs, mail-order writing classes, and finally take the plunge becoming full-fledged publishers with STORY Press. The publishing house had distribution through Harper, but the venture was checkered, at best—their only bona fide success being Ignazio Silone, the author of *The Abruzzo Trilogy*. The second novel in the series, *Bread and Wine*, came out in 1937.

With the war coming, articles and editorials thickened the issues, but nothing at this time in fiction was half as electrifying as the thunderbolt which had struck, ten years earlier, smack in the middle of *STORY*'s February 1934 issue: *Horizontally wakeful amid universal widths, practising laughter and mirth, satire, the end of all, of Rome and yes of Babylon...*
Those were the first words of "The Daring Young Man on the Flying Trapeze," a dazzling improvisation on George Leybourne's 19th-century song, which marked William Saroyan's literary debut. Martha Foley always claimed that after this coup, the author of "70,000 Assyrians" had sent her a story a day for a full month—not counting his letters to her, a few of which she published as well ("Dear Martha Foley, I want you to know that it is very cold today in San Francisco...").

By 1945, Saroyan himself estimated that he'd written more than 500 short stories. He was famous for sending them several times to the same editor, barely changed, even after consecutive rejections. One day, Martha

Scoundrels & Spitballers: Writers and Hollywood in the 1930s

Prolific storyteller William Saroyan was one of Whit Burnett and Martha Foley's great discoveries

Foley asked him if he knew this other Armenian, who appeared so gifted, who was publishing stories in *Hairenik* (fatherland), the Boston Armenian daily newspaper—a man named Tessiad, about whom Edward O'Brien kept raving. The two editors even had a friendly rivalry and ongoing bet, as to which of the two Armenians, the one from Fresno or the one from Boston, had the most genius and would first become famous. Saroyan, for one, claimed this Tessiad was a cousin of his in Fresno who picked his rejected stories out of the paper bin and mailed them to Boston. It was pretty obvious, however, that Saroyan himself sent the stories to *Hairenik* under the pseudonym.

But the miracle of the multiplying Armenians was not due solely to Saroyan's transparent ruse. There *was* another Armenian writer in Fresno, a legitimate one, publishing under the name of Sirak Goryan, as well as a swarthy, cantankerous Turkish Armenian who was laying siege to the same magazine offices as Saroyan. To top it all, this one had been to school with him in Fresno. To sort out this silly mess, Foley decided to publish two of Albert Issok Bezzerides' letters, in which the semi-Armenian revendicated his right to work on the same subjects as Saroyan:

> I was born in Samsun, in Turkey, but my parents met in Istanbul. My father was Greek, from Talas, and my mother Armenian – Hourani Kuludjian was her maiden name. One year after I was born, in 1909, they came to Fresno with one dollar in their pocket. I suppose this makes me Greek-Armenian, but as my mother was the one wearing the pants in our home, I'd rather consider myself Armenian-Greek...
>
> I am thoroughly disgusted. You'll see why when you read what follows. Up till now I'd refused to read Saroyan's book because I thought he and I were writing pretty much on the same things and I wouldn't feel too good reading it. Of course I've read his stories in *STORY*, the *Mercury*, and the one in *Esquire*.

But tonight my wife brought his book from the public library and brought my attention to a story of his called "Big Valley Vineyard." In it he mentions certain things I also write about in my story "Passage Into Eternity" (published in this issue). Why must they look so similar?

Bezzerides at the time was an electrical engineer and a movie-camera repairman working out of a shop in downtown Los Angeles. He was still three years from publishing his first novel, *Long Haul*, and thirty years from writing the pilot and "bible" of the vastly popular television series *The Big Valley*, starring Barbara Stanwyck. In her response, also published along with his letter, Foley had tried to lighten things up: "The more the merrier. If we must have a Levantine Renaissance, so be it. Two Armenians are enough to start things rolling…But wait only one or two months until our Syrian from Dayton, Ohio, is ready for the printer! We'll hear no end of talk about Syrians."

Saroyan's main strength at the time was his arrogance, and the refreshing way he had of doing everything as if he'd just invented it. Everything that crossed his mind he considered worthy of interest to be broadcast to the world at large. To funnel this flow of unsold stories and scraps, he even talked Stanley Rose and another friend of theirs, lawyer-historian Carey McWilliams, into founding the Stanley Rose Press—a project that fizzled when the two enlisted partners realized nothing else would be issued from that press but the Saroyan *Nouveau*.

One cannot stress enough how seriously writing was taken in the 1930s. And in Hollywood, a magazine like *STORY* was held in almost ridiculous reverence by the overpaid writers toiling at the studios. Such was the chasm between the two worlds (the "serious" writers and the dissipated ones), that one day, at a Salka Viertel party, Austrian author Vicki Baum cornered Martha Foley (who'd just left *STORY* and Burnett) to ask her very seriously if, in her opinion, she could send a piece to *STORY* with any chance of it being published. Foley assured her that she could, whereupon the famous author of *Grand Hotel* and *Ladies Lake* asked, incredulously: "With my name on it?"

The four Warner brothers, in more fraternal times: Sam, Harry, Jack, and Albert

DEAR BROTHER JACK

F　**ILM HISTORIANS LIKE TO DECLARE** Warner Bros. the most liberal and socially conscious of all the Hollywood studios. Yet except for *I Am a Fugitive from a Chain Gang*—a picture so emotionally powerful it helped reform the penal systems in some Southern states—it is fair to say, in retrospect, Warner mostly chose targets that were already fair game, like lynching and the Ku Klux Klan (*They Won't Forget* and *Black Legion*). Jack Warner was the only studio chief to support Roosevelt, however briefly, during the 1932 Presidential elections (so did W. R. Hearst, for that matter). Darryl Zanuck and Hal Wallis, his successive heads of production, were Republicans to the core, but even they knew a good story when they saw one. Ideologically, however, it never went beyond good business and showmanship. As for the Warner brothers themselves, the letters one can find in the studio's archives, concerning now-famous films or controversial proposed projects, show how deeply schizoid the Warner machine was.

Harry Warner, in particular, was easily alarmed and timorous, ceaselessly advising his younger brother Jack not to make waves. Harry was based on the East Coast, in charge of the corporate side of the business, and as soon as he heard of a "delicate" subject being considered in Burbank, he literally flooded his brother with apprehensive messages, mostly concerned with coddling his political allies. Should a story touch upon or, God forbid, *cross* the Mexican border, Harry was immediately sick with concern for "our Mexican friends" (read "our Mexican market"). Should he hear of a story taking on mine owners and union organizers, Harry blew a gasket while he tried desperately to reassure senators from targeted states and all "our friends from the bitumous industry," that the picture would not be about *them*, or better still, that it would not be made. As soon as a congressman or a senator sneezed in Washington, Harry got chills; and he hastily relayed them to the Other Coast.

A case in point is the letter he wrote J. L. upon learning that he had writers developing a picture about Huey Long called *Kingfish*—the nickname bestowed on the Governor of Louisiana by his adoring constituency. A screenwriter by the name of William Rankin pitched the subject as early as 1932, claiming he was good friends with Long. From March until June 1933, Carl Erickson toiled on a first draft, but on June 12, a pair of letters put the project in jeopardy: one was from the Kingfish himself, the other from Harry Warner. Huey Long claimed to be scandalized by the tenor of the script (it is not known how he could possibly have read it, and he also claimed he did not know "this Rankin fellow"). Long was by now in the U.S. Senate and could hardly be ignored. He quickly countered, however, by proposing to the studio that he would, in two months time, personally write a script about his sensational career and charge very little for it. His offer was immediately rejected. But Harry Warner's letter, which arrived the same day, was more serious, and even more revealing:

Dear Brother Jack,
    You will get into a lot of trouble if you make a picture about Huey Long. I do not feel like being audited again and I don't want to go up against such an unpredictable anti-Semite – as you know, a guy like him can cause us a lot of grief. My advice to you is to throw this story into the incinerator. If you go with this, you'll be sorry.

Lovingly,
Brother Harry

Nevertheless, Hal Wallis persisted for a few more months, writing to Jack Warner on July 3: "As you know, I gave a copy of *Kingfish* to E. G. Robinson. I just got a call from his wife; she reads for him. She tells me she had him read pieces of it and that they are both very enthusiastic. So, do we go on and send Rankin to New Orleans?"

Wallis picked Robert Lord, a recently promoted writer, to supervise the project for what would have been his first production. Lord was young and hard-driving, but by September his reports were discouraging: Erickson and Rankin had been hard at work trying to incorporate Long's changes and wishes, but they would need at least another month before they could send Rankin to see the Senator with a workable script, while the Kingfish was bombarding Burbank with threatening letters and telegrams. Wallis put a third writer on the script: Brown Holmes, who had done the early work on the superb and groundbreaking *I Am a Fugitive from a Chain Gang*. But to no avail: on October 11, Roy Obringer, head of the legal department, cabled Warner: "Long will never approve the present script, in any shape or form." The project was shelved.

In April 1935, however, story department head Fred McEwen brought up the matter again to Warner and Wallis, and with good reason: Senator Long had just announced his candidacy in the 1936 Presidential race. Moreover, a "March of Time" documentary on the populist politician was currently being shown all over the country, smashing all attendance records. In his memo, McEwen suggested contacting the "March of Time" people and finding out how they managed to protect themselves against libel and lawsuits. Wallis, for one, wrote his boss that they should pick up where they left off and revive the script they had. "William Keighley read it and is crazy about it." Wallis went on speculating that now that he was a Presidential candidate, Long would be more amenable to publicity—"any kind of publicity." He also suggested sending a certain Grad Sean to Washington and discuss all this with Long. "He speaks his language and may be more successful than we have been."

A month later, on September 10, 1935, Huey Long got his publicity all right, as the son-in-law of a political opponent shot him in the belly at the Louisiana State Capitol, an oversized monstrosity that Long had proudly built with taxpayers' money and which he viewed as one of his greatest achievements. Carl Weiss, his assassin, was immediately shot dead by Long's bodyguards. The Senator died two days later in the hospital. News of his demise was heard around the world, and 200,000 people attended his State funeral in Baton Rouge.

A motion picture about Huey Long was, it now appeared, possible. Help came from unlikely quarters, no later than one day after the assassination. A distant relation, one James Long Wright, contacted McEwen to offer his services: "As soon as Mrs. Long will have recovered from the shock of her husband's death," he wrote, "I will be officially authorized to negotiate a filmed version of Senator Long." Still, McEwen warned his employers that this boondocks hustler also had screenwriting ambitions as well as the gall to pitch the studio a story idea completely filched from an old Warner movie. Wallis was for dropping the whole matter, even after McEwen came back with another option: the studio could acquire, for $30,000, all rights to Huey Long's autobiography, *Every Man a King*. For this price, his widow would relinquish any control or veto power over the enterprise, provided Warner hired one Earle J. Christenberry, author of something called "A Brief Outline of the Accomplishments in Louisiana of the Late United States Senator Huey P. Long," as a consultant, at a weekly salary of $125. "He was apparently very close to Long," McEwen went on, "and his widow does everything he says. Are you interested?"

The big *NO* slashed in grease pencil across McEwen's letter is proof that by this point Wallis, and everybody on the lot, was eager to drop this hot potato. Or maybe the spud was too cold: legally, nothing prevented the studio from cooking up their own film, along the lines of what they had had in mind three years earlier. In the interim, however, Huey P. Long's brand of strong-armed populism began to smell different to the American public. As late as 1933, Columbia had distributed a documentary on Benito Mussolini, with unexpectedly strong box-office returns. Many movie moguls and personalities were fascinated by Il Duce's domestic successes. Capra kept a bust of Mussolini on his desk, as did his boss Harry Cohn. Zanuck was an early fan, and Hal Roach went so far as entertaining a juicy proposition from Mussolini's 21-year-old son Vittorio to take over the Italian movie industry and make it a competitor to Hollywood. But when Vittorio came to California to close the deal, he and Roach were met by violent protests in the press and from the fledgling Hollywood Anti-Nazi League. Mussolini Jr. was wined and dined by Roach and had his picture taken with the *Our Gang* kids. At 20th, he had his picture taken with Shirley Temple—

but that was as far as it went. Roach finally had second thoughts and regretfully—for a time, that is—declined the deal.

Ironically, the Huey P. Long story would not reach the screen until 1949, and then under Columbia's banner. By that time, Robert Penn Warren had published *All the King's Men*, his extraordinary novel on the politician's life. The film version was produced and directed by ex-Warner Bros. writer Robert Rossen, who'd had a hand in writing the script for *They Won't Forget*, a picture featuring a feckless prosecutor with political ambitions. Griffin, the Southern district attorney played by Claude Rains, had a little bit of Huey Long in him. But when it came to make *All the King's Men*, the Long legacy and his persistently strong base support, forced Columbia to avoid filming in Louisiana, as considered. Most of the location work was done in Stockton, California, an area that often substituted for Southern locales in Hollywood movies. (Jean Renoir had filmed *The Southerner* near Stockton four years earlier.)

For all Zanuck's bluster about making movies from newspaper headlines torn "hot from the press," Warner Bros. often proved timid in the clinches. Michael Curtiz's *20,000 Years in Sing Sing* is a powerful film, and Spencer Tracy's breakthrough performance cannot be ignored, but reformer Warden Lewis E. Lawes, on whose book the movie was based, weighed so much on the production that today the picture feels generic and sanctimonious, as does the performance of Arthur Byron, the usually fine actor who played him. The ending especially feels like a tidy wrap-up, a replay of the opening with all the years being served in Sing Sing flying off from the calendar. A pre-release review in *Variety* (Oct. 28, 1932) described a much more sardonic ending, showing Tracy's electrocution broadcast on the air, coast to coast, concluding with radio bandleader Ted Lewis asking, "Is Everybody Happy?"—a line familiar to every American home in 1932, but also echoing the gallows humor of the men seen earlier on death row. The original release, according to the *Variety* preview, ran 95 minutes. All extant prints of the picture today run 78 minutes, and there is no indication that the picture was not originally released at that length. The Warner brass must have feared public sentiment and had the negative recut in the pat way we know it today. It ends abruptly with the condemned Tracy holding the Warden's unsteady hand as he is giving him a light for his last cigarette. Then follows an awkward reprise of the film's opening montage, with the years ticking off for each prisoner.

Of all the hard-hitting socially minded Warner pictures of this period, however, Mervyn LeRoy's 1932 *I Am a Fugitive from a Chain Gang* remains the most striking. Zanuck had a right to take it as a personal triumph, given the in-house opposition he had to overcome. In his autobiography, LeRoy typically takes all the credit, but the Warner archives indicate that he came late to the production, and wasn't even Zanuck's first choice for the assignment. The young Warner production chief had bought Robert E. Burns' biography as early as June 1931 when it had been serialized in *True Detective Mysteries*. He paid $12,500 for the rights, a very high sum for a story nobody in Hollywood wanted to touch. When his story was finally published in book form by Vanguard in March 1932, Robert E. Burns was still a fugitive and liable to be returned to the Georgia penitentiary from which he'd escaped a few years before. Zanuck's faith in the story took guts, as many in the studio thought the project misguided at best. Even Roy Del Ruth, given first crack at directing, turned it down, calling it "too morbid." Even earlier, when Zanuck had circulated the serial in 1931, a reader from the Warner story department, one Esme Ward, recommended a pass, with the following objections (which must have mirrored Harry Warner's very own sentiments):

1/ This penitentiary system has been abolished in most States.
2/ The few States still running chain gangs will ban the picture.
3/ Officials and important people are involved.
4/ The story shows corrupt practices by various law officers and lawmakers.
5/ This will only accentuate antagonism between North and South.
6/ Rough on lawyers, elected law officers and local government members.
7/ There is a vindictive tone throughout this book that is certainly understandable, but probably exaggerated.

With one sweep of his already famous polo mallet, Zanuck brushed aside these objections from the rank and file, which were even lamer than Brother Harry's apprehensions. Zanuck immediately hired an ex-prison warden as consultant, and put no less than three writers on the script: Sheridan Gibney for construction, Brown Holmes for the actual writing of the script, and Howard J. Green for the polish. Zanuck's eagerness and impatience may have had something to do with his old pal Rowland Brown making a picture on a similar subject at RKO. Brown was already shooting *Hell's Highway* in a canyon not far from Warner's Burbank lot, where the *Fugitive* script was still being constructed. That was the beginning of July 1932, and Zanuck wanted to start shooting his convict film by the end of the month. It took much longer, but the studio head should not have worried about Brown's picture. Although similarly themed, *Hell's Highway* was too episodic and laconic to cast a shadow over *I Was a Fugitive from a Chain Gang*. Brown's film had delicious moments, but its pace was too slow, its tone too prosaic, and its cast a bit too over-the-hill to entertain any serious chance against the punch of Paul Muni's performance. In addition, the script of the LeRoy picture was infinitely superior: its indictment of antiquated prison rules is so powerfully hard and violent it still shocks today. The last shot, with Muni shouting from the darkness of an alley the famous line, "I steal!" (his wife has just asked how he survived on the run), has almost as much impact as Chaplin's awful smile at the end of *City Lights*. In his autobiography, LeRoy claims that the darkness was an accident due to an electrical failure, and that he had chosen to go with it, finding it more powerful. Maybe so. But it is Zanuck who decided to end the picture on this striking line, which in the script was followed by a shot of a road map indicating Muni's progress towards the Mexican border, with stock shots of the border itself and road signs announcing it. The picture faded out on a silhouette of the fugitive walking over a hill, having finally made it. Zanuck cut all of this, an example of "The Zanuck Touch" at its best.

Robert E. Burns saw the picture in Trenton, New Jersey, and did not have to disguise himself to do so. A luncheon followed the screening, to which State dignitaries and policemen were also invited. Burns had become a *cause célèbre*—but this did not prevent the FBI from arresting him as a fugitive some time later. Three consecutive New Jersey governors refused his extradition to Georgia, and Burns remained free until, finally, in 1945 the Georgia Pardons Board absolved him of any crime. In the meantime, he had vindicated at least one of the Warner reader's objections, confessing to *Time* magazine that he had never been whipped, nor chained, while he was incarcerated in Georgia.

THE LAST OF THE HARD-ASSES

I find him in a West Hollywood enclave surrounded by gyms, gay bars, and stucco apartment buildings. It's 1986, and his hovel is one of the last remnants of the 1930s in this unincorporated municipality already developed beyond reclaim. 826 Westbourne Drive is now just a row of shabby single-room apartments that must have been part of a court, its patio and other half having long ago been gobbled by real estate greed. Next door, a four-story building is under construction, so John Bright's front door now opens on a cyclone fence, as if the old man's grouchy volleys and verbal abuse had to be constrained by steel netting.

He is 79-years old, and a ratty beige polo shirt barely covers his distended belly. He wears black chinos that have turned yellow and shiny, not necessarily through washing. He also sports the most extraordinary Turkish slippers, curling at the toes. Charlie, his dog, is difficult to miss because of the smell. Instinctively you want to scratch yourself, which is something the host does openly, vigorously and incessantly. When he interrupts the conversation to relieve himself, he does so without closing the bathroom door, splashing merrily while he keeps on talking.

John Bright is a survivor of many fights. You can't make out the thinning mustache within the lines and crevices of his face. A few years ago, a stroke left him semi-paralyzed and incapable of writing. He lives mainly on potato chips, water, and lethal doses of television news. He still has two sons left in this world, one making out like a bandit with a rock club in Costa Mesa, the other a building contractor in Malibu. Bright has a "gal friend" who drops in occasionally. His eyes light up when he pronounces the words, and he watches closely for my reaction. Recently, the *gal friend* brought him a photograph as a present, one she found in the files of the defunct *Hollywood Citizen-News*. She had it framed, and it now sits on top of the television set. Bright knew the picture well, but had not seen it in more than forty years. In it one sees a rounder, almost cherubic John Bright, dressed to the nines. "Oh, I was a dude!" he crows, "a real clotheshorse." And this much is true. George Raft, sitting alongside, has nothing on him, except maybe the actor's easy grace, and that supremely indifferent German shepherd gaze. Sitting with them on the same steps of the Paramount wardrobe department is "the guy who directed Raft in *If I Had a Million,* at least the sketch I wrote," says Bright, who can't recall the director's name. But then, nobody remembers anything about the movie except for Charles Laughton's performance in Ernst Lubitsch's sketch. Raft's turn, however, as a forger on the lam who can't cash a check if his life depended on it (and it does), is very fine. Bright wrote the piece with Lester Cole, a fellow blackballed Commie who Bright will, typically, be badmouthing to me within the hour.

The disorder in the room is staggering, books cascading everywhere and covering every piece of furniture—books mostly on politics, psychology, history, and movie making, along with a smattering of novels (among which I am not a little surprised to find a first edition of Leonard Gardner's *Fat City*). The volumes are stacked so high along the walls that you can barely make out the yellowing and frayed poster for *Brooklyn, U.S.A*, the Bright play that opened on Broadway in December 1941, just before Pearl Harbor. "Not a good time for a play or anything else," he says. I've heard that one before, but about the 1929 crash.

His memory fogs up at times, but you can talk to him. He answers in a thin, almost exhausted voice, a long murmur sometimes punctuated by a dry, unpleasant, mirthless laugh. "My problem," he says, "is that I've scattered myself everywhere. I wrote novels, movie scripts, tons of reviews, and no less than six plays. And I wrote on a lot of different things. If I had glommed onto a genre and stayed on it, if I'd dug my row, written in depth about one place, like O'Hara with Bucks County, for instance ... There is a type of writer who is like a doctor building a practice. But I wasn't one of them."

Scoundrels & Spitballers: Writers and Hollywood in the 1930s

I had come to talk about the book of memoirs he had written some years back, to see if I could get it published, if not in the United States, at least in France. At that point, in April of '86, I had not quite finished reading *Arsenic and Old Faces*, as he was calling his manuscript. In it, he settles accounts with various employers in a sardonic (if relentless) way that seemed to come naturally to him. "If only this book could come out, hopefully not posthumously," he murmurs. I proffer lame reassurances, but avoid looking him straight in the eye. At the time, I did not know to what extent his book was unreliable and factually perverse, but the tone alone, the vindictive drone, made me suspicious. It reminded me of another book of memoirs, by one of his old comrades who, like him, helped start the Screen Writers Guild in 1933 in opposition to the studio bosses and producers, and, like Bright, had ended up being blacklisted in the late 1940s. Sure enough, as soon as Lester Cole's name comes up, Bright knocks him down: "He sent me his book to blurb or to review, I don't really know which. I had to decline because I don't like his book. He's a friend and I did not want to badmouth him publicly."

One could say the same thing about Bright's book, its artfully composed vignettes etched in acid. They were entertaining enough to read, but all too obviously written for effect, and for effect only. Why did some of these people, who had put the truth above all else and paid a heavy price for it, so often take liberties with the truth? Why were there so many unreliable sources among the victims of the blacklist and their relatives?[1]—as if you needed to blacken the lily, instead of gilding it (which some of them did as well).

But, of course, I do not tell him this. Instead, I listen to him recount (for the third time) how he arrived in Hollywood through the Panama Canal on the "S. S. Ecuador" on the day of the 1929 Stock Exchange Crash, having lost at the ship's gambling tables all of the advance he and his partner had been paid to come out and adapt a book they'd just written, *Beer and Blood*. As if the John Bright and Kubec Glasmon story needed spiking. In their time, the pair would be so successful, the pictures they wrote would make so much money for the studio, that Warner used their

---

1 A glowing exception to this rule is Walter Bernstein's *Inside Out: A Memoir of the Black List*, Alfred A. Knopf, 1996.

names on publicity material, in type as big as some stars rated. This was unprecedented in 1931, especially for a pair of writers the studio paid a paltry $100 a week. Their travails on *Beer and Blood* resulted in *The Public Enemy*, their own title having been deemed too startling and vulgar. It had not yet reached the screen when Zanuck put them to work on a quickie called *Smart Money*, a mediocre picture but a smart move, as it cashed in on the breakthrough successes of star-of-the-moment Jimmy Cagney and Little Caesar himself, Edward G. Robinson (even if, in this picture, Cagney was merely a foil to Robinson). Within a year, the Bright and Glasmon team would churn out four scripts for Warner Bros., until Zanuck split them up.

As a teenager, John Bright had been an errand boy for Ben Hecht at the *Daily News* desk in Chicago. After being fired, he found employment as a soda jerk in a drugstore. The pharmacist there was named Jakob Glasmon (born Jakobek Glasmann). Glasmon was ten years older than Bright, but the difference in experience was far greater than that. Glasmon, the son of Polish Jews, had truly lived. As a pharmacist, he had legal access to alcohol, which inevitably put him in contact with the Chicago underworld. He knew bootleggers, racketeers, gambling joints and whorehouses—a world Bright had no inkling of in 1929. Nevertheless, Glasmon supported his young friend financially while he wrote his first book, a fawning biography of Chicago Mayor "Big Bill" Thompson. When Bright's publisher later advanced him a small sum against a book on the Chicago underworld, tentatively called *Beer and Blood*, Glasmon decided to throw in his lot with Bright.

A Chicago theatrical acquaintance, Rufus LeMaire, managed to sell the book to Warner Bros. (the title, at least), and the two partners took a slow boat to California. Bright's avowed reason for going was that he was pursuing a girl (whom he "unfortunately ended up marrying," in his words). Glasmon, for his part, simply wanted to take to the air and shed the family and business ties that rooted him to the Windy City. *Beer and Blood* told the story of a small-time Irish hood Glasmon had known in Chicago, set against a background of bootlegging and racketeering the former pharmacist knew well. Their novel was a much stronger brew than the movie eventually made from it—in fact, its vulgarity is still shocking today, with lines like "A slit is a slit, even if it's a cow's," or "You make such a racket when you get your ashes hauled." Warner had bought the story for $1,000 and hired Bright and Glasmon to fashion a script under the supervision of an experienced screenwriter named Harvey Thew. As Bright said, "Zanuck was quick to get rid of LeMaire and take credit for finding us; he promoted him [to] head of casting at the studio, which was good for pussy, but not so good for his career. He stayed in casting a very long time."[2]

The Public Enemy remains famous for two things: James Cagney and his electrifying performance, and the breakfast scene in which he pushes half a grapefruit into Mae Clarke's face. The actress' part was brief, not even earning her an on-screen credit, but the bit gave her more durable fame than the later fine turns she had in James Whale's *Waterloo Bridge* and *Frankenstein*. Zanuck, director William Wellman, and a few others later claimed credit for the grapefruit scene in their respective memoirs or interviews, but the truth is that it's already in both the novel *Beer and Blood* and in the Bright-Glasmon script. Warner Bros. pictures would be rife with grapefruit references for years to come, as in *Hard to Handle* (1933), in which fast-talking promoter Cagney quips, "What do I know about grapefruit? I never even saw a grapefruit," which of course brought the house down at every showing, evidence of *The Public Enemy*'s popularity.

As for Cagney, even if we are to believe that Glasmon and Bright convinced Wellman to switch parts between Cagney and weakling Eddie Woods (originally pegged to play the leading role of Tom Powers), it is undoubtedly true that Cagney's career was launched not by *The Public Enemy*, or by Wellman, but by Rowland Brown and *The Doorway to Hell* (1930). Zanuck was certainly aware of Cagney before Wellman got the assignment, and, contrary to what John Bright claimed in a 1985 interview with Lee Server, Cagney on *The Public Enemy* wasn't earning the same paltry weekly salary as Bright ($100), but $400.

As soon as they hit Hollywood, the balance in the relationship between Glasmon and Bright quickly tipped; the latter wasn't looking up to his mentor any longer. While Glasmon advised, Bright did the actual writing. Once, when Bright pleaded sick and hid out in Palm Springs waiting for a

---

2 Zanuck brought LeMaire with him to 20th-Century Fox, where LeMaire was head of the casting department for many years.

salary offer better suited to his sudden notoriety, Glasmon stayed in Burbank and kept on working. The studio finally relented, adjusting Bright's salary to $500 a week, and Glasmon's went up as well. Resentment festered between the two former friends, and by late 1932, when they both were making $7,000 each writing *Three on a Match*, they no longer were on speaking terms. Age difference, temperament, politics—everything now separated the two men, but office intrigues and Zanuck's animosity were even more responsible for splitting up their profitable association. An incident occurred between Bright and Zanuck concerning the casting of Loretta Young in a Bright-and-Glasmon vehicle called *Taxi*. Bright is only one of several writers who have claimed to have almost thrown Zanuck through an office window. In this particular case, Bright maintains that he was prevented from doing so by Zanuck's personal secretary. As a result, Bright's option was not picked up and Zanuck spread the rumor that Glasmon had been the brains of their partnership. Regardless, none of this prevented Glasmon and Bright from having healthy separate careers for a while, although sometimes they'd work at the same studio, such as Paramount and MGM. Bright soon found in jailbird-turned-scriptwriter Robert Tasker the soul mate Glasmon had never truly been for him: a younger, more handsome and adventurous man. Later, Bright wrote a few interesting pictures in Mexico, including several adaptations of B. Traven novels. He was also, if you're inclined to believe him, instrumental in bringing Dalton Trumbo's *Johnny Got His Gun* to the screen, when he was employed as story department head somewhere.

Glasmon, for his part, married Joan Blair, a two-bit actress, and fashioned a small career for himself. He worked at Paramount on *The Glass Key* (1935), the intriguing but ultimately ghastly first adaptation of Dashiell Hammett's novel, directed by Frank Tuttle. Better was another Raft vehicle, *Bolero*, an enjoyable drama in which the actor died on stage while dancing. If any movie star deserved such a kiss-off, it was the generally unloved Raft, who, at least in his younger days, made up with grace and dancing skill what he lacked in acting technique. Another curiosity Glasmon wrote was a picture made at 20th Century Pictures, Zanuck's fledgling company after he left Warner. *Show Them No Mercy*, a kidnapping yarn vigorously directed by George Marshall, rounded up as rough a bunch of no-goods as you'd ever want to see: Cesar Romero, Bruce Cabot, Warren Hymer, and the ever-smiling, truly scary Edward Brophy, here playing a crumb called "Buzz." The kidnapping story was original enough to hold interest, most of it taking place after the ransom has been paid and the scion of the rich Hansen family is released. An unlucky couple and their baby girl get cooped up with the gangsters in their farm hideout for the duration of the story. The picture, made and released in 1935, is also interesting for measuring how far the movies had veered from the gangster glamour of the early 1930s. Here the G-Men are supposed to rule supreme, and lip service is paid to the Bureau of Investigation (not yet called the FBI), but the head of the Feds, played by Frank Conroy, is so wooden all one remembers is how lively the gangsters are. Rarely has a bunch of hoods been depicted this casually and this endearingly. We see them cutting up, mercilessly teasing Edward Brophy, or taking pot-shots at the dog. They often are seized by bellyaching laughing fits. Cesar Romero, regal in his high-waisted zoot suit trousers, dances the cha-cha while shaving. Brophy has an unexplained hatred of woodpeckers, and horrid Bruce Cabot wants to rub out everybody (he does in Romero for his measly $300 at the end). All these engaging performances completely nullify the moralistic slant of the picture—which might have been the idea all along. The credits are presented as the front page of the *"Daily Bulletin"* with SHOW THEM NO MERCY! the screaming headline. Glasmon gets a prominent place ("by Kubec Glasmon"), reminiscent of the earlier stature he'd had with Bright at Warner Bros. In contrast, Henry Lehrman, who wrote an early draft, gets buried on page four. Photography is nimbly handled by newly promoted cameraman Bert Glennon, who would be the director of photography of 1954's *Crime Wave*. All in all, it was not a bad picture to end Glasmon's writing career.

In 1938, the battered Screen Writers Guild attempted to rise from its ashes and fight off its rival, a pro-employer organization called Screen Playrights. According to John Bright (and let's not forget he was a story spinner), it was decided that each SWG member would visit a colleague and persuade him to switch sides. Bright surprised his fellow members when he volunteered to call on Kubec Glasmon, who, like him, was currently employed at MGM. By Bright's account, Glasmon had been warm and receptive. The bosses had separated the two men, and Glasmon realized he had never shed his atavistic fear of authority. As the son of immigrant Jews, he had no sense of entitlement and never dared to go head-to-head against the bosses. But no more, he swore. "The next day," Bright pungently writes in his memoirs, "two things happened to Kubec Glasmon: he bought his Screen Writers Guild membership, and in the evening he died of a massive heart attack."

John Bright died on September 14, 1989, three years after I visited him on Westbourne Drive. He was 81.

A DUCK DINNER AT THE MONTECITO

THE FIRST THING JAMES M. CAIN saw when he arrived at the Santa Fe station in Los Angeles on a November morning in 1933 was a man crossing the street paddling a canoe. Under a driving rain and wearing rubbers, Cain was taken by a Paramount flunky in a company car to the Knickerbocker Hotel in Hollywood, where he was to stay until he could find proper lodging.

The first familiar figure Niven Busch spotted on the night of his arrival in Hollywood, two weeks later in this same month, was the tall, lanky frame of James M. Cain sticking out of a booth at Musso & Frank. The two men knew each other from New York, where they had been just a few weeks before, both having left newspaper and magazine careers behind on the East Coast. Cain had long written for W. R. Hearst's *World*, Busch had been a sportswriter for *Time*. Recently, both had been toiling at the *New Yorker* under the exacting rule of Harold Ross. If Busch looked up to Cain, older than he was by ten years, it was also because he saw Cain as something of an institution. At 39, James M. Cain already had spent most of his lifetime in the newspaper business: reporter, editorialist at *The American Mercury*, then the *World*, Cain seemed to have had ink running in his veins. He spoke from the corner of his mouth in a blustery voice without looking at you, like a City Desk editor in the movies, minus the cold cigar. At the *New Yorker*, Cain had edited Busch's copy (if anybody but the irascible Ross could be called an editor at the magazine). A fit young Princeton graduate, Busch had come to the *New Yorker* with the notion of writing about golf, boxing, hockey and college football—all things Ross found deeply repugnant. But Cain, whom Ross had hired as managing editor, was largely responsible for the "back-of-the-book" content, and he'd managed to sneak in quite a few of Niven Busch's sports pieces. Because of Ross' notoriously volatile temper, the managing editor post had been a revolving door for years, and Cain had no illusions about his future at the magazine. Instead of waiting to be sacked, he had made arrangements on the sly, secured a job in Hollywood, and left town without so much as a week's notice.

I met Niven Busch in the summer of 1982 at the second (and last) edition of the Santa Fe Film Festival, which that year was dedicated to the Western film. I knew he had worked on the MGM adaptation of *The Postman Always Rings Twice* in 1945, and after introducing myself I asked him about it. He threw his head back and, after one of his peculiar donnish laughs, said: "If you want to know about Jim Cain, you came to the right place." It was the first time I'd heard Cain refered to as "Jim." I was to find out later that Busch had never been interviewed by Cain's first biographer, Roy Hoopes, whose 1982 book was, and still is, the authoritative work on the novelist. In Santa Fe, Busch took me back to those first days he and Cain shared in Hollywood.

"In New York, Jim had always been courteous to me, but we didn't see each other socially. One day I went to see him at the *New Yorker* to tell him I was turning in my last article because I was leaving for Hollywood. I had waited until the last moment to tell him because I didn't want it to be known around town. I could already hear the sarcasm around me, about my 'selling out.' I wasn't going to wait for this. And Jim was great about it, he just asked what studio I was going to work at. I told him Warner, and he wished me good luck. Three weeks later I am in Hollywood, and the first time I go out for dinner, who's the first guy I see sitting in a booth but Jim Cain! He'd been there just a few weeks before me. He hadn't told me, he hadn't told anybody, because he didn't get along very well with Harold Ross—they were two very strong personalities. Actually, Cain had a superior training as a newspaperman. He'd been with [Walter] Lippmann, and he was great friends with Herbert Swope, the editor-in-chief of the *New York World*. But Ross had hired him away at a greater salary and for much easier work. I don't know how much notice he gave Ross, but it couldn't have been much. Well, anyway, he was working for

Paramount, on a three-month try-out contract, and I don't think they took up his option. I was a bit luckier because I picked up one or two credits right away, one for *The Crowd Roars*, a car-racing picture with Cagney. So, that wasn't so bad because with those credits I knew I could go back working eventually. But I don't know that Jim had screen credits at that time, I don't think so. I was making $300 or $400 a week, which was pretty good

James M. Cain

money during the Depression, but I was already making about that much as a journalist in New York. What brought me to Hollywood was the feeling that I had topped out in New York. I can still see the memo Zanuck sent Hawks about me. His secretary was a friend of mine and he showed it to me. It said: 'Niven Busch is a marvelous dialogue-writer, and he'll be a great help.' Well, I'd never written dialogue, I was a magazine writer, not one line of dialogue! But Hawks took it pretty much as if it came from the tablets of Moses, or else he didn't give a damn. Anyway, he liked and respected my dialogue. But the actors didn't show the same respect because when I showed them the dialogue they said, 'Jesus, I can't say this crap!' And I'd ask them, 'Well, what do you want me to have you say?' I must have worked three or four months at Warner before they let me go. I lasted a bit longer than Jim at his studio, but we both ended up like everybody else in 1932: unemployed and pretty skint. Studios at that time were going bankrupt one after another, crisis was everywhere. It was even worse for Jim. I was a bachelor, but Jim had brought his wife with him; she was a Finn, I believe, and a pretty odd woman. She also had a little boy and a little girl. Jim had taken two apartments on the same floor of the Montecito, a residential hotel on Franklin, just behind Musso & Frank. This was a pretty swell place, Art Deco and all that. He was paying $300 just in rent. And he was like me, all his professional contacts were 3,000 miles away on the East Coast: Mencken, Walter Lippmann, all those guys. Here in Hollywood, he was just another journalist who tanked out on his first try. On top of this, he had serious digestive trouble; he wasn't healthy. But he seemed resigned to stay in California. His wife liked it here, and I think he got used to it himself. Elina, his wife, was a weird sort of fish, kind of a hard cookie. Later, I think she had a lover on the side. But at the time, she was a pretty good companion for Jim.

"It was in spring of 1933, I believe, that we saw each other again. Like me, he had a few jobs here and there, but things were pretty dismal. But one day, he had come around to my apartment and left a note: he had four wild ducks, some hunter friend had brought them to him, and he was inviting me to dinner that evening. So I went there, to the Montecito, and I brought a date along. The duck was delicious, of course. As you may know, Cain had two passions in life, good food and opera music. He was a gourmet and a very good cook. He even wrote cooking articles for *Esquire*, later on. And here in his two-room apartment at the Montecito, he had all the stuff, all the cooking gear. He even had a duck press, you know, to press out the blood from the duck after it's roasted. He probably was the only person in Hollywood who had a duck press! But anyway, dinner was delicious. The girls were doing the dishes and we were having a last drink. I asked him what he was doing at the moment, and he gave me a queer look, like he was wondering whether he should tell me. But I guess he wanted or needed to talk about it because he said, 'Well, I've just written a novel.' Apparently, he'd had a hell of a time with it because from 200,000 words he had cut it down to something like 60,000. Alfred Knopf had refused it the first time, but Walter Lippmann persuaded Blanche Knopf to change her mind. Finally, they took it and gave him a $500 advance, which was the lowest that they could give. But anyway, he had a publisher for it. So I said, 'Jim! That's wonderful news, I always knew you'd write a book someday, but what's it about?' And he answers: 'It's about the insurance business.' I took that in while sipping my drink, thinking Oh my god, here is this poor guy who hasn't got a job, got a family to feed, and we've just had a feast with his ducks, and he wrote a novel about the *insurance business*? But then he started to tell me the story of *The Postman Always Rings Twice*—he was a good storyteller I remember, he got into the details, he took at least three-quarters of an hour to tell me the story. And when he was finished I said, 'Jim, this is the goddamnest story I've heard in years, maybe ever. This is going to be a big hit, you'll make lots of money with it, but for God's sakes, why do you say it's about the insurance business?' And he said, 'Well, you know, my father was in the insurance business.'

"Apparently, Jim got part of his story from cases his father told Jim about, years before. I have to say that his novel was not yet called *The Postman Always Rings Twice*, but—get this—he called it *Bar-b-Que*! I can't figure why. Maybe the cat who gets fried on the power line! But Jim was funny that way. He was intelligent, but his mind functioned only a certain way. He had to reason out everything, and to have justification for everything. For instance, he couldn't start a novel until he found a justification as to how he knew the story, who was telling it. This is why you have all kinds of dictating machines, or telephone confessions, in his novels. These things used to drive him crazy, but all these hurdles were of his own making, nobody else worried about things like that in fiction.

"Of course, *Postman* was a smash hit, it stayed several weeks on the *New York Times* bestseller list. Cain was going to make money after all; even a lot of money because after this he wrote quite a few books. Meanwhile, things hadn't turned bad for me either. I'd started writing novels as well, books that earned me much more money than what I'd been making as a scriptwriter. And when I wrote *Duel in the Sun* I sent Jim a copy. He wrote a wonderful blurb for the publicity people, and after this I made a habit of sending him what I'd just written. After two or three commercial successes, I wrote one that was pretty heavy in the socio-political department. It was called *Day of the Conquerors*. He sent me a note when I sent him that one: 'Dear Niven, if you want to do something big, go wash yourself an elephant.' That was his main comment. The novel was actually interesting; it took place during one day in San Francisco, with the United Nations in town and all that, but Jim didn't go for the social commentary stuff at all. Anything that smacked of pretension, he detested. And he was right because the novel did not sell. So much for messages.

"Now, we are in 1945. I write book after book, two of which I sold to the movies within the same year. I am married to a famous actress [Teresa Wright]. So, I wasn't doing badly, either. I was offered a lot of assignments. But if I was asked to adapt *The Postman Always Rings Twice*, it was pure coincidence. Now, my agent had been H. N. Swanson—he had represented me for *Duel in the Sun*—but now I was with Victor Orsatti, who was very well connected at MGM. It was pure chance, he didn't even know Jim and I were friends. I accepted because I felt I was qualified. Of course, everybody involved knew we couldn't do the book because of censorship, and we had no illusions about that, Jim included. But after all, I had written *Duel in the Sun*, which had pretty torrid sex scenes as well. And in David Selznick's picture of it they don't say the girl was fourteen. She's as old as the woman they pick to play the part and that's that. So, yes, I was interested, on top of the $20,000 the job represented for me. But MGM put Carey

Wilson on the project as the producer, and Carey Wilson was very boring. An old-timer, he had been a writer during the silents, and at the time he produced most of the Andy Hardy movies. They had a saying about him at Metro: if you asked Carey Wilson what time it was, he'd tell you how to make a watch. At work, he was the same: demanding story conference after conference. Well, I like to work fast, and alone. I didn't like to be pestered this way. Plus, the Breen Office was giving us all kinds of headaches, sending us list after list of stuff we couldn't put in or even hint at, not just the sex. For instance, the husband could not be a Greek as he was in the book, for fear of hurting the Greek community's feelings. No overt love scenes either, especially not after they've just murdered the husband. No 'Rip me! Rip me!' in the ravine right next to the husband's body in the wrecked car, as in the novel! You've got to remember that this book was hot, hot, hot, even fifteen years after its publication. It had taken all that time for MGM to get the nerve to try and adapt it. They'd had the rights all along. And the war may have changed attitudes about sex somewhat, but I'll tell you, that passage when Frank gets his hands on Cora down that ravine, it was torrid!

> I ripped her. I shoved my hands in her blouse and jerked. She was wide open, from her throat to her belly ... She was right down there at my feet, her eyes shining, her breasts trembling, drawn up in tight points, and pointed right at me ... "Yes! Yes, Frank, yes!" ... Hell could have opened for me then, and it wouldn't have made any difference. I had to have her, if I hung for it. I had her.

"I don't know why I never talked to Jim about the problems we were having with the censors; maybe he wasn't in Hollywood at the time, or maybe I didn't want to talk to him because I was afraid we wouldn't do justice to the book because of all the inhibitions we were having from all sides. But anyway, that guy Carey Wilson was very boring, and finally he put another guy on it, a pal of his named Harry Ruskin, a hack writer who was doing all the "Dr. Kildare" movies at the time. Ruskin took my dialogue and added a few cruddy jokes and that was all. They previewed the picture in Glendale, and it didn't go too well. I believe Jim saw that version. So they cut the scene when Frank goes to Mexico with the girl who's a lion tamer, and they cut the cat getting fried in the power lines. Later on, I learned that Jim Cain hated the movie, but at the time he was very happy with it. Probably he was mostly happy to have sold a book everybody thought was unfilmable. At least, we never mentioned the picture when I saw him next. As a matter of fact, I hired him for a few weeks. This was on a Victorian detective picture called *Moss Rose*. The producer was Leland Hayward.[1] And when I bogged down on it, Leland told me to hire who I wanted, and I hired Jim Cain! It was not a very satisfactory collaboration, I must say. It was up his alley, and he was very fertile with his ideas. We were writing in my apartment and each day we'd arrive at a story line we found satisfactory, but the next morning Jim would come in and destroy it, saying, 'It's no good, I got a better one,' and so on and so on, until one day I told him we'd better call it off because we weren't making any headway. But at least I got him a couple weeks' salary, which I don't think he needed, but anyway...

"He was then back living at the Knickerbocker; I think he had divorced Elina. I was shocked when I saw him: he had nearly doubled in volume. He'd turned from an eagle-faced lean man into rather a fleshy man. He'd had a gall bladder operation, and it completely changed his metabolism. He also had stopped drinking and smoking, although when we were together he always had a pack of cigarettes he was toying with in his pocket. One day I took one off it and it was stale like you wouldn't believe. I think he managed to go back to his old frame and shape, but by that time he had left Hollywood for good. We had drifted apart little by little, but that certainly was not because of *The Postman Always Rings Twice*."

When I met Niven Busch in 1982, he was in his seventies and in remarkable shape. He still cut the figure he had in the forties, that of the westernized East Coast intellectual—an unlikely but convincing Man of the West: sportcoats or blazers, an ascot casually knotted under open shirt collars, he spoke in a gravelly radio voice and had a peculiar brayish laugh that could have belonged to an Oxford don or a prospector's donkey. Busch

---

[1] Busch must have meant Gene Markey, who co-wrote and produced *Moss Rose* in 1947, starring Vincent Price, Victor Mature, and Peggy Cummins.

Scoundrels & Spitballers: Writers and Hollywood in the 1930s

was also a notable exception to the rule among writers of his time: a man who most probably would never have written a novel, let alone fifteen, had it not been for Hollywood. Besides his most well-known, *Duel in the Sun*, there are *They Dream of Home*, *The Furies*, *The Hate Merchant*, *The Actor*, *California Street*, *The San Franciscans*, *The Gentleman from California* (about the selling of Richard Nixon), and *Continent's Edge*.

When I next paid him a visit, at his home in San Francisco, he was finishing a novel about industrial espionage and the Silicon Valley. He lived on a steep Pacific Heights street opposite the Soviet Consulate, and often joked about the diplomatic personnel he saw coming and going, and the surveillance. There were so many high-powered microphones, cameras and other high-tech gizmos at the consulate that more than once the microwave in his kitchen or the TV remote in his living room would start on their own and other household electronics would go berserk.

Busch spoke of Hollywood without any trace of nostalgia, like a man whose life had been full and well lived. He'd gone from being a lowly-paid beginner at Warner Bros. to a $1,000-a-week writer who adapted literary classics like *Babbitt* and *The Westerner*, not to mention his friend James M. Cain's most famous novel. He had also been Samuel Goldwyn's story editor for several years, where he mostly looked out for the career of his wife, Goldwyn contract player Teresa Wright. He wrote or adapted so many Westerns in Hollywood that he got drawn to life on the range, at least to the extent of becoming a cattle man himself. For years, he owned a substantial outfit near Hollister, south of San Francisco, and at the 1980 Santa Fe Film Festival dedicated to the Western, I heard him talk knowledgeably with other writer-ranchers like Jack Schaefer (author of *Shane*) and Thomas McGuane, about modern-day stockmen problems, such as the financial drain caused by chainsaw rustling (McGuane had written a movie about it, 1975's *Rancho Deluxe*, directed by Frank Perry).

"I worked in Hollywood for twenty years, at practically every studio: Universal, Paramount, RKO, and at Warner a long time. In Burbank, the writers lunched in the Green Room. We'd gamble for the check, I remember; we played the matchstick game. It could get to be expensive. If you paid for the lunch, then you didn't have to play the game for a week. At

Paramount, they had another thing—a word game. A bit like Scrabble, but just on bits of paper. They had blanks and they scribbled on those while eating their sandwich. One day, a banker came from New York, a VIP visitor, and he asked: 'What are they doing?' indicating the guys scribbling away. 'Oh, they're the writers,' he was told. The banker was very impressed. 'Hell, do they always work so hard?'

"There was this mob of writers back then, new battalions that came every year from the East from the world of publishing, the world of the theater, and the world of journalism. They learned the trade pretty quick and got very good at it. I was rather young when I worked at Warner, and I looked even younger, so a lot of the old guys liked to give you advice and help you along. I remember this one big red-headed guy named Courtenay Terrett. He was a famous by-line writer for the *New York World*. He had his office right above me. I'd just done my first picture and I still didn't know what I was doing because, on *The Crowd Roars,* Hawks had helped me along. So, I told Terrett I didn't know the first thing about writing pictures. He said, 'Look, as often as you can, get a script of one of their successful pictures and have it screened for you.' You could have a private showing of any picture you wanted, day or night. So you read the script, screen the picture, read the screenplay again, understand the dynamics of the thing, understand why it works. The theater people who came to Hollwood scoffed at such an idea. They thought writing a script was easy as pie. Well, it isn't. You had to learn how to do it."

Busch remembered other writers, now forgotten, but who were probably more representative of the species than the "legends." Gene Towne and Graham Baker, then a famous writing team, were among them. Towne started early in Hollywood, writing cards for silent films. Baker had been a newspaperman in the Midwest. In the 1930s, they worked principally for producer Walter Wanger, but freelanced just about everywhere. The pair is noted for the marvelous *History Is Made at Night*, which they wrote for Wanger and Frank Borzage in 1937.

"They had a very funny routine," Busch remembered. "They sold so many originals in those days. Baker was the writing man. He was a rather austere, soberly dressed man who looked like a small-town bank president.

Writer Niven Busch with his bride, actress Teresa Wright

And Gene Towne was a little bald-headed Jew with a sunburned nose who wore the most garish clothes. They would go into the office of the victim producer, and Towne would start telling the story they had. He would leap into the room and would start acting out all the scenes. From time to time, Baker would interject a criticism, an objection, and pretty soon they'd start arguing in front of the producer. And they made sure Baker's objections were nothing too serious or unfair. So, the producer, already caught up in the story, would invariably side with Towne and defend the story. And, magnanimous, Baker would yield, and the producer would sign the contract. They called this 'spitballing,' in those days."

At the other end of the spitballing spectrum was director Eddie Goulding, who often worked as a story man and screenwriter. "He made a lot of money, but Eddie was always short of cash. So, one day he went up to see Thalberg, and he told him a story. Thalberg liked it, called a clerk and had him cut a check for $10,000. They agreed on a tentative title, and Goulding would get another ten grand on delivery of the screenplay. Eddie had been up to the occasion that day because he was up to his neck in debt. He had a 60-day delivery date on the contract. Of course, Eddie didn't remember a thing he'd said to Thalberg, so he thought up a story and wrote it, but it was another story. Thalberg read it and he said, 'This is a marvelous story, and your $10,000 advance applies to this one. But what I'd like you to do now is write the story you told me the first time, and I'll pay you another $20,000.' So, Eddie is dancing on one foot, kind of embarrassed. And Thalberg smiles and asks him, 'Would you like me to tell you what you told me the first time?' He remembered, you see, and he had the girl read it aloud, because she had taken it all down in her book. That was Thalberg for you. He hardly brushed up against the real world. He thought in motion picture captions, he wooed women in motion picture gallantry. He was thoughtful when he thought of you, but he rarely thought of you unless you could be useful to a picture project. Thalberg picked brains, that's what he did all day."

From 1937 on, things started to change for Niven Busch. He got an Oscar® nomination for writing *In Old Chicago* and his salary jumped to $700 a week. "Then I went to work for Goldwyn, who did not have anything for me just yet, but loaned me out to my old studio, 20th Century–Fox. And right after this, I married Teresa. So, I told my agent, Leland Hayward, that I thought I could do better than writing on assignment, that I wanted to be an executive because I didn't want to waste time writing scripts. So, he took me to Goldwyn and I became his story editor, in 1941. Leland told Sam that I was a great organizer. Leland could talk anybody into anything. Nevertheless, I did become Goldwyn's story editor, and nobody had anything to complain about that I know of. I bought stories from my friends and hired them to write scripts, but I also brought some good projects to Goldwyn. I edited Lillian Hellman's play, *The Little Foxes*, and saved him a lot of money. I sat down with Wyler and made him take a lot of stuff out. I started *Ball of Fire* with Hawks, and *Pride of the Yankees*, for my girlfriend Teresa Wright. In fact, I mostly looked out for her interest—as later Selznick did with Jennifer Jones, but, I want to believe, with better results. I had it down in my contract with Goldwyn that he could not call upon me to write for him, but he had no trouble loaning me out on writing jobs, like he did with his contract actors or actresses. It was a very lucrative arrangement.

"But in general Goldwyn's organization was excellent. He made only two or three pictures a year. He had the best people in all the different departments, he had them under contract, year-round: Gregg Toland, Alfred Newman, William Wyler, Merle Oberon, Teresa Wright, Walter Brennan ... That was quite a roster. Walter was a character, in films of course, but also in life. He had a knack for immitating Goldwyn's voice, it was downright scary. One day, he was in some office on the lot, and there was a call from the gate, on Formosa Avenue, announcing the arrival of Mrs. Goldwyn. So Walter grabs the phone and tells the guard, speaking in Goldywn's voice, not to let her in, under no pretext! There was a lot of commotion after this, I tell you, because the Goldwyns were very serious people; they were snobs, in fact. But there was something in Goldwyn, a very aristocratic taste, a nose for artistic achievement. Some of it he might have gotten from his wife, who gave great dinner parties. He was a *grand seigneur*, although he could make off-color jokes and terrible, tasteless mistakes sometimes—all those musicals, for instance. That was his *nouveau riche* side; he always wanted the best in everything. He'd hire famous ballerinas or opera singers, like he wanted to educate the great unwashed, but the pictures would still be lousy because he'd hire the Ritz Brothers to make the sauce.

"But his tantrums and famous malaproprisms, the 'Include me outs,' those were purely a put-on. Just like Louis B. Mayer crying in front of you. Those guys were all hams, and the beauty of the thing was they put it across: their victims laughed and told those jokes about them, but they got rooked just the same. A good part of the Goldwyn legend was the work of Howard Dietz, his publicist in the early days. I know for a fact that Dietz invented the famous exchange between Goldwyn and George Bernard Shaw, 'The trouble, Mr. Goldwyn, is that we don't speak the same language; you want to hear me talk about art, I want to hear you talk money.'—That was Dietz. He's also the guy who founded the MGM motto, under Leo the Lion, '*Ars Gratia Artis.*' He stayed on as publicity chief at MGM when Goldwyn left Mayer and the others. Frankly, he was one of their best assets. But to go back to Goldwyn: he was good and bad with writers. He always wanted writers with big reputations, but he'd watch them like a hawk to see if they would deliver, even if they were good and knew what they were doing. The result of all that pressure was that often the writers were paralyzed from fear, but also sometimes from irritation or even anger."

Los Angeles Times | October 6, 1946

SCREEN COUPLES LEARN TO COMBINE TALENT

by HEDDA HOPPER

Leland Hayward manages Margaret Sullavan. Walter Wanger produces Joan Bennett's pics. DeToth directs Veronica Lake. Lucien Ballard photographs Merle Oberon. And Niven Busch scripts Wright.

"Goldwyn's wife, Frances," said Busch, "was a formidable woman in many ways. She was very clever, socially. This is how I got screwed with *Till the End of Time*. I had written this novel, my second, on discharged soldiers returning to their homes in America, and about the problems they met adapting to peacetime. The book was called *They Dream of Home*. And at a Goldwyn dinner one evening, I had to shoot off my big mouth about it. The novel was not out yet, but I told Frances about it. It didn't fall on deaf ears because, by the time I sold the rights of my book to RKO, Goldwyn had put someone to work on *The Best Years of Our Lives*.[2] Our picture was released before his, but of course it couldn't compete with Wyler's, its cast and even its script, which were all superior to ours.

"I had left Goldwyn by then, but Teresa was still under contract there, and the hell of it was that she was in *The Best Years of Our Lives*! It was a very Hollywood situation. Every year she was nominated for an Oscar®, and that year she was, too. She won a Best Supporting Actress once, for *Mrs Miniver*. Yet, after a few years, although she was still with Goldwyn, I managed to get her contractually to do two pictures a year outside the studio. This is when we launched Hemisphere Pictures, our independent production company, which in reality was just to have an outlet for the both of us. I wrote vehicles for Teresa, and she starred in them. This was during that period that I renewed with Jim Cain, when I produced *Moss Rose*.

"Of course, the Hemisphere picture I'm most proud of is the Western I made with Mitchum, *Pursued*. I wrote it, and it really launched a new genre, as you know—the 'psychological Western.' Stylistically, it was very close to film noir. Mitchum was great in this, of course, but the funny thing is, we nearly hired somebody else for the part. Teresa had been in a play in New York in which a young man had impressed her. His name was Montgomery Clift. He was totally unknown in Hollywood. We brought him over to make a test. And he was very good, he read very well, but nobody expected someone so thin and so frail. To make matters worse, the person in charge of putting him in costume had done it in a hurry. After all, this guy was an unknown, so why make an effort? When we saw poor Monty coming in with these big heavy calfskin chaps and two huge six-shooters knocking about his knees, we had a hard time not laughing him out of the

---

2 The writer was Midwestern author MacKinlay Kantor. The intricate and real story behind *that* picture is to be found in Eddie Muller's *Gun Crazy: The Origin of American Outlaw Cinema* (2015, Black Pool Productions).

room. So we thanked him, and he went back to New York. A year later, he was starring opposite John Wayne in one of the greatest Westerns of all times, *Red River*."

Retrospectively, Busch had come to be of two minds regarding the genre he had helped spawn, the "Freudian Western." His reservations stemmed less from his own further stabs at it (*The Furies*, for example, superior in many respects) than from the excesses he saw in other people's attempts to put an Oedipus complex under every rock, as Arthur Penn did in his *The Left-Handed Gun*. "My objective," he said, "when I started this, was only to make the characters more real, give them three dimensions in modern terms—something you did not see very often in Westerns at that time. But in doing so, maybe I gave these characters psychological makings they did not really have in those days. Perhaps I just applied modern concepts that did not apply. I've always wondered about this."

Like Cain, Busch got tired of the Hollywood game and ended up dedicating his time to ranching and writing novels. His separation from Teresa Wright in 1951 may also account for it (they divorced a year later; she went on to marry New York playwright Robert Anderson, author of *Tea and Sympathy*). But Busch was also a rarity in this, leaving as early as he did; at least it was his own decision, and he quit at the top of his game. He liked the isolation of the Hollister ranch, even though he soon would move to San Francisco when he married Carmencita Baker in 1956. About Hollister, he once wrote *Publisher's Weekly* columnist Paul Nathan: "Clipping services are not rightly understood in local areas. The gal who did my income tax accounting listed Romeike Clipping Service under 'Veterinary Services.'" This was the kind of humor he could only share with fellow writer-ranchers like McGuane or Schaefer.

James M. Cain, on the other hand, always allowed that in Hollywood he had "hit the deck like a watermelon that has rolled off the stevedore's truck," as he once wrote in the introduction to his most famous collection of novellas, *Three of a Kind*. He just didn't like pictures, and he liked writing them even less. In reality, his movie career was longer and more lucrative than he admitted, but only because of the sales of his novels to the studios. Yet Cain liked California, in a way, and less than a year after the dinner at the Montecito, he was serving duck again, this time in the glossy pages of the fledgling *Esquire* magazine. Arnold Gingrich's publication was then the most vital in America, if not yet the best paying. Cain's article was featured between pieces by Ernest Hemingway, George Nathan, and Ezra Pound. The same January 1935 issue had short stories by F. Scott Fitzgerald, Erskine Caldwell, and Michael Fessier. Cain had started his hardboiled culinary series almost immediately following publication of *The Postman Always Rings Twice*. In the December 1934 issue, he wrote about the only way (his way) to carve a holiday turkey, wedged between a Hemingway bottom-drawer article, Fitzgerald's take on insomnia, and Saroyan's "Little Miss Universe." Two months later, Cain would outdo himself in a piece called "Oh, Les Crêpes Suzette!" By then, he played a heavier hand and the hardboiled tone was openly comical, opening with this leery lead: "*Brother, it's none of my business why you want to make crêpes suzettes, but you can't blame me for having my suspicions about it.*" He follows with the peremptory advice that the things are only worth the trouble if you're entertaining a lady with one thing on your mind: "*Serves 2.*"

"Them Ducks," on the other hand, was a lavish affair, with *Esquire* trying to match Cain in the he-man department. "*Take your stop-watch in your hand, gather your stags 'round your duck-press and—surprise!*"

> The first thing you must get through your head, if you are plotting a wild duck dinner, is that there is something silly about the whole rite. You simply cannot get away with it if you do it as you would do an ordinary dinner, with your wife at one end of the table, yourself at the other, and rows of politely dressed ladies and gentlemen in between. You try that, and you are in for a flop. The reason is that some of those people will show their manners by ignoring your hocus-pocus, others will show their sense of humor by giggling at it, and all of them will show a lamentable ignorance as to what it is all about. Bow your head, then, to reality. Banish dressing. Banish politeness. Banish women. In other words, keep your eye on this central principle: when it comes to something faintly absurd, as this is, the male gender has a much greater capacity for punishment than

the female, a much greater inclination to accept it with becoming solemnity—so that you should make the thing stag. ...

So much, then, for the general approach: we shall now take up the thing itself. I warn you that this is appallingly expensive, at least in initial outlay, although once that has been made, game ducks don't cost much more than any other kind of ducks. First, then, you will have to go to a restaurant supply house and get yourself a duck press. This will cost you about $20 and you have to have it. Ducks without a duck press is like turkey without cranberry sauce: possible, but hardly conceivable. You will have to get a chafing dish, if you do not have one already, and this will set you back something too. And of course you will have to get the ducks. If you have friends who shoot, they will often give you some, just to make you feel like a poor relative; if not, a few discreet inquiries at your favorite restaurant will usually put you on the track of some. They have laws about ducks, you see, and sometimes a little money has to pass, but if you mean it, you can get them....

Now, then, for the ducks. The whole trick here is in timing, and as the maid figures in it just as importantly as you do, you will have to coach her patiently, so that she knows every move she has to make. This is the way the thing goes:

Maid comes in with paraphernalia for sauce, as soon as she has poured wine and removed soup plates, and places it on the table, to your left.

Ducks, on word from you, go into the oven.

You make the sauce at the table, all except for blood, which goes in last.

Ducks come in, and you carve them.

Carcasses go into press, blood is pressed out, add to sauce.

Carved portions go into sauce, are put on plates, and passed.

The maid, obviously, is the key to all this. ...

There is no cook in the world, except the chefs in the very best restaurants, who really believes that nine minutes are enough for ducks. If you don't hold your own watch on them, they will be cooked twelve, fifteen, or even twenty minutes, and then you are sunk. They won't have any taste, and worse, they won't have any blood; all your press, your sauce and everything else will look completely ridiculous, and you will wish to God you had never started this thing at all. ...

All right, now you are pretty near home. The maid, all this time, is at your elbow. You take those carcasses with the fork and you clap them into the duck press. Under the spout, the maid has placed a saucer. She now turns the press while you hold its legs, and the blood begins to run. When you have most of it, pick up the saucer and have her take the press away, and come back with the hot plates. Add the blood to the sauce a very little at a time, shaking the chafing dish gently as before. If you don't get panicky and dump the blood in all at once, so that it curdles into the worst mess you ever saw in your life, the sauce will steadily thicken and gain color and smell. When the saucer of blood is all in, spoon the few puddles of blood that remain on the platter. Your sauce is now ready. Leave the flame burning low, and dip each portion of duck smartly into the sauce, so that it is well soaked. Serve on the hot plates. Have the maid get busy with the hominy, the wild rice and the sweet potatoes. That is your wild duck dinner ... Pat yourself on the back. Quaff your Burgundy. Accept your plaudits. Reflect that you are probably a crack-brained fool, but then, who isn't?

Edward Anderson

THIEVES LIKE US

In 1949, Edward Anderson worked for the Fort Worth *Star-Telegram* as either a reporter or deskman, no one seems to remember which. As a tramp newspaperman with two published novels to his credit—one of them just reprinted under a new title as a Bantam paperback—he had no better prospects than his $25-to-$30-a-week newspaper wages in the Texas city that liked to advertise itself as "Cowtown—Where the West Begins." Anderson's opportunity for success had already come and gone in the 1930s, and he seems to have recognized that fact with a combination of resignation and bitterness. One October day in 1949 at the grimy *Star-Telegram* newsroom above Seventh Street, writing on the paper's letterheaded stationery, Anderson composed a letter to Howard Hughes, the owner of RKO Radio Pictures in Hollywood.

Dear Mr. Hughes:

I appeal to the largesse of RKO.

The picture scheduled to be released in November is based on my work, THIEVES LIKE US and with the screen title of WE LIVE BY NIGHT. I sold the screen rights to the book for $500 plus promises, including work on the picture, that were not fulfilled.

The book was reprinted under RKO auspices and was on the newsstands under the title YOUR RED WAGON before I knew anything about it and, if nothing else, showed contempt for my interest in the book.

Meanwhile, the editor of *Movie Story* magazine asked for permission to "fictionize" the book in order to publicize the picture, offering no money, and I appealed to Mr. Liebing of RKO, in charge of publicity I understand, and was answered by – silence. *Movie Story* insisted for the rights, paralleling the picture to *The Snake Pit* and other big hits, and while it put nothing in my pocket and only took out a postage stamp, I consented rather than feel a heel.

I live in a rickety house full of offspring in need of clothing and work on a newspaper and skip dinners to get by and that is the truth of my situation. In the event WE LIVE BY NIGHT lives up to its preview heralding (as Louella Parsons'), could I not have the hope of a bonus that would fix the foundation of our house on the railroad track and paper it?

I thank you.

EDWARD ANDERSON
Editorial
The Star-Telegram
Fort Worth, Texas

The "rim-rat," as these itinerant newspapermen were called, had signed his pitiful letter in proofreader's grease pencil. In the Texas of his day, Anderson embodied the fast-disappearing figure of the tramp newspaperman, but there was little to romanticize in the work he and his colleagues performed. As a group, they were self-educated men who often ran down stories, took photos, wrote copy and cut-lines, and, if necessary, set their own pieces in type. The work was grueling, monotonous, sometimes hazardous, and always low paying. But it was the collective dream of the tramp newsmen to get around the press barons, if necessary, and bag the Big Scoop that would deliver to them riches and glory. In 1951, Kirk Douglas would impersonate such a man in Billy Wilder's acrid *Ace in the Hole.*

By this time, Anderson had already had his shot at the movies and had "come a cropper," as his cotton-planting relatives might have put it. Born in Weatherford, Texas, in 1906, Edward Ewel Anderson was of Irish descent, with a trace of Cherokee Indian on his mother's side. His father was a printer. In his senior year at high school, he left home to take a cub reporter's job on a small daily newspaper in Ardmore, Oklahoma. He also served an apprenticeship as a printer. For the next ten years, he worked on newspapers in ten different towns scattered across Oklahoma, Arkansas, and Texas. Sometimes he would walk off a job, joining a carnival as a slide trombone player, or trying his luck as a professional prizefighter. His build and handsome black Irish features drew crowds, but he soon gave it up. Instead, he tried to write fiction, selling his first story—not surprisingly, a prizefighting yarn—to a pulp magazine. In 1930, he left a copyreader's job in Houston to become a deck boy on a cotton freighter running out of New Orleans. He spent six months in the North Atlantic. When he came back, the Depression had set in across the country and he spent the next few years riding freight trains and looking for work—an experience he related in his short stories and in his first book, *Hungry Men*.

In New Orleans, he met and made friends with John H. Knox, "a preacher's son who lived in a shack and wrote introspective poetry for nothing and horror stories with plenty of action for two cents a word," as Anderson relates in a 1935 autobiographical sketch for *Wings*, the Literary Guild newsletter. Under John Knox's influence, Anderson started to write a variety of genre stories for the pulps, with little success. He wanted to write about the "gentlemen hoboes" he knew first-hand, "but the pulp editors want only cowboy heroes. Or detectives. The mothers of juvenile readers won't tolerate hobo heroes."

In early 1934, Anderson was in Abilene, Texas, working in a printer's shop. After a short courtship, he married Polly Anne Bates in August. She was the daughter of a Texas Department of Justice agent. The newlyweds were broke. "My mother gave us the choice between some silver and a hundred dollars in cash," Mrs. Anderson recalled when I contacted her by mail. "We took the money and went to New Orleans."

There, Anderson "worked on the paper"—probably the *New Orleans State*—while Polly Anne kept house. They had a daughter, Helen. Mrs. Anderson was soon haunting the police stations in order to get stories for her husband, who would then write them up for *True Detective* magazine. One of the news features he wrote in this period profiled an elderly executioner for the State of Louisiana. The paper spiked it as too morbid and horrifying.

Anderson sent it to *True Detective*, whose editors suggested he try again as fiction. He did, under the title "The Hangman." On the pulp front, he also wrote for *Murder Stories*. But, as always with him, "only the prizefighting stories seemed to sell"—things with titles such as "The Little Spic."

Anderson adjusted his literary sights upward and started sending material to the low-paying but seminal *STORY*, co-edited by Whit Burnett and Martha Foley. He had his first work published there in October 1934, joining company with other fledgling writers such as William Saroyan, Alvah Bessie, Nelson Algren, and John Fante. Never would vanguard writing brush closer to the world of the prize ring than during these Depression years. Contenders from all over the country were showing their fanciest footwork in material submitted from Fresno, Los Angeles, Vermont, Chicago, Oklahoma. In the May 1935 issue of *Wings*, Martha Foley explains how Anderson ended up sharing first prize in a novel contest organized by *STORY*. The other winner was Dorothy McCleary, and both were awarded $1,000 and saw their novels published by the Literary Guild. Anderson's novel was *Hungry Men*. "Among the thousand-odd manuscripts which come to *STORY*'s office every week have been many dealing with drifting men, hoboes and the unemployed. One of the most able of those we published was 'The Guy in a Blue Overcoat' by Edward Anderson. It, too, brought many letters from readers who said they wanted more of his work. In *Hungry Men* they will have their wish."

And indeed they had, since *Hungry Men* amounts to little more than a rambling succession of scenes and stories (with a great deal of editorializing thrown in). "Bare Legs," the other Anderson short story published in the magazine, could, for instance, be easily inserted between any two chapters of his first novel.

The *Saturday Review*, which two years later would also review *Thieves Like Us* and hail Anderson as "the most exciting new figure to appear in American writing since Hemingway and Faulkner," dismissed his first effort out of hand. In the arch tones of a literary commissar, reviewer Ben Ray Redman wrote that, though he had turned in a fairly competent job of superficial reporting, Anderson should "turn his inquiring eye away from the road and towards the universities, the magazines, business houses and factories. Revolutions are never made by down-and-outers..." He went on pompously (but truthfully) to declare that Anderson's story was "as monotonous as the life that it describes, and his characters are as uninteresting on the printed page as most of their originals are in reality."

If anything, the excesses and ultimate failure of the whole proletarian movement in American literature is encapsulated in Redman's raw condemnation. Still, leaving aside the critic's transparent bias, *Hungry Men* does not hold up very well today compared to similar works such as *Waiting for Nothing* by Tom Kromer, published by Knopf that same year. And it has almost nothing in common with the control one finds in *Thieves Like Us*, which Anderson would publish later, with its utter felicity of language and characterization.

The prize money and publication of *Hungry Men* in 1935 had a liberating effect on Anderson. "It was our first money," recalled his wife Polly Anne, "Our first car..." With what was left of the money, they went straight to Kerrville, a small resort town in the Texas Hill Country west of San Antonio. Known for the quality of its air and its game-hunting, Kerrville was favored by sportsmen and tuberculosis patients, and it would become the inspiration for the town called "Antelope Center" in *Thieves Like Us*. As the young fugitives would do in the novel, the Andersons took rooms in an old sanitarium converted into an auto camp. According to Polly Anne, Anderson wanted peace and quiet in order to write his second book. "As soon as we checked in, he started pounding on the typewriter like a madman."

It is often assumed by contemporary readers that Anderson based the characters of "Bowie" and "Keechie" on Clyde Barrow and Bonnie Parker. According to Mrs. Anderson, this was not the case at all. Back in 1933, Anderson had handled public relations for William McCraw in his winning bid for the post of Texas Attorney General. Two years later, Anderson used this connection to obtain permission to conduct extensive interviews with one or more bank robbers at Huntsville Prison. Although his checkered work history was about to broaden once again, Anderson at heart remained a reporter.

When their bank roll ran out, the Andersons returned to Abilene, to Anne's mother's home, where she wanted to deliver her second baby. It was there Anderson waited for *Thieves* to be published (first in Canada, then in New York by Frederick A. Stokes)[1] and for his son Dick Edward to be born. In 1936, they were all in Denver, where Anderson once again "worked on the paper." They did not have a phone, so it was by wire that Anderson learned there was a job for him in Hollywood. The offer came from Ade Schulberg, mother of Budd Schulberg, who had recently become an agent after separating from her husband, Paramount chief of production B. P. Schulberg. The family of four took the train to Los Angeles and settled in a little apartment near Paramount, where Anderson was to be employed. The Seaforth, a tawdry yellow brick building, still stands today, just behind the old Enterprise (now Raleigh) Studios, which in 1937 housed B. P. Schulberg Productions (he had, in the meantime, been sacked by Paramount). Just a few blocks away, running west along Melrose, was RKO studios—where many years later the first film version of *Thieves Like Us* would be made.

Anderson started work at Paramount. Polly Anne only remembered the story editor there—one George Auerbach—"a foul-mouthed, insulting man who said Ade Schulberg had sneaked Anderson through her ex-husband's backdoor." After B. P. Schulberg left Paramount to set up shop across the street, Anderson joined him. He was given William Saroyan's former office.

Anderson soon left Schulberg to work at Warner Bros. The first project he was put to work on never made it to production, but its title—*Siberia*—seemed appropriate to Anderson's stint at the Burbank studio. A shy man, he detested Hollywood—his colleagues as well as his employers. As a seasoned newspaperman, he had no patience or taste for the confections he was supposed to turn out. One cringes picturing him slaving over the script of the Warner programmer *Nancy Drew, Detective*.

Still, the pay was $150 a week—pratically the bottom of the barrel by Hollywood standards, but a fortune for a newsman in 1938. Anderson, who had always been a drinker, began hitting the bottle heavily during this period. When the last of his studio jobs lapsed, he went back to report-

---

1 *The American Mercury* published exerpts of the novel under the title "Twenty Grand Apiece" in its February 1937 issue.

Anderson in the mid-1930s, flush with optimism and ready to take on Hollywood

ing—first at the *Los Angeles Examiner*, then for the *Sacramento Bee*. Polly Anne stayed behind when he moved to Sacramento because the children had the whooping cough. Also, Hollywood had made Anderson more and more difficult to live with. "When I need a drink I need it," says one of his characters in "Bare Legs." "There is no stopping me. That's the way I am about it."

Anderson was rooming alone in Sacramento when he sold the rights to *Thieves Like Us* to Rowland Brown in March 1939. The terms ("$250 upon signing and $250 within thirty days thereof") may today seem like highway robbery, but everything indicates that Brown had more in mind than a quick killing. He was certainly an operator and liked to fancy himself a wheeler-dealer, but he was also passionate about motion pictures. When he bought Anderson's novel, he had started a partnership with Joel McCrea, who was to play "Bowie." *The Hollywood Reporter*, dated April 21, 1941, carried the following notice: "Joel McCrea will play the leading role in "Thieves Like Us," which will be the first picture for New World Productions, headed by Rowland Brown and himself. Brown, who wrote the original story [!], is now revising the script to fit the role to McCrea."

When Paramount would not release the actor from his contract, or allow him any outside work, Brown sought to sell the project elsewhere. On May 2, 1941, he offered the property, along with the fine script he had fashioned, to RKO for $10,000. He even suggested an intriguing approach to casting that included Edmond O'Brien, Richard Barthelmess, and Harry Carey. RKO bought *Thieves Like Us*, but nobody at the studio wanted anything to do with Brown. At 43, his turbulent career as a writer-producer-director and general hellraiser was pretty much behind him. In the early 1930s, he had made perhaps the best gangster pictures in Hollywood, if not the most successful: *Quick Millions*, *The Doorway to Hell*, and *Blood Money*, casting Spencer Tracy, James Cagney and Frances Dee in their first meaningful parts.

Brown was regarded as a dream collaborator for any producer, provided he did not get too big for his britches: a writer who thought visually. His script of *Thieves Like Us* proves without a doubt the empathy he felt for the book and its characters. Not only does his script follow Anderson's story very closely, sometimes incorporating dialogue lifted straight from the novel, but his added touches and details only emphasized Anderson's bleak view of the world. Brown even amplified the author's accusations against a society whose greed produced the Depression, and against the hypocrisy of "those dirty capitalists" pulling all the strings. The finale imagined by Brown, with Bowie playing a shellac record of Mother Goose songs, was worthy of Fritz Lang or Sam Fuller. One thing Brown did not achieve, however, was making his script palatable to the Breen Office. Even in peacetime, Anderson's story would have had to be considerably softened to get past the censors—but in late 1942, with the United States finally at war, it was inevitable that a decree would come down banning the production of any films critical of the system or showing public officials—judges, wardens, bankers—as outright crooks. This was not, Washington opined, what the country needed to win this war.

Thieves Like Us was effectively shelved for years, even though the RKO records indicate that Dudley Nichols worked on a script of it for what was supposed to be his directorial debut. Nothing came of it. In 1944, Rowland Brown once again approached the studio, this time offering to co-produce the picture in Mexico. It was only upon the arrival at RKO in March 1946 of producer John Houseman, who was in search of material, that the *Thieves Like Us* file was once again dredged up. Houseman's memoirs (*Front and Center* and *Final Dress*) should be taken with a grain of Romanian salt, but there is no doubt that as soon as he learned of *Thieves Like Us*, he intended it to be his friend and protégé Nicholas Ray's entry to the cinematic world.

Ray was no writer; in daily conversation, or even on a set, he was inarticulate at best. But he wrote no less than one treatment and two early drafts of *Thieves Like Us*, before Houseman hired Charles Schnee to do the final. At the end of his 176-page script, dated August 6, 1946, Ray had written, in pencil: "This is NOT a gangster picture, not a sordid bloody story. It is tender, not cynical. Tragic, but not brutal. This is a love story. It is also a morality tale, in the rhythm of its time."

Ray, whose salary had jumped to $300 a week for his writing assignment, also had long conversations at Lucey's, the Paramount-RKO watering hole right across the street from the studios, with Robert Mitchum, an early admirer of Anderson's novel. When I asked Mitchum about this in 1986, the actor typically replied, "What of it?" only to gruffly concede that he'd wanted to play the hardened Indian thief Chickamaw "with my hair greased back and flat like a Cherokee. But the front office at the time absolutely refused to have me die in a movie. Remember, for those people I was the cash cow—their male Jane Russell. So, Nick Ray was pissed at me, and this is one of the reasons I made *The Lusty Men* with him, so he'd forgive me. I die in that one, I know, but that was a bit later. *Thieves Like Us* could have made a good movie if we had made it together, Nick and I, because we were both familiar with that part of the country and that sort of rural criminal type."

Ray's film was more romantic than the novel—the story had been re-centered on the young fugitive lovers. Thankfully, Ray's initial psychological explanations and backstories had been eliminated from the script by the time he started shooting, and the censors also helped make *They Live by Night* a picture strangely devoid of real violence. The opening prison break was striking for 1947, showing the escapees from the sky, not from inside the prison camp as in earlier scripts; it was one of Hollywood's first helicopter shots (at least with actors in it), and certainly the most arresting. Three separate holdups are melded into two in the picture, and only seen from outside the banks; T-Dub's death was now unseen, something Chickamaw related to Bowie. Initially, Ray wanted to "explain" or exonerate Keechie by making her uncle, Mobley, responsible for her indifference to either sex or lawlessness. In one of his notes, Ray wrote: "I think the *Romeo and Juliet* aspect of the story must be reinforced by making Mobley a bad parent, completely responsible for Keechie's behavior."

Nicholas Ray's first film suffered greatly from censorship, studio infighting, and no less than three title changes. It was not successful at the box office when it was finally released in early November 1949, almost two years after completion. Needless to say, Edward Anderson's pathetic "appeal to the largesse of RKO" fell on deaf ears. At the time of the picture's release, the addressee, Howard Hughes, was in the process of selling the studio to a tire company from which he'd make a handsome profit.

One could say Anderson was twice rooked by Hollywood, although it was done legally in both cases. When the author died in 1969, he had been living in reduced circumstances for years and was resigned to it. He could not have known that four years earlier, independent producer Jerry Bick had negotiated a deal to buy back *Thieves Like Us* from RKO. To save a few dollars, the studio had not renewed the copyright on the novel, which fell into the public domain. RKO's lawyers argued that the studio still owned the motion picture rights in all territories. Bick finally bought the rights from RKO for the modest sum of $7,500. He first tried to fashion a script with the help of Southern novelist Calder Willingham, then he let director Robert Altman turn it into a much more personal and idiosyncratic project. According to the producer, with whom I talked in 1986, nothing of Willingham's script was used by Altman. The remake of *Thieves Like Us*, finished in 1974, is the great exception to the rule that only inferior novels can be made into superior pictures. This is the miraculous book of a man who once—and only once—hoisted himself up to the level of his subject, a man who wouldn't necessarily be capable of writing another one this good. In this sense, Raymond Chandler was right when he called Anderson a "one-book writer," even if he did publish another.

The story Anderson's novel tells about his two-bit *desperados* is strangely different from both film versions, but is in no way inferior to either. The novel is as naive and disarming as the romantic motion picture Nicholas Ray made of it, and it's as hard and laconic as Altman's version, which is stripped of all sentimentality. The films couldn't be more different in tone and sensibility, yet it is fascinating to see how close to the book they remain, in details as well as dialogue and characterizations. If Anderson's novel managed to serve as a springboard for Ray's intimate lyricism as well as Altman's revisionism (which markedly distanced itself from a movie that had been made in the interim called *Bonnie and Clyde*), it is because *Thieves Like Us* contains all these remarkably authentic elements.

Altman, in his approach, was faithful to the book and its time, although for financial reasons he had to shoot most of the movie in Louisiana, instead of Oklahoma. The only point where Altman veers from the novel is at the end, when he shows Keechie surviving the hail of bullets shot into the motor court cabin. "I just did not want her to die with Bowie," Altman told me when I asked about it years later. "I wanted to keep away from the *Romeo and Juliet* aspect as much as possible. I wanted to see the girl board that bus, pregnant with her baby." This last scene is possibly more poignant than even the director intended. When Keechie (played by Shelley Duvall), sitting on a bench in the station, asks a woman next to her (played by Joan Tewkesbury, who co-wrote the script with Altman) where the next bus is headed, the woman replies, "Fort Worth." The filmmakers likely did not know that Texas city had been Edward Anderson's last known address. At any rate, Jerry Bick hadn't tried very hard to find Anderson, if he ever did. The producer did reveal to me, however, that prior to Altman's film, none other than John Ford had shown interest, in the 1960s, in retelling the story. According to Bick, Ford admitted he couldn't very well avoid the social message it contained, even if the idea horrified him. He claimed he just wanted to film a train robbery—a typical John Ford remark, as there is no train robbery anywhere in the book.

It is impossible to know if Anderson liked Ray's picture when he saw it in 1949. Elston Brooks, a *Star-Telegram* columnist, remembers sitting next to the author when he saw the picture one afternoon at the Hollywood Theatre in downtown Fort Worth, just a few blocks from the newspaper's offices. Brooks recycled his memories in several columns over the years, including in 1974 when Altman's version came out. Incredibly, the scribe never bothered asking Anderson what he thought of the picture they'd watched together.

Anderson did not live long enough to see Altman's version. In 1949, after receiving the predictable answer to his letter to Hughes from an underling from the RKO legal department, the author had only two paths left to pursue: drifting and drinking. His tracks can be followed through many Texas towns, with the exception of San Antonio. He worked several years "on the paper" in El Paso, then Laredo, then for the McAllen *Monitor*, in what was not yet called Magic Valley in South Texas. He had a stint at the Harlingen *Valley Morning Star,* before landing in Brownsville at the *Herald*. Brownsville might be seen as the end of the line by most, but there would be many more stations of the cross on the way down.

At the *Herald*, where he worked from 1960 to 1963, Anderson covered local politics. In the summer of 1985, when I made my inquiries and found the paper's editor-in-chief at his desk, Don Duncan was not much help. He knew who "Eddie" was, of course, but had not the slightest recollection to impart. The man who knew Anderson in Brownsville—enough to call him "Eddie" at any rate—was slinging hamburgers in a narrow storefront on E. Washington Street. Martin Rutledge had inherited this grease emporium in the 1920s, and the place hadn't changed much since then. The gumball dispenser on the sidewalk was chained to a parking meter and still took pennies. In the incredibly cluttered corridor reeking of fried onions, the proprietor offered me a seat atop a stack of Fresca cases and told me how he knew Anderson in the sixties:

"He came here every day, either before lunch, or right after the rush hour. He never ate here, he only came to talk. He was a very bitter man. Angry at the whole world. He thought he hadn't got the recognition he deserved for his books, even though he rarely mentioned or discussed them with anyone. He was obsessed by Fidel Castro at the time I knew him. He feared the American government would push him into the arms of the Russians—which is what happened. He also was into the philosophy of Swedenborgianism—now don't ask me why, I never understood this part. But then, Eddie was not an easy man to understand, or know. He did not drink with just anybody, or just anywhere. For this, we went to my place or else to the Pilot Bar, which was just down the street from here. It is closed now. Anderson was a drinking man, but not a drunk. He was never pathetic. He had long periods when he stopped drinking, but when he fell off the wagon, he went the whole hog. You could see it on his face, the drinking—it looked like a big prune. Otherwise, he kept fit. It was almost remarkable, the way he kept his body trim. And he liked to show it, too: he wore these short-sleeved shirts, to show his biceps. And this little jaunty hat, even when they became out of fashion and nobody wore hats anymore. He didn't care.

"He had met this Mexican woman at a dancing club. She was a taxi-girl, or something like that, you could dance with her for a roll of tickets. Name of Lupe. He surprised many when he married her. Here on the border almost everyone has a Mexican mistress on the side, or even lives with a Latina. But marrying one. ... Although we later understood better when he wrote this series of articles in the *Herald* about social security fraud, which was rampant at the time. He had learned a thing or two with those stories. He quit the paper right after that and for a few years he lived off social security benefits, his, Lupe's, and her numerous family members. Anyway, they lived together, they even had a daughter, named Serita. He did not seem particularly happy with this woman, but at least she did not put heavy demands on his lifestyle. He was always his own man in this respect, and could be wild at times. Once, during the Cuban missile crisis, he really went over the edge. He was telling anybody who would listen that he'd buried the manuscript of a book he'd been working on for ten years in his garden, behind the little clapboard house he rented on E. Washington Street. After Eddie died, an FBI agent named Clay Zachary even tried to help Lupe find that manuscript, as she was destitute, but they never did dig up anything. I myself doubt it ever existed."

On this, Martin Rutledge may be wrong. The magazine writer Grover Lewis, who at the time of my inquiries was both my friend and my mentor in Los Angeles, had been taken by my findings and soon followed up with his own investigations. One bit of information he uncovered, after he found Anderson's old agent Alex Jackelson, was that the agency had several manuscripts in its files by Anderson—including a novel. Alternatively titled *Seven Hundred Wives* or *One Hell and Many Heavens*, this novel seems to have been started by the author about fifteen years before he died. He reshaped it several times. It took place along the South Texas border at the time of Pancho Villa (who makes a cameo appearance), and was the story of a group of disenfranchised indigents. In a later version, the ending had been rewritten, its Swedenborg-inspired optimism in jarring contrast with the rawness of the rest. A synopsis of it still exists in the Warner Bros. files, proof that the novel had been submitted to the studios, and that Anderson had not completely given up hope on that front. The WB reader's report, though, is crushing.

After his few years at the *Brownsville Herald,* Anderson seems to have lived—as Rutledge told it—on combined social security benefits. Then, for almost a year leaving Lupe and Serita behind in a furnished apartment, he took over a small country gazette, the *Cuero Record*, in the cotton harbor of Cuero, south of Corpus Christi. At the *Record,* he did everything, including writing columns that for once carried his own byline. He copyedited and sometimes even did the layout himself. Al Gonzales, the gazette's editor at the time I paid a call in 1989, remembered Anderson as "the best newsman Cuero ever had." But Cuero, besides cotton, had only a Coca-Cola bottling factory for its economic prospects, and Anderson soon pulled up stakes once more. Today, Cuero does not have much more, even if it proclaims itself the "Turkey Capital of the World." In Cuero, even the elbow-rests of public benches are in the shape of pig-iron turkeys, and the flyblown town could only have found favor with an old roustabout like T-Dub Mansfield—albeit to hit his thirtieth bank there, not live in it.

Edward Anderson returned to Brownsville once more, this time for good. He was only 64 when he died of a ruptured aneurysm at Mercy Hospital in September 1969. His passing was not noted in the *New York Times* nor in *Variety*, but instead in publications befitting his stature: a man who died broke and unrecognized. Obits appeared in papers he'd once worked on, such as the Harlingen *Valley Morning Star* and the *Brownsville Herald.* The way these notices get it wrong, on almost every crucial point of his life, is the bane of the hard-luck writer: "Anderson," says one, "retired author and journalist, wrote a best-selling novel, *The Hungry Men*, which later was made into a film. In the thirties and the beginning of the forties, Anderson worked in Hollywood as a scenario writer. He contributed to the filmed version of his novel, *They Drive by Night*."

The irony of these uninformed tidbits is even greater when you know what went on behind the making of that 1940 Warner Bros. picture starring Humphrey Bogart, George Raft, and Ida Lupino—or the life story of its author, yet another man rooked by Hollywood, the perennially discontented A. I. Bezzerides.

A. I. "Buzz" Bezzerides

THIEVES LIKE THEM

Sometime in the late 1930s, a young electrical engineer fresh out of U. C. Berkeley began working nights mixing programs for the CBS Radio Network. The orchestra played in a nightclub on Wilshire Boulevard, the studio was on Sunset. The man was powerfully built, with a head like a hawk's. He wore thick-framed glasses with thick lenses and had hair all over: on his hands, coming out of his nose and ears. A mat of the stuff overflowed through the collar of his shirt, which he always wore open. His skin was dark, almost swarthy. His father was Greek, his mother Armenian; he was born in the Turkish town of Samsun and had arrived in California when he was nine-months old. His name was Albert Issok Bezzerides. Albert Isaak on his passport, "Al" or "Buzz" to his friends and family. After the radio stint, there were good-paying jobs at the Los Angeles Department of Water and Power, then at Mitchell Cameras where he worked in maintenance and later in the research department. He always left these jobs for the same reasons: he and his peers did all the work, but the bosses got the promotions and raises. There was no end of injustice and bad manners in the world.

"When I quit Mitchell, I earned $40 a week. I'd asked them for a raise because I had invented something for them, which made them save a lot of money. They asked me how much I wanted and I said $45. They told me, 'You should have asked before you gave us your invention, not after.' I would never have done such a thing, as I thought it immoral. I was working for them, they were paying me, I thought it normal they profit from what I knew, then reward me. Apparently, it didn't work that way. So, they turned me down. Not long after that, I told them I was quitting. If they had given me the raise, I never would have left. I had just sold my book to Warner Bros. and they were hiring me as a screenwriter on a tryout. Two months later, the Mitchell people called me at the studio and told me they wanted to see me. I went down there and they said they had made a big mistake about me. They had four fellows to do the work I did, and even so, they couldn't make it. They wanted me back. They would pay me up to $125 a week. I told them I was making $300 at Warner. They did not understand; they thought I meant $300 a month. In their world, $300 a week was inconceivable. No, no, gentlemen, I told them, you better sit down: I said $300 a *week*, and in two weeks it goes up to $900 because the first script I worked on was being filmed. In a way, Warner was my deliverance, but the irony of it is they gave me that job because they swindled me when they bought my novel!"

The irony was compounded by the fact that the novel in question, *Long Haul* (as would his later *Thieves' Market*), drew largely on the experiences of Bezzerides' father who, according to the author, was cheated all his life hauling produce to market. In his teens, Bezzerides often rode with his father in the beat-up half-ton Ford (later there would be a three-ton Reo Speedwagon), hauling the oranges or apples they bought in the orchards around Fresno, where they lived, to the produce markets of San Francisco and Los Angeles. His father had started in the produce business selling fruit door-to-door from a horse-drawn cart. He then bought a farm, working it for nine years until it went under. He parlayed what he had into an old beat-up truck held together with wire and rope. Each "long haul" was an adventure, each load a matter of life and death. Bezzerides' first novel succeeded wonderfully in conveying this sense of all-or-nothing, the life of the independent trucker. At the end of the game, the dice are always loaded in the middleman's favor. The trucker may score a few lucky breaks, but in the end the wholesale broker always wins, often forcing the independent to either quit the game or take a job with his own in-house trucking fleet. According to Bezzerides, his father always wanted to bring him along because the kid had a knack for repairing things. Once, young Bezzerides was able to fix a broken driveshaft with his belt, just long enough to get the truck to the nearest garage.

Scoundrels & Spitballers: Writers and Hollywood in the 1930s

In Fresno, Bezzerides had been an exceptional student, winning a scholarship to study engineering at Berkeley. But his father wanted him to stay home. "This was his way of keeping me under his thumb. Here was a man who had been nearly ruined, who was discredited with his own family—my mother wouldn't speak to him for years, and he slept on the porch in back of the house, not in her bed. But still, he expected his kids to serve him hand and foot; he thought he was back in the old country, master in his home, after God. Except that this didn't wash with us kids—we were Americans, for Chrissakes. One day he ordered me to fetch his slippers and I told him to go fuck himself. I was still hesitating about going to Berkeley because of him, but that clinched it. After this, I never stopped working, but never in Fresno. Nothing kept me there—certainly not this family that was like a lid over me. I'd always been writing, since high school. I wrote in Berkeley, too; I even took a writing course. And once I was married, I still wrote after work because my wife, Yvonne, believed in me. She encouraged me. Without her, I never would have written *Long Haul*, I would not have had the will. In Fresno, my mother never encouraged me. And yet, she was a reader. I remember some afternoons when she'd read pages and pages of Thomas Hardy aloud, translating them into Armenian for my grandmother. And later, I discovered she'd been sending my stories and sketches to the Fresno newspaper. She found them in *Hairenik*, the Armenian newspaper in Boston. This is where I started publishing my stuff, and in *The New Republic*, from 1935 on. And then I published in *STORY*. I wrote a lot for *STORY*, and this led to my being published in *Esquire* later on."

In the February 1936 issue of *Esquire*, Bezzerides' story "The Man Who Was Not Killed" shared the honors with a fishing yarn by Hemingway and F. Scott Fitzgerald's infamous confessional "The Crack-Up"; there also was Dos Passos on Rudolph Valentino and W. R. Burnett on dog racing. And yet at this stage, Bezzerides did not consider himself a writer, not fully.

"I'd been writing for a long time, but I still didn't know what to write *about*. All my stories had something to do with feelings. When I'm asked what I'm trying to do with writing, I always answer that I try to *touch*. Touch what? Touch the heart? Of course, what else is there to touch? In a sense, I was doing what Saroyan was doing at the time, except that he wanted to touch the heart to make you smile. I didn't give a damn if you smiled or if you wept, as long as you were touched. Saroyan and I lived close to each other in the same part of Fresno, south of town near the Cosmos Playground—which you might say was the wrong side of the tracks. We fought for the same books at the library. At first, it was the Russians, mostly: Dostoyevsky, Chekhov, Andreyev, Babel ... These guys tried to touch you, too. Later there was Sherwood Anderson, the master; and Hemingway—mostly the short stories. And also the authors who wrote for *STORY*, like Alvah Bessie before he became a Communist. But as soon as he got motivated by his political ideas and his going to Spain to fight the fascists, his writing wasn't worth a damn. It's like Steinbeck, whom I never liked as a man. He was very good in the beginning—*The Red Pony*, his Cannery Row stories, *The Pastures of Heaven*, all wonderful. Somebody must have had a good influence on him, or read his stuff and advised him. Maybe his first wife, I don't know. When I met him, he was divorcing. Right after this, he started going bad. Like Saroyan, who changed his manner to become more commercial. He even rewrote the stories he published in *Hairenik* when he collected them to make *My Name Is Aram*. He made them sweeter, more pleasant. Whereas you wept standing up when you read something like "Seventy Thousand Assyrians," the way he'd written it in *Hairenik*. Even this one he made sweeter, when he included it later in *The Daring Young Man on the Flying Trapeze*.

"One day, Saroyan and I drove to Salinas to see Steinbeck, and right off the bat I found him to be a big phony. He was acting the great writer for us. He knew Saroyan slightly, me not at all, and I spent the whole afternoon with a half-smile on my face, not saying anything. He ignored me completely. Come evening, we went to an orchard, where there was a barn. We were under a tree, each chewing on an apple, and then he finally looked at me. He sighed and he says, 'OK, I suppose we'll have to talk a little about art...' And I interrupted him and snarled, 'The art of what?' And he said, 'The art of writing, what else?' And I cut him off again: 'What is there to say? Either it comes or it doesn't.' Steinbeck, that shut him up but good. Not because he was taking me seriously, I was a nobody to him, but because now he couldn't blabber about art and writing and all that stuff. Saroyan had to go hide behind the barn, he was laughing so much. Steinbeck wrote about all the great human themes, the big universal questions, and you might think he was a generous man. But I found him to be a shit, and a very uptight character."

In 1942, Bezzerides wrote the following biographical sketch on the back cover and flaps of his second novel, *There Is a Happy Land*:

> My name is pronounced Buzz-air-uh-dees. I won't go into my complicated background except to say that I can swear and pray in Armenian and Turkish. I seldom pray. ...
>
> After quitting school, I drove a truck for a while. Truckers don't make much money but they do pick up a lot of experience. I did, anyhow, and eventually put it into my first novel, *Long Haul*, which was made into the movie *They Drive by Night*.
>
> I write on the wrestling plan, catch as catch can. I am impatient, and if a piece does not come out right the first time, I try to ditch it, but my wife prods me on. She's a first class prodder. As soon as *Long Haul* was finished, she started me on *There Is a Happy Land*. I'm in Electrical Engineering, and I like working at it. More and more I realize the similarity between designing an electrical job and doing a story. They require the same discipline and give the same satisfaction when they are done.

Forty years later, he recalled, more simply: "I wrote *Long Haul* and sent it to Ann Watkins, a New York agent. She sold it on the first try to Carrick & Evans. I got a $500 advance, a good review in *Time*, and sold 400 copies. They always say that Hollywood is the writer's demise, but the truth is that in my case, I would not have written a second book, let alone a third one, had it not been for Hollywood. In spite of my desire to write, I would have stayed at Mitchell Cameras fixing projectors, or inventing things for them. At the time of *Long Haul*, I was living near the beach, in Redondo. I was broke and had no telephone. One day, I get a telegram from William Dozier, saying I should call him. Bill Dozier was still an agent at the time, he was not story editor at Paramount, he was not the big producer he became later on. At the time, he was working for the Phil Berg agency. So, he asks me what I'm doing with my novel, and I say, nothing, it didn't sell. And that's when he tells me that maybe he could sell it to Warner for $1,500. Like I was supposed to get real excited on hearing this. But even to me it didn't seem like much money, and I told him so. Then he said, 'Let me see what I can do.' Two days later, he comes to see me and announces that he could get me two grand. This still didn't seem like much money, but I was strapped for dough, so I said yes. Only when I went to the studio to sign the contracts did I realize that Dozier, big agent that he was, was seeing to the interests of the buyers, more than to his own client. His successful career in the film business proves that he was richly rewarded by the studio bosses. And I really should never have found them out, but they were very stupid about it. One day they introduced me to Mark Hellinger, who was going to produce the picture based on my book, and we said hello, and he had to leave his office for a minute. I spotted a script he had by his desk set. I read two pages of it; it was *Long Haul*. They had started on it even before buying the rights to my book. Dozier knew this, naturally, and the studio must have greased his paw on the other end because his commission on $2,000 was peanuts. Later, someone told me he could have gotten me $30,000 for it because the studio was stuck: they had selected something called *The Patent Leather Kid* to be the next George Raft picture, a prize-fighting story, but when they put those satin boxing trunks on old George, they realized he had a potbelly and love handles and looked ridiculous as a fighter. He just couldn't do the movie, and the brass at Warner needed a story quick, to get him something to play, because here he was costing them a lot of money, doing nothing. This is when Jerry Wald, who was very clever, got the notion of cobbling an old story they had, *Border Town*, which they'd already made years before, to my novel. And they needed the realism of the trucking stuff that was in my book. Wald and his writing partner, Richard Macaulay, had already cooked up this treatment, or script, with bits of my novel, and that became *They Drive by Night*. They saw me reading the script and that was embarrassing, even for them. So, to make me swallow the bitter pill easier, they offered me a tryout contract as a writer on the lot—thinking that would be the last they'd hear of me."

If *They Drive by Night* retained the tone and the authenticity of Bezzerides' novel, it veered off it when it came to the plot: Raft doesn't die in the end, falling asleep at the wheel and driving off the road; instead, he becomes the company manager. Nevertheless, the movie was a good operation for all concerned, in spite of early worries from Albert Warner, supported by brother Harry in New York, who tried to dissuade brother Jack from making it ("The American Trucking Association is not pleased...."). Or in spite of Hal Wallis constantly fuming after seeing Raoul Walsh's dailies because he did not provide enough establishing shots of market stalls and buildings ("Where is the $13,500 I sunk into those sets?" Wallis asks in an apoplectic memo). Yet upon its release in July 1940, the picture was a success. Raft was very pleased to play, for a change, someone more wholesome than a gangster or a rat. Bogart kept up his string of more rounded and complex characterizations. As for Ida Lupino, her bravura court scene at the end of the picture so impressed Warner's front office they put her under contract soon after the film's release.

The budget sheet corresponding to Production #510, April 1940, for *They Drive by Night* reveals that Lupino's fee exceeded that of all other players (except top-billed Raft) because she was not on the Warner payroll, as were Bogart and Ann Sheridan. One must consider these budget sheets for the sake of comparison only, as studios typically spread the overhead to the more successful productions, which paid for the flops.

Possibly to assuage "our friends from the American Trucking Association," the studio publicity department mounted an unusual campaign: Embarking on the promo trail from Chicago on July 25, trouper Ann Sheridan was ceremoniously given a semi-truck, officially "From the Teamsters to the Ooomph Girl" or "To Ann with the beautiful pan" or on another whistle stop, "To Cassie with the chassis." When the caravan got back to California, it headed from San Francisco to Los Angeles, purposefully following the same route used by the truckers in *They Drive by Night*. It all ended with a cocktail party at the Burbank studio. Typically, good-natured Ann Sheridan took it all in stride and even joked about keeping the truck on the lot and using it as her dressing room. The poster and other publicity material, on the other hand, did nothing to emphasize the hard-hitting, realistic tone of the picture; on the contrary, the three-sheet showed Raft and Bogart nattily dressed in suits, complete with display handkerchiefs in breast pockets; as to "the chassis," Ann Sheridan showed hers off in a flimsy negligee.

If the Warner brass felt remorse for swindling Bezzerides on the price of his novel, as the author believed, they took almost a year to act on it. For the first job on his tryout contract, in May 1941, they put him to work on a lost cause, perhaps to intentionally discourage him. The project seemed doomed for three reasons: one, the original story by Theodore Pratt, a tomato-picking yarn set in Florida, wasn't much good; two, Bezzerides had been teamed with Ken Gamet, an experienced but lazy scriptwriter who usually worked on Westerns and didn't give two hoots about tomatoes (the edible kind at any rate); three, the project had been assigned to the notoriously bad-tempered German émigré Curtis Bernhardt. The former Kurt Bernhardt, an A-list director in the UFA days, had only been in America for two years, but was already known on the Burbank lot for his autocratic ways and raging fits. He had already said in no uncertain terms that this story was "shit." Gamet, knowing which way the wind blew, refused to touch a word of this sorry-ass story of tomato pickers, drifters, and conniving bosses. Bezzerides, on the other hand, was immediately intrigued. The engineer in him had to know why the story went wrong, and how it could be fixed.

"So, I started writing scenes, and Gamet was mocking me but let me do it. When the time came to let Bernhardt see what we had, the director shouted, in that imperious way he had: 'Who wrote this?' He didn't really shout, but that was the impression he gave. So, I said, 'We did,' because I wanted to be a good scout. But Gamet immediately denied it: 'No, he did, alone.' And Bernhardt told the producer: 'Let him write the script, you can fire the other one.' And they did, which prompted Gamet to spread the word around the studio that I had intrigued with my communist friends to get the assignment alone. Which was of course ridiculous, as I was new there and did not know a soul, communist or not. But anyway, this is how I got my first credit, on my first assignment. I stayed four years at Warner."

This is also how Al Bezzerides tried for the first time (but certainly not the last) to turn a sow's ear into a silk purse. *Juke Girl* is a sunny (and certainly less solemn) cut-rate version of *The Grapes of Wrath*, featuring Ronald Reagan as an unlikely champion of the downtrodden. But more importantly, this was terrain Bezzerides knew first hand, and it shows in the zippy dialogue. You sense his hairy paw and quirky humor behind almost every exchange, in lines like "Kinda living in a hurry, ain't you?" And with Yippy, the truculent character played by Alan Hale, the writer inaugurates the series of incongruous, added-on characters that stand out in almost all of his scripts—usually Italians or Greeks—that would culminate in *Kiss Me Deadly*, a picture chock full of them, and not just Nicky, the grease monkey of "Va-Va-Voom" fame. *Juke Girl* already has the kind of salty dialogue the writer would become famous for, as when Ann Sheridan asks a pesky suitor, "When do you change your oil?" Today it may seem piquant to find Reagan defending the rights of workers against capitalists—even though Bezzerides noted that the actor's politics were to the left at the time—and the end of the picture is particularly lame. But *Juke Girl* was successful in certain markets, mostly Midwestern and rural. Bezzerides, who was at the sneak preview in San Bernardino, remembered only two things of that night: a little old lady coming out the theater on the arm of her husband and telling him, "Whoever wrote this sure knew his folks," and Jack Warner, perusing some of the reaction cards, asking himself aloud how anyone could like "shit like this."

Apart from this first try, the pictures Bezzerides worked on between 1942 and 1948, at Warner and at Paramount, do not stand out in any way. A single project with producer Jerry Wald seemed promising: *Tough Road*, a trucking story involving the transport of dynamite, which would have predated *The Wages of Fear* by years. But the picture was shelved, and Bezzerides was still trying to get the story idea back from the studio when he left for Paramount in 1945. At the Burbank lot, he was known mostly for his audacity and luck at craps, more than his screenwriting talent. W. R. Burnett remembered vividly, when I talked to him, a long game of craps in somebody's office with everyone on their knees shooting the dice. "There wasn't a dollar left in the whole Writers Building," claimed Burnett, admiringly. Typically, Bezzerides only remembered those who did not honor their gambling debts, Irving Stone being on top of the list. But what mystified other writers the most about Bezzerides was his close association with William Faulkner. The shy Armenian with the stevedore manners made a curious pair with the polite, aloof Southerner. But there it was: during the war years, Bezzerides became for Faulkner a combination guardian angel, chauffeur, and male nurse, saving his friend many times from scraps at the studio, whisking him out of the lot when he was too drunk to stand up—no small favor, as drunkenness was a capital offense at Warner, usually resulting in an immediate pink slip.

One colleague who still had vivid memories of Bezzerides on the Warner lot when I met her was Catherine Turney. She'd had a scrap with Jerry Wald over her adaptation of *Mildred Pierce*, following which she worked under the mild-mannered Henry Blanke, who supervised the "women's pictures" for the studio. They were very lucrative, and Turney wrote many of them, including *My Reputation* for Stanwyck, *The Man I Love* for Lupino, and the remake of *Of Human Bondage* for Eleanor Parker. Turney often worked for Curtis Bernhardt, notably on the lurid Bette Davis melodrama *A Stolen Life*, and she remembered witnessing epic shouting matches between the director and Bezzerides, then working on some other project. "They were like two bulls in the ring," she told me. "But Curt tolerated him, I think because he considered him a good writer—and Buzz *was* a good writer. But what I remember the most is the strange carpool we had driving to Musso's for lunch. If you didn't find the Green Room food to your taste, but mostly if you wanted to drink your lunch, you went to Musso's. The war was on and gas was rationed, so we'd pile up into Buzz's car, and I must say we were a rather motley bunch. Really a crazy mix. There was Buzz, Faulkner, Albert Maltz, sometimes Stephen Longstreet, and also the Baroness, as we all called Lili Hatvany. She never had many credits that I know of, but she was a character. According to her, she had been 'Queen of Budapest' and she'd come to America with Molnár, the great playwright—she was one of his mistresses. Anyway, she was very chic and tony, gave parties for the upper crust of the social register, and it was very funny to see her squeezed between us in Buzz's car."

Bezzerides, as would be his wont, only remembers the bad side of the carpool, namely Albert Maltz's infuriating habit of asking to be let out at a certain traffic light in the Cahuenga Pass "without ever letting me finish the story I was telling. Once, I could not contain myself and I threw him out, telling him never to come back. We drove on to Musso's parking lot, and Faulkner, who usually never uttered a word during the whole trip, pulled on his pipe and told me, 'Ahm glad you did that, Budd.' He called everybody Budd when he wanted to be friendly, but I think they all do this in the South."

The very first time Bezzerides walked into Musso's famed backroom, he was told off by Frederick Faust—who wrote Westerns under the professional name of Max Brand. He had been drinking his lunches there for years, and did not take kindly to strangers. But that day Faulkner spoke up for Bezzerides, vouching for him, adding that Buzz was his friend, and a good writer. From then on, he was part of the club, but he did not owe this acceptance to his job at Warner. At the time, Bezzerides was still writing novels, and he was respected as such by the other backroom patrons. He was employed at Warner when he published his second, and possibly best, novel, *There Is a Happy Land*, the story of an Okie loafer squatting with his family on some farmer's land in the San Joaquin Valley. A mix of George Sessions Perry's *Walls Rise Up* and *Hold Autumn in Your Hand*, which inspired Jean Renoir's film *The Southerner* in 1945, with a little of *The Pastures of Heaven* from Steinbeck thrown in, *There Is a Happy Land* is one of the great "lost" fictions of the Depression. The loafer of the novel is thought of by everyone as a good-for-nothing moocher too lazy to support his family—until he asks the farmer to give him a piece of land to prove his mettle by working for himself, not wages. This was not a story that would likely sell to the movies, and it never did.

Bezzerides was luckier with his third novel, *Thieves' Market*, published by Scribner in 1949. Not only did that novel sell to 20th Century–Fox, but the studio hired Bezzerides to adapt it for the screen, at a rather high salary. During his time at Fox, he also worked on André De Toth's fine and unusual *Slattery's Hurricane*, a sunny noir filmed in Florida. You can spot his goofy sequences, as when Richard Widmark comes home drunk, bellowing the lyrics to "Home on the Range"—a typical Bezzerides touch. *Thieves' Highway*, as his picture was finally called, was the best deal Bezzerides ever made in Hollywood, but it also went to show that no story is safe in the hands of a studio, even when the author himself does the quartering. Jules Dassin's picture superficially possesses the gritty naturalism for which he was starting to gain a reputation, but it comes up well short of the novel's bruising frankness. (At the 1996 edition of the Amiens International Film Festival where he was being honored, I happened to sit beside Bezzerides at the screening of *Thieves' Highway*. It was an excellent print and the audience was clearly engrossed, but I could hear the writer gnashing his teeth throughout muttering, "Lies, lies" and "Phony line" on occasion.) In 1949, though, Bezzerides surely was experienced enough as a screenwriter to know he could not put some of the most gruesome scenes from his novel into the script, such as the book's opening in which the central character, Nick, threatens to have his mother cremated upon her death if she doesn't turn over her husband's life insurance to him. That's how Nick is able to buy an Army surplus truck to try his luck as an independent operator. The movie version did worse than omitting such scenes—it resurrected the dead father, Bezzerides going so far as writing a scene of gross pathos, with actor Morris Carnovsky hamming it up with a theatrical, almost comical, Slouvaki accent. With this scene, the Richard Conte character buys himself a new conscience, becoming the "good guy" Nick certainly isn't in the novel. Similarly, the girl isn't as clearly a prostitute as she was in the book. For this last fudging, Bezzerides blamed Dassin specifically, claiming that at the time the director was having an affair with Italian import Valentina Cortese. Not only did the writer have to change her into an Italian refugee, but he had to soften her character considerably. Zanuck was busy with other productions at the time and Dassin's film wasn't high on his priority list. But he still had two or three story conferences (some recorded) that show he was the complete showman and could spot script weaknesses a mile away. "I liked her better as a whore," he simply said. But Zanuck did not push it further. According to Bezzerides, Dassin was in a spot. "He did not want to go back to his girlfriend and have to tell her she was playing a whore." Which of course the Breen Office would never have permitted anyway.

"Zanuck always spotted these things," Bezzerides said about the stu-

Bezzerides, Nick Ray, Ida Lupino, Ward Bond, and Robert Ryan during production of *On Dangerous Ground*

dio boss he'd work for several times. "He had an innate sense of what worked and what didn't in a character, but although he also understood feminine characters just as well, on the page, he had a blind spot when it came to casting women. He was almost always wrong. And his blind spot did not just concern the actresses he bedded."

As a screenwriter, Bezzerides had his best run during the 1950s. By that time, he was freelancing all over town. He made a great, unforgettable cameo appearance in *On Dangerous Ground*, one of the most personal among the pictures he wrote. Early in the film he appears, playing a greasy-looking bookie in a diner, telling a joke to the violent policeman played by Robert Ryan. He tells the cop his horse has won, a hint at possible corruption. Bezzerides told me he had written this character (not in the original novel by British writer Gerald Butler, *Mad with Much Heart*) with the hope of getting a friend of his hired for the role. The friend was a Greek with ugly features who spoke from one corner of his mouth, like Bezzerides himself. "The Greek played the scene several times," the writer told me, "but Nick Ray wasn't happy. He asked me to put on the guy's suit (a vile wide-striped double-breasted number) and play the scene. 'Just so I can see it,' he said. 'Just one take.' So, I did, and, of course, that's the take he kept. I got along with Ray, and yet he was never able to communicate with you verbally. He'd say, 'It should be more, er, er...' He never finished a sentence. And yet, I always knew what he meant. But put him with an actor, then he'd light up, it was magical the way he understood actors and could help them. Some of the scenes I wrote he treated with an understanding and a sensitivity you rarely find in a film director—like the one with the kid who molested a little girl. I understood that scene, it came from my guts, because something of this nature happened to me when I was a teen in Fresno. On the playground I approached a girl, totally innocently, but because of my ugly puss she got scared and ran away. It crushed me, I always remembered how I felt, I could have hurt her too, by pure accident. But I did not have to explain this to Nick Ray, he understood. He was also very sensitive in the way he treated Ida Lupino in this. She played a blind girl, and it took a while for the audience to realize it. Did you know she was bald? True fact. So, in *They Drive by Night*, you had three wigs or toupees: hers, Bogart's, and Raft's! I liked *On Dangerous Ground*, but it really was two films. It only really starts to kick in once you get to the open country, and in the snow. Ray kept adding and adding scenes explaining why Ryan was so bitter and violent, his visceral hatred of the hoods. But there is no story in this long city part. And what Houseman writes in his memoirs, that Ray and I spent nights and nights in patrol cars with the LAPD to learn the cops' manners and lingo, this is bullshit; I was alone riding with them."

In 1953, Bezzerides wrote *Track of the Cat* for William Wellman, a strangely vapid adaptation of the Walter Van Tilburg Clark novel. The film was not only marred by Wellman's conceit of making a black-and-white picture in color, but the impressive outdoor sequences were too few to salvage the oppressive Freudian gabfest taking place in the family's cabin.

None of the actors could save this, not even Mitchum, and certainly not Beulah Bondi. But one senses that Bezzerides had poured into her character all the gloomy hardness he'd found in his mother when growing up.

Around this time, he also wrote a vigorous action picture for Fox, set in Florida amongst two sets of sponge fishermen, Conch and Greek. It was called *Beneath the 12-Mile Reef* and was right up Bezzerides' alley. Then, of course, in 1955 he adapted Mickey Spillane's *Kiss Me Deadly* for Robert Aldrich. He had a field day with this one, one of the rare occasions when he was left completely alone while writing a picture, and his script was left intact by the director. Aldrich couldn't understand the plot, but that didn't seem to matter to him. Spillane's cold war ideology and his popular creation, private eye Mike Hammer, were repugnant to Bezzerides, who amused himself by turning the story into a wild ride peopled with strange and lurid characters. The main clue in the plot was now contained in a Rossetti poem (that may say it all), and the "MacGuffin" was changed from a cache of drugs to a Pandora's Box that unleashes nuclear furies. Aldrich obliged by casting the film almost perfectly: hard-edged and narcissistic Ralph Meeker was a good fit for Hammer, aided by all sorts of fifties' gadgets, some invented by electrical engineer Bezzerides (he claims Hammer's reel-to-reel phone answering machine was not yet on the market). Cloris Leachman exited early, but she stayed in your mind way after her final exhortation to Hammer: "Remember me." Gaby Rodgers, as Lily Carver, was properly kooky, her pasty round face the perfect picture of greed ("I want half."). On the male side, Aldrich rounded up an incredible array of favorite screen villains and creeps: Percy Helton got his fingers crushed in a desk drawer, Paul Richards was a hapless knife assailant who tumbles to the bottom of a long Bunker Hill stairway, Jack Lambert and Jack Elam played brain-dead thugs, and Paul Stewart was his usual smooth, grinning, menacing self. The only hitch in the casting was the actress playing Hammer's secretary, Velda. Maxine Cooper was slatternly enough for the part, but not pretty enough, with greasy skin and a runty build. It was hard to understand why Bezzerides had written all those scenes for her in front of the ballet bar and full-length mirror. He explained, with his usual vehemence: "I had written this part with a friend of mine in mind. I had become friendly with Gwen Verdon—this was before she was with Bob Fosse. But she was a very troubled person then, even though she was a terrific dancer. Anyway, we were friends and I tried to help her; we both were in analysis. And I thought she'd be terrific in that part of Velda. But for some reason, Aldrich wanted that other girl, who couldn't dance for shit, and he kept the scene as I'd written it. So that was not so good. Apart from that, I liked the picture, even though I did not take it seriously. Nobody did, at the time."

This was the period—before he started in television, writing for shows like *The O. Henry Playhouse*, *The Barbara Stanwyck Show*, and *Bonanza*, and before he created and wrote the "book" for the long-running Stanwyck series *The Big Valley*—when Bezzerides got heavily into psychoanalysis. The crisis was prompted by his divorce from his first wife, Yvonne, a split that caused him great anguish and guilt. She lived on her own near the beach with their two children. Bezzerides, at least in retrospect, took all the blame for the separation: "I had never associated my wife to my movie work. I don't think I ever brought her once to the studio when I was at Warner. She had pushed me and nurtured me through all those years; she had read and edited my work, and all of a sudden she was not part of any of it any more. I never understood how she must have suffered from this—because at that time, the movie work for me was like my work at Mitchell Cameras, nothing to brag about. But Yvonne, she thought I spent all my time screwing secretaries." This, and possibly his financial success at a job he did not think much of, led to a period of intense self-examination. Psychoanalysis colors all of Bezzerides' scripts during and after this period, even his action pictures. This bent was reinforced after he met and courted another screenwriter with similar interests, and an even heavier sense of guilt. Silvia Richards was from Colorado; she had been a model before marrying New York radio producer Bob Richards. She started writing for radio and quickly built a reputation. Once, she adapted Lovecraft's *The Dunwich Horror* for William Spier's tony radio show *Suspense*, which got her noticed in the business. Hollywood soon beckoned, and the couple settled in Santa Monica in quest of better and more financially rewarding careers. Instead, they ended up feuding and splitting. An acrimonious divorce followed, culminating with Richards testifying against her former husband in front of the HUAC

Silvia Richards

witch hunters. In 1947, a few years before this, she felt vindicated in her wrath. As she told a journalist for the *Daily News*, "I found myself with a drunk and a brute for a husband, two kids on my hands and a ruined career. I felt all alone and bitter. But I had a neighbor, a little old guy who didn't look like much, but was always telling me that maybe he could help me. I did not take him seriously, but one day, out of desperation, I asked for his help. It turned out that this old immigrant knew all the agents and studio executives in town. In no time, he got me a job with Warner, and I adapted *Possessed* with Ranald MacDougall. One day I was with my two kids, the wolf at my door, and the next I was writing for Joan Crawford."

At Warner, through Curt Bernardt, Richards met Fritz Lang. He was taken by the young woman, who possessed all the physical attributes Lang went for: a strong chin and long copper-colored hair that made her look like Lizabeth Scott. But what cinched it for Lang was the young woman's knowledge of Santa Fe and of Western lore and songs, which came in handy when he worked on an early version of what would become Anthony Mann's *Winchester 73*. Lang put Richard's knowledge to even greater use when he made *Rancho Notorious* a few years later—a picture he originally wanted to articulate around a song, "The Legend of Chuck-a-Luck." Lang and Richards often took trips to desert destinations and Indian lands, and were fond of square-dancing. The first thing Lang did after he created Diana Productions, an independent company he formed with Walter Wanger and his wife, actress Joan Bennett, was to hire Richards. The first picture they worked on together was *Secret Beyond the Door*, a preposterous psychoanalytic version of the Bluebeard tale based on a Rufus King short story. It's about an architect who collects rooms, like others collect paintings. His theory is that architecture can predispose, or even induce, people into killing. Richards hated "that idiotic story" and did everything she could to dissuade Lang from making it, but her infatuation with him curbed her vehemence. The real secret behind the door, the reason the script took over a year to write, was perfectly clear to Lang's increasingly annoyed partners. The director had once been enamored of his star, when he and Bennett made *Manhunt* in 1940, and two subsequent pictures, *The Woman in the Window* and *Scarlet Street*. But now he had grown tired of her, and of what he saw as a movie star's capricious demands. He attributed the slowness of the shoot to director of photography Stanley Cortez, who had been imposed on him by Bennett. Although Lang later decried the picture as a mistake, it is hard to believe he was not thinking of Joan Bennett when he and Richards wrote the scene at the beginning of *Secret Beyond the Door* in which Bennett and Michael Redgrave meet. Looking at this almost middle-aged woman, he tells her: "You are not what you appear to be... Something in your face...I have seen in South Dakota, in the wheat lands. The trembling calm just before a tornado. The first gust of wind that creases the golden wheat...I know that behind this smile there is a...turbulence." Nobody ever qualified better the actress' "atmospheric" appeal—an arousing mix of placid dowdiness and unfathomable sexual depth.

At any rate, the *Secret Beyond the Door* fiasco sealed the fate of Diana Productions. Lang had tasted the felicities of independent production and tried it again with Howard Welsch's Fidelity Pictures, with lesser pleasure but better films; at least *House by the River* and *Rancho Notorious* garnered better reviews and now enjoy a higher reputation in the Lang canon. Richards had been Lang's mistress for a few years, and, according to her, he even proposed marriage. "I did not work very long on *Rancho Notorious*. Fritz wanted us to live together, but on his own terms. He did not want to leave Lili Latte and the convenient domestic arrangement he had with her. He proposed to rent me a house slightly below his, on Summitridge Drive. The fact that I had my two children weighed in, too. In the end, I chose to go with Buzz, whom I'd known for some time and was more accommodating. But Fritz and I had a good run of it."

Richards went on working, notably for King Vidor on *Ruby Gentry*, before going to work in television. Soon she and Bezzerides settled in a house in Woodland Hills, built by Rudolph Schindler on a dirt street in what was still predominantly a citrus grove. Bezzerides bought it for a song in the mid-1960s from actor Albert Dekker—he and his two-toned shoes had played a crucial role in *Kiss Me Deadly*, that of the sinister Dr. Soberin. The house still had an unfinished look when I began visiting the writer regularly in the mid-1980s. As is the case of many famous mid-century architect-designed houses, the one at 19950 Collier Street had its quirks and peculiarities. Everything was built of rough-hewn redwood or pine planks, a stairway to the upper bedroom had no bannister whatsoever, making it especially perilous when drunk, or for small children. But the main problem was the copper roof Schindler had insisted on, a folly in this stretch of the San Fernando Valley where summer temperatures often soar into triple digits. Frequently, I would call the house and Silvia would pick up saying that Buzz was "working on the roof," as the copper plates kept expanding under the heat, creating major leaks.

But the writer was always repairing something: old cars (he had a dozen wrecks, including a Jaguar, in his yard), old typewriters, telephones. Once he hauled in two very soiled chairs he'd found on the street. They were vintage Eames plywood chairs. "All you need is stripping them," he said. Except that he never actually got down to repairing anything, except scripts. In the 1980s, and well into the '90s, his skill at this was still in demand. When we first met, he was "fixing" (his favorite word) a script for Sam Peckinpah, a cop thriller set in Amsterdam. As with almost every story he wrote or "fixed," Buzz tried to inject some sort of guilt into the cop, something to do with his father, of course. When they started living together, Al and Silvia mostly pooled their paranoia and various guilts. Richards', of course, had to do with her finking on her husband in front of HUAC. Buzz's had more to do with his first wife (he still repaired her roof when needed) and his son's illness. The kid had become a schizoid paranoiac after doing too many drugs at school, something Bezzerides attributed to his not being there for him. When I knew them, Al and Silvia endlessly talked of their respective analyses, between the sacrosanct watching of the evening news—sure to send at least one of them into a ballistic fit about something or other. Silvia collected stray animals the way Buzz gathered junk and wrecked cars. They lived in the stench of at least a dozen cats and two dogs, and later even took in and raised two small children that belonged to a couple of junkies they'd befriended. The boy was a promising writer, according to them. After two years "away" in San Francisco, the junkie couple came back for the kids, seemingly straightened out. Buzz was especially proud of the boy. Before leaving with the kids, they asked Buzz to drive them to the bank so they could withdraw their money and close the account. Off they went in Buzz's wheezy yellow VW bug. "I kept wondering why those two had accounts in so many banks, until it dawned on me I was their getaway driver. Nobody could have suspected us in such a slow car. ... They got caught of course and went back to prison, so we had the kids for a couple more years."

Things like this seemed to happen to him all the time. Once, after I helped publish a translation of *Long Haul* in France, I organized a small promotional tour that involved several TV and press interviews, as well as a showing at the Amiens International Film Festival, where he was being honored. He stayed for two weeks, and it was clear he got a charge at this revival of interest in his work. But he was also anxious to go home, as he had left behind an ailing Silvia and felt bad about it. He had shown up in Paris in a corduroy coat, thick corduroy pants, sensible shoes, and he wore the same outfit the entire time. He only carried with him what looked like a leather bowling bag. When at last I took him to the Charles de Gaulle Airport for the trip home, there was a panicky moment. The young border control officer looked at Bezzerides' passport, then looked up, visibly puzzled. "*Monsieur, comment avez-vous fait pour venir ici?*"

Buzz looked at me. "What's he saying?"

"His passport expired seventeen years ago," said the border guy. He had to go fetch his supervisor, as he had never before dealt with a case like this. The supervisor took one look at the old man in his rumpled outfit, clutching his satchel, and said with a shake of his head: "Get him out of here. See that he doesn't come back!" I'll always remember Buzz that way, scampering away through security, not looking back or saying goodbye.

Buzz kept on going for some time after Silvia died. The cars were hauled away, Buzz finally yielding to a city summons after too many neighbors complained. He kept hammering away on his massive typewriter, which he had long ago set up under the stairway, away from the domestic madness upstairs. He still worked on scripts and stories. One that particularly seemed to engage him was called "First Kill," about a boy's initiation to hunting with his father. In January 1995, I was living in France and trying to get another of his novels published, when he wrote me this note—the only one I ever got from him:

Dear Philippe:

Here I go, writing you a note. I thought I might hear from you by now, but I guess nothing has developed that would stimulate that.

So be it.

But let me know what's going on, no matter how negative it is, so I'll know. I don't mind. Whatever it is. Just knowing is what's important, instead of stewing about it.

I'm working on First Kill. I avoided writing, because it got better and better as I thought about it. It's not just a simple story, like it was in the script I showed you. I won't go into details, because it keeps shaping itself, all by itself, which wouldn't have happened if I had started too soon.

I'm not writing it, it's writing itself, now that I know all the characters as intimately as I do, or begin to. And the real world they all live in.

Anyway, I've begun to put it down.

What else? Ah, the rain storms that have been coming our way. Breaking 100 year records.

Just drop me a note, about how things that pertain to me are going. At 86, I'm tough, I can take anything.

Greetings to your wife!

Buzz

The last time I saw the old man, who invariably answered "I'm still breathing" when you asked him "How are you?," he was standing in the unpaved street in front of his house, waving goodbye with a small hand gesture, smiling that youthful grin of his. Here was a man who somehow had spent the last half of his existence repairing his life, rebuilding himself a family by scavenging bits of his old life, which had long ago been hauled to the wrecking yard with his cars. A still-bitter first wife, a mentally fragile son, brothers and cousins all left behind in Fresno, all having lived first under the father's thumb, then under the still more formidable shadow of women, the kind he'd always known growing up in the San Joaquin Valley—dragons of love and cupidity, three hundred pounds of motherhood as fiercely vocal as he was, and just as hairy. In the novels and stories he never ceased honing and polishing during his later years, Buzz went on wondering about them, about other women he'd met since, about the human race he found so insane and yet so fascinating. Reading these family sagas of abusive fathers and insensitive mothers, one is reminded that, if Bezzerides is mostly known for the outrageously entertaining scenes of sadism displayed in *Kiss Me Deadly*, he is also the man who substituted the nuclear Pandora's Box for the more banal Spillane MacGuffin, leaving us with the immortal line, when Lily Carver is warned about the dangers of nuclear fission: "I want half."

"I want half" could also serve as the *cri du coeur* of every screenwriter. No writer has deplored the lack of parity in Hollywood contracts more than Al Bezzerides, or at least as raucously. He never stopped grouching about the way he was rooked at the beginning of his career with the sale of *Long Haul* to Warner, or how he let the producer of *The Big Valley*, Lou Edelman, take advantage of him. The TV series enjoyed an incredibly popular run that benefited Barbara Stanwyck as well as Edelman. Bezzerides, too trusting (according to him), was talked into selling his points to Edelman for $100,000—peanuts for a show that lasted four seasons, and decades more in syndication. When Edelman died of a heart attack years later, Bezzerides immediately attributed it to remorse—an extravagant claim, no doubt, but typical of someone who always viewed life as a Freudian version of *Crime and Punishment*.

Lionel Stander as PR flak
"Matt Libby" in *A Star Is Born*

THE MATT LIBBY SCHOOL OF SCREENWRITING

JULIUS J. EPSTEIN, an ex-NCAA bantamweight champion, was working as a press relations man for a boxing promoter in New York when he received a telephoned SOS call from another press agent who'd recently gone Hollywood. It turned out that this friend, who reportedly could sell ice to Eskimos, had sold a story idea to Warner Bros. for a musical. The studio had then hired him and still another mutual friend to write the script. The trouble was, they hadn't the slightest idea how to go about it. Would Epstein come to the rescue and write the thing? And for which the two "writing partners" would be only too happy to give him their combined salaries, in full!

So that's how Julius Epstein who went to Hollywood on October 14, 1933, and scripted the immortal *Twenty Million Sweethearts* for its "writers," Paul Finder Moss and Jerry Wald. It became Wald's first movie credit. Wald's contract option was picked up by Warner and he kept on writing for them, usually paired with Richard Macaulay—notably on *They Drive by Night*, as related in the preceding chapter. Wald then parlayed this into a prolific and impressive career as a producer—whose achievements included *Objective, Burma!*, *Mildred Pierce*, *Dark Passage*, *Johnny Belinda*, and *Flamingo Road*. He left Warner in 1950 and formed an independent unit at RKO with Norman Krasna, then became Production Vice President at Columbia producing increasingly ambitious and tony projects like *An Affair to Remember* or *The Sound and the Fury*, although one might prefer his more gritty offerings, such as *The Lusty Men*, *Clash by Night*, and *The Harder They Fall*.

Julius Epstein, for his part, didn't waste any time bringing his twin brother Philip in on a good deal. The twins rapidly became the in-demand writing team for a certain type of sophisticated comedy, such as *Strawberry Blonde*, *The Bride Came C.O.D*, or *Arsenic and Old Lace*. Most famously, the brothers performed the principal script work on *Casablanca*. When I spoke with him in the mid-1980s, Julius Epstein typically declared himself infinitely prouder of his later Peter De Vries adaptations like *Pete 'n' Tillie* and *Reuben, Reuben* than of his and his brother's contribution to *Casablanca*—or any other Warner Bros. concoction, for that matter. The most surprising credit in his prestigious career might be his contribution to the script of Sam Peckinpah's nihilist war picture *Cross of Iron*, released in 1977.

Among other press agents who accessed the screenwriting profession through this needle's eye were Daniel Mainwaring, Norman Krasna, Owen Francis, and Claude Binyon. Binyon, rather improbably a close friend of Nathanael West, had also been a desk reporter at *Variety*. According to Hollywood lore, he's the one who came up with the famous headline announcing the 1929 crash: WALL STREET LAYS AN EGG. Binyon had an interesting career at Paramount in the '30s, and writing the amusing comedies *Take a Letter, Darling* and *No Time for Love* for Mitchell Leisen in the early 1940s. Then, Binyon became a rather mediocre producer-director.

Norman Krasna, who started his long career as a copy-boy at the *New York World* (James M. Cain's alma mater) and then as a legman for the *Exhibitors Herald and Motion Picture World*, also did a stint in Warner Bros.'s New York publicity department before becoming one of the best and most prolific screenwriters of the 1930s and 1940s. Strangely enough, Krasna had preceded all this with long years studying for the bar at Northwestern University, Columbia, and St. John's University Law School. According to him, seeing *The Front Page* in 1931, when he was in publicity for Warner, prompted him to become a playwright and screenwriter. He wrote his first play that same year, and *Louder, Please* was running on Broadway by that November. Soon, he was in Hollywood, first at Columbia, then at RKO and MGM, quickly earning a reputation as a writer of clever comedies and crackling dialogue, sometimes just breezy-witty, as in *Hands Across the Table* and *Bachelor Mother*, sometimes more profound like *Wife versus*

Jerry Wald (left) with his writing and producing partner Norman Krasna

Secretary, directed by Clarence Brown. But Krasna wasn't just confined to comedy: he wrote the script for Fritz Lang's 1936 American debut, *Fury*. He remains best known for *The Devil and Miss Jones* (1941), and for writing Marilyn Monroe's last completed picture, *Let's Make Love* (1960).

Owen Francis' filmography is as bare and spotty as Norman Krasna's was solid and prolific: *Good Time Charley* (1927), *No Other Woman* (1933), *Magnificent Brute* (1937), *Pack Up Your Troubles* (1939). One of his last credits, a Western comedy reuniting child actor Jane Withers and singing cowboy Gene Autry, was called *Shooting High*, a title that evidently did not apply to him. Born in Pennsylvania before the turn of the 20th century, Francis became orphaned when he was two-years old. He worked in a Carnegie Steel foundry in Clairton until war was declared. He shipped to France and Flanders with the "Iron Division," 28th Infantry Regiment. He was gassed and sent home, where he began a drifter's life common to many at the time: he picked melons in California's Imperial Valley, sold spark plugs in Washington, insurance in Pittsburgh. His meager disability pension finally enabled him to study at USC in Los Angeles. He started writing stories for *The American Mercury* around this time, mostly about steelworkers and the mills he knew first-hand. One such story is "A Prodigal Returns," written in 1929.

While honing his craft, he became a press agent for a number of movie stars around Hollywood. In that capacity, he was known both for his meanness and his rampant alcoholism. Sam Brown, as well as many others, claimed that Francis was the model for the "demon press agent" Matt Libby, played by Lionel Stander in the first *A Star Is Born* (1937). In his later years, John Fante remembered Owen Francis with uncharacteristic fondness and admiration: an amiable drunk who once stole a Pacific Electric streetcar on the north end of Vermont Avenue and drove it almost to San Pedro. In a biographical sketch he wrote for *The American Mercury*, Francis himself revealed: "I was living the drifting life until one day Warner bought a story of mine and made a motion picture of it called *Good Time Charley*. They wanted me to write plenty others, but I soon grew tired of those Hollywood boys, so I went back to Pittsburgh." This was likely written to please Mencken more than anything else.

Good Time Charley happens to be a very good picture, one of the best of Michael Curtiz's early American films—which are often harder to see than his silent European output. In this 1927 silent, Warner Oland played a good-natured but self-centered vaudevillian who criss-crosses the country with his wife and child—all in all a happy family. One day the mother is killed backstage while fighting off the producer's advances. Someone in the troupe witnesses the murder, but keeps it to himself for seventeen years. Oland leaves the troupe and goes his own way, the rest finally make it on Broadway solely on the talent and looks of the daughter. The son of the murderous producer ("A chip from the old block," reads a card), takes her for a ride, marries her and ruins her. Meanwhile, Oland has gone blind. He sends his daughter the money he has been saving for an eye operation, all the while assuring her by wires that he is doing splendidly on the road. He and his cronies end up at an old folks' home for carny people. The daughter (played by a radiant Helene Costello), now a star and doing charity work across the country, finds her father there. The story is openly melodramatic, but in just the right amounts. It works completely.

It is not known whether Owen Francis "went back to Pittsburgh," as he claimed, but many pictures based on his stories are set in steel mills, such as *No Other Woman* (1933), in which Irene Dunne and Charles Bickford play a steelworker and his wife who make a fortune partnering in a dye works, to their constant sorrow. *Magnificent Brute* (1936) featured Victor McLaglen and William Hall as two brawling hunks fighting over the same girl, and was also set in the steel mills, based on a Francis story called "Big." But the lackadaisical writer also toiled for the Ritz Brothers and lowly programmers on occasion. His last story, *They Made Me a Killer*, in 1946, was also an early Daniel Mainwaring screenplay.

Sam Brown told me a story about Owen Francis that just about sums up the man. Brown met him in New Orleans in 1932, where Francis had just married a society girl, if not for long. "My brother Rowland and I were great admirers of his and of his stories set in the steel fields of Pennsylvania. There was one, especially, that we liked called "Disaster." When we went back to Hollywood, we managed to have Selznick buy the story and hire Owen to adapt it. But he never did because all he did was drink. I remember he lived in an apartment on Vine Steeet, just opposite the Hollywood

Market. Which must have been convenient at least for one thing."

By contrast, Daniel Mainwaring (pronounced "Mannering") was born in 1902 to a patrician Oakland, California, family that went as far back as the 1849 Gold Rush. After graduating from Fresno State, he became a crime reporter for a series of Los Angeles newspapers such as the *Herald Examiner*, *Daily News* and *Evening Express*. In 1933, he wrote a proletarian novel published by an obscure house called Ray Long & Richard R. Smith, Inc. *One Against the Earth* told the story of a widow and her three sons trying to survive on a barren farm. Typical of the proletarian novels being written at the time, it was hardly a promising start. The author must have sensed this, as he promptly got a job in the Warner publicity department at a salary of $85 a week. Three years later, he was only making double that and he quit the studio to write, under a pseudonym, a series of crime novels with a recurring journalist hero named Robin Bishop. He wrote four of these, starting with *The Doctor Died at Dusk*, before going back to publicity hack work, this time at RKO. But he continued writing, inaugurating a new series with a detective named Humphrey Campbell, who only drinks milk and relaxes by playing the accordion. *No Hands on the Clock, Finders Keepers, Forty Whacks* were some of the titles, followed by other non-Campbells like *The Street of the Crying Woman, The Hill of the Terrified Monk*. Every year, William Morrow published a Mainwaring novel, under the rather effete *nom de plume* Geoffrey Homes. The books were popular, often reprinted as Bantam paperbacks. In reprint, the titles invariably were made more muscular: *Stiffs Don't Vote, Dead as a Dummy*, etc. Some of these sold to the pictures as B-movie fodder.

At this time, Mainwaring's life crossed with John Fante's—who was also looking to make his way as a novelist. Fante had just gotten married and had published his first novel. The young couple moved back to Los Angeles from Roseville, the bride's hometown, and although their address kept changing, it was never far from Mainwaring: first on Temple St., then North New Hampshire Ave., and finally S. Berendo St. It is on S. Berendo, in the back of a Victorian house, that Fante would write most of his second and most celebrated novel, *Ask the Dust*. At this time, Fante had stopped writing for the studios, and the couple lived exclusively on the $94 a month

Joyce Fante earned from the Writers Project Administration. As a published poet, she had applied as a writer for the Los Angeles Book Project. In the mid-1980s, when I frequently saw her, Joyce Fante many times spoke of Dan Mainwaring:

"He often came to see us. He lived near us, on Ocean View, and he would walk over. His wife Peggy was an ex-dancer and actress who had become obese. He was completely devoted to her. She died in 1940 from peritonitis, and he remarried. His new wife was called Sally, and she was Mayo Methot's best friend. Dan already knew Bogart because of his publicity work at Warner, but they became closer at that time, even though it was not always easy to be friends of the "Battling Bogarts," as they were known around Hollywood. We liked Dan a whole lot. He was not tall, but wide, with blue eyes and light brown hair cut very short, like in the military. He smoked a pipe, and with his tweeds he looked more like an Englishman than a reporter, or a press agent. The Mainwarings had a lot of dinner parties, and the guests were sometimes from the tony set. Once, I remember, there was a rather well known British author. Dan was five or six years older than John, and the two of them often talked shop. But literary craft, not movies. For the movies, John always deferred to Frank Fenton, who had been his mentor in the early scriptwriting days. But Dan Mainwaring was one of the first persons to read *Ask the Dust* in manuscript. And he is the one who advised John to switch his first chapter and put it at the end of the novel. As John had it, it started with the Mexican girl Camilla walking into the desert with the little dog, presumably to their death, and then we flashbacked. Dan maintained that he had to keep it in continuity, make it more linear, and John immediately saw the soundness of his advice. John could be ornery and touchy about his work, but he also was merciless. And he respected Dan, although he hadn't written much of anything yet. He hadn't written *Build My Gallows High*, for instance, and hadn't started writing for the movies. We saw a lot of Dan at this time, and then not at all, when we moved to Manhattan Beach."

Mainwaring would break with his soul-killing bread-and-butter work in 1943, leaving RKO. He didn't, however, exactly enter into movie work through the main gate. The producing team of Thomas-Pine at Paramount were the only ones to offer him jobs, most of them no-budget Westerns or crime programmers like the previously mentioned *They Made Me a Killer*. He wrote six of these for Thomas-Pine, all of which he later derided. In the winter of 1945, tired of the grind at Paramount, Mainwaring quit and repaired to Lake Tahoe. There he tried something new, a departure from his crime capers, something more in the hardboiled genre. William Dozier, an astute story editor at Paramount who was now an executive at RKO, bought the rights to *Build My Gallows High* (by "Geoffrey Homes") when it was published in 1946. Mainwaring was hired to adapt it for the screen, with Warren Duff in charge of production. In an interview for *The Velvet Trap*, Mainwaring later revealed that he had personally brought the finished script to Bogart on his yacht in Newport Beach. According to the author, Bogart wanted to play Jeff Bailey, but Warner refused the loan-out, and Mitchum donned the trenchcoat instead. Mainwaring also noted that Warren Duff hired James Cain to do a rewrite, since Mainwaring was a novice at movie writing. "They wasted $20,000 for nothing, as Jim Cain ruined the thing; he took out all the scenes in the mountains and at Lake Tahoe, brought everything back to the city!" recalled a still-rattled Mainwaring. "Frank Fenton also worked on the script, but finally we went back pretty much to what I had written, and this is what Jacques Tourneur shot, more or less. He had come aboard almost at the last minute, as they did at the time. They only changed the title. Mine came from a poem or from a Negro spiritual I must have heard or read one day, but that I never found again. The publicity department changed *Build My Gallows High* to *Out of the Past* instead."

Our sentimental investment in the picture today is such that we prefer to believe that *Out of the Past* represented the stunning debut of a very good screenwriting career, one that included *The Big Steal* (1949), the unmatched *Invasion of the Body Snatchers* (1956) and the sensational *Baby Face Nelson* (1957). Nevertheless, contemporary critic Jeff Schwager's examination of successive script versions seems to indicate that Mainwaring may have minimized the contributions of script doctor Frank Fenton, and possibly even Cain's. The latter's two passes at the script are not much good, it is true (too Manichaean, with a lame ending), but Cain's two-part structure was kept in the final version. Still, he made the characters far too unpleasant and inhuman: Jeff Bailey was a dullard at best, and Kathie (whom Cain renamed Maisie for some reason) was a calculating natural born killer who could make *Double Indemnity*'s Phyllis Dietrichson pass for a candy striper. On the other hand, Schwager is reasonably convincing in demonstrating that the final shooting script greatly benefitted from a myriad of Fenton touches. This English transplant to Hollywood was an experienced fixer whose movie credits do not account for the many polish jobs he was known for around town. His name figures nowhere in the *Out of the Past* credits.

Fenton died in 1971, which still would have given him ample time to claim part authorship for what in the meantime had become a cult classic, possibly the best film noir ever made. But he must have been quite indifferent to this sort of thing. He earned $8,333 for his contribution to the picture. Cain, who still had quite a reputation in the mid-1940s, pocketed $16,666. Mainwaring, on top of the $20,000 price he got for his novel, earned $11,083 for the adaptation. And, in spite of his later gripes, Mainwaring was the first to admit that Tourneur's picture was infinitely superior to his novel. Schwager's meticulous comparisons suggest that Fenton had a lot to do with this. Many one-liners are his, like the famous "Just get out. I have to sleep in this room," as well as crucial changes, like Jeff and Kathie fleeing Mexico for San Francisco, or the deadly finale, with Kathie shooting Jeff in the getaway car even if it means joining him in death. Other crusty exchanges are Fenton's, like the one between the two lovers on the lam: "Is there a way to win?" Kathie asks. "There's a way to lose more slowly," Jeff replies. It would appear that Fenton's main contribution was in reinforcing Jeff's laconic nature and basic fatalism, which, of course, fit the Mitchum persona like an well-worn shoe. And yet, maybe Schwager made too much of it, as any hound dog would with a choice bone to gnaw. In what circumstances, for instance, was Fenton brought in on the picture? Did he not benefit from all the work done before him? Or did he work independently, straight from the novel? None of this is made clear in Schwager's *Film Comment* article, nor are producer Warren Duff's reasons for hiring three writers. But, as a former screenwriter himself, didn't he know what he was doing? This only goes to show that, especially at that time in Hollywood, no writer ever had a clear vision of the whole picture. Only the producer knew what was going on, and he often kept the different writers ignorant of what the other collaborators were doing. Still, Daniel Mainwaring wrote the basic story of *Out of the Past*, and came up with the lure that was sure to hook any studio. In his interview for the *The Velvet Light Trap* (Fall 1973), Mainwaring acknowledged that: "I consciously hooked the studio with that scene in the book. Joe, Kirk Douglas' heavy [played by the wonderfully spry and smiling henchman Paul Valentine], has followed Jeff to the river where he is fishing. And I had the deaf-mute kid following *him*, making Joe fall into the torrent by hooking him with his fishing rod. No studio executive or producer could have resisted that!" And in truth, this is precisely what made William Dozier buy the rights to the book.

FIFTY GRAND: THE REAL MCCOY

THE HORACE MCCOY PAPERS, donated by his widow Helen to UCLA Special Collections, hold several versions of his *Kiss Tomorrow Goodbye* manuscript; *Night Cry*, one of his last finished scripts, revealingly written in several small accounting books, as well as the Brazilian edition of his first novel (*Mas não se matam cavalos?*) whose translator has the reassuring name Érico Lopes Veríssimo. The collection is more poignant, however, for what it doesn't hold: his paintings (the ones he bought and the ones he painted); his famed library; a collection of 78 rpm jazz records that another serious shellac aficionado, W. R. Burnett, qualified as "the best in the country"; or the scrapbook he kept when he was making waves in the Dallas Little Theatre scene of the 1920s.

The paintings were dispersed, the library went for a mere $700, as did the records, sold immediately after his death to pay his considerable debts. As for the scrapbook, McCoy disposed of it himself in the backyard incinerator, like his hero Ralph Carston burned his in McCoy's novel *I Should Have Stayed Home*. His prized Lincoln Continentals and Cadillacs were long gone, but there are WWII gas ration cards in the Special Collections cartons; an unused ticket for a Detroit Lions-Green Bay Packers game at the old Gilmore Stadium; a press-pass from the LAPD, unsigned; a coupon for free chips at a gambling joint in Ocean Park called La Boule; a mysterious phone message left for Ernest Hemingway in room 106 of an unidentified hotel; and countless membership cards: Rolling Hills Country Club, Hillcrest Country Club, Bel-Air Country Club, Virginia Country Club (Long Beach), Beverly Hills Tennis Club, Wilshire Country Club (notoriously off-limits to actors and Jews). There are golf scores aplenty,

Horace McCoy

memories of sunny days on the links. McCoy was a good golfer, and an even better tennis player. He would have been a champion had it not been for an old knee injury from his varsity football days in Dallas. Instead, McCoy worked for a time as a press agent for Walter Hagen, the golf champion, a position that facilitated his entry into Southern California society without making him entirely acceptable. He could play tennis with them on their private courts, he could elbow his way to the Musso's back room bar, or even dine at Chasen's with Dorothy Parker and her husband Alan Campbell. But for the writers on the Boulevard and the Stanley Rose literary crowd, Horace McCoy would always remain "Horses" McCoy—the "big fellow," the flashy movie hack.

The pathetic remnants of a furiously *nouveau riche* life found in the UCLA collection are in many ways more revealing than any manuscript, letter, or novel. McCoy saved his golf scores the same way he had saved every scrap of hyperbolic praise he received from *Saint-Germain-des-Prés* intellectuals in the late 1940s. McCoy was competitive in everything, seeing himself successively as an actor, a writer, a filmmaker, a documentarian, even as a painter—never really as a screenwriter, which nevertheless is what he truly was for thirty years, and rather successfully. His story is possibly the saddest of all Hollywood writers, not because he was a casualty (he earned *a lot* of money in the movies), but because his meager literary output was fueled by envy, by a rage to make it big, with all the attendant resentment when it failed to happen. It's also sad because he knew this rage was mostly unwarranted, merely the result of the aggrandized view of himself he had acquired very early on—an image he projected in his writings, in interviews, and on tennis courts. His misery was an entirely self-imposed, fabricated dilemma, stemming at the beginning from unfettered ambition, but in the end poisoning his life in the worst way.

At the root of this fundamental unhappiness was the fact that Horace McCoy regarded himself as a bad writer. Fear of failing, of not making the grade as a serious writer, or as a family provider, or as anything worthwhile, informs almost all his career moves—right up to the publication of his last book in 1952, *Scalpel*, his penultimate prostitution, a novel in which he cynically watered down his usual spleen and acrid sharpness with plenty of

McCoy (left) with his bride, heiress Helen Vinmont, whom Hammett called "my dream girl"

drugstore-friendly purple prose. With *Scalpel,* he realized his dearest wish (in both senses of the word); he at last had a commercial success—the only one he ever "enjoyed"—but *Scalpel* was not merely a compromised novel, it was a sellout before it was even written: Hal Wallis had bought the movie rights to it before McCoy had written a word. It represents the ultimate dissolution between literature and cinema: *Scalpel* was not written to become Horace McCoy's fifth novel, but expressly to become *Bad for Each Other*, a mediocre Irving Rapper movie starring Charlton Heston and Lizabeth Scott. Bad for everyone concerned.

Born on April 14, 1897, near Nashville, Tennessee, Horace McCoy left school early for a drifter's life, working odd jobs in Dallas and New Orleans. In 1917, he enlisted in the Texas National Guard, soon transferring to a fledgling aviation outfit in Georgia, training as an aerial photographer. He went to war in France in 1918 and, from bomber planes, photographed enemy lines. He also served as a gun-turret man, decorated for several kills and for bringing back his damaged plane to safety. Before returning to civilian life in the States, he briefly toured Europe with an Army USO troupe, the "Romo Follies of 1919." Back in Texas, he worked as a sports writer for the *Dallas Dispatch*, soon graduating to the tonier *Dallas Journal*. It was there he started writing for the pulps, publishing his first story, "The Devil Man," in the December 1927 issue of *Black Mask*. He had some success with a series of airmen stories featuring a central character named Jerry Frost, leader of "Hell's Stepsons," a daredevil squad of former Air Force pilots. The Depression squeezed him out of his newspaper jobs, and he first came to Hollywood in May of 1931, in the company of Oliver Hinsdell, whom MGM had just hired as a drama coach for its talkies. Hinsdell was director of The Dallas Little Theater, where a Metro talent scout named Ben Piazza had noticed McCoy, not so much for his talent as a thespian as for his self-assurance and handsome physique. At the Little Theater, McCoy had played the title role in Ferenc Molnár's *Lilith*.

Later, in spite of the rancor that irrigates *I Should Have Stayed Home*—McCoy's own account of his struggling days as an actor in Hollywood—he dedicated the novel to Piazza and Hinsdell, as well as to Joseph T. Shaw, his early champion at *Black Mask*. McCoy actually made more headway than his hero does in the novel: at MGM, he was given a screen test opposite Walter Huston and Billy Bakewell (who had played the Sun King and his twin brother in Allan Dwan's *The Iron Mask*), and joined the studio Charm School for a time, along with more promising prospects like Robert Young, Clark Gable, and Robert Taylor. Of that bunch, he was the only one not signed to a contract, which may explain why seven years later McCoy had his *I Should Have Stayed Home* doppelgänger, Ralph Carston, threaten to beat up Bob Taylor when he spots him leaving the Mocambo on the arm of Barbara Stanwyck (to the anguished cry of "What has he got I don't have?"). Just like his hero, the author never used his paid return train ticket to Dallas, where he had left behind only creditors and outraged readers. But his early salaries in Hollywood barely matched his Dallas newspaper wages: he earned $17.50 a day when he could find a small part to play, which was rarely. Later, McCoy claimed to have done all sorts of menial jobs during this period, like picking the usual lettuce in Imperial Valley, working as a soda jerk in a drugstore, or substituting on boxing cards at the Hollywood Legion; he also, supposedly, worked as a bodyguard for a politician and as a dance marathon bouncer. But of course, he hadn't done any of this. McCoy had been a war hero, a flyer, a newspaperman, and a press agent—and that was it.

Hoping to improve on his strictly-from-hunger movie and pulp revenues, McCoy called on H. N. Swanson at RKO, a *College Humor* editor who had just come in as a producer, tasked with creating a "junior writers pool" at the studio. "Radio," as RKO was known around town, had always been too cash-poor to buy prominent Broadway plays or big novels and, at least according to Pandro Berman who was the Number Two Man at the studio, finding stories to produce had always been RKO's primary problem. David Selznick, after taking over as chief of production, wanted to remedy this by creating a kind of in-house story incubator, hiring Swanson from his job in Chicago to write and produce cheap musical comedies for the studio. Swanson did it for a while, in great numbers, creating comedies that often featured varsity football stars and blonde co-eds, stories so insipid that even Swanson grew tired of them and left RKO to become one of the most durable agents in town—representing the likes of James M. Cain,

Raymond Chandler (ever so briefly), W. R. Burnett, F. Scott Fitzgerald, Cornell Woolrich, and later Elmore Leonard. "Swanie," as he was known, was famous for always wearing a white carnation on his lapel, and for being tight with a dollar in true Scandinavian fashion. But he claimed[1] he let McCoy sleep on his office couch a few times, and had even negotiated the sale of *They Shoot Horses, Don't They?* But that was forty years later, after McCoy was dead. Transactions regarding this title were complicated by the fact that McCoy at the time had stupidly crossed his agents and sold the theatrical rights behind their back for a paltry $250. Swanson's memory has always been suspect, even in his published memoirs, but Sam Marx, who was story editor at MGM in the thirties and played tennis with McCoy, also described him as being "technically on the fritz" during this period. Still, Swanson found a few jobs for McCoy as a junior writer at RKO. McCoy always claimed he worked with experienced screenwriter James Ashmore Creelman on *King Kong*, but this can't be verified. He definitely wrote an original for Tim McCoy (no relation) in which he played a newspaperman, a departure for the cowboy star. It was called *Hold the Press*, was directed by Phil Rosen, and released in October 1933. McCoy also claimed to have played a bit part as a salty newsman, but no written proof or movie still has ever been found to substantiate this.

McCoy was living at the time in a shoebox apartment at the El Rey, 660 S. Cloverdale Ave. In New York, "Captain" Shaw at *Black Mask* would sometimes receive humorous cables co-signed by Dashiell Hammett and McCoy, and the occasional story, usually something imitative and characteristic of his mood, like "Death in Hollywood." 1932 was a very hard year for him, although by January of '33 he'd managed to hire on at Columbia for $50 a week. Now hopeful, he moved to a bungalow on Beachwood Canyon to be nearer the studio. His first original story credit at Columbia was *Dangerous Crossroads* (1933)—a Charles "Chic" Sale picture about a railroad engineer, with a young Preston Foster in the lead. He was then cowriter on *Soldiers of the Storm*, also '33, a Regis Toomey B-picture about drug-running and border police. McCoy even acquired a movie agent (Joy

---

[1] Interviewd in his Sunset Boulevard office in West Hollywood in 1987. I talked to Sam Marx around the same time.

& Polymer, offices on Sunset) and stopped writing for the pulps.

And then, momentously, things seemed to turn for the better: on November 4, 1933, he married Helen Vinmont, a prominent heiress then living on Los Feliz Blvd. Irving Briskin, one of the countless Briskins toiling at Columbia, was his best man. Dashiell Hammett gave him as a wedding present a signed copy of *The Thin Man*, with the cryptic inscription: "To Horace McCoy, who married my dream girl." Jacques Vinmont was sufficiently rich for his daughter's wedding to rate a notice in the society pages of the *Los Angeles Daily News*, including a photo. In it, Helen looked pretty and vivacious with darkly made-up mouth and nails, her short dark hair curled close to the skull; she wore an orchid corsage on her satin wedding dress. In contrast, McCoy looked ill at ease in his wedding suit, almost strangled by a striped ascot. He sports one of those little "in-the-know" smiles of which actor Edward Everett Horton made a life-long trademark. But the groom, above all, mostly looks guilty.[2]

This was his third (and last) marriage, but not the first time he'd married money. In 1921, he had wed Loline Scherer, the first woman radio announcer in Texas, with whom he had a son, Stanley, born in 1924. The couple divorced four years later, and soon after McCoy eloped with a rich socialite, as was often done at the time—or at least in Hollywood screwball comedies. And just as in a Capra caper, Loline's parents sent the cops after them and promptly obtained an annulment, paying off McCoy (who would give a romanticized version of the escapade in *Kiss Tomorrow Goodbye*). At least that book's hero, Ralph Cotter, earned a better profit than McCoy. This business was one of the reasons the writer left Dallas in a hurry in 1931, the other being that he owed money all over the place; a more pressing reason than the purported crusade against the Ku Klux Klan which he published in the short-lived *Dallasite*, a sort of backwoods version of the *New Yorker*. McCoy would give a romanticized version of this in his second novel, *No Pockets in a Shroud*.

According to Yetive Moss, who saw the couple occasionally in Stanley Rose's bookstore, Helen walked with a pronounced limp, the result of a

---

2 At the legendary antiquarian bookstore of Maurice Neville in Santa Barbara (Neville Books), I once saw a copy of Dashiell Hammett's *The Thin Man* dedicated by the author to "Horace, who stole my dream girl."

malformation at birth. She also appeared classy and resourceful, and apparently loved her husband. They had two children and stayed married until McCoy's death in 1955. But neither discussed whether it had been a marriage of convenience, which, for a man who put appearances above all else, was a constant embarrassment. This fear of being perceived a moocher was all the more ironic, in that for most of their married life the McCoys lived largely on his earnings as a screenwriter and novelist, since Jacques Vinmont never approved of his daughter marrying this fortune-seeker. The newlyweds didn't go any further than Santa Barbara on their honeymoon.

As Columbia was paying him only $50 a week, and McCoy spent money like a rich man in any circumstances, by July 1934 the couple were forced to declare bankruptcy to avoid creditors. The furniture was impounded and they moved under a cloud of opprobrium. They found refuge at the Montecito, where a year earlier James M. Cain had lived during similar economic straits. And just as Cain had done at this felicitous Hollywood address, McCoy wrote his first novel at the Montecito.[3] Meanwhile, his agent sold his old Jerry Frost aviation stories to Harry O. Hoyt, a silent-era buzzard who had placed a serial at Columbia called *The Eagle's Brood*—about a crew of daredevils patrolling the Mexican border, more or less like Jerry Frost did in McCoy's *Black Mask* and *Battle Aces* stories. In October 1934, Hoyt announced in the trades that although production had been delayed, McCoy would assist him in directing. This was one of the writer's gnawing ambitions, which may explain why Robert Syverten, in *They Shoot Horses, Don't They?* often pontificates about von Sternberg, Boleslawski, and Mamoulian.

It has often been said, especially given the savagery and terse prose of *Horses,* that the novel must have been honed and polished to a nub (going from 90,000 words to 45,000, according to one account). But Michael Fessier, a friend of McCoy's who had sold a Hollywood hardboiled novel about this same time (*Fully Dressed and in his Right Mind*), and to whom *Horses* is dedicated, maintained that McCoy's main worry was that his book would never be long enough to qualify as a novel. As it was, *They Shoot*

---

[3] George Carrol Sims, who wrote for *Black Mask* under the name Paul Cain and for the screen as Peter Ruric, also stayed at this decidedly inspirational apartment house.

Horses, Don't They? was still, by far, the longest piece of writing McCoy had ever done. It sold reasonably well, for a work of its kind, and was even more successful in England. Simon & Schuster had promoted the novel as a "hard-boiled shocker" in the vein of *The Postman Always Rings Twice*, and if it did not enjoy the same phenomenal success as Cain's book, it had on McCoy the same effect as *Postman* had on the previous prisoner of the Montecito: not only could he move to nicer digs, the novel actually made him semi-famous. Barely two months after it was published in August of 1935, Walter Wanger put McCoy under contract and *Esquire* asked him to write a piece called "The Grandstand Complex"—a condition he knew something about. Meanwhile, the McCoys moved through a succession of Beverly Hills addresses: a house on Sierra Drive, where he wrote *I Should Have Stayed Home*, then two others on Roxbury Drive.

For Wanger, McCoy first worked on a story for Fred Astaire which was never produced, called *Prince of Rhythm*, followed by a big three-strip Technicolor production, Henry Hathaway's *The Trail of the Lonesome Pine* (1936), based on the John Fox novel, which had already been made once as a silent. McCoy was brought in presumably because of his Tennessee origins, although his rather genteel upbringing (his parents were "book-rich and land-poor," he used to say) was very far from the backwoods blood-feuding families in the picture. Starring Henry Fonda, Fred MacMurray, and Sylvia Sidney, its script was credited mostly to Harvey Thew. That same year, still for Paramount and still uncredited, McCoy worked on another Fonda picture, a racing yarn broadly directed by Raoul Walsh, called *Spendthrift*. He rarely wrote alone, often collaborating with an experienced scripter named William R. Lipman. Together they penned no less than 16 pictures, with titles that leave little doubt as to their bread-and-butter character: *Parole!, Hunted Men, Persons in Hiding, Parole Fixer, Undercover Doctor, Women without Names,* and *Queen of the Mob*. These were made either at Paramount or Universal, later at Republic.

One of them, a 1938 Paramount production, was more entertaining than most. Indifferently directed by Robert Florey and based on an Edgar Wallace play, *Dangerous to Know* featured Akim Tamiroff as a gangster and political boss named Stephen Recka who loves playing J. S. Bach on a monumental organ in his living room. His refined tastes are not appreciated by everyone, especially the craven WASP old-money businessmen who have to toadie up to him. The only one who appreciates him is his assistant-servant, Lan Ying (Anna May Wong), widely but incorrectly believed to be his mistress. She secretely loves him, and warns him repeatedly against his infatuation with one of the businessmen's socialite daughters, played by Gail Patrick at her bitchiest. Tamiroff manages to make his character both grotesque and moving, and Anna May Wong shines in her best Hollywood part after *Shanghai Express.*

McCoy did not write for the screen in 1937, at least nothing that was produced. He was busy adapting *They Shoot Horses, Don't They?* with and for Dudley Murphy—an incredibly watered-down version of the novel with an upbeat ending that is revealing about the author and his sell-out complex. The script reads: "*We leave Robert and Gloria convinced that now he will be able to make his short, which will get attention from the studios, which will lead, who knows, to even bigger and better things; maybe he will become the greatest movie director in the world.*" ... No pistol, no blood, no mercy killing.

Soon the trades reported that Bette Davis was "very eager" to play the female lead in *Life Is a Marathon*, Dudley Murphy's next production for Associated Artists. But there would be no follow-up to that story. Meanwhile, McCoy finished his second novel, *No Pockets in a Shroud*, a hastily written and aggrandized account of his Dallas muckracking days at the *Dallasite* and other Texas newspapers. The book was immediately rejected by Simon & Schuster. Alfred Knopf, who the year before had come personally to Los Angeles to see McCoy during the hoopla caused by *Horses*, also passed on *Shroud*. Finally, Arthur Baker, who had published *Horses* in England, agreed to take the new book, "provided the pornography was considerably toned-down." *No Pockets in a Shroud* would not be published in the United States until ten years later, in paperback, by Signet—and then in a revised version; it was almost another book.

But in 1938, as McCoy started on the movie grind again, Knopf renewed his pressure and encouragements to get a new novel out of him. When McCoy finally delivered, Alfred and Blanche Knopf declared themselves "enchanted" by the novel. They objected, however, to his original title and the ending. "Looks Like They'll Never Learn," judged as too literal, became *I Should Have Stayed Home*, and its dim hero, Ralph, no longer turned on the gas to end it all, but instead returned to working at the studios as an extra. Such fine-tuning was largely wasted, however, on a novel in which characters barely exist. Instead of the hallucinatory allegory that was *They Shoot Horses, Don't They?*, here we get almost non-stop editorials and rancid resentment against the movie business and its callow capital. Even the accusations are vague and ineffectual. McCoy mostly goes against the fan magazines and the glamour press, rather easy targets. But, as flimsy as it is, the short novel is representative of what gnawed at McCoy, even when he became flush with Hollywood money, and which had hounded him since those traumatic first years in the movie business: his conviction that he was a phony and his fear of failing (no greater than his fear of success, which, in his eyes, could only be achieved by selling out). His first novel had been a volley, executed in a startling voice (if a bit rough) and it had a totally nihilistic view of the world which would appeal to French intellectuals in years to come. But the books that followed had no such impact and held no such views. Instead, they became incredibly narrow and narcissistic.

During the brief notoriety after the publication of *Horses*, McCoy wrote to a friend in Dallas that he hoped to put aside $50,000 of his movie money so he'd be able to tell off the Hollywood vultures. Typically, in the letter he writes "fifty grand," as if it's a prizefighter's payday or a Hemingway title. McCoy wouldn't be the first writer of his time to measure himself against the big man—they all did in those days—even when badmouthing him. Hemingway was secretly envied by his peers for having accomplished, right from the start, the feat of earning good Hollywood money without ever setting a foot in a studio. But McCoy must have made that fifty grand at least ten times over during his long Hollywood career. He has more than forty credits to his name. And yet, he never went back to "serious writing." In this, of course, he was far from being alone. But in this he is also the archetypal "Hollywood victim," the prototype of the sell-out writer who stuck it out for more than half a century.

His Hollywood output is mostly undistinguished, concoctions about airmen, postal inspectors and Western bandits. Once or twice, he achieved something better. In 1942, with Vincent Lawrence (James Cain's mentor in film and fiction construction, who gave him the title for his breakthrough novel), McCoy wrote one of Raoul Walsh's most beloved pictures, *Gentleman Jim*, a heartfelt evocation of boxer Jim Corbett and his wild days on the Barbary Coast, perfectly played by Errol Flynn. After this job at Warner, the studio offered him the usual seven-year step-deal, starting at $850 a week. Even though this was low for a man who had been writing scripts for ten years and had amassed 26 screen credits, McCoy accepted the terms, provided he was allowed to work at home. "Apparently," explained agent Paul Nathan to Roy Obringer, of WB's legal department, "McCoy writes very fast and performs his work only at night and cannot, in any circumstances, function under studio discipline—but I am certain that Mr. Warner knows this and will be agreeable." When Jim Geller, the studio's new story editor, asked for confirmation from Jack Warner, the boss answered with a terse scrawl on the memo, written in proofreader's grease pencil: "LET HIM GO." McCoy wouldn't return to the Burbank lot until 1954, by then all washed-up, to write on a picture called *Bimini Run*, which would never be produced.

After the succession of Beverly Hills addresses, the McCoys finally settled in a big ranch house at 608 N. Alpine Drive, in the Beverly Hills flats. Alpine was a quiet street bordered by carob trees so dense and so high they formed a sort of green tunnel above the pavement. There, in 1945, the McCoy's last child, Peter, was born. Now there was a family of six to provide for. A year later, however, McCoy was broke once again. This sort of financial rollercoaster would go on until his death. According to one of his friends, fellow pulp writer P. J. Wolfson—who sometimes toiled with him in the studios—McCoy "always lived well, in any circumstances, and always above his means. He had his table at Chasen's, he bought three or four pairs of shoes at $50 a pop, shirts by the dozens. Nothing was too fine for him. He was the first person I ever saw behind the wheel of the new Lincoln Continental, and I lived in Beverly Hills! He never learned from the Depression: whenever he hit the jackpot, he immediately spent insanely."

So, the image he projected in Hollywood was certainly not that of an *artiste maudit*, as the French say. He was the first to confess (in a letter to a friend in 1948): "I had as much success in this business as anyone, in everything except intrinsically [sic]." And in an article in the September 1949 issue of *Esquire*, McCoy wrote: "To be successful in Hollywood is no accident—it's like everywhere else." His piece, "Hollywood, Hometown," played against another, on the same page, penned by publisher-story editor (and not-yet agent) Donald Friede, called "Sleeping Pills, Inc." The dueling essays were displayed under the title "Benzedrine or Oranges." Friede could afford to be flip, as he announced from the get-go: "I have turned my back on Hollywood, after thirteen years in those lush and tasteless fields. Wild horses wouldn't drag me back now." He added: "The measure of a Hollywoodian's success is his ability to take insults and rebuffs." McCoy, on his side of the page, had earned the right to take the high road, having most likely taken much more rebuffs in twenty years than had a well-heeled heir and not so successful publisher. After describing his daily life (he worked at home and describes his street in detail, noting that his neighbors are all at work in their respective offices or studios), McCoy quietly states: "My lot as a Hollywood writer is not very hard, but why should it be after twenty years of learning my business—a slight advantage that the fly-by-night frustrates do not seem to consider ... There was a day when a writer was a somehow magician who was paid a thousand dollars just to stand around and look superior. But not anymore. Nowadays you have to produce. In these days you have to know your business. Is that what's eating these guys?"

By the end of the war, he had begun work on a novel he clearly felt was decisive for him—a deliberate attempt to put his writing career back on track, or at least to regain his self-esteem. On the surface, the story was more removed from McCoy's own experience than his other books, but *Kiss Tomorrow Goodbye* may actually be the most sincerely autobiographical novel he wrote, and also (given the ambitious nature of the project) his most fundamental failure. There is a lot of McCoy in the central character, Ralph Cotter, even if he is a Depression-era gangster: just as the writers or actors in his previous books couldn't help putting down the competition (Gene Fowler, Hemingway), this intellectual gangster wants to prove to the world that Dillinger and Baby Face Nelson were mere chicken thieves compared to him. But the writing did not come easily, and in his letters he never ceased to fret about not being up to writing seriously anymore, moaning that he wanted to quit this imbecilic life and go to Connecticut or somewhere "to write in earnest."

And then, all of a sudden, he learned that in France the post-war existentialist writers and philosophers had discovered him, that they were placing him on the same level as Camus and Hemingway, seeing him as the leading figure of the American nihilist novel. Strangely enough, *No Pocket in a Shroud* had been the only book of his published in France before the war, under the title *Un suaire n'a pas de poches*, and it had been translated from the watered-down British edition. But in 1947, Marcel Duhamel published *On achève bien les chevaux* (*They Shoot Horses, Don't They?*) in his fledging but seminal hardboiled collection *Série Noire* at Éditions Gallimard, as well as *J'aurais dû rester chez nous* (*I Should Have Stayed Home*). McCoy was in such demand that Duhamel also reprinted *No Pockets in a Shroud* under the new title *Un linceul n'a pas de poches*.

Needless to say, this was enough to raise the Great McCoy from the ashes of despair, and he finished *Kiss Tomorrow Goodbye* in a flash. There were also pressures from New York, as the French hoopla over McCoy had occasioned a small bidding war between Bennett Cerf and Alfred Knopf. The latter had an option for McCoy's next two books. Cerf, on the other hand, while in California on Random House business, practically forced his way through the door at Alpine Drive, his curiosity aroused by a recent article on McCoy published in *Vogue* in which the new book was mentioned. After a few acrimonious exchanges with Harold Matson, McCoy's literary agent, Alfred Knopf wrote him off with almost palpable disdain:

...given our good personal relationship, and also because we had been far from impressed by the first 80 pages Mr. McCoy sent us, and trusting you will in return find us something we really care for, we shall amiably withdraw from the whole McCoy business...

After the heady French smell of success, McCoy fell from even greater

106 NORTH FLORES STREET
LOS ANGELES, CALIFORNIA

5th Feb. 1938

Dear Alfred Knopf —

The books have come; and I think they are lovely. The jacket is swell and certainly arresting. Please thank Messrs. Salter and Dwiggins for me.

And my best to Blanche and yourself and when are you coming out? Good luck with the book.

Sincerely —
Horace McCoy

Alfred Knopf, Esq.
New York, N.Y.

McCoy pens a satisfied note to Alfred Knopf celebrating the publication of his Hollywood novel *I Should Have Stayed Home*

heights once Random House published *Kiss Tomorrow Goodbye* in 1948. The reviews—noting the dated subject and mocking McCoy's lyrical flights and catastrophic shifts in tone—were absolutely savage. In *The Philadelphia Inquirer*, young turk Nelson Algren sharpened his teeth on *Kiss Tomorrow Goodbye*: "Yet another of those hard-boiled, badly written books representing a world only peopled by cardboard psychopaths, paper-paste gargoyles and two-bit Frankensteins." The *Time* critic was even more ferocious: "If the Dead-End Kids had set to writing a book using a dictionary, the result would probably look like this novel, one of the most unpleasant ever published in this country." He went on, calling McCoy a "literary caveman," and his novel "a cop-and-copulation extravaganza."

Responding, McCoy immediateley put the blame not on his writing, but on the way Random House had launched the novel, complaining bitterly to Cerf that he was treated shabbily on a short promotional trip to New York, after he had rolled out the red carpet for Cerf a few months before in Hollywood. But mostly he resented the fact that Random House did not seem to believe in his book. In this, at least, he was quite right.

Still, on that same trip to New York, McCoy had been introduced to two fervent admirers, Victor Weybright and Kurt Enoch, both editors at Signet, who would soon turn his fortunes around. Signet reprinted *Kiss Tomorrow Goodbye* in an unprecedented initial run of 300,000, and *reissued* his older novels in pocket editions as well, including the true first American publication of *No Pockets in a Shroud*—which no longer had much to do with the original version, so extensive were the revisions McCoy made for the occasion. All reference to the character of Myra was rubbed out. For instance, the original *Myra takes her orders from Moscow, she did time in Texas for distributing subversive leaflets*, became simply *She's a goddamn sex-maniac* in the new version—a woman who has done time for corrupting a minor. In the same vein, the pocket edition of *Kiss Tomorrow Goodbye* had been "improved" (according to the author himself), with the jettisoning of no less than 35,000 words.

Over the following years, these Signet editions combined would sell 1,600,000 copies, *Kiss* especially selling better than the older titles. It was of course a far cry from the 35,000,000 copies sold by Erskine Caldwell in similar paperback Signet reprints, or James M. Cain's phenomenal reissues of his older books. And although the Signet edition of *Kiss Tomorrow Goodbye* made a big deal of McCoy's reputation in Europe, the company was more pragmatic about its cover art, a painting by James Avati that showed a girl in a black bra beside an unmade bed, beneath a banner blaring: LOVE AS VICIOUS AS A BLOW TORCH! The sums advanced by Signet varied from book to book, between $1,500 and $2,500, and McCoy used some of that to repay the original publishers of the novels to compensate for poor sales. The royalty rate at Signet was one-and-a-half cents for each 25¢ copy sold. Even if *Kiss Tomorrow Goodbye* had been the success he'd hoped for, McCoy would not have been able to make a living from his books alone—especially given his lifestyle. Ironically, McCoy had confessed to a friend in a letter that he did not see a movie in his last novel. *Kiss Tomorrow Goodbye* would, however, be the only novel he sold to Hollywood in his lifetime (*Scalpel* cannot really qualify, as it was sold to the movies *before* it was written). Warner bought the rights to *Kiss Tomorrow Goodbye* for James Cagney's company, and director Gordon Douglas made a mediocre movie of it. Cagney was too old for his familiar bantam rooster act to be convincing, and scenarist Harry Brown compounded the story's mistakes, weighing the picture down under a cumbersome flashback structure and tedious courtroom sequences. The girls are plain, the action scenes indifferent, and Cagney a shadow of his old self. The only character showing a bit of life is the disbarred lawyer Cherokee, played by Luther Adler, who sees in Ralph Cotter a way to get back at a world that spurned him.

From 1950 on, McCoy would eke out a comfortable life in Hollywood. His rates were now higher than $1,000 a week. Occasionally, he got a plum assignment, as when producer Jerry Wald hired him at RKO to write a rodeo picture, which would eventually become one of director Nicholas Ray's best pictures: *The Lusty Men*. For this, McCoy claimed to have spent several months on the rodeo circuit, and even boasted to *Los Angeles Daily News* journalist Horace Greenletter that "For once, I have the chance to write a screenplay exactly as I want it, without interference." The article is the usual puff-piece, written in the breezy manner of its time:

Horace McCoy is a big, affable, gray-haired writer who has put more words in actors' mouths than Shakespeare and more unconventional ideas in housewives' heads than Kinsey ... He specializes in red-blooded, raw meat stories, and to prepare them for picturization he frequently goes in search of local color—at studio expense.

"I can't go to the public library, get a few expressions, and write a script about it," he says. "If I am to deal with rodeo-ers, for instance, I want to be right there among them."

When producer Jerry Wald commited him to "The Lusty Men," McCoy insisted on hitting the road immediately. Wald agreed and McCoy joined the circuit at El Centro (Calif.). For five months he traveled with hard-riding, hard-fighting, hard-living bronco busters through Salinas, Livermore, Denver, DeMoines, Cheyenne, Omaha, Phoenix, Tucson, Yuma, Pendleton and Puyallup. [He probably only went to Pendleton, Oregon where the rodeo scenes were filmed, and possibly Spokane] ... Loaded with firsthand information, McCoy got off the wheel at the Cow Palace in San Francisco. He wrote his screenplay in 12 weeks ... "I used to do 15 or 20 scripts a year for Universal," he says. "I guess I've passed the 100 mark, all told...."

Having completed the rodeo run, McCoy is fixing to leave Hollywood again. He is heading for Glacier Park in Montana, where he will write an on-the-spot draft of his newest assignment, "The Glacier Story" for RKO Radio. Its heroes are America's Park Rangers.

"Looks like I'll be on horseback again," he concludes.

Robert Mitchum famously gave another account of this in numerous interviews, including one I conducted (if one can ever claim of "conducting" anything with Mitchum, especially interviews) for a French television show in the summer of 1982. It was one of the actor's favorite stories in his repertoire of tall tales. Mitchum railed against McCoy's and producer Jerry Wald's pretentions, claiming that he and director Nicholas Ray just "talked the picture" over drinks at Lucey's, a favorite watering trough for movie folks right across Melrose from the RKO and Paramount lots. As actress Susan Hayward was pressing them for a script, or at least to be told the story, "We just made one up," Mitchum said. In all of his versions, the actor makes reference to "old Horace," and the many writers Wald had put on the picture, all of them (including Wald) grabbing as much credit as they could. "I don't know what happened, but old Horace at the time had started to wear those *polo shirts*, and he had grown *tits*, you know…"

At least one thing is certain about this picture: as was his wont, Howard Hughes cast his long slim shadow over it, first because he detested the original title, *Cowpoke*; then, as Hughes' personal interest in Susan Hayward grew, so did her part—with old Horace receding even further into the background. In his biography of Nick Ray, Bernard Eisenschitz amply demonstrated that the preparations for *Cowpoke*, as it was called during production, were even more complicated and haphazard. Originally, Wald had intended to make a rodeo picture with Robert Parrish, based on a *Life* article by Claude Stanush, starring, he hoped, Gary Cooper. When Ray came into the picture, he discovered that the scripts had no human conflicts, and almost no story; just impressionistic vignettes and atmosphere. To remedy that, McCoy was hired in September 1951. When he turned in his script for *Cowpoke*, the story ended before the last third of the picture we now know, before the Hayward character becomes more prominent. Stanush, after reading it, only objected to McCoy's dialogue, which in his opinion was more Southern than Western. But the "You Can't Go Home Again" first scene—as fine and striking as the helicopter shots in the opening of Ray's first feature—were already in McCoy's first draft. With extraordinary performances by both Mitchum and old-timer Burt Mustin (whom Ray knew from his radio days in Pittsburgh), this is easily the best scene in the picture, one Ray would riff on in Wim Wender's *Lightning Over Water* while watching a screening of the *The Lusty Men* at a college campus. Short as it is, this scene is easily the best cinematic counterpart to Thomas Wolfe's *You Can't Go Home Again*—a book Ray claimed Susan Hayward was reading at the time, and which he used to break the ice with the actress, who was both wary and irritated by the he-men club formed by Ray, Mitchum, and Arthur Kennedy; Ray suggested Wolfe poems she might like to read.

But as soon as Hughes demanded the beefing up of Hayward's part, McCoy ceased to be useful. Besides, he had other things on his mind by then, having contracted with Hal Wallis to write *Scalpel*, a book for which he got a $50,000 advance (which included the film rights)—his famous "fifty grand" all in one lump sum. He also had received a $3,000 advance from publisher Archie Ogden at Appleton-Century-Crofts for the book version.

All through the summer of 1952, as he papered his walls with unread memos from Jerry Wald, McCoy finished his 394-page *Scalpel* manuscript. As for *The Lusty Men,* Ray groped his way through the movie from day to day, writing as he went and improvising a great deal. Two more writers were brought in to flesh out scenes, and director Robert Parrish came back on the project for a few days while Ray was bedridden with intestinal flu. Accidents to stars, director and crew abounded, and it is a miracle that the picture turned out as well as it did. When it came time to send a second unit to Pendleton, Oregon, to shoot rodeo scenes, McCoy was called back in—to write the funny rodeo accounts we see in fake newspaper sports pages.

Maybe the haste in which he whipped up *Scalpel* accounts for the compromised nature of the novel. Written in the first person, no attention is paid to point of view, plausibility, or anything else. It should really have been titled *Fifty Grand.* Ironically, McCoy would get some of the best reviews of his career for this book, which even figured for a few weeks on the *New York Times* bestseller list. Yet his colleague and good friend W. R. Burnett could not resist a few jabs when he reviewed the book in *The Saturday Review* (June 21, 1952), under the cheeky title "Under the Knife." He gently mocked McCoy and his central character, über-surgeon Tom Owen, but in ways that were not only damning, but cut to the root of Horace McCoy's character beneath the showy attitude:

> Mr. McCoy's new novel is a far cry from that excellent, terse, and well-known stunner of the Thirties, "They Shoot Horses, Don't They?"—and I am not certain that I feel at ease with the new Mr. McCoy and his leisurely, mannered course. "Scalpel," basically, is the story of a man in search of his soul. That he happens to be a high society doctor who has made a painful upward climb from the poverty and dirt of a small Pennsylvania coal town, is merely incidental to the main theme; as is the somewhat over-elaborate and rather too neatly worked-out plot.
>
> Let me tell you about him. He is big, strong, handsome, vir-

ile. He is a graduate of the University of Pennsylvania, a fraternity man and a great athlete—he personally defeated Cornell once with a well placed place-kick. Not only that, but he is an amateur poet, well versed in literature, and can quote obscure passages from some of Baudelaire's lesser known works. He is an expert on expensive automobiles, from Cadillacs to Hispano-Suizas. He can quote Skira on Utrillo—and it appears that he was once a personal friend of Picasso's. He was awarded the DSC for extraordinary bravery in World War II, and presented a pair of pearl-handed pistols by General Patton—a pal. He is a gourmet; he is knowledgeable about women's clothes, well aware of the difference between a Mainbocher and a Dior; and he is a connoisseur not only of women and wine—he drinks Heidsick '38 and Moet & Chandon in his most expansive moments. On top of all this he is a great surgeon, a genius with a scalpel, and is ultimately invited, in fact, implored, by the august Dean of Medicine, to become a full professor at Harvard.

When I inform you that this rather amazing protagonist tells the story in the first person I think you will see that here we have something very unusual indeed. In novels told in the first person, the narrators are almost without exception vague, colorless figures, modest, retiring. But our narrator, Dr. Tom Owen, makes Sir Willoughby Patterne seem like a very humble and self-effacing fellow. And yet this magnificent Renaissance figure suffers badly, intermittently, from self-doubt: he has qualms; he even considers himself to be a dubious character at times, a hustler, a name-dropper, in short, he is frightened that he is a "phony"… and from this weird disparity arises the real, it might even be said the hidden drama of this strange and at times vivid and compelling book.

Of most current novels it can be said that there is less in them than meets the eye, with Mr. McCoy's novel it is definitely the reverse: and what is below the surface is the most important; but the difficulty seems to be that Mr. McCoy can never quite succeed in making us understand precisely what it is.

During one of our conversations in the 1980s, Burnett told me he didn't think he had been unkind—the novel deserved much worse—but McCoy was incensed by the review, and when they next saw each other he called him on it. "Lucky we were really good friends," said Burnett, "because for a moment I thought he would beat me up. Which he certainly was physically equipped to do." Here Burnett was certainly relying on memories of his dead friend because Stanley McCoy, during a visit home from college in 1953, found his father "flabby, fat and tired." Not so tired he couldn't pull another fast one that year—flogging Marcel Duhamel a "new novel" for his *Série Noire*, which in reality was a hastily reshaped version of a story he had sold to Paramount three years before for Alan Ladd. *The Turning Point* (1952) eventually starred William Holden and Edmond O'Brien and was directed by William Dieterle. The "new French novel" was called *Pertes et fracas*, and its American version was published four years after the author's death as a Dell original under the title *Corruption City*.

It was at this point that McCoy's career took yet another tack, possibly its most bizarre—he started dedicating all his creative hours to painting. His son Stanley remembers seeing him one day returning to the house on Alpine Drive with a station wagon full of artist's supplies and equipment—with another load following behind on the store's truck. The Great McCoy had availed himself of a complete artist's studio with one strike of the checkbook. "Picasso could not have had better gear," his son said. The family also remembers that he was rather gifted; sufficiently so to at least paint honest copies of Utrillo, his favorite artist. Needless to say, McCoy owned a complete library of expensive art books.

Come 1955, McCoy seemed to have roused himself once again from his doldrums. He signed contracts like a bandit, including one for *Night Cry*, which he not only completed, but clearly intended to direct himself, judging from the scenario's numerous notes and asides, precise camera angles and other indications, things that never before figured in his scripts. Another contract was for a new novel called *The Hard-Rock Man*, of which McCoy would only write 46 pages.

On December 5, 1955, he died of a massive heart attack at the age of 58. His widow had to reimburse all the advances and sell the record collection. She even had to sell McCoy's personal library for the paltry sum of $750. Among the volumes was a copy of *The Great Gatsby* in which Fitzgerald, in 1939, had inscribed one of the doggerels he loved writing so much. It read:

> FROM SCOTT FITZGERALD
> Of doom a herald
> FOR HORACE MCCOY
> No harbinger of joy

Unlike Fitzgerald, McCoy never published his "Crack-Up," never owned defeat publicly. But in a 1953 letter to a friend, he stated his inner conflicts with heartrending lucidity, in his usual brutal way: "All my life I tried to bluff my way through, with my pose and apparent assurance. But this was all flash, just exhibitionism—not the least trace of truth and honesty in it. I was never fooled, and I guess I didn't fool the people around me either."

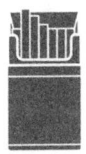

THE ROAD TO CALAMITY

Ann Arbor, Michigan
20 July 1938

Dear Pep,
Should you hear of a job for me in Hollywood, even temporary, do not hesitate giving me the call. There is a little dear there I'd like to see again. This strictly between us, be careful!
For the *Locust* review in the *Saturday Review*, there should be no problem.
Send news.

Your friend,
George Milburn

MILBURN HAD MET NATHANAEL WEST in 1935 when he was a guest of Josephine Herbst at the Erwinna, Pennsylvania, farm she was sharing with the Perelmans. Two years later, Milburn found a lucrative, if soul-killing, job in radio; he'd write for CBS on the *Scattergood Baines* program until 1941. All those years, five days a week, Milburn wrote episodes and dialogue for this show, centered around a jovial hardware store clerk, which would eventually be made into five movies starring the insufferable Guy Kibbee. Radio work paid well, but was easily as deadening as movie writing, if not more.

But who was George Milburn? And what promising literary career was he leaving behind for Hollywood money? Milburn rarely figures in schoolbooks or even histories of the Depression. He figures prominently,

George Milburn > me

715 S. Forest Av
Ann Arbor, Mich
March 12, 1939

Dear Pep,

Just got yr letter of the 6th after it had been shunted back & forth to Chicago a couple of times. Believe it or not, I had already got George Stevens' promise to let me review yr novel for The Saturday Review, two or three weeks ago. He asked me if I was a friend of yrs, but I'm keeping mum on that point because it wont have anything to do with my review. I'm reviewing George Leighton's "Five Cities" for him this wk. Cowley, you know, wouldnt let me have yr novel because he said I was too close to you.

Is there any excuse you can invent for me to take a plane trip out to the coast within the next week or so? There is a girl in Pasadena I'm crazy to see; telephoning leaves so much to be desired. *Confidential*

I have written a thing since the first of the yr except one short short story (toyed with & rejected by Colliers) and a book review for the New Republic ($7.50). Apparently I can go on writing "Scattergood Baines" @ $250 a wk as long as I like, but I dont think I'm going to like it much longer. Too many stories I have to write & it's my deplorable habit to work on a story straight through for hrs without thinking of anything else -- so I cant combine the two jobs.

Your letter was fine. I think I understand. We are together. I'll give the book my best, but I have some qualms about my adequacy as a critic. So be lenient with me when the review appears. Meanwhile, not for backscratching but for auld lang syne, cant you find some reason for me to fly out there even for a few hrs. Yours, George

Letter from George Milburn to Nathanael West

however, on a literary blog called *Writers No One Reads* (http://writersnoonereads.tumblr.com). In the 1930s, however, he was as respected a writer as he was popular, possibly the greatest author ever to come out of Oklahoma, along with Jim Thompson. His two short story collections, *Oklahoma Town* and *No More Trumpets*, as well as his novel *Catalogue* (all published by Harcourt, Brace and Co. between 1931 and 1936) seem strikingly fresh and original even today. But these titles are rarely seen, not even in used bookstores—the man has simply disappeared.

Discovered by folklorist Ben A. Botkin and popularized by H. L. Mencken, in his time George Milburn enjoyed a far greater reputation than Nathanael West or John Fante, and certainly was more widely read. His stories appeared in *Harper's, Scribner's,* even the *New Yorker* and later *Esquire*. And yet, as early as June 1934, Mencken was already writing him off in a letter to his old friend Harry Leon Wilson:

> Whatever happened to George Milburn, you ask? I don't know. I agree with you, he's an authentic talent. And not just for fiction, he was real good with articles as well. I used to publish him all the time in the *American Mercury*, whenever I could get my hand on something from him. Unfortunately, he is rather eccentric. One time I saw him in New York, he had a wife, a baby and a goatee. The wife and the baby seemed reasonably legitimate, but the goatee gave me such a shock I managed to talk him into shaving it. Then he seems to have fallen under the sway of Greenwich Village, always nefarious for a young writer, as can be a family, as a matter of fact. In any case, his *Oklahoma Town* is unmatched in the genre.

Mencken was a bit premature about the demise of George Milburn (*Catalogue*, one of his best books, would be published the following year), but he had every reason to worry. What happened to Milburn was a bigger calamity than a goatee or a baby: it was the surefire kiss of death for any writer—a Guggenheim. After two tries, he finally received a John Simon Guggenheim Memorial Fellowship to help him travel in Europe. Others had applied for the same grant that very same year: John Fante and Nathanael West, for instance, both in vain.

Being turned down by the Foundation was what prompted West to go to Hollywood, and one wonders what turn his career would have taken had he been accepted and had he slid down the cushy but slippery chute of endowed art, careening from Yaddo to New Hope, remaining at the tit of patronage. Allen Tate, Katherine Anne Porter, Kay Boyle, James Ross, Carson McCullers, Josephine Herbst, all followed that path, and with few exceptions this sheltered life led them to produce a kind of hothouse literature, at best.

Nevertheless, as so many had done before him, Milburn in the fall of 1934 crossed over with wife and child, first to London, then to Spain. But his wife Vivian's sudden illness made him shorten his stay, and they were back in New York by February 1935. In a way, his soul had been spared for the time being, but you can already see his life and career tilting during this year. Strangely enough, Milburn seemed fully conscious of it. Like many artists of his day, he went for the "back to the land" fad, and we find the couple in Pineville, Missouri, in the Ozark Mountains, where Milburn writes a short story called "The Road to Calamity." There actually is a town called Calamity in the region, but the story is very close to Raymond Chandler's "A Couple of Writers," minus the gallows humor. Milburn's story would be published the following year in *The Southern Review*. Like Chandler's funny but ultimately chilling tale, it featured a couple at the end of their tether, but in this one there is only a single blocked writer. He is first seen on a dirt road, vainly looking for the last jug of white lightning he has buried somewhere, all the while lamenting the dilemma confronting every writer: how to earn a living and still remain true to one's vision. The slicks are the only publications that pay well, but they only go for the glib and the trivial. Literary reviews (like the one which would eventually publish "The Road to Calamity") want art but pay nothing, or too little. Searching for his booze is just another way to fudge the problem, and Milburn's writer, finding his jug in the end, albeit almost empty, has to rinse the bottle to get the last drops of alcohol. Diluting one's vision and principles seems to be the only recourse—and Milburn will do plenty of that in years to come.

Though still living in Missouri a year later, his prospects didn't seem all that dire, however, as he wrote to Charles Miles, a friend from the University of Oklahoma in Norman.

Pineville, Missouri, 1936 September 2

Dear Charlie,

Your letter was one of the most pleasant surprises I've had out of this whole *Catalogue* furor. I began a long letter to you right after Joe Brant [an agent] was over here and I urged you to stock up on first editions of *Catalogue*. But it all sounded a little too much like I was trying to sell you a pup, so I tore it up. I wish now that I had sent it. "Catalogue" went into its third printing the first week [after its initial run of 2,500]. Harcourts are being very cautious about it though. If Simon & Schuster had had it they would have had it on the best-seller lists by now. But I don't care. I don't believe that ballyhoo and advertising and all that really count in a book's success. It's the people who have read it telling other people that makes a book sell. And there is no reader I'd rather please than Charlie Miles. Did you see the review in last week's *Times* (NY) Book Review section? Best one I've seen so far with the exception of the one Wm. McFee wrote in the *New York Sun*. Harcourts have signed a contract with Eddie Dowling the New York producer for a dramatization & NY stage production of the book. This also covers moving picture rights. There is another play option out on one of my stories and has been for several months so I'm not getting too hepped up over this. No cash money as yet. But I am hoping at least that *Catalogue* will pull me out of debt this winter. That will be something, too. I have had a terrible struggle to keep my head above water this last year. ... This novel I'm working on now is about 10 times better than *Catalogue*. I was just practicing on *Catalogue* & I don't regard that as a finished piece of work at all. Unfortunately we boys who depend on squeezing a living out of words can't destroy our experiments. We have to foist them on the Public if publishers will take them. And I haven't the least complaint about the way the Public is taking this one of mine—although I would have liked it if the reviews, instead of giving *Catalogue* so much space had given more indication that the reviewers had given the book something more than a hasty, superficial reading. ... I don't believe I'll be coming to Norman any more, much as I regret it. But every time I come there I get sued. I try conscientiously to pay all my honest debts. But they keep slipping up on me, with piddling little bills I've never even heard of. ... Next time they'd probably have me up for playing tiddlywinks with Norman manhole covers. This makes me feel that I should never set foot within Norman city limits again. There are about a dozen people there, you among them, whom I care a great deal for, but I hope to God I can see them all outside Norman—a place which by actual head count has more sons of bitches per square foot than any other town in the United States. Well, Charlie, I stand in a way to make some money for the first time in my life. I am being deluged with offers from the movies (if you can call seven offers a deluge). The highest yet is $500 a week. I am holding out for $750. ... I may be making a mistake to hold out for more money, but I'm not going out there until I can command a salary that will put me in a position to command a certain amount of respect. The vogue for this book may die out before long and then there won't be any anxiety about getting me out to Hollywood. (I must admit that $500 has a strong pull and that if I hadn't set my head I'd probably snap it up; but I've got a troublesome conscience and I'd just as soon lose the money altogether as to have to put up with that once I got out there). Anyway I've got a few more tricks up my sleeve. This book I'm working on now is close to my heart and I believe it's going to be a good one. ... You know me well enough to know that I'm not an egotist, Charlie, but I can promise you that *Catalogue* is not a patchin to the books I'm going to write and that I am now where Mark Twain was about a hundred years ago.

With gratitude and best wishes,

Yours,
George

His boasts to friend Charlie notwithstanding, "The Road to Calamity" would prove to be prophetic: after the publication of *Catalogue*, Milburn would produce nothing worth reading. His radio serial would take all his working hours from 1937 to 1941. The war years would be spent in similar dissipations between New York and Hollywood, where he toiled for Paramount, Warner and 20th Century–Fox, in equal obscurity. In Los Angeles, his alcoholism and artistic block became such that he was forced to briefly hold a job in the emergency room of St. Vincent's Hospital, as a safety valve. His last published hardcover book, *Flannigan's Folly* (1947) was just a pleasant yarn about a farmer in Eastern Oklahoma, almost mocking the grace and incisiveness of his earlier writings.

In 1949, he moved to New York for good, divorced Vivian, worked for a time as a receptionist in a hospital before landing a rewrite job at the *New York Telegram*. The 1950s looked better for him: a four-line notice in the *New York Times*, dated May 14, 1950, claimed Paramount took an option on *Catalogue* to become Bing Crosby's first foray into drama. But the crooner would instead make his debut as a serious thespian in George Seaton's adaptation of Clifford Odet's play *The Country Girl*, co-starring William Holden and Grace Kelly. The Paramount option on *Catalogue* was not renewed, and Milburn returned to his professional drifting: a tryout contract as editor-in-chief of the *Organic Farmer*, in Pennsylvania; a little freelancing here and there; a short teaching job at the University of New York, a think-piece in *The Nation* called "Sex, Sex and the World Crisis." Milburn would finish his days working for various New York State administrations, including the DMV.

In the early 1950s, he lived in Greenwich Village on W. Eighth Street, corner of MacDougal, near Washington Square Park. There, he befriended a vague acquaintance from the Depression and the University of Oklahoma in Norman: Jim Thompson. The two men had started on very different paths, Thompson writing proletarian novels and stories, eventually becoming executive secretary of the Southwest Writers Congress (Oklahoma City 1937) and subsisting on his modest Federal Writers' Project paychecks, while Milburn squandered his talent on trips, scholarship applications, and artist colonies. Yet, Thompson had been influenced by Milburn's "heartless sketches," as a *New York Times* review had once called his early work. Like Milburn, Thompson had alighted in New York after a calamitous decade mostly spent in drunk tanks and detox wards. But, contrary to his new friend, Thompson was then enjoying the most creative years of his writing life. Between September 1952 and March 1954, he wrote no fewer than 12 books, including some of his best novels: *The Killer Inside Me, A Hell of a Woman, A Swell-Looking Babe,* and *The Nothing Man*. Most of these were published by Lion Books, the lower-rung of the paperback ladder, and Thompson tried to help his pal by persuading Lion's editors, Jim Bryans and Arnold Hano, to reprint Milburn's *Oklahoma Town* and *No More Trumpets*. "No more strumpets" would have been more like it, for, following company policy, the two collections were retitled *Sin People* and *Hoboes and Harlots,* with lurid covers to match. Later, in 1956, Hano and Bryans would assign Milburn to a modernization of a Chaucer tale, "The Miller's Wife," which would become *Julie,* Milburn's last published book. He had been doing the same kind of piecework elsewhere: on Dell's 1952 list, for instance, there is a pocket book edition of *The Human Beast* "by Emile Zola and George Milburn." And Zenith Books, an even baser paperback outfit than Lion, reprinted *Catalogue* as *All Over Town,* its cover showing scantily dressed country gals galavanting in the bushes with moonshine-guzzling yokels. "*Small town girls with big city notions—and hell to pay over the difference...*" was the come-on.

Milburn and Thompson remained great drinking buddies during the first part of the 1950s, spending many nights at the kitchen table of the Milburn's W. Eighth Street flat in the Village, talking about their home state and the Indian reservation from which both of them had fled at the earliest chance. Other nights were spent at the Minetta Tavern, on MacDougal, where Hemingway, e.e. cummings, and Dylan Thomas once hung out. Mary Milburn, the author's second wife, claimed that no two men drank more than Thompson and Milburn when they were together. The former often showed up early at the Milburn's, and after a long evening and several Chianti bottles, Alberta Thompson would come on the underground to fetch her husband. But, if drinking affected Thompson's writing very little at this stage, Milburn was clearly coasting. His DMV job was followed by a similar one at the unemployment bureau. His health and his heart were bad, and finally a cancer of the liver finished him off on September 22, 1966. According to Mary Milburn, on his hospital bed he kept repeating, "I've got to get Oklahoma off my mind."

If this sounds like a song title, it was more than appropriate for a man who was above all a folklorist, having debuted as such—his first published book was a collection of songs, *The Hobo's Hornbook*. Milburn was born April 27, 1906 in Coweta, Indian Territory; a year later, the area would be incorporated into the Union as the State of Oklahoma. After campaigning in Cuba with Teddy Roosevelt, his father had come west to practice law in an area that had none. Spending too much time defending Indians or colored folks against those who sought to dispossess them, he never prospered, and finally took a position in Coweta as Postmaster. In young George's eyes, his father always cut quite a figure in this small town, a model of tolerance and intelligence among a mob of bigots and hypocrites. There is a lot of Downey Milburn in *Catalogue*'s Postmaster Shannon. His father was also a raconteur, and liked to read. Books became a similar passion for young George: all of his jobs would have something to do with printing or writing, from the very first one at age eleven (as a go-fer at the printing plant of the *Coweta Times*) until his last as a Lion Books ghost writer. When he was 16, he distinguished himself by sending an article to the *Pawhuska Daily Capital*, the country gazette of the burg where he held a summer job at the telegraph office. Milburn had followed the National Guard maneuvers near Fort Sill and had seen non-coms and officers drunk as skunks on the train. His piece, describing in lurid detail the troops' gastric distress, made some noise in Oklahoma. The boy was still in school when he was appointed correspondent for the *Tulsa Tribune*. Late in 1925, he went to Chicago, riding on a freight car. Like many, he claimed to have been a hobo at this time, but in fact a job was waiting for him in the Windy City as editor and factotum for the Haldeman-Julius Publishing Company's Little Blue Books. These cost 5¢, were no bigger than three x five inches, its pages crudely stapled together, with covers mostly pale blue, sometimes yellow. They contained brutally abridged versions of the classics—*Hamlet* in thirty small pages, for example—biographies, manuals and joke books. Milburn had to tackle things like *How to Play Baseball, Best Rube Jokes, How to Become a U. S. Citizen*, or *How to Tie All Kinds of Knots*. These little books were treasured by cowboys and laborers all over the American West: you could read them in the saddle, store them inside a boot or back pocket. These Little Blue Books also spread like prairie fire in a unique way when the Arbuckle Coffee Company in Chicago started buying up all the unsold Haldeman-Julius backstock and putting a booklet in every Arbuckle coffee can, making it a favorite brand around the camps. Arbuckle—a very dark roast, cut with no small amounts of chicory—was the kind of coffee thick enough to pass the cowboy test: floating a shoehorn. Later, Milburn would pitch *The American Mercury* a piece about the creator and first editor of the Little Blue Books. The proposed article would be called "Voltaire from Kansas," as Haldeman had started his popular-culture empire in Girard, Kansas.

Come 1927 Milburn was in New Orleans (like everyone else, it seemed), starving agreeably among the local bohemians and trying to "write seriously" for the first time. It is during this winter that he wrote his first sketches, when not peddling tout-sheets at the Fair Grounds Race Course. The next year, in order to be closer to his gravely ill father, Milburn enrolled at the University of Oklahoma, paying his way by editing the student newspaper. There he met Ben Botkin, the folklorist, who published Milburn's first pieces in his influential *Folk-Say* magazine. He also introduced Milburn to the literary editor of *The Times-Picayune*, who in turn recommended him to Mencken. The Sage of Baltimore really took to him, buying practically everything Milburn had managed to salvage from his drifting years. The first seven *Oklahoma Town* sketches were published in the November 1929 issue of *The American Mercury*, and 21 more over the following eight months. These were Milburn's most creative years, living in Norman, the campus town near Oklahoma City. Physically he looked barely more than a boy, bantamweight and five-foot three, but with twice as much gumption and explosive energy as when he was prowling the country gazette offices. His letters to Mencken grew in number, as did his pitches for articles. He wanted to write about the socialist paper *Appeal to Reason*, which at one time, he claimed, had a bigger circulation than *The Saturday Evening Post* (apparently, even Mencken did not believe him[1], as he turned him down). Milburn also wanted to cover the epic fight for the post of Oklahoma Governor, which pitted "Bolivia Bill" in the Democratic corner against the incumbent "Alfafa Bill" on the Republican side. Menck-

---

1 *Appeal to Reason* had a circulation of 500,000 in 1910, when *The Saturday Evening Post*'s was two million by 1913.

en, always fond of local curiosities and the absurdities of the boondocks, lapped it up of course, even when Milburn proposed a comprehensive story on the origins of the song "Frankie and Johnny". The unrelenting Milburn also alerted Mencken to the existence of *The New Menace*, "the big anti-Catholic weekly published in Aurora, Kansas," not to mention *Whiz Bang*, a chapbook of dirty jokes for travelling salesmen, edited and published in Robbinsdale, Minnesota. Mencken may have been reluctant to publish anything on the "billy-goat gland peddler" who was nearly elected Governor of Oklahoma, but the affection between the two men is almost palpable in their correspondence. Milburn stopped writing for the *Mercury* after its co-founder left it in 1934, but he was one of the rare contributors, with Fante, who always sent the old man a card or a letter on his birthday, even after the war when Mencken, now a paraplegic, was out of the loop.

Oklahoma Town was finally published by Harcourt, Brace & Co. in January 1931. The cocky outsider writes tellingly to Mencken: "I have no idea whether it is selling or not. The *New York Times* lead its book pages with it, but the review was condescending. All those comparisons with *Winesburg, Ohio*... Why not *The Pickwick Papers*, while they're at it?"

It was a year later that Milburn met his proud mentor in New York. Mencken took him to lunch at Lüchow's. The young writer walked on air during the whole visit, forgetting that his editor once turned down his beginner's novel, *A Sack of Sugar*. "Just as well," he would judge later. He kept writing sketches and short stories, most of which would become *No More Trumpets*, but he became restless, ruinously attracted to bohemia and the artist's life. On the recommendation of Lewis Mumford, he spent the summer of 1932 at Yaddo, the Saratoga Springs, NY, artist's retreat, reporting to Mencken: "You were right, Waldo Frank is here, but you were wrong, I regret to say, about the three fat dolls who would come to my bed on the first night. Only one made vague allusions to it, and she is not as fat as that."

Meanwhile, *Oklahoma Town* was translated into German, published as *Die Stadt Oklahoma* in 1932, with pungent cover art by George Grosz. There was also a Russian translation, and the French made inquiries. Milburn appeared to be launched on a solid writing career. But now he was talking of going back to the land, or at least of spending the winter at Josephine Herbst's farm in Pennsylvania. And he filled out his Guggenheim application like he did every year. As early as May 1933, Mencken for the first time turns down one of his articles. "I detect a certain vagueness in all this," writes Mencken, still in shock from the goatee Milburn sported when he last saw him. "I am starting to suspect some debilitating effect of your pilosity…" A year later, however, after he had relinquished editorship of the *Mercury,* Mencken wrote to his protégé : "Believe it or not, your stories were the best stuff I published in fiction in all the years at the magazine."

Milburn was essentially a teller of short stories. Even his novel *Catalogue* is fragmented, each story linked by the ingenious conceit of the work: it is the portrait of a small Oklahoma town, almost a photograph of its population, on the highly anticipated day when the Sears & Roebuck catalogues arrive at the railway station. The book starts exactly at the moment the postmaster receives them, before they are sent along. The catalogue's appearance was a big event, as for decades it was the only window on the world people had in these small towns. Milburn then follows the catalogues into people's homes, revealing a thousand comic traits and turpitudes of the town. The catalogue causes trouble, jealousy, but also is a springboard for dreams and escape. One surmises this is how Milburn once escaped the doldrums of small-town living, eager to leave as soon as possible. Through the catalogue's fashion or furniture illustrations he sensed what lay beyond the prairie horizon, beyond the county and state lines, all the way across the Atlantic.

Milburn was a comic writer, but there was nothing folksy about him, and his satire of small-town life was so cutting and dead-on that, instead of enjoying fame in the state he helped putting on the literary map, he became the brunt of a lasting hatred in Oklahoma. When he left it behind, he thought he was on the road to fame and recognition, when in reality his roaming and dissipation deprived him of what had made him original in the first place. Rooted deeper in his native mulch, even if it was loathsome mulch, he could have become a greater and more imaginative writer. George Milburn's destiny, as obscure and poignant as it is, illustrates like that of no other how no middle ground existed for writers at that time: there was no way to make a living, no possible salvation, outside of New York, Hollywood, or the faculty.

POLO, ANYONE?

Work and Leisure in Burbank and Elsewhere

ACCORDING TO THOSE WHO TOILED at practically every studio in town, Warner Bros. was, by consensus, not only the leanest and meanest of them all, but also the best managed. There was less waste at Burbank; once the studio decided upon a project, and one or several screenwriters had worked on it, a movie would emerge at the end of the assembly line. Almost always. Jack Warner may have famously called his scribes "Schmucks with Underwoods," and he may not have tolerated their cars parked on the lot, but they were not treated more harshly than others. As W. R. Burnett once told me with a wry smile: "You should have heard what he thought of *directors*!"

At Warner Bros., as at most studios, no writer would have considered it a promotion to be made into a director. Some were kicked upstairs and became producers ("supervisors," they were called at Warner), but never directors. Paramount was the studio where uppity writers sometimes took over, as with Preston Sturges and Billy Wilder. But even there, they were a rarity. A lot of stories have been told over the years about the harshness of the brass at Warner, and it is true that few employees who left the studio remained amiable with Jack Warner. Producers, heads of production, directors, and even screenwriters all left behind long, amusing letters enumerating their grievances with the studio: Jerry Wald, Hal Wallis, Delmer Daves, to name only a few. Only André De Toth thanked "The Colonel" upon his departure. Jack Warner had even offered to pay his not inconsiderable debts and renew his contract, for which the Hungarian was grateful. De Toth declined the offer, wanting to test himself on unknown paths, but he left behind a warm note to the boss. But then, De Toth was a contrarian with a rather warped sense of humor. Most found Jack Warner brutal. Locks were changed overnight on office doors, parking spaces repainted and reassigned. Wallis had to sneak off the lot like a thief. The loftier the position, the harsher the treatment: Paul Muni had been the studio's biggest star for years and he was sent packing like a bum.

This is lore, but it also happened, most of it. What was it really like to work at Warner? I asked Niven Busch, who had been there in the 1930s. He was as qualified as anyone to tell us about Stalag Warner, its rules, and the proper way to jump its walls.

"You arrived 'round nine in the morning. Nine-thirty, you could pass. Later than that, you received a note from Jack Warner, always the same—polite but firm. At the employees' entrance, there was a pretty blonde girl ticking your name on the list. I even remember her name. Her name was Grant. The fellows always tried to date her, in the hope she would be a little more lenient with them in case they arrived late one day. You couldn't see her face behind the window. Standing up she was less attractive, but the guys didn't mind. She had the list!

"So, the rules were rather strict, as compared to Paramount, for instance, where it worked more on an honor code. They liked to see the place as a gentleman's studio. And the regulations at Warner were a little stupid, when you think of it, because who can really write from nine to five? Nobody. Three, four hours, that's the maximum, after that you go flat. So, of course, the fellows had their ways to kill time. After they'd done their pages, they'd play cards. Others tipped quietly from hidden bottles. Others called their agents or their bookies. Frederick Faust got rid of his studio work in three hours in the morning. After that, he wrote for himself. He wrote incredibly fast. He had to, he was churning out all those Westerns under the name Max Brand. He also drank hard in the backroom at Musso's during lunch hours."

There was also gambling at the studio. A. I. Bezzerides told me about that one year at the studio in the mid-forties where he had incredible luck shooting craps. When I asked whether it was condoned, he told me that once, as he and several writers were kneeling on the floor of his office shooting craps, Jack Warner came to the window and said, 'Who's win-

Musso & Frank Grill, legendary watering hole for Hollywood writers

ning?' I thought he'd be pissed off, but he wasn't. One night, Bill Burnett had a birthday. We'd been shooting craps, and as we wanted to throw him a party we went to his house and celebrated his birthday—a bunch of writers and I. John Fante was there with us, too. Then Fante said, 'And now we're going to a place and have some fun.' I didn't ask any questions, 'cause I was kind of naive about this kind of thing. We ended up in a place on Sunset, a second floor that looked like a small auditorium. And there were some odd-looking people in there. And, all of a sudden, they brought out the dice. And these strange-looking guys also played dice with us, they were in the game. I could see they had a lot of money. But I kept winning, I won several thousand dollars. And one of the guys says, 'You can't win, he's hot.' And they all quit. And suddenly I realized they were professional gamblers. Fante, who'd been watching, said, 'I'll take him on.' That night I won $80,000 from him. I *couldn't* lose. It broke my heart to do that, I couldn't imagine *him* owing *me* $80,000. As a matter of fact, at one point he wanted to quit, and I said, 'No, let's keep shooting until you win all the money back.' And we shot and shot, people started leaving, Burnett and all of them, we wore them out! By three or four o'clock in the morning,

Fante had won back the whole $80,000. And I said, 'OK? You've got your money back.' He'd given me an IOU and everything. That's when he said, with an evil glint in his eye, and a voice I had never heard before, 'NOW, WE PLAY!' So, I said to him, 'John, if you win $80,000 from me, will you let me play until I win it all back?' And his eyes shifted, and I said, 'This is it, we quit.' I remember leaving that place alone, not with him. I realized then that he hadn't understood *for one moment* that I'd saved his ass by letting him play. I didn't see him for a long time after that. But that was when my lucky streak stopped, after that whole year of winning everything."

Niven Busch never mentioned the gambling in his conversation about Warner. But he had things to say about playing hooky. "The fellows all had their ways to leave the studio in the afternoon. A few had stepladders hidden in the shrubbery near the wall, and hop! Of course, you had to push back the ladder before you hopped over so it would disappear again, flat with the grass; and you had to find another way to come back. The best trick was to walk back through the Olive Avenue entrance, where the extras came in and out, on the west side of the studio. You waved at the guard, pretending to go to the casting office. Six o'clock came, you walked out with the others, said hello to Grant, and she checked you off. It was after my time, but I was told that the only ones who could do as they pleased were the Epstein brothers because they were identical twins and Grant never could tell them apart. I couldn't prove it because I wasn't there at the time. In the thirties, I had my own recreative way to leave the studio in the afternoon. Zanuck was still head of production then, and he had started a polo team at the studio. 'Los Indios' we were called. It was not a very good team, and the grounds were pretty poor, dirt instead of grass. But the stables were great, old-fashioned, lining up Riverside Drive near the polo grounds, which were across the river where they still shot Westerns. Forrest Lawn bought it all up long ago and it is now a cemetery[1]. You didn't have to be very good to be on the team, just flush enough to keep two or three ponies at the stables. You signed a paper, saying you were knocking off to play polo. You were supposed to

---

[1] In November 2002, André De Toth's ashes were interred at Forest Lawn Memorial Park – Hollywood Hills in a paper grocery bag (according to his last wishes), to the tune of "Don't Fence Me In" and "Home on the Range."

work an extra hour the next morning, but nobody cared about that. Jack Dorman was on the team, he had been a captain in Her Majesty's cavalry back in England. He was our coach. He also rode pretty well, which was of course the only reason Zanuck kept him on the rolls, first at Warner, then at 20th Century–Fox. There were a lot of these guys. Not much good at scriptwriting, but good riders. Courtenay Terrett was another one, and a real character. "Brick" Terrett, we called him, because of his red complexion and his military manners. He had written a book early on in his life that pretty much summed up his philosophy, it was called *Only Saps Work*. His shtick was crusty newspapermen stories or prison stories. He worked on *20,000 Years in Sing Sing*. Warner brought him over in 1930, but at this time many other studios wanted him, mainly for his knowledge of gambling, prostitution, bootlegging and extortion rackets. He wrote a film for Universal that was particularly sordid, about speakeasies and gambling, with Mae Clarke and Ricardo Cortez. It was called *Reckless Living*[2].

"Anyway, when Zanuck went over to 20th, he took Dorman and Terrett with him. The polo team over there was called Los Amigos. Zanuck had managed to get rid of the mediocre players on our team, but Los Amigos were not much better. Zanuck was a very weak polo player anyway; he was better with the mallet in his office: he constantly waved that thing, pacing and making his points. We played on the lot along Pico Boulevard, where they built the definitive studio later. But the best polo team in Hollywood was by far Frank Borzage's team, the Uplifters. He had Big Boy Williams and Charlie Farrell in it. He also headed a more informal team that played on Sundays at the Riviera Country Club in Brentwood. There he played against the likes of Spencer Tracy, Will Rogers, Walt Disney, Dick Powell, and Walter Wanger.

"But there were far less physical entertainments as well in Hollywood. You must have heard of the fanatical croquet games that took place at Samuel Goldwyn's home—they were absolutely deadly. They played for incredibly high stakes there—because all these moguls were gamblers to the bone: poker, horses, croquet, movies, it was all the same to them. Personally, I belonged to a more timorous group, a bowling team that gathered one night

---

2 Universal title, considered a lost film.

20th Century–Fox's polo-playing prince, Darryl F. Zanuck, at his leisure

a week at the Vendome, Billy Wilkerson's restaurant on Sunset, just opposite his paper, the *Hollywood Reporter*. I still remember the address of the Vendome, 6666 Sunset Boulevard. There was a gourmet grocery shop and a restaurant next to it, and of course Wilkerson used his joint as a magnet for his paper. You dined at the Vendome, you had a tidbit in the *Reporter* the next day. He sold the Vendome, at the height of its popularity, for a lot of money. And then in the 1940s, he opened Ciro's, higher on Sunset. But anyway, we got together at the Vendome, had a gourmet dinner—or at least what passed for one in Hollywood in those days—then we'd drive to the bowling alley on La Cienega. I could hold my own at polo, but I was a very bad bowler. But the group was organized by Preston Sturges, who was a very funny guy, life of the party and all that; and he was rather good at bowling. On the team was Eliot Gibbons, Cedric's brother. Eliot was a very obscure screenwriter and he later married Irene when she replaced Adrian to head the wardrobe department at MGM. I think Eliot and Irene's was a marriage of convenience, as he was gay, always scooting off to Mexico, while she kept pining for Gary Cooper. Cedric Gibbons was the arbiter of almost everything in Hollywood, socially speaking. He was married to Dolores del Río, had a tremendous house in Beverly Hills and all that. He sometimes came along with us, but of course bowling was all too déclassé for him; he didn't want to muss his beautiful suits. We also had Jules Furthman, whom I'd seen in *The Crowd Roars*. Hawks appreciated him a great deal, always used him to give his script some "finish," as he called it. Furthman was frightfully gaunt and sickly looking, not the athletic type at all. He could barely lift the ball, so you can imagine how many pins he could strike. Come to think of it, our team was nothing but misfits. Furthman was notoriously antisocial, verging on nasty. And Preston ... You have to admit that bowling as a game is pretty limited. But we had fun. It was a fad of the period, a sort of inverted snobbism. And with Sturges, you were sure to have many laughs. I also went to the fights with him on the odd Friday night. Either at the Olympic Auditorium or at the Legion, behind the Hollywood Brown Derby. There it was mostly the Mick mafia—Pat O'Brien, George Raft, sometimes Cagney, Frank McHugh. Preston liked the fights. As a matter of fact, he liked going out at night in general. Anything but stay home, was my impression..."

STRANGER IN PARADISE

"**IT'S THE QUALITY OF THE AIR** that got me, soon as I got off the train. A clean feeling. Everything sharp. I was from the Middle West and had always known the bad weather they have over there. I was immediately smitten by the West, soon as I got there."

William Riley Burnett had stepped off the train not in Los Angeles or Pasadena, as one would expect for a man who had caused such a stir with his 1929 novel *Little Caesar*, but in Tucson, Arizona. Intrigued by what he had read about Wyatt Earp, Burnett had come to research the events that made Tombstone famous for what would become *Saint Johnson*, one of the first novels to take on Wyatt Earp, Doc Holliday, and the famous Gunfight at the O.K. Corral. He had come alone, leaving his wife behind in Chicago. After the sensation caused by his first novel, published eight months prior, Burnett felt he deserved a holiday.

"Tombstone at that time was not the tourist trap it is today, practically nothing had changed since the days of Wyatt Earp [Earp had died earlier that year, 1929, in Los Angeles]. I slept in the only hotel they had there, and at night I could hear coyotes tumbling the trashcans over, right under my window. I managed to speak to two or three ranchers there who had known all the participants in what I quickly identified as a political battle between Republicans (the Earp brothers) and Democrats (Johnny Behan, the County Sheriff, and the Clanton Gang). I took to Tombstone so much that I telegraphed my wife to join me. But soon it was summer and it started to get beastly hot, so we pushed on to Los Angeles. And right away the climate there enchanted me, so much so that I stayed nearly fifty years.

"But my relocating to Los Angeles had nothing to do with the movies, which interested me not at all. I was having too much fun to bother. Money was literally dripping from above. Because at the beginning of my career, I sold everything I wrote: novels, stories, articles, the studios bought everything."

Of all modern authors, Burnett may be the one whose books sold best to Hollywood, some even twice or three times, like *High Sierra*, *The Asphalt Jungle*, *Iron Man*, or *Saint Johnson*. No less than 29 motion pictures were based on his novels or stories. His literary output numbers 33 volumes. But in these early years of the 1930s, when *Little Caesar* had created a tremendous demand for gangster stories—and when producers like Howard Hughes and Jack Warner insisted on filling his pockets (despite his minimal expertise) to help craft gangster pictures he generally despised, Burnett was deemed certifiably cuckoo when he announced that his next book would be a Western. The man was truly marching to his own drummer, a writer without a star, career be damned.

This attitude may also stem from the fact that, even if he did launch the gangster vogue in popular literature and pictures (at least ones showing the underworld from the point of view of the hoods, without any moral commentary or bias), and if he did go on to write a few more good books on racketeers, Burnett did not see himself as a specialist of the genre. Steeped in French literature (of which he was remarkably knowledgeable) with Guy de Maupassant and Prosper Mérimée his avowed masters, Burnett's secret ambition was to become the American Balzac, to paint as wide a panorama as he could of the America of his century. So, for him to write about the West was just a logical extension of this grand, secret project.

In Hollywood, on the other hand, Burnett cut a figure akin to his books' heroes: a fish out of water, who brought to every script he touched a down-to-earth sensibility solidly anchored in Middle America—particularly Ohio, where he was born two months before the turn of the 20th century. This singularity also explains why Burnett never really ran with the Hollywood crowd, even if he resided and toiled among them for nearly 50 years, and even if he had durable friendships with the likes of the Hustons (father and son), George Raft, Raoul Walsh, Stuart Heisler, and John Sturges—not to mention the inevitable Howard Hughes.

With the notable exception of Rico in *Little Caesar*, whom he saw as an unavoidable canker feeding on society's less visible but even more noxious political and business corruption (as shown in the remarkable *The Beast of the City*, which he wrote in 1932), Burnett's gangsters were closer to Western desperadoes than to Chicago cockroaches: Roy Earle in *High Sierra*, in spite of his innate hardness, nurtures the narrow middle-class aspirations of his native Middle West. Dix Handley in *The Asphalt Jungle* dreams of horses and his native Kentucky. They are rebels, but still belong to an agrarian society (like deadly loners Bonnie Parker, Clyde Barrow, or John Dillinger), more than organization men like Capone or Luciano. Burnett himself had known those mobsters only peripherally, and he never claimed otherwise. In fact, in 1927, the few criminal events he had witnessed in Chicago shocked him—but the police sirens and smell of cordite also were as bracing and inspiring to him as was, later, clean Arizona air.

"What a difference it made to find yourself in Chicago, when you came from Columbus, Ohio! People got run over in the streets and nobody even turned his head to watch. I couldn't believe my eyes. But the only hood I knew, even slightly, was a Sicilian who was about my age, who was a barber. He was also known as Barber, wherever he went. The job was obviously a cover for him, so he could claim legitimate revenues and not be ridden out of town, thrown in jail or even deported on a vag rap. In the beginning, he was wary of me because I'd told him I was a writer. In his mind, this could only mean one thing: I was a reporter. He couldn't even conceive that you could write for something other than the newspaper. But when he understood what I was trying to do, he got a little looser with me. He worked for Terry Druggan; he was a bagman who was giving the payoffs all over the North Side. Druggan was "Bugs" Moran's second in command. And Barber helped me not so much with his anecdotes as with solving a problem I'd been having from the start with this: that of point of view. From the beginning, I wanted to write a novel from the criminal's point of view. Trouble was, I did not understand these guys at all. For me, they were all animals. Barber amused me sometimes, but most of the time I found him repulsive, like the night we went on the roof of our hotel on a Fourth of July and he started to shoot his gun every which way. He was drunk, he and his prostitute girlfriend. That time I was a bit scared, but I couldn't escape either. But it is Barber who opened my eyes. Every time I read about a gang killing in the paper I was horrified. Yokel that I was, I thought these birds must have been wracked with guilt for what they did. That's what you read in novels, Dostoyevsky, *Crime and Bloody Punishment*! Barber, on the other hand, thought I was crazy. He asked me if a soldier who killed asked himself questions or had remorse. For him it was like that. War. And once I got that, I had the book, it came easily.

"I wrote *Little Caesar* in a suite of the Hazel Crest Hotel, a ritzy place that was totally empty. I was poor as a church mouse, but I lived there. Truth be told, my father had the place in trust, he worked for the Chicago Title and Trust, and because of the Crash the company suddenly found itself with a lot of bankrupt hotels and apartment buildings on receivership. But before this, I had stayed in a little flyblown hotel in the North Side which my father also had in trust—the Northmere. This is where I met Barber. I also rode along with a *Chicago Tribune* reporter when he went to the crime scene of the St. Valentine's Day Massacre. He went in, but I stayed out; I didn't have the stomach for this sort of thing. But even from outside you could see it had been a carnage.

"But to go back to *Little Caesar*, it was really do-or-die for me. I had my back to the wall because I'd already written five novels which I either threw to the wastebasket or that were refused everywhere. Once I got a note of encouragement from Max Perkins at Scribner's, the editor who worked with all the big authors there—Thomas Wolfe, Fitzgerald, Hemingway. He was telling me to rewrite the thing, or something of the sort. I did not follow his advice, but I was flattered, it mattered a lot to me. So, encouraged by that, he was the first person I sent *Little Caesar* to. He sent it back within a week, a real saloon swinging door! The greatest editor of my generation... I was so devastated I kept the novel in a drawer for months. But in the end, I couldn't stand it because I was really in a fix: I had come to Chicago to write, to get out of this routine job that had been mine in Columbus, where I worked as a statistician for the State—a job I owed to my family. For generations they controlled the Democratic machine in Ohio. My grandfather had been Mayor of Columbus many times,

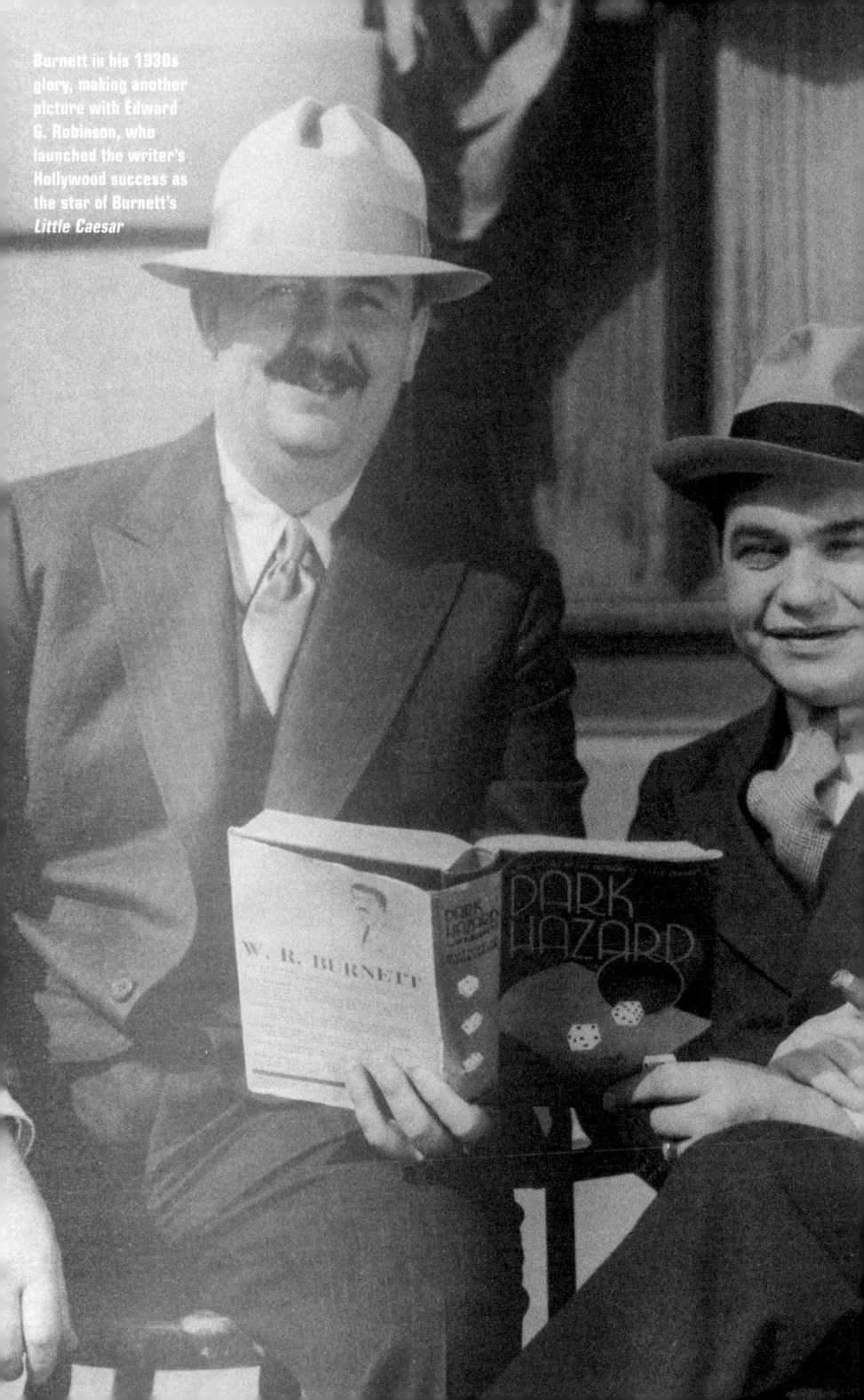

Burnett in his 1930s glory, making another picture with Edward G. Robinson, who launched the writer's Hollywood success as the star of Burnett's *Little Caesar*

my father was Cox's right-hand man, the Governor of Ohio. My wife Marjorie was also at the tit of the State bureaucracy, she had a job in Acquisitions and had a lot to do with building roads and bridges and such. We got married in 1920. I got home at night and after dinner wrote till 4 a.m. At 7, I went to work. I did that for seven years. That was an impossible situation. So, I had come to Chicago to make it—it was do or die. My wife encouraged me at first, but she soon got tired of my little game, so we separated. She kept the job and stayed in Columbus.

"So, I could not admit defeat. Besides, I knew deep down that this novel was by far better than the others I had written. I knew what I had accomplished. It was sort of a revolt against the way novels were written at the time, against a certain literary style with a lot of descriptions, a lot of adjectives and similes. I threw all that through the window, only kept very naturalistic dialogue. And for the rest, I aimed at a very simple, spare style. I saw Rico as a product of society, as an archetype. I showed his actions, but I never explained them."

When *Little Caesar* was finally accepted by Dial Press and became a phenomenal success, Marjorie called Burnett from Columbus to congratulate him, intimating her desire to live together again. According to what his second wife told me, Burnett wasn't exactly enchanted with the prospect of resuming married life. He was like a gambler who had finally won big and sensed new horizons, fresh riches in front of him. He had broken the chains, was out of the doldrums and into fame and freedom. He saw himself in California, wearing short-sleeved shirts, living at racetracks. But his family, as well as his wife's family, wanted the couple to get back together. And so, reunited with Marjorie, Burnett started his new life. But, contrary to the Marg in his 1933 novel *Dark Hazard*, who is the standard-issue kill-joy wife, Marjorie seems to have been more of an accomplice than anything else, at least when it came to gambling and the high life. As Whitney, Burnett's second wife, told me: "She had her interests, and he had his. They led almost separate lives for a number of years. Only gambling seemed to unite them."

As soon as he arrived in California, Burnett got the dog-racing bug, big time. Soon he was the owner of one of the best kennels in the country (with a farmer in Kansas who raised greyhounds for him) and a small ranch in Arcadia, close to Los Angeles, where he trained and conditioned them. One year, he had up to eighty dogs. In 1932, his champion greyhound War Cry was widely considered the fastest dog on the circuit, valued at $7,500 for claiming races. The big black dog stars in Warner Bros.'s film version of *Dark Hazard*, and Burnett can be seen with him and Edward G. Robinson in publicity pictures. Robinson played a gambler loosely based on Burnett himself. But the writer had other prize dogs, like Traffic Court, My Laddie, and Silvia's King. The Los Angeles dogtrack was called the Culver City Kennel Club and it was on Washington Blvd., between the MGM lot and the ocean. Culver City was an unincorporated municipality that already harbored bootleggers and gambling joints, Los Angeles being fiercely against these types of establishments. But even so, a consortium of movie mavens killed the dog-racing business for good in 1934, once they'd founded the Santa Anita horse-racing track.

Los Angeles had not had a genuine horse-racing track since old "Lucky Baldwin" built a makeshift one on his Rancho Santa Anita in 1907. Even then, Baldwin ran his racetrack as a passionate hobby, not a commercial enterprise. And even though old Baldwin's thoroughbreds regularly beat those from the established stables, the Other Coast kept being snubbed by the horse-racing establishment anchored round Saratoga (NY), Belmont (NY), and Louisville (KY). Even the San Francisco track was ostracized by the East Coast.

After Baldwin closed his track, the Hollywood swells had to trek to Agua Caliente to go to the races, all the way to the Mexican border. In 1933, Hal Roach had tried to start a Turf Club in Culver City, where his studios were, but he was refused a license. The official reason given was lack of funds, but lack of respectability was more like it. To the bluenoses in the state capital, movie money was barely more legitimate than what flowed through the gambling ships and casinos. In spite of Hollywood and its glamour, Los Angeles remained largely a community of yokels uprooted from the Bible Belt. But the following year, the tenacious producer of "Our Gang" and Laurel and Hardy slapstick comedies tried again, this time with the solid backing of Charles H. Strub, president and partner of the San Francisco Seals baseball club. This ex-dentist had turned the sport around by being the first to offer decent salaries to his players. He was famous for getting exorbitant figures for players whose contracts he sold to major league teams—like Lefty Gomez and Joe and Dom DiMaggio. But "Doc" Strub, mostly, had a knack for lining his companies' boards with bankers, judges, philanthropists and unimpeachable pillars of society, which made the Los Angeles Turf Club practically untouchable from leagues of decency or gambling commissions. But before opening their fabulous track at Santa Anita, it was essential to get rid of the competition.

"Dog racing had no chance against these guys," said Burnett. "They had the pols in their pocket. Hollywood was also against it, as the greyhounds were a popular attraction, exactly like the movies, we were competing for the same dollar. And the horse crowd wanted only one type of action in town. So, I quickly was out of business. At one time, I'd earned more money from the dogs than from my book and movie revenues. But Santa Anita broke me cold. I had to take my dogs to Florida and New York, where they still ran them. You can imagine the expense. And a greyhound is a delicate dog. It took about two hundred dollars to condition a greyhound. Females have no problems with their litters, but the pups are very delicate, get sick like they breathe: parasites, tape worms, canine distemper, chorea... And then you have those who can't stand being put in starting gates. I had one who always found himself in reverse in the box. Finally, I told the groom to put him tail first in the box, and I never had a problem after that. Still, you had to have major money to feed and keep those dogs. In the early thirties, money was no problem; I must have run through half-a-million dollars during that period. I have to say that Marjorie helped in the spending department. She was no slouch when it came to burning money. In our house in Glendale, she had twenty-seven cabinets for her wardrobe only. As for the races and the felt tables, we made a good pair..."

Burnett's first wife, in spite of her bloodline and respectable Ohio family, seems to have been something of a hellion, resembling in equal parts the "Valery" of *Dark Hazard* as well as "Marg": a woman who liked society, pleasure, and was always game to follow her husband on the dog-racing circuit. A photo taken at that time shows Burnett and Marjorie holding the leash of their champion Sergeant Troy, a fair-haired greyhound. She is on the plump side in her white linen suit, with heavy features and the nose of a Pekingese. But her jaunty hat gives her an attractive, almost saucy look. She barely reaches Burnett's shoulder in height. He squints into the sun and looks ill at ease in an absurdly tight-fitting dark suit, almost strangled by a spotted tie. He sports a dark mustache and a head of lighter hair, with the same part on the side as on the line portrait used on the *Dark Hazard* dust jacket. Burnett had a story about this pen drawing: one morning, he mentioned to his wife that *Harper's* had requested a portrait or an author's photo for the jacket of his next book. Marjorie, who to his knowledge had never drawn before, spent the whole day on it, surprising him with it in the evening. "Best portrait ever done of me," he told me, still amazed after all these years. This bemused, casual remark also gave me a sense that these two didn't know each other very well, or could not be bothered to try. They only were together when it was time to play. And for several more years this is what they did; it looked like the party would never end.

Come October 1929, *Little Caesar* had passed the 100,000 mark in sales. Burnett's second novel, *Iron Man*, was already written, but wouldn't be published until the following year, an automatic selection of the Book of the Month Club. Meanwhile, Burnett had set to work on his Tombstone book, *Saint Johnson*. The couple resided in a snazzy Los Angeles neighborhood at 729 S. St. Andrews Place. In November of the next year, Burnett was awarded the O. Henry Prize for a short story he'd published in *Harper's* called "Dressing-up"—one of the rare ones that wasn't snapped up by the studios. Ironically, Burnett at that time considered himself done with the difficult art of the short story, which he never thought of as his forte. But, contrary to the four apprentice novels he had destroyed, he still had a pile of essays and stories which publishers had refused in leaner days, but which he was now selling like hotcakes to the biggest magazines in the land, as well as to Hollywood.

His novels fared just as well with the studios: *Iron Man*, a boxing novel, was given the lavish treatment by Carl Laemmle Jr.—who at 21 had just taken the reins of production at Universal and started a short but artistically fructuous association with two distinctive directors, James Whale and Tod Browning. *Iron Man*, the movie, starred Lew Ayres and Jean Harlow in an early role, and is today one of the hardest Browning pictures to find. It's not one of Browning's best; clocking in at barely an hour, it showed little boxing, even though Ayres was often seen shirtless or even in the buff. It was scripted by Francis Edward Faragoh, a writer Burnett already loathed for his work on the film version of *Little Caesar*, which he found ludicrous.

With *Saint Johnson*, Burnett's unlikely career and its close ties to Hollywood began taking shape, as Universal bought the rights to the novel before publication. Both the book and the picture were released the same month. The film version, titled *Law and Order*, boasted a winning cast for a Western of that time: it starred two men who had personnally known Wyatt Earp when the law-and-order man was living in Los Angeles. Harry Carey played a Doc Holliday-inspired character and looked a little foolish under a stovepipe hat. But Walter Huston was completely authentic in the part of Earp/Johnson, looking like one of those itinerant thespians who worked the rough circuit of boom towns, peddling Shakespearean sonnets and medicinal liniments in the same barker spiel. Thanks to a little nepotism, young John Huston (who had only written one script before) was hired to adapt the novel, which started a felicitous collaboration with Burnett (Huston was to serve well two later Burnett novels, *High Sierra* and *The Asphalt Jungle*).

Law and Order was one of these laconic and stark Universal Westerns of the early thirties (young Wyler's *Hell's Heroes* is another one), well directed by Edward L. Cahn, a recently reappraised Hollywood figure whose career is all but mystifying, as it started so strong and then plumetted, although it endured, in a prolific if uneven way, until the early sixties. Cahn started his career as an editor[1] working on big arty pictures by Eastern European

---

1 One could say Edward L. Cahn started as an imposter, as he got his first job impersonating his brother, Philip Cahn, an experienced cutter already established in Hollywood. Edward quickly learned on the job.

imports like Paul Fejos and Paul Leni, and he worked on *All Quiet on the Western Front*, a pet project of Carl Laemmle Jr. So, it is not surprising that the often-reviled young production chief would call on Cahn a year or two later to direct cheaper but still distinctive pictures like *Law and Order*, the ball-and-chain *Laughter in Hell* (from an odd-ball Jim Tully novel), and *Afraid to Talk*, as bleak and desperate a depiction of political corruption as anything that reached the screen at that time. Burnett never talked about *Law and Order*, but he surely must have been more satisfied with it than with either *Iron Man* or *Little Caesar*.

In March 1930, Warner Bros. had bought the rights to the runaway hit novel for $15,000, also hiring Burnett as "consultant" at $1,000 a week during the shoot. He also collaborated with big-time scribbler John Monk Saunders (*Wings*) on an original scenario titled *The Mob*—which eventually would be made into *The Finger Points* a year later, starring Fay Wray, Richard Barthelmess, and featuring a very young and feckless Clark Gable. Howard Hughes then upped the ante when he asked Burnett to help on *Scarface*. But when you asked the writer his opinion of these films, he just shrugged and replied: "They paid heavy on Wednesdays." Even if the enormous success of Mervyn Leroy's film version of *Little Caesar* helped his novel's numbers in no small measure, Burnett still scoffed, forty years after the fact, about the ridiculous casting and the mediocrity of *Little Caesar*. "This was a story about Sicilians, and look at the stars: Eddie Robinson, a respected figure of the Yiddish Theatre in New York. For the rest, Ivy League anglos like Douglas Fairbanks Jr., William Collier Jr., Stanley Fields, Ralph Ince... And the script Faragoh turned in was a disaster; he made my story very conventional, like having Rico arrested by a Mick cop. And in a fleabag hotel, on top of that. Imagine Rico staying in such a place. Not on your life! And this old fence lady who tells him off! He would have murdered her on the spot. The picture is a success only because of Robinson's performance, and also because they kept everything of Rico. The background is a disaster, but Rico was so alive in that film, it was enough. When they previewed the film in New York without advance publicity, they had to bring in the mounted police and finally play the movie continuously, around the clock. And here, in Los Angeles, I'll never forget the premiere.

They had everyone and his brother-in-law on that stage, and after they finished preening out there, from the director to the last actor, the radio announcer said, 'Oh yes, the author. Because, you have to have an author, haven't you?' That gall! So when he tried to present me to the audience I told him to go screw himself. This is when I understood what they thought of writers in Hollywood, and for a long time I made them pay dearly for it because I didn't give a hoot about their pictures. On *Scarface*, Hughes paid me $2,000 a week. I won't say I wrote on the script because they already had so many, a dozen or more when I arrived. And mine was no better than the others, nor was it the last. Finally, Ben Hecht saved Hughes' ass, and Howard Hawks', I suppose. Hecht earned much more than I did, but he was worth every suitcase full of money Hugues was paying him every night. Hugues had paid $25,000 to that guy Armitage Trail, only because he wanted to use the title of his book. An absolutely worthless novel, horrible. Armitage went on a binge and never got sober. Two years later, he was dead of a heart attack, right in front of the Grauman Chinese Theatre. Another Hollywood story. Hecht saved the day all right, but that incest stuff lifted from the Borgias, what stupid crap that was. The only good thing in the film is Raft and him flipping his coin. I'm sure he was the least paid of them all, and yet that coin was George's idea, no one else's, in spite of what all those guys have written later in their books.

"Strangely enough, there never was a good film made about Capone at that time[2]. They were always casting a Jew or a Hungarian in the part. Mind you, I wrote one for MGM with John Lee Mahin that didn't turn out not too bad, *The Beast of the City*. Jean Hersholt was properly savage and repugnant in a Capone-inspired role. There were also Jean Harlow, Walter Huston as a hardass Mick cop, and his little brother was played by

---

2 One of the first was written by Frances Marion, directed by her husband George Hill in early 1931, just when Capone was being sent to prison on Federal income tax evasion charges. *The Secret Six* had a Capone-like character played by Wallace Beery called "Slaughterhouse," a reference to his former job as a pig-sticker. He sported his scar on the chin, not his cheek. This movie was produced by W. R. Hearst's Cosmopolitan production company, and like his other film of the period, *Gabriel Over the White House*, carried populist overtones verging on fascism. The Secret Six, a consortium of wealthy businessmen in Chicago who financed the effort to put Capone out of commission on tax charges, really existed, and were known to the public and the press by that name, but their depiction in the film was particularly farcical with their black masks and all. A tenacious Irish police chief is also most implausible, if only by his longevity.

Wallace Ford. They gave this to a limey to direct—Charles Brabin, a guy from Liverpool. He didn't do too bad a job of it."

This is a euphemism, as the picture is one of the most striking of the period, a bleak indictment of municipal corruption attacking public indifference, as most were justifiably too craven to testify against the "beasts," all swarthy in comparison to the lily-white Irish lawmen who, in the end, take the law into their own hands in a speakeasy shootout to exterminate the pests that no judge will put behind bars. The finale, predating *The Wild Bunch* and its carnage by decades, is as grim and smoky as Peckinpah's is baroque and flamboyant.

Hollywood's loot was just pocket money to Burnett, at least until the end of the thirties. The novelist was more gratified by the esteem in which Howard Hughes seemed to hold him personally than by the salaries he paid—like the time when the millionnaire, very shyly, asked Burnett to sign his copy of *Goodbye to the Past*, his favorite among the writer's novels. Tellingly, this was the story of an industrial dynasty, something Hughes knew well. Burnett's narrative started in 1929 and ended in 1865. The author always liked to experiment with structure, and this was his most extreme tweaking—and not a success with the general public.

As for *Dark Hazard*, he had nothing to do with the picture, except lending the studio his top dog, War Cry, to play the canine hero. Once again, Warner Bros. had bought the novel before publication for $15,000. The picture, directed by the nimble Alfred E. Green, is barely above the level of a tidy little programmer, but it moves right along and is critical of Midwestern kill-joy hypocrisy (personified by the mother-in-law). The adaptation is faithful to the book, with the exception of a less depressing ending. The picture is "pre-code" in many ways: Robinson keeps telling old flame Glenda Farrell that she hasn't "disappointed him yet" (read: in bed). There is also a belabored but outrageously brazen thing about bamboo: in the film as in the book, Turner (Robinson) is gaga over what he finds in his California garden. "Imagine," he keeps marveling to his wife, "to have one's own bamboo..." Later, when he gets a drubbing from her after he's spent the night out, he offers the lame excuse: "The weather was so nice this morning, I thought I'd water the bamboo." "Yeah," replies his wife bitterly, "you watered it all right. All night long."

In his autobiography, Robinson refused to speak of that "abominably scripted dog they forced me to play in." Burnett, who was not too crazy about the picture either, was adamant about the actor's bad faith in this case. "Robinson was badly miscast, it's true, but Eddie loved playing the flashy gambler, and he insisted to get the part. The studio people just gave in." Robinson does ham it up in most of the picture, resorting to the same loverboy ways and leprechaun smiles he exhibited in *Smart Money*, another Alfred E. Green[3] quickie, which suffered from an infinitely flatter and more tawdry script (written underhandedly by the winning team of the day, John Bright and Kubec Glasmon). Still, one hasn't lived until seeing Edward G. Robinson kiss a greyhound; or worse, try his hand at hitchhiking with one. Alfred E. Green's picture is also full of nice surprises, like a shot of the dogs running on the track of the Culver City Kennel Club, taken from the perspective of the mechanical rabbit they pursue. Warner made another picture around the same time, *The Crowd Roars*, directed by Howard Hawks (and car-racing sequences probably filmed by ace stunt photographer Carl Akeley)—which is no more exciting than the dumb dogs of *Dark Hazard*. And Burnett's story is infinitely more original.

Burnett once again didn't have much imput on two major pictures adapted from stories of his, both released in 1935. *The Whole Town's Talking* and *Dr. Socrates* share the writer's jaundiced take on small-town America and its narrow-minded Midwestern mentality. For the former, Burnett spent two days at Columbia trying to help John Ford and his scenarists out of a fix they'd landed in by over-tweaking the plot of his story "Jail Breaker." The novelist was still burning about it forty years later: "At one stage, the producer, Sam Briskin, had the nerve to give me a hard time for having written a story with a bad ending. I told him to go screw himself; I asked him if that was the case, why did they buy it in the first place? I wasn't

---

3 Green is often unfairly lumped with hack directors like Archie Mayo or George Archainbaud. But, like many Warner employees, he was always as good as the script he was given to direct; he displays vigor and humor in almost everything he tackles. He may have suffered from not being associated with a specific genre, or star, but he was not unlike Raoul Walsh, without the latter's grace. An exception is the marvelous and underappreciated Western *Four Faces West* (1948) in which the hero, Joel McCrea, actually leaves an IOU behind at the bank window after making an unavoidable "small withdrawal" at gunpoint.

taking any guff from those Hollywood guys, especially in those days."

Dr. Socrates is a whole other story, and tracing its development in the Warner archives through letters and memos is very instructive about how things worked at the studio, and especially about the star system there. It also confirms that at the time Warner Bros. bought the property, Paul Muni was their biggest star. Although Hal Wallis was interested from the start in Burnett's short story as a vehicle for Muni, the studio had missed out on it and later had to buy it from Paramount for a great deal of money. The idea was to have Muni in the role of the misanthropic doctor ostracized by the narrow-minded, bigoted inhabitants of a small Ohio town, and Edward G. Robinson as "Red Bastian," a gangster on the lam who becomes his first patient. The doc ministers to the crook at gunpoint, while also plotting to rescue a young hitchhiker who was in the gangsters' getaway car and is mistakenly taken for one of the hoods.

As early as March 8, 1935, a meeting was held on the project, four months before director William Dieterle became associated with it. An experienced screenwriter, Mary C. McCall Jr., was assigned the task of "following closely Burnett's book" [sic]. After this decision, Robert Lord, a screenwriter recently bumped up to the position of "supervisor," wrote Wallis:

> Bastian's part is tailor-made for Robinson; he can play this better than anyone in the business, and my feeling is that we should do everything so that he accepts the role. Because there is no denying the obvious: Robinson is no longer the star he once was. The public has already decided this. But he is a very good actor, and his way of playing gangsters is unique. He would help the picture and would also greatly help himself if he accepted the part, of this I am absolutely certain.

This is a stunning evaluation: only four years after Robinson's breakthrough performance in *Little Caesar*, he is already viewed by his employers as a glorified character actor. History (and the witch-hunters of the fifties) would come to validate Robinson's star status, but a memo from Hal Wallis dated June 11 indicates what a dilemma he has on his hands—and the weight Muni carried on the Burbank lot. "Is Muni really serious when he says he wants to play Bastian? If this is the case, we are all for it. Obviously, his part should be rewritten and developed." Eventually, veteran heavy Barton MacLane played the gangster, and the delicious Ann Dvorak was chosen as Muni's foil, the damsel in danger.

But all the feverish correspondence in the Warner archives concerning this project indicates Muni's power at the studio, and to what lengths the front office was willing to go to satisfy his every whim. Having chosen William Keighley as director of *Dr. Socrates*, the brass held off on signing him until the choice was okayed by Muni. Eventually, William Dieterle got the job, presumably for his reputation of being receptive to actors' needs and contributions. Dieterle had been an actor in Germany, and a director of note, before he moved to California and directed his initial film for First National Pictures in 1931, ironically titled *The Last Flight*. This magnificent effort is the era's best depiction of the "Lost Generation," soon to be written about by the likes of Fitzgerald and Hemingway; it's the story of a group of ex-WWI soldiers who chose to remain in Paris and more or less die of high living, rather than return to the dull existence which awaits them in America.

Muni was notorious for his meddling, and Wallis soon got irritated by the star's interference in matters that, in the producer's eyes, did not concern him. Muni even had opinions about scenes in which he didn't figure. The always reasonable Lord tried to assuage his boss:

> I agree that this is all a bit irritating and absurd. Yes, these changes would be detrimental to the structure, but what we lose in continuity we'll gain a hundred-fold in Muni's performance. Let me repeat what I've been saying for years: there is no worse actor in the world than Muni when he's forced to play a scene he doesn't "feel" or agree with. Once you embark on a picture with him, you have to accommodate him, at least to a point, otherwise he will be so bad you won't even be able to release the picture. Up till now, Muni and Dieterle are very happy with what I have rewritten for them on the script. They are in high spirits and try sincerely to make the best picture possible. I feel that it would be madness, at this stage, to insist on going back to the things in the original script we decided to bypass or change.

Philippe Garnier

The "original script" was by Mary McCall Jr., a veteran of too many movie wars to be offended by what was going on. She nevertheless sent a revealing letter to Wallis a bit later, which sheds light on how writers were treated at Warner. We already know that Jack Warner didn't want any of these "schmucks" to park their cars on the lot. But, more incredibly, they were not even invited to movie previews, even for pictures they had written. Not until 1939, that is. It took an improvised strike in support of Seton I. Miller to effectively break this blatant ostracism. Casey Robinson said in an interview that on that day, in a show of support, most of the writers had crossed the street to have lunch with him at the Lakeside Country Club. Fueled by many cocktails, the spontaneous gesture soon turned to outright sedition. Wallis was sent over by the studio to negotiate, and since the head of production was leaving on vacation the next day, he yieldied completely, allowing not only "Hap" Miller to attend his picture's preview, but extending the privilege to all the other writers as well.[4] This was a few years before Mary McCall wrote the following witty letter to Wallis, which indicates a certain measure of familiarity and assurance in their boss-employee relationship.

Dear Hal,

Obviously I am disappointed not being able to write the changes demanded by Muni. Given the fact that I was the only one, besides you, to see the possibilities in Burnett's story, and given the speed at which I delivered the screenplay to help out the studio, I was hoping to be able to at least oversee my work through the whole process. To tell me a woman can't write dialogue for this type of characters is ridiculous. Before coming to this studio, I worked for years and with much success for big magazines, often on stories about men ...

As a salve to soothe my wounded self-esteem—and I can assure you it is wounded, and how—I would like to attend tomorrow's screening of *A Midsummer Night's Dream* at the Beverly Hills Theatre [McCall co-wrote the adaptation of this big Warner production,

---

[4] Interview of Casey Robinson by Joel Greenberg, in *Backstory 1: Interviews with Screenwriters of Hollywood's Golden Age*, 1986.

directed by William Dieterle]. I have not yet seen the picture with the music. I know that they don't admit anybody for these sort of sales people screenings, but I also know that a pass from your office would solve the problem. I promise you not to use any profanity that would make your salesmen blush, and not park my chewing-gum on the swank velvet seats.

Wickedly yours,
Mary McCall Jr.

Finally, in spite of all the Hollywood windfalls, the dogs, the gambling and the high-life broke the Burnetts financially, and the day came when they had to declare bankruptcy to protect themselves from creditors. But, just as with Lonnie Drew in Burnett's 1946 novel *Tomorrow's Another Day*, it didn't take the writer long to rebound. Dogs and dice may not have favored him any longer, he still had his trusty typewriter. And he toasted the coming decade by writing *High Sierra*, a fresh start for him.

Burnett was still working at Warner when he conceived the basic idea of the novel. In March, he was assigned to write a screenplay on John Dillinger. "They put me on this with Charley Blake, the reporter who had followed Dillinger throughout his career in crime. Blake was with the Chicago cops when they shot down Dillinger in front of the Biograph Theater. But as soon as Warner announced they were preparing this picture, all hell broke loose in the opinion pages: we were about to glorify a gangster once again. So, Jack Warner shelved the project. Meanwhile, we had all this research, which I found fascinating. And one day, I was fishing in the Sierras, just above Bishop, California—at June Lake—and it came to me all at once. I just saw what we could do with a character like this, who is on the lam, a little past his time, but mostly a man who is out of his element: Roy Earle is a city guy, with a Middle West mentality, and here he is in the West, in this light, in this virgin beauty, surrounded with very open and welcoming people. This is what interested me in the story, and here I was, in that fishing camp, in one of those log cabin camps they have up there. There even was a dog! A smart little mongrel so smart and so cute he would soon lead you by the nose if you weren't careful."

Knopf published *High Sierra* on March 5, 1940. *Redbook* also published it in installments, beginning with its March issue. On the 13th of the same month, Warner bought the rights for $12,000, a rather high price for the time (Paramount was also after it). Wallis had a number of supervisors on the lot give it a read, including Warren Duff, Mark Hellinger, and John Wexley. Only Hellinger expressed enthusiasm for the material; although considerably less than the writer he'd eventually hire to adapt the novel—that old Burnett fan, John Huston.

March 21

Dear Hal,

I just finished reading *High Sierra* and I think it is terrific. But first I have to admit I have a weakness for everything Burnett writes.

It would be very easy to make it into a routine gangster film, and this is exactly what we shouldn't do. With the exception of *Little Caesar*, all of Burnett's books have suffered in adaptations. In my opinion, both *Iron Man* and *Dark Hazard* are little masterpieces—between two cardboard covers—but on the screen they are nothing, I suppose because they just followed their plot and not their spirit. Take the spirit out of Burnett's books, this strange inevitability that comes from our growing understanding of their characters and of the forces that move them, and you have nothing but the shell of the story.

This could easily happen to *High Sierra*. On the other hand, if one goes about it a little seriously—the seriousness that Burnett deserves—I think we could make an excellent picture that would stand out.

John Huston

March 28

Dear Mr. Wallis,

I am happy that you recognized the possibilities in *High Sierra* and that you want to make it into a picture with such a great actor as Paul Muni. The book received good notices, my best since *Little Caesar*. I am sure you will give it to adapt to someone quite qualified, but for once I would like to be on it, even for only a few weeks. As was the case for the Dillinger project, this is the type of things I'd like to do in pictures, and I am willing to work at the same salary rate, which is quite low, as you can verify …

W. R. Burnett
926 Hillcroft Rd.,
Glendale

Wallis answered the novelist that Huston was already on it. At this point, Wallis and Hellinger were already convinced that the approach suggested by Huston was what *High Sierra* needed—the same he would apply to Dashell Hammett's *The Maltese Falcon*, i.e. follow the novel to the letter and lift the dialogues whole. Meanwhile, on May 4, a telegram sent from the North Hollywood Western Union branch and signed Humphrey Bogart reminds Wallis that he already left a note on his desk two weeks before concerning the lead role in *High Sierra*, "seeing as there seems to have [been] doubts about Muni."

A memo dated July 5 confirms, on the other hand, that Burnett had gotten his wish and joined Huston to polish the script, as Muni had rejected an earlier draft. According to Burnett, there'd been bad blood between the actor and Huston. One night, at a cocktail party, a very drunk Huston had insulted Muni, calling him a pompous ass. The star had not forgotten. Wallis offered to put the author of the novel in charge of the changes on the new script, as a way to assuage his star's feelings. In fact, unbeknownst to Muni, Wallis had him backed against the wall. Come the end of July, the actor—as Wallis expected—refused Burnett and Huston's script changes. As a result, Jack Warner fired his biggest star, and in his inimitable style: that very afternoon Muni was refused entrance to the lot, like any no-account. No notice was served. It was the biggest palace upheaval since Warner had moved to Burbank, comparable only to Wallis' own sacking a few years later.

Bogart eventually got the part he was after, which would change his fortunes at the studio forever. But he was never to become the untouchable diva Muni had been at Warner only weeks before. The following message about the now-finished *High Sierra* made this clear:

September 18

MEMO : WALLIS TO JACK WARNER

Why not inverse the names on the posters and put Lupino's above Bogart's? After all, he was in B pictures for years, this could hurt *High Sierra*'s success, or at least affect it.

Lupino's name *would* be above Bogart's on all the original posters in 1941. The picture was a big success, and it would be remade twice by the studio. Burnett was long gone from Warner by 1949 when they made it into an excellent Western, *Colorado Territory*, directed (again) by Raoul Walsh and starring Joel McCrea and Virginia Mayo—it's almost a better picture than *High Sierra*. Burnett agreed, as he had his own gripes about the 1941 film's mawkish scenes with Joan Leslie, who played the ungrateful cripple Roy Earle falls for and tries to help by paying for an operation to surgically repair her clubfoot.

"That was all Hellinger's doing—his own sentimental approach to everything," said Burnett forty years later. "I had another crack at it much later, in 1955, when I returned to Warner. I wrote a much better script, and Stu Heisler was a good director. But they gave it to Jack Palance and Shelley Winters as the leads—two of the most repulsive people in pictures, so *I Died a Thousand Times* never stood a chance!" William Riley Burnett never was anything but an outspoken man.

As for Muni, the material in the Warner archives plainly contradicts what Raoul Walsh wrote in his 1974 book *Each Man in His Time*, a version which has since become one of the more perdurant Hollywood stories, as cinema and film noir specialists endlessly repeat it over the years. *High Sierra* was, from the start, bought and conceived as a Muni vehicle, and neither Jimmy Cagney, George Raft, nor Edward G. Robinson were ever considered for the part of "Mad Dog" Roy Earle. The famous anecdote about Raft refusing the part, leading directly to Bogart's big breakthrough is most certainly apocryphal. Among film historians, only Bernard Eisenschitz, in his book *Humphrey Bogart* (Eric Losfeld, 1967), bothers to grant Raft a comeback to the story, while still quoting Walsh on the incident. Walsh, in fact, seems to be the sole source for a story that has forever characterized the amiable Raft as a dunderhead. But then, why would Walsh have stooped to telling the plain boring truth in his autobiography, when he could instead apply to it the same nonchalance he did to just about everything, including the direction of motion pictures?

BURNETT WORKED FIVE YEARS AT WARNER in the early 1940s, his weekly salary increasing from $750 to $1,500. He quickly acquired a reputation as a script fixer, but also as a man you could dispatch on an uppity star like Bogart or Raft to make them listen to reason—they both respected and liked him. More than these services, however, the studio appreciated that Burnett could generate original material. They even gave him a contract that separated him from any other denizen of the Writers Building. Due to his bad eyesight, Burnett couldn't drive, so a studio car arrived each morning at his Glendale house to take him to the lot, and it returned him home each evening. Later, he was even allowed to work at home, a very rare derogation from Warner rules (Julius Epstein was the other exception). And his contract was peculiar. "I don't think anyone else had one like mine," he explained. "In fact, there were a series of contracts. They were paying me to write my novels. Of course, Jack Warner knew what he was doing, I was a good risk. I didn't drink, I worked fast. And my stories were generally the kind you could adapt, sometimes several times in different genres. The only advantage they had, and it was a big one, was that the price for the novel's rights was fixed in advance. Of course, I could have sold the book somewhere else and probably gotten a higher price. But these conditions suited me fine, mainly because I never had a problem generating material. In fact, my problem was that I was too prolific, and later I had so many books ready for publishing, I had to use pseudonyms for some of them! But here, I had an outlet."

In fact, the "unique" kind of contract Burnett boasted about happened only once, for *I Wasn't Born Yesterday*, mainly because it turned out to be a fiscal nightmare for the accounting department. And this so-called ideal arrangement had mixed results, not always good, but always complicated. One of these typical contracts, dated sometime in the summer of 1941, stipulated that for an advance of $8,000 Warner was buying a story called "Nobody Lives Forever." In addition, Warner would pay Burnett to write the adaptation, at $750 a week, four weeks minimum. The author reserved literary and legitimate theatre rights. Two years later, having sold another story to Warner under similar conditions (the advance was $10,000 this time), Burnett wrote Hellinger:

> As the title I gave my story, *I Wasn't Born Yesterday*, supposedly belongs to the Lee Furthman-Macaulay Cie, I suggest, to avoid any litigation, to call it *Nobody Lives Forever*. It is the title of a story I sold to Warner a few years back, which was never made. To my mind, it is a good title, and if you agree this is the one *Collier's* and Knopf will use when the novel is published as a serial and in book form—which will be good promotion for the picture.

The ever-accommodating Hellinger seconded this proposal in front of Jack Warner, and Knopf published the novel in 1943. The picture would not be completed (by Jean Negulesco) until November 1944, and not released until the end of WWII. It was markedly different from the book, although not much better. Garfield reportedly accepted the lead part because he wanted to play opposite the famous Irish-American theatre actress Geraldine Fitzgerald. But, even though we see her briefly running on the beach in a white one-piece swimsuit, there was no spark approaching what had made his picture with Lana Turner a success. Garfield sleepwalks through this, one of his weakest performances. *Nobody Lives Forever* is only memorable for George Coulouris' truly malevolent presence. His character in the book, "Doc," was a junkie, on top of being a has-been confidence man. Coulouris didn't need this to make each of his entrances striking and toxic.

As for the change of title, Burnett was familiar with this kind of pragmatic recycling: in 1945, for instance, he dusted off a story he'd written for Errol Flynn about a racetrack gambler and turned it into a novel, *Tomorrow's Another Day*, tailoring it for the new couple of the day, Lauren Bacall and Humphrey Bogart. But they made *The Big Sleep* instead. Still, one can't help thinking that this novel, one of Burnett's best, would have produced the same kind of sparks the two actors struck in *To Have and Have Not*. There is the same sexy antagonism, the same fire passing between gambler Lonnie Drew and the society girl he can't help pursuing, Mary Donnell. There was a lot of Whitney, Burnett's new wife, in this affectionate character, and a lot of Burnett in Lonnie Drew, the retired gambler, just as there had been a lot of the new Mrs. Burnett in Gladys Halvorsen in *Nobody Lives Forever*. It is easy to read between the lines: a man used to having his own way falls for his "mark," a young rich widow who is inexperienced, clinging and almost motherly. Just like Whitney, the widow had been a secretary before marrying into money. As Jim Farrar muses, "It's a new one on me." But he is not quite resigned to give up the much more lively and dangerous "Tony," a girl "strictly on the chisel," but a lot of fun. As we'll see, Burnett in his private life was confronted by a similar quandary.

This was the second time Burnett had missed out on Bogart, as he had also written *Nobody Lives Forever* with the star in mind. But the studio brass decided to give the lead to rising star John Garfield instead. Was this the straw that broke the camel's back, as Burnett grew increasingly irritated by Warner? Maybe not. But Burnett had offers from other studios, and on Spetember 15, 1945, he asked for and got an annulment of his Warner contract. The local press spoke of the "real epidemic of independence" that struck Burbank at this time. Hal Wallis and Jerry Wald would soon follow

Burnett through the door. According to a *Los Angeles Herald* article reporting on Burnett's departure, the writer had in store a novel he intended as a vehicle for Joan Crawford and intended to offer it, as a package, to the highest bidder. He described the story, "Romelle," as a "psychological crime novel, set in a residential area of the San Fernando Valley, that featured bizarre events never seen before in pictures." One immediately thinks of *Mildred Pierce*, the James M. Cain novel Jerry Wald and Mike Curtiz were making that year on the Burbank lot. But here the comparison ends. Burnett, who at that time had the same Hollywood agent as Cain, H. N. Swanson, remembered vividly Swanie's reaction when he brought him the manuscript for *Romelle*. "You and Cain!" exploded the Swede, slamming the heap of pages against his desk. "He puts faggots in everything, and *you*, YOU, you take the cake! What are you bringing me here? A guy who likes dressing as a woman!"

True, crossdressing had been spotted in Hollywood pictures before (think Cary Grant, for one), but always as comedy, never as a serious psychological study. And what exactly was Crawford supposed to play? A man dressing as a woman? Since the star was known for wearing the pants in most of her relationships, it's easy to see why this scheme never got anywhere. Alfred Knopf published *Romelle* in 1946, probably trying to look the other way, and this head-scratcher remains a mystery both in Burnett's résumé and in his personal life—which in this period took a turn as decisive as his leaving Warner for MGM.

One can track the changes by looking at the successive dedications in his books: *The Quick Brown Fox*, a 1942 novel, was "Once again for Marjorie." But *Nobody Lives Forever*, in 1943, as well as *Tomorrow's Another Day*, two years later, were "To Whitney."

Burnett met Whitney Forbes Johnstone at 20th Century–Fox, where she worked in the secretarial pool. They married some time later and had two sons together. She was still with him when he died on April 25, 1982. Ten months after his passing, tall, still very beautiful, with a lot of gold around her neck and wrists, she received me in their Marina del Rey apartment, which by then I knew well, having visited her husband many times. But this was the first time I really talked to her. Sitting under Burnett's large oil portrait, which showed him with a thin Howard Hughes mustache, hair combed back, shirt collar open, Whitney Burnett attempted for the first time to explain—obviously to herself as well as to me—how her relationship with him differed from the one he had with Marjorie for so many years.

"After we got married, the first thing he proposed was to take me to the track with him at Santa Anita. There was a horse he wanted to buy in a claiming race. And I said, 'And what if we bought a house instead?' This is what we did, we found and bought one on top of a hill in Northridge, way out in the San Fernando Valley. But you see, Marjorie would never have talked to him this way. She never said no, especially if it meant going out for fun. They had this enormous pile of a house in Glendale, but this was mostly for Bill's parents. Otherwise, they were gypsies. Bill never cared for anything but his dogs. He liked to gamble, but that life would never have been for me.

"When they divorced, Marjorie got the kennel in Arcadia; Bill got the house in Glendale, but there was only his mother left, and it was way too big. She talked us into selling it, and she settled in a nice hotel for the rest of her life. She was a wonderful woman, very smart. When he moved to California, Bill soon brought his parents, and they never had to work a day in their life. He supported them, and Marjorie's folks as well. As her mother loved entertaining, it was non-stop parties at their place. Bill told me that one evening, on a Fourth of July, he stayed up all night to finish a book. There were nearly a hundred and fifty people milling about in the house, drinking heavily. Finally, he left and got himself a room some place. You see, Marjorie and I differed in just about everything, physically as well as temperamentally. I never liked socializing, bridge nights or other parties bore me. I never liked having people over, except a few friends, quietly. So, this was a big change for Bill, but after a while he got to like his home as well. Nothing mattered any longer except his books, his children, and me. This happened as soon as we bought our house on Stradella, in Bel-Air. It was built in the English style, bricks and peaked roofs. David Huntington had it built this way—he was heir to the Huntington fortune in Pasadena, railroad and real estate money—and truth to tell, this was more his taste than Bill's, or even mine. But Bill never cared for things like this. He never spent anything on himself, except for books and jazz records, which he loved. On the other hand, he never refused anything to his wife or children.

"We had more than half an acre, mostly steep. The view was stunning. At this time, 1946, you could see all the way through downtown, City Hall, and Santa Monica. Smog was not so bad then. We lost everything in the [1961] Bel-Air fire. It happened suddenly. At 11 a.m., everybody was on the run, cars going every which way. When we decided to leave, we just grabbed what clothes we could, the five dogs and two kids and we ran down the hill all the way to Sunset. We went back in the evening. It was strange, some houses were absolutely intact, untouched, others completely destroyed. Walking up Bellagio, we started hoping. But our home was burned down, there were only the two chimneys left. I never went back, but I heard that on the lot, Marlo Thomas' father had a very modern house built, all white, for her and Phil Donahue. I don't know if they are still there.

"We had invested a bit in antiques—that was my thing—and of course, even with the insurance, the money never makes up for the loss. Bill only regretted his library—he had over five hundred books in there—and his jazz records. Other than that, he never cared for possessions. Unlike me. And the funny thing was, he got to be even more homebound than I was. In the fifties, Rank made him an offer to go to England and write a script there. At the time it was just us, the children were gone. We could have gone, and I wanted it badly. I think this is the only thing he ever refused me. He felt good at home, he said you'd have to be crazy to risk the discomfort of travel, when you had a house like we had on Stradella. He never went anywhere. He traveled in his mind, through books. Myself, I never ever went further than San Francisco or Catalina!

"Bill was always in good health. He only started to have problems with his sight in his last year, when you knew him. And I must say it irritated him a great deal. And he had reason to be depressed, as reading was his life, as much as writing. He still wrote. He wrote to the end. He had one of those contraptions, like an enormous magnifying lens, above his typewriter. It was always something to watch him write a story or a novel. He took a long time mulling about it, sometimes up to three years, but when he was ready he wrote very fast. It was all first draft, never a typo. And he never revised, never edited. He took enormous pride in that. Except for his first years, he never had an editor at any of his publishers who asked him to rewrite. He sent the thing out, and that was it.

"The day he turned down the big bowl of chocolate ice-cream he always gobbled down in the middle of the night [he worked at night], I knew something was wrong. If he knew anything, he never let on. He always hated doctors and the sight of hospitals. He went only once, for a benign sinus condition, and he never came back alive. They did a procedure on him and he had a heart attack. Three packs of cigarettes a day mustn't have helped, mind you.

"We had a very solid marriage, and I appreciate how lucky I was because when I worked in the studios, before the war, I had seen what went on there, especially with secretaries. My best friend worked at Metro, and for many months her assignment had been to go see Dashiell Hammett at the Beverly Wilshire penthouse he rented. On the first day, he laid on a sofa, not saying anything. She waited four hours like this. Then he told her to come back the next day. This went on for three months, exactly the same routine. And one day he told her to be ready the next day because they were going to work in earnest. Of course, they had an affair. They were all the same. Not Bill, though. For one thing, he would never have dictated anything! As for women, he had a thing once for Zizi Jeanmaire, he was so crazy about her I started to get jealous. But this remained fantasy, in his head—like his way of traveling through his books."

Here, Whitney twirls one of her heavy bracelets around her wrist, thinking. There is a short silence. Then, as if it occured to her for the first time, and as if she had not said what she just said: "Of course, Bill was very private. You could never really tell with him, what he thought of things, or people. But many writers are like this. They express themselves through their novels, not in life."

Listening to her thinking aloud, trying to sort out her feelings, I kept seeing Burnett in the kitchen, the moles on his chin, his short-sleeved shirts or polo pull-overs, his total lack of affectation. And his sense of self-worth, which was almost rueful. "I always had a plan, a design. I wanted to do with the modern American scene what Balzac had done with nineteenth-century France. A social panorama. Trouble is, I seem to have been the only one thinking this because nobody noticed!"

There was no bitterness in his words, only wistfulness, and a bit of sadness. His books had always given him a good life, he said, so he could not complain. It was also a marvel to hear him speak of French writers with the familiarity you'd discuss contemporary authors. He was very set in his tastes. He didn't like Celine, for instance—not at all. But he would mention a forgotten writer like Eugene Dabit, and his *Hôtel du Nord*, and then, as if stating the obvious: "The novel was great, not the picture. The picture was awful." He admired Maupassant, Arthur Conan Doyle, and Simenon above all else, but spoke even more often of Prosper Mérimée, who, except as the author of *Carmen*, is forgotten today, even in his own country. Burnett kept coming back to him: "I discovered Mérimée when I was twenty years old. Up till then, I had absolutely no taste in my reading, I read everything and anything. But with Mérimée, I started to understand what was good and what was trash. I read everything I could find by him, and I re-read him all my life. Some of his stuff, you'd think it was written yesterday."

He even wrote a screenplay based on a Mérimée story, *Vendetta*, an ill-fated venture if there ever was one. "It was for Hughes, who had all the wrong people on it, starting with himself. He wanted a vehicle for Faith Domergue. Both Max Ophüls and Preston Sturges were fired as directors on the first version. Then Stu Heisler took over, but he got sick. Oh, it was a mess!"[5]

Maybe it was this foundation, his profound fondness for European literature, that set him apart and allowed him to remain for so long, if not a stranger in paradise, at least indifferent to Hollywood.

His wife told me that over time, Burnett had come to take Hollywood as a given. He thought its windfalls would go on forever.

"Jack Warner was very fond of Bill," she said, "and I think it went both

---

5 Preston Sturges was actually going to produce the film for his and Hughes' independent company. He hired Ophüls, and a week later Hughes told him to "get rid of that man." The film was originally called *Columba*, after Mérimée's title.

ways. He could have remained at Warner for twenty years if he had wanted. But somehow, somebody talked him into moving to Metro, where he sat there for nearly two years, doing nothing. Producers kept saying, 'What are you griping about? You get paid, don't you? Come on, come with us to the track.' So, he took a few jobs with Hughes at RKO, and then went back to Warner—but it was not the same then. He said it was like going to work in a ghost town. Everyone was gone. Only Horace was there from the good days. Horace McCoy, whom we saw socially from time to time. Bill liked him. Then there was John Sturges; he worked [not always credited] on *Sergeants 3*, *The Great Escape*, and *Ice Station Zebra*. That was his last film. Of course, he wrote on a ton of TV series, but he hated it. He hates writing in committees. He liked to be left alone when he wrote something. And then even publishing books became difficult. Editors and publishers started to change. He sometimes wrote paperback originals. Or books under another name. Some of these books were as good as the old ones, but there was no demand any more. It's funny—because I always associate this with the fire. It is true that after we lost the house things were not the same for Bill. You are popular and in demand for years, and suddenly the studios do something else, at least not the kind of stories Bill was associated with. One day you're on top of the hill, like we were in Bel-Air. The next morning. . . He never complained, and we were never in dire straits, but no longer on top of the hill, either."

The author of 33 books, including the celebrated *Little Caesar* and others that have been turned into almost-perfect crime pictures, like John Huston's *The Asphalt Jungle*, W. R. Burnett, even when going downhill, would never have believed that one day his work would practically disappear, and would only abide in a few people's memories, his name only rated in the book collectors' market. When he died in 1982, and as late as 1992, only *High Sierra* and *Little Caesar* were still available in the country he had taken such great pains to depict in his work.

CHRONOLOGIES

NATHANAEL WEST

1903: Nathan Weinstein is born October 17 on the Upper East Side of Manhattan. He grows up in Harlem, goes to the DeWitt Clinton High School (Bronx, NY), then Brown University.

1926: Legally changes name to Nathanael West in August. Trip to Paris, October to January the following year.

1927: Starts working as assistant manager of the Kenmore Hotel, NYC.

1931: Publishes first book, *The Dream Life of Balso Snell*; contributes to *Contact*.

1933: Liveright publishes *Miss Lonelyhearts*, but immediately falls into bankruptcy. Novel is reissued by Harcourt, Brace & Company at the end of the year, but too late to ride on the original good notices. First trip to Hollywood. West works briefly as a junior writer at Columbia. Laid off.

1934: In June, Covici-Friede publishes *A Cool Million*.

1935: Due to failure of his latest novel, West goes to Hollywood in the spring, in search of work. Lives at the Parva-Sed Apta apartment building on Ivar Street. Difficult period.

1936: Employed in January by Republic studios at $200 a week. Stays until January 1938. Among produced titles he writes or collaborates on are

Ticket to Paradise, The President's Mystery, Gangs of New York, Rhythm in the Clouds, Born to be Wild, and *It Could Happen to You.*

1938: Returns to New York for *Good Hunting,* a play written with MGM screenwriter Joseph Schrank, opened at the Hudson Theatre on November 21. It closes after two performances. West returns to Hollywood, driving cross-country with George Milburn. Writes *Five Came Back* for RKO (Dalton Trumbo and Jerry Cady also credited). The John Farrow picture is an unexpectd success and will be remade many times.

1939: In May, Random House publishes *The Day of the Locust.* Less than 1,500 copies are sold, out of a first run of 3,000. Resumes screenwriting career. Burt Kelly gets West a job at Universal writing on *The Spirit of Culver* and *I Stole a Million.* Works with Boris Ingster on *Before the Fact* at RKO, which will become Alfred Hitchcock's *Suspicion.* Meets Eileen McKenney in the fall.

1940: Marries Eileen McKenney in April. Still at RKO, writes *Men Against the Sky* (a Richard Dix vehicle) and *Let's Make Music* (for Bob Crosby, brother of Bing). Polishes script of *Stranger on the Third Floor* for friend Boris Ingster, who directs the picture, starring Peter Lorre. On December 22, dies with his wife in a car crash outside of El Centro, California, the day after friend F. Scott Fitzgerald dies of cardiac arrest in Hollywood.

JOHN SANFORD

1904: Julian Lawrence Shapiro born May 31 in Harlem; attends DeWitt Clinton High School in Bronx, NY. After graduation, studies law.

1930–1931: Trip to Europe.

1933: The Dragon Press publishes first novel, *The Water Wheel.*

1935: Changes legal name to John Sanford. *The Old Man's Place* is published by Albert & Charles Boni. Leaves for Hollywood at the end of the year.

1936: Works briefly at Paramount as a contract writer, chiefly on an adaptation of Humphrey Cobb's WWI novel *Paths of Glory*, decades before the Kubrick picture.

1938: Works a few weeks on *The Shining Hour* for Joseph Mankiewicz at MGM. Dismissed. Joins American Communist Party. Marries MGM screenwriter Marguerite Roberts.

1939: Alfred A. Knopf publishes *Seveny Times Seven*, his third novel.

1941: Bogus collaboration with his wife on *Honky Tonk* (MGM, starring Clark Gable).

1943: Harcourt, Brace & Company publishes *The People from Heaven*.

1951: Marguerite Roberts blacklisted, stops working at MGM. Sanford self-publishes *A Man Without Shoes* at Marguerite's expense. Long trip to Europe.

1953: *The Land that Touches Mine* (Jonathan Cape/UK, Doubleday/U.S.)

1957: He and Roberts move to Montecito, near Santa Barbara, CA.

1964: *Every Island Fled Away* (W. W. Norton & Company).

1967: *The $300 Man* (Prentice-Hall).

1975: *A More Goodly Country: A personal history of America* (Horizon Press).

1976: *Adirondack Stories* (Capra Press).

1984: *The Winters of That Country* (Black Sparrow Press). *William Carlos Williams / John Sanford: A Correspondence* (Oyster Press).

1985: *The Color of the Air: Scenes from the Life of an American Jew*/Vol. 1 (Black Sparrow Press).

1986: *The Waters of Darkness: Scenes from the Life of an American Jew*/Vol. 2 (Black Sparrow Press).

1987: *A Very Good Land to Fall With: Scenes from the Life of an American Jew*/Vol. 3 (Black Sparrow Press). Writes part of a book on HUAC informant Martin Berkeley called *Judas and Inquiry*. Berkeley was the Hollywood screenwriter who gave up more than 150 names during HUAC inquiries, including Roberts' and Sanford's.

1989: *A Walk in the Fire: Scenes from the Life of an American Jew*/Vol. 4 (Black Sparrow Press). Marguerite Roberts dies.

1991: *The Season, It Was Winter: Scenes from the Life of an American Jew*/Vol. 5 (Black Sparrow Press).

1993: *Maggie: A Love Story* (Barricade Books).

1994: *The View from Mt. Morris: A Harlem Boyhood* (Barricade Books).

1995: *We Have a Little Sister, Marguerite: The Midwest Years* (Capra Press).

2003: *A Palace of Silver: A Memoir of Maggie Roberts* (Capra Press). Dies on March 5, at 98.

MARGUERITE ROBERTS

1905: Marguerite A. Roberts is born September 21 in Nebraska.

1927: Begins work at Fox as secretary to production chief Winfield Sheehan.

1930-1932: Continues secretarial work at Fox, then got a job in the reading department, then became a screenwriter.

1933: Co-scripts the bawdy if sometimes tedious *Sailor's Luck* for Raoul Walsh, and *Jimmy and Sally* (with Claire Trevor).

1935: *The Last Outpost* (with Cary Grant, Claude Rains; Louis Gasnier, director).

1936: Signed by Paramount as a contract writer. *Florida Special* (with Sally Eilers), *Forgotten Faces* (with Herbert Marshall; E. A. Dupont, director), *Hollywood Boulevard* (with Robert Cummings, Marsha Hunt; Robert Florey, director).

1940: Starts long stint at MGM. *Escape* (with Robert Taylor, Norma Shearer; Mervyn LeRoy, director).

1941: *Ziegfeld Girl* (with James Stewart, Judy Garland; Robert Z. Leonard and Busby Berkeley, directors), *Honky Tonk* (with Clark Gable, Lana Turner; Jack Conway, director).

1942: *Somewhere I'll Find You* (with Clark Gable, Lana Turner; Wesley Ruggles, director).

1944: *Dragon Seed* (with Katharine Hepburn and Walter Huston; Jack Conway, director).

1947: *The Sea of Grass* (with Katharine Hepburn, Spencer Tracy; Elia Kazan, director), *Desire Me* (with Greer Garson, Robert Mitchum; George Cukor/Melvyn LeRoy/Jack Conway, directors), *If Winter Comes* (with Walter Pidgeon, Deborah Kerr; Victor Saville, director).

1949: *The Bribe* (with Robert Taylor, Ava Gardner; Robert Z. Leonard, director), *Ambush* (with Robert Taylor, Arlene Dahl; Sam Wood, director).

1951: *Soldiers Three* (with Stewart Granger; Tay Garnett, director). In April, summoned to appear before HUAC. Refuses to answer. MGM lets her go, despite contractual obligation to pay her regardless.

1952: *My Man and I* (with Ricardo Montalban, Shelley Winters; William Wellman, director). Co-scripted by John Fante; Roberts' credit does not appear due to blacklisting.

1961: Signs contract with Columbia.

1963: *Rampage* (with Robert Mitchum, Elsa Martinelli; Phil Karlson, director).

1965: *Love Has Many Faces* (with Lana Turner, Cliff Robertson; Alexander Singer, director).

1968: Works at Paramount. *5 Card Stud* (with Robert Mitchum, Dean Martin; Henry Hathaway, director).

1969: *True Grit* (with John Wayne; Henry Hathaway, director).

1971: At Universal. *Shoot Out* (with Gregory Peck; Henry Hathaway, director), *Red Sky at Morning* (with Richard Thomas, Claire Bloom; James Goldstone, director).

1989: Dies of cancer, February 17.

ROBERT TASKER

1903: Born November 13 in Albee, South Dakota. Raised in Canada, finished high school in Portland, Oregon.

1922: Moves to Northern California.

1924: Arrested for armed robbery of a dance hall in Oakland, May 24. Sentence: five years to life, incarcerated at San Quentin in October.

1927: Debut story ("The First Day") published in March issue of *The American Mercury*. "A Man is Hanged" follows soon after.

1928: Prison novel *Grimhaven* is published by Knopf

1929: December 8 leaves San Quentin on parole. Employed in Hollywood by fan magazine *Photoplay*. Terms of release forbid him to write about his criminal career or prison life for two years or to associate with criminals.

1930: Helps Frances Marion write *The Big House*. In 1931, Marion wins Oscar® for Writing (Best Screenplay).

1931: In January, plays bit-part in Rowland Brown's *Quick Millions* in which he "kills" George Raft and is nabbed by the police—in effect, breaking his parole. Knopf turns down his second novel. Starts screenwriting career. Marries Lucille Morrison, heiress to Fletcher's Castoria laxative fortune.

1932: Under contract at RKO. Collaborates with Rowland Brown on *Hell's Highway*. Also writes with Samuel Ornitz on *Secrets of the French Police* and *The Great Jasper*.

1933: At Paramount, works uncredited with John Bright on *Luxury Liner* (Lothar Mendes, director).

1934: Divorces Lucille Morrison.

1936: *The Accusing Finger* (James Hogan, director).

1937: Works on *San Quentin* with John Bright at Warner (uncredited). Hired along with Bright by B. P. Schulberg. *John Meade's Woman* (with Edward Arnold; Richard Wallace, director).

1939: Works with Bright on *Back Door to Heaven* (William K. Howard, director).

1942: Went to Mexico to do nominal work for Nelson Rockefeller's goodwill program. Resides in Mexico City.

1944: Writes adaptations of French classics *La Dame aux Camélias* and *Les Misérables*. Dies on December 7 at 41 years of age. Probable cause: suicide.

JOHN BRIGHT

1908: John Milton Bright born January 1 in Baltimore. Raised in Lake Forest and Chicago. Credits father, a clerk and an amputee, for his early radicalism. Although conventional in every other way, father was a fierce opponent of racism.

1921-1928: Works as go-fer and various jobs at the *Chicago Daily News*. Claimed to have been Ben Hecht's office boy. Travels to Europe in 1928 with a friend.

1929: Fired from the *Daily News*. Employed as soda jerk in Chicago drugstore owned by Jakob Glasmon (born Jakobek Glasmann) who underwrites Bright's book on the mayor, *Hizzoner Big Bill Thompson: An Idyll of Chicago*. Gets advance to write a novel on Chicago gangsters, *Beer and Blood*, and receives ticket to Hollywood from Rufus LeMaire. Glasmon burns down drugstore for insurance money and throws in his lot with Bright. They arrive in Los Angeles, via the Panama Canal, October 29, 1929.

1930: Through LeMaire, they sell *Beer and Blood* to Zanuck in galley form and are hired to write a toned-down adaptation, which becomes *The Public Enemy* (dir. William Wellman). Bright and Glasmon put under contract by Warner Bros. Pair shares nomination for Best Original Story at Academy Awards in 1932.

1931: *Beer and Blood* published (according to Bright in a 1988 interview) in a bowdlerized version.

1931-1932: Bright and Glasmon quickly become studio's hot team, writing *Smart Money* (Alfred E. Green, director), *Blonde Crazy* (Roy Del Ruth, director), *Taxi* (Roy Del Ruth). Bright claims authorship of three Joan Blondell vehicles, *Three on a Match* (Mervyn LeRoy, director), *Union Depot* (Alfred E. Green, director) and *Convention City* (Archie Mayo, director). Also writes George Raft sketch for *If I Had a Million*. End of year, Bright quarrels with Zanuck and is fired.

1933: At Paramount, co-writes *She Done Him Wrong* for Mae West (Lowell Sherman, director). Becomes one of the 10 founders of the fledging Screen Writers Guild.

1934: Claims co-credit for *Crimson Romance*, produced by Nat Levine's Mascot Pictures. Works on Upton Sinclair's California gubernatorial campaign.

1936: Becomes one of four original members of the Hollywood American Communist Party cell. Partners with Robert Tasker, shares with him writing credit on *Girl of the Ozarks*. Writes *The Accusing Finger* (James Hogan, director) with Tasker at Paramount.

1937: With Tasker, writes on *San Quentin* (Lloyd Bacon, director) at Warner Bros. They also work for producer B. P. Schulberg on *John Meade's Woman* (Richard Wallace, director).

1939: *Back Door to Heaven* with Robert Tasker (William K. Howard, director).

1942: With two others, writes George Raft vehicle, *Broadway* (William A. Seiter, director), at Universal. Also, with Lynn Riggs, from a story by Arthur Conan Doyle, gets credit on *Sherlock Holmes and the Voice of Terror* (John Rawlins, director) for same studio.

1944: Joins Coast Guard in New York.

1948: Co-writes *Close-Up* (Jack Donohue) for independent producer Harry Brandt. Also co-credit on *I Walk Alone* (Byron Haskin, director) for producer Hal Wallis at Paramount.

1951: Adapts Tom Lea's *The Brave Bulls* for Robert Rossen at Columbia. Officially put on the blacklist.

1952-1959: Lives in Mexico with his activist wife Josefina Fierro ("My best wife," he used to say. He had four.) Writes screenplays under pseudonym, among those produced, an adaptation of B. Traven's *The Rebellion of the Hanged* (Alfredo B. Crevenna, director) and *Canasta de cuentos mexicanos*, produced by José Kohn. Helped by actor Pedro Armendáriz.

1960: Returns to United States.

1969: Becomes story editor and advisor to Bill Cosby and his production company for 18 months. Recommends to Cosby's partner Bruce Campbell that he buy the rights to Dalton Trumbo's novel *Johnny Got His Gun*, which Trumbo will eventually adapt and direct in 1971.

1989: Dies at Kaiser Hospital in Panorama City, September 14, at 81 years of age.

ROWLAND BROWN

1900: Chauncey Rowland Brown is born in Cleveland, Ohio, November 6. Raised in Canton, where father Samuel Gilson Brown is a contractor.

1917: At 16, attempts to enlist in Army for WWI service and is rejected.

1918: Serves one week of active duty in November at the Great Lakes Naval Training Station.

1919-1920: Attends art school in Detroit.

1921: Marries Rhea Widrig, a commercial illustrator.

1922: Makes first trip to Los Angeles to visit wife's family.

1925: Returns to Los Angeles to join his elder sister. Begins getting odd jobs at studios. Works as ditch digger, then a gagman for Reginald Denny. Also sells cars.

1929: Under contract at Universal for nine months. First credit on Hoot Gibson Western *Points West* (Arthur Rosson, director).

1930: Sells *A Handful of Clouds* to Zanuck at Warner Bros.; it becomes *The Doorway to Hell* (with Lew Ayres and James Cagney; Archie Mayo, director).

1931: While working as a gagman at Fox, writes and directs *Quick Millions* (with Spencer Tracy, Sally Eilers, George Raft). Gets bonus, takes a trip to Paris.

1932: Under contract to Universal. Loaned to RKO and David Selznick to write (with Gene Fowler) *What Price Hollywood* (with Lowell Sherman, Constance Bennett; George Cukor, director). Also writes *State's Attorney* for Selznick and John Barrymore. Quarrels with Selznick and walks away, replaced by George Archainbaud. With Samuel Ornitz and Robert Tasker, writes *Hell's Highway*, which he also directs. Quarrels with RKO and refuses to shoot added scenes he finds "phony." John Cromwell replaces him.

1933: Zanuck, now at 20th Century Pictures, calls on Brown to write and direct a picture, as he has a six-picture slate and only six months to make them. *Blood Money* stars George Bancroft, Frances Dee, and introduces Judith Anderson.

1934: In London to direct *The Scarlet Pimpernel* for Korda. Quits after one week. Sells screen stories to American studios making quota films in England, among them *Leave It to Blanche* and *Widow's Might*.

1935: Works for Thalberg, now an independent producer at MGM. Scheduled to direct *Stealing Through Life*, based on ex-con Ernest Granville Booth's prison memoir; nothing comes of it.

1936: Still at MGM, writes and directs *The Devil Is a Sissy*. Fired after three weeks. The picture is completed by W. S. Van Dyke. Learning the studio will give Van Dyke sole credit, Brown assaults executive Benny Thau (with a telephone book or a script, depending on the storyteller).

1938: Brown's story *Angels with Dirty Faces* is made at Warner, directed by Michael Curtiz. It is nominated for a 1939 Academy Award for Best Writing (Original Story).

1939: Buys screen rights to Edward Anderson's *Thieves Like Us*. Adapts it to direct himself, with Joel McCrea starring. Once this falls through, sells rights and script to RKO for $10,000. Sells original story, *The Lady's from Kentucky* to Paramount. Film made with George Raft and directed by Alexander Hall.

1940: Marries Marie ("Sugar") Helis, daughter of Greek immigrant-turned-multi-millionaire oilman William George Helis. Writes for Zanuck at 20th Century–Fox on *Johnny Apollo* (with Tyrone Power).

1942: In New York, writes and produces play *Johnny 2x4*, featuring Barry Sullivan and Lauren Bacall in their first starring roles. Has affair with Karen Van Ryn, who plays "Maxine" and is also Bacall's understudy. Play runs only eight weeks, hurt by an especially bad review from the *Times*' Brooks Atkinson.

1943: Brings a pregnant Van Rhyn back to Hollywood. Divorces Marie Helis.

1946: Writes original story for *Nocturne*, a George Raft vehicle for RKO directed by Edwin L. Marin.

1950: *The Nevadan* (Gordon Douglas, director), a Randolph Scott Western for Ranown, Randolph Scott and Harry Joe Brown's production company.

1952: Sells original story of *Kansas City Confidential* to independent producer Eddie Small. Phil Karlson directs.

1963: Dies of a stroke in Costa Mesa, California, May 6.

SAM BROWN

1904: Samuel Gilson Brown born in Canton, Ohio, April 13.

1919: Studies at Colorado School of Mines, Golden, CO.

1925: Joins brother Rowland in Los Angeles. Works as propman around the studios before becoming mainstay at Fox. Works principally for Tom Mix and F. W. Murnau (first on *Sunrise*, then *4 Devils*).

1929-1930: In Tahiti with Murnau and producer Robert Flaherty working on *Tabu*. With his brother, attempts to secure distribution for the film through their connection to Zanuck. Paramount eventually will distribute *Tabu*.

1934: Writes *Dinky* with Frank Fenton and John Fante. Joins brother in London to help with *The Scarlet Pimpernel*. Fante and Fenton sell *Dinky* to Warner, earning Sam Brown his first story credit. Stays in England after brother leaves. Meets furture wife Nora. Works in Europe shooting newsreels and transparency plates.

1937: Claims screenplay for MGM's *Navy Blue and Gold*, although Hungarian writer George Bruce has sole credit (Sam Wood, director). Writes script for *Boys of the Street* at Monogram (William Nigh, director).

1944 -___: Effectively blacklisted in Hollywood, but not for political reasons. Works as a cutter, first at Technicolor, Inc., then at Columbia. Ends his professional career as an editor of trailers for National Screen Service (NSS).

1991: Dies of pneumonia on September 10 at the hospital of the Motion Picture Home in Woodland Hills, California.

NIVEN BUSCH

1903: Born in New York City, April 26. His father becomes treasurer to Lewis J. Selznick's production company after his own bank fails. Befriends Selznick's two boys, David and Myron.

1921: Begins at Princeton.

1924: Leaves Princeton. Bankruptcy of father's law firm ends tuition, forces him to drop out.

1924-1931: Journalist in New York City. Cinema reviewer for *Time*, sportswriter at the *New Yorker*. Leaves for Hollywood in November with prospective job at Warner Bros.

1928: Marries Sonia Alexandra Frey (divorced in 1934).

1932: Writes on *The Crowd Roars* (Howard Hawks, director), *Alias the Doctor* (Michael Curtiz, Lloyd Bacon (uncredited), director), *Scarlet Dawn* (William Dieterle, director) and *Miss Pinkerton* (Lloyd Bacon, director).

1933: Writes *College Coach* (William Wellman, director).

1934: Adapts Sinclair Lewis' *Babbitt* for First National Pictures. Mary McCall Jr. writes final screenplay (William Keighley, director). With Tom Reed, writes screenplay for *The Man with Two Faces* (Archie Mayo, director) from the play *The Dark Tower* by George S. Kaufman and Alexander Woollcott, starring E. G. Robinson and Mary Astor. Also collaborates on *He Was Her Man* (Lloyd Bacon, director) and *The Big Shakedown* (John

Francis Dillon, director). Laid off at the end of year.

1935: Mostly jobless. Works, uncredited, on *3 Kids and a Queen* (Edward Ludwig, director) at Universal and *Lady Tubbs* (Alan Crosland, director).

1936: Marries Phyllis Cooper, "Los Angeles Society Girl" (*L. A. Times*) in January.

1937: His story on the Chicago fire, *In Old Chicago*, is adapted by Lamar Trotti at 20th Century–Fox, (with Tyrone Power; Henry King, director). Big success; nominated for a 1938 Best Writing (Original Story) Oscar®.

1939: Back at Warner, co-writes *Off the Record* (James Flood, director), a Joan Blondell–Pat O'Brien picture. Also on *Angels Wash Their Faces* (Ray Enright, director), an attempt to capitalize on success of *Angels with Dirty Faces*.

1940: Shares credit with Jo Swerling on Sam Goldwyn's production *The Westerner*. Four others wrote on it, including W. R. Burnett, Dudley Nichols and Lillian Hellman. Divorces Cooper.

1941: Becomes Goldwyn's story editor. Works unofficially on *The Little Foxes* (William Wyler, director). Sells his story on *Belle Starr* to 20th Century–Fox, made by Irving Cummings and scripted by Lamar Trotti (starring Gene Tierney and Randolph Scott.) William Morrow and Company publishes his first novel, *The Carrington Incident*.

1942: Marries Goldwyn contract actress Teresa Wright.

1944: Publishes *Duel in the Sun* (Morrow). RKO buys it, has Oliver H. P. Garrett adapt it for John Wayne, with Teresa Wright for the female lead. When RKO Chief Charles Koerner instead goes to Selznick for Jennifer Jones, Busch rewrites the script—not to Selznick's satisfaction. RKO in November sells *Duel in the Sun* package to Selznick's Vanguard Films, Inc. The picture was released in 1946 starring Jones and Gregory Peck, and was directed by King Vidor. Appleton-Century publishes his novel *They Dream of Home*.

1945: Adapts friend James M. Cain's *The Postman Always Rings Twice* for MGM (with John Garfield and Lana Turner; Tay Garnett, director).

1946: *Till the End of Time*, from his 1944 novel *They Dream of Home*, is adapted by Allen Rivkin (with Guy Madison, Dorothy McGuire, Robert Mitchum; Edward Dmytryk, director). Harper & Brothers publishes his novel *Day of the Conquerors*. Starts his own independent production company, Hemisphere Films, Inc., with Teresa Wright and Milton Sperling.

1947: Through Hemisphere, produces and co-writes period thriller *Moss Rose* (Gregory Ratoff, director) and psychological Western *Pursued* (Robert Mitchum, Teresa Wright; Raoul Walsh, director).

1948: The Dial Press publishes his Western novel *The Furies*.

1950: Anthony Mann directs *The Furies* for Hal Wallis at Paramount (scripted by Charles Schnee, starring Barbara Stanwyck, Wendell Corey and Walter Huston). Busch writes and produces *The Capture* for his new company, Showtime Properties, Inc. (with Lew Ayres and Teresa Wright; John Sturges, director). Distributed through RKO.

1951: With Martin Rackin, from his own story, writes *Distant Drums* for Warner (with Gary Cooper; Raoul Walsh, director). Leaves Hollywood to raise cattle on a ranch in Northern California—an effort, he said, to save his marriage.

1952: Divorces Teresa Wright.

1953: Co-writes *The Man from Alamo* for Budd Boetticher at Universal. *The Moonlighter* (with Barbara Stanwyck, Fred MacMurray, Ward Bond; Roy Rowland, director) is based on his ranching experiences.

1955: Writes script of *The Treasure of Pancho Villa* for producer Edmund Grainger Productions. Filmed in Mexico (with Shelley Winters, Gilbert Roland; George Sherman, director). Simon & Schuster publishes his novel *The Actor*.

1956: Marries Carmencita Baker (divorced in 1968). For the next two decades, while still ranching, continues to publish novels: *California Street: A Novel* (1959), *The San Franciscans* (1962), *The Gentleman from California* (1965), *The Takeover* (1973).

1974: Marries Suzanne de Sanz.

1980: Moves to San Francisco. Simon & Schuster publishes *Continent's Edge*.

1989: Random House publishes final Niven Busch novel, *The Titan Game*.

1991: Dies of congestive heart failure on August 25 at the age of 88.

JAMES M. CAIN

1892: James Mallahan Cain is born July 1 in Annapolis, Maryland.

1903: Cain family settles in Chestertown, Maryland, where his father is principal at Washington College, a private liberal arts college.

1910: Graduates from Washington College at 18-years old.

1910-1915: Series of random jobs. Reporter for the *Baltimore American*, then *The Baltimore Sun*.

1916: Drafted by U.S. Army; rank of private, mustered into the 70th Infantry Division. Works for military newspaper *The Lorraine Cross*. Brother dies in a plane crash over enemy lines.

1919: Returns to Baltimore, reclaims previous job at *The Sun*.

1920: Marries Mary Rebekah Clough.

1922: Produces articles for *The Nation* and *Atlantic Monthly*. Meets H. L. Mencken.

1923: First novel fails, decides to change career. Teaches journalism at St. John's College, Annapolis, Maryland.

1924: Places several pieces in Mencken's *The American Mercury*. Separates from wife. Moves to New York, hired by Walter Lippmann at the *New York World*.

1926: First play produced, *Crashing the Pearly Gates*. Crashes.

1927: Divorces Clough, marries Elina Sjöstedt Tyszecka, a Finn with two young children.

1928: First story published in *The American Mercury*, "Pastorale."

1930: Knopf publishes *Our Government*, a collection of articles and editorials.

1931: Loses job at the *New York World*. From February–September, works as managing editor at the *New Yorker*. Arrives Hollywood in November, with a tryout contract at Paramount.

1932-33: Briefly employed at Columbia. Publishes "The Baby in the Icebox" in *The American Mercury*, which sells to Paramount and is released in '34 as *She Made Her Bed* (with Richard Arlen, Sally Eilers; Ralph Murphy, director).

1933: Starts writing editorials for the Hearst newspaper syndicate.

1934: Knopf publishes *The Postman Always Rings Twice*. Enormous success. Employed at MGM.

1935: Stops writing for Hearst. Employed at Paramount, loaned to Warner, writes five weeks on a Paul Muni picture, *Dr. Socrates*, directed by William Dieterle.

1936: "Double Indemnity" is published in *Liberty* magazine. Adapts *Postman* for the stage. The play runs 72 days on Broadway.

1937: Knopf publishes *Serenade*.

1938: Additional dialogue on *Algiers* (John Cromwell, director) for producer Walter Wanger and United Artists. *Algiers* was a remake of Julien Duvivier's *Pépé le Moko*. Story "Two Can Sing" published in *American Magazine*. Will be made into two movies at 20th Century–Fox: 1939's *Wife, Husband and Friend* (Gregory Ratoff, director), and, ten years later, *Everybody Does It* (Edmund Goulding). Writes another play, called *7-11*. A flop. Employed at MGM.

1939: Sells unpublished novella "The Modern Cinderella" to Universal, made as *When Tomorrow Comes* (with Charles Boyer, Irene Dunne; director John M. Stahl). Remade in 1957 as *Interlude* (with June Allyson, Rossano Brazzi; Douglas Sirk, director).

1940: "Money and the Woman" published in *Liberty* magazine. Sold to Warner, turned into film of the same title (William K. Howard, director). Works at Universal. Separates from wife Elina.

1941: Five weeks on *The Shanghai Gesture* (Joseph von Sternberg, director) for producer Arnold Pressburger. Knopf publishes novel *Mildred Pierce*. Big Success. Undergoes operations for ulcers and gallstones.

1942: Knopf publishes *Love's Lovely Counterfeit*.

1943: Knopf publishes *Three of a Kind*, a collection of Cain's most succesful stories, "Double Indemnity," "Career in C Major," and "Money and the Woman" (here retitled "The Embezzler"). Works three weeks on *Gypsy Wildcat* (Roy William Neill, director), a Maria Montez vehicle for Universal, and seven weeks on a remake of *The Bridge of San Luis Rey* for United Artists.

1944: Paramount releases *Double Indemnity*, co-written by Billy Wilder and Raymond Chandler, directed by Wilder. Huge success. Spawns similarly themed films. Script nominated for Oscar®. Cain marries Aileen Pringle, an actress from the silents and an old friend of H. L. Mencken.

1945: Warner releases *Mildred Pierce*, produced by Jerry Wald, starring Joan Crawford. Huge success for everyone involved. Cain employed at MGM and Paramount. Warner buys rights to Cain's 1937 novel *Serenade*.

1946: Employed at RKO for five months. MGM releases *The Postman Always Rings Twice* (Tay Garnett, director). Knopf publishes *Past All Dishonor*, a Civil War novel. Works a few weeks on the script for *Out of the Past* at RKO.

1947: Knopf publishes *The Butterfly*. Cain divorces Pringle, marries ex-opera singer Florence Macbeth. Avon publishes *Sinful Woman* as a paperback original. Jerry Wald plans to produce movie version of *Serenade*, with Ann Sheridan and Dennis Morgan. Production aborts, sabotaged by director Michael Curtiz.

1948: Knopf publishes *The Moth*. Cain leaves Hollywood for good and settles in University Park, Hyattsville, Maryland, on outskirts of Washington, D.C.

1950: Avon publishes *Jealous Woman*, a paperback original.

1951: Avon publishes *The Root of His Evil*, a paperback original.

1953: Knopf publishes *Galatea*. Never adapted, strangely.

1956: Independent producer Benedict Bogeaus releases *Slightly Scarlet* (with Rhonda Fleming, Arlene Dahl, John Payne; Allan Dwan, director), adapted from Cain's *Love's Lovely Counterfeit*.

1962: The Dial Press publishes *Mignon*, a New Orleans novel.

1965: The Dial Press publishes *The Magician's Wife*.

1966: Death of wife Florence.

1976: Mason/Charter publishes *The Institute*.

1977: Dies on October 27 in Hyattsville at the age of 85.

2012: *The Cocktail Waitress*, an unfinished Cain manuscript, is pieced together by editor and publisher Charles Ardai and released in hardcover by Hard Case Crime.

A. I. BEZZERIDES

1908: Albert Issok Bezzerides born in Samsoun [Samsun], Turkey, August 9.

1910: Family moves to Fresno, California, where "Buzz" will grow up.

1925-1934: Drives his father's truck while still in high school. Wins a grant to study electrical engineering at U. C. Berkeley. Writes his first stories, published in the Boston Armenian newspaper *Hairenik*.

1934-1939: Works for the Los Angeles Department of Water and Power, then at Mitchell Cameras. Marries Yvonne Von Gorne. In 1938, Carrick & Evans publishes *Long Haul*, his first novel.

1940: *Long Haul* bought by Warner Bros., made as *They Drive by Night* (with George Raft, Humphrey Bogart, Ida Lupino; Raoul Walsh, director).

1941: Given tryout contract by Warner. Writes *Juke Girl*.

1942: Release of *Juke Girl* (Curtis Bernhardt, director). Henry Holt and Company publishes *There Is a Happy Land*.

1943: Works on *Action in the North Atlantic* (Lloyd Bacon, director) with three others, including W. R. Burnett. Writes on *Northern Pursuit* (Raoul Walsh), uncredited, along with Alvah Bessie and William Faulkner. Writes original story about convoy transporting explosives, which will remain unproduced. Moves to Paramount.

1945: Contract writer at Paramount.

1946: Writes on *Desert Fury* (uncredited) for Hal Wallis at Paramount.

1949: Charles Scribner's Sons publishes *Thieves' Market*. Sells rights to 20th Century–Fox. Hired to adapt his own book and write script as *Thieves' Highway* (with Richard Conte, Valentina Cortese; Jules Dassin, director). Writes a few scenes on *Slatterly's Hurricane* (André De Toth, director) at Fox. Writes on *Sirocco* (Curtis Bernhardt, director) at Warner.

1951: Adapts *On Dangerous Ground* (Nicholas Ray, director) for producer John Houseman at RKO.

1952: Scripts *Holiday for Sinners* for Houseman at MGM.

1953: Writes *Beneath the 12-Mile Reef* at Universal (with Robert Wagner, Gilbert Roland, Richard Boone; Robert D. Webb, director). Starts living with writer Silvia Richards. Adapts Walter Van Tilburg Clark's *The Track of the Cat* for Warner's William Wellman; 1954 film stars Robert Mitchum.

1955: Co-writes *A Bullet for Joey* (Lewis Allen, director) with Daniel Mainwaring for independent producer Sam Bischoff (United Artists). Adapts Mickey Spillane's *Kiss Me Deadly* for Robert Aldrich, also for UA.

1959: Adapts *The Angry Hills* for director Robert Aldrich, starring Robert Mitchum. Co-writes *The Jayhawkers!* (Melvin Frank, director) with Frank Fenton at Paramount.

1961: Writer on *The Barbara Stanwyck Show* (6 episodes).

1961-1962: Writer on *The Detectives* TV show (2 episodes).

1962: Writer on *77 Sunset Strip* TV show (2 episodes).

1963: Adapts, with Hugo Butler, Mickey Spillane's *Vengeance Is Mine* for Aldrich. Never produced. Writes one episode of *Bonanza*.

1965: Writes one episode of *The Virginian*. Creates pilot and bible for *The Big Valley*, long-running TV series (1965-1969) starring Barbara Stanwyck.

1968: Pressed for cash, Bezzerides is persuaded by Louis F. Edelman, producer of *The Big Valley*, to sell him his points for $100,000, a mistake that will rankle the writer to the end of his life.

1979: Scripts documentary *Faulkner: A Life on Paper* for PBS.

1996: Éditions Gallimard publishes *Le Marché aux voleurs*, French translation of *Thieves' Market*.

2001: Éditions Gallimard publishes *La longue route*, French translation of *Long Haul*.

2005: *The Long Haul of A. I. Bezzerides*, documentary by Fay Efrosini Lellios.

2005: *Buzz*, documentary by Spiro Taraviras.

2007: Dies January 1 at 98 years of age.

HORACE McCOY

1897: Born in Pegram, Tennessee, April 14

1917: Enlists and becomes a pilot. Fights in France for 18 months. Wounded and decorated by France (*Croix de Guerre* recipient).

1922: In Dallas, works as a sportswriter and a columnist at local newspapers.

1925: Active in The Dallas Little Theater as an actor.

1927: Sells first story to *Black Mask*, "*The Devil Man*".

1928-1931: Press agent for golf champion Walter Hagen.

1931: Goes to Hollywood with Oliver Hinsdell, head of The Dallas Little Theater, on the recommendation of MGM talent scout Ben Piazza. Joins the Metro "Charm School" with the likes of Clark Gable, Robert Young, and Robert Taylor. Turned away months later without a contract. H. N. Swanson hires him briefly at RKO as a writer and bit-player.

1933: Hired as a junior writer at Columbia. Writes story for *Dangerous Crossroads* (Lambert Hillyer, director) and works uncredited on a Tim McCoy Western, *Man of Action* (George Melford, director). Marries Helen Vinmont in November.

1934: Couple declares bankrupcy to avoid creditors. Moves to the Montecito apartments in Hollywood on Franklin Avenue. Sells Jerry Frost aviation stories to Harry O. Hoyt, who has a serial at Columbia, "The Eagle's Brood." Writes *They Shoot Horses, Don't They?* while at the Montecito.

1935: Simon & Schuster publishes *They Shoot Horses, Don't They?* in August. Walter Wanger puts him under contract. Works on *The Trail of the Lonesome Pine* (Henry Hathaway, director) and other pictures.

1936: Co-writes (with Kubec Glasmon and two others) *Parole!* at Universal (Lew Landers, director). Also, *Fatal Lady* (Edward Ludwig, director) for Walter Wanger at Paramount.

1937: Tries to set up adaptation of *Horses* with producer-director Dudley Murphy at Associated Artists, with Bette Davis attached. Deal falls through. British publisher Arthur Baker releases *No Pockets in a Shroud* in England, in bowdlerized version.

1938: Knopf publishes *I Should Have Stayed Home*. With William R. Lipman, writes *Dangerous to Know* (Robert Florey, director) at Paramount, starring Akim Tamiroff and Anna May Wong. Also *Hunted Men* (Louis King, director) and the story *King of the Newsboys* (Bernard Vorhaus, dirietor) for Republic.

1939: At Republic. *Persons in Hiding* (Louis King, director), *Undercover Doctor* (Louis King, director). Also, *Island of Lost Men* (Kurt Neumann, director) at Paramount, starring Anna May Wong and Broderick Crawford.

1940: At Paramount writes *Parole Fixer* and *Women Without Names* for director Robert Florey (the latter based on the play by ex-con Ernest Booth). Also *Queen of the Mob* (James P. Hogan, director).

1941: Still partnered with Lipman, writes *Texas Rangers Ride Again* (James P. Hogan, director) at Paramount. Adapts *Wild Geese Calling* (John Brahm, director) at 20th Century–Fox. Provides dialogue on *Western Union* (Fritz Lang, director). Co-writes *Texas* (with Glenn Ford, William Holden; George Marshall, director) at Columbia.

1942: Under contract to Warner Bros. (at $850 a week). Writes *Gentle-*

man Jim (with Errol Flynn; Raoul Walsh, director). Opts out of his contract when studio refuses his request to work at home. Writes comedy Western for RKO, *Valley of the Sun* (with Lucille Ball and James Craig; George Marshall, director).

1943: Co-writes *Appointment in Berlin* at Columbia (with George Sanders; Alfred E. Green, director). Story credit for *Flight for Freedom* (Lothar Mendes, director), and original screenplay for *There's Something About a Soldier* (with Evelyn Keyes, Tom Neal; Alfred E. Green, director).

1946: Tries to revive career as novelist by writing *Kiss Tomorrow Goodbye*.

1947: Learns of sudden popularity in France. With Lawrence Hazard, co-writes a "Wild Bill" Elliott Western for Republic, *The Fabulous Texan* (Edward Ludwig, director).

1948: Random House publishes *Kiss Tomorrow Goodbye*. Reviews are savage. Signet reissues McCoy's old titles in paperback, including thoroughly rewritten *No Pockets in a Shroud*, essentially the first American edition of the novel.

1950: *The Fireball* (Tay Garnett, director), a roller-skating vehicle for Mickey Rooney, from a story by Garnett. James Cagney's company produces *Kiss Tomorrow Goodbye* (Gordon Douglas, director).

1951: Sells *Scalpel* to Hal Wallis before writing it. Works on *The Lusty Men* (Nicholas Ray, director) for Jerry Wald at RKO. Writes *Scalpel*.

1952: Appleton-Century-Crofts publishes *Scalpel*. Robust sales. With Lillie Hayward, shares writing credit for *Bronco Buster* (Budd Boetticher, director) at Universal. Credited for dialogue on *The World in His Arms* (Raoul Walsh, director,) with a script by Borden Chase. Also, *Montana Belle* (Allan Dwan, director) for RKO. Writes original story for *The Turning Point* (William Dieterle, director) for Paramount. Warren Duff writes screenplay.

1953: *Bad for Each Other* (Irving Rapper) made from *Scalpel*, to which Hal Wallis had bought the movie rights before the book was written. McCoy sells *The Turning Point* in novel form to Éditions Gallimard *Série Noire*. Published posthumously in English years later as a Dell original paperback titled *Corruption City*.

1954: For RKO, works on *Dangerous Mission* (with Victor Mature, Piper Laurie, William Bendix; Louis King, director).

1955: Writes screenplay *Night Cry*, which he intends to direct himself and will star William Bendix. Signs deal for new novel, *Hard Rock Man*. Dies of heart attack December 15.

1969: Screenplay by James Poe and Robert E. Thompson for *They Shoot Horses, Don't They?* (with Jane Fonda, Michael Sarrazin, Gig Young; Sydney Pollack, director).

1974: Actor-director Jean-Pierre Mocky makes *Un linceul n'a pas de poches*, from McCoy's *No Pockets in a Shroud*. A very Frenchified version, with comic actors like Francis Blanche, Michel Galabru, Jean Carmet, and French noir regular Michel Constantin.

1995: Scott McGehee and David Siegel writer-directors of *Suture* and *The Deep End*, write a dusted-up version of McCoy's *Night Cry* for Sydney Pollack's company, intending it to be a feature film. The film was never made.

W. R. BURNETT

1899: Born in Springfield, Ohio, November 25. Family deeply involved in state and local politics. Burnett will attend Ohio State University.

1920: Marries Marjorie Louise Bartlow. Works as a statistician for the State of Ohio while trying to become a writer.

1927: Goes to Chicago alone to write seriously, working as night clerk in various hotels.

1929: The Dial Press publishes smash success *Little Caesar*. Travels to Tombstone, Arizona. Pushes on to Los Angeles.

1930: The Dial Press publishes *Iron Man* in January and *Saint Johnson*, his novel on Tombstone, AZ, and Wyatt Earp, at end of year. Works as well-paid consultant on gangster pictures, including *Scarface* (1932) for Howard Hughes. Wins O. Henry Award for his story "Dressing-up," published in November 1929 issue of *Harper's*.

1931: The Dial Press publishes *The Silver Eagle*. Burnett and John Lee Mahin write original screenplay of *The Beast of the City* for MGM (with Walter Huston, Jean Hersholt as the Capone-like "Beast."; Charles Brabin, director).

1932: Harper & Brothers publishes *The Giant Swing*, filmed by 20th Century–Fox in 1941 as *Dance Hall* (with Carole Landis, Cesar Romero; Irving Pichel, director).

1933: Harper & Brothers publishes *Dark Hazard*, adapted by Warner in early 1934 starring Edward G. Robinson (Alfred E. Green, director).

1934: Harper & Brothers publishes *Goodbye to the Past* and the historical novella *The Goodhues of Sinking Creek*.

1935: At Columbia, works briefly on *The Whole Town's Talking* (John Ford, director), based on his short story. At Warner, works on *Dr. Socrates* (with Paul Muni; William Dieterle, director), based on his story.

1936: Harper & Brothers publishes *King Cole*.

1938: Knopf publishes *The Dark Command*. No less than four writers turn it into a screenplay two years later at Republic, starring John Wayne and Claire Trevor, directed by Raoul Walsh.

1939: Dog-racing business tanks out; Burnett in dire financial straits.

1940: Knopf publishes *High Sierra*.

1941: Raoul Walsh makes *High Sierra* at Warner, scripted by John Huston, once intended for Paul Muni, but eventually starring Humphrey Bogart and Ida Lupino. Starts screenwriting in earnest: with Albert Maltz adapts for Paramount Graham Greene's *This Gun for Hire* (with Alan Ladd, Veronica Lake; Frank Tuttle, director). With Wells Root writes *The Getaway* (Edward Buzzell, director) for MGM.

1942: Knopf publishes *The Quick Brown Fox*. Works on war propaganda movie *Wake Island* (John Farrow, director) for Paramount. New contract at Warner Bros. where he is paid to write novel *I Wasn't Born Yesterday*. Works 14 days on *Action in the North-Atlantic* (Lloyd Bacon, director), and a month adapting Eric Ambler's *Background to Danger* (Raoul Walsh, director). Both Warner films release in 1943.

1943: Finishes and publishes novel *I Wasn't Born Yesterday* under the title *Nobody Lives Forever* (Knopf), as former title was owned by another company. Divorces Marjorie, marries Whitney Forbes Johnstone.

1945: Adapts *San Antonio* (David Butler, director) from an Alan Le May story. In September, his Warner contract is canceled and he moves to MGM, where he will do nothing for two years. Knopf publishes *Tomorrow's Another Day*.

1946: Knopf publishes *Romelle*, his most mystifying novel (about cross-dressing).

1949: Knopf publishes *The Asphalt Jungle*. Raoul Walsh makes *Colorado Territory*, a Western remake of *High Sierra* (with Joel McCrea, Virginia Mayo).

1950: John Huston makes a near-perfect movie of *The Asphalt Jungle* at MGM. Fawcett publishes *Stretch Dawson* as a Gold Medal original. Works for Howard Hughes on *The Racket* (John Cromwell, director) and *Vendetta* (Mel Ferrer, director) from the Prosper Mérimée novella *Columba*.

1951: Knopf publishes *Little Men, Big World*.

1952: Knopf publishes *Vanity Row*.

1953: Knopf publishes *Adobe Walls: A Novel of the Last Apache Rising*. Filmed as *Arrowhead* (with Charlton Heston, Jack Palance; Charles Marquis Warren, director). Fawcett publishes *Big Stan* as a Gold Medal original, under the pseudonym John Monahan.

1954: Scripts *Dangerous Mission* (Louis King, director) for RKO. His friend Horace McCoy also works on it. Knopf publishes *Captain Lightfoot*.

1955: *Captain Lightfoot* made at Universal (with Rock Hudson, Barbara Rush; Douglas Sirk, director). Burnett returns to Warner, co-writes *Illegal* (Lewis Allen, director), as well as the remake of *High Sierra*, under the title *I Died a Thousand Times* (with Shelley Winters, Jack Palance; Stuart Heisler, director).

1956: Knopf publishes *Pale Moon*. Random House publishes Burnett's jazz novel *It's Always Four O'Clock* (under the pseudonym James Updyke). Joe Kane makes *Accused of Murder* at Republic, from Burnett's 1952 novel *Vanity Row*.

1957: Knopf publishes *Underdog*.

1958: Knopf publishes *Bitter Ground*.

1959: Knopf publishes *Mi Amigo: A Novel of the Southwest*.

1960: Writes *September Storm* (Byron Haskin, director) from a Steve Fisher story, for independent producer Edward L. Alperson. Shot and presented in Stereo-Vision, a rare 3D variation of the widescreen format.

1961: Popular Library publishes *Conant* as a paperback original. Gold Medal publishes *Round the Clock at Volari's* as a paperback original. November 1961 Bel-Air fire destroys the Burnett home.

1962: Writes *Sergeants 3* (John Sturges, director). Doubleday publishes *The Goldseekers*, and Macdonald & Co. publishes (in England only) *The Widow Barony*.

1963: Writes on *The Great Escape* for John Sturges. Contributes to script of *4 for Texas* (Robert Aldrich, director). Pocket Books publishes *The Abilene Samson*, a paperback original.

1964: C.N. Potter publishes *The Roar of the Crowd*.

1965: Bantam publishes *The Winning of Mickey Free*, as a paperback original.

1968: Writes his last script, *Ice Station Zebra*, for John Sturges. Gold Medal publishes *The Cool Man* as a paperback original.

1981: St. Martin's Press publishes *Good-bye, Chicago*, Burnett's final novel.

1982: Dies in Los Angeles, April 25, at the age of 82.

ACKNOWLEDGMENTS

Leith Adams (Warner Bros. Chief Archivist) and Ned Comstock (Cinematic Arts Library, USC) have been accomplices and friends from way back. Abraham Polonsky, interviewed in his Beverly Hills apartment and on the Raleigh Studio lot in 1983, was as thoughtful and funny in private as he was contrarian in public. The following people have shielded me from real life and its unpleasantness from the beginning: Bernard Eisenschitz, Jean-Luc Fromental, Lili Stajn, Michel Aphesbero and Danielle Colomine, Philippe Grenier, Patrick and Arlette Raynal, Vincent Toledano. More recently, Laurent Chalumeau, Manuel Chiche, Philippe Ghielmetti, Gian Luca Farinelli, Maelle Arnaud, and Thierry Frémaux.

Throughout the researching and writing of this book in the 1990s, the late Grover Lewis was an invaluable friend, sounding board, and supporter. The Edward Anderson chapter was mostly rewritten by him and figures in this book as both communion and homage.

Honi Soit Qui Malibu was the first book of mine published by Jean-Claude Fasquelle, then director and founder of Éditions Grasset. He kept me alive for many years and allowed me to write on whatever I fancied, the way I wanted, no matter how low the sales. No writer can ask for more than this, for which I remain deeply grateful, over the span of years and estrangement that followed.

Mention in the early chapters of title writers like Ralph Spence and Robert Hopkins owes a great deal to a talk historian Kevin Brownlow gave at the Cinémathèque française on March 26, 1999. He furnished me with the transcript, as he has done with unfailing generosity over the years, notably concerning my two-decade long obsession with director Charles Brabin. His support and kindness have been invaluable to me.

Pat McGilligan's books of interviews (the *Backstory* series, University of California Press) and Lee Server's *Screenwriter: Words Become Pictures* (Main Street Press, 1987) were published after my own research was over; nevertheless, they were precious to me for comparing and cross-checking, but above all, since they interviewed some of the same writers I did, they alerted me to the vagaries of human memory—which became the watermark of this book, and its true theme.

John Burke in *Rogue's Progress* (G.P. Putnam's Sons, 1975) and Sidney Phillips (in *Los Angeles* magazine) have both written on Wilson Mizner. Jim Heimann's delicious *Out with the Stars* (Abbeville Press, 1985) is the principal source on restaurant and nightclubs in Los Angeles.

William Saroyan in *Places Where I've Done Time* (Praeger, 1972), Budd Schulberg in *The Four Seasons of Success* (Doubleday, 1972), and John Fante in *Dreams from Bunker Hill* (Black Sparrow Press, 1982) all mention Stanley Rose and his Hollywood Boulevard bookstore. The chapter on booksellers owes much of its content to several interviews I conducted in the early 1980s: Eddie Gilbert (February 1982) spoke to me in his bookshop across from the Pantages Theatre on the boulevard east of Vine, which would close down soon after. Milton Luboviski was questioned around the same time during one of his trips back to Hollywood (he had sold Larry Edmunds Bookstore and was living in Paris). Yetive Moss, in June 1982, was still working in a bookstore (this one in Westwood) when she talked with me and revealed the snapshot of Stanley Rose's front window. Louis Epstein, truly the Memory of the Boulevard at that time, was the most helpful and generous, when he received me in his home in March 1983. Joyce Fante also shared her memories of Rose's bookstore during many visits at her Point Dume home.

Nathanael West, The Art of His Life (Farrar, Straus and Giroux, 1970), remains the main reference on West. Its author, Jay Martin, generously allowed me to pore over his notes and listen to his tape recordings deposited in the Huntington Library Special Collections. He also let me read the letters Sid Perelman left with him. In July 1986, for a short documentary on West's death for the French TV show *Cinéma cinémas*, I interviewed John Sanford at his Montecito house, as well as Wells Root in Brentwood, and Burt Kelly's widow. Thank you Brian Light for the picture.

Background on jailbird screenwriters Ernest Booth and Robert Tasker comes mainly from newspaper articles of the period (including the *San Quentin Bulletin* and the *San Quentin News*), but, more importantly, from the H. L. Mencken papers deposited at the New York Public Library, which include a massive correspondence between the Sage of Baltimore and his various protégés: John Fante, Robert Tasker, Jim Tully, and Ernest Booth, among others. John Bright and Sam Brown also provided precious details on Tasker when I interviewed them. Randy Davis is to be thanked for the arcane information concerning the "Porfirio Laredo" incident, and for sharing his depthless curiosity about *anything* with me over the years.

The chapter on Sam and Rowland Brown would not have been possible without the help, patience and generosity of the entire Brown family. Karen Brown Mower talked to me on the phone about her husband. Daphne and Barry Bernstein let me pore over the unproduced scripts of Daphne's father, Rowland Brown. Above all, Moya Brown not only let me reproduce many family photographs, she also shared personal memories about her uncle and father. I thank all of them for their trust, and hope I did both justice. The three interviews with Sam Brown were held at his San Dimas home in the spring of 1986, then later in July in a rest home, also in San Dimas, California. To my knowledge, Don Miller was the only person who wrote in depth about Rowland Brown before I started my research (*Notes on a Blighted Career,* in *Focus on Film #7,* 1971). His Brown filmography is used by Frank Thompson in his book *Between Action and Cut* (Scarecrow Press, 1985). I also thank Yves de Peretti and Solera Films for sharing with me a few of Rose Kearin's letters to F. W. Murnau, and details on the filming of *Tabu.*

Martha Foley published *The Story of STORY Magazine* in 1980 (W. W. Norton), and my chapter owes a great debt to her. In 1989, a magazine bearing the same name and vocation appeared on the newsstands, revived by publisher Richard Rosenthal and editor Lois Rosenthal. It ran until the winter of 2000, after winning two National Magazine Awards for fiction.

I interviewed John Bright at his West Hollywood home in April 1986. His memoir *Arsenic and Old Faces,* which I read at the time, was published in 2002, after his death, by Scarecrow Press, under the title *Worms in the Winecup.* I thank Max Lamb, professor at USC, for giving me his rare copy of *It's Cleaner on the Inside,* Bright's fictionalized book on his friend and writing partner Robert Tasker.

Niven Busch talked to me about James M. Cain and his ducks at the second (and last) edition of the Santa Fe Film Festival in August 1980. I met him again a year later at his Pacific Heights home in San Francisco. Articles on Cain and interviews with the author are too numerous to list here. Roy Hoopes (Holt, Rinehart and Winston, 1982) wrote the only Cain biography extant at the time I researched my book. He never once spoke to Niven Busch. There have been other books on Cain since then.

The Edward Anderson track goes far back. In 1982, Nicholas Ray's first biographer, Bernard Eisenschitz, delved into the RKO Archives to research his subject. As he was staying at my house, I tagged along. The RKO Archives were then at 129 N.Vermont Avenue, near a Korean church. This is where the late great John Hall, West Coast General Manager of RKO Pictures, let us run amok with the files and the Xerox machine. This is where I read Rowland Brown's script of *Thieves Like Us*. This is where I found Anderson's letter to Howard Hughes, which opens my chapter. The collection was impeccably organized and preserved (mostly thanks to Hall's predecessor, Vernon Harbin), and staffed almost exclusively with sashaying bodybuilders. The collection did not fare as well after it was donated to UCLA, especially when Ted Turner bought what remained of RKO and dispersed the archives in at least five different institutions. A few years after this initiation in archival delights, Polly Anderson, of Fort Myers Beach, Florida, wrote me letters about her husband, after Eisenschitz had put me in touch with her. Her daughter Helen sent photographs. I also exchanged letters with producer Jerry Bick about his version of *Thieves Like Us*. I spoke to Robert Altman about it in the summer of 1982 on the set of *O. C. and Stiggs* in Phoenix, Arizona. In the spring of 1985, I went to the Rio Grande Valley and to Brownsville, Texas, to retrace Anderson's last years and places of employment. My main sources there were hamburger slinger Martin Rutledge, and a crusty ex-newspaperman named Chuck Schwanitz. The results of this quest were published in several installments in the French daily newspaper *Libération* in July 1985, under the title "Loin de Dallas." Since then, Patrick Bennett published *Rough and Rowdy Ways: The Life and Hard Times of Edward Anderson* (Texas A&M University Press, 1988). I have mentioned already Grover Lewis' contribution, and his life-long obsession and identification with Anderson. One year before he died, he went to South Texas to find more about Anderson and had hoped to write about him in the *Texas Monthly*.

My first contacts with A. I. Bezzerides go back to 1981 and ceased only six or seven years before his death in January 2007. I wrote two articles on him for *Libération* and had French publisher Éditions Gallimard translate two of his novels in the late 1990s. I also interviewed him for *Cinéma cinémas* in the summer of 1982. I thank the late Silvia Richards, who after years of reticence reminisced about her collaboration and affair with Fritz Lang. I met Catherine Turney at the Huntington Library, where she was researching a novel, and she spoke about her time at Warner as a scriptwriter in the 1940s, and about Bezzerides, Faulkner, and the famous carpool to Musso & Frank. Joyce Fante and Milton Luboviski also told me stories and anecdotes about Bezzerides and Fante, a few off the record. I have respected their wishes.

I interviewed Julius Epstein for *Cinéma cinémas* in the summer of 1986. John Fante wrote about Owen Francis in a letter to Carey McWilliams. Don Siegel spoke about Daniel Mainwaring in an interview for *Cinéma cinémas* filmed in Cambria in July 1986. Joyce Fante also had a lot to offer about Mainwaring.

Thomas Sturak's unpublished 1960s thesis (at UCLA) still remains the principal source on Horace McCoy and is a precious guide through the considerable archives left by the author to UCLA's Special Collections. Yetive Moss and W. R. Burnett were also invaluable as direct witnesses.

Steven Turner wrote on George Milburn (Southwest Writers Series, Steck-Vaughn Company) as well as Ben Botkin. Charles Angoff, an old collaborator of Mencken's at *The American Mercury*, also wrote on Milburn in *H. L. Mencken: A Portrait from Memory* (Thomas Yoseloff, 1956). Robert Polito wrote the definitive Jim Thompson biography, *Savage Art: A Biography of Jim Thompson* (Knopf, 1995), and the passage about his boozing with George Milburn in the Village in the later part of their lives comes from that book. The Milburn letter to Nathanael West comes from Sid Perelman via Jay Martin.

Andy Dowdy, bookseller *extraordinaire* at Other Times Books in West Los Angeles, sold me a soiled copy (*sans* dust jacket) of Tom Kromer's

Waiting for Nothing. He is also responsible for some of my more giddy interest in this kind of marginal literature. I have missed him ever since he disappeared from our lives (without even dying) twenty years ago. Since then, Arthur D. Casciato and James L. W. West III gathered all of Kromer's writings in one volume (University of Georgia Press, 1986).

Niven Busch is the principal source for the chapter "Polo, Anyone?" I owe the information on the "Uplifters" team to Hervé Dumont and his indispensable *Frank Borzage, Sarastro à Hollywood* (Cinémathèque française/Mazzotta, 1993).

Two serious biographies on Malcolm Lowry have been published: Douglas Day's (Oxford University Press, 1973) owes its existence and perspective to Lowry's second wife, Margerie Bonner. The most recent bio, Gordon Bowker's *Pursued by Furies* (St. Martin's Press, 1997), presents the view of Lowry's first wife, Jan Gabrial. Two sides of the same man's story, seen through the eyes of the women in his life.

I interviewed W. R. Burnett several times at his Marina del Rey condo in January 1982, three months before his death. Claude Benoit's filmography of Burnett and J. J. Schleret's article, both published in *Polar #5*, were very useful. I interviewed Whitney Burnett about her husband in 1984. Leith Adams lent me a print of *Dark Hazard*, and was generally indispensable for all this research.

Finally, I want to thank, once again, my friend and publisher Eddie Muller for the editing and for giving me a voice in this country.

And Eva for being Eva.

NOTES

NOTES

NOTES